Lecture Notes in Artificial Intelligence   1495

Subseries of Lecture Notes in Computer Science
Edited by J. G. Carbonell and J. Siekmann

Lecture Notes in Computer Science

Edited by G. Goos, J. Hartmanis and J. van Leeuwen

Springer
Berlin
Heidelberg
New York
Barcelona
Budapest
Hong Kong
London
Milan
Paris
Singapore
Tokyo

Troels Andreasen   Henning Christiansen
Henrik L. Larsen (Eds.)

Flexible Query Answering Systems

Third International Conference, FQAS'98
Roskilde, Denmark, May 13-15, 1998
Proceedings

 Springer

Series Editors

Jaime G. Carbonell, Carnegie Mellon University, Pittsburgh, PA, USA
Jörg Siekmann, University of Saarland, Saarbrücken, Germany

Volume Editors

Troels Andreasen
Henning Christiansen
Henrik Legind Larsen
Roskilde University, Computer Science Department
P.O. Box 260, DK-4000 Roskilde, Denmark
E-mail: {troels,henning,hll}@ruc.dk

Cataloging-in-Publication Data applied for

Die Deutsche Bibliothek - CIP-Einheitsaufnahme

Flexible query answering systems : third international conference ;
proceedings / FQAS '98, Roskilde, Denmark, May 13 - 15, 1998.
Troels Andreasen ... (ed.). - Berlin ; Heidelberg ; New York ;
Barcelona ; Budapest ; Hong Kong ; London ; Milan ; Paris ;
Singapore ; Tokyo : Springer, 1998
   (Lecture notes in computer science ; Vol. 1495 : Lecture notes in
   artificial intelligence)
   ISBN 3-540-65082-2

CR Subject Classification (1991): H.3, I.2, H.2, H.4, H.5

ISBN 3-540-65082-2 Springer-Verlag Berlin Heidelberg New York

Typesetting: Camera ready by author
SPIN 10638902   06/3142 ~ 5 4 3 2 1 0   Printed on acid-free paper

Preface

This volume constitutes the proceedings of the Third International Conference on Flexible Query Answering Systems held at Roskilde University, Denmark, 13–15 May, 1998.

The conference addresses problems and aspects of users posing queries and (electronic) systems producing answers. In order to recognize a query-answering system as being flexible, we expect it to produce answers which correspond to the users' needs, and that cannot in general be obtained by a strictly logical interpretation of the query. The latter often leads to empty answers, too large answers, or even irrelevant answers. We see no sense in giving a precise definition of this notion of flexibility as it relates to the way a user experiences the system.

Flexibility in query-answering can be touched upon at several levels where we identify the following three as central. Firstly, the *query interface*; do the linguistic and other means make it possible to express ones needs in an easy way? Is it possible to indicate vagueness or leave choices open to the system? Secondly, *representation*; what are the underlying formalism and semantics applied for representing information? Can knowledge, domain knowledge, and metaknowledge be integrated in some way? And thirdly, *query evaluation* which does not necessarily have to comply with the semantics but can extend or restrict this in several ways. The quality of answers produced should be measured for usefulness before classical virtues such as soundness and completeness.

Taking a broad view of the contributions to this conference, they cover conceptual definitions and requirements as well as implemented systems and theoretical models in which flexibility is or can be exemplified. The conference theme overlaps naturally with several established research areas but is distinguished by a particular focus. We can mention logic, fuzzy logic, various database "schools" (deductive, fuzzy, extensions to the relational model, object-oriented etc.), linguistics, philosophy, human-computer interfaces, and information retrieval.

We are grateful to have invited contributions from distinguished and experienced researchers: Patrick Bosc, Jack Minker, and Ami Motro. By their talks at the conference, they provided a higher level of abstraction, drawing attention to the central issues, and gave the future propects and historical background of the field. We would also like to express our thanks to the members of the program committee, particularly to Hendrik Decker, Fosca Giannotti, and Robert Demolombe for their great efforts as invited session chairs. Finally, we greatly acknowledge the support of the sponsoring organizations (listed below) which made the conference possible.

Roskilde
July 1998

Troels Andreasen
Henning Christiansen
Henrik Legind Larsen

Organization

FQAS'98 is organized by members of the Intelligent Systems Group at the Computer Science Department, Roskilde University, Denmark.

Organizing committee

Troels Andreasen
Henning Christiansen (Chair)
Henrik Legind Larsen
— all of Roskilde University, Denmark
  E-mail: {troels,henning,hll}@ruc.dk

Secretariat and practical assistance

Birthe Nielsen
Anne-Lise Roed
Thomas Hald Frandsen

Program committee

Troels Andreasen
Bernadette Bouchon-Meunier
Rita De Caluwe
Henning Christiansen (Chair)
Laurence Cholvy
Hendrik Decker
Robert Demolombe
Didier Dubois
Jørgen Fischer-Nilsson
Fosca Giannotti

Janusz Kacprzyk
Henrik Legind Larsen
Amihai Motro
Jose Nuno Oliveira
Olivier Pivert
Olga Pons
Henri Prade
Amparo Vila
Ronald R. Yager

Sponsoring organizations

STVF, The Danish Technical Research Council

PDC, Prolog Development Center, Copenhagen, Denmark

COMPULOG, Network of Excellence in Computational Logic

DBC, Danish Library Centre, Ballerup, Denmark

ERUDIT, European Network in Uncertainty Techniques Developments for Use in Information Technology

Table of Contents

CHR$^\vee$: A Flexible Query Language

Slim Abdennadher and Heribert Schütz

Universität München, Institut für Informatik, Oettingenstr. 67, D-80538 München
{Slim.Abdennadher|Heribert.Schuetz}@informatik.uni-muenchen.de

Abstract. We show how the language Constraint Handling Rules (CHR), a high-level logic language for the implementation of constraint solvers, can be slightly extended to become a general-purpose logic programming language with an expressive power subsuming the expressive power of Horn clause programs with SLD resolution. The extended language, called "CHR$^\vee$", retains however the extra features of CHR, e.g., committed choice and matching, which are important for other purposes, especially for efficiently solving constraints. CHR$^\vee$ turns out to be a very flexible query language in the sense that it supports several (constraint) logic programming paradigms and allows to mix them in a single program. In particular, it supports top-down query evaluation and also bottom-up evaluation as it is frequently used in (disjunctive) deductive databases.

1 Introduction

Constraint Handling Rules (CHR) is a high-level logic language for the implementation of constraint solvers [7]. Its operational semantics differs from SLD resolution in various ways. Most of these differences are extensions, but there are also two incompatible differences:

- While SLD resolution performs full unification between goals and rule heads, CHR performs a one-sided unification ("matching"). That is, CHR only allows the variables of a rule to be instantiated in order to match the rule head with some part of the goal.
- While SLD resolution tries to apply all appropriate rules to a goal (usually implemented by backtracking), CHR applies only one, i.e., it follows the committed-choice approach.

These incompatibilities make CHR difficult to use as a general-purpose logic query language, especially for search-oriented problems.

We show, however, that only a small and simple extension to CHR is needed in order to reach an expressive power that subsumes the expressive power of Horn clause programs with SLD resolution: We allow disjunctions on the right hand sides of CHR rules.

We will give formal operational semantics for the resulting language, which we call CHR$^\vee$, and show how any Horn clause program can be converted into an equivalent CHR$^\vee$ program. The central idea is to move unification and non-committed choices to the right hand sides of rules. The required transformation turns out to be Clark's completion of logic programs [5].

So while currently CHR is used as a special-purpose language for constraint solvers and CHR programs are typically supplements to Prolog programs, CHR$^\vee$ allows to write the entire application in a uniform language. But it is not only possible to merge constraint solving and top-down query evaluation: CHR (and, of course, also CHR$^\vee$) allow also to write logic programs for bottom-up evaluation as it is frequently used in (disjunctive) deductive databases. Together with disjunction, it is even possible to implement disjunctive logic databases and to evaluate them in a bottom-up manner in the style of Satchmo [9] (formalized as PUHR tableaux [4]) and CPUHR tableaux [2].

The paper is organized as follows: In Section 2 we define the CHR language and calculus and SLD resolution as far as we need them for our work. Section 3 contains the formalization of the language CHR$^\vee$ and details on the expression of Horn clause programs in CHR$^\vee$. In Section 4 we give examples for the use of CHR$^\vee$ with multiple logic programming paradigms. Some comparisons to related work conclude the paper in Section 5.

2 Preliminaries

In this section we give some definitions for SLD resolution and CHR, which we will use in the following sections.

2.1 SLD Resolution

Even though we expect the reader to be familiar with Horn clause programs and SLD resolution, we give some definitions in order to introduce our terminology and notation, which we will need for comparisons with CHR and CHR$^\vee$.

Syntax A *Horn clause program* is a set of *Horn clauses*, also called *rules*, which are formulas of the form $H \leftarrow B$, where H is an *atom*, i.e., an atomic first-order formula and B is a conjunction of atoms. We call H the *head* and B the *body* of the rule.

Declarative Semantics The logical meaning of a Horn clause program P is given by its *completion* [5]: The *completed definition* of a predicate p is a formula of the form $\forall \bar{v}(p(\bar{v}) \leftrightarrow (\exists \bar{x}_1(\bar{v} \dot{=} \bar{t}_1 \wedge B_1) \vee \ldots \vee \exists \bar{x}_n(\bar{v} \dot{=} \bar{t}_n \wedge B_n)))$,[1] where $p(\bar{t}_1) \leftarrow B_1, \ldots, p(\bar{t}_n) \leftarrow B_n$ are all the clauses with head predicate p in P, every $\bar{x}_i$ is the list of variables occurring in the ith such clause, and $\bar{v}$ is a list of fresh variables of appropriate length. The *completion* of P consists of the completed definitions of all the predicates occurring in P and a theory defining $\dot{=}$ as syntactic equality.

---

[1] Here $\bar{v} \dot{=} \bar{t}_i$ stands for the conjunction of equations between respective components of the lists $\bar{v}$ and $\bar{t}_i$.

Operational Semantics The operational semantics can be described as a state transition system for *states* of the form $<G, \theta>$, where G (the *goal*) is a conjunction of atoms and θ is a substitution. Transitions from a state $<G, \theta>$ are possible if for some fresh variant[2] of a rule $H \leftarrow B$ in the given program P and some atom A in the goal G the head H and $A\theta$ are unifiable. In the resulting state, A is replaced by B in the goal and the substitution is composed with the most general unifier of H and $A\theta$.

This computation step is also given in Figure 1. Here and in the rest of the paper conjunctions are considered to be associative and commutative.[3] We are

> **Unfold**
> $(H \leftarrow B)$ is a fresh variant of a rule in P
> β is the most general unifier of H and $A\theta$
> $$\overline{<A \land G, \theta> \mapsto <B \land G, \theta\beta>}$$

Fig. 1. SLD resolution step

looking for chains of such transitions from the initial state, which consists of the user-supplied query and the identity substitution, to some final state, where the goal must be the empty conjunction $\top$.

Given some state $<A \land G, \theta>$, there are two degrees of nondeterminism when we want to reduce it to another state:

- Any atom in the conjunction $A \land G$ can be chosen as the atom A.
- Any rule $(H \leftarrow B)$ in P for which B and $A\theta$ are unifiable can be chosen.

In order to achieve certain completeness properties of SLD resolution we have to try all possibilities w.r.t. the second degree. But it is a fundamental property of SLD resolution that w.r.t. the first degree it suffices to choose an arbitrary atom A. So the first degree of nondeterminism is of "don't-care" type, while the second is of "don't-know" type.

We leave the don't-care nondeterminism implicit in the calculus as usual, whereas we note the don't-know nondeterminism in a refined version of the **Unfold** computation step in Figure 2. With this modified rule we construct trees of states rather than sequences of states. The root is the initial state as given above. Every inner node has children according to some application of **UnfoldSplit**. Leaves are either *successful* leaves, where the goal has become empty, or *failing* leaves if there are no appropriate rules in P for the chosen goal atom A.

---

[2] Two formulas or terms are variants, if they can be obtained from each other by a variable renaming. A fresh variant contains only new variables.

[3] We will, however, not consider conjunctions to be idempotent.

UnfoldSplit

$(H_1 \leftarrow B_1), \ldots, (H_n \leftarrow B_n)$ are fresh variants of all those rules in P
for which H_i $(1 \leq i \leq n)$ is unifiable with $A\theta$
β_i is the most general unifier of H_i and $A\theta$ $(1 \leq i \leq n)$

$<A \wedge G, \theta> \mapsto <B_1 \wedge G, \theta\beta_1> \mid \ldots \mid <B_n \wedge G, \theta\beta_n>$

Fig. 2. SLD resolution step with case splitting

2.2 CHR

Constraint Handling Rules (CHR) [7] is a declarative high-level language extension especially designed for writing constraint solvers. With CHR, one can introduce *user-defined* constraints into a given host language, be it Prolog, Lisp or any other language.

CHR consists of guarded rules with multiple heads that replace constraints by simpler ones until they are solved. CHR defines both simplification of and propagation over user-defined constraints. Simplification rules replace constraints by simpler constraints while preserving logical equivalence (e.g., $X > Y \wedge Y > X \Leftrightarrow false$). Propagation rules add new constraints, which are logically redundant but may cause further simplification (e.g. $X > Y \wedge Y > Z \Rightarrow X > Z$). Repeated application of rules incrementally solves constraints. For example, with the two rules above we can transform $A > B \wedge B > C \wedge C > A$ to $A > B \wedge B > C \wedge A > C \wedge C > A$ and to *false*. Multiple atoms in a rule head are a feature that is essential in solving conjunctions of constraints.

We now give the syntax and the semantics of CHR.

Syntax A *constraint* is a first order atom. We use two disjoint sorts of predicate symbols for two different classes of constraints: One sort for *built-in* constraints and one sort for *user-defined* constraints.[4] Built-in constraints are those handled by a predefined constraint solver. User-defined constraints are those defined by a CHR program.

A *CHR program* is a finite set of rules. There are two basic kinds of rules[5]. A *simplification rule* is of the form $H \Leftrightarrow C \mid B$ and a *propagation rule* is of the form $H \Rightarrow C \mid B$, where the *head* H is a non-empty conjunction of user-defined constraints, the *guard* C is a built-in constraint and the *body* B is a conjunction of built-in and user-defined constraints. A guard *"true"* is usually omitted together with the vertical bar.

Declarative Semantics The logical meaning of a simplification rule is a logical equivalence provided the guard holds $\forall \bar{x}$ $(C \rightarrow (H \leftrightarrow \exists \bar{y}\ B))$. The logi-

---

[4] When CHR is used as an extension language for another logic programming language such as Prolog (the host language), then constraint predicate symbols are also distinguished from other predicate symbols handled by the host language.

[5] There is also a third hybrid kind of rule called simpagation rule [3].

cal meaning of a propagation rule is an implication provided the guard holds $\forall \bar{x} \ (C \to (H \to \exists \bar{y} \ B))$. Here $\bar{x}$ is the list of variables occuring in H and C and $\bar{y}$ are the variables occuring in B only. The logical meaning of a CHR program is the union of the logical meanings of its rules and a constraint theory CT that defines the built-in constraints. We require CT to define the predicate $\doteq$ as syntactic equality and *true* (*false*) as predicates that are always (never) satisfied.

Operational Semantics The operational semantics of CHR is again given by a transition system. A *state* is a triple $<G, C_U, C_B>$. G is a conjunction of user-defined and built-in constraints called *goal store*. C_U is a conjunction of user-defined constraints. C_B is a built-in constraint. C_U and C_B are called *user-defined* and *built-in (constraint) stores*, respectively. An empty goal or user-defined store is represented by $\top$. The built-in store cannot be empty. In its simplest form it is the built-in constraint *true* or *false*.

The aim of the computation is to incrementally reduce an initial state $<G, \top, true>$ with a user-supplied query G to a state that contains no more goals in the goal store and a maximally simplified user-defined constraint store (with respect to a given program P). Given a CHR program P we define the transition relation $\mapsto$ by introducing four kinds of computation steps (Figure 3).

Notation: Capital letters denote conjunctions of constraints. An equation $c(t_1, \ldots, t_n) \doteq d(s_1, \ldots, s_n)$ of two constraints stands for $t_1 \doteq s_1 \wedge \ldots \wedge t_n \doteq s_n$ if c and d are the same predicate symbol and for *false* otherwise. An equation $(p_1 \wedge \ldots \wedge p_n) \doteq (q_1 \wedge \ldots \wedge q_m)$ stands for $p_1 \doteq q_1 \wedge \ldots \wedge p_n \doteq q_n$ if $n = m$ and for *false* otherwise. Note that conjuncts can be permuted since our conjunction is associative and commutative.

In the **Solve** computation step, the built-in solver normalizes the constraint store C_B with a new constraint C from the goal store. To normalize the constraint store means to produce a new constraint store C'_B that is (according to the constraint theory CT) equivalent to the conjunction of the old constraint store C_B and the new constraint C.

Introduce transports a user-defined constraint H from the goal store into the user-defined constraint store. There it can be handled with other user-defined constraints by applying rules.

To **Simplify** user-defined constraints H' means to remove them from the user-defined store and to add the body B of a fresh variant of a simplification rule $(H \Leftrightarrow C \mid B)$ from the program to the goal store and the equation $H \doteq H'$ and the guard C to the built-in store, provided H' matches the head H and the resulting guard C is implied by the built-in constraint store C_B.

Note that "matching" means that it is only allowed to instantiate variables of H (say, with a substitution β) but not variables of H'. Also C_B must imply $C\beta$ in full generality and not only an instance of it. In the logical notation this is achieved by existentially quantifying only the fresh variables $\bar{x}$ in the condition. The other variables are implicitly universally quantified.

The **Propagate** transition is similar to the **Simplify** transition, but retains the user-defined constraints H' in the user-defined store. Trivial nontermination

---

Solve

$$C \text{ is a built-in constraint}$$
$$CT \models C_B \wedge C \leftrightarrow C'_B$$
$$\underline{C'_B \text{ is simpler than } C_B \wedge C}$$
$$<C \wedge G, C_U, C_B> \mapsto <G, C_U, C'_B>$$

Introduce

$$\underline{H \text{ is a user-defined constraint}}$$
$$<H \wedge G, C_U, C_B> \mapsto <G, H \wedge C_U, C_B>$$

Simplify

$$(H \Leftrightarrow C \mid B) \text{ is a fresh variant of a rule in } P \text{ with the variables } \bar{x}$$
$$\underline{CT \models C_B \rightarrow \exists \bar{x}(H \doteq H' \wedge C)}$$
$$<G, H' \wedge C_U, C_B> \mapsto <G \wedge B, C_U, C \wedge H \doteq H' \wedge C_B>$$

Propagate

$$(H \Rightarrow C \mid B) \text{ is a fresh variant of a rule in } P \text{ with the variables } \bar{x}$$
$$\underline{CT \models C_B \rightarrow \exists \bar{x}(H \doteq H' \wedge C)}$$
$$<G, H' \wedge C_U, C_B> \mapsto <G \wedge B, H' \wedge C_U, C \wedge H \doteq H' \wedge C_B>$$

Fig. 3. CHR computation steps

caused by applying the same propagation rule again and again is avoided by applying a propagation rule at most once to the same constraints. A more complex operational semantics that addresses this issue can be found in [1].

In contrast to SLD resolution, CHR is a committed-choice language. That is, whenever more than one transition is possible, one transition is chosen nondeterministically in the sense of don't-care nondeterminism, i.e., without backtracking.

3 CHR$^{\vee}$ as a Logic Programming Language

It is obvious that there are similarities and differences between CHR computation and SLD resolution. As we have mentioned in the introduction, while some of the differences between CHR and SLD resolution extend the expressive power of CHR w.r.t. SLD resolution (+), others are incompatibilities ($\neq$) or mere technical differences ($\bullet$):

+ While variable bindings are accumulated in a substitution by SLD resolution, a CHR computation uses equality constraints in the **built-in constraint store** for this purpose. Obviously every substitution can be expressed by equality constraints, but not every built-in constraint can be simulated by substitutions. **Solve** computation steps allow direct use of arbitrary built-in constraints in user-supplied queries and bodies of CHR rules.

- Since CHR does not handle all constraints through rules, but is able to use a built-in constraint solver, there is a distinction between user-defined and built-in constraints. For technical purposes it is useful to **split the goal store** of SLD resolution into a goal store (containing a mixture of built-in and user-defined constraints) and a store for user-defined constraints only. The two stores communicate via **Introduce** computation steps.
+ Horn clauses are used by SLD resolution in a way similar to simplification rules in CHR, since the atom A that is unified with the rule head is removed from the goal. However, there is nothing like **propagation rules** for SLD resolution.
+ CHR allows for **multiple atoms in rule heads.**[6] So a rule application may need to match (and, in the case of a simplification rule, consume) several atoms in the user-defined constraint store.
≠ CHR performs **committed choice**, i.e., it does not generate more than one child state from any given state. That is, only a linear computation is performed instead of a traversal of some tree.
≠ A rule head is **matched** rather than unified with some part of the user-defined constraint store. The restriction to matching is needed in order to retain certain completeness properties in the presence of committed choice [8].
+ CHR allows adding **guards** to rules. This is also needed as a consequence of committed choice: Guards must frequently be used to avoid application of inappropriate rules, which cannot be backtracked as in SLD resolution.

In the rest of this section we will show how the two incompatibilities above can be eliminated by a simple extension of CHR.

3.1 Adding Disjunction to CHR

Consider the Horn clause program $\{p \leftarrow q, \ p \leftarrow r, \ r \leftarrow \top\}$ and the query p. SLD resolution will generate a tree as in Figure 4. Note that the left and right

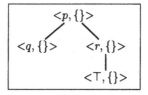

Fig. 4. An SLD tree

leaf are failing and successful, respectively.

---

[6] Multi-headed rules have not only been investigated for CHR, but according to [6] also for variants of logic programming languages, mainly for coordination languages.

A naïve transformation into a CHR program might lead to: $\{p \Leftrightarrow q, \; p \Leftrightarrow r, \; q \Leftrightarrow false, \; r \Leftrightarrow \top\}$. As we have discussed above, Horn clauses are converted to simplification rules because these consume the selected constraint from the user-defined constraint store. Notice that the rule $q \Leftrightarrow false$ has been introduced because a CHR computation would not fail just because the constraint q cannot be reduced. An evaluation of this program essentially follows one of the two branches in Figure 4, where the choice is performed nondeterministically.

So the query may either fail or succeed, which is, of course undesirable. The CHR program is said to be non-confluent. From a logical point of view, the reason for this behavior is that the program's meaning $(p \leftrightarrow q) \wedge (p \leftrightarrow r) \wedge (q \leftrightarrow false) \wedge (r \leftrightarrow true)$ is inconsistent.

The intended logical meaning of the original Horn clause program is $(p \leftrightarrow q \vee r) \wedge (q \leftrightarrow false) \wedge (r \leftrightarrow true)$. In order to express this in a CHR program we must allow disjunctions in rule bodies. So we extend the syntax of CHR: In a simplification rule $H \Leftrightarrow C \mid B$ the body B is now a formula that is constructed from atoms by conjunctions and disjunctions in an arbitrary way. For the sake of uniformity the syntax of propagation rules is extended in the same way and also user queries may be of the same form as a rule body. We call the extended language "CHR$^\vee$".

In CHR$^\vee$ we can express the above Horn clause example in a more appropriate way than in CHR: $\{p \Leftrightarrow q \vee r, \; q \Leftrightarrow false, \; r \Leftrightarrow \top\}$.

The computation steps from Figure 3 will be used for CHR$^\vee$ programs in the same way as they have been used for CHR programs. However, with the extended syntax disjunctions make their way into the goal store. In order to handle these, we introduce the **Split** computation step (Figure 5). This step can

---

Split
$$<(G_1 \vee G_2) \wedge G, C_U, C_B> \mapsto <G_1 \wedge G, C_U, C_B> \mid <G_2 \wedge G, C_U, C_B>$$

Fig. 5. Computation step for disjunctions

---

always be applied if the goal store contains a disjunction. No other condition needs to be satisfied. The step leads to branching in the computation in the same way as we had it for SLD resolution. So we will again get a tree rather than a chain of states. In the two children of the state containing a disjunction in the goal store this disjunction will be replaced by one or the other alternative of the disjunction, respectively.

Leaves in the state tree can be *successful*, *failing* or *blocking*:

- A leaf of the form $<\top, \top, C_B>$ where C_B is satisfiable is called *successful*.
- A leaf of the form $<G, C_U, C_B>$ where C_B is unsatisfiable is called *failing*.
- Other leaves are called *blocking*.

The evaluation of a query p w.r.t. this program leads to the tree given in Figure 6, which is similar to the one in Figure 4.

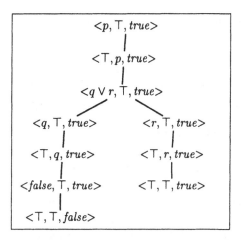

Fig. 6. A CHR$^\vee$ tree

3.2 Expressing Horn Programs in CHR$^\vee$

In the previous subsection we have seen how to circumvent the committed choice incompatibility using disjunction as a new language construct. We have essentially moved case splitting to the right hand sides of rules. In this subsection we will see that also (full) unification can be performed on the right-hand sides of rules, thus circumventing the matching/unification incompatibility. Altogether we essentially replace the Horn clause program by its completion.

Consider for example the well-known ternary *append* predicate for lists, which holds if its third argument is a concatenation of the first and the second argument. It is usually implemented by these two Horn clauses:

$$append([], L, L) \leftarrow \top.$$
$$append([H|L1], L2, [H|L3]) \leftarrow append(L1, L2, L3).$$

The corresponding CHR$^\vee$ program consists of the single simplification rule

$$append(X, Y, Z) \Leftrightarrow (\ X \doteq [] \land Y \doteq L \land Z \doteq L$$
$$\lor X \doteq [H|L1] \land Y \doteq L2 \land Z \doteq [H|L3] \land append(L1, L2, L3)\ ).$$

According to the declarative semantics of CHR$^\vee$ (which is the same as for CHR) the logical meaning of this rule is

$$\forall X, Y, Z\ (\ append(X, Y, Z) \leftrightarrow$$
$$\exists L, H, L1, L2, L3\ (\ X \doteq [] \land Y \doteq L \land Z \doteq L$$
$$\lor X \doteq [H|L1] \land Y \doteq L2 \land Z \doteq [H|L3] \land$$
$$append(L1, L2, L3))).$$

This is trivially equivalent to the completed definition

$$\forall X, Y, Z \ (\ append(X, Y, Z) \ \leftrightarrow$$
$$(\ \exists L \ (X \doteq [] \wedge Y \doteq L \wedge Z \doteq L)$$
$$\vee \ \exists H, L1, L2, L3 \ (X \doteq [H|L1] \wedge Y \doteq L2 \wedge Z \doteq [H|L3] \wedge$$
$$append(L1, L2, L3)))).$$

of *append* in the original Horn clause program.

Note that for a predicate that appears only in bodies of Horn clauses, the right hand side of its completed definition is the empty disjunction, which we equivalently represent by the built-in constraint *false*.

It can be shown that also the operational semantics of a Horn clause program with SLD resolution is equivalent to the operational semantics of the corresponding transformed program with CHR$^\vee$-style evaluation in the following sense: For every successful leaf $<\top, \sigma>$ in the SLD tree there is a corresponding successful leaf $<\top, \top, C_B>$ in the CHR$^\vee$ tree where C_B is an equality constraint representing the substitution σ, and vice versa. Furthermore there are no blocking leaves in the CHR$^\vee$ tree. The central observation in the proof is as follows:

> The CHR$^\vee$ computation steps corresponding to an **UnfoldSplit** step in the SLD tree may produce more branches than the **UnfoldSplit** step: They produce a branch for every Horn clause in the original program whose head predicate coincides with the predicate of the selected atom of the **UnfoldSplit** step, even if the clause head and the selected atom do not unify. Nevertheless the superfluous branches will only lead to failing leaves due to the equality constraints in the body of the completed predicate definitions, which have been introduced in order to replace the unification with the clause head.

4 Mixing Logic Programming Paradigms using CHR$^\vee$

4.1 Bottom-up Computation and Constraint Solving

With propagation rules one has a similar behavior as in deductive databases: A fact is not consumed by applying a rule. There is a simple transformation from deductive databases in which all derivable atoms are ground to propagation rules that compute the same set of atoms. A bottom-up rule of the form $H \leftarrow B$, where the body is non-empty, has to be converted to the propagation rule $B \Rightarrow H$. Since CHR is query-driven, a rule of the form $H \leftarrow \top$ (usually called a *fact*) has to be converted to $start \Rightarrow H$. With the query $start$ the evaluation of the corresponding CHR program begins, computing its least Herbrand model.[7]

---

[7] It is even possible to avoid the dummy predicate *start* if we allow empty heads in propagation rules and modify the definition of final states slightly.

Example 1. The following standard ancestor program

$$anc(X, Y) \leftarrow parent(X, Y).$$
$$anc(X, Y) \leftarrow anc(X, Z) \wedge par(Z, Y).$$
$$par(a, b) \leftarrow \top.$$
$$par(b, c) \leftarrow \top.$$
$$par(c, d) \leftarrow \top.$$

can be converted to an operationally equivalent CHR program

$$par(X, Y) \Rightarrow anc(X, Y).$$
$$anc(X, Z) \wedge par(Z, Y) \Rightarrow anc(X, Y).$$
$$start \Rightarrow par(a, b).$$
$$start \Rightarrow par(b, c).$$
$$start \Rightarrow par(c, d).$$

With (disjunctive) propagation rules, it is now also possible to write disjunctive logic programs and to evaluate them in a bottom-up manner in the style of Satchmo [9]. Satchmo expects its input to be given in clausal form. In a way similar to the CPUHR-calculus [2], $CHR^{\vee}$ can handle even disjunctive logic programs with existentially quantified variables and constraints as shown in the following example.

Example 2. Consider the following informations that we have about a university and a student: If a student S is enrolled in a course C at some time T and C has another course C' as a prerequisite, then S must also be enrolled in C' at some time T' before T. *john* has only taken courses before 1994 and from 1996 onward. These informations can be formalized by the following propagation rules:

$$enrolled(S, C, T) \wedge prereq(C, C') \Rightarrow enrolled(S, C', T') \wedge T' < T.$$
$$enrolled(john, C, T) \Rightarrow T < 1994 \vee T \geq 1996.$$

The following rules define a part of the constraint solver for "<", and "$\geq$", that is able to handle constraints even with variable arguments. "$<_B$" is a simple built-in constraint that compares two numbers and cannot deal with uninstantiated variables.

$$X < Y \wedge X < Z \Leftrightarrow Y <_B Z | X < Y.$$
$$X < Y \wedge X \geq Y \Leftrightarrow false.$$
$$X \geq X \Leftrightarrow \top.$$

The first rule means that the constraint $X < Z$ (with a given number Z) can be omitted if there is another constraint $X < Y$ (with a given number Y) provided that Y is smaller than Z. The second rule means that some value X cannot be smaller and greater-or-equal to a value Y at the same time. The last rule means that a constraint of the form $X \geq X$ is trivially valid and can be omitted.

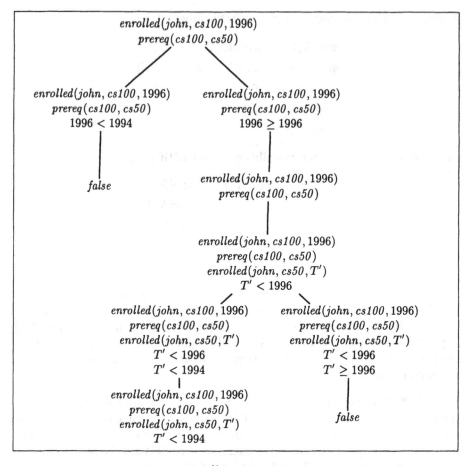

Fig. 7. CHR$^\vee$ Tree for Example 2

Facts are brought into the computation by a CHR$^\vee$ query. The facts that *john* has taken course *cs100* in 1996 and *cs100* has prerequisite *cs50* lead to the initial state

$$< enrolled(john, cs100, 1996) \wedge prereq(cs100, cs50), \top, true>.$$

The computation is given in Figure 7 in a simplified form. The atom *enrolled*(*john*, *cs100*, 1996) activates an instance of the second propagation rule and CHR$^\vee$ distinguishes two cases corresponding to the disjuncts on the right hand side of the rule. In the left case, we get a contradiction (1996 < 1994). In the only successful leaf we see that *john* must have taken *cs50* some time before 1994.

4.2 Combining don't-care and don't-know Nondeterminism

CHR$^\vee$ combines don't-know and don't-care nondeterminism in a declarative way. This can be used for implementing efficient programs as in the following example.

Example 3. The CHR$^\vee$ program for *append* defined above

$$append(X, Y, Z) \Leftrightarrow (\; X \doteq [] \land Y \doteq Z$$
$$\lor \; X \doteq [H|T] \land Z \doteq [H|TY] \land append(T, Y, TY) \,).$$

can be improved by adding the following rule

$$append(X, [], Z) \Leftrightarrow X \doteq Z.$$

With this rule the recursion over the list X in the initial definition of *append* is replaced by a simple unification $X \doteq Z$ if Y is the empty list. In order to achieve the efficiency advantage, the inference engine for CHR$^\vee$ should of course choose the latter of the two overlapping definitions of *append* whenever possible. This can be enforced by adding a guard $Y \dot{\neq} []$ to the original rule, which makes the program deterministic again.

5 Conclusion

We have introduced the language CHR$^\vee$, a simple extension of CHR. It supports a new programming style where top-down evaluation, bottom-up evaluation, and constraint solving can be intermixed in a single language.

The implementation of CHR$^\vee$ was the most pleasant aspect in our research: Prolog-based implementations of CHR are already able to evaluate CHR$^\vee$ programs. It happens that even the non-logical features of Prolog such as negation as failure "not", cut "!", assert/retract and ground work in these implementations in a reasonable way.

We briefly compare CHR$^\vee$ to some other logic programming languages:

Prolog: We have seen that it is possible to rephrase any pure Prolog program as a CHR$^\vee$ program in such a way that the evaluation of the two programs is equivalent. CHR$^\vee$ provides a clear distinction between don't-care nondeterminism (committed choice) and don't-know nondeterminism (disjunction), whereas Prolog only supports don't-know nondeterminism in a declarative way. Don't-care nondeterminism is typically implemented in Prolog in a nondeclarative way, e.g., using cuts.

MixLog [10] generalizes Prolog in several simple ways:
- Among other things, MixLog provides multiple heads and rules not consuming atoms. This way it supports bottom-up logic programming in a way similar to CHR.
- Furthermore, MixLog can be configured to use committed choice instead of backtracking, but not both in the same program.

In general, it appears that the design of MixLog is mainly driven by the question which features can be supported by simple modifications of the implementation. Thus it looses the close correspondence between the operational semantics and a logic-based declarative semantics, which we think is an important property of logic programming and which is preserved in CHR and CHR$^\vee$.

Sisyphos [11] also adds support for bottom-up logic programming to Prolog. Sisyphos uses separate engines for bottom-up and top-down evaluation. It therefore requires that it is explicitly specified in which direction a rule is to be evaluated. In contrast to this, CHR, CHR$^\vee$ and MixLog allow more gradual transition between rules for the two evaluation directions. The Sisyphos approach, however, has the advantage that it supports calling predicates defined by top-down rules from the antecedents of bottom-up rules.

References

1. S. Abdennadher. Operational semantics and confluence of constraint propagation rules. In *Third International Conference on Principles and Practice of Constraint Programming, CP'97*, LNCS 1330. Springer, 1997.
2. S. Abdennadher and H. Schütz. Model generation with existentially quantified variables and constraints. In *6th International Conference on Algebraic and Logic Programming*, LNCS 1298. Springer, 1997.
3. P. Brisset, T. Frühwirth, P. Lim, M. Meier, T. L. Provost, J. Schimpf, and M. Wallace. *ECL^{i}PS^e 3.4 Extensions User Manual*. ECRC Munich, Germany, 1994.
4. F. Bry and A. Yahya. Minimal model generation with positive unit hyper-resolution tableaux. In *5th Workshop on Theorem Proving with Tableaux and Related Methods*, LNAI 1071. Springer, 1996.
5. K. Clark. *Logic and Databases*, chapter Negation as Failure, pages 293–322. Plenum Press, 1978.
6. J. Cohen. A view of the origins and development of Prolog. *Communications of the ACM*, 31(1):26–36, 1988.
7. T. Frühwirth. Constraint handling rules. In *Constraint Programming: Basics and Trends*, LNCS 910. Springer, 1995.
8. M. J. Maher. Logic semantics for a class of committed-choice programs. In *Proceedings of the Fourth International Conference on Logic Programming*. The MIT Press, 1987.
9. R. Manthey and F. Bry. SATCHMO: A theorem prover implemented in Prolog. In *9th Int. Conf. on Automated Deduction (CADE)*, LNCS 310. Springer, 1988.
10. D. A. Smith. Mixlog: A generalized rule based language. In *VIèmes Journées Francophones de Programmation en Logique et programmation par Contraintes*. Hermes, 1997.
11. J. E. Wunderwald. *Adding Bottom-up Evaluation to Prolog*. PhD thesis, Technische Universität München, 1996.

Query Answering by Means of Diagram Transformation[*]

Jaume Agustí[1], Jordi Puigsegur[1,2**], and W. Marco Schorlemmer[1]

[1] Institut d'Investigació en Intel·ligència Artificial
Consell Superior d'Investigacions Científiques
Campus UAB, 08193 Bellaterra, Catalonia (Spain), EU
[2] Indiana University
Visual Inference Laboratory
Lindley Hall #215, Bloomington IN 47405, USA
{agusti,jpf,marco}@iiia.csic.es

Abstract. In previous work we presented a diagrammatic syntax for logic programming which clearly 'resembles' the semantics of predicates as relations, *i.e.* sets of tuples in the Universe of Discourse. This paper shows diagrams as an alternative formal notation for pure logic programming which not only emphasizes some structural features of logical statements, but could also be useful to conduct visual inferences and to communicate them. This paper describes the current state of our research on a visual inference system for answering visually posed queries by means of diagram transformations. Although the transformations are shown by example we point to their correctness and formal character. We explore two interesting features provided by its diagrammatic nature: First, the ability of intuitively keeping track —within a diagram— of the proof that is built while solving a query, and second, the possibility to represent within a unique diagram the several different alternatives to answer a query.

1 Introduction

We are interested in intuitive forms of problem description and resolution within a complete formal language. We believe that the understanding and pragmatics of formal logic and automated deduction are sensitive to the syntax used to express statements. For instance, it has been shown that the taxonomic syntax of many knowledge representation languages facilitates the inference [13]. This paper explores the somehow informal claim that a diagrammatic syntax not only can be an alternative formal notation which emphasizes some structural features of logical statements [1], but it could be useful to conduct visual inferences [2] and communicate them. In the next section we present the intuitions on which

---

[*] Supported by project MODELOGOS funded by the CICYT (TIC 97-0579-C02-01)
** On leave from the IIIA supported by a doctoral grant from the *Direcció General de Recerca*

we base our claim. The rest of the paper presents the state of our research on a diagrammatic logic for pure logic programming based on set inclusion and set membership, putting special emphasis on its visual operational semantics for answering diagrammatically posed queries. Although the operational semantics is based on standard resolution inference mechanisms, its diagrammatic nature provides us with some interesting features, namely the ability of keeping track, within a diagram, of the proof that is built while answering the query, and the possibility to represent within a unique diagram the different alternatives to answer a query. Of course this advantages carry with them some additional complexity.

2 Visual Horn Clause Programs

We are after a formal syntax for logic programming which clearly 'resembles' the corresponding semantics. The standard form of symbolic logic was set by mathematicians in linear form, patterned after Boolean algebra. This syntax favors the interpretation of predicates as truth functions and connectives as truth operators. Nothing in it suggests the more usual interpretation by logic practitioners of predicates as relations, that is, sets of tuples of individuals from the Universe of Discourse. In the following paragraphs we will stepwise transform a predicate definition in standard Horn logic syntax into a diagram which we believe better conveys its meaning. Then we will show the visual syntax and its fitness to represent automated deduction in it.

To define who the ancestors of a person are, we could write the following Horn clauses,

$$ancestor(X, Y) \longleftarrow person(X) \land parent(X, Y)$$
$$ancestor(X, Y) \longleftarrow person(X) \land parent(X, Z) \land ancestor(Z, Y)$$

in which as we said previously, the interpretation closest to the syntax is by considering *person*, *ancestor*, and *parent* as truth valued functions. However, if we want to suggest their interpretations as a set of tuples of individuals, then a better notation could be set notation using membership ($\in$) as unique predicate and write the previous expressions as follows:

$$\langle X, Y \rangle \in ancestor \longleftarrow X \in person \land \langle X, Y \rangle \in parent$$
$$\langle X, Y \rangle \in ancestor \longleftarrow X \in person \land \langle X, Z \rangle \in parent \land \langle Z, Y \rangle \in ancestor$$

The next step in order to make the syntax better convey the intended operational meaning of logical expressions could be to somehow make explicit the wanted directionality of some arguments as input or output. The importance of directionality was stressed for instance in [8]. In our example, both, *ancestor* and *parent*, are better understood as non-deterministic functions, which give for each individual the set of its ancestors and parents respectively. Then we can transform the previous expressions into the following ones,

$$Y \in ancestor(X) \longleftarrow X \in person \land Y \in parent(X)$$
$$Y \in ancestor(X) \longleftarrow X \in person \land Z \in parent(X) \land Y \in ancestor(Z)$$

where we use the conventional linear syntax for functional application. This new functional notation allows us to show syntactically two other structural features of the definition of relations: First, relation composition by successive applications, and second, logical implication by set inclusion. In the standard syntax, relation composition is expressed by means of the 'and' connective ($\wedge$), see for instance the composition of *parent* and *ancestor* in the second of the previous clauses. However, relation composition could be noted more directly by successive function applications. Then we can write the previous expressions as follows:

$$Y \in ancestor(X) \longleftarrow X \in person \ \wedge \ Y \in parent(X)$$
$$Y \in ancestor(X) \longleftarrow X \in person \ \wedge \ Y \in ancestor(parent(X))$$

Now we are ready to represent logical implication by means of set inclusion. In most Horn clauses we can distinguish a main implication, which connects the head of the clause with conditions in the body sharing the same output variable. For instance, the previous clauses can be written as follows,

$$(Y \in ancestor(X) \longleftarrow Y \in parent(X)) \longleftarrow X \in person$$
$$(Y \in ancestor(X) \longleftarrow Y \in ancestor(parent(X))) \longleftarrow X \in person$$

making explicit the main implication. Then it can be more directly represented by set inclusion ($\subseteq$), leaving the other implications as conditions. For instance, in our example instead of the implications, we represent the inclusion of *parent* into *ancestor* and of *ancestor_of_parent* into *ancestor* as follows:

$$parent(X) \subseteq ancestor(X) \longleftarrow X \in person$$
$$ancestor(parent(X)) \subseteq ancestor(X) \longleftarrow X \in person$$

Up to now we have transformed the initial Horn clauses into a new type of Horn clauses with two predicates only, inclusion ($\subseteq$) and membership ($\in$) between terms composed with predicates (relations) of the initial syntax. We call them *inclusional Horn clauses*.

Notice that the transformations, although explained by means of an example are completely general, and could be applied to any standard Horn clause definition of a predicate. However, the real interest in using this set notation for Horn clauses comes from its natural representation by means of diagrams. To do so we exploit two well known visual formalisms: Venn/Euler diagrams in order to emphasize set inclusion and membership, and directed acyclic graphs in order to describe structured terms. For instance, each one of the previous inclusional Horn clauses can be represented by a different diagram as shown in Figure 1(a).

Diagrams

The correspondence between an inclusional Horn clause and the corresponding diagram is as follows: Variables are represented as circles. Each n-ary relation

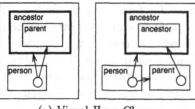
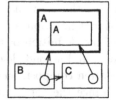

(a) Visual Horn Clauses   (b) Pattern Diagram of Recursion

Fig. 1.

(seen as an $(n-1)$-ary non-deterministic function whose result is the nth argument of the original relation) is represented by a square box labeled with the name of the relation, and is pointed by $n-1$ arrows coming from its arguments. The argument order of the relation may be disambiguated by labeling the arrows if necessary. The square box denotes the set of results corresponding to the nth argument of the n-ary relation not represented with an incoming arrow. The relation being defined is distinguished by drawing its box with thick lines, and it contains the box corresponding to the left-hand side of the inclusion in the inclusional Horn clause. The memberships in the body of the clause are represented by circles contained in boxes denoting the corresponding relations. Then each clause is represented by a set of graphical containments circumscribed by an unlabeled box to note the scope of the diagram.

We claim that the 'degree of homomorphism' or 'resemblance' [5] between a diagram and the relation it describes is higher than with linear formulas. Another structural feature of relation definition highlighted by diagrams is recursion. The structure of recursion is represented by the visual metaphor of a picture reproduced inside itself, as can be seen in the right diagram of Figure 1(a). Furthermore, 'pattern diagrams' labeled with variable symbols could be useful to record different patterns of recursion like the one in Figure 1(b). It is a simple recursive pattern common to many definitions, as for instance the one of ancestor given in Figure 1(a). A library of diagrammatic patterns recording different styles of description could become a pragmatic tool to support the use of logic. However, the utility of this diagrammatic language to a particular community of users can only be claimed after serious empirical testing, which still has to be done. Currently we are implementing a prototype system that will allow us to carry out this experimentation.

In the previous diagrams we only represented relation and variable symbols. In general we also need to represent terms built from function and constant symbols. These terms denoting individuals are represented by directed acyclic graphs (DAGs). Their nodes are either round boxes labeled by the name of a function (or of a constant) or circles. As usual, arrows in a DAG represent function application. The advantage of representing terms as DAGs compared to linear textual terms is well known. Figure 2 shows a more complex Horn clause in standard syntax, inclusional syntax, and the corresponding diagram. Notice that there is no need to name variables —we denote them simply by circles. The graph structure allows us to represent variable sharing or correference.

$$p(f(X), Z) \longleftarrow q(f(X), g(X, Y), Z) \land r(g(X, Y)) \land s(Y, g(X, Y))$$
$$\Downarrow$$
$$q(f(X), g(X, Y)) \subseteq p(f(X)) \longleftarrow g(X, Y) \in r \land g(X, Y) \in s(Y)$$
$$\Downarrow$$

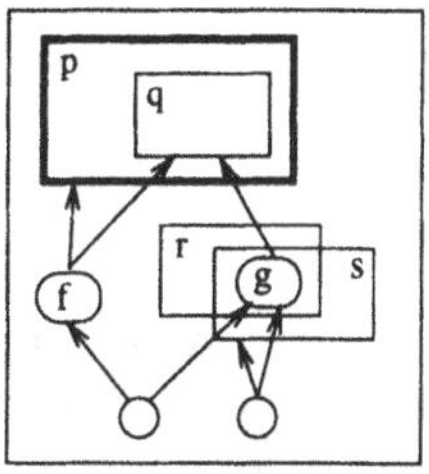

Fig. 2. From Horn Clause to Diagram

In general, each diagram has a special predicate —marked using thick lines to draw its box— which is the predicate we are defining (in Figure 2 it is predicate p), and which contains one or more graphical items, either a round box, a circle, or another square box free of other containments. All other square boxes (drawn with thin lines) may contain at most one graphical item, and these can only be round boxes or circles, never other square boxes. Nonetheless overlapping of different square boxes is allowed (e.g., in Figure 2, boxes r and s). A diagram defines a predicate by stating the subsets or elements of the graphical set associated to the predicate. Let us insist once more that diagrams can be viewed as conditional subset or membership assertions, where the conditions are the rest of membership relations of the diagram. A collection of the kind of diagrams of Figures 1 and 2 form a visual logic program (or visual logic database) like the one given in Figure 3.

The fully formal definitions of the syntax and semantics of visual programs are found in [17, 1, 18, 15]. There is also a simple algorithm to produce the inverse translation from a diagram to a standard Horn clause [16]. This allows a heterogeneous logic programming environment where both, textual and diagrammatic Horn clauses are used.

Our visual notation is close to Venn diagrams, but two important differences are worth noticing: First, the graphical sets of our diagrams do not have a unique physical existence, i.e. the same set may appear in various places of the diagram. Second, in a diagram only graphical containment information is relevant, the absence of graphical containment is not taken into account, which means that graphically non-overlapping sets may still have elements in common.

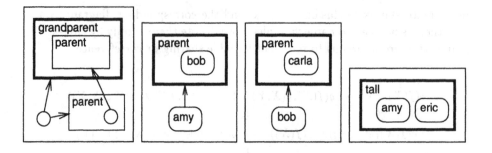

Fig. 3. A Visual Program

Visual inference

The conventional textual syntax not only is not indicative of the semantics of relations as sets, but tells nothing about the inference with Horn clauses. We believe diagrammatic syntax is more fit to make intuitive the resolution inference rule with Horn clauses, which corresponds directly to the transitivity of inclusions, given for free in the diagrammatic notation. This is called a 'free ride' by Shimojima [20]. For instance, the resolution inference rule applied to the two Horn clauses defining the *ancestor* relation considered above is made intuitive by the transitivity of box containment in the visual inference depicted in Figure 4. The inferred clause corresponds to the special case of ancestors which are grandparents. Here we are not interested in visual inferences in general which could become too complicated diagrammatically, but in query answering by means of diagram transformation.

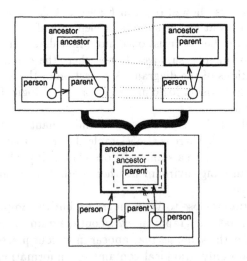

Fig. 4. Visual Inference

Query diagrams

We provide a way to ask questions about a visual program as the one of Figure 3 by means of 'query diagrams' (see below), and we define a diagram transformation mechanism that captures visual inferences operating on those query diagrams. In addition we explore and highlight the advantages of using a visual syntax for answering queries.

A *query diagram* is actually a standard diagram as described in Section 2, with the difference that no box is marked with thick lines, and no box is contained within another, since no predicate is being defined. Instead it expresses a set of existential memberships to be proved. Suppose, given the visual program of Figure 3, we want to know if there is some grandparent of a tall person. We will draw a query diagram as the one in Figure 5.

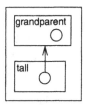

Fig. 5. Query Diagram: $\exists X, Y \; tall(X) \land grandparent(X, Y)$?

Queries are answered by transforming *query diagrams* into *answer diagrams* applying visual inference rules. The idea behind this diagram transformation is to complete the query with the trace of its proof, while instantiating circles (*i.e.* variables) by unification.

3 Query Answering by Diagram Transformation

As in conventional logic programming, we answer a query by exploring the definitions given in the program. We look for a definition diagram whose thick-line box has the same label as one of the boxes of the query diagram and whose overall structures unify, and merge it into the query diagram. This will become clear by looking at an example. Let's answer the simple query represented in Figure 5. Figure 6 shows the whole transformation tree which we now comment in detail:

Solving boxes by unification

The first transformation step of Figure 6 corresponds to the visual inference which, by unifying the *grandparent* box with its definition in Figure 3, transforms the query diagram by unifying the two circles —the argument of each

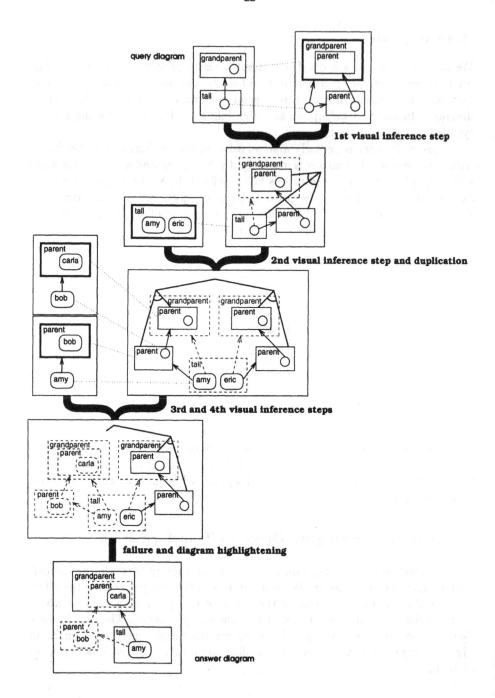

Fig. 6. Diagram Transformation

grandparent box—, and by adding to the query diagram all boxes of the definition of *grandparent*.

This inference step captures the idea that we are going to proof the existence
of an element in the *grandparent* box by means of its membership in the *parent*
box contained in it. Therefore we place the circle contained in the *grandparent*
box also within the *parent* box.

In general we merge a definition diagram into the query diagram by unification. A square box of the query diagram unifies with a thick-line box with
identical label of a definition diagram if all their arguments unify. Two arguments
unify whenever

- they are two circles (the result will be another circle),
- they are two round boxes with identical labels,
- they are a circle and a round box (the result is the round box).

In Figure 6 we have shown where unifications take place by drawing a dotted
line between unifying components of query and definition diagrams respectively.

Tracing the proof

At this point the first advantage of a visual syntax with respect to a textual
one arises. Note that the resulting query diagram reflects both the new inferred
membership of the goal variable into the *parent* box and the old one into the
grandparent box. This way we can keep track of the original query and its proof
during subsequent diagram transformations. The transitivity of the membership
relation with respect to subset inclusion is clearly visualized by the diagram:
The circle contained in the parent box is obviously also within the *grandparent*
box! This captures directly a basic kind of computational logic reasoning.

Keeping track of the original query forces us to distinguish goals that still
need to be solved from the already solved ones. That is why we have drawn
the solved *grandparent* box with dashed lines. This is how we represent solved
goals. Boxes representing goals still to be solved —we call them *active boxes*—
remain drawn by solid lines.

Textual equivalent of visual inference rules

The diagram transformation process resembles closely the refutation of negated
queries by means of a standard, but visual, resolution-based inference mechanism. Since our syntax is based on graphical containment between graphical
items, visual programs are actually Horn theories involving subset relations or
memberships (recall the discussion of Section 2). Levy and Agustí noticed that
rewrite techniques can be applied to the deduction with inclusions in a similar way they have been used for the deduction with equality relations [11, 12].
Bachmair and Ganzinger generalized these techniques by means of their *ordered
chaining calculus for transitive relations* within the context of resolution-based
theorem proving [3]. The operational behavior of visual query answering in our
language is rooted on their work.

Therefore, the visual inference applied so far actually corresponds to the *negative chaining* inference of the above mentioned chaining calculus, where conditional membership or subset statements are expressed as logically equivalent inclusional Horn clauses:

$$\text{(negative chaining)} \quad \frac{s \notin t \quad u \subseteq v \ \vee \ C}{\sigma(s) \notin \sigma(u) \ \vee \ \sigma(C)}$$

where σ is the most general unifier of t and v. C is the body of the Horn clause.

The other basic visual inference rule we are going to use in subsequent diagram transformations is actually *resolution*:

$$\text{(resolution)} \quad \frac{s \notin t \quad u \in v \ \vee \ C}{\sigma(C)}$$

where σ is the most general unifier of s and u, and t and v, respectively.

Simultaneous representation of several alternatives

During the second transformation step of Figure 6 we choose to solve the *tall* box, which is unified with its definition in Figure 3[1]. Since in this definition diagram *two* graphical items are contained in its thick-line box, we have two alternatives to instantiate the circle within *tall*, either by round box *amy* or *eric*.

A new additional advantage of our visual syntax is that it easily allows us to represent both alternatives seen previously (*amy* and *eric*) in one single diagram (see the result of the second visual inference step of Figure 6). Keeping several alternatives simultaneously is actually 'multiply instantiating' the circle within *tall* with *amy* and *eric*. Whenever such a multiple instantiation occurs we will have to duplicate all those boxes that also contained or had as arguments the variable (or term containing the variable) where the multiple instantiation has occurred. And again when we duplicate these boxes we might have to duplicate other boxes that share variables with them. A formal definition of this duplication operation is outside the scope of this paper but can be seen in [15].

AND-OR annotation tree

Different alternatives due to multiple instantiation introduce disjunction in the query, and consequently we need to make explicit the logical relations between active boxes of the query diagram. In our case both *parent* boxes and the *tall* box need to be solved — they form a *conjunction*. But their duplications are different alternatives and therefore form a *disjunction*. It is well known in the diagrammatic reasoning community that disjunction is a representationally 'thin'

---

[1] In the current state of our research we do not consider specific deduction strategies and therefore do not consider the possible orders in which active boxes may be solved.

concept, a concept that is difficult to capture diagrammatically [5]. We choose an *AND-OR annotation tree* for this purpose, where the active boxes of the query diagram are its leaves.

Unless multiple instantiation occurs, all active boxes form a conjunction: we need to solve them all in order to succeed with the query diagram transformation. We will therefore connect them all to an AND-node of our annotation tree (see the transformed query diagram of Figure 6 after the first visual inference step). When a visual inference step is performed we will connect all the new boxes introduced from merging the definition diagram into the query diagram to the same AND-node where the solving box was attached. But, as soon as a multiple instantiation of a circle occurs, and some fragment of the query diagram has to be duplicated to introduce disjunction of different alternatives, we will need to create an OR-node and connect to it all the duplicated fragments of the AND-OR tree to this OR-node (see the transformed query diagram of Figure 6 after the second visual inference step).

Success and failure

Further transformation steps in our example of Figure 6 do not add new boxes to the query diagram, but solve the *parent* boxes by applying visual inferences that unify them with their definitions given in the visual program of Figure 3.

In our example during the third and fourth visual inference steps we are able to solve all the active boxes attached to the AND-node of the left OR-branch (see Figure 6). Every time a box is solved and marked as solved its branch is deleted, since only active boxes are leaves of the annotation tree. In the resulting query diagram only the *parent* boxes of the right OR-branch remain active (see Figure 6). Unfortunately we cannot solve this branch: One of its AND-branches fails, because we do not dispose of a unifying definition diagram for finding a parent of *eric*. The box fails and has to be erased from the diagram. Since the box was attached to an AND-node, the whole node fails and all other boxes attached to the same AND-node are erased, too (see the transformed query diagram of Figure 6 after the failure). In general not only the active boxes, but of course also all those previously solved boxes that once were active boxes of that AND-node will have to be erased. In our example the failing AND-node was attached to an OR-node, so that, at the end, this failure doesn't affect the solvability of the whole query.

In general we will deal with disjunction of different alternatives within a single diagram and therefore we need to distinguish between success or failure in OR-nodes from success or failure in AND-nodes of the annotation tree, and carefully record all these situations. Since, we have chosen to show diagrammatically only how active boxes are logically related (by means of the AND-OR tree), we need to associate somehow to the AND-node the solved boxes that once were attached to it, in case this node fails and the boxes need to be erased. For the same reason, whenever a whole node succeeds, we need to copy its associated solved boxes to its ancestor node in the tree. In addition, when a box attached to an OR-node has been solved then the OR-node is 'marked' (though not visually) so that if the other branches do not succeed the node will nonetheless succeed.

Finally, if the root node fails, the whole diagram fails, *i.e.* the query cannot be answered.

Answer diagram

The answer we have obtained to the original query is that Carla is a grandparent of Amy, who is tall. In order to make the answer more readable we may highlight the boxes of the original query diagram given in Figure 5, by drawing them with solid lines, though they are not active boxes anymore (see Figure 6). We call such a diagram an *answer diagram*: The original query diagram plus a trace of its proof.

Features of visual with respect to textual query answering

Although the rules are formally based on the chaining calculus, the visual inference mechanism is intrinsically different. Visual queries differ from textual ones, since they involve different kinds of query transformations, providing a new and interesting framework for exploring and developing visual inference systems. The main difference with regard to a conventional calculus is that in our diagrams we do not erase boxes (predicates) that have already been refuted, because we want to keep track of the trace of the proof. In a standard resolution process, every time we solve a goal it disappears from the query, finishing the inference process when the query is empty. For this reason in our queries we need to distinguish solved from unsolved goals by means of dashed and solid lines respectively. Another difference is when we are applying diagrams whose thick-line boxes contain more than one graphical item, and therefore various alternatives for solving a goal arise. As shown in this section, in this case we can represent all alternatives in one single query diagram by duplicating parts of it, and annotating it with an AND-OR annotation tree.

4 Related Work

The starting point of our research in the visual languages area was diagrammatic reasoning as presented by Jon Barwise's group (see [4, 2]). However our goal differs from those of the diagrammatic reasoning community. Our use of Venn/Euler diagrams is centered on its computational aspects. We want to focus on simple diagrams with a clear computational interpretation, avoiding as many logical symbols as possible. There exist other visual declarative programming languages like CUBE [14], VEX [7] and SPARCL [23], but none of them uses sets, Venn/Euler diagrams, and graphical containment as its foundations. In the Database field, most visual formalisms are applied to what is known as visual query languages and we do not know of any other formal visual language devoted to deduction in deductive databases. Visual Query languages are languages designed to be similar to the content of the database. An interesting example is NQS [10], a graphical system for models with binary relation types.

The graphical schemes representing conceptual models in [6], do not attempt a formal and systematic visual representation of deduction. On the other hand, the existential graphs of Charles S. Peirce (see [9, 19]), a diagrammatic reasoning system for full first-order predicate logic, are of great interest and —although bared on different intuitions— they are a source of inspiration of our research; together with John Sowa's *conceptual graphs* (see [21, 22]) modeled after Peirce diagrammatic approaches to predicate logic.

5 Conclusions and Future Work

In this paper we have presented the current state of our research on a visual logical language, putting special emphasis on its visual inference system for answering visually posed queries by means of diagram transformation. In [17, 1] we first designed a formal logic programming language and more recently [18] we showed that it was possible to derive a fully visual operational semantics for it.

The operational semantics presented in [18] was incomplete and did not take into account the difficulties arising when keeping track, within a diagram, of the proof that is built while solving a query, and, when we represent within a unique diagram the several different alternatives to answer a query. This paper has gone a little bit further in exploring these features, and we are currently working in completely formalizing the visual inference system presented here, together with its additional features [15].

Immediate work is going to focus on proving the completeness of the inference system presented in this paper —soundness is obvious—, and enhancing it in order to cope with other features of the visual language like predicate composition. We would also like to explore the use of other programming constructions, like for instance partitioning constraints [23] or richer element representations, to improve the expressive power of the language. Other work we contemplate is to perform larger experimentation and to develop a specific programming methodology for this visual logic programming language.

Finally, we are also interested in studying how the use of a visual syntax changes the formal properties of the operational semantics. We want to know if there are other advantages —apart from the obvious visual ones— of using visual syntax in declarative programming.

Acknowledgments

We are grateful to Dave Robertson with whom we initiated this work on visual logic programming, and to Hendrik Decker for his helpful comments on previous versions of this paper.

References

1. J. Agustí, J. Puigsegur, and D. Robertson. A visual syntax for logic and logic programming. *Journal of Visual Languages and Computation*, 1998. To be published.
2. G. Allwein and J. Barwise, editors. *Logical Reasoning with Diagrams*. Oxford University Press, 1996.
3. L. Bachmair and H. Ganzinger. Rewrite techniques for transitive relations. In *9th Annual IEEE Symposium on Logic in Computer Science*, pages 384–393, 1994.
4. J. Barwise and J. Etchemendy. *Hyperproof.* CSLI Publications, 1993.
5. J. Barwise and E. Hammer. Diagrams and the concept of logical system. In *Logical Reasoning with Diagrams*, chapter III, pages 49–78. Oxford University Press, 1996.
6. M. Borman, J. A. Bubenko, P. Johannensson, and B. Wangler. *Conceptual Modelling.* Prentice Hall, 1997.
7. W. Citrin, R. Hall, and B. Zorn. Programming with visual expressions. In *Proc. of the 11th IEEE Symposium on Visual Languages*. IEEE Computer Press, 1995.
8. Y. Deville. *Logic Programming.* Addison Wesley, 1990.
9. E. M. Hammer. *Logic and Visual Information.* CSLI Publications & FoLLI, 1995.
10. H. J. Klein and D. Krämer. NQS – a graphical query system for data models with binary relationship types. In S. Spaccapietra and R. Jain, editors, *Proc. of the 3rd IFIP 2.6 Working Conference on Visual Database*, 1995.
11. J. Levy and J. Agustí. Bi-rewriting, a term rewriting technique for monotonic order relations. In C. Kirchner, editor, *Rewriting Techniques and Applications*, LNCS 690, pages 17–31. Springer, 1993.
12. J. Levy and J. Agustí. Bi-rewrite systems. *Journal of Symbolic Computation*, 22:1–36, 1996.
13. D. A. McAllester and R. Givan. Natural language syntax and first-order inference. *Artificial Intelligence*, 56:1–20, 1992.
14. M. A. Najork. Programming in three dimensions. *Journal of Visual Languages and Computation*, 7:219–242, 1996.
15. J. Puigsegur and J. Agustí. Towards visual declarative programming. Research report, Institut d'Investigació en Intel·ligència Artificial (CSIC), 1998.
16. J. Puigsegur, J. Agustí, and J. A. Pastor. Towards visual schemas in deductive databases. Research report, Dep. LSI, Universitat Politècnica de Catalunya, 1998.
17. J. Puigsegur, J. Agustí, and D. Robertson. A visual logic programming language. In *12th Annual IEEE Symposium on Visual Languages*. IEEE Computer Society Press, 1996.
18. J. Puigsegur, W. M. Schorlemmer, and J. Agustí. From queries to answers in visual logic programming. In *13th Annual IEEE Symposium on Visual Languages*. IEEE Computer Society Press, 1997.
19. D. D. Roberts. *The Existential Graphs of Charles S. Peirce.* Mouton and Co., 1973.
20. A. Shimojima. Operational constraints in diagrammatic reasoning. In *Logical Reasoning with Diagrams*, chapter II, pages 27–48. Oxford University Press, 1996.
21. J. F. Sowa. Conceptual graphs. *Information Processing in Mind and Machine*, 1984.
22. J. F. Sowa. Relating diagrams to logic. In G. W. Mineau, B. Moulin, and J. F. Sowa, editors, *Conceptual Graphs for Knowledge Representation, Proc. of the First Int. Conf. on Conceptual Structures, ICCS'93*, LNAI 699. Springer, 1993.
23. L. Spratt and A. Ambler. A visual logic programming language based on sets and partitioning constraints. In *Proc. of the 9th IEEE Symposium on Visual Languages*. IEEE Computer Press, 1993.

Query Subsumption

Mohammad Al-Qasem , S. Misbah Deen

Department of Computer Science, University of Keele, Keele, Staffs, ST5 5BG, UK
e-mail: {mohammad, deen}@cs.keele.ac.uk

Abstract. Subsumption between queries provides valuable information, for example in an interoperability environment when there is a need to convert queries over different systems especially when the query conversion is very expensive or unavailable. In this paper we develop algorithms to test query subsumption as well as an algorithm to write filter queries. Our algorithms cover both conjunctive and disjunctive queries. The algorithm deals with function free queries and it does not take integrity constraints into account.

1 Introduction

Subsumption checking is very important in many areas such as schema integration, terminology management, query optimisation, reuse of materialised views, cooperative question-answering and retrieval systems. However, there is no general solution covering all aspects in different areas, or at least it is computationally intractable.

In this paper we will not discuss subsumption of concepts to determine whether a term is more general than another [12]. Also we will not talk about subsumption of relationships over a schema [3] and [8]. Our focus in this paper is to tackle the problem of query subsumption (containment problem). In short the problem is : From the definition of two queries Q_i and Q_j can we know if all answers to Q_j are also included in the answers to Q_i for all possible states.

Our algorithm covers both conjunctive queries as well as disjunctive queries. The algorithm will decide if a query can be subsumed from another query or not. If yes then the algorithm will build a query filter if there is any. The limitations of our algorithm will be discussed later in this paper.

Query subsumption is a very important technique in many situations. In the multi-system environment, query subsumption becomes a vital technique to answer some queries which are unanswerable without subsumption. For example a system with limited query facilities, in which the direct answer of some queries does not exist, so another query (which subsumed the wanted one) can be used instead. This can be seen in systems based on Boolean queries [7]. In other cases, some systems provide a very limited set of queries which can be answered (parameterised query templates), and for any query to be sent to that system it has to be semantically equal to at least one of the provided query templates or at least can be then subsumed from one of them [4] [13].

Subsumption is also important in an interoperability environment when there is a need to convert queries over different systems especially when the query conversion is very expensive or unavailable. In these cases subsumption can be used to reduce the conversion mechanisms by using one of the already converted queries.

SQL dominates relational database query languages and most database query languages are similar to SQL with some differences such as LOREL (Lightweight Object REpository Language) which is used in TSIMMIS project [10] and OEM-QL (Object Exchange Model Query Language) which adapts existing SQL-like languages for the Object-Oriented model to OEM. We will use COAL (Co-Operating Agent Language) which is similar to SQL in its concept but it is a very flexible language for multi-agent systems (See section 1.2 for the details).

The organisation of this paper is as follows : related work is next then COAL language is discussed in the end of this section. Notations that we will use and the limitations of our algorithm are presented in section 2. Section 3 describes the containment checking between predicates. The algorithm for checking subsumption between two queries is described in section 4. Section 5 deals with the building of the filter query, if any is existed. Finally, Section 6 is the conclusion and further work.

1.1 Related work

The subsumption (containment) problem has been studied by many researchers. Ullman [16] has produced the QinP (Query in Program) algorithm to determine the containment between a conjunctive query and a datalog program. His algorithm is very abstract and deals with a datalog program and a conjunctive query. Chan [5] has proposed an algorithm that handles negation in conjunctive queries in the context of restricted object based data and query models only. But Staudt and Thadden [15] have proposed an algorithm that covers the negation and the exploitation of semantic knowledge. Hariuarayon and Gupta [11] have proposed an algorithm for deciding efficiently when a tuple subsumes another tuple for queries that use arbitrary mathematical functions.

The TSIMMIS project [4] [13] [14] uses an algorithm to check the subsumption between a description D as a datalog program and a query Q. In [13] they have extended Ullman's QinP algorithm to check if there is a filter query to the existing query in order to return the exact answer without any additional information. Because of the goals of their project, they do the checking with query templates, i.e. parameterised queries. Subsumption has also been used in Boolean queries in digital libraries, but with a query language with very limited features [6] [7].

1.2 Language facility

Because this work is a part of a large project in the development of an ontology model for legacy systems using an agent based approach [1] we need a good language to suit our purpose; even though our algorithm can be modified for any other language.

The language that we will use is called COAL (Co-Operating Agent Language). COAL is currently under development in the DAKE Centre, as an extension of an earlier language DEAL which provided a relational facility, fortified with some Prolog like predicates. COAL supports nested relations as a superset of normalised relations and lists, backed by extended relational operations, first-order deduction, recursive functions, parameterised macros, triggers and extensibility [9].

COAL is a very flexible language and one of its advantages is the concept of link-elements. In COAL, predicates for every relation are written between two brackets [ ]. In the case of a predicate concerning attributes from two relations we use a link-element.

COAL Syntax :

   ? [A1, A2 ...]
    : R1 [tuple-predicates],
     R2 [tuple-predicates],
     Sys [predicates]

? implies Retrieve (equivalently Select of SQL)
: implies the Where predicate.
[...] after ? includes output attribute list. If empty output list, is interpreted all the attributes.
[...] after : and thereafter include tuple predicates related to relation which its name preceding the brackets. Or system predicates when Sys. Precede the brackets. Predicates are separated by :

   (,) for logical AND.   (|) for logical OR.   (~) for logical NOT.

Example. From now on we will use the following relations to illustrate examples in this paper. These relations are :

   Pi - pilot   (p-no, empl-no ,months, tel-no, hours, flights, salary....)
   Em - empl (empl-no, name, city, ...)
   Pa - pilot-aircraft (p-no, aircraft-type, hours, flights, ...)
   Pb - pilot-bonus (p-no, bonus)
   Ai - Aircraft (model, no-engine, size, ...)

Example :

A query in COAL :   The equivalence SQL query :
   ? [Pi.p-no, name, X3]   SELECT Pi.p-no, name, salary
   : Pi [p-no = X2, salary = X3],   FROM Pi, Em
    Em [p-no = X2]   WHERE Pi.p-no = Em.p-no

2 Notations and Limitations

Comparison between two queries written in COAL or any other high level query language, is very difficult. Therefore we need to transform queries to another form which can be dealt with easily. So, first we classify predicates and transform COAL queries to a new formalism, then two functions related to link-elements will be defined.

2.1 Predicates : Classification, Limitations and Functions

Classification. Predicates are classify as follow: β be a general predicate, α is an atomic predicate, ω is a disjunction predicate and σ is a conjunction predicate.

a. Atomic predicate (α) : An atomic predicate (α) is a single predicate with a variable on one side, a comparison operator followed by another variable or a value. From now on by variable we mean an attribute of a relation and by value we mean a real value or a variable equal to one value.

Each α can be in one of the following formats :

    1. α type #1 is a predicate with a variable or a link-element on the left hand side, and a value on the right hand side.

    2. α type #2 is a predicate with two variables or two link-elements.

    3. α type #3 is predicate with a variable and a link-element (joining two or more relations).

b. Disjunction predicate (ω). In this paper we represent each ω by a set of (αs) and (σs); (see next paragraph for a description of σ). ω is in the following format:

$$\omega \equiv (\alpha_1 \vee .. \vee \alpha_i, \vee .. \vee \alpha_n \vee \sigma_1 \vee .. \vee \sigma_i \vee .. \vee \sigma_m)$$

c. Conjunction predicate (σ). In this paper we represent each σ by a set of (αs) and (ωs). σ is in the following format:

$$\sigma \equiv (\alpha_1 \wedge .. \wedge \alpha_i \wedge .. \wedge \alpha_n \wedge \omega_1 \wedge .. \wedge \omega_i \wedge .. \wedge \omega_m)$$

Limitations. As a limitation of our algorithm we will deal only with atomic attributes which means that all variables are of single values.

Functions. From the above classification it is obvious that α is basic to any predicate. So we define the following functions related to αs :

$T(\alpha)$: returns the type of the α which can be #1, #2 or #3.

$VL(\alpha)$: returns the variable on the left hand side of the α.

$VR(\alpha)$: returns the variable on the right hand side of α (only α of type #2 and #3).

$O(\alpha)$: returns the operator of the α.

$V(\alpha)$: returns the value on the right hand side of the α (only α of type #1).

     In addition we need a function to check if two βs are literally identical or not.

$E(\beta_1, \beta_2)$: returns true if both β_1 and β_2 are literally identical and returns false otherwise.

Examples :

    1. $\alpha \equiv$ (flights > hours) $\Rightarrow T(\alpha) = 2$

    2. $\alpha \equiv$ (flights > hours) $\Rightarrow VL(\alpha) = $ flights

    3. $\alpha \equiv$ (flights > hours) $\Rightarrow O(\alpha) = $ ">"

    4. $\beta_1 \equiv$ (flights > hours) and $\beta_2 \equiv$ (flights $\geq$ hours) $\Rightarrow E(\beta_1, \beta_2) = $ False.

2.2 Formalism of Queries in COAL

In this section we will explain the new formalism, but first we will explain some restrictions of writing COAL queries.

Rewriting COAL Queries. We will assume that we have a program to rewrite users' queries in COAL to follow the following restrictions (the new query is in COAL too) :

1. For αs, if there is a value it is always on the right hand side of the predicate. And if there is a link-element and an attribute, the link-element must be on the right hand side of the predicate.

Examples : $\alpha \equiv (2000 < \text{empl-no})$ becomes $\alpha \equiv \text{empl-no} > 2000$

$\alpha \equiv (X1 = \text{empl-no})$ becomes $\alpha \equiv (\text{empl-no} = X1)$

2. Link-elements can not be used to rename variables. So a link-element can not be used in one relation only.

Example : $Q \equiv ? [\text{P-no}, X1]$ 　　　　　　　becomes $Q \equiv ? [\text{P-no}, \text{name}]$

　　　　　 : E [P-no > 2000, name = X1] 　　　　　　: E [P-no > 2000]

3. Once an attribute is equal to a link-element, then the link-element is used instead of that attribute. For example :

Pi [empl-no=X1, empl-no $\geq$ 2100] 　　　becomes 　Pi [empl-no = X1, X1 $\geq$ 2100]

4. Remove the negation. To simplify predicate checking, every predicate with negation is replaced by an equivalent predicate without negation :

$\neg (a = b)$ ≡ $a \neq b$, 　　$\neg (a \neq b)$ ≡ $a = b$, 　　$\neg (a > b)$ ≡ $a \leq b$

$\neg (a \geq b)$ ≡ $a < b$, 　　$\neg (a < b)$ ≡ $a \geq b$, 　　$\neg (a \leq b)$ ≡ $a > b$

Where a and b can be attributes, link-elements, variables or values.

The equivalent of $\neg \omega \equiv \neg (\beta_1 \vee \beta_2 \vee .. \beta_n) \equiv (\neg \beta_1 \wedge \neg \beta_2 \wedge .. \wedge \neg \beta_n) \equiv \sigma$

The equivalent of $\neg \sigma \equiv \neg (\beta_1 \wedge \beta_2 .. \wedge \beta_n) \equiv (\neg \beta_1 \vee \neg \beta_2 \vee .. \vee \neg \beta_n) \equiv \omega$

Examples :

　$\beta \equiv \text{Pi} [\sim (\text{empl-no} \geq 2100)]$ 　becomes $\beta \equiv \text{Pi} [\text{empl-no} < 2100]$

　$\beta \equiv \text{Em} [\sim (X1 > 2100 \,|\, X2 = 4)]$ 　becomes $\beta \equiv \text{Em} [(X1 \leq 2100 , X2 <> 4)]$

　$\beta \equiv \text{Em} [\sim (X1 \leq 2100 , X2 > 4)]$ 　becomes $\beta \equiv \text{Em} [(X1 > 2100 \,|\, X2 \leq 4)]$

The New Formalism of COAL Queries. Each COAL query transforms to four basic functions in addition to two functions for each link-element used by the query. The result of each function is a set, the following abbreviations will be used in the formalism definition: Q for a query, R for a relation, X for a link-element.

The functions are :

1. Rel(Q)　　: returns all relations used by Q.

2. Att(Q)　　: returns all attributes and link-elements selected by Q.

3. P(Q)　　　: returns all predicates in all relations in Q excluding the join predicate.

4. Link(Q)　: returns all link-elements used in Q.

5. E(X,Q)　　: returns all attributes from all relations in Q where X=Attr$_i$.

6. PL(X, Q)　: returns all αs (all of them from type #3) concerning X in Q excluding those in the ωs.

From now on, we will deal only with queries in the above format. Example of query transformation can be seen in [2].

2.3 Link-elements and Functions that Deal With them

Link-elements are very important and they can be replaced by their corresponding attributes without affecting the predicate. For example if (Attr1=X1) and (X1>30) then (Attr1>30) is equivalent to (X1>30).

Unlike attributes, link-elements are query dependent. For example, attribute R1.Attr1 in Q_1 is the same as R1.Attr1 in Q_2, but X2 in Q_1 is different from X2 in Q_2; for this reason we need some functions to deal with the conversion between link-elements and attributes in the same query as well as in different queries. These functions are :

Conv1(Set, Q). Converts every link-element in Set (set of αs) to its equivalent attributes in the same query Q.

Conv2(β, Q_i, Q_j). Converts all attributes and link-elements in β in Q_i to their corresponding link-elements in Q_j. In the case of a link-element equal to one attribute without a corresponding link-element in Q_j, this function converts that link-element to its attribute in Q_i.

3 Check Subsumption (Containment) between Predicates

In order to check subsumption between queries, we need first to check subsumption, containment, between predicates. Assume both β_1 and β_2 concern attributes in R1, R2 and R3, β_1 contains β_2, if all tuples satisfy β_2 are also satisfy β_1 regardless the values of the tuples. The algorithm for the containment checking is dependent on the type of the predicates. Follow is the algorithms for the needed cases. Each algorithm represented by a function of two input arguments, it returns true if the first β contains the second β, and returns false otherwise.

3.1 The Containment Between two αs. Contain1(α_1, α_2)

Contain1(α_1, α_2) returns true if both α_1 and α_2 are from the same type, they deal with the same variables and α_1 contains α_2. For simplicity we divide this checking into three cases; two αs of type #1 (Contain1a) (see the algorithm below), two αs of type #2 (Contain1b) and two αs of type #3 (Contain1c) (the algorithm of the last two cases can be found in [2]). The containment between two αs from different types returns false.

$$
\begin{aligned}
\textbf{Contain1}(\alpha_1, \alpha_2) \Leftrightarrow \\
\textsc{t}(\alpha_1) = \textsc{t}(\alpha_2) \quad \wedge \quad (\ (\ \textsc{t}(\alpha_1) = 1 \wedge \text{Contain1a}(\alpha_1, \alpha_2) \ ) \\
\vee \ (\ \textsc{t}(\alpha_1) = 2 \wedge \text{Contain1b}(\alpha_1, \alpha_2) \ ) \\
\vee \ (\ \textsc{t}(\alpha_1) = 3 \wedge \text{Contain1c}(\alpha_1, \alpha_2) \ ) \ )
\end{aligned}
$$

Contain1a $(\alpha_1, \alpha_2) \Leftrightarrow$

  $VL(\alpha_1) = VL(\alpha_2)$

  $\wedge \quad E(\alpha_1, \alpha_2)$

  $\vee \quad (O(\alpha_1) = "\neq" \wedge \quad (\ (O(\alpha_2) = "=" \wedge V(\alpha_2) <> V(\alpha_1))$

  $\vee (O(\alpha_2) = ">" \wedge V(\alpha_2) \geq V(\alpha_1))$

  $\vee (O(\alpha_2) = "\geq" \wedge V(\alpha_2) > V(\alpha_1))$

  $\vee (O(\alpha_2) = "<" \wedge V(\alpha_2) \leq V(\alpha_1))$

  $\vee (O(\alpha_2) = "\leq" \wedge V(\alpha_2) < V(\alpha_1))))$

  $\vee \quad (O(\alpha_1) = ">" \wedge V(\alpha_2) > V(\alpha_1)$

  $\wedge (O(\alpha_2) = "=" \vee O(\alpha_2) = ">" \vee O(\alpha_2) = "\geq"))$

  $\vee \quad (O(\alpha_1) = "\geq" \wedge V(\alpha_2) \geq V(\alpha_1)$

  $\wedge (O(\alpha_2) = "=" \vee O(\alpha_2) = ">" \vee O(\alpha_2) = "\geq"))$

  $\vee \quad (O(\alpha_1) = "<" \wedge V(\alpha_2) < V(\alpha_1)$

  $\wedge (O(\alpha_2) = "=" \vee O(\alpha_2) = "<" \vee O(\alpha_2) = "\leq"))$

  $\vee \quad (O(\alpha_1) = "\leq" \wedge V(\alpha_2) \leq V(\alpha_1)$

  $\wedge (O(\alpha_2) = "=" \vee O(\alpha_2) = "<" \vee O(\alpha_2) = "\leq"))$

3.2 Check the Containment between two βs (except two αs).

For α_1 to contain ω_1, all βs in ω_1 must be contained in α_1. For ω_1 to contain α_1, at least one predicate in ω_1 must contain α_1. For α_1 to contain σ_1, at least one predicate in σ_1 must be contained in α_1. For σ_1 to contain α_1, every predicate in σ_1 must contain α_1. For ω_1 to contain ω_2, they must be equal or every predicate in ω_2 must be contained in at least one predicate in ω_1. Finally for σ_1 to contain σ_2, they must be equal or every predicate in σ_1 must contain at least one predicate in σ_2.

Contain2 $(\alpha_1, \omega_1) \Leftrightarrow$

  $\forall \alpha_2 \ (\alpha_2 \in \omega_1) \Rightarrow \text{Contain1}(\alpha_1, \alpha_2) \wedge \forall \sigma_1 \ (\sigma_1 \subseteq \omega_1) \Rightarrow \text{Contain4}(\alpha_1, \sigma_1)$

Contain3 $(\omega_1, \alpha_1) \Leftrightarrow$

  $\exists \alpha_2 \ (\alpha_2 \in \omega_1) \wedge \text{Contain1}(\alpha_2, \alpha_1) \vee \exists \sigma_1 \ (\sigma_1 \subseteq \omega_1) \wedge \text{Contain5}(\sigma_1, \alpha_1)$

Contain4 $(\alpha_1, \sigma_1) \Leftrightarrow$

  $\exists \alpha_2 \ (\alpha_2 \in \sigma_1) \wedge \text{Contain1}(\alpha_1, \alpha_2) \vee \exists \omega_1 \ (\omega_1 \subseteq \sigma_1) \wedge \text{Contain2}(\alpha_1, \omega_1)$

Contain5 $(\sigma_1, \alpha_1) \Leftrightarrow$

  $\forall \alpha_2 \ (\alpha_2 \in \sigma_1) \Rightarrow \text{Contain1}(\alpha_2, \alpha_1) \wedge \forall \omega_1 \ (\omega_1 \subseteq \sigma_1) \Rightarrow \text{Contain3}(\omega_1, \alpha_1)$

Contain6 $(\omega_1, \omega_2) \Leftrightarrow$

  $E(\omega_1, \omega_2) \vee (\ \forall \alpha_1 \ (\alpha_1 \in \omega_2) \Rightarrow \text{Contain3}(\omega_1, \alpha_1)$

  $\wedge \ \forall \sigma_2 \ (\sigma_2 \subseteq \omega_2)$

  $\Rightarrow \exists \alpha_3 \ (\alpha_3 \in \omega_1) \wedge \text{Contain4}(\alpha_3, \sigma_2) \vee \exists \sigma_3 \ (\sigma_3 \subseteq \omega_1) \wedge \text{Contain7}(\sigma_3, \sigma_2))$

Contain7 $(\sigma_1, \sigma_2) \Leftrightarrow$

  $E(\sigma_1, \sigma_2) \vee (\ \forall \alpha_1 (\alpha_1 \in \sigma_1) \ \Rightarrow \text{Contain4}(\alpha_1, \sigma_2)$

  $\wedge \forall \omega_2 \ \ (\omega_2 \subseteq \sigma_1)$

  $\Rightarrow \exists \alpha_3 \ (\alpha_3 \in \sigma_2) \wedge \text{Contain3}(\omega_2, \alpha_3) \vee \exists \omega_3 \ (\omega_3 \subseteq \sigma_2) \wedge \text{Contain6}(\omega_2, \omega_3))$

3.3 Examples.

$\alpha_1 \equiv$ hours $> 10, \alpha_2 \equiv$ hours > 20	$\Rightarrow$ Contain1a$(\alpha_1, \alpha_2) =$ T.
$\alpha_1 \equiv$ hours $\geq$ flights, $\alpha_2 \equiv$ hours $<$ flights	$\Rightarrow$ Contain1b$(\alpha_1, \alpha_2) =$ F.
$\alpha_1 \equiv$ p-no $\geq$ X1, $\alpha_2 \equiv$ p-no $=$ X2	$\Rightarrow$ Contain1c$(\alpha_1, \alpha_2) =$ T.
$\alpha_1 \equiv$ hours > 10, $\omega_1 \equiv$ (hours $= 3 \vee$ hours > 20)	$\Rightarrow$ Contain2 $(\alpha_1, \omega_1) =$ F.
$\omega_1 \equiv$(hours$\geq$flights$\vee$hours$=3\vee$hours>20), $\alpha_1 \equiv$ hours$=$flights	$\Rightarrow$ Contain3 $(\omega_1, \alpha_1) =$ T.

$\alpha_1 \equiv$ flights>35, $\sigma_1 \equiv$(hours$>30\wedge$ (flights$=31\vee$ flights>40)) $\Rightarrow$ Contain4 $(\alpha_1, \sigma_1) =$ F.

$\sigma_1 \equiv$ (hours $> 5\wedge$ hours < 30), $\alpha_1 \equiv$ hours $= 10$ $\Rightarrow$ Contain5$(\sigma_1, \alpha_1) =$ T.
$\omega_1 \equiv$(hours$\geq$flights$\vee$ hours$=3\vee$ hours$>20\vee$ flights>8),

$\omega_2 \equiv$ (hours$=$flights $\vee$ hours$=5$ $\vee$ hours > 30) $\Rightarrow$ Contain6$(\omega_1, \omega_2) =$ F.

$\sigma_1 \equiv$(flights$>20 \wedge$ hours>40), $\sigma_2 \equiv$ (flights$>30 \wedge$hours>60) $\Rightarrow$ Contain7$(\sigma_1, \sigma_2) =$ T.

4 An Algorithm to Check Subsumption Between Two Queries

For two queries, Q_i and Q_j, Q_i subsumes Q_j if A_j, the answer of Q_j, is contained in A_i, the answer of Q_i, in all database states. So, the predicates of Q_i must subsume the predicates of Q_j. In another word, for Q_i to subsume Q_j, for every predicate in Q_i there must be a predicate in Q_j where the predicate in Q_i contains the predicate in Q_j. The algorithm should take link-elements into account when checking Q_i's predicates. From the new formalism of our query (see section 2.2) we need to check for :
Every β in $P(Q_i)$) and all α in $PL(X_n, Q_i)$). So we check normal predicates in Q_i and join elements. Note that all join elements in Q_i must exist in Q_j. Also all relations used by Q_i must be used by Q_j. And all attributes selected by Q_j must be selected by Q_i. The attributes check is presented below and the three following sections contain algorithms dealing with predicate checking, and finally the full algorithm is presented in section 4.5.

4.1 Check the Attributes Selected by Q_i and Q_j

Superset($\text{Att}(Q_i)$, $\text{Att}(Q_j)$) : This function deals with specific type of sets ($\text{Att}(Q)$). It returns true if all attributes and link-elements selected by Q_j are selected by Q_i taking into account link-element conversion. See [2] for the details.

4.2 Check for all αs of type #3 in Q_i

Subsume1(Q_i, Q_j) : This function returns true if all join attributes in Q_i exist in Q_j and returns false otherwise. For every link-element used as a join element $(PL(X,Q_i))$ in Q_i there must be a link-element in Q_j where for every β in $(PL(X, Q_i))$ there must be at least one β in $(PL(X, Q_j))$ where the first β contains the second one. In some cases with no equijoin, the straight forward checking does not work, therefore the checking will deal with βs not in $(PL(X, Q_i))$ but it will deal with them after converting the link-element to all its equivalent attributes $(\mathrm{Conv}1(\mathrm{PL}(X, Q_i)))$ for all link-elements in Q_i. Of course we will ignore nonsense predicates such as $(a = a)$.

$$
\begin{aligned}
&\mathrm{Subsume}1(Q_i, Q_j) \Leftrightarrow \\
&\forall\, l_1\ (l_1 \in \mathrm{Link}(Q_i)) \wedge \mathrm{size}(\mathrm{PL}(X_1, Q_i)) > 1 \\
&\quad \Rightarrow \exists\, l_2\ (l_2 \in \mathrm{Link}(Q_j) \\
&\qquad \wedge \forall\, \alpha_1\ (\alpha_1 \in \mathrm{Conv}1(\mathrm{PL}(X_1, Q_i)) \\
&\qquad\quad \Rightarrow \quad \mathrm{VL}(\alpha_1) = \mathrm{VR}(\alpha_2) \\
&\qquad\qquad \vee \exists\, \alpha_2 \quad (\alpha_2 \in \mathrm{Conv}1(\mathrm{PL}(X_2, Q_j))) \wedge \mathrm{Contain}1(\alpha_1, \alpha_2))
\end{aligned}
$$

Examples :

$Q_i \equiv ?\,[\,............\,]$
   : Pa [aircraft-type = X1]
    Ai[model = X1]
$\mathrm{Link}(Q_i) = \{\ X1\ \}$
$E(X1, Q_i) = \{\ \mathrm{Pa.aircraft\text{-}type}\ \}$
$P(Q_i) = \{\}$
$\mathrm{PL}(X1, Q_i) = \{(\mathrm{Pa.aircraft\text{-}type} = X1),$
      $(\mathrm{Ai.model} = X1\ )\}$

$Q_j \equiv ?\,[\,............\,]$
   : Pa [aircraft-type = X2]
    Ai[model = X2, no-engine > 2]
$\mathrm{Link}(Q_j) = \{\ X2\ \}$
$E(X2, Q_j) = \{\ \mathrm{Pa.aircraft\text{-}type}\ \}$
$P(Q_j) = \{\ (\mathrm{Ai.no\text{-}engine} > 2\ )\}$
$\mathrm{PL}(X2, Q_j) = \{(\mathrm{Pa.aircraft\text{-}type} = X2),$
      $(\mathrm{Ai.model} = X2\ )\}$

4.3 Check for all αs in Q_i

$\mathrm{Subsume}2(Q_i, Q_j)$: This function returns true if every α in $P(Q_i)$ contains at least one β in $P(Q_j)$ and returns false otherwise. Because of link-elements, searching for β in $P(Q_j)$ is not enough; a β in $P(Q_j)$ may be contained in an α in $P(Q_i)$ even if they have different attribute names. So the algorithm checks for every $\mathrm{Conv}2(\alpha, Q_i, Q_j)$ for all αs in $P(Q_i)$ to contain at least one β in Q_j.

$$
\begin{aligned}
&\mathrm{Subsume}2(Q_i, Q_j) \Leftrightarrow \\
&\forall\, \alpha_1\ (\alpha_1 \in P(Q_i)) \\
&\quad \Rightarrow \quad \exists\, \alpha_2 \quad (\alpha_2 \in P(Q_j)) \wedge \mathrm{Contain}1(\mathrm{Conv}2(\alpha_1, Q_i, Q_j), \alpha_2) \\
&\qquad \vee \exists\, \omega_1 \quad (\omega_1 \subseteq P(Q_j)) \wedge \mathrm{Contain}2(\mathrm{Conv}2(\alpha_1, Q_i, Q_j), \omega_1)
\end{aligned}
$$

examples :

$E(X_i, Q_i)$ and α in $P(Q_i)$	$\mathrm{Conv}2(..)$	$E(X_i, Q_j)$ and β in $P(Q_j)$	T or F
Pi.p-no > 10	X2 > 10	$E(X2, Q_j) = \{$ Pi.p-no, Pa.p-no$\}$ $P(Q_j) = ((X2 = 20 \vee X2 = 30))$	T
$E(X3, Q_i) = \{$Pi.p-no, Pa. p-no $\}$ X3 > 10	X1 > 10	$E(X1, Q_j) = \{$Pi.p-no, Pa.p-no $\}$ $P(Q_j) = X1 > 20$	T
$E(X3, Q_i) = \{$Pi.p-no, Pa. p-no $\}$ X3 > 10	X2 > 10	$E(X2, Q_j) = \{$Pi.p-no,Pa.p-no $\}$ $P(Q_j) = ((X2 = 2 \vee X2 > 10))$	F

4.4 Check for all ωs in Q_i

Subsume3(Q_i, Q_j) : This function returns true if every ω_l in $P(Q_i)$ contains at least one β_j in $P(Q_j)$ and returns false otherwise. Similar to the checking of αs, the algorithm checks for a β_j in $P(Q_j)$ which is contained in Conv2(ω_l, Q_i, Q_j) for all ωs in $P(Q_i)$. Also we need to check if an α of type #3 in ω_l contains any β_j in Q_j; to check this we need to check all $PL(X_n, Q_j)$ after converting their link-elements to attributes in the ω_l and check for one element in Conv1$(PL(X_n, Q_j))$. α of type #3 become α of type #2 after the conversion. Because every join element in Q_i exists in Q_j we will not have a problem of a link-element in Q_j which has more than one link-element in Q_j, therefore the Conv2 function always works.

Subsume3$(Q_i, Q_j) \Leftrightarrow$
$\forall \omega_l \ (\omega_l \subseteq P(Q_i))$
$\Rightarrow \ (\exists \alpha_1 \quad (\alpha_1 \in P(Q_j)) \wedge \text{Contain3}(\text{Conv2}(\omega_1, Q_i, Q_j), \alpha_1))$
$\quad \vee (\exists \omega_2 \ (\omega_2 \subseteq P(Q_j)) \wedge \text{Contain6}(\text{Conv2}(\omega_1, Q_i, Q_j), \omega_2)))$
$\quad \vee (\exists \alpha_2, \alpha_3, l_1 \,(\alpha_2 \in \text{Conv1}(\omega_1)) \wedge (l_1 \in \text{Link}(Q_j)) \wedge (\alpha_3 \in \text{Conv1}(PL(X_1, Q_i)))$
$\qquad \wedge \text{Contain1}(\alpha_2, \alpha_3))$

---

examples :

$E(Xi, Q_i)$ and ω in $P(Q_i)$	$\text{Conv2}(\omega, Q_i, Q_j)$	$E(Xi, Q_i)$ and β in $P(Q_j)$	T or F
(Pi.flights > 5$\vee$ Pi.hours > 10)	(X2>5$\vee$ Pi.hours>10)	$E(X2 \ Q_j) = \{$ Pi.flights, ...$\}$ $P(Q_j) = X2 > 7$	T
$E(X1,Q_i) = \{$Pi.p-no, Pb.p-no$\}$ $E(X3, Q_i)=\{$Pi.salary, ..$\}$ (Pb.bonus > 100 $\vee$ X3 > 2000 $\vee$ X1 > 130)	(Pb.bonus>100 $\vee$ X3 > 2000 $\vee$ X4>130)	$E(X4 \ Q_j)=\{$Pi.p-no, Pb.p-no$\}$ $P(Q_j) = X4 > 200$	T

4.5 The Full Algorithm

Is A_j included in A_i? In order to answer this question we need first to minimise both Q_i and Q_j by removing all redundant predicates (see [16]), then apply the following function :

Subsume(Q_i, Q_j) : Returns true if A_j is included in A_i; and returns false otherwise. For this function to be true, five functions must be true as we will see below, but once one of these functions return false the algorithm stops and Subsume(Q_i, Q_j) returns false.

Subsume$(Q_i, Q_j) \Leftrightarrow$
$\quad$ Supset $(\text{Rel}(Q_i), \text{Rel}(Q_j))$
$\quad \wedge$ Superset $(\text{Att}(Q_i), \text{Att}(Q_j))$
$\quad \wedge$ Subsume1(Q_i, Q_j)
$\quad \wedge$ Subsume2(Q_i, Q_j)
$\quad \wedge$ Subsume3(Q_i, Q_j)

5 Deciding the Predicates of the Filter Query

Once we decide that query Q_i subsumes another query Q_j, then we need to decide what is the filter query (Q'_j) such that when we apply it to A_i, we get A_j. The problem is not to check if there is a filter query or not, but the problem is to find the best filter query and then to decide if it applicable to A_i or not.

First we need to decide the predicates of the filter query. So we will define a new set, Filter(Q), which will contain all required predicates for the filter query Q'. To decide what predicates should be included in the filter, every β in Q_j is checked, if it exists in Q_i, we ignore it, otherwise we add it to Filter(Q_j). We need to check all predicates of Q_j, which are distributed in several sets; these are $P(Q_j)$ and $PL(X_i, Q_j)$ for all X_n, where $X_n \in \text{Link}(Q_j)$. Following are two different functions, one for individual α in Q_j and one for individual ω in Q_j; and then an algorithm to build Filter(Q_j).

Exist1(α, Q_j, Q_i) returns true if α in Q_j has at least one semantically equivalent β in Q_i, and returns false otherwise.

$$
\begin{array}{l}
\text{Exist1}(\alpha_1, Q_j, Q_i) \Leftrightarrow \\
\quad \exists\, (\alpha_2\ (\alpha_2 \in P(Q_i)) \\
\qquad \wedge \text{Contain1}(\alpha_1, \text{Conv2}(\alpha_2, Q_i, Q_j))) \wedge \text{Contain1}(\text{Conv2}(\alpha_2, Q_i, Q_j), \alpha_1)\,) \\
\quad \vee\, (\,\exists\, \omega_1\ (\omega_1 \subseteq P(Q_i)) \\
\qquad \wedge \text{Contain2}(\alpha_1, \text{Conv2}(\omega_1, Q_i, Q_j)) \wedge \text{Contain3}(\text{Conv2}(\omega_1, Q_i, Q_j), \alpha_1)\,)
\end{array}
$$

Exist2(ω, Q_j, Q_i) returns true if ω in Q_j has at least one semantically equivalent β in Q_i, and returns false otherwise.

$$
\begin{array}{l}
\text{Exist2}(\omega_1, Q_j, Q_i) \Leftrightarrow \\
\quad \exists\, (\alpha_1\ (\alpha_1 \in P(Q_i)) \\
\qquad \wedge \text{Contain3}(\omega_1, \text{Conv2}(\alpha_1, Q_i, Q_j)) \wedge \text{Contain2}(\text{Conv2}(\alpha_1, Q_i, Q_j), \omega_1)\,) \\
\quad \vee\, (\,\exists\, \omega_2\ (\omega_2, \subseteq P(Q_i)) \\
\qquad \wedge \text{Contain6}(\omega_1, \text{Conv2}(\omega_2, Q_i, Q_j)) \wedge \text{Contain6}(\text{Conv2}(\omega_2, Q_i, Q_j), \omega_1)\,)
\end{array}
$$

5.1 The Algorithm to Decide Predicates of the Filter Query

The goal of the algorithm is to find the best filter query, which contains the minimal number of predicates. The first statement in the algorithm is to initialise Filter(Q_j) as an empty set. Then we check all αs and ωs in Q_j to build up Filter(Q_j). Finally we add to the filter all join elements of Q_j which do not exist in Q_i. Because we need to apply the filter to A_i, we convert all predicates to be compatible with Q_i before adding them to the filter.

$$\text{Filter}(Q_i) = \{ \}$$
$$\forall\, \alpha_1\ \text{Member}(\alpha_1, P(Q_i)) \land \neg\, \text{Exist1}(\alpha_1, Q_j, Q_i)$$
$$\Rightarrow\ \text{Adjoin}(\text{Conv2}(\alpha_1, Q_j, Q_i), \text{Filter}(Q_i))$$

$$\forall\, \omega_1\ \text{Subset}(\omega_1, P(Q_j)) \land \neg\, \text{Exist2}(\omega_1, Q_j, Q_i)$$
$$\Rightarrow\ \text{Adjoin}(\text{Conv2}(\omega_1, Q_j, Q_i), \text{Filter}(Q_i))$$

$$\forall\, X_1, \alpha_2\,(l_1 \in \text{Link}(Q_j)) \land (\alpha_2 \in \text{Conv1}(\text{PL}(X_1, Q_j))) \land \neg\exists\, X_2, \alpha_3\,(X_2 \in \text{Link}(Q_j))$$
$$\land (\alpha_3 \in \text{Conv1}(\text{PL}(X_2, Q_j))) \land \text{Contain1}(\alpha_1, \alpha_2) \land \text{Contain1}(\alpha_2, \alpha_1)$$
$$\Rightarrow \text{Adjoin}(\text{Conv2}(\alpha_2, Q_j, Q_i), \text{Filter}(Q_i))$$

5.2 Check if the Filter is applicable to the Answer of the Subsume Query then Write the Filter Query

We can apply the filter query to A_i only if all variables in the filter exist in the header of Q_i, ($\text{Att}(Q_i)$).

Following are three functions to check the existence of variables of the three different types of β (α, ω and σ); each returns true if all variables in β exist in $\text{Att}(Q_i)$, and returns false otherwise. And then we present the filter query.

$$\text{Check1}(\alpha_1, Q_i) \Leftrightarrow$$
$$T(\alpha_1) = 1 \land (\text{VL}(\alpha_1) \in \text{Att}(Q_i))$$
$$\lor\, T(\alpha_1) <> 1$$
$$\land (\text{VL}(\alpha_1) \in \text{Att}(Q_i)) \land (\text{VR}(\alpha_1) \in \text{Att}(Q_i))$$
$$\lor (\text{VL}(\alpha_1) = \text{VR}(\alpha_1) \land (\,O\,(\alpha_1) = "=" \lor O\,(\alpha_1) = "\geq" \lor O\,(\alpha_1) = "\leq"\,))$$
$$\text{Check2}(\omega_1, Q_i) \Leftrightarrow$$
$$\forall\, \alpha_1\,(\alpha_1 \in \omega_1) \Rightarrow \text{Check1}(\alpha_1, Q_i) \land \forall\, \sigma_1\,(\sigma_1 \subseteq \omega_1) \Rightarrow \text{Check3}(\sigma_1, Q_i)$$
$$\text{Check3}(\sigma_1, Q_i) \Leftrightarrow$$
$$\forall\, \alpha_1\,(\alpha_1 \in \sigma_1) \Rightarrow \text{Check1}(\alpha_1, Q_i) \land \forall\, \omega_1\,(\omega_1 \subseteq \sigma_1) \Rightarrow \text{Check2}(\omega_1, Q_i)$$

The full Algorithm. Now we check for all βs in $\text{Filter}(Q_j)$

$$\text{Yes-filter}(Q_i) \Leftrightarrow$$
$$\forall\, \alpha_1\,(\alpha_1 \in \text{Filter}(Q_i)) \Rightarrow \text{Check1}(\alpha_1, Q_i)$$
$$\land\ \forall\, \omega_1\,(\omega_1 \subseteq \text{Filter}(Q_i)) \Rightarrow \text{Check2}(\omega_1, Q_i)$$

Writing up the Filter Query. The final step now is to write the filter query only if Yes-filter(Q_j) is true. And because predicates in Filter(Q_j) use attributes and link-elements with respect to Q_j we need to convert the requested (selected) attributes by Q_j, i.e. $\text{Att}(Q_j)$, to those used in the header of Q_i i.e. $\text{Att}(Q_i)$. We define $\text{Att}(Q'_j)$ as a header of the filter query, Q'_j.

$$\text{Att}(Q'_i) = \text{Conv2}(\text{Att}(Q_i), Q_j, Q_i)$$
$$\text{The filter query is}: Q'_i \equiv\ ?\,[\text{Att}(Q'_i)]$$
$$: A_i\,[\text{Filter}(Q_i)]$$

6 Conclusion and Further Work

In this paper we have presented an algorithm for subsumption between two queries. We have shown the importance of such subsumption. Our algorithm can be applied to conjunctive and disjunctive queries with the following limitations, all attributes are atomic, all queries are function free and the algorithm does not take integrity constraints into account. Another algorithm is included to write a filter query if there is any applicable one. Also a brief explanation about COAL, the query language we use, has been presented.

As for further work, we may make some changes and extend the algorithm to includes systems' predicates, aggregation functions and integrity constraints.

We are currently developing an ontology model for legacy systems using an agent-based approach; query subsumption is a part of our model and we will improve the algorithm according to the needs of the model.

References

1. Al-Qasem, M., "An Implementation of an Ontology Model for Legacy Systems Using an Agent-Based Approach", Dake Centre Technical Report, Keele University, 1996.
2. Al-Qasem, M., "Query Subsumption", Dake Centre Technical Report, Keele University, 1997.
3. Beneventano, D. et al, "Using Subsumption in Semantic Query Optimization". IJCAI Workshop on Object-Based Representation System, Chambery , France, August 1993
4. Bergamaschi, S., "Extraction of Informations from Highly Heterogeneous Sources of Textual Data". Proceeding of the First International Workshop of Cooperative Information Agents(CIA'97), Kiel, Germany, February 1997.
5. Chan, Em., " Containment and Minimization of Positive Conjunctive Queries in OODB's". In Proceeding of 11th ACM SIGACT-SIGMOD-SIGART Symposium on Principle of Database Systems. PP 202-211, 1992.
6. Chang, K. et al, "Predicate Rewriting for Translation Boolean Query in a Heterogeneous Information System". available at http://www-db.stanfors.edu/pub/papers/pred_rewriting.ps.
7. Chang, K. et al, "Boolean Query Mapping Across Heterogeneous Information Sources". IEEE Transaction on Knowledge and Data Engineering, Vol. 8, NO. 4, 1996.
8. Chu, W. and Q. Chen, "A Structure Approach for Cooperative Query Answering". IEEE Transaction on Knowledge and Data Engineering, Vol. 6, NO. 5, pp738-749, 1994.
9. Deen, S., "An Architectural Framework For CKBS Applications". IEEE Transaction on Knowledge and Data Engineering, Vol. 8, NO. 4, 1996.
10. Garcia-Molina, H. et al, "The TSIMMIS Approach to Mediation: Data Models and Languages". Journal Of Intelligent Information Systems 8, pp 117-132, 1997.
11. Harinarayan, V. and Ai. Gupta, "Optimization Using Tuple Subsumption". In Database Theory - ICDT'95, 5th International Conference Proceeding, edited by G. Gottlob and M. Vardi. Prague, Czech Republic, January 1995.
12. Mena, Em. et al, "OBSERVER : An Approach for Query Processing in Global Information Systems Based on Interoperation Across Pre-existing Ontologies". Proceedings of the First IFCIS International Conference on Cooperative Information Systems (CoopIS'96), Brusseles, Belgium, June 1996.

13. Papakonstantinou, Y. et al, "A Query Translation Schema for Rapid Implementation of Wrappers". available at : ftp://db.stanford.edu/pub/papakonstantinou/1995/querytran-extended.ps.
14. Papakonstantinou, Y. et al, "Object Exchange Across Heterogeneous Information Sources". available via anonymous FTP from host db.stanford.edu, file: /pub/papakonstantinou/1994/object-heterogeneous-is.ps.
15. Staudt, M. and V. Thadden, "A Generic Subsumption Testing Toolkit for Knowledge Base Queries". In 7th International Conference, DEXA'96, Proceeding, edited by R. Wagner and H. Thoma. Zurich, Switzerland, September 1996.
16. Ullman, J., "Principles of Database and Knowledge-Base Systems", Volume 2. Computer Science Press, 1989.

Partial Answers for Unavailable Data Sources*

Philippe Bonnet[1] and Anthony Tomasic[2]

[1] GIE Dyade, INRIA Rhône Alpes, 655 Avenue de l'Europe, 38330 Montbonnot,
France; Philippe.Bonnet@dyade.fr
[2] INRIA, Domaine de Voluceau, Rocquencourt, BP 105, 78153 Le Chesnay Cedex,
France; Anthony.Tomasic@inria.fr

Abstract. Many heterogeneous database system products and prototypes exist today; they will soon be deployed in a wide variety of environments. Most existing systems suffer from an *Achilles' heel*: they ungracefully fail in presence of unavailable data sources. If some data sources are
unavailable when accessed, these systems either silently ignore them or
generate an error. This behavior is improper in environments where there
is a non-negligible probability that data sources cannot be accessed (e.g.,
Internet). In case some data sources cannot be accessed when processing
a query, the complete answer to this query cannot be computed; some
work can however be done with the data sources that are available. In
this paper, we propose a novel approach where, in presence of unavailable data sources, the answer to a query is a *partial answer*. A partial
answer is a representation of the work that has been done in case the
complete answer to a query cannot be computed, and of the work that
remains to be done in order to obtain this complete answer. The use of
a partial answer is twofold. First, it contains an *incremental query* that
allows to obtain the complete answer without redoing the work that has
already been done. Second, the application program can extract information from a partial answer through the use of a secondary query, which we
call a *parachute query*. In this paper, we present a framework for partial
answers and we propose three algorithms for the evaluation of queries in
presence of unavailable sources, the construction of incremental queries
and the evaluation of parachute queries.

1 Introduction

Heterogeneous databases provide declarative access to a wide variety of
heterogeneous data sources. Research into improving these systems has
produced many new results which are being incorporated into prototypes
and commercial products. A limiting factor for such systems however,
is the difficulty of providing responsive data access to users, due to the
highly varying response-time and availability characteristics of remote

---

* This work has been done in the context of Dyade, joint R&D venture between Bull
and Inria.

data sources, particularly in a wide-area environment [1]. Data access over remote data sources involves intermediate sites and communication links that are vulnerable to congestion or failures. Such problems can introduce significant and unpredictable delays in the access of information from remote sources.

In cases data from a remote source is delayed for a period of time which is longer than the user is willing to wait, the source can be considered unavailable. Most heterogeneous database systems fail ungracefully in presence of unavailable data sources. They either assume that all data sources are available, report error conditions, or silently ignore unavailable sources.

Even when one or more needed sites are unavailable, some useful work can be done with the data from the sites that are available. We call a *partial answer* the representation of this work, and of the work that remains to be done in order to obtain the complete answer. In this paper, we describe an approach [2], where in presence of unavailable data sources, a *partial answer* is returned to the user.

The use of partial answers is twofold. First, a partial answer contains an incremental query that can be submitted to the system in order to obtain the complete answer efficiently, once the unavailable data sources are again available. Second, a partial answer contains data from the available sites that can be extracted. To extract data, we use secondary queries, which we call *parachute queries*. A set of parachute queries is associated to each query and can be asked if the complete answer cannot be produced.

In the rest of the section, we discuss an example that illustrates a practical use of partial answers.

1.1 Example

To be more concrete, let us illustrate the problem and our solution with the following example, concerning a hospital information system.

Consider an hospital that consists of three services: administration, surgery, and radiology. Each service manages its own data and is a data source. A mediator system provides doctors with information on patients. The mediator accesses the data sources to answer queries. Figure 1 contains mediator schema; three service data sources are integrated: administration, surgery, and radiology. The schema contains a relation identifying patients (*patient*), a relation associating the local identifiers of patients (*map*), and two relations identifying medical treatments (*surgery* and *radiology*). The data from the *patient*, *surgery* and *radiology* relations are located respectively on the local data sources. The *map* relation is located

id	name	age	address
1	Durand	56	Paris
2	Dupont	38	Versailles
3	Martin	70	Suresnes

(a) patient

patient_id	radiology_id	surgery_id
1	r_1	s_1
2	r_2	s_2
3	r_3	s_3

(b) map

id	date	description
s_1	10/03/96	appendicitis
s_2	23/07/97	broken arm
s_3	30/05/96	appendicitis
s_3	23/10/97	broken leg

(c) surgery

id	date	description	xray
r_2	22/07/97	right arm	$\heartsuit_1$
r_3	23/10/97	right leg	$\heartsuit_2$

(d) radiology

Fig. 1. Hospital Information System Schema. Figure (a) is the *patient* relation from the administrative service. Figure (b) maps the identifiers from the data sources – this relation is contained in the mediator. Figure (c) is the *surgery* relation from the surgery service. Figure (d) is the *radiology* relation from the radiology service. The symbol $\heartsuit$ represents a digitized x-ray.

in the mediator. (We assume there is no semantic heterogeneity between data sources; this problem is tackled in [4].)

A typical query that a doctor may ask is the following, *select the date, type and description of surgeries and the X-ray for the patient named Martin, that occur on the same date*:

```
Q: select surgery.date, surgery.description,
       radiology.date, radiology.xray
   from patient, surgery, radiology, map
   where patient.name = "Martin" and
       patient.id = map.patient_id and
       map.surgery_id = surgery.id and
       map.radiology_id = radiology.id and
       surgery.date = radiology.date;
```

The answer to this query is:

surgery.date	surgery.description	radiology.date	radiology.xray
23/10/97	broken leg	23/10/97	$\heartsuit_2$

Each service administrates its own data source. In particular, the administrator of the data source in, say the radiology service, can decide at any time to shut down its system to perform maintenance. In the meantime, this data source is unavailable when the mediator tries to access it. Using a classical mediator system, the query described above, which involves radiological data cannot be answered when maintenance is performed in the radiology service. Now, with a mediator providing partial answers, parachute queries may be associated with the original query. In our example, we could consider two parachute queries: (1) for the case where the radiology source is unavailable and (2) for the case where the surgery source is unavailable.

```
PQ1: select surgery.date, surgery.description
     from patient, surgery, map
     where patient.name = "Martin" and
         patient.id = map.patient_id and
         map.surgery_id = surgery.id;

PQ2: select radiology.date, radiology.xray
     from patient, radiology, map
     where patient.name = "Martin" and
         patient.id = map.patient_id and
         map.radiology_id = radiology.id;
```

Suppose the radiology data source is unavailable when the doctor asks query Q. The complete answer cannot be computed; the system can however obtain data from the administration and surgery data sources. The system returns a partial answer which notifies the doctor that the query cannot be answered because the radiology data source is down. The parachute queries that are associated to the query can be evaluated using the obtained data. The doctor obtains the following answer to the parachute query PQ1;

date	description
30/05/97	appendicitis
23/10/97	broken leg

Using the same obtained data, the system also generates an incremental query that will efficiently compute the complete answer once the radiology data source is available again. The incremental query retrieves data from the radiology data source and reuses data already obtained from the administration and surgery data sources (this incremental query is described in Section 2)

1.2 Contributions

In summary, this paper describes a novel approach to handling unavailable data sources during query processing in heterogeneous distributed databases. We propose a framework for partial answers; an algorithm for the evaluation of queries in presence of unavailable sources; an algorithm for the construction of incremental queries; and an algorithm for the evaluation of parachute queries. We have implemented part of these algorithms in the Disco prototype [10].

We present in Section 2 an overview of our approach, and in Section 3 our algorithms. We discuss related work in Section 4. We conclude the paper in Section 5 by summarizing our results and discussing future work.

2 Overview of Partial Answers

Let us consider again the initial query described in the introduction. If all sites are available, then the system returns a complete answer. The complete answer is the set of tuples obtained from the root of the execution plan.

Let us suppose now that site radiology is unavailable, while the other sites are available. A complete answer to this query cannot be produced. We propose a solution that, in such a case, does the following:

phase 1 each available site is contacted. Since the radiology site is unavailable neither the join between the *radiology* relation and the data obtained from the administration site, nor the join with the *surgery* relation can be performed. The data from the administration site, i.e. the result of the sub-query SQ1 *select * from patients, treatments where patient.name = "Martin" and patient.id = treatment.patient_id*, and the *surgery* relation, i.e. the result of sub-query SQ2 *select * from surgery*, can however be obtained and materialized on the site where query processing takes place. SQ1 and SQ2 denote data materialized locally in relations R1 and R2.

phase 2 an incremental query, Qi, semantically equivalent to the original query, is constructed using the temporary relations materialized in phase 1 and the relations from the unavailable sites. In our example Qi is:

```
select radiology.date, radiology.description,
       R2.date, R2.description
from R1, R2, radiology
where R1.radiology_id = radiology.id
  and R1.surgery_id = R2.id ;
```

Qi is semantically equivalent to the original query under the assumption that no updates are performed on the remote sites.

A partial answer is returned to the user. It is a handle on the data obtained and materialized in phase 1, as well as on the query constructed in phase 2. In the next section we propose two algorithms that implement these two phases for the construction of partial answers.

A partial answer can be used in two ways. First, the incremental query Qi, constructed in phase 2, can be submitted to the system in order to obtain the final answer. Evaluating Qi only requires contacting the sites that were unavailable when the original query was evaluated. In the example, R1 and R2 denote data materialized locally, only *radiology* references data located on a remote site.

When Qi is evaluated, the system returns either a complete answer, or another partial answer depending on the availability of the sites that were previously unavailable[1]. When Qi is submitted to the system, the query processor considers it in the same way as a plain query, and it is optimized. The execution plan that is used for Qi is generally different from the execution plan used for the original query. If the sources that were unavailable during the evaluation of the original query are now available, then a complete answer is returned. Under the assumption that no relevant updates are performed on the remote sites, this answer is the answer to the original query.

Submitting Qi, instead of the original query, in order to obtain the complete answer presents two advantages. A complete answer can be produced even if all the sites are not available simultaneously. It suffices that a site is available during the evaluation of one of the successive partial answers to ensure that the data from this site is used for the complete answer. Moreover, Qi involves temporary relations that are materialized locally; evaluating Qi is usually more efficient than evaluating the original query.

Second, data can be extracted from a partial answer using parachute queries. Parachute queries are associated to the original query; they may be asked in case the complete answer to the original query cannot be produced. In the next section, we propose an initial algorithm for the evaluation of parachute queries.

3 Algorithms

3.1 Architecture

For our algorithms, we consider an architecture that involves an application program, a mediator, wrappers, and data sources. During query

---

[1] Possibly, successive partial answers are produced before the complete answer can be obtained.

processing, the application program issues a query to the mediator. The mediator transforms the query into some valid execution plan consisting of sub-queries and of a composition query (the algorithms we propose are independent of the execution plan). The mediator then evaluates the execution plan. Evaluation proceeds by issuing sub-queries to the wrappers. Each wrapper that is contacted processes its sub-queries by communicating with the associated data source and returning sub-answers. If all data sources are available, the mediator combines the sub-answers by using the composition query and returns the answer to the application program. In case one or several data sources are unavailable, the mediator returns a partial answer to the application. The application extracts data from the partial answer by asking a parachute query.

3.2 Query Evaluation

The algorithm for query evaluation follows the iterator model. The query optimizer generates a tree of operators that computes the answer to the query. The operators are relational-like, such as `project`, `select`, etc. Each operator supports three procedures: `open`, `get-next`, and `close`. The procedure `open` prepares each operator for producing data. Each call to `get-next` generates one tuple in the answer to the operator, and the `close` procedure performs any clean-up operations.

The new operator `submit` contacts a remote site to process a sub-query. During the `open` call to `submit` a network connection to the remote site is opened. In this paper, we assume that if the `open` call to the wrapper succeeds, then the corresponding data source is available and will deliver its sub-answer without problems. If the `open` call fails, then the corresponding data source is unavailable. This behavior implies that each data source can be classified as *available* or *unavailable* according to the result of the `open` call.

We assume that no updates relevant to a query are performed between the moment the processing of this query starts and the moment where the processing related to this query ends, because the final answer is obtained, or because the user does not resubmit the incremental query.

We describe a two-step evaluation of queries. The first step, the `eval` algorithm, performs a partial evaluation of the execution plan with respect to the available data sources. If all the sources are available, the result of the first step is the answer to the query (a set of tuples). If at least one source is unavailable, the result of the first step is an annotated execution plan. The second step, the `construct` algorithm, constructs the incremental query from the annotated execution plan. A partial answer

```
eval(operator) {
  for each subtree in children of operator {
    eval(subtree)
  }
  if source is available or all subtrees are available then {
    mark operator available
  } else {
    mark operator unavailable
  }
}
```

Fig. 2. The evaluation algorithm.

is then returned to the user. It is a handle on both the data materialized during the first step and the query constructed in the second step.

Eval algorithm The eval algorithm is encoded in the **open** call to each operator. The implementations of **get-next** and **close** are generally unchanged from the classical implementations. Evaluation commences by calling **open** on the root operator of the tree. Each operator proceeds by calling **open** on its children, waiting for the result of the call, and then returning to its parent. We consider two cases that can result from calling *open* on all the children of an operation. Either all the calls succeed, or at least one call fails. In the former case, the operator marks itself as *available* and returns success to its parent. In the latter case, the operator marks itself as *unavailable* and returns failure to its parent. The traversal of the tree continues until all operators are marked either available or unavailable. Note that by insisting that each operator opens all its children, instead of giving up with the first unavailable child, we implement a simple form of query scrambling [1]. See Figure 2 for an outline of the algorithm.

After the open call finishes, the root operator of the tree has marked itself either available or unavailable. If it is marked available, then all sources are available and the final result is produced in the normal way. If at least one data source is unavailable, the root of the execution plan will be marked unavailable and the final result cannot be produced. In the latter case the tree is processed in a second pass. Each subtree rooted with an available operator *materializes* its result. Materialization is accomplished by the root operator of the subtree repeatedly executing its

```
construct(execution_plan) returns Incremental Query {
  if available() then {
    return the temporary relation containing the intermediate result
  } else {
    S := ∅
    for each subtree in children(execution_plan) {
      S := S ∪ construct( subtree )
    }
    return the query for execution_plan using S
  }
}
```

Fig. 3. Construction of the incremental query.

get-next call and storing the result. The resulting tree is passed to the construct algorithm.

Construct algorithm We construct a declarative query from an annotated execution plan by constructing a declarative expression for each operator in the tree in a bottom-up fashion. The declarative expressions are nested to form the incremental query.

Operators marked available generate a declarative expression that accesses the materialized intermediate result. It is an expression of the form **select * from** x **in** r, where x is a new unique variable and r is the name of the temporary relation holding the materialized intermediate result. Operators marked unavailable generate a declarative expression corresponding to the operator. For example, a **project** operator generates an expression of the form **select** p **from** x **in** arg, where p is the list of attributes projected by the operator, x is a unique variable, and arg is the declarative expression that results from the child operator of the project operation. The association between the operators we consider and declarative expressions is straightforward.

The construction of the incremental query, see Figure 3, consists in traversing recursively the tree of operators, stopping the traversal of a branch when an available operator is encountered (there is an intermediate result), or when an unavailable leaf is reached (a **submit** operator associated to an unavailable data source), and in nesting the declarative expression associated to each traversed node.

The incremental query, together with the annotated execution plan is used to return a partial answer.

3.3 Extraction Algorithm

We present an algorithm for extracting information from a partial answer, using a parachute query. The algorithm traverses the annotated execution plan searching for an intermediate result that *matches* the parachute query.

The algorithm proceeds as follows, see Figure 4. First, a query is generated for each intermediate result materialized in the annotated execution plan using the construct algorithm. We obtain a set of queries whose result is materialized in the annotated execution plan. Then, we compare the parachute query to each of these queries. If the parachute query is contained by one of these queries, then we can obtain the answer to the parachute query: it is the result of evaluating the parachute query on one materialized relation. Otherwise, we cannot return any answer to the parachute query. Query containment is defined in [11]. This problem is exactly the same as matching a query against a set of materialized views; an algorithm similar to this one is implemented in ADMS [5].

```
extract(execution_plan, parachute_query) returns Answer {
   S := materialized_subqueries(execution_plan)
   for each subquery in S {
     if parachute_query ⊆ subquery then
        return parachute_query evaluated on intermediate result of subquery
   }
   return null
}
```

Fig. 4. The extraction algorithm.

An improvement in the evaluation of parachute queries would consist in using a more elaborate evaluation algorithm. We can utilize for this problem, the results of [7] where an algorithm for answering queries using views is proposed. This algorithm would allow to combine several materialized views to evaluate a parachute query.

4 Related Work

Multiplex [9] tackles the issue of unavailable data sources in a multi-database system and APPROXIMATE [12] tackles the issue of unavailable data in a distributed database. Both systems propose an approach based on approximate query processing. In presence of unavailable data, the system returns an approximate answer which is defined in terms of subsets and supersets sandwiching the exact answer.

Multiplex uses the notions of subview and superview to define the approximate answer. A view V1 is a subview of a view V2 if it is obtained as a combination of selections and projections of V2; V2 is then a superview of V1. These notions can be a basis to define the relationship between a query and its associated parachute queries. APPROXIMATE uses semantic information concerning the contents of the database for the initial approximation. In our context, we do not use any semantic information concerning the data sources. None of these system produce an incremental query for accessing efficiently the complete answer.

References [6] and [8] survey cooperative answering systems. These systems emphasize the interaction between the application program and the database system. They aim at assisting users in the formulation of queries, or at providing meaningful answers in presence of empty results. Reference [8] introduces a notion of partial answer. When the result of a query is empty, the system anticipates follow-up queries, and returns the result of broader queries, that subsume the original query. These answers are offered in partial fulfillment of the original query. This notion of partial answer is different from the one we have introduced. For [8], a partial answer is an answer to a query subsuming the original query. For us, a partial answer is the partial evaluation of the original query.

5 Conclusion

We have proposed a novel approach to the problem of processing queries that cannot be completed for some reason. We have focused on the problem of processing queries in distributed heterogeneous databases with unavailable data sources. Our approach offers two aspects. First, in presence of unavailable data sources the query processing system returns a partial answer which is a handle on data obtained and materialized from the available sources and on an incremental query that can be used to efficiently obtain the complete answer. Second, relevant information can be extracted from a partial answer using parachute queries. We have implemented our approach [10].

The use of parachute queries provides a very flexible and familiar interface for application programs. However, formulating parachute queries may be a burden for the application programmer. We suspect that relevant parachute queries can be automatically generated given the original query. We have started investigating interesting classes of parachute queries and algorithms to generate them [3]; we have also studied performance trade-offs in a system dealing with parachute queries.

Acknowledgments

The authors wish to thank Laurent Amsaleg, Stéphane Bressan, Mike Franklin, Rick Hull, Tamer Oszu and Louiqa Raschid for fruitful discussions, and Mauricio Lopez for comments on previous drafts of this paper.

References

1. L. Amsaleg, Ph. Bonnet, M. J. Franklin, A. Tomasic, and T. Urhan. Improving responsiveness for wide-area data access. *Bulletin of the Technical Committee on Data Engineering*, 20(3):3–11, 1997.
2. Philippe Bonnet and Anthony Tomasic. Partial answers for unavailable data sources. Technical Report RR-3127, INRIA, 1997.
3. Philippe Bonnet and Anthony Tomasic. Parachute queries in the presence of unavailable data sources. Technical Report RR-3429, INRIA, 1998.
4. S. Bressan and C.H. Goh. Answering queries in context. In *Proceedings of the International Conference on Flexible Query Answering Systems, FQAS'98*, Roskilde, Denmark, 1998.
5. C.M. Chen and N. Roussopoulos. The implementation and performance evaluation of the ADMS query optimizer: Integrating query result caching and matching. In *Proceedings of the 4th International Conference on Extending Database Technology*, 1994.
6. T. Gaasterland, P. Godfrey, and J. Minker. An overview of cooperative answering. *Journal of Intelligent Information Systems*, 1(2):123–157, 1992.
7. A.Y. Levy, A. Mendelzon, Y. Sagiv, and D. Srivasta. Answering queries using views. In *Proceedings of the 14th ACM SIGACT-SIGMOD-SIGART Symposium on Principles of Database Systems, PODS-95*, San Jose, California, 1995.
8. A. Motro. Cooperative database systems. In *Proceedings of the 1994 Workshop on Flexible Query-Answering Systems (FQAS '94)*, pages 1–16. Department of Computer Science, Roskilde University, Denmark, 1994. Datalogiske Skrifter - Writings on Computer Science - Report Number 58.
9. A. Motro. Multiplex: A formal model for multidatabases and its implementation. Technical Report ISSE-TR-95-103, George Mason University, 1995.
10. A. Tomasic, R. Amouroux, Ph. Bonnet, Olga Kapitskaia, Hubert Naacke, and Louiqa Raschid. The distributed information search component (DISCO) and the World-Wide Web. In *Proceedings of the ACM SIGMOD International Conference on Management of Data*, Tucson, Arizona, 1997.
11. Jeffrey D. Ullman. *Principals of Database and Knowledge-Base Systems*, volume 2. Computer Science Press, 1989.
12. S. V. Vrbsky and J. W. S. Liu. APPROXIMATE: A query processor that produces monotonically improving approximate answers. *Transactions on Knowledge and Data Engineering*, 5(6):1056–1068, December 1993.

On Diverse Answers Issued
from Flexible Queries *

Patrick BOSC

IRISA/ENSSAT
Technopole ANTICIPA
BP 447 22305 Lannion Cedex France
E-mail: bosc@enssat.fr

Abstract. The notion of flexible queries covers different meanings depending on the authors. Here, it is assumed to stand for queries involving preferences and the fuzzy set framework is advocated as a general tool for supporting the expression of preferences. If fuzzy queries can apply to regular databases where information stored is precisely known, one can wonder about the case where the database contains some ill-known data (represented as possibility distributions) and this issue is the heart of the paper. Two significantly different approaches are suggested. In the first one, any condition concerns the values themselves and its interpretation is based on a fuzzy pattern matching mechanism. Then, the answer of a query is uncertain, i.e., any element is associated with a possibility and a necessity degree. In the second approach, a condition relates to the representation of values, and, as such, returns a truth value which is certain.

1 Introduction

This paper investigates different types of flexible queries addressed to regular databases as well as to databases where some pieces of information may be tainted with imprecision. By flexible queries, we mean queries whose results are discriminated and then, it is assumed that a flexible (or gradual) query involves some kind of preference with respect to the objective of discrimination. The term imprecision covers situations where the value taken by a single-valued variable cannot be assigned for sure, and then, it is necessary to make use of a representation mechanism to describe candidate values (which strongly depends on a model for uncertainty, e.g., probability theory, OR-sets, possibility theory). Incompletely known information as well as flexible query handling capabilities are expected to extend the range of applications for future database management systems.

The notion of a gradual query is first recalled and situated in the context of fuzzy set theory since fuzzy set membership functions are convenient tools for

---

* Invited Paper, Flexible Question Answering Systems, May 13-15, 1998, Roskilde, Denmark

modeling user's preference profiles and the large panoply of fuzzy set connectives can capture different attitudes concerning the way the different criteria present in a query compensate or not. Then, we consider the case where such queries are addressed to a regular database. In this context, any element returned by the system is assigned a grade expressing the extent to which it complies with the preferences of the request. A second situation is then taken into account, namely the case where the database may contain ill-known information. At that point, it is worth noticing that one can distinguish between two types of conditions: i) those whose target is the value itself, which are indeed identical to conditions addressed to precise values (e.g., age = 'young', salary = 'very high'), but whose result is in general uncertain (if we are uncertain about the precise value of John's age, we cannot always be sure that John satisfies a given requirement on the basis of the age value) and ii) those taking into account the representation of an imprecise value, which make sense only because a new level appears (that of the representations of values), such as: people whose age representation is such that 40 (years old) is much more preferred than 30.

2   Gradual Queries and Regular Databases

Here, we consider the situation where a regular database is queried, i.e., the database contains precise data and this case is particularly important since it corresponds to most of presently available information. The objective is to extend Boolean queries into gradual queries, whose responses are no longer a set of undifferentiated elements, but rather discriminated ones. If Boolean conditions fit many traditional database domains (especially business applications), they turn out to be restrictive, in particular when users want to express that some elements are better then others, due to preferences at the level of atomic conditions and/or importances between these atomic conditions.

These limitations have been pointed out in some research works dealing with flexible querying frameworks where the objective of a query is no longer to decide whether an element is selected or not, but rather to determine the extent to which it is an acceptable answer, thus a rank-ordering of the answers is provided. Some of the proposals [8, 12, 15, 19, 21] aim at a remedy by extending existing relational DBMSs without calling on fuzzy sets through a two-stage process: 1) a subset of elements is selected by means of a regular relational query handled by a usual relational DBMS and 2) these elements are ordered thanks to a dedicated module. An alternate solution is based on fuzzy set theory and is a natural way of doing since a fuzzy set represents a gradual concept and the more an element belongs to it, the more preferred it is.

An analysis and comparison [2] of these two approaches show that fuzzy sets offer a more general framework, where selection and ranking are mixed in a single mechanism. The modeling of non fuzzy set-based approaches in a unique framework enables a better understanding of their behaviors and three main points may be mentioned: 1) the typology of queries based on a selection (intended for the identification of a "reasonable" subset) followed by an ordering, 2) the specificity of the preferences taken into account (for instance, the relaxation of the equality into a resemblance does not allow for the expression of conditions such as "young", "well-paid" or "salary much greater than commission" which cannot be expressed as distances with respect to an ideal value) and 3) the discontinuity caused by the sequence selection - ordering (an element which is poorly satisfactory on all criteria is retained whereas another which is ideal for all criteria except one for which it is not at all satisfactory, is excluded).

Moreover, fuzzy sets provide a framework where fairly general gradual predicates are expressible. Atomic predicates correspond to elementary terms (adjectives) or to comparisons involving a fuzzy operator such as "much more than", etc. An elementary term can be associated with a linguistic modifier (corresponding most often to an adverb) intended for altering the initial semantics of the term, according to different interpretations (e.g., power or translation of the characteristic function).

Atomic and modified predicates can be combined thanks to the use of binary or n-ary connectors such as conjunction, disjunction and mean operators allowing for the expression of various trade-offs expressing for instance preferences between conditions. They can also be aggregated using a quantifier [14] as illustrated in:

almost all (age = 'young', salary = 'high', position' = 'interesting' , country = "France").

The regular relational algebra can be extended to fuzzy relations and most of the usual properties are maintained, in particular the compositionality principle. Beyond the algebraic point of view, the extension of an SQL-like query language has been proposed [3], which would enable SQL programmers to write gradual queries in the same way as they write regular queries. With such languages, the result of a query is a fuzzy (weighted) relation where each tuple is assigned a grade expressing the extent to which it fits the preferences involved in the query.

Example. Let us consider the relations EMP(num, e-name, salary, age, dep) and DEP(nd, d-name, budget). The query aiming at retrieving the pairs <department name, employee's name> where the employee has a high salary and works in this "high-budget" department can be expressed by:

select distinct e-name, d-name **from** EMP, DEP

where salary = 'high' **and** budget = 'important' **and** dep = ndep

and any resulting pair <e-name, d-name> has a grade of satisfaction with respect to the compound condition salary = 'high' **and** budget = 'important'◊

3 Queries on Imperfect Data

3.1 Introduction

Now, we consider the situation where some of the data stored in the base are imperfectly known. Different formalisms such as probability theory [1, 10], possibility theory [20, 23, 24] and OR-sets [13, 16, 17] can be considered depending on the nature of the available knowledge and their main characteristics will be given.

As far as querying is concerned, two completely different types of (flexible) queries can be envisaged. The first category, which is the one commonly considered, involves queries identical to those considered previously and which concern the values taken by attributes (e.g., age > 45, salary = 'important', salary much greater than commission). It is of prime importance that the model considered for representing imperfect data be compatible with fuzzy (gradual) queries and this is why we will focus on the possibilistic model. However, it is also possible to devise a second (fairly new) family of queries exploiting the fact that ill-known values make use of a representation model (i.e., a value is not the same as its representation as it is for a precise value). The conditions involved in this second type of queries are no longer a matter of value of an attribute, but concern the representation of the (possibly) ill-known value taken by an attribute. In this case, any model of uncertainty can be chosen, and it will only influence the semantics of some conditions. For instance, in the probabilistic setting, one will use a criterion asking for values which are more probable than others and in the possibilistic one for values more possible, or for the presence of a level of uncertainty. In fact, when ill-known data are considered, conditions inside queries can concern either the level of the values or that of their representations. As it will be shown , the differences between these two categories lies in the nature of both the conditions and the results returned, which are potentially uncertain in the first case, whereas there is no room for uncertainty in the other one.

3.2 A Brief Overview of Imperfect Data Representations

OR-sets OR-sets (or disjunctive sets) generalize existential null values. An existential value represents an attribute whose actual value is in a database domain. An OR-set represents an attribute whose value is in an explicit, smaller set. An ordinary atomic value can be viewed as a singleton. An existential value corresponds to an OR-set containing the entire attribute domain (it is indeed a disjunction of all the values of the domain). OR-sets can also contain a special value Ø to represent the possibility that there is no value for a given attribute.

Example. The relation given in Table 1 contains OR-sets values. In this relation, the second tuple represents that Thomas teaches one of the courses of the set {Physics, Chemistry, Biology}. The third tuple represents that either Susan teaches Algebra, or that Martha does, or that the course is not taught◊

Professor	Course
Marc	Databases
Thomas	{Physics, Chemistry, Biology}
{Susan, Martha, Ø}	Algebra

Table 1. An example of relation containing OR-sets

The Probabilistic Model A probabilistic database contains probabilistic information about data values in the following way. Probabilistic relations have key attributes that are deterministic, as in classical relations. Thus each tuple represents a known entity or relationship. The other attributes may be deterministic or stochastic. The latter are described with the help of probabilistic sets. An example of such a probabilistic relation drawn from [26] is shown in Table 2.

Takes	Student	Course
	John	{Algebra/0.5, Calculus/0.4}
	Ann	{Physics/0.5, Calculus/0.5}

Table 2. A relation with probabilistic attribute values

The semantics of this relation can be expressed in terms of possible worlds as follows. The first tuple represents three possibilities: John takes Algebra, John takes Calculus, or John takes no course. For the second tuple, since the probabilities of the course taken by Ann add up to 1.0, there are only two possibilities. Therefore, the relation has six possible worlds (with their respective probability):

$$W1 = \{(John, Algebra), (Ann, Physics)\} \quad P(W1) = 0.25$$
$$W2 = \{(John, Calculus), (Ann, Physics)\} \quad P(W2) = 0.20$$
$$W3 = \{(John, \bot), (Ann, Physics)\} \quad P(W3) = 0.05$$
$$W4 = \{(John, Algebra), (Ann, Calculus)\} \quad P(W4) = 0.25$$
$$W5 = \{(John, Calculus), (Ann, Calculus)\} \quad P(W5) = 0.20$$
$$W6 = \{(John, \bot), (Ann, Calculus)\} \quad P(W6) = 0.05$$

The Possibilistic Model On the other hand, possibility theory provides a purely ordinal model for uncertainty where imprecision is represented by means of a preference relation coded by a total order over the possible situations. This constitutes the fundamental difference between this theory and probability theory which is quantitative. Possibility theory is structurally more qualitative, but is better suited to the representation of imprecise information. More generally, possibility theory allows to model uncertain information which is not of a stochastic but rather of a subjective nature.

The concept of possibility distribution in a universe X, introduced by L.A. Zadeh [25], concerns an application π of X to [0, 1] which is interpreted as a restriction of the possible values of a variable taking its values in X. We denote $\pi(a)$ the degree of possibility that the actual value of x is a.

The possibilitic approach can be applied for representing uncertain values in a relational database and the available information about the value of a single-valued attribute A for a tuple x is represented by a possibility distribution $\pi_{A(x)}$ on D $\cup$ {e} where D denotes the domain of attribute A and e is an extra-element which stands for the case when the attribute does not apply to x. There should exist a value in D $\cup$ {e} for A(x), which leads to the normalization condition $\max_d \pi_{A(x)}(d) = 1$ (i.e., at least one value in D $\cup$ {e} is completely possible). For instance, the information "Paul is young" will be represented by: $\pi_{Age(Paul)}(e) = 0$ and $\pi_{Age(Paul)}(d) = \mu_{young}(d), \forall d \in D$. Here, μ_{young} is a membership function which represents the vague predicate "young" in a given context. It is important to notice that the values restricted by a possibility distribution are considered as mutually exclusive. $\Pi_{A(x)}(d) = 1$ only means that d is a completely possible value for A(x), but does not mean that it is certain that d is the value of A for x (or in other words that d is necessarily the value of A for x), except if $\forall d' \neq d, \pi_{A(x)}(d') = 0$.

From a normalized possibility distribution ($\exists x_0 \in X$ such that $\pi(x_0) = 1$), one can build a measure of possibility which is an application Π of the powerset of X ($\mathcal{P}(X)$) in [0, 1]:

$$\forall A \in \mathcal{P}(X), \Pi(A) = \sup_{x \in A}(\pi(x))$$

such that : $\Pi(\emptyset) = 0, \Pi(X) = 1, \forall A, B \in \mathcal{P}(X), \Pi(A \cup B) = \max(\Pi(A), \Pi(B))$.

This last axiom constitutes the fundamental difference between probabilities and possibilities. In particular it allows us to deduce :

$$\forall A \in \mathcal{P}(X), \max(\Pi(A), \Pi(\bar{A})) = 1$$

which says that from two opposite events at least one is totally possible. With probabilities, one passes from the knowledge of $P(A)$ to that of $P(\bar{A})$ or vice versa ($P(A) = 1 - P(\bar{A})$), whereas here the knowledge of $\Pi(A)$ says nothing about $\Pi(\bar{A})$. Consequently, a measure of necessity N has been defined as:

$$\forall A \in \mathcal{P}(X), N(A) = 1 - \Pi(\bar{A})$$

which says that the necessity (certainty) of an event corresponds to the impossibility of the opposite event.

Possibility and necessity measures can be extended to fuzzy events:

$$\forall A \in \tilde{\mathcal{P}}(X) \text{ (set of fuzzy parts of X)}, \Pi(A) = \sup_{x \in X} \min(\pi(x), \mu_A(x))$$

$$\forall A \in \tilde{\mathcal{P}}(X), N(A) = \inf_{x \in X} \max(1 - \pi(x), \mu_A(x))$$

3.3   Value-Based Querying of Possibilistic Databases

Here, we are concerned with the querying of databases containing ill-known values represented by possibility distributions. The type of querying considered hereafter is called "value-based" since it relates to the same general philosophy as crisp database querying, in the sense that the conditions allowed reduce to a comparison (crisp or fuzzy) between an attribute and a value (which can be a linguistic term), or between two attributes. The criteria considered here only concern the *value* that the data can take, and not its representation.

When a condition applies to imperfectly known data, the result of a query evaluation can no longer be a single value. Since we do not know the precise values of some attributes for some items, we may be uncertain about the fact that these items satisfy or not the query (to some degree). It is why two degrees (attached to two points of view: the extent to which it is possible that the condition is satisfied and the extent to which it is certain that the condition is satisfied) are used. The result is thus a pair of fuzzy sets $\tau\Pi$ and τN where each element (tuple, for example) is linked to the degree of possibility (resp. necessity or certainty) that it satisfies the criterion. These two degrees are comparable to an optimistic and a pessimistic limit of the degree to which the condition, considered in the presence of imprecise data, is satisfied. It should be noted that a relation is not obtained and that the usual principle of compositionality is not preserved. Compound conditions involving connectives and negation can be defined (see [4] for details).

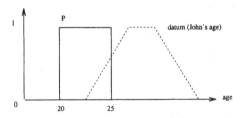

Fig. 1. The characteristic functions of "age $\in$ [20,25]" and John's age

Example. Hereafter, we illustrate the matching mechanism in the case where the data is imprecise and the predicate is Boolean (for the sake of clarity of the figure). If John's age and the predicate P: "age $\in$ [20, 25]" are represented according to Figure 1, the computation of "John's age $\in$ [20, 25]" will be based (according to Figures 2 and 3) on the computation of the values: $\min(\pi_{John's\ age}(d)$, $\mu_P(d))$ for which the supremum (α) will be taken to obtain Π and: $\max(1 - \pi_{John's\ age}(d), \mu_P(d))$ for which the lowest value (0) corresponds to $N\Diamond$

It is easy to show that when the data is precise, Π and N are identical and correspond to the grade of satisfaction (or membership) defined in section 2.

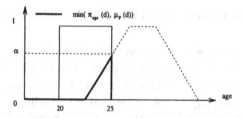

Fig. 2. Possibility representation

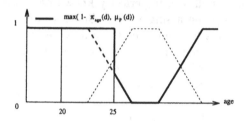

Fig. 3. Necessity representation

3.4 Representation-Based Querying of Possibilistic Databases

An alternate querying approach (called representation-based querying) consists in exploiting some concepts of the data model which concern the representation of imprecision/uncertainty. This idea can be illustrated in the framework of a database containing disjunctive information (an attribute value being represented as a disjunctive set of domain values). For example we know that the price of house H1 is $80,000 or $100,000 or $120,000. Whereas an example of a usual (value-based) filtering criterion is: "find the houses whose price is higher than $90,000" (in this case, H1 belongs to the set of possibly satisfactory elements, but not to the set of certain answers because of the price value $80,000), an example of a representation-based criterion is: "find the houses whose price representation contains at least three possible values". This type of filtering criterion corresponds to a querying approach of a different nature, the objective being to be able to exploit some available knowledge which is not taken into account by the previous querying approach.

In the preceding example (regular disjunctive sets), the representation-based criteria that can be envisaged remain quite simple, and a more interesting situation, from a semantic point of view, corresponds to the case where graded models of uncertainty are used. The framework used can be possibilistic or probabilistic, but for the sake of brevity we only consider the possibilistic model.

One can distinguish several kinds of conditions involving one or two representations. In the first case, such conditions can refer in particular to:

i) the possibility degrees of some values of the domain. Let A be an attribute, D the domain of A, and $X = \{d_1, \cdots, d_n\}$ a crisp subset of D. Let us denote poss(A, X) a function returning the truth value of the statement "all the values in X are possible for A". Formally, we have:

$$\text{poss}(A, \{d_1, \cdots, d_n\}) = \min(\pi_A(d_1), \cdots, \pi_A(d_n)).$$

Using this function, one can express conditions such as:

- the values a_1 and a_2 are possible over a degree λ for attribute A: poss(A, $\{a_1, a_2\}) \geq \lambda$,
- the value a_1 is preferred to the value a_2 for attribute A: poss(A, $\{a_1\}) \geq$ poss(A, $\{a_2\}$).

ii) the cardinality of a given λ-cut. Let us introduce the function card_cut(A, λ) (resp. card_supp(A)) giving the number of D-values whose possibility degrees for A are greater than λ (resp. are strictly positive). We have:

$$\text{card\_cut}(A, \lambda) = |\{d \in D \,|\pi_A(d) \geq \lambda\}|$$
$$\text{card\_supp}(A) = |\{d \in D \mid \pi_A(d) > 0\}|.$$

Using these functions, one can express conditions such as:

- at least n values are possible over λ for attribute A: card_cut(A, λ) $\geq$ n,
- the support of attribute A contains at least n values: card_supp(A) $\geq$ n.

iii) the imprecision of an attribute value. For example, let us consider the query: "find the houses whose price value is not precisely known". It is possible to express the corresponding condition in a straightforward manner using the predicate card_supp defined above (a value which is not precisely known is a distribution whose support contains more than one domain value) and we get:

$$\text{card\_supp}(A) > 1$$

where A denotes the considered attribute. Nevertheless, if one wants to qualify more accurately the amount of imprecision attached to an attribute value, one has to use a specific measure indicating the extent to which a value is imprecise (defined for example as the ratio between the area of the possibility distribution and the size of the domain).

iv) the uncertainty level attached to a given attribute value. For example, let us consider the query: "find the houses whose price value is uncertain at a degree less than .3". The level of uncertainty λ attached to an attribute value A defined on a domain D can be defined in the following way: λ is the largest value α in the unit interval such that $\forall d \in D$, poss(A, $\{d\}) \geq \alpha$. In other words, we have:

$$\lambda = \sup \{\alpha \in [0, 1], \text{card\_cut}(A, \alpha) = |D|\}.$$

From a query language point of view, one needs to define a
function unc_level(A) returning the uncertainty level attached to A, in order
to allow for the expression of such conditions.
v) the shape of the possibility distribution representing a given attribute value.
For example, let us consider the query: "find the houses whose price value
is represented as an interval (resp. a triangular distribution, a trapezoidal
distribution, etc)". Here again, some specific predicates must be defined to
extend the considered query language.

The conditions described above being Boolean, the result of a query will be
a non-weighted relation. However, such criteria can also take a fuzzy form. For
example, one can imagine to transform some of the preceding conditions into
"a_1 is *much* preferred to a_2", "all the values $\{a_1, ..., a_n\}$ have a *high* degree of
possibility", "*many* values are possible over a degree λ", etc. Then, the result
would be a fuzzy relation i.e., a relation where a membership degree is assigned
to each tuple.

When two representations are used, the key point is to define the way they are
compared. Several methods have been proposed to compare possibility distributions (or fuzzy sets), but the approach appropriate in our context is to measure
the extent to which two *representations* are globally close to each other [5, 7, 18,
22] which significantly differs from a possibilistic measure [9, 20]. In [22], Raju
and Majumdar define the fuzzy equality measure, denoted EQ, in the following
way:

$$\mu_{EQ}(\pi_{A(x)}, \pi_{A(y)}) = \min_{u \in D} \psi(\pi_{A(x)}(u), \pi_{A(y)}(u))$$

where ψ is a resemblance relation (i.e., reflexive and symmetric) over [0, 1]. A
similar method is advocated in [11]. These approaches are suitable when strict
equality is the only way to compare domain values. However, there are many
circumstances which reveal the necessity of specifying a resemblance relation on
domains. In this case, the comparison consists in estimating the extent to which
the respective representations of A(x) and A(y) are interchangeable with respect
to the considered resemblance relation. In this spirit, a measure of interchange-
ability, generalizing Raju and Majumdar's measure of fuzzy equality, is defined
in [5].
Such representation-based measures can be used, of course, to compare two
ill-known attribute values. In the representation-based querying framework, two
data D1 and D2 are viewed as linguistic labels and what we measure is the
approximate synonymy of their respective representations. On the second hand,
these measures can be used to compare an ill-known attribute value D and a fuzzy
predicate P. The basic idea is the same: one evaluates the extent to which the
predicate and the value represent the same concept. For example, let us consider
a possibility distribution D representing John's age and a fuzzy predicate P =
"middle-aged" (represented by a fuzzy set). While the fuzzy pattern matching
method allows to measure the extent to which John is possibly (resp. necessarily)
middle-aged, the new querying approach proposed can be used to measure the

extent to which the representation of John's age and the fuzzy set representing the concept "middle-aged" are close to each other. The value computed will then correspond to the synonymy of the representation of John's age and "middle-aged".

It must be noticed that representation-based criteria can be evaluated against regular (precise) data. As a matter of fact, a crisp value x can be seen as a possibility distribution $\{1/x\}$, and thus, the different conditions introduced above will make sense in this case too. It has been shown [6] that the expression of representation-based conditions in the querying framework based on fuzzy pattern matching is quite problematical: either these conditions require multiple queries, or they are not expressible at all. This result justifies the need for a specific querying framework well-suited to this kind of selection conditions.

4 Conclusion

This paper has been devoted to the issues of flexible database querying and the handling of ill-known data through different types of user queries. First, we have considered the case where the data are precise. It has been recalled that, in such a context, fuzzy sets provide a general sound framework for dealing with preferences which are the basis for gradual queries. The regular relational algebra can be extended to fuzzy relations and most of the usual properties are maintained, in particular the compositionality principle. The basic idea underlying the extension of an SQL-like query language has been outlined. In fact, if the features of querying languages and the bases are now correctly mastered, a significant amount of work has to be devoted to implementation of such systems in the near future. This is clearly a crucial point which is a key for promoting fuzzy querying.

The remainder of the paper has been devoted to the representation and the handling of ill-known values in relational databases. Different frameworks for the modeling of imperfect data have been presented, and we have focused on the possibilistic framework which proves to be the best suited to the representation of imprecise and/or uncertain information. We have considered two different ways of querying a database containing ill-known values represented as possibility distributions.

The first one, called value-based querying, uses a fuzzy pattern matching mechanism and allows for evaluating queries of the same kind as in the usual case (i.e., when the data is precise) in the sense that the conditions refer to the values of the data. Two degrees are computed for each item, corresponding respectively to the level of possibility and the level of necessity that the item satisfies the query. In the special case where the data is precise, we come back to the situation described above: the two degrees are then equal and correspond to a gradual degree of satisfaction. It is important to point out the fact that the definition of extended algebraic operators in the possibilistic framework is a much more complex issue than it is in the gradual relation framework. The fuzzy pattern matching mechanism is the basis of a sound definition of the extended algebraic operator of selection, however some problems appear when one wants to give a sound semantics to operations involving several relations, such as the Cartesian product and the join. As a matter of fact, it would necessitate to be able to recognize that two disjunctions in the result correspond to a same fact, which means that the model should be extended with some semantics in addition to the representations of ill-known values. It must be noticed that this problem is not tied to the possibilistic model, its source being rather in the values handled which are represented as disjunctions. Another problem lies in the non-compositionality of the operators, which is due to the fact that the relations resulting from a selection have a different format than the initial ones (one gets twofold relations in the sense that two degrees are computed for each tuple). This makes it impossible to define a set of operators constituting an algebra in the usual sense. This problem, as well as the one mentioned above, should give rise to further research works in a near future.

In the last part of the paper, we have considered an alternate way of retrieving ill-known data, involving conditions on the representations of the data. Contrary to the preceding one, this querying approach does not introduce uncertainty in the results but provides regular or gradual relations, which should allow to define a formal querying framework more easily than in the value-based case.

References

1. Barbará, D., Garcia-Molina, H., and Porter, D. The management of probabilistic data, IEEE Trans. on Knowledge and Data Eng., 4, 487-502, 1992.
2. Bosc, P., and Pivert, O. Some approaches for relational databases flexible querying, Int. J. of Intell. Inf. Syst., 1, 323-354, 1992.
3. Bosc, P., and Pivert, O. SQLf: A relational database language for fuzzy querying, IEEE Trans. on Fuzzy Syst., 3, 1-17, 1995.
4. Bosc, P., and Prade, H. An introduction to the fuzzy set and possibility theory-based treatment of flexible queries and imprecise or uncertain databases, In "Uncertainty Management in Information Systems: From Needs to Solutions" (A. Motro, P. Smets, Eds.), pp. 285-324. Kluwer Academic Publishers, 1997.
5. Bosc, P., and Pivert, O. On the comparison of imprecise values in fuzzy databases, Proc. 6th IEEE Int. Conf. on Fuzzy Syst. (FUZZ-IEEE'97), Barcelona (Spain), 707-712, 1997.
6. Bosc, P., and Pivert, O. On representation-based querying of databases containing ill-known values, Lecture Notes in Artificial Intelligence, 1325 (Z. Ras, A. Skowron, Eds.), pp. 477-486. Springer Verlag, 1997.
7. Bouchon-Meunier, B., Rifqi, M., and Bothorel, S. Towards general measures of comparison of objects, Fuzzy Sets and Syst., 84, 143-153, 1996.
8. Chang, C.L. Decision support in an imperfect world, Research report RJ3421, IBM San José, CA, USA, 1982.
9. Cubero, J.C., and Vila, M.A. A new definition of fuzzy functional dependency in fuzzy relational databases, Int. J. of Intell. Syst., 9, 441-448, 1994.
10. Dey, D., and Sarkar, S. A probabilistic Relational model and algebra, ACM Trans. on Database Syst., 21, 339-369, 1997.

11. Gasos, J., and Ralescu, A. Adapting query representation to improve retrieval in a fuzzy database, Int. J. of Uncertainty, Fuzziness and Knowledge-Based Syst., 3, 57-77, 1995.

12. Ichikawa, T., and Hirakawa, M. ARES: a relational database with the capability of performing flexible interpretation of queries, IEEE Trans. Soft. Eng., 12, 624-634, 1986.

13. Imielinski, T. Incomplete information in logical databases, IEEE Trans. on Data Eng., 12, 29-40, 1989.

14. Kacprzyk, J., and Ziolkowski, A. Database queries with fuzzy linguistic quantifiers, IEEE Trans. Syst., Man and Cybern., 16, 3, 474-478, 1986.

15. Lacroix, M., and Lavency, P. Preferences: putting more knowledge into queries, Proc. 13th VLDB Conf., Brighton (GB), 217-225, 1987.

16. Libkin, L., and Wong, L. Semantic representations and query languages for or-sets, Proc. 12th PODS Conf., 37-48, 1993.

17. Lipski, W. On semantic issues connected with incomplete information databases, ACM Trans. on Database Syst., 4, 262-296, 1979.

18. Liu, W. The fuzzy functional dependency on the basis of the semantic distance, Fuzzy Sets and Syst., 59, 173-179, 1993.

19. Motro, A. VAGUE: a user interface to relational databases that permits vague queries, ACM Trans. on Office Inf. Syst., 6, 187-214, 1988.

20. Prade, H., and Testemale, C. Generalizing database relational algebra for the treatment of incomplete/uncertain information and vague queries, Inf. Sc., 34, 115-143, 1984.

21. Rabitti, F. Retrieval of multimedia documents by imprecise query specification, Lecture Notes in Computer Science, 416, 202-218, 1990.

22. Raju, K.V.S.V.N., and Majumdar, A.K. Fuzzy functional dependencies and lossless join decomposition of fuzzy relational database systems, ACM Trans. on Database Syst., 13, 129-166, 1988.

23. Umano, M. FREEDOM-0: a fuzzy database system, In "Fuzzy Information and Decision Processes" (M.M. Gupta, E. Sanchez, Eds.), pp. 339-347. North-Holland, Amsterdam, 1982.

24. Vandenberghe, R., Van Schooten, A., De Caluwe, R., and Kerre, E.E. Some practical aspects of fuzzy database techniques: An example, Inf. Syst., 14, 465-472, 1989.

25. Zadeh, L.A. Fuzzy sets as a basis for a theory of possibility, Fuzzy Sets and Syst., 1, 3-28, 1978.

26. Zimanyi, E., and Pirotte, A. Imperfect information in relational databases. In "Uncertainty Management in Information Systems: From Needs to Solutions" (A. Motro, P. Smets, Eds.), pp. 35-87. Kluwer Academic Publishers, 1997.

Answering Queries in Context*

Stéphane Bressan[1] and Cheng Hian Goh[2]

[1] Sloan School of Mgt, MIT, Cambridge, USA
steph@context.mit.edu
[2] Dept of Info Sys & Comp Sc, NUS, Singapore
gohch@iscs.nus.edu.sg

Abstract. The emergence of the Internet as the de facto *Global Information Infrastructure* enables the construction of decision support systems that leverage on the panoply of on-line information sources. This highly dynamic environment presents a critical need for a flexible and scalable strategy for integrating the disparate information sources while respecting their autonomy.

The *Context Interchange* strategy addresses above concerns with an emphasis on resolving problems arising from *semantic heterogeneity*, i.e. inconsistencies arising from differences in the representation and interpretation of data. This is accomplished using three elements: a shared vocabulary for the underlying application domain (in the form of a *domain model*), a formal object-relational data model (COIN), and an object-deductive language (COINL). Semantic interoperation is accomplished by making use of declarative definitions corresponding to source and receiver contexts; i.e. constraints, choices, and preferences for representing and interpreting data. The identification and resolution of potential semantic conflicts involving multiple sources are performed automatically by the *context mediator*. Users and application developers can express queries in their own terms and rely on the context mediator to rewrite the query in a disambiguated form.

1   Introduction

While the Internet (and the World Wide Web) provide the *physical connectivity* and the first level of *logical connectivity* to thousands of potentially useful information sources [10, 18, 2, 21], heterogeneity of data semantics and representation among these sources continues to elude the seamless integration of these data sources into practical decision support applications [14]. Consider the following information sources that exemplify the idiosyncrasies that prevail among these sources:

---

* This work is supported in part by ARPA and USAF/Rome Laboratory under contract F30602-93-C-0160, the International Financial Services Research Center (IFSRC), the PROductivity in Information Technology (PROFIT) project at MIT, and ARF RP970628 at the National University of Singapore.

- The NASDAQ stock exchange recently decided to report stock quotes in fractions at the 32nd (previously at the 16th). Most non-American stock exchanges, on the other hand, chose to report stock prices in decimals.
- A French company, in its registration statement (Form S-8) to the American Securities and Exchange Commission, reports a nominal value of shares in French Francs and a maximum offering price in US Dollars. A footnote on the statement explains: *"Amounts represented on an as converted basis from French francs to U.S. dollars. The noon buying Rate for French francs used for such conversion was 5.71 francs per U.S. dollar on March 20, 1997."*

These disparate reporting conventions in the above information sources came about for a variety of reasons (for example, cultural or regulatory). In most of the cases, they are legitimate and are in line with the requirements for which the information is collected. However, the disparities *between* these different sources makes the task of data integration across disparate systems a most difficult task. For example, a smart investor with her assets distributed in stocks and bonds in her country as well as in foreign markets may want to know her "net asset." Although most of the information she needs can be obtained from the variety of information sources on the Internet, the collation of this information is a non-trivial task given the idiosyncrasies present in different sources.

Most sources exhibiting heterogeneity (and potential conflicts) are easy to comprehend and resolve when taken individually. For example, in the registration statement of the French company mentioned above, information pertaining to the necessary currency conversions is easily available. In the financial reporting domain, these problems often reduce to scaling factors, unit conversions, or naming conventions. Furthermore, for a given application domain, the different types of data heterogeneity can reasonably be modeled by the use of a shared vocabulary – which we call the *domain model* – consisting of the set of common concepts manipulated by the information sources and the various applications. In our investment example, such concepts may be company names, company "financials" (including revenues, stock prices or total assets), different types of currencies, and currency conversion rates.

Although the reconciliation of the above conflicts can be manually performed by a user, this task may become unbearably cumbersome with increasing number of information sources (and potential conflicts). Our research stems from the premise that applications and users ought to focus on specifying what information is needed and how the results should be presented, *but should not have to worry about different representation and interpretation of the same information in disparate systems*. We suggest that this latter task can be taken care of by a *Context Mediator*. *Context mediation* refers to the process whereby a query formulated under one *context* (the set of assumptions concerning how data is represented or how it ought to be interpreted) is transformed to a semantically equivalent query for accessing information present at sources having disparate contexts, such that all potential conflicts can be identified and resolved. To this end, we propose a deductive and object-oriented data model (COIN) and language (COINL) for the definition of contexts, and show that context mediation can be automatized provided that a *domain model* and *context definitions* for the sources and receivers are available. The overhead of defining the domain model for an application domain and of defining contexts for the sources and receivers is justified by the observation that the information sources made accessible under this Context Interchange framework remain loosely coupled to one another. This means that new information sources can be added (or existing ones withdrawn) without any adverse impact on the other systems. As we have pointed out elsewhere [14], this approach allows us to achieve interoperation on a large-scale despite the rapid pace of changes that take place on the Internet.

Our goal in this paper is to present a concise description of the logic-based object-relational data model as well as the underlying query rewriting strategy that allow queries formulated in one context to be meaningfully evaluated on disparate sources that may have conflicting interpretation or representation of data. Specifically, the data model makes provisions for the same data object to have different representations in different contexts, and allows different conversion functions to be introduced when converting data between different contexts. These features collectively offers a sound (logical) basis for making inferences as to *when* data conflicts may occur, and *how* a query can be rewritten to take these conflicts into consideration.

The remainder of this paper is organized as follows. In the next section, we introduce the crucial elements of our data model with the aid of a series of examples. we describes how the data model is used in supporting our integration strategy. Then we present the inference mechanism underlying query transformation arising from conflicting data representations. The last section summarizes our contributions.

2 A Logic-Based Object-Relational Data Model

The essence of our integration strategy can be summarized as follows. We assume the existence of a shared vocabulary in the form of a *domain model* consisting of a collection of "rich types" that are meaningful to some underlying application domain. Every information source wanting to make its data available must provide a declarative description of the conventions or assumptions adopted in data reporting with reference to the types defined in this domain model. This description is referred to as the *context* for the corresponding information source. Similarly, every user has associated with him or her a context which captures the implicit assumptions that the user adopts in interpreting the data received. Whenever information is exchanged between a source and a receiver (or between two sources, as in a "join" operation), the contexts are compared to determine if a conflict may exist. If so, the query may have to be rewritten to include additional data operations that allow the conflicts to be mitigated. The detection of potential conflicts and the accompanying query rewriting is accomplished by a middleware component which we refer to as a *context mediator*.

We describe in this section features of the data model COIN that are instrumental in supporting the integration approach which we have adopted. These include (1) a notion of semantic-objects distinct from "printable" primitive-objects; (2) the ability to annotate semantic-objects using tags which are assigned different values in different contexts; and (3) a novel concept of semantic-equivalence which allows objects to be compared while taking into account the possibility that the same object may have different symbolic representations.

2.1 Primitive- versus Semantic-Types and Objects

Information units in our data model are modeled as *objects*. Every object is an instance of some type; the latter can either be a *primitive-type* or a *semantic-type* (but not both). Primitive-types correspond to printable data types (e.g., strings, real numbers, and integers) whereas semantic-types correspond to complex types pertaining to a given application domain (e.g., stock-price, return-on-investment). Every object has both a *print-value (pval)* and an *object-identity (oid)*. The pval and oid of *primitive-objects* (i.e., instances of primitive-types) are identical and furthermore is invariant across distinct contexts. This is not the case for *semantic-objects*: although a semantic-object has an immutable oid, it may have distinct pval depending on the *context* in which the pval is reported. We denote the pval of an object o in context c by $pval(o; c)$. (We use a functional notation for *pval*. It must be clear that $X = \text{pval}(o; c)$ is a syntactic variant of $\text{pval}(o, c, X)$).

Example 1 Consider a semantic-type `stockPrice`. The statement

o_1 : `stockPrice`

introduces an instance of `stockPrice` which is referred to using the oid o_1. Although this object may correspond to a uniquely identifiable piece of information in the real world, it may be represented in a number of ways in different systems. For example, suppose c and c' denote two distinct contexts, it may happen that $pval(o_1; c) = 10$ whereas $pval(o_1; c') = 1500$. (In this particular instance, stock price is presented in thousands of US Dollars in context c, but in ones using Singapore currency in c', where the exchange rate is given by 1 USD = 1.5 SGD). Loosely speaking, the same information (corresponding to the object o_1) is reported differently because of the disparate assumptions underlying their representation in different systems. The same anomaly is *not* exhibited by primitive objects; for instance, the data objects 10 and 1500 are primitive-objects of the primitive-type `integer` and have no distinct pval apart from their oid. Moreover, the primitive object 10 has the value 10 regardless of context: i.e., $pval(10; c) = 10$ for any context c. $\square$

2.2 Annotations in Context

As was illustrated in Example 1, the same object may have different representations or pval in disparate systems by virtue of the different assumptions arising from various social or organizational practices. To capture these variations, each semantic-type is allowed to have zero or more *meta-attributes* (also called *modifiers*). A meta-attribute is in essence a *single-valued method* which returns another semantic-object. It is a *parameterized method* because it is allowed to return different semantic-objects for different contexts.

Example 2 Consider the semantic-type `stockPrice` as introduced earlier. Suppose we now associate two meta-attributes `currency` and `scaleFactor` with this semantic-type. These meta-attributes can now be assigned different semantic-objects in different contexts. For example, suppose o_{USD} and o_{SGD} denote semantic-objects corresponding to the currency US-Dollar and Singapore-Dollar respectively, we may write[1]

$$\text{currency}(o_1; c) = o_{USD}$$
$$\text{currency}(o_1; c') = o_{SGD}$$

These statements allow us to associate different objects with the modifier **currency** (corresponding to the semantic-object o_1) in contexts c and c'. □

Notice that instead of assigning primitive-objects (i.e., printable values) to meta-attributes, we have chosen to use semantic-objects instead. For example, the value assigned to the semantic-object o_1 (with respect to context c) in the preceding example is yet another semantic-object denoted by o_{USD}. The reason for this convoluted representation is because *meta-data are often present as data in source systems and are susceptible to the same curse (of having different representations in disparate systems).* This "recursive" structure of semantic-objects presents a challenge in reasoning about data conflicts since data elements in two distinct information sources may have the same meta-attribute-value (e.g., both are represented in the same currency), but the symbolic representation of the currency in use may be different (e.g., USD in one source, and US\$ in another[2]).

2.3 Semantic Equivalence

The phenomenon of semantic-heterogeneity suggests that a naive comparison of the values of data elements in disparate information sources is not adequate. With reference to Example 1, the value 10 and 1500 corresponding to a particular `stockPrice`-object are "equivalent" even though they appear to be vastly different. Conversely, two data elements having the same value in two contexts may mean very different things.

The above anomaly is circumvented in the Context Interchange framework by transforming all comparisons between data elements to be those between

---

[1] We have chosen to use a Datalog-ish syntax here as opposed to an "object-oriented" syntax *a la* F-logic [16], say $o_1[currency(c) \rightarrow o_{USD}]$. However, it should be clear that the differences between the two syntactic forms are merely cosmetic.

[2] In a the formulation of a meta-data model [19] that is precursor to the one reported here, this problem was overlooked resulting in a representation language that is overly restrictive.

semantic objects. Specifically, if θ is a relational operator (say, of the set $\{=, <, >, \geq, \leq, \neq, \ldots\}$) and o_1 and o_2 are semantic-objects, then we say that $o_1 \theta_c o_2$ if and only if $pval(o_1; c) \, \theta \, pval(o_2; c)$. More concretely, we say that semantic-objects o_1 and o_2 are *semantically-equivalent with respect to context* c (a condition we denote by $o_1 \doteq_c o_2$) if and only if $pval(o_1; c) = pval(o_2; c)$.

Example 3 Suppose o_1 and o_2 are both semantic-objects of the type `stockPrice`, and contexts c and c' correspond to those introduced in Example 1. If $pval(o_1; c) = 10$ and $pval(o_2; c') = 1500$, then o_1 and o_2 are semantically-equivalent with respect to context c since $pval(o_1; c) = pval(o_2; c) = 10$. Similarly, o_1 and o_2 are semantically-equivalent wrt context c'. □

In the Context Interchange framework, every semantic-object o has a reference context $\mu(o) = c$ for which $pval(o; c)$ is known. (The reason for this will become apparent in the next section.) The pval of o corresponding to a context c' (distinct from c) is determined via the application of a unique *mapping function* corresponding to the semantic-type T of o. This mapping function is in turned defined (explicitly or implicitly) through the composition of *conversion functions* corresponding to modifiers of T. Conversion functions exist in one-to-one correspondence to modifiers: i.e., a semantic-type with k modifiers will have k conversion functions, the composition of which yields the mapping function.

Example 4 Consider again Example 1. The semantic-type `stockPrice` has two modifiers `currency` and `scaleFactor`. The conversion function associated with `scaleFactor`, in a Datalog-like syntax, may be defined as follows:

```
cvt(scaleFactor,o,v,c') = v' ←
    c = μ(o),                          % c is the reference context for o
    f' = pval(scaleFactor(o;c'); c'),  % f' is the pval of o's scaleFactor
                                       % in context c'
    f = pval(scaleFactor(o;c);c'),     % f is the pval of o's scaleFactor in c
    v' = v * f/f'.                     % v' is the scaleFactor of o in c'
```

The mapping function for the semantic-type *stockPrice* can be defined as

```
map(stockPrice,o,c') = v' ←
    c = μ(o),
    v = pval(o;c),
    cvt(scaleFactor,o,v,c') = v_0,
    cvt(currency,o,v_o,c') = v'.
```

The conversion function for `currency` has been omitted here for brevity. □

2.4 Semantic-Relations

We introduce the notion of a *semantic-relation*, which is used for representing relationships that exists between different semantic-objects. Let $D_1, \ldots, D_n$ be semantic-types, not necessarily distinct. A semantic-relation defined on $D_1, \ldots, D_n$ is a subset of $dom(D_1) \times \cdots \times dom(D_n)$ where $dom(D_i)$ denotes the set of all instances of the type D_i. Hence, a semantic-relation is simply a collection of tuples for which constituent elements are semantic-objects.

In the Context Interchange framework, semantic-relations are introduced via view definitions. Semantic-objects and semantic-relations are never instantiated and they exists only "virtually" for the purpose of reasoning about the semantics of underlying data elements. We refer to these view definitions as *elevation axioms*, since we can think of actual information sources as existing at a representational-level which is rooted in the idiosyncrasies of the underlying context, whereas semantic-relations are insulated from these quirks and exists at a "higher" level of abstraction.

For a given extensional relation r, the corresponding semantic-relation r' (or textually, r_p) is defined via the axiom:

$$\forall x_1, \ldots, x_k \exists y_1, \ldots, y_k \text{ such that } r'(y_1, \ldots, y_k) \leftarrow r(x_1, \ldots, x_k).$$

To avoid having to deal with the existentially quantified variables $y_1, \ldots, y_k$, we introduce the Skolem-objects

$$f_{r\_A1}(x_1, \ldots, x_k), \ldots, f_{r\_Ak}(x_1, \ldots, x_k)$$

where f_{r_Ai} denotes Skolem functions for the relation r corresponding to attribute Ai. This allows us to rewrite the elevation axiom to the following:

$$r'(f_{r\_A1}(x_1, \ldots, x_k), \ldots, f_{r\_Ak}(x_1, \ldots, x_k)) \leftarrow r(x_1, \ldots, x_k).$$

For each of the Skolem object (semantic-object) introduced in the elevation axiom, we need to (1) associate it with a semantic-type defined in the domain model; and (2) identify its value for its reference context c (associated with the relation r).

Example 5 Consider the relation given in the following schema

```
cnn(Ticker, Date, LastPrice)
```

The lifting axiom for this relation is as follows:

```
cnn_p(f_cnn_ticker(W,X,Y), f_cnn_compname(W,X,Y)
      f_cnn_lastPrice(W,X,Y)) ← cnn(W,X,Y).
```

The typing information is introduced via the following statements which are akin to F-logic typing statements:

```
f_cnn_ticker(_,_,_) : ticker
f_cnn_date(_,_,_) : calendarDate
f_cnn_lastPrice(_,_,_) : stockPrice
```

The semantic-types `ticker`, `calendarDate`, `stockPrice` will have to be defined in the domain model. (The underscore '_' used above correspond to "anonymous variables" as in Prolog.)

Finally, the values of each semantic-objects for the reference context c (the context corresponding to the relation cnn) has to be established. For example, we can write

```
Y = pval(f_cnn_closing(W,X,Y); c) ← cnn(W,X,Y).
```

This completes the integration of the extensional relation cnn into the Context Interchange system. □

This construction, based on skolem functions is similar to the general mechanism discussed in [11] for answering queries using views. Indeed, in our case, the extensional relations can be seen as views over the semantic relations where objects have been reified into primitive values.

3 Reasoning about Semantic Conflicts

Context Mediation is essentially a view rewriting process. However, unlike standard federated systems [20], the views in the Context Mediation system are not statically defined but are dynamically (and incrementally) determined through the comparison of source contexts (i.e., those corresponding to data sources) and receiver context (i.e., that of the application or user issuing the query). Because context definitions and the functions which implement conversions between contexts are kept independent of specific views, this information can be reused, introducing flexibility and scalability to the integration process.

3.1 Example

Let us consider a query retrieving stocks prices in the New York Stock Exchange (NYSE) for the stocks in the portfolio, as well as analysts' latest recommendations. The initial portfolio data is stored in a relation in a local database (`local`). The necessary information is available from various sites on the World Wide Web[3]. The NYSE Web site (`http://www.nyse.com`) provides general data about the stocks such as ticker symbols, company names, industry sectors, or number of outstanding shares. Among many other Web sites, the CNN Financial Network (`http://www.cnnfn.com`) provides, free of charge, 15 minutes delayed stock last prices and related data (high, low, P/E ratio, etc). Zacks Investment Research publishes quantified recommendations for stocks in the American stock exchanges on its Web site (`http://www.zacks.com`).

Consider the SQL query:

---

[3] See [3] for a discussion on the access to Web data.

```
SELECT local.ticker, nyse.companyName, local.qty * cnn.last,
    zacks.rec
FROM local, cnn, nyse, zacks
WHERE nyse.ticker = local.ticker AND cnn.ticker = nyse.ticker AND
    zacks.ticker = nyse.ticker;
```

The literally equivalent Datalog query is:

```
query(Ticker, Name, Total, Rec) ←
    local(Ticker, _, _, Qty), cnn(Ticker, _, LastPrice),
    nyse(Ticker, Name, _, _), zacks(Ticker, Rec),
    Total = Qty * LastPrice
```

When submitted to the Context Mediator, this query is first compiled into a Datalog query. The references to the relations in the sources are replaced by references to the corresponding semantic relations, and the values projected in the results are rewritten into the print values of the semantic objects in the receiver context.

Suppose the investor is French. In her context, stock prices are assumed to be expressed in French francs. If we denote her context by c_french, this will allow us to rewrite the query into the following:

```
query(Ticker, Name, Total, Rec) ←
    local_p(STicker, _, _, SQty), cnn_p(STicker, _, SLastPrice),
    nyse_p(STicker, SName, _, _), zacks_p(STicker, SRec),
    Total = Qty * LastPrice,
    Ticker = pval(STicker; c_french),
    Qty = pval(SQty; c_french),
    LastPrice = pval(SLastPrice; c_french),
    Name = pval(SName; c_french),
    Rec = pval(SRec; c_french).
```

The Context Mediator then rewrites the query by incrementally testing for potential semantic conflicts and introducing conversion functions for their resolution when necessary. This may involve references to additional information sources which are not found in the original query. The context definition chooses as a valid currency conversion function the (historical) conversion rates provided by the Olsen Associates Web site (http://www.oanda.com). This Web site is treated as a data source that exports a relation olsen with the attributes To, From, Rate, and Date, to represent the exchanged currency, the expressed currency, the exchange rate, and the date for which the rate is valid, respectively. Notice however, that a date format conflict we may not have anticipated has been detected by the Context Mediator. In order to produce a timely result for the rate, the ancillary source requires date to be in the European format (DD/MM/YY). However, CNN reports dates in the American Format (MM/DD/YY). This information was found in the respective contexts of Olsen and CNN. An additional conversion is introduced by means of a conversion function (seen as a relation) us2eur. Finally, the mediated query in Datalog is:

```
query(Ticker, Name, Total, Rec) ←
    local(Ticker, _, _, Qty), cnn(Ticker, Date1, LastPrice),
    nyse(Ticker, Name, _, _), zacks(Ticker, Rec),
    olsen('USD', 'FRF', Date2, Rate), us2eur(Date1, Date2),
    Total = Qty * LastPrice * Rate.
```

The query can be translated back into SQL:

```
SELECT local.ticker, nyse.companyName,
       local.qty * cnn.last * olsen.rate, zacks.rec
FROM local, cnn, nyse, zacks, us2eur, olsen
WHERE nyse.ticker = local.ticker AND cnn.ticker = nyse.ticker AND
      zacks.ticker = nyse.ticker AND cnn.date = us2eur.aDate AND
      olsen.date = us2eur.eDate AND olsen.to = 'FRF' AND
      olsen.from = 'USD';
```

3.2 The Abductive Framework

A COINL program – formed from the collection of all the relevant clauses in a Context Interchange system, but excluding extensional facts which are part of extensional information sources – constitutes a Horn clause theory T. The Context Mediation of a query Q is defined as the abductive inference [15] of the sub-queries from the query Q and the theory T under some additional integrity knowledge about the sources. Indeed, as administrators of the mediation network are creating contexts and integrating new sources, it is reasonable to provide them with a means to express integrity knowledge about the sources. Currently such knowledge is expressed as Datalog rules of the form: $\neg(l_1, ..., l_n)$, i.e. a Horn clause containing only negative literals.

The abductive framework for Context Mediation is defined by the following elements:

- the COINL program (domain model, context, conversions, etc) expressed as a theory T of Horn clauses;
- the set P of all predicate symbols used in T composed into the disjoint union of two sets P_c and P_a. P_c contains the predicates corresponding to context axioms and to views. P_a contains the predicates corresponding to the relations exported by the sources, the ancillary relations used to resolve the conflicts (e.g. olsen), and other predicates evaluable at execution time (e.g. arithmetic). P_a is called the set of *abducible* predicates. We say that a literal is abducible if the literal's predicate symbol is in P_a.
- the set of integrity constraints IC describing integrity knowledge about the sources and ancillary relations.

Q' is defined to be inferred from Q and T by abduction under IC if and only if:

- Q' is a conjunction of abducible literals.
- Q is a logical consequence of $T \cup Q'$
- T, IC, and Q' are consistent

3.3   The Mediation Procedure

We now describe the principles behind the procedure implementing the inference discussed above. Such a procedure is comparable to the procedures proposed in [13] and [9]. A generic framework where an abductive procedure is combined with CLP constraint propagation has been proposed in [23, 22, 24].

Because we do not allow recursive view definitions, the inference can be implemented by a slightly modified SLD-resolution of the query Q against the program T. In this modified SLD-resolution, no attempt is made to resolve abducible literals; instead they are removed from the resolvent when selected by the selection function and placed in a special data structure local to each branch of the resolution, we call the *store*. The store, at the leaf of one branch of the resolution leading to an empty resolvent, contains literals whose conjunction is an abductive answer w.r.t. the abductive framework described in the previous section.

Intuitively, the algorithm can be described as the top-down resolution of the query against the view definitions and the context knowledge where the evaluation of sub-queries to remote sources is left to a subsequent phase.

The integrity constraints are used to detect inconsistencies in the store. Each integrity constraint $(\neg(l_1, ..., l_n))$ is compiled into a series of propagation rules (using the new symbol $\Rightarrow$) of the form:

$$l_1, .., l_{j-1}, l_{j+1}, l_n \Rightarrow \overline{l_j}$$

where $\overline{l_j}$ stands for the positive counterpart of the negation of l_j[4]. Propagation consists in adding the literal in the right hand side of a rule if the left hand side subsumes part of the store content.

For instance, a functional dependency $X \rightarrow Y$ expressed by the integrity constraint:

$$\neg(p(X, Y), p(Z, T), Y \neq T, X = Z)$$

is compiled into the two propagation rules:

$$p(X, Y), p(X, T) \Rightarrow X = Y$$

$$p(X, Y), p(Z, T), Y \neq T \Rightarrow X \neq Z$$

If the store contains $p(a, X), p(a, Y)$, the first propagation rule is triggered and adds the literal $X = Y$ to the store. We also assume that duplicates (syntactically identical literals) are eliminated from the store. In addition, equalities are evaluated immediately as they are added. In the above example, as $X = Y$ is added to the store, X and Y are unified. The variable bindings are propagated back into the resolution branch. Inequalities and disequalities are evaluated if they are ground. If the unification resulting from an equality literal, or the evaluation of a disequality or inequality literal fail, an inconsistency is detected in the

---

[4] Notice that variables shared among several literals need to be previously translated into explicit equalities.

store. In such a case, the resolution branch is abandoned. Abandoned branches correspond to inconsistent sub-queries, i.e. queries which would return an empty result if evaluated.

Pragmatically, the completeness of the consistency test is not essential to the procedure since it mainly implements a form of semantic optimization, which rules out sub-queries whose subsequent evaluation would return an empty result.

Store propagation has been primarily introduced to perform the natural duplicate elimination needed when syntactically equivalent literals are added to the store and to detect such duplicates under the knowledge of functional dependencies. Immediately it occurred to us that this form of propagation could be generalized, following the abductive framework, and be used to optimize the mediated query according to additional integrity knowledge.

The query transformation achieved by the propagation of the integrity constraints in the store is similar to various forms of Semantic Query Optimization. Semantic Query Optimization, as described in [8], is the process of increasing the potential for an efficient evaluation of database queries using semantic knowledge expressed by integrity constraints. For example, in the simplest case, a query may be answered without accessing a particular data source if it is known, a priori, that all data at that source is inconsistent with the constraints (i.e. the answer to the query is the empty set). Integrity knowledge can also be used to augment the query with additional selections, which may restrict the amount of data retrieved from individual relations or enable the use of keys and indices. These examples correspond in the classification of King [17] to the cases of "detection of unsatisfiable conditions", "scan reduction", and "index introduction," respectively.

Example 6 In order to illustrate the query rewriting process, let us consider a simple example program.

```
Rules:  q(Z) ← r1(a, Z), Z > 2500.
        r1(X,Y) ← r3(X, Y), r4(Y).      r1(X,Y) ← r5(X, Y).
        r5(X, Y) ← r6(X, Y).            r5(X, Y) ← r7(X, Y).
        r6(a, Y) ← r8(Y).               r7(b, Y) ← r8(Y).
IC:     r4(X) → X < 1000.
```

Figure 1 shows the SLD tree for the query q(X). The abducible literals in this example are: r3, r4, and r8. The arrows above such literals signify their posting into the store. The leftmost branch illustrate the triggering of the integrity constraints introducing the new literal X < 1000 in the store. This branch fails because an inconsistency is detected in the store as X > 2500 is abducted. The right most branch illustrates a standard case of failure of the plain SLD-resolution. The central branch succeeds after several abducible literals have been posted to the store. After the resolvant is emptied, the store contains one (the only) component of the mediated query. If several branches succeed the mediated query is the union of the queries for each branch.

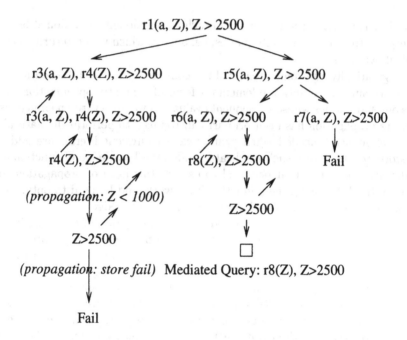

Fig. 1. SLD Tree with abducible and store propagation

3.4 Implementation

We have implemented the Mediator and the abduction procedure using the ECLiPSe parallel constraint logic programming platform [12]. The store, is implemented using coroutining as a constraint store .

The propagation rules generated from the integrity constraints are directly implemented as Constraint Handling Rules (CHRs) [7, 1]. In addition to the propagation rules stemming from the integrity constraints, a set of CHRs implements the propagation of inequality and disequality constraints, and possibly, as required by the application, of specific constraints such as, for instance, linear equations.

4 Conclusion

The approach we have discussed has been implemented in a prototype called MINT [4, 6]. Figure 2 shows one possible front-end interface of the system: a specialized ODBC driver allows the results of queries to be integrated into an Excel spreadsheet. The spreadsheet on the figure present in tables and pies the market value of a simplified portfolio composed of stocks from the New York Stock Exchange (NYSE) as well as analysts' latest recommendations for the stocks in the portfolio. The market value of the portfolio can be monitored in various currencies.

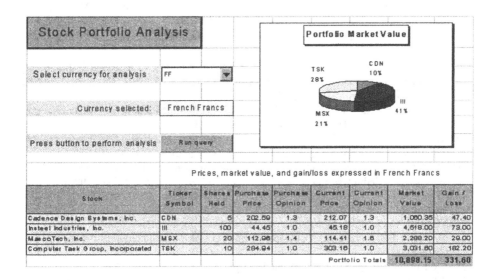

Fig. 2. Excel Spreadsheet

We have described in this paper an object-relational model – COIN – in which information objects are modeled as complex objects having different representation in different contexts. An interesting feature of COIN is that it does not mandate the physical materialization of information objects; instead, these exists only as virtual objects (views and Skolem-objects) for making inferences that accounts for their different representations in different contexts. The semantics of information objects are specified in a declarative manner, with the aid of the language which we call COINL. We have also demonstrated how this declarative approach can facilitate the incremental detection and resolution of conflicts as data are exchanged among different contexts. Further details on the underlying reasoning can also be found in a companion paper [5].

References

1. ABDENNADHER, S., AND SCHÜTZ, H. CHRv: A flexible query language. In *this volume* (1998).
2. BONNET, P., AND TOMASIC, A. Partial answers for unavailable data source. In *this volume* (1998).
3. BRESSAN, S., AND BONNET, P. Extraction and integration of data from semi-structured documents into business applications. In *in Proceedings of the Intl. Conference on Industrial Applications of Prolog* (1997).
4. BRESSAN, S., FYNN, K., GOH, C., JAKOBISIAK, M., HUSSEIN, K., KON, H., LEE, T. MADNICK, S., PENA, T., QU, J., SHUM, A., AND SIEGEL, M. The context interchange mediator prototype. In *Proceedings of the ACM SIGMOD Intl. Conf. on Management of Data* (1997). (see also http://context.mit.edu/demos/sigmod).

5. BRESSAN, S., GOH, C. H., LEE, T., MADNICK, S., AND SIEGEL, M. A procedure for mediation of queries to sources in disparate contexts. In *Proceedings of the International Logic Programming Symposium* (Port Jefferson, NY, Oct 12–17 1997).

6. BRESSAN, S., PENA, T., FYNN, K., AND AL. Overview of a prolog implementation of the context interchange mediator. In *Proc. of the Intl. Conf. on Practical Applications of Prolog* (1997).

7. BRISSET, P., AND FRÜWIRTH, T. High-level implementations of constraint handling rules. Tech. Rep. ECRC-90-20, ECRC, 1995.

8. CHAKRAVARTHY, U. S., GRANT, J., AND MINKER, J. Logic-based approach to semantic query optimization. *ACM Trans. on Database Sys. 15*, 2 (1990).

9. DECKER, H. An extension of SLD by abduction and integrity constraints for view updating in deductive databases. In *Proc. JICSLP'96, MIT Press* (1996).

10. DUSCHKA, O., AND GENESERETH, M. Query planning in infomaster. http://infomaster.stanford.edu/, 1997.

11. DUSCHKA, O., AND GENESERETH, M. Answering recursive queries using views. In *Proceedings of the International Conference on Principles Of Database Systems (PODS)* (1998).

12. ECRC. *ECRC parallel constraint logic programming system*, 1996.

13. FINGER, J., AND GENESERETH, M. Residue: A deductive approach to design synthesis. Tech. Rep. TR-CS-8, Stanford University, 1985.

14. GOH, C. H., MADNICK, S. E., AND SIEGEL, M. D. Context interchange: overcoming the challenges of large-scale interoperable database systems in a dynamic environment. In *Proceedings of the Third International Conference on Information and Knowledge Management* (Gaithersburg, MD, Nov 29–Dec 1 1994), pp. 337–346.

15. KAKAS, A. C., KOWALSKI, R. A., AND TONI, F. Abductive logic programming. *Journal of Logic and Computation 2*, 6 (1993).

16. KIFER, M., LAUSEN, G., AND WU, J. Logical foundations of object-oriented and frame-based languages. *JACM 4* (1995), 741–843.

17. KING, J. *Query Optimization by Semantic Reasonning*. PhD thesis, Stanford University, 1981.

18. LEVY, A., RAJARAMAN, A., AND ORDILLE, J. Querying heterogenous information sources using source descriptions. In *Proc. of the 22nd Conf. on Very Large Databases.* (1996).

19. SCIORE, E., SIEGEL, M., AND ROSENTHAL, A. Using semantic values to facilitate interoperability among heterogeneous information systems. *ACM Transactions on Database Systems 19*, 2 (June 1994), 254–290.

20. SHETH, A. P., AND LARSON, J. A. Federated database systems for managing distributed, heterogeneous, and autonomous databases. *ACM Computing Surveys 22*, 3 (1990), 183–236.

21. TOMASIC, A., AMOUROUX, R., BONNET, P., KAPITSKAIA, O., NAACKE, H., AND RASCHID, L. The distributed information search component (DISCO) and the world-wide web. In *Proceedings of the ACM SIGMOD Intl. Conf. on Management of Data* (1997).

22. WETZEL, G., KOWALSKI, R., AND TONI, F. A theorem proving approach to CLP. In *Proc . of the 11th workshop on Logic Programming* (1995).

23. WETZEL, G., KOWALSKI, R., AND TONI, F. Procalog: Programming with constraints and abducibles in logic. JICSLP Poster session, 1996.

24. WETZEL, G., AND TONI, F. Semantic query optimization through abduction and constraint handling. In *this volume* (1998).

Effective Reformulation of Boolean Queries with Concept Lattices

Claudio Carpineto and Giovanni Romano

Fondazione Ugo Bordoni
Via Baldassarre Castiglione 59, 00142, Rome, Italy
{carpinet, romano}@fub.it

Abstract. In this paper we describe an approach, implemented in a system named REFINER, to combining Boolean information retrieval and content-based navigation with concept lattices. When REFINER is presented with a Boolean query, it builds and displays a portion of the concept lattice associated with the documents being searched centered around the user query. The cluster network displayed by REFINER shows the result of the query along with a set of minimal query refinements/enlargements. REFINER has two main advantages. The first is that it can be used to improve the effectiveness of Boolean retrieval, because it allows content-driven query reformulation with controlled amount of output. The second is that it has potentials for information exploration, because the displayed network is navigatable. We compared information retrieval using REFINER with conventional Boolean retrieval. The results of an experiment conducted on a medium-sized bibliographic database showed that the performance of REFINER was better than unrefined Boolean retrieval.

1 Introduction

Most large-scale retrieval systems and on-line information services are based on the Boolean model. The user queries the system using a set of terms connected by the Boolean operators and, or, and not, and the system returns the set of documents that match the query. Boolean retrieval systems have become popular in operational situations for two main reasons. The first is that they are easy to implement and computationally efficient. The second is that they allow high standards of performance, mainly due to the clarity and expressive power of their underlying model. Furthermore, the retrieval effectiveness of the Boolean model can be improved through various additional facilities usually provided by modern systems, such as truncation and proximity operators, co-occurrences information, and ranking heuristics.

It is well known, however, that Boolean retrieval systems have several limitations, some of which are addressed in this paper. One problem is that only documents that satisfy a query exactly are retrieved; in particular, the and operator is too strict because it fails even in the case when all its arguments except one are satisfied. Another problem is that users are often faced with the null-output or the information overload problem (e.g., [17], [14]) because they cannot control the number of documents produced in response to a query. A third limitation is that Boolean systems, like other query-based retrieval systems (e.g., vector-space and probabilistic), are not suitable for causal users and for exploration of new domains. As the user must specify a query perfectly (or partially) matching some description of the documents, this approach requires the user to have some specific goal in mind and to have some knowledge about the content of the database. This seems to be an important limitation of current query-based retrieval systems, especially in the light of the continuously growing amount of Internet accessible information resources.

In this paper we present an approach, implemented in a system called REFINER, that helps overcome these problems. Given a set of documents described by a set of terms, the approach is based on a mapping between the set of Boolean queries that can be defined over the terms and the nodes of a particular cluster lattice built from the terms/documents, called concept (or Galois) lattice. When the user formulates a query, the system computes a small portion of the lattice centered around the user query; it turns out that the nodes determined by REFINER are a complete set of minimal refinements/enlargements of the query with respect to the document/term relation. By using a visual interface, the user may exploit the information contained in the displayed region to refine a submitted query or may navigate through it; in the latter case, the displayed region is built dynamically as the user moves from one node to another. We argue that the integration of conventional Boolean querying with lattice-based refinement may result in better retrieval performance over unenhanced Boolean retrieval. In addition we show that REFINER is also suitable for information exploration, because the user may readily mix browsing and searching styles of interaction with the system.

The rest of the paper is organized in the following way. We first introduce the model underlying the clustered representation of a document/term relation. Then we present an algorithm for building the portion of lattice relevant to a given query, and describe REFINER, a retrieval interface for combining conventional Boolean querying with lattice-based query refinement and navigation. Next, we report the results of an experiment on subject searching in a reasonably-sized database where REFINER compared favourably with a conventional Boolean retrieval system. Finally, we compare our approach to related work and offer some conclusions.

2 Concept lattice

We first give an informal characterization of a concept lattice and then describe it more formally. As an illustration, Table 1 shows a very simple bibliographic database consisting of four documents described by four binary terms, while the concept lattice built from it is illustrated in Figure 1. Each node of the lattice is a pair, composed of a subset of the documents and a subset of the index terms; in each pair, the subset of terms contains just the terms shared by the subset of documents, and, similarly, the subset of documents contains just the documents sharing the subset of terms. The set of pairs is ordered by the standard set inclusion relation applied to the set of documents and terms that describe each pair. The partially ordered set is usually represented by a Hasse diagram, in which there is an edge between two nodes if and only if they are comparable and there is no other intermediate concept in the lattice (i.e., each node is linked to its maximally specific more general nodes and to its maximally general more specific nodes). The ascending paths represent the subclass/superclass relation; the bottom concept is defined by the set of all terms and contains no documents, the top concept contains all documents and is defined by their common terms (possibly none).

Table 1. A simple document/term relation with four terms (*a*, *b*, *c*, and *d*) and four documents (*1, 2, 3*, and *4*).

	1	2	3	4
a	x	x		x
b	x	x		
c			x	x
d	x		x	x

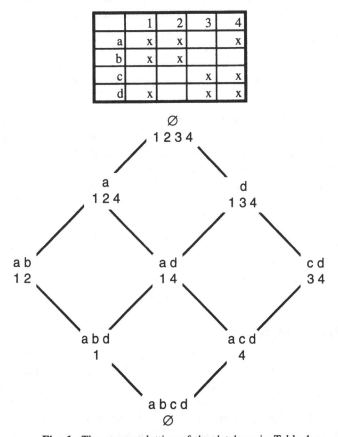

Fig. 1. The concept lattice of the database in Table 1.

More formally, consider a binary relation between a set of documents (D) and a set of terms (T), called *context*. Therefore a context is a triple (D, T, I) where $I \subseteq DxT$. We write *dIt*, meaning the document *d* has the term *t*. For $X \subseteq T$ and $Y \subseteq D$, define:

$X' = \{ d \in D \mid (\forall t \in X)\, dIt \}$, $Y' = \{ t \in T \mid (\forall d \in Y)\, dIt \}$.

X' is therefore the set of all documents possessing all the terms in X and Y' is the set of all terms common to all documents in Y. Then a concept of the context (D,T,I) is defined to be a pair (X, Y) where

$X \subseteq T$, $Y \subseteq D$, and $X' = Y$, $Y' = X$;

X and Y are called the *intent* and the *extent* of the concept, respectively. Note that a subset A of D is the extent of some concept if and only if $A''=A$ in which case the unique concept of which A is an extent is (A', A). Therefore only some pairs (X,Y), i.e., the pairs that are complete with respect to I according to the given definition, represent admissible concepts. For instance, in the lattice relative to the context in Table 1 there cannot be any pair having an intent equal to b, because all documents having b have also a. The set of all concepts of the context (D, T, I) is denoted by $C(D, T, I)$. An ordering relation $(\leq)$ is easily defined on this set of concepts by

$(X_1, Y_1) \leq (X_2, Y_2) \leftrightarrow X_1 \supseteq X_2$ or, equivalently, by
$(X_1, Y_1) \leq (X_2, Y_2) \leftrightarrow Y_1 \subseteq Y_2$.

$C(D, T, I)$ along with $\geq$ form a partially ordered set, that turns out to be a complete lattice [22].

A more thorough treatment of concept lattices and further theoretical and computational results are contained in [8] and [4]; in this paper we concentrate on their interpretation and application in the information retrieval domain. Each node can be seen as a query formed of a conjunction of terms (the intent) with the retrieved documents (the extent). The lattice allows gradual enlargement or refinement of a query. More precisely, following edges departing upward (downward) from a query produces all minimal conjunctive enlargements (refinements) of the query with respect to that particular database. In other terms, given a node it is not possible to delete (add) terms in such a way to obtain an intermediate concept between the node and its fathers (children). In the next section we show how this clustering model can be used to support Boolean querying refinement.

3 Description of REFINER

REFINER is based on a two-step procedure. In the first step it maps a Boolean query on some node in the lattice; in the second step it builds and display the set of parents and children of the node determined in the earlier step. The first step is carried out by computing the set of documents that satisfy the query (i.e., the extent of the lattice node corresponding to the query) and then by determining the set of terms possessed by all previously found documents (i.e., the intent of the lattice node corresponding to the query). For the simple and very common case when the query consists of a conjunction of terms, the lattice node associated with the query, assuming that V is the set of query terms, is given by (V'', V'), where $V'= \{d \in D \mid (\forall t \in V)\, dIt \}$, $V'' = \{t \in T \mid (\forall d \in V')\, dIt\}$. For instance, if we take the context shown in Table 1, for the query *b* AND *d*, we get: V={b, d}, V'={1}, V"={a, b, d}. It may happen that in the lattice there are no nodes that contain all the terms specified in the query (i.e., there are no documents exactly matching the query). In this case REFINER adds a virtual node to the lattice, as if the query represented a new document, and applies the second step of the algorithm, described below, to it.

The second step is computationally more complicated. Here we consider only the problem of finding the parents of a given node, because the determination of its children is a dual problem. The candidate parents are all the nodes whose intent is more general than the intent of the node. However, it is not necessary to generate all such possible intents. Given a node (X, Y), it is sufficient to generate, for each document *d* that does not belong to Y, the set of documents $Z = Y \cup \{d\}$, then find $Z' = \{t \in T \mid (\forall d \in Z)\ dIt\}$, $Z" = \{d \in D \mid (\forall t \in Z')\ dIt\}$. The set of parents is then obtained from the set of nodes $(Z', Z")$ generated in this way, by selecting all the most specific of them (i.e., those whose intent is not contained in the intent of some other node in the same set). Following the example introduced above, once the the query *b* AND *d* has been mapped on the lattice node < a b d, 1 >, REFINER computes three candidate parents, i.e., < a b, 1 2 >, < a d, 1 4 >, < d, 1 3 4 >, the third of which is removed because it is more general than the second one. The resulting two concepts are the parents of the given node (see Figure 1). The time complexity of the described algorithm is proportional to $\|D\| \cdot p$, where p is the average number of parents, which is usually proportional to the size of the query node's intent. In practice, the efficiency of the algorithm can be further improved by sorting the set of documents in the outer iteration in such a way that the documents having the largest intersections with X are examined first.

It is important to note that the method that we have just described can be applied not only to conjunctive queries with atomic arguments, as in the examples, but to any Boolean query. The procedure is the same, provided that there is some document that satisfies the query; the only difference is that the intent of the mapping node, which will be described by the (possibly empty) set of terms common to the extent's documents, may not contain some of the query terms while containing terms other than those present in the query.

REFINER, implemented in Common Lisp on a Power Macintosh, combines Boolean querying and lattice-based refinement with a visual interface. In Figure 2 we show an example screen of REFINER. The screen example was produced during an experiment described below, where a user was searching the documents of the CISI collection - a widely used, electronically-available bibliographical collection of 1460 information science documents described by a title and an abstract - relevant to the following question: *Computerized information systems in fields related to chemistry.* As shown in Figure 2, the user may formulate Boolean queries in a window placed in the left upper corner of the screen. REFINER allows full-text Boolean retrieval, with stop-wording and word-stemming; it also maintains a history of user queries and a history of the nodes visited for each query. In the example shown in Figure 2, the query input by the user was: *computer* AND *chemistry*. REFINER mapped the user query on to the lattice node with intent: {chemistry, computer, result, search}; i.e., all the documents in the database that had *computer* and *chemistry* had also *result* and *search*. The relevant portion of the lattice is displayed by REFINER on the main window. The node matching the query is shown in bold; for each node, it is shown its intent and the cardinality of its extent. Usually, the number of parents and children is limited; in any case, the number of adjacent nodes displayed on the screen cannot exceed a user-supplied threshold. Figure 2 shows also the list of documents associated with one of the nodes on the screen (encircled by REFINER) and the text of one of them.

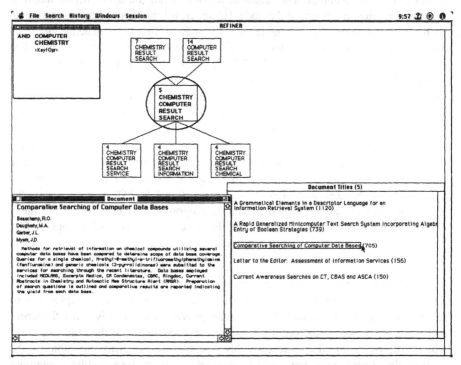

Fig. 2. Display screen of REFINER relative to the search of the CISI documents relevant to the question: *Computerized information systems in fields related to chemistry.*

The display in Figure 2 reveals much information relevant to the specific user question that would have been otherwise difficult to acquire. On one hand, it shows two query refinements that would produce manageable outputs, whereas in the absence of this kind of information the user might be tempted to enlarge the initial query by deleting either computer or chemistry, which would result in an output list containing hundreds of documents. The display also reveals other terms in the database (e.g., *chemical*) that index documents that are likely to be of interest to the user.

One interesting feature of REFINER is that the procedure described above can be recursively applied to each of the nodes displayed on the screen. When the user clicks on a node, the system builds the region corresponding to the query contained in the intent of the selected node. In this way, it is as if the user were navigating through the lattice, with the advantage that we do not need to build the entire lattice in advance.

4 Evaluation

The goal of our experiment was to evaluate how the retrieval effectiveness of Boolean retrieval changes when it is enhanced with a lattice-based refinement facility. To obtain the basic Boolean retrieval system with which to compare REFINER, we simply turned off the query-refinement component of REFINER. In this way we minimized as much as possible the effect that having different interfaces has on performance: both systems ran on the same machine and used the same interaction devices. In our experiment we used the database CISI described above, where ranking methods usually perform poorly. Each document was automatically indexed; we excluded words on CACM's stop list of common words, and we mapped word variants into the same root by using by using a very large *trie*-structured morphological lexicon for English [13], that contains the standard inflections for nouns (singular, plural, singular genitive, plural genitive), verbs (infinitive, third person singular, past tense, past participle, progressive form), adjectives (base, comparative, superlative). At the end of this treatment, each document was described by an average of 47.1 terms. Along with the CISI database comes a set of 35 linguistic queries with their relevance judgements.

For the experiment we randomly selected 20 queries among them; the average number of relevant documents for the 20 queries was 32. We tested four subjects in the experiment. The subjects were computer science students with little knowledge of the document domains and no prior knowledge about the systems. The two subjects were asked to retrieve the documents relevant to the 10 queries using the two retrieval methods. For assigning the queries to the methods we used a repeated-measures design, in which each subject searched each query using each method. To minimize sequence effects, we varied the order of the two methods. During each search the user, who was not asked to finish within a certain time period, could see the abstract of the documents returned in response to Boolean queries or associated with the nodes displayed on the screen. The documents scanned during the search were noted as retrieved. We have to emphasize that in evaluating the effectiveness of interactive retrieval systems the definition of the retrieved set of documents is usually not obvious. Our choice is consistent with that of [20] and [21], where a document is rated as as a retrieved document as soon as its full description (the abstract, in our case) is recovered. For each search we considered four measures: recall, precision, number of Boolean queries, and search time (i.e., the time taken by the user to perform his task). The results are displayed in Table 2.

The table shows that searching with REFINER obtained better evaluation scores for recall, precision and search time. To see if these differences can be considered statistically significant we performed a paired t-test for each measure. The test revealed no effect of the method on precision ($p = 0.235$) and recall ($p = 0.289$).

However, it did reveal the superiority of REFINER with respect to search time ($p =$ 0.011). These results seem to suggest that the use of content-based query refinement may reduce user search time without reducing retrieval effectiveness. These results are not surprising, because REFINER complements the basic capabilities of a Boolean retrieval system with other useful features. In particular, as explained above, REFINER allows smooth query refinement/enlargement, which is likely to be the key factor for obtaining the search time improvement. Another advantage of REFINER, as opposed to strict Boolean retrieval where this kind of information is not available, is that the user may exploit the feedback obtained from the structure to facilitate selection of relevant terms in the database or to discover unwanted senses of words [7], for instance when an intent contains two words that were not expected to appear together. Also, REFINER's AND operator would always produce a non-null output (unless none of the AND's arguments are satisfied), while the strict Boolean AND operator fails whenever there is at least one argument that is not satisfied. A further useful observation for justifying the marked superiority of REFINER over Boolean retrieval is that most (85%) of the queries submitted in our experiment were simple conjunctions of terms[1], whose refinements are more intuitive to the user.

Table 2. Average values of retrieval performance measures

Method	recall	precision	number of Boolean queries	search time (sec)
Boolean	0.366 (σ=0.098)	0.289 (σ=0.077)	13.2 (σ = 2.212)	1901 (σ =265)
REFINER	0.419 (σ=0.107)	0.330 (σ=0.085)	6.00 (σ = 2.44)	1467 (σ = 263)

5 Related work

This research is closely related to work done in four areas: reformulation of Boolean queries, hybrid approaches to information retrieval, applications of concept lattices to information browsing, and cooperative database systems. In this section we examine the relation to each of them in turn.

- Cleverdon [6] has proposed an approach to supporting interactive reformulation of Boolean queries named quorum-level searches. Starting from an AND clause containing n terms, the user may choose a new query from a n-level query hierarchy where each level is a disjunction of AND clauses obtained by removing 1, 2, ...n-1 terms from the original top AND clause. The query hierarchy may therefore drive the user from narrow to broader formulations of an initial conjunctive query[2]. In the same vein, Spoerri [19] has proposed a more systematic and powerful approach. He describes INFOCRYSTAL, a system that computes

---

[1] That users prefer simple conjunctive queries is also suggested by other studies [2]
[2] A similar technique has also been used in [1] with a different goal, namely to help assessors evaluate recall on large databases.

and display the result, in terms of number of documents, of all possible Boolean queries in a normal form that involve the terms present in a user query. This method has the advantage that it can be applied to any Boolean expressions, not only to conjunctive queries as quorum-level searches. However, in both of these approaches the meaning of the proposed reformulations may be difficult to understand for the user. While in REFINER each reformulation is obtained by deleting terms (query enlargement) or adding new terms (query refinement), each reformulation shown by INFOCRYSTAL (or quorum-level search) contains only and all of the terms present in the user query, connected with different operators and with different precedences. Thus, the queries displayed by the latter two systems may be semantically distant from the search query, and their utilization may be not obvious for the user. For instance, the set of reformulations produced by INFOCRYSTAL in response to the query "a AND b AND c" would also contain the query "(NOT a) AND (NOTb) AND (NOT c)". This raises the question of the system's retrieval effectiveness, for which no experimental evidence has been in fact reported. Another limitation of INFOCRYSTAL is that it does not scale up well, because if a query contains N terms it must build and display 2^{N-1} queries. Finally, unlike REFINER, both quorum-level search and INFOCRYSTAL cannot help user select other relevant terms present in the document collection.

- A third more recent approach to supporting users in Boolean retrieval is FIRE [3]. FIRE provides two main kinds of support: terminological help and strategic help. The terminological help consists of new system-generated terms for expanding or refining a user query. However, in FIRE the source of the terms proposed to the user is a (manually-constructed) thesaurus with no explicit relation to the content of the database being searched. This contrast with REFINER, where the new queries suggested by the systems are actual refinement/enlargements of the user query with respect to the given database. The strategic help provided by FIRE is based on a set of rules for modifying the constituents of a Boolean expression, including terms, operators, and precedence, when the users faces an adverse situation. Under this respect, FIRE is more powerful than REFINER, although certain kinds of strategic help can be easily deduced from REFINER's display screen. For instance, when a query produces an empty output, REFINER shows all the minimal query enlargements with a non empty answer set (if any). Finally, Brajnik et al. [3] compared the performance of automatic support for query reformulation versus non-automatic support (such as printed thesaurus or human expert), whereas we are more interested in evaluating whether an enhanced Boolean retrieval system can perform better than a basic Boolean system.

- A great deal of the research on hybrid approaches has concentrated on the combination of browsing and querying styles of interaction. Browsing is generally seen either as an aid for conventional query-based retrieval or as an alternative search method. The first approach is described by [9] and [16] where a search through a *term* space is used to improve query formulation in a distinct *document* space. An example of the second approach is [15] where a hierarchical browsing system supplements a Boolean query system. In these systems, the network that supports browsing is usually developed and maintained as a distinct component. The main drawback of these retrieval architectures is that the user must map different concept representations and data spaces. REFINER, by contrast, integrates browsing and querying into a single term/document space. This has the advantage that the user may combine query refinement with direct inspection of the document database. Users, therefore, do not have to commit themselves to one specific retrieval mode; rather, they may exhibit a continuum of behaviors varying between querying and browsing that is characterized by the level of specificity of their information seeking goals.

- The application of concept lattices to information retrieval has been explored by [11] and [5]. These systems build the concept lattice associated with a document/term relation and then employ various methods to access the relevant information, including the possibility for the user to search only those terms that the user has specified [5]. These systems, however, are severely affected by their computational requirements: since they build an entire concept lattices, they can only be applied to databases of modest size, where each document is described by a small number of index terms. By contrast, REFINER builds only a relevant portion of the lattice, and therefore allows full-text indexing even for reasonably-sized databases. Furthermore, REFINER combines the potentials of lattice-based inspection with the great expressive power of Boolean retrieval, while the query mode of the systems described in [11] and [5] is inherently limited.

- Much work on improving cooperative behaviour of information systems has been done in the fields of database query answering systems, logic programming, and deductive databases (see [10] for a review). One common concern is to recover from a failing query, (i.e., a query producing an empty answer set) by extending relational and deductive database systems with facilities to find minimal failing, maximal succeeding, and minimal conflicting subqueries [12]. Compared to our approach, work done in this area relies on different assumptions (structured data with powerful query languages versus unstructured data with simple query languages) and has also a different scope. While for library searches it is convenient to consider both query enlargement and query refinement, for database querying it seems more useful to concentrate on ways to recover from failing queries (which can be seen as a special case of query enlargement), considering also implicit causes of failure, such as violation of integrity constraints.

6 Conclusion

We have presented REFINER, an approach to combining Boolean retrieval and content-based navigation with concept lattices. The main advantage of the system is that it suggests controlled ways for refining/enlarging a conjunctive Boolean query. An additional distinguishing feature of REFINER is that it combines querying and browsing styles of interaction: the user may choose a hybrid retrieval strategy from a continuum ranging from casual inspection to highly-specific information seeking goals. We compared REFINER's retrieval effectiveness with that of a conventional Boolean retrieval system on a subject searching task. The results suggest that the performance of query-refinement enhanced Boolean retrieval may be better than unrefined Boolean retrieval, especially with respect to search time, and for databases of non trivial size.

This research can be extended in several directions. One fundamental design choice in REFINER is the size and the topology of the lattice region that is built and displayed in response to a query. The current version of REFINER shows the set of parents and children of a focus node, but one could use advanced visualization techniques, such as fisheye views [18], to show more distant ancestors and descendants, as well as nodes that are not directly comparable with the focus (e.g., its siblings). It is clear that a small region is more efficient to build, while a large region shows more refinements/enlargements and contains more information on the content of the database. On the other hand, it is not clear whether using a larger region will automatically result in better retrieval performance, because this may also increase the cognitive overload and the user disorientation. We are currently exploring these fundamental trade-offs.

Another related research issue concerns the scope of this approach. The experiment that we performed provides some insigths, but its results can only be taken as indicative. As suggested above, one factor that needs be controlled to evaluate the system's efficiency and effectiveness is the characteristics of the lattice region displayed by the visual interface. However, in operational situations there may be other important parameters that need be controlled. One direction for future work is to perform further experiments to evaluate how the performance results change when controlling a wider range of factors including database scale, indexing strategies and characteristics of domain and users.

Acknowledgments

We thank three anonymous reviewers for pointing out relevant work in the field of cooperative databases and for many useful comments and suggestions. This work has been carried out within the framework of an agreement between the Italian PT Administration and the Fondazione Ugo Bordoni.

References

1. Blair, D. (1996). STAIRS Redux: Thoughts on the STAIRS evaluation, ten years after. *Journal of the American Society for Information Science*, 47 (1), 4-22.
2. Borgman, C. L., Meadow, C. T. (1985). Designing an information retrieval interface based on user characteristics. *Proceedings of the Eight Annual International ACM SIGIR Conference on Research and Development in Information Retrieval*, 139-146.
3. Brajnik, G,, Mizzaro, S., Tasso, C. (1996). Evaluating User Interfaces to Information Retrieval Systems: A Case Study on User Support. *Proceedings of the 19th Annual*

International ACM SIGIR Conference on Research and Development in Information Retrieval, 128-136.

4. Carpineto, C., Romano, G. (1996a). A Lattice Conceptual Clustering System and Its Application to Browsing Retrieval. *Machine Learning*, 24, 1-28.

5. Carpineto, C., Romano, G. (1996b). Information retrieval through hybrid navigation of lattice representations. *International Journal of Human-Computer Studies*, 45, 553-578.

6. Cleverdon, C. (1974). Optimizing convenient on-line access to bibliogrphic databases. Information Services and Use, 4 (1), 37-47.

7. Cooper, J., Byrd, R. (1997). Lexical navigation: visually prompted query expansion and refinement. *Proceedings of the Second ACM Digital Library Conference*, 237-246.

8. Davey, B., Priestley, H. (1990). *Introduction to Lattices and Order*. Cambridge, Great Britain: Cambridge University Press.

9. Frei, H., Jauslin, J. (1983). Graphical presentation of information and services: a user oriented interface. *Information Technology: Research and Development*, 2, 23-42.

10. Gaasterland, T., Godfrey, P., Minker, J. (1992). An Overview of Cooperative Answering. *Journal of Intelligent Information Systems*, 1(2), 123-157.

11. Godin, R., Missaoui, R., April, A. (1993). Experimental comparison of navigation in a Galois lattice with conventional information retrieval methods. *International Journal of Man-machine Studies*, 38, 747-767.

12. Godfrey, P. (1997). Minimization in Cooperative Response to Failing Database Queries. *International Journal of Cooperative Information Systems*, 6(2), 95-149.

13. Karp, D., Schabes, Y., Zaidel, M., Egedi, D. (1992). A freely available wide coverage morphological analyzer for English. *Proceedings of the 14th International Conference on Computational Linguistics (COLING '92)*, Nantes, France.

14. Lesk, M. (1989). What to do when there is too much information. *Proceedings ACM-Hypertext'89*. Pittsburgh, PA, USA, 305-318.

15. Maarek, Y., Berry, Kaiser, G. (1991). An Information Retrieval Approach For Automatically Constructing Software Libraries. *IEEE Transactions on Software Engineering*, 17(8), 800-813.

16. Pedersen, G. (1993). A browser for bibliographic information retrieval based on an application of lattice theory. *Proceedings of the Sixteenth Annual International ACM SIGIR Conference on Research and Development in Information Retrieval*, Pittsburgh, PA, USA, 270-279.

17. Salton, G., McGill. (1983). *Introduction to Modern Information Retrieval*. New York: McGraw Hill.

18. Sarkar, M,, Brown, M. (1994). Graphical Fisheye Views. *Communications of the ACM*, 37(12), 73-84.

19. Spoerri, A. (1994). InfoCrystal: Integrating exact and partial matching approaches through visualization. In *Proceedings of RIAO 94: Intelligent Multimedia Information Retrieval Systems and Management*, New York, USA, 687-696.

20. Tague-Sutcliffe, J. (1992). The pragmatics of information retrieval experimentation, revisited. *Information Processing & Management*, 28(4), 467-490.

21. Turtle, H. (1994). Natural language vs. Boolean query evaluation: a comparison of retrieval performance. *Proceedings of the Seventeenth Annual International ACM SIGIR Conference on Research and Development in Information Retrieval.*, Dublin, Ireland, 212-220.

22. Wille, R. (1984). Line diagrams of hierarchical concept systems. *International Classification*, 2, 77-86.

Different Ways to Have Something in Common

Marco Colombetti

Politecnico di Milano, Piazza Leonardo da Vinci 32
I-20133 Milano, Italy
Marco.Colombetti@polimi.it

Abstract. Agent technology is rapidly gaining favor among computer scientists. In typical applications, agents are not viewed as isolated systems, but rather as individuals living in a complex society of other agents and interacting with them, in order to cooperate to the achievement of tasks and negotiate solutions to conflictual situations. Social agents of this kind must be able to entertain mental states not only about their application domain, but also about other agent's mental states; information sharing and communication thus become issues of primary importance. In this paper I define formally a number of mechanisms through which social mental states can be established, and then I analyze such definitions in search of criteria for designing artificial agents.

1 Introduction

Agent technology is rapidly gaining favor among computer scientists. According to a fashionable vision, autonomous agents are soon going to dwell in our workstations and move across the web to retrieve information and access services on our behalf. Instead of following a rigidly pre-programmed strategy, agents are expected to generate their own rational behavior with a high degree of autonomy. Before this dream can come true, however, many problems have to be solved. In particular, a better understanding must be gained of what we mean by "rational behavior".

There are, in fact, two independent notions of rationality, one typical of theoretical economics and behavioral ecology, and one more common in cognitive science. According to the economical point of view, an agent is rational if it strives to maximize some form of payoff. The cognitive notion of rationality is quite different, in that it does not rely on maximizing a quantitative criterion: rather, an agent is regarded as rational if it entertains beliefs and goals, and uses its beliefs to generate behavior plans which will achieve its goals in diverse situations. Both notions of rationality have found their ways into agent technology. Economical rationality, for example, is central to the subfield of machine learning known as reinforcement learning, which has been successfully applied to the development of robotic agents able to carry out tasks in a physical environment (see for example Dorigo and Colombetti, 1998). On the other hand, the cognitive point of view is typical of the approach to agents based on classical artificial intelligence techniques. In particular, a promising approach is to regard agents as systems able to entertain propositional *mental states,* like beliefs and

This research has been funded by the CNR (Italian National Research Council), through grant No. 95.04063.CT11 to Marco Colombetti for the years 1995–96.

goals, as a basis for rational behavior. This paper is concerned only with the cognitive perspective.

In typical applications, agents are not viewed as isolated systems, but rather as individuals living in a complex society of other agents and interacting with them, in order to cooperate for the achievement of tasks and to negotiate solutions to conflictual situations. Social agents of this kind must be able to entertain mental states not only about their application domain, but also about other agent's mental states; information sharing and inter-agent communication thus become issues of primary importance. Since the beginning of the eighties, various models of communicative interaction based on mental states have been proposed in the fields of artificial intelligence and cognitive science. The new challenge is to implement them as parts of autonomous agents able to produce effective behavior in realistic application domains.

Two types of mental states which are deeply involved in human social interactions are *common beliefs* (also known as mutual beliefs) and *communicative intentions*. Let me clarify these concepts with a couple of examples. In some situations, for instance during a talk, raising one's arm counts as a request for the permission to ask a question. It seems appropriate to say that this behavior is effective because everybody knows[1] the meaning of raising one's arm: more technically, such a meaning is *shared knowledge*. Note however that this is not enough. Suppose you are part of a group, all members of which know the meaning of raising one's arm. But now also suppose *you do not know* that all other members know the meaning of raising one's arm, which is indeed compatible with the previous assumption. In such a case, raising your arm to ask a question would not be rational, because you would have no reason to assume that your request will be correctly understood. So, in order to plan rational interactions with other agents, it is not enough that information be shared, in the sense of being known to every agent. It is also necessary that all agents share that information is shared; and so on *ad infinitum*. When information has such a status, it is called *common*.

In the following sections I shall analyze different ways in which a piece of information can become common. As we shall see, one of these is intentional communication: indeed, to communicate means to make something common. However, as it has been argued by the philosopher Paul Grice (1957), intentionally making a piece of information common not necessarily counts as communication. For example, suppose that you want it to become common belief in a group of people that you are very rich, but that you do not want to appear as publicizing this. Then you may park your Rolls-Royce in such a way that everybody can see you doing this, even if it seems that you do not want to be seen. This behavior would not count as communication, because your intention that a piece of information becomes common is not overt. Precisely this notion of "overtness" seems to play an important role in intentional communication. Later on, we shall see how all this can be captured in formal terms, and what function overtness might have.

The above examples concern human interaction. However, there are good reasons to believe that the interaction of social artificial agents might raise similar problems, and

---

[1]   In this paper, "to know" is used as a synonim of "to believe".

require similar solutions. Moreover, interactions will often involve both artificial and human agents, and it is reasonable to assume that artificial agents will be able to understand the behavior of human agents only if they can reason about human mental states (see for example Sadek, Bretier and Panaget, 1997). A first step in this direction is to give formal accounts of social mental states and related entities, including common beliefs and intentional communication. Typically, this is done using modal logic tools. Doing so does not involve a commitment to *implement* agents as symbolic manipulators; rather, logical accounts of mental states can be viewed as *specifications* of rational agents, which can be implemented using whichever technique suits a specific application. In particular, my approach in this paper will be define formally a number of processes through which social mental states can be established, and to analyze such definitions in search of criteria which may help to design artificial agents.

The rest of this article is organized as follows. In Section 2, I introduce a modal logic of individual beliefs, intentions, common belief, and communication. In Section 3, I give a formal definition of four basic mechanisms by which a piece of information can became a common belief in a group of agents. In Section 4, I analyze such definitions in more detail, and show that they suggest a number of criteria for agent design. Finally, in Section 5 I draw some conclusions.

2   Individual and Social Mental States

In a recent paper (Colombetti, in press), I have suggested a possible way to introduce common belief and intentional communication within a propositional modal logic of individual belief and intention. Here I shall briefly describe a formal system which provides a possible sound and complete formalization of such concepts.

2.1 Individual Beliefs

Let A be a group of agents. If agent $a \in A$ individually entertains the belief that proposition φ is true, I write $B_a\varphi$. For individual belief, I shall adopt the modal system known as $KD45_n$ (or Weak $S5_n$). This includes the following axioms and inference rules:

(Prop) *All propositional tautologies,*

(K_B) $B_a\varphi \wedge B_a(\varphi \supset \psi) \supset B_a\psi,$

(D_B) $B_a\varphi \supset {\sim}B_a{\sim}\varphi,$

(4_B) $B_a\varphi \supset B_aB_a\varphi,$

(5_B) ${\sim}B_a\varphi \supset B_a{\sim}B_a\varphi,$

(RMP) $\dfrac{\varphi, \varphi \supset \psi}{\psi},$

(RN_B) $\dfrac{\varphi}{B_a\varphi}.$

This modal system is quite standard and extensively studied in the specialized literature (see for example Halpern and Moses, 1992; Lismont and Mongin, 1995;

Meyer and van der Hoek, 1995). It describes formally the belief system of an agent which has unlimited inferential resources (Prop, K_B, RMP, RN_B), is coherent (D_B), and has both positive (4_B) and negative (5_B) introspection of its own beliefs. Most of the considerations contained in the rest of the paper, however, would still be valid under weaker assumptions.

2.2 Intention

Contrary to the case of belief, no commonly accepted treatment of intention is available in the literature. Let us write $I_a\varphi$ for "a intends to bring about that φ". Here is a rather weak set of axioms and inference rules, which however will suffice for our current purpose:

(K$_I$) $I_a\varphi \wedge I_a(\varphi \supset \psi) \supset I_a\psi$,

(D$_I$) $I_a\varphi \supset \sim I_a\sim\varphi$,

(4$_{IB}$) $I_a\varphi \supset B_a I_a\varphi$,

(5$_{IB}$) $\sim I_a\varphi \supset B_a \sim I_a\varphi$,

(RN$_I$) $\dfrac{\varphi}{I_a\varphi}$.

This logic presupposes that intentions propagate to logical consequences (K$_I$, RN$_I$) and are coherent (D$_I$), and that agents have both positive (4$_{IB}$) and negative (5$_{IB}$) introspection of their own intentions. The system including all the above axioms and inference rules for belief and intention turns out to be sound and complete (Colombetti, in press).

Let us now have a look at possible formal treatments of common belief and intentional communication. In the following I shall only provide a quick overlook of the main points; the interested reader is referred to the specialized literature.

2.3 Common Belief

If all agents in A individually believe that φ is true, I write $B_A\varphi$. In many cases of practical interest, A will be a finite set (often it will contain exactly two agents); in such a case, $B_A\varphi$ is equivalent to a finite conjunction of individual beliefs:

(A) $B_A\varphi \equiv \bigwedge_{a \in A} B_a\varphi$;

otherwise, it will be necessary to define $B_A\varphi$ through first-order quantification:

(A') $B_A\varphi \equiv \forall x\,(A(x) \supset B_x\varphi)$,

where $A(x)$ means that x belongs to the group A of agents. The latter definition is less innocent than it may look. In fact, it is quite unusual to index a modal operator by a first-order term, like an individual variable (but see Lomuscio and Colombetti, 1997). In this paper, however, I do not want to go into fine-grained technical details, and at times I shall use modal logic formulae with some liberty.

When a proposition is believed by everybody (in A), it is called a *shared belief*. As I have already pointed out, shared beliefs are insufficient as a basis for social interactions. Let me now be more precise about this. Suppose a number of agents have to cooperate to carry out a given task. To do so, it is necessary that all of them share a number of beliefs about various aspects of the task. However, this is not sufficient. Suppose for example that in order for cooperation to be successful φ must be true, and assume that all agents believe that φ, but that a does not know that everybody believes that φ. In such a case, a cannot rationally rely on φ being known to all agents, and this will typically impede cooperation. It is fairly easy to see that agents need not only to share that φ holds, but also that φ is shared, and so on *ad infinitum*. If this is the case, we say that φ is a *common belief* (of A). Remarkably, it is possible to express this requirement in finitary terms. If we write $B_*\varphi$ for "it is common belief (in A) that φ", we have:

$$(\mathrm{F}_{B_*}) \quad B_*\varphi \equiv B_A(\varphi \wedge B_*\varphi).$$

That is: it is common belief that φ, if and only if it is shared that φ, and that it is common belief that φ. The modal formula F_{B_*} is known as a *fixpoint axiom*, and its origin can be traced back to works by Lewis (1969), Harman (1977), and Barwise (1989). The underlying idea is to define common belief in a circular way. A well known alternative definition of common belief, due to Schiffer (1972), is based on an infinite conjunction of nested individual beliefs. Schiffer's definition cannot be directly represented into classical logic; it is however possible to show that it is semantically equivalent to the circular definition given above, at least within the realm of normal modal logic.

It is possible to show that the fixpoint axiom, F_{B_*}, does not characterize common belief unambiguously. Technically, what we need is the *forward fixpoint axiom*,

$$(\mathrm{FF}_{B_*}) \quad B_*\varphi \supset B_A(\varphi \wedge B_*\varphi),$$

and an inference rule, called the *rule of induction*:

$$(\mathrm{RI}_{B_*}) \quad \frac{\psi \supset B_A(\varphi \wedge \psi)}{\psi \supset B_*\varphi}.$$

If these assumptions are added to a classical modal logic of individual belief (like the one presented in 2.1), we obtain a sound and complete logic in which the fixpoint "axiom", F_{B_*}, can be proved as a theorem. It is interesting to note that, contrary to other applications of modal logic in the field of computer science, common belief cannot be formalized at the level of nonmodal first-order logic. In fact, the logic of common belief is not *semantically compact* (see for example Lismont and Mongin, 1995); that is, such a logic allows for an unsatisfiable set of statements, Ω, such that every finite subset of Ω is satisfiable. Given that we know that every nonmodal first-order theory is semantically compact, it follows that our modal logic of common belief cannot be translated into nonmodal first-order logic.

To assume that a group of agents entertain a common belief is a strong requirement. In fact, within an appropriate modal logic of individual belief, the common belief that φ logically entails every finite nesting of individual beliefs that φ:

$$\vdash B_*\varphi \supset B_{a_i}...B_{a_k}\varphi, \quad \text{for every nonempty sequence } \langle a_i,...,a_k \rangle \text{ of agents.}$$

For this reason, states of common belief have strong inferential power. The back of the coin, as we shall see, is that to infer that a common belief holds, agents need to rely on very strong assumptions.

2.4 Intentional Communication

The term "communication" is used with different acceptations in different disciplines. When human communication is involved, it is common to rely on some definition related to Grice's concept of non-natural meaning (Grice, 1957). Here is my favorite one. Suppose that a group A of agents is given. The idea is that a *speaker*, $a \in A$, intends to communicate that φ to his or her *audience*, $A - \{a\}$, if and only if a intends it to be a common belief (of A) that φ, and that a intends to communicate (to $A - \{a\}$) that φ. If we write $C_a \varphi$ for "a communicates that φ to his or her audience", we have:

(F_C) $\quad C_a \varphi \equiv B_* (\varphi \wedge I_a C_a \varphi)$

Again, the proper technical formulation of this idea involves a forward fixpoint axiom,

(FF_C) $\quad C_a \varphi \supset B_* (\varphi \wedge I_a C_a \varphi)$,

and a rule of induction,

(RI_C) $\quad \dfrac{\psi \supset B_* (\varphi \wedge I_a \psi)}{\psi \supset C_a \varphi}$.

If such assumptions are added to the modal logic of individual belief, common belief and intention presented in Sections 2.1–2.3, we obtain a sound and complete modal system (Colombetti, in press). As in the case of common belief, communication will have strong inferential power; but again, as we shall see, to infer that an event of communication took place requires strong assumptions.

We now come to the main point of this article. Common beliefs are fundamental for social interaction, but where do they come from? I shall try to answer these questions in Section 3.

2.5 Interpreting Modal Axioms, Theorems and Inference Rules

The use of formal logic as a specification language is quite standard in many areas of computer science. However, many computer scientists are not familiar with modal logic, and may therefore misunderstand modal axioms, theorems and inference rules. I shall spend a few words about the matter, but of course the interested reader is referred to a basic textbook of modal logic (e.g. Chellas, 1980; Hughes and Cresswell, 1996).

All modal operators considered in this paper are *normal*; this implies that the semantics of modal statements can be given in terms of *possible worlds* which, at an intuitive level, can be regarded as possible situations. Therefore, a statement will be considered true or false with respect to a given situation; and a statement will be considered as logically valid if and only if it is true in all possible situations (more technically, at all possible worlds of all models).

All axiomatizations given in this paper are sound and complete (Colombetti, in press), and this means that theorems coincide with valid statements. As a consequence, a theorem of the form

$$\vdash B_a\varphi$$

means that agent a believes φ in all situations. Now consider a theorem of the form

$$\vdash \psi \supset B_a\varphi.$$

This means that in all possible situations, the truth of ψ implies that a believes φ. But this is equivalent to saying that a believes φ in every situation in which ψ is true. In this way, we can use implicative statements to say that an agent has a belief under given conditions. Most theorems discussed in the following will have this form.

Given a formal system, defined in terms of axioms and inference rules, one can derive not only theorems, but also new inference rules. More precisely, a *derived inference rule* is an inference rule which can be added to a formal system without affecting the set of theorems. Typically, derived inference rules are introduced to make formal proofs shorter, or because they shed light on important relationships among logical constructs. This is the case, for example, with the two derived rules introduced in Section 3.4.

Implicative axioms should not be confused with inference rules. In classical propositional logic one can always derive an implicative theorem from an inference rule, thanks to the deduction theorem; for example, from the inference rule

$$\frac{\psi}{\varphi}$$

one can derive the implicative theorem

$$\vdash \psi \supset \varphi.$$

The same is true in first-order logic, provided ψ is a sentence (i.e., a closed formula). This is not possible in modal logic: for example, from rule RN_B of Section 2.1 one *does not* derive a theorem of the form

(1) $\qquad \varphi \supset B_a\varphi,$

which by the way would make epistemic logic completely useless. In fact, RN_B and (1) say two quite different things. According to RN_B, if a sentence φ is true in all situations, then any agent will believe φ in all situations – an assumption which is justified if we want to model idealized rational agents. On the contrary, (1) says that any agent will believe any statement φ in every situation in which φ is true: indeed a much stronger, unwarranted claim.

Finally, let me point out that in this paper axioms and theorems are typically formulated from an "objective" standpoint (i.e., the standpoint of an external, omniscient observer), but admit also of a weaker, "subjective" formulation (i.e., from the standpoint of a specific agent). Take for example a theorem of the form

(2) $\qquad \vdash \psi \supset B_a\varphi,$

This theorem can be viewed as a statement of an omniscient observer, able to find out whether ψ is objectively true in a situation. Most often, however, we are interested in what an agent believes as a consequence of what the agent itself knows about the situation, and not of what is objectively true. In such a case, we need a weaker version of (2). Given that B_a is a normal modal operator, we can rely on the derived inference rule of *monotonicity*:

$$(\text{RM}_B) \quad \frac{\varphi \supset \psi}{B_a\varphi \supset B_a\psi}.$$

Applying this rule to (2), we obtain:

$$\vdash B_a\psi \supset B_aB_a\varphi.$$

From this, given that our formal system has the theorem $\vdash B_aB_a\varphi \supset B_a\varphi$, we can derive:

$$(3) \qquad \vdash B_a\psi \supset B_a\varphi,$$

which makes no reference to objective truth. Analogous considerations hold for the other modal operators used in this paper.

In many cases of practical interest, the weaker, subjective statement will more immediately useful than the stronger, objective one. In any case, their significance as formal specifications is quite different. For example, theorem (2) defines a requirement on agent beliefs with respect to what is objectively true in a given, concrete situation. On the contrary, theorem (3) defines a requirement on an agent's cognitive architecture, with no reference to what is true in the external world. All such considerations should be kept in mind in order to appreciate the possible impact of logical specification on actual agent design.

3 Different Ways to Have Something in Common

There seem to be four basic mechanisms by which a common belief can be established in a group of agents, which I shall now briefly analyze.

3.1 Deduction in the Space of Common Beliefs

The simplest mechanism by which a common belief can be derived is based, so to speak, on pure logical reasoning. In fact, B_* turns out to be a normal modal operator, which implies that the K_{B_*} scheme is a theorem:

$$(K_{B_*}) \quad \vdash B_*\varphi \wedge B_*(\varphi \supset \psi) \supset B_*\psi.$$

This means that reasoning based on Modus Ponens can be "transferred" into the space of common beliefs. However, while the use of this theorem allows an agent to generate common beliefs from previous ones, it does not shed any light on the origin of "brand new" common beliefs.

3.2 Displayed Information

The second mechanism which brings in common beliefs is related to the notion of public information, a notion which is already implicit in a pioneering note on common knowledge by Aumann (1976). Let me start from a more general concept. If, for given propositions φ and ψ, one can prove that

(S) $\vdash \psi \supset B_A \varphi,$

I say that ψ *displays* φ. This means that ψ cannot hold without φ being recognized by all agents. By itself, this does not guarantee common belief of φ. However, if ψ also displays itself, that is:

$$\vdash \psi \supset B_A(\varphi \wedge \psi),$$

by RI_{B_*} we can derive that

$$\vdash \psi \supset B_* \varphi.$$

Therefore, $B_* \varphi$ is true in every situation in which ψ holds:[2] a genuine case of a brand new common belief. Now, if a proposition ψ displays itself, it is said to be *public*:

(P) $\vdash \psi \supset B_A \psi.$

This means that φ is so evident that it cannot hold without everybody realizing that it holds. If P can be proved for some ψ, that we can immediately derive

$$\vdash \psi \supset B_* \psi$$

by the rule of induction for B_* (with $\varphi = \psi$).

3.3 Mutual Observation

The third mechanism which allows us to derive a common belief is *mutual observation*, a notion which, as far as I know, has been used for the first time in the artificial intelligence community by Perrault (1990), who in turn was probably inspired by the concept of copresence conditions introduced by Clark and Marshall (1981). This case cannot be appropriately accounted for at the level of propositional modal logic, to which I have kept so far. I shall therefore use a first order modal notation at an intuitive level, without defining it rigorously (a technical report on this subject is in preparation). Let $A(x)$ mean that x is an agent belonging to group A, and $O(x)$ mean that agent $x \in A$ observes all agents belonging to A (including itself). I say that a fact φ is *observable* if:

$$\vdash O(x) \wedge \varphi \supset B_x \varphi.$$

The following axiom seems to capture an ideal property of observation, that is, that the activity of observing is itself observable:

$$O(x) \wedge O(y) \supset B_x O(y).$$

From this, given that every observer also observes itself, we have in particular that observation is introspective:

$$\vdash O(x) \supset B_x O(x).$$

---

2 Remember that this paper is concerned with modal systems which are sound and complete: we can therefore switch freely from the syntactic notion of theoremhood to the semantic notions of truth and validity.

Now, let us assume that we can exploit a suitable induction rule analogous to RI_{B_*}. Then we can prove that

$$\vdash \forall x \, (A(x) \supset O(x)) \supset B_* \forall x \, (A(x) \supset O(x)),$$

which means that mutual observation (by all agents in A) implies the common belief that mutual observation takes place. We can now go on and prove that under mutual observation, every observable property becomes common belief.

3.4 Communication

Finally, we have a fourth mechanism by which information can become common, that is *intentional communication*. As defined through FF_C and RI_C, communication has a number of interesting properties. The first one, which by now should be hardly surprising, is that communication implies common belief:

$$\vdash C_a \varphi \supset B_* \varphi.$$

Therefore, as I have already argued, an act of communication can bring in brand new common beliefs.

The second important property is that communication is an *intentional action*, which in our system is expressed by the following theorem:

$$\vdash C_a \varphi \supset I_a C_a \varphi.$$

A third property is that communication is public:

$$\vdash C_a \varphi \supset B_A C_a \varphi.$$

Also the converse implications holds:

$$\vdash B_A C_a \varphi \supset C_a \varphi.$$

This property is very interesting, because it shows that there is nothing really "objective" in communication: if all agents individually believe that communication takes place, then communication does take place! This is by no means a general property of intentional action: for example, a group of people might believe they are going to win the lottery, without this event actually taking place.

It is also possible to show that $C_a \varphi$ is the weakest intentional and public action which implies the common belief that φ. That is, if there is a statement ψ for which the following theorems can be proved:

$$\vdash \psi \supset I_a \psi,$$
$$\vdash \psi \supset B_A \psi,$$
$$\vdash \psi \supset B_* \varphi,$$

then it follows that:

$$\vdash \psi \supset C_a \varphi.$$

We can restate this condition in the form of a derived inference rule:

$$\frac{\psi \supset I_a \psi, \; \psi \supset B_A \psi, \; \psi \supset B_* \varphi}{\psi \supset C_a \varphi}.$$

We have here an interesting characterization of communication as the weakest intentional and public action that entails the common belief that φ. Taking into account our logic of common belief, we can further weaken the conditions of this inference rule, to obtain what I call the *rule of communication*:

(RC) $$\frac{\psi \supset I_a\psi,\ \psi \supset B_A\psi,\ \psi \supset B_A\varphi}{\psi \supset C_a\varphi}.$$

Rule RC says that if an intentional action ψ is public and displays φ, for φ to be communicated it is sufficient that ψ is performed.

4   The Four Mechanisms at Work

So far with pure modal logic. The issue now is: can all the machinery I have introduced be exploited to design and implement artificial agents? If we try to use our modal axioms, rules and theorems as they are, we immediately face a difficulty. Let me take for example the concept of public information (the other mechanisms have similar problems, and allow for similar solutions). If, for some proposition φ, we can prove

(P) $\vdash \varphi \supset B_A\varphi$,

then we know that φ can be taken as common belief. However, what does P actually mean? It means that φ *logically entails* $B_A\varphi$; in other words, all agents necessarily recognize φ to be true *in every possible situation* in which φ happens to hold. This is indeed a very strong requirement.

P can be proved easily if φ is itself a theorem; but this is not interesting in practical applications: in fact, we would like to know how a *contingent proposition* (i.e., one which is sometimes true and sometimes false) can possibly be public. In general, we shall need to add *specific axioms* to our system. Suppose for example that the atomic formula Broadcast(a,x) means that a message, x, has been broadcast by a to all other agents in A. If this operation is successful, we can safely assume that within a suitable time interval all agents will believe that x has been broadcast by a; this can be captured by the specific axiom:

(B)   Broadcast(a,x) $\supset B_A$Broadcast(a,x),

which is an instance of P. From this, we can immediately derive that any event of broadcasting is common belief. However, this axiom rules out the possibility of failures in sending or receiving messages, which is indeed a nonrealistic assumption. We might think that the problem is not too severe. Maybe, even if axiom B is not always true, we can assume that in *every particular situation* in which Broadcast(a,x) implies B_ABroadcast(a,x), an event of broadcasting will be common belief.

But this is not the case: such an inference assumes it to be a theorem that

$$(\varphi \supset B_A\varphi) \supset (\varphi \supset B_*\varphi),$$

which is definitely not the case. (For an intuitive counterexample, consider that even if Broadcast(a,x) does in fact imply B_ABroadcast(a,x) in some situation, an agent might not know this, and in such a case no common belief could arise.)

Modal logic allows us to derive theorems only if these are true in all possible situations. However, it seems that we should be concerned not with what is universally true, but with what is *typically* or *normally* true. So, if broadcast is normally successful, agents will typically take every broadcast event to be common belief. However, this conclusion cannot be taken for granted. Indeed, communication failures are possible, and in order to carry out interactions safely it is necessary to take the possibility of failure into account. So, if we really want to implement agents as symbolic reasoners, we will have to rely on some kind of nonmonotonic logic. The problem is that no universally accepted approach to nonmonotonic logic has been proposed yet, in particular for modal systems.

There is, however, another possibility. We might regard logical theories of mental stated as abstract descriptions, which we should try to approximate rather than implement directly. Of course, this does make the problem vanish. But, by careful design, we can try to minimize practical difficulties. Following this line of thought, in the rest of this section I shall try to extract useful design criteria from the formal definitions given so far.

4.1 Deduction in the Space of Common Belief

As we have seen in Section 3.1, an agent can perform inferences in the space of common beliefs. It is interesting to remark that inferences in such a space seem to be very natural for human beings; in particular, it has been argued that children initially assume all beliefs to be common, and only later come to discover that the beliefs of different individuals may not coincide (Clark and Marshall, 1981).

Deduction in the space of common beliefs suffers from all the difficulties of deduction in general. The worst such difficulty is a particularly bad version of the problem of logical omniscience: performing an inference in the space of common belief involves the assumption that all agents will perform the same inference. If this is not the case, an agent may consider as common a piece of information which is not. Unfortunately, it does not seem to me that there is any obvious way out of this impasse. Possibly, the only reasonable approach is to put a strict limit on the complexity of the inferences performed by an agent and, at least in critical cases, to plan communicative acts to establish whether certain propositions are actually entertained as common beliefs.

4.2 Displayed Information

The basic intuition is that a piece of information, φ, is "normally displayed" by some event, ψ, if φ is so evident that it will be perceived by all agents when ψ takes place, unless some malfunction occurs. To establish which facts can be safely considered to be normally displayed, we need a few hypothesis on the agent's perceptual interfaces. Consistently with standard technology (for example in the field of robotics), I shall assume that perceptual routines fall into two categories: *passive* (or mandatory), and *active* (or optional). Passive perception is directly controlled by the external event which is perceived: for example, if its sensors work properly, a robot endowed with sonars cannot fail to perceive a wall in front of it. Active perception is under the agent's control: an active perception event has to be planned and executed under the control of a supervisor. For example, measuring the exact distance from a specific obstacle can be viewed as an act of active perception.

In my opinion, the distinction between passive and active perception is meaningful for all kinds of agents, and not only for robots. A fact can be considered as normally displayed if its perception involves only passive perceptual routines; on the contrary, we cannot consider as normally displayed any piece of information that may require an active perceptual event. Suppose for example that all agents in A are designed so that they always receive all broadcast messages and process them to extract their content. Then, under the assumptions that all agents work properly, the content of a broadcast messages is displayed by the broadcasting event, which is in turn public. This implies that the content of a broadcast messages can be taken to be common belief. On the other side, the information contained in a database cannot be assumed to be common belief of all agents accessing the database, since accessing a database is an instance of active perception.

4.3 Mutual Observation

Mutual observation comes in naturally when active perception is involved. First, we must suppose that the fact that an agent is performing an act of active perception is itself either public, or accessible to active perception by the other agents. From the point of view of agent design, this means that an agent will have to display its acts of active perception. For example, an agent, a, might be able to (optionally) inspect certain types of data local to another agent, b. If a and b are to consider such data as common belief, agent a should display that it has accessed b's data.

It goes without saying that all this presupposes the definition of suitable standards. In the previous example, if a is to display that it accessed b's data, it will have to produce an observable output to which b can give the appropriate meaning, and this presupposed the definition of some standard. This need has been already recognized, as demonstrated by the activity of such organizations as the Foundation for Intelligent Physical Agents (FIPA, http://drogo.cselt.it/fipa/).

4.4 Intentional Communication

An analysis of human intentional communication makes it clear that human beings carry out fairly complex behavioral patterns just in order to be reasonably sure that their communicative acts are successful. Such behavioral patterns include the control of eye contact and different ways of addressing one's audience. In turn, members of an audience typically perform various actions (like nodding one's head, uttering contact expressions, etc.), whose function is to indicate that communication is being received properly. The indication for artificial agent designers is that similar procedures have to be implemented; again, this will require appropriate standards to be defined.

With communication, however, securing the successful reception of a message is only part of the story. In fact, there is a fundamental difference between what an agent perceives and what it is told: while, in normal conditions, perception is truthful, assuming the same for communication involves a hypothesis on the *sincerity* of the speaker: of course, when an agent is insincere the result of an act of communication cannot be a common belief, because at least the speaker does not believe what has been said!

The issue of agent sincerity is still badly understood. Most applications in the field of plan-based communication are build on the hypothesis that agents are actually sincere. But it is not obvious why it should always be so, for example in competitive situations. The fact is that an agent cannot assume that all other agents are always sincere just because they should be taken a priori to be "good guys"; some more complex mechanism must be at work. My opinion is that performing a communicative act creates some sort of *commitment* by the speaker with respect to its audience. For example, asserting a proposition φ creates a commitment for the speaker; more precisely, at least in the near future the speaker is committed to act *as if* it believes φ to be true. This allows the agents in the audience to form expectations about the speaker's future behavior.

This view of communication is coherent with its circular definition. It seems reasonable to assume that only intentional actions should create commitments; the circularity of communication then suggest that when agents perform communicative acts, they intend the implied commitment to become common belief. So far, however, I have not developed this idea formally.

5   Conclusions

Modal logic allows us to produce formal definitions of important concepts involved in the specification of autonomous agents. Among these are concepts related to the social interaction of agents, like common belief and intentional communication.

A problem with classical (monotonic) modal logic is that interesting theorems involve very strong assumptions. In particular, modal logic formulations do not allow us to deal with what is not universally true, but only normally or typically true in practical situations. On the other hand, nonmonotonic logic has not yet reached the level of development required by realistic applications.

In my opinion, it is very unlikely that agents will routinely be implemented as "abstract reasoners", that is, as inference engines implementing pure deduction on logical expressions. However, logical descriptions of different aspects of agency are likely to suggest important ideas to agent designers. In particular, an analysis of the processes by which a piece of information can become common to a group of agents indicates that agents should implement a number of mechanisms critically involved in information sharing.

References

Aumann, R.J. (1976). Agreeing to disagree. *The Annals of Statistics*, 4, 1236–1239.

Barwise, J. (1989). On the model theory of common knowledge. In J. Barwise, *The situation in logic*, CSLI, Stanford, CA, 201–220.

Chellas, B.F. (1980). *Modal logic*, Cambridge University Press, Cambridge, UK.

Clark, H.H., and C.R. Marshall (1981). Definite reference and mutual knowledge. In A.K. Joshi, B.L. Webber, and I.A. Sag, eds., *Elements of discourse understanding*, Cambridge University Press, Cambridge, UK, 10–63.

Colombetti, M. (in press). A modal logic of intentional communication. *Mathematical Social Sciences.*

Dorigo, M., and M. Colombetti (1998). *Robot shaping: An experiment in behavior engineering*, MIT Press, Cambridge, MA.

Grice, P. (1957). Meaning. *Philosophical Review*, 67, 377–388.

Halpern, J.Y., and Y. Moses (1992). A guide to completeness and complexity for modal logics of knowledge and belief, *Artificial Intelligence*, 54, 319–379.

Harman, G. (1977). Review of *"Linguistic behaviour"* by Jonathan Bennett, *Language*, 53, 417–424.

Hughes, G.E., and M.J. Cresswell (1996). *A new introduction to modal logic*, Routledge, London, UK.

Lewis, D.K. (1969). *Convention: A philosophical study*, Harvard University Press, Cambridge, MA.

Lismont, L., and P. Mongin (1995). Belief closure: A semantics of common knowledge for modal propositional logic. *Mathematical Social Sciences*, 30, 127–153.

Lomuscio, A., and M. Colombetti (1997). QLB: A quantified logic for belief. In J.P. Müller, M.J. Wooldridge and N.R. Jennings, eds., *Intelligent Agents III*, Springer, Berlin, 71–85.

Meyer, J.-J. Ch., and W. van der Hoek (1995). *Epistemic logic for AI and computer science*, Cambridge University Press, Cambridge, UK.

Perrault, C.R. (1990). An application of default logic to speech act theory. In P.R. Cohen, J. Morgan and M.E. Pollack, eds., *Intentions in communication*, MIT Press, Cambridge, MA, 161–193.

Sadek, D, P. Bretier and F. Panaget (1997). ARTIMIS: Natural dialogue meets rational agency. *Proceedings of IJCAI '97*, Nagoya, Japan, 1030–1035.

Schiffer, S. (1972). *Meaning*, Oxford University Press, Oxford, UK.

A Schema-Based Approach to Modeling and Querying WWW Data*

Sara Comai[1], Ernesto Damiani[2], Roberto Posenato[3], and Letizia Tanca[1,3]

[1] Politecnico di Milano, Dipartimento di Elettronica e Informazione
[2] Università degli Studi di Milano, Polo di Crema
[3] Università degli Studi di Verona, Facoltà di Scienze MM. FF. NN.

Abstract. The steady growth of the amount of data published on the World Wide Web has led to a number of attempts to provide effective Web querying, as a complement to conventional navigation techniques. In this paper, we propose to support WWW querying by specifying both logical and navigational aspects of a Web site through the unifying notion of schema. Schemata are a powerful tool for classifying and maintaining WWW data as well as for semantics-aware search on the Web. Moreover, schema availability is the basis for an effective flexible querying mechanism.

Following the style of such languages as Good and G-Log, the WG-Log language described in the paper uniformly represents site schemata, instances and queries as graphs. Gracefully supporting schemata that are huge or subject to change, WG-Log adequately represents data whose structure is less rigid than that of traditional databases; moreover, it allows for a uniform representation of flexible queries and views, the latter expressing customized access structures to the site information.

1 Introduction

Access to the huge amount of data available on the World Wide Web is being made awkward by the fact that to this date the only way to extract Web information is to browse individual pages. Nevertheless, while the advantages of schema-aware query formulation are widely recognized in the database context, this technique has seldom been tried on the WWW, on the grounds that Web sites are considered too loose and dynamic to allow schematization [19].

Of course, Web site data may sometimes be fully unstructured, consisting of scarcely organized collections of images, sound and text. Other times, especially on Intranets, WWW data are extracted on-the-fly from traditional relational or object-oriented databases, whose completely specified semantics is exactly mirrored by the site structure.

However, often the structure of WWW information lies somewhere in between these extremes. In fact, the availability of effective design tools for hypermedia

---

* This work has been partially supported by the INTERDATA project from Italian Ministry of University and Scientific Research, 1997.

has profoundly affected the design of Web sites. Several methodologies such as HDM or RMM [6, 8] provide the Web site designer with more or less formal, but quite effective means to express data semantics during site design. Based on these methodologies, research prototypes of Web site generators [4] and many commercial Web authoring environments are currently available and widely used.

Unfortunately, the semantic information produced during the hypermedia design process gets eventually lost when this process is ended. As a result, no explicit representation of semantics is usually associated with the semi-structured, hypertext-style information of the WWW and no query support is generally offered for Web sites.

It is a moot point how database-style support for Web querying should be provided, and three main WWW query languages have been proposed so far: Web3QL [9], WebSQL [11] and WebLog [10]. The first two languages are modeled after standard SQL used for RDBMS, while the third is inspired by the Datalog language. However, all these three languages refrain from the explicit representation of semantics. Indeed, Web3QL and WebSQL offer a standard relational representation of Web pages, based on which users can present SQL-like queries to Web sites. Content-related queries are mapped in free-text searches using a conventional search engine. In addition to similar query capabilities, Web3QL offers an elementary graph pattern search facility, allowing users to search for simple paths in the graph representing the navigational structure of a Web site. Finally, WebLog (and similar languages [7]) propose an O-O instance representation technique which leads to a complete deductive query language; but again it lacks any representation of data semantics.

In other approaches, a representation of semantics is computed as an afterthought from the data instance. The *Tsimmis* system [5] proposes to use the OEM object model to represent semistructured information, together with a powerful query language, *Lorel*. For each Web site, the user defines OEM classes to be used in its Tsimmis representation. Then, an extraction technique based on a textual filter is applied, initializing objects from Web pages' data. An additional facility allows to identify regularities in the extracted instance representation to produce a *DataGuide*, carrying some of the information of a fully fledged site schema.

A representation of semantics based on a standard relational schema is used in the *Araneus* project [1] where Web site crawling is employed to induce schemata of Web pages. These fine grained page schemata are later to be combined into a site-wide schema, and a special-purpose language, *Ulixes* is used to build relational views over it. Resulting relational views can be queried using standard SQL, or transformed into autonomous Web sites using a second special-purpose language, *Penelope*.

A distinct though related approach is given by *Strudel* [2], that provides a single graph data model and a query language for data integration. This approach defines a loose, virtual schema, not much different from DataGuide, and maps on it the contents of the data sources.

In this paper we follow a different line of research introducing *WG-Log*, a graph-oriented language supporting the representation of logical as well as navigation and presentation aspects of hypermedia. This data description and manipulation language for the Web gracefully supports schemata that are huge or subject to change. Moreover, it easily retains the representation of semantics created during the design process, allowing Web users to exploit this semantics by means of a database-like querying facility. In our opinion, the availability of a fully fledged schema is the key for providing effective, flexible query execution and view construction mechanisms.

WG-Log has its formal basis in the graph-oriented language G-Log [16], where *directed labeled graphs* are used to specify database schemata, instances and queries. WG-Log extends G-Log by including some standard hypermedia design notations ([6, 8]) as, for example, navigational links: WG-Log descriptions cleanly denote both *logical* and *structural* (navigational) concepts, with the additional possibility to specify some typical hypermedia features like index pages or entry points, which are essentially related to the hypertext *presentation style*.

The advantages of this approach are many, the first one being the immediate availability of a uniform mechanism for flexible query and view formulation. Uniform graph-based representations of schemata and instances are used for query processing, while Web site data remain in their original, semi-structured form. Thus, WG-Log does not require Web site contents conversion to a fully structured format to allow for database-style querying, as it is the case, for instance, of the Araneus approach.

Schema availability supports flexibility allowing users to build queries that are partially specified w.r.t. the schema; the expressive power of WG-Log, which is fully equipped with recursion, is another powerful resource to this effect. Flexibility is also supported by WG-Log's ability of building custom views over semi-structured information.. When a new *view* over a site is established, clients can formulate queries to include additional information and a good deal of restructuring to the result. In fact, this mechanism can be exploited to reuse existing sites' content as well as schemata to produce new sites.

This paper is organized as follows: in Sect. 2 we present an outline of our approach, with a preliminary description of the system architecture. Section 3 presents the data model and language of WG-Log, while Sect. 4 discusses flexible querying in the WG-Log environment, introduces a computation algorithm for a simple class of queries and investigates its execution complexity. Section 5 draws the conclusions and briefly discusses our future research.

2 An Outline of Our Approach

Our approach to Web querying involves five basic steps: 1) schema identification, 2) schema retrieval, 3) query formulation, 4) result retrieval and restructuring, 5) presentation of results. These steps, together with the basic system modules needed to perform them, will be briefly described in the following.

The *schema identification* and *retrieval* steps involve a dialogue between the client module and a distributed object-oriented server called *Schema Robot*. Essentially, a Schema Robot is a *trader object* which provides Web site schemata, stored and presented in *WG-Log* form, to clients in execution over the Net. Users can either query Robots by using keyword search in the schema repository or adopt more sophisticated styles of interaction. Interacting with Schema Robots, users identify Web servers holding the information they need on the basis of their schema, i.e. on the semantics of their content.

After helping the user in schema identification, clients must provide facilities for easy and effective *query formulation*. Since many Web users are well acquainted with graph-like representation of the hypertextual structure of Web sites, the main purpose of our client module is to provide user-friendly visual tools for query formulation, based on graph-like schema and query representations. Novice users rely on a "cut-and-paste" approach to put together ready-made basic blocks, together with schema parts, to compose their queries, while experts retain the power of a fully expressive query language.

An effective support for query execution and *results retrieval* is essential in the development of Web-based applications. In our approach, queries specify both the information to be extracted from a site instance, and the integration and *results restructuring* operations to be executed on it. This is especially useful in constructing *site views*, i.e. queries whose result is not volatile but forms a new, independently browsable Web site. Views to be stored at the client side are a powerful tool for reusing Web sites' content as well as structure.

Queries are delivered to object-oriented servers called *Remote Query Managers*, which are in execution at target Web sites. Remote Query Managers use an internal lightweight *instance representation* to execute queries and to return results in the format selected by the user. There are two basic modes for the remote Query Manager to return results: as a *list of handles* (e.g. URLs), in order to keep network traffic at a minimum; and as a *result instance graph* which includes complete restructuring of hypertextual links inside the set of HTML pages.

The partial result computed by the Remote Query Manager is processed *at the client site* by the *Local Query Manager* module, which has access to the additional information requested by the user, and produces the complete query result.

The Presentation Manager provides facilities for the *presentation of results*. This mechanism allows the client to require customized presentation styles on the basis, for instance, of constraints on the resources available at the user location.

Finally, we are designing other components of the system, aimed at exploiting the site content information obtained by means of site crawling techniques employed by several current research projects [1, 5]. An interesting possibility is translating such information about the sites content in a WG-Log schema form, to be classified and stored by the Schema Robots system [14].

3 The Data Model and Language

In this section we introduce the data model and the language of WG-Log; formal presentations of this material can be found in the papers on G-Log [16] and in previous papers on WG-Log [3].

In WG-Log, *directed labeled graphs* are used as the formalism to specify and represent Web site schemata, instances, views (allowing customized *access paths or structures*), and queries. The *nodes* of the graphs stand for objects and the *edges* indicate logical or navigational relationships between objects. The whole lexicon of WG-Log is depicted in Fig. 1.

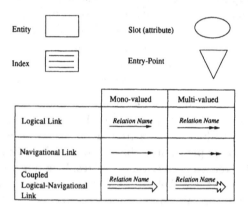

Fig. 1. WG-Log lexicon

In WG-Log schemata, instances and queries we distinguish four kinds of nodes:

- *slots* (also called *concrete nodes*), depicted as ellipses, indicate objects with a representable value; instances of slots are strings, texts, pictures;
- *entities*, depicted as rectangles, indicate abstract objects such as monuments, professors, or cities;
- *collections*, represented by a rectangle containing a set of horizontal lines, indicate collections or aggregates of objects, generally of the two types above;
- *entry points*, depicted as triangles, represent the unique page that gives access to a portion of the site, for instance the site home page. To each entry point type corresponds only one node in the site instance.

It is worth noticing that entry points, like collection nodes, are very useful when a complex query is issued that requires an appropriate *access structure* to alternative, customized presentations of Web portions, or when designing a new view of the site.

We also distinguish three kinds of graph edges:

- *structural edges*, representing navigational links between pages;
- *logical edges*, labeled with relation names, representing logical relationships between objects. The presence of a logical relationship does not necessarily imply the presence of a navigational link between the two entities at the instance level;
- *double edges*, representing a navigational link coupled with a logical link.

At the schema level, each kind of edges may have a single or a double arrow: double arrows indicate that the represented link is multi-valued. As an example of use of these lexical elements, Fig. 2 shows the WG-Log schema of a Restaurant Guide.

3.1 WG-Log Schemata

A (site) *schema* contains information about the structure of the Web site. This includes the (types of) objects that are allowed in the Web site, how they can be related and what values they can take. Logical as well as navigational elements can be included into a site schema, thus allowing for flexibility in the choice of the level of detail.

Formally, a schema contains the following disjoint sets: a set *EP* of *Entry Point labels*, a set *SL* of *concrete object (or Slot) Labels*, a set *ENL* of *ENtity Labels*, a set *COL* of *COllection Labels*, a set *LEL* of *Logical Edge Labels*, one *Structural Edge Label SEL* (which in practice is omitted), a set *DEL* of *Double Edge Labels* and a set $\mathcal{P}$ of *productions*[1].

Sometimes we refer to the first four kinds of labels as *object labels*. The *productions* dictate the structure of WG-Log instances (which represent the actual sites); the productions are triples representing the types of the edges in the instance graph. The first component of a production always belongs to $ENL \cup COL \cup EP$, since only non-concrete objects can be related to other objects; the second component is an edge label and the third component is an object label of any type.

A Web site schema is easily represented as a directed labeled graph, by taking all the objects as nodes and all the productions as edges.

Finally, we assume a function π associating to each slot label a set of *constants*, which is its domain; for instance, the domain of a slot of type *image* might be the set of all *jpeg* files.

3.2 WG-Log Instances

A (Web site) *instance* over a schema $\mathcal{S}$ represents the information that is stored in the Web site pages. It is a directed labeled graph $I = (N, E)$. N is a set of labeled nodes. Each node represents an object whose type is specified by its label. The label $\lambda(n)$ of a node n of N belongs to $EP \cup SL \cup ENL \cup COL$. If $\lambda(n)$

---

[1] We require that the productions form a *set* because we do not allow duplicate productions in a schema

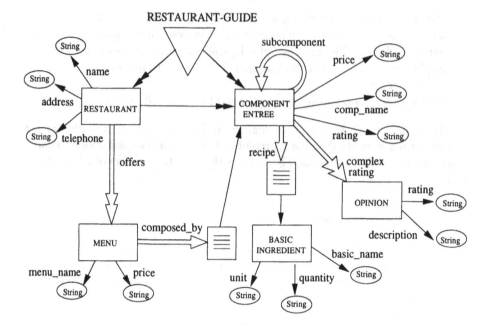

Fig. 2. The WG-Log schema of the Restaurant Guide site

is in EP, then n is an entry point node, and is the only one with label $\lambda(n)$; if $\lambda(n)$ is in SL, then n is a concrete node (or a slot); if $\lambda(n)$ is in ENL, then n is an abstract object, that can coincide with one or more site pages; otherwise n is a collection node. If n is concrete, it has an additional label $print(n)$, called the *print label*, which must be a constant in the domain $\pi(\lambda(n))$ of the label $\lambda(n)$; $print(n)$ indicates the value of the concrete object, for instance an image file or a text. Thus, all the instance nodes must *conform* to some schema node.

E is a set of directed labeled edges with only one arrow. An edge e of E going from node n to n' is denoted (n, α, n'). α is the label of e and belongs to $LEL \cup \{SEL\} \cup DEL$. The edges must conform to the productions of the schema.

3.3 WG-Log Rules and Queries

A WG-Log query is a (set of) graph(s) whose nodes can belong to all four node types used in the schema; moreover, a *dummy* node is allowed, whose purpose is to match all the node types of the schema. The edges can be logical, double or navigational. This allows for purely logical, mixed or purely navigational queries; in all three cases, in fact, the query results in a *transformation* performed on the instance.

WG-Log queries use *rules, programs* and *goals* to deduce or restructure information from the information contained in the Web site pages. Rules and goals are themselves graphs, which can be arranged in programs in such a way that new views (or perspectives) of (parts of) the Web site be available for the user. WG-Log rules are constructed from patterns.

A *pattern* over a Web site schema is similar to an instance over that schema. There are three differences: 1) in a pattern equality edges may occur between different nodes, having the same label, 2) in a pattern concrete nodes may have no print label, and 3) a pattern may contain entity nodes with the *dummy* label, used to refer to a generic instance node. The purpose of the last two elements is allowing incomplete specification of the information when formulating a query. Such partial specification allows a high degree of flexibility.

A WG-Log *rule* is a *colored pattern*, representing an *implication*. To distinguish the body of the rule from its head in the graph (pattern) P representing the rule, the part of P that corresponds to the body is colored red, and the part that corresponds to the head is green. Since this paper is in black and white, we use thin lines for red nodes and edges and thick lines for green ones.

The application of a rule r to a site instance I produces a *minimal superinstance* of I that *satisfies* r. Informally, an instance satisfies such a rule if every matching of the red part of the rule in the instance can be extended to a matching of whole rule *in the instance*. The matchings of (parts of) rules in instances are called embeddings.

Rules in WG-Log can also contain negation in the body: we use solid lines to represent positive information and dashed lines to represent negative information. So a WG-Log rule can contain three colors: red solid (RS), red dashed (RD), and green solid (GS).

To express more complex queries in WG-Log, we can combine several rules and apply them simultaneously to the same instance: a WG-Log set A is a finite set of WG-Log rules that work on the same instance. The generalization of satisfaction to the case of WG-Log rule sets is straightforward. Let A be a WG-Log set; an instance I *satisfies* A if I satisfies every rule of A.

Figure 3(a) contains a WG-Log query over the Web site schema of Fig. 2, formed by two rules. The query is: *find all restaurants whose rating is "great"*.

Note that in the site schema ratings can have two forms: either they are expressed as complex *Opinion* nodes, or as simple values. The query does capture both the situations: in the result, the node 'Rest-list' will be linked to Restaurant entities having either of the two properties. If we were to select only one of the possible rating formats, we should use only the rule pertaining to it.

WG-Log allows also the expression of *goals*, in order to filter out non-interesting information from the instance obtained from the query. A *goal* over a schema S is a subschema of S, and is used combined with a query. The effect of applying a goal G to an instance I is called I *restricted to* G (notation: $I|G$) and is the maximal sub instance of I that is an instance over the schema G. The definition of satisfaction of a WG-Log rule is easily extended to rules with goals. If R is a WG-Log rule, then an instance I over G *satisfies R with goal G* if there exists an instance I' satisfying R such that $I'|G = I$.

There is a strong connection between G-Log and first order predicate calculus. In [16] G-Log is seen as a graphical counterpart of logic. WG-Log is only a

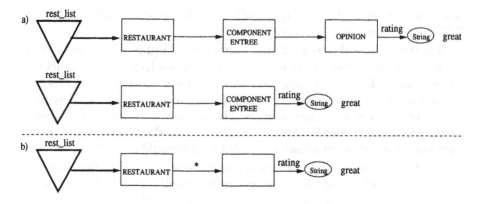

Fig. 3. WG-Log flexible queries.

syntactic variant of G-Log, whose semantics we want to retain in order to keep its expressive power and representation capability; thus the same correspondence holds for WG-Log. Consider for instance the query of Fig. 3(a). This may be expressed in First Order Logic as the conjunction of the following two formulas:

$$\forall r \, \forall ce \, \forall o \, \exists Rest\text{-}list : \mathrm{SEL}(r, ce) \wedge \mathrm{SEL}(ce, o) \wedge \mathrm{rating}(o, \text{``\textbf{great}''})$$
$$\Rightarrow \mathrm{SEL}(Rest\text{-}list, r)$$
$$\forall r \, \forall ce \, \exists Rest\text{-}list : \qquad \mathrm{SEL}(r, ce) \wedge \mathrm{rating}(ce, \text{``\textbf{great}''})$$
$$\Rightarrow \mathrm{SEL}(Rest\text{-}list, r)$$

By examining the logical counterpart of WG-Log, we get an intuition of the meaning of a WG-Log rule; however, in order to use WG-Log as a query language we need to define its *effect*, i.e. the way it acts on instances to produce other instances.

Informally, the *semantics Sem(A)* of a WG-Log set A is the set of instance pairs (I, J) (a relation over instances), such that J satisfies A and J is a minimal superinstance of I. In general, given an instance, there will be more than one result of applying a WG-Log set of rules, which corresponds to the fact that WG-Log is non-deterministic and the semantics is a relation and not a function [16, 3].

In WG-Log, it is allowed to sequence sets of rules. A *WG-Log program P* is a finite list of WG-Log sets to be applied in sequence according to a specified order. The semantics $Sem(P)$ of a WG-Log program $P = \langle A_1, \ldots, A_n \rangle$ is the set of pairs of instances (I_1, I_{n+1}), such that there is a chain of instances $I_2, \ldots, I_n$ for which (I_j, I_{j+1}) belongs to the semantics of A_j, for all j. If a number of WG-Log rules are put in sequence instead of in one set, then, because minimization is applied after each rule, fewer minimal models are allowed: thus sequencing can be used to achieve deterministic behavior. The notion of goal is straightforwardly extended to be applied to the results of WG-Log rule sets or of whole WG-Log programs. The use of all the complexity levels (rules, sets and programs), possibly in conjunction with a goal, guarantees that WG-Log is computationally complete [16], i.e., it can produce any desired superinstance of a given instance.

To give another idea of the expressive power of WG-Log, let us consider the transitive closure query. Figure 4(a) shows the transitive closure of the relationship *subcomponent* of the Restaurant Guide site schema. The rule of Fig. 4(b) uses this definition to construct non-vegetarian menus, each containing a restaurant and the list of the restaurant's entrees containing meat.

The transitive closure of the SEL edge (denoted by *) can also be used to specify the flexible query of Fig. 3(a) in an alternative way (see Fig. 3(b)).

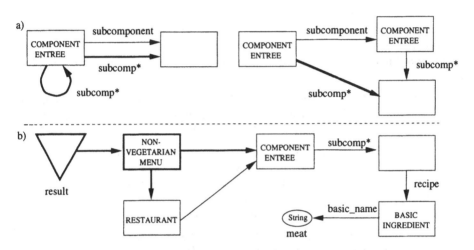

Fig. 4. A WG-Log program using Transitive Closure.

4 Query Evaluation

In order to express a rich set of queries, we have conceived WG-Log as a language with a complex semantics; this gives rise to a computation algorithm that, in the general case, is quite inefficient. However, in many cases the queries on the Web are expressed by only one or two rules, and possibly a goal which contributes to improving the efficiency of program computation. In this section we present a computation algorithm for the most frequent WG-Log queries, and show its complexity.

For the sake of simplicity, from now on we call "objects" the abstract objects, while concrete objects will always be referred to as "slots".

4.1 General Query Evaluation

The general algorithm *GenComp* [15] computes the result of a generic WG-Log set. Suppose we are given a set of rules $A = \{r_1, \ldots, r_k\}$ on schema $\mathcal{S}$, and a finite instance I over S. The procedure *GenComp* will try to extend the instance I to an instance J, in such a way that J is finite and $(I, J) \in Sem(A)$. If this is impossible, it will print the message: "No solution". *GenComp* calls a function *Extend*, which applies graph matching to find embeddings of the red parts of the rules into the instance J. Then, it recursively adds elements to J until J satisfies A, or until J cannot be extended anymore to satisfy A. In this last case, the function backtracks to points where it made a choice among a number of minimal extensions and continues with the next possible minimal choice. If the function backtracks to its first call, then there is no solution. In this sense, *GenComp* reminds the "backtracking fixpoint" procedure that computes stable models [18][2].

The result of the application of a WG-Log program is obtained by sequencing several applications of the algorithm for sets. The result of a program with goal is computed by pruning the result instance of the nodes and edges not specified by the goal.

In [15] we proved that the *GenComp* algorithm is sound and finitely complete for every WG-Log set A, that is, for every input instance I, *GenComp* produces every finite instance J such that $(I, J) \in Sem(A)$.

The problem of graph matching has been widely studied in different forms. For example, [12] studies the complexity of matching graph paths to a generic graph (instance). The problem is found to be NP-hard in the general case, while the authors show that it is polynomial in the case of conflict-free instance graphs, i.e. graphs where each instance node does not belong to more than one pattern.

In this paper we focus on a particular structure of the rule graph, which induces a class of (very frequent) queries: a *simple query* is composed by a single rule having a connected RS part of any form, a (possibly unconnected) RD part formed by lists of length 1, and a connected GS part formed by a single node linked to the rest of the graph by an edge. We study simple queries applied to any kind of instance graph topology.

Simple queries are rather expressive and allow to formulate the most common queries on the Web. The GS part formed by a single node expresses a frequent situation, since it allows to organize in a list the information which satisfies the red part of the query (more complex GS parts are instead generally used in views to restructure the information); moreover, RD parts formed by lists of length 1 are sufficiently expressive, since generally we want to negate some relations directly linked to the information to be extracted, while a whole list of dashed object nodes becomes even difficult to understand.

The two rules of Fig. 3(a) are examples of simple queries. Being positive they can be equivalently applied simultaneously or in sequence, thus the result can be obtained by two applications of the algorithm we are going to present.

---

[2] It is interesting to note that the algorithm reduces to the standard fixpoint computation for the sub language of WG-Log that is the graphical counterpart of Datalog, i.e. sets of rules that consist of a red solid part and *one* green solid edge.

4.2 The Simple-Query Computation Algorithm

We now present the *SA (Simple Algorithm)*, that computes the result of a WG-Log *simple query* by using a kind of depth-first search technique.

Suppose we are given a rule R on schema S and a finite instance I over S. The algorithm *SA* will produce a graph J' in such a way that $J = I \cup J'$ is finite and $(I, J) \in Sem(R)$. Intuitively, J' is an instance over the schema represented by the solid part of the rule; J' is thus obtained by setting a kind of "implicit goal" on the query in order to prune the final instance of all the information that is not mentioned in the query itself. This allows a significant amount of optimization, because during computation the algorithm will only retain query-related information. In case the user be interested in the whole final instance, it is always possible to eliminate the implicit goal by merging the output J' with the input instance I.

The algorithm *SA* tries to determine J' by finding *all* the embeddings of the RS part of the rule in the instance graph and verifying that these embeddings are not extendible in the instance with the RD part of the query. The search of all the embeddings is made by a depth-first search in the graph of I guided by a depth-first search in the graph of R. Starting from an object node x in R, the algorithm searches all the *corresponding* object nodes in I and, for each of these, tries to search the embeddings for the rest of RS part by means of the *Depth_First_Search* recursive procedure. We say that an instance node is *corresponding* to x if it has the same label as x, and the same or a superset of the slots of x.

The *Depth_First_Search* procedure, given an object node x of the graph rule and an object node y of the instance graph, after verifying that y is correspondent to x, executes a recursive depth-first search on the rest of the query graph for each object node adjacent to y corresponding to the object nodes adjacent to x. If any of these searches ends successfully, y is added to the instance solution.

The algorithm uses four auxiliary functions: *Starting_Node(R)* returns the RS node with fewest corresponding nodes in the instance; *Corresponding_Instance_Nodes(I, x)* returns the set of the nodes of I that *correspond* to the node x of the rule; *Create_Green_Node(Y)* creates a new instance node of the same type of the rule green node and links it to the nodes in the set Y. *Corresponding(x, y)* verifies the correspondence of x and y according to the color of x (it is used by *Depth_First_Search*): if the node x is RS, the function returns *true* if the instance node y has the same slots as x, or a superset thereof, *false* otherwise; if the node x is RD, the function returns *true* if all the slots of the instance node y are different from the slots of x, *false* otherwise.

```
SA(I, R)                              {Input: I=instance graph, R=rule graph}
begin
    J' := null;                                     {candidate solution}
    to_green := null;          {set of instance nodes connected to green node}
    x := Starting_Node(R);
```

```
    set_of_y := Corresponding_Instance_Nodes(I, x);
    for y ∈ set_of_y do
        Make_Unvisited_Nodes(R);                    {Prepare for a depth-first search}
        J" := null; candidate_to_green := null;
        if Depth_First_Search(I, J", R, x, y, 1, candidate_to_green)
            then {there is one embedding: add the embedding(s) to instance solution}
                    to_green := to_green ⋃ candidate_to_green;
                    J' := J' ⋃ J";
        fi od
    if (J' ≠ ∅)                                          {if there is a solution}
        then
            if (to_green ≠ ∅) then        {and the green node isn't in the instance}
                    set_of_y' = Create_Green_Node(to_green);
                    J' := J' ⋃ set_of_y';
            fi
            output(J');
        else output("No solutions");  fi
end
```

Soundness, Finite Completeness and Time Complexity

Given the input instance I and a simple rule R, let $J' = SA(I, R)$ be the output of SA. By $FComp(R) = \{(I, J) \mid I$ is a finite instance and $J = I \cup J'\}$ and $FSem(R) = \{(I, J) \mid (I, J) \in Sem(R)$ and $|J| < \infty\}$ we denote, respectively, the finite relation computed by the algorithm and the finite semantics of WGLog on rule R.

The aim of SA is to answer to a user's query as soon as possible, so it outputs only one instance J such that $(I, J) \in FSem(R)$. Therefore the algorithm is not finitely complete in the sense defined above, since given a rule R and an input instance I, there can be other, different J'' such that $(I, J'') \in FSem(R)$.

Nevertheless, it is straightforward to show that, for each I, all the J such that $(I, J) \in FSem(R)$ are *equivalent up to bisimulation* [17, 13], and that $J = I \cup SA(I, R)$ is the instance with the smallest number of nodes among those belonging to the same equivalence class w.r.t. bisimulation. We could say that the algorithm computes the "most interesting representative" of the equivalence class.

Let us consider the quotient set of $FSem(R)$ w.r.t. bisimulation, and let us take as the class representatives just the pairs where the output instance has the smallest number of nodes. We sketch the finite completeness w.r.t. this relation. It is easy to show that the *Depth_First_Search* procedure examines *all* the instance nodes corresponding to the query nodes (essentially, it executes a depth first search of the query graph) and adds an instance node y to the list constructed in J' if there is an embedding of the query graph that contains y (in other words, if there is a depth first search starting from y that ends successfully). The well-known completeness of depth-first search technique guarantees that all the possible embeddings are examined. Eventually, node(s) that correspond to green nodes are created and added at the end by the main algorithm.

The SA algorithm is sound, i.e. $FComp(R) \subseteq FSem(R)$ for every rule R. Let $(I, J) \in FComp(R)$. We show that J satisfies the two conditions for (I, J) to belong to $FSem(R)$.

1. J satisfies R. The algorithm essentially determines the embeddings of the rule making a depth-first search of the query graph for every n-ple of corresponding instance nodes. Therefore the algorithm ends the search with J' that contains *only* the embeddings of the RS part. By the addition of the green node(s), if they are not already present, we construct J' (and consequently J) satisfying R.

2. J is a minimal superinstance of I. Note that, by construction (see point 1.), we add at most *one* node corresponding to the green query node; therefore J is a minimal superinstance of I.

The time complexity of algorithm SA can be determined by evaluating the number of comparisons between the query object nodes and the instance object nodes (function $Corresponding()$) because this is the most expensive operation of the algorithm. The order of the number of comparisons is essentially a function of the length of the simple paths in the query graph.

Let $R = (V, E)$, with $|V| = n$, be the rule graph and $I = (V', E')$, with $|V'| = m$, the instance graph. Without loss of generality, let x_1 be the starting node of the algorithm and $x_1, x_2^1, \ldots x_{j_1}^1; \cdots; x_1, x_2^k, \ldots, x_{j_k}^k$ be k $(0 < k < n)$ simple paths with common starting point x_1 such that $j_1 \geq j_2 \geq \cdots \geq j_k$ and $\bigcup x_i^j = V$ and they are different in the end part $(\forall i, j \ i \neq j \ 0 \leq i, j \leq k \ \exists l \ s.t. \ \forall h \ h > l, \ x_h^i \neq x_h^j)$.

An upper bound to the comparisons made by the algorithm is

$$\#comparisons \leq \sum_{i=1}^{k} \prod_{l=1}^{j_i} m_{\lambda(x_l^i)}$$

where m_i $(\sum_j m_j = m)$ is the number of the instance object nodes of type i and λ is the label function (Ref. Sec. 3.2).

The worst case for the algorithm is given, for example, when the rule is a list of n nodes of the same type and the instance has m nodes of this type; it is simple to show that in this case the time complexity is $O(m^n)$. However, if we consider the most probable star topology for the red part of the rule, even if the nodes are of the same type, the time complexity already reduces to $O(nm^2)$ that is polynomial in the size of the two graphs.

5 Conclusions and Future Work

In this paper we have presented WG-Log, a new approach to querying Web sites which is based on the specification of site semantics by the use of a notion of site schema. In WG-Log, graph-based instance, schema and query representations are used, while Web site data remain in their original, semi-structured form, thus allowing the system to coexist with conventional searching and browsing mechanisms.

This approach is particularly suited for Intranets, but our future research will address its smooth extension to the Internet, providing the possibility to express and evaluate flexible queries across federated or totally unrelated sites.

Our current research addresses also further optimizations of the most general computation algorithm.

Acknowledgments

We like to thank Riccardo Torlone and Agostino Dovier for some useful discussions on Web site querying; moreover, we thank all the students of the WG-Log team of Verona University.

References

[1] P. Atzeni and G. Mecca. To Weave the Web. In *Proceedings of VLDB'97*, pages 206–215, 1997.

[2] P. Buneman, S. Davidson, M. Fernandez, and D. Suciu. Adding structure to unstructured data. In *Proc. of the ICDT 1997*, pages 336–350. Springer Verlag, 1997.

[3] E. Damiani and L. Tanca. Semantic Approach to Structuring and Querying the Web Sites. In *Procedings of 7th IFIP Work. Conf. on Database Semantics (DS-97)*, 1997.

[4] P. Fraternali and P. Paolini. Autoweb: Automatic Generation of Web Applications from Declarative Specifications. http://www.ing.unico.it/Autoweb.

[5] H. García-Molina, Y. Papakonstantinou, D. Quass, A. Rajaraman, Y. Saviv, J. Ullman, V. Vassalos, and J. Widom. The TSIMMIS Approach to Mediation: Data Models and Languages. In *Proceedings of JIIS*, volume 2, pages 117–132, 1997.

[6] F. Garzotto, L. Mainetti, and P. Paolini. Hypermedia design, analysis, and evaluation issues. *Commun. ACM*, 38(8):74–86, Aug. 1995. http://www.acm.org/pubs/toc/Abstracts/0001-0782/208349.html.

[7] F. Giannotti, G. Manco, and D. Pedreschi. A deductive data model for representing and querying semistructured data. In *Proceedings of the ILCP 97 Post-Conference Workshop on Logic Programming Tools for Internet Applications*, Leuwen, 1997.

[8] T. Isakowitz, E. A. Stohr, and P. Balasubramanian. RMM: A methodology for structured hypermedia design. *Commun. ACM*, 38(8):34–44, Aug. 1995. http://www.acm.org/pubs/toc/Abstracts/0001-0782/208346.html.

[9] D. Konopnicki and O. Shmueli. W3QL: A Query System for the World Wide Web. In *Proceedings of the 21th International Conf. on Very Large Databases*, pages 54–65, Zurich, 1995.

[10] L. V. S. Lakshmanan, F. Sadri, and I. N. Subramanian. A declarative language for querying and restructuring the Web. In IEEE, editor, *Sixth Int. Workshop on Research Issues in Data Engineering, February, 1996, New Orleans*, pages 12–21. IEEE Computer Society Press, 1996.

[11] A. O. Mendelzon, G. A. Mihaila, and T. Milo. Querying the World Wide Web. In IEEE, editor, *Proceedings of the Fourth International Conference on Parallel and Distributed Information Systems: December 18–20, 1996, Miami Beach, Florida*, pages 1–10. IEEE Computer Society Press, 1996.

[12] A. O. Mendelzon and P. T. Wood. Finding regular simple paths in graph databases. In *Proceedings of the 15th Conference on Very Large Databases, Morgan Kaufman pubs. (Los Altos CA), Amsterdam*, pages 185–193, Aug. 1989.

[13] R. Milner. Operational and algebraic semantics of concurrent processes. In J. van Leewen, editor, *Handbook of Theoretical Computer Science*, volume B: Formal Models and Semantics, chapter 19, pages 1201–1242. The MIT Press, New York, N.Y., 1990.

[14] B. Oliboni, L. Tanca, and D. Veronese. Using WG-Log to represent semistructured data: the example of OEM. In *Proocedings of the Italian National Conference "Sistemi evoluti per Base di Dati (SEBD98)"*, Ancona, June 1998.

[15] J. Paredaens, P. Peelman, and L. Tanca. G-log: A declarative graphical query specification language. Technical report, Antwerpen, 1991.

[16] J. Paredaens, P. Peelman, and L. Tanca. G-Log: A graph-based query language. *IEEE Transactions on Knowledge and Data Engineering*, 7(3):436–453, June 1995.

[17] D. Park. Concurrency and automata on infinite sequences. In P. Deussen, editor, *Theoretical Computer Science: 5th GI-Conference, Karlsruhe*, volume 104 of *Lecture Notes in Computer Science*, pages 167–183, Berlin, Heidelberg, and New York, Mar. 1981. Springer-Verlag.

[18] D. Saccà and C. Zaniolo. Stable models and non-determinism in logic programs with negation. In *Proceedings of the 9th ACM SIGACT-SIGMOD-SIGART Symposium on Principles of Database Systems*, pages 205–217, Nashville, TE, Apr. 1990. ACM Press.

[19] D. Suciu. Management of semistructured data. In *Foreword to a special section of the ACM Sigmod Record*, volume 26. ACM Press, Dec. 1997.

Querying Multimedia Documents
by Spatiotemporal Structure

Vasilis Delis[1], Dimitris Papadias[2]

[1]Computer Engineering and Informatics Department, University of Patras, Computer Technology Institute, Kolokotroni 3, 26221, Patras, Greece - delis@cti.gr
[2]Department of Computer Science, Hong Kong University of Science and Technology, Clear Water Bay, Hong Kong - dimitris@cs.ust.hk

Abstract. Interactive multimedia documents are rapidly becoming available on the WWW. Navigating in such large document repositories requires flexible retrieval techniques based on spatiotemporal structure. In this paper we address this issue by extending the notion of *conceptual neighborhood* (a concept describing similarity among relations between time intervals) to various resolution levels and higher dimensions. We propose a binary string encoding of relations which allows the automatic derivation of similarity measures and apply our framework for effective support of multimedia queries.

1 Introduction

There is nowadays an abundance of multimedia documents on the WWW, from simple HTML pages to complex multimedia presentations. Current IT users are confronted with huge amounts of information, originating from various sources and containing several forms of data ranging from text to sounds, slide shows etc. In the sequel, the term "multimedia document" (or simply document) will be overloaded to refer to any kind of the above information structures, presented on a computer screen. The specification of such a document entails definitions of its *content* (semantic information), *interactivity* (control flow based on user interaction) and *structure* (which refers to spatiotemporal relations among the document's objects).

Research conducted in the information retrieval field so far mainly focuses on content-based retrieval, covering many types of data forms, like text [13], images [4] and video [14]. However there is an increasingly evident demand[1] for a new paradigm for querying and navigating in the available document repositories: users should be allowed to ask for documents based on their structure and metainformation, in addition to content [7]. For example, a traveller may be interested in getting all

---

[1] This paradigm shift in information retrieval involves a series of research steps, from building conceptual multimedia models able to capture structure, to developing intelligent search engines able to retrieve documents according to structure and metainformation. The importance of handling this type of advanced information can be also demonstrated by the recent efforts to establish sophisticated mark-up languages like SGML and XML.

in [12,13,14,15]. A rule-based methodology for the transformation of the user query prior to its execution is presented in [16].

The COBASE system [17,18] makes use of structures for knowledge representation known as *type abstraction hierarchies*. The *Carmin* project [19] aims at developing a general framework for cooperativeness. A natural language based cooperative interface - named COOP - is described in [20]. The work [21] includes an algorithm, named ISHMAEL, for enumerating both minimal failing subqueries and maximal succeeding subqueries of a query, when the query fails. Other relevant works with a view to structuring question-answering systems are [22,23,24,25].

The NICE system [26,27,28] introduces a methodology for cooperative access to data and knowledge bases based on the modification of the user request - query or update, by means of the systematic application of request-modification rules (RM-rules) against the request. The methodology adopted in the NICE project allows the investigation of several research aspects, with a view to proposing and developing extensions to the system. The kernel of the question-answering model discussed in this paper is essentially a NICE-based methodology for cooperative question-answering. We will restrict ourselves to query requests in this paper.

The paper is organized as follows. In section 2 we present a brief description of the methodology. Next, in section 3, we give simple query examples illustrating the methodology. Section 4 concludes the paper. For a more formal description of the system as a whole, the interested reader should consult [29].

2 Description of the System

We describe in this section the main aspects of our system including the way of describing applications, the basis of the request modification methodology, the provided cooperative query-execution commands, and the way of processing the users' requests.

2.1 The Concepts of a NICE Application: Clausal Specification

We will present, in this section, the concepts that are relevant to the development of applications in the context of our system. In the appendix we explore some of the syntactical aspects of the specification. The reader is referred to [26,28] for a more formal discussion.

The conceptual model is essentially the Entity Relationship Model [30] with *is_a* hierarchies. Therefore, at the conceptual level, the application designer must introduce clauses for the *entity* and *relationship* classes, and for relating entity classes through *is_a* hierarchies. For each of the specified entity and relationship classes, one can introduce clauses defining its *attributes*. Domain values, which define the values for the attributes, should be introduced in specific *domain* clauses. Next, at the object level, *facts* can be specified. Each introduced fact corresponds to either an entity or a relationship class instance.

Consistent with the abstract data type approach, the operations allowed upon a DB are predefined. Each application-oriented operation is specified by a set of clauses indicating:

- the effects of the operation, i. e., the facts that are added to or removed from the DB as a consequence of the application of the operation;
- the preconditions of the application of the operation in terms of the facts that should hold or not in the DB.

Related to the application operations are the clauses of the definition of a predicate named *imposs*, used to specify a list expressing a conjunction of goals which must not hold in any state of the application, as it implies the violation of some of the integrity constraints.

The application designer can introduce, in the application specification, clauses characterizing the user classes of the application. In addition the designer may specify restrictions with respect to the operations allowed to each user class.

As it will be clear later, an important aspect of the current work is to allow the system to propose new questions, from the query submitted by the user. To identify possible subsequent queries, the system must know how the concepts are related among themselves. A natural and immediate way of constructing such queries is through the structure adopted for the knowledge base, more specifically, taking into account, mainly, the relationships explicitly stated in the knowledge base. The problem with this strategy is that the resulting number of queries can become really large. Thus, it is essential to try to constrain the set of possible following queries.

In the current prototype implementation, the constraining is done implicitly by the system - through the consideration of domain restrictions, and explicitly, through the introduction of clauses defining the predicate *constraining_rule*, whose general form is:

```
constraining_rule(RId,CF,UC,OQC,FQC,CC)  :- condition.
```

where: *Rid*: is an identification of the rule; *CF*: is a constraining fact: it must be true at the time the rule is called into use; *UC*: provides the identification of the user class for which this rule is to be applied; *OQC*: is the original query concept, from which other queries will be proposed by the system; *FQC*: is a list of the following query concepts to structure the subsequent queries; and *CC*: is the constraining class, which could be either *complete* or *partial*, the first option meaning that only the concepts on the list FQC can be used to structure new queries, and the second one meaning that the system may consider additional concepts in the process of structuring the queries.

For example, in an academic database application, if a student, at the enrollment period, presents a question about *subject*, then the system may propose other questions related to the concepts included on a list of follow-up concepts. That list, which corresponds to the parameter *FQC*, could include, for instance, the concepts *prerequisite_of*, *subject_classes*, and so on.

There are situations in which it is reasonable that a fact is not present in the knowledge base. In those cases, one should not deal with the absence of the fact as an ordinary failure. Instead, it could be the case that only an appropriated message should be displayed. (On the contrary, the system would try to carry out a complete f_post processing (see section 2.2 below), in the sense of the NICE methodology.) To characterize such situations, one should introduce clauses defining the predicate *missing_info*, whose general form follows:

```
missing_info(Pred, Cond, Msg)  :- condition.
```

where: *Pred*: corresponds to the undefined predicate; *Cond*: specifies a condition which must be true at the time the rule is invoked; and *Msg*: is a message which will explain why the absence of *Pred* is reasonable in the context of the application of the rule.

For instance, in the academic database application, a specific *missing_info* clause may used to indicate that, at the enrollment period, a *teacher* has not yet been assigned to a specific *class* (of a *subject*).

2.2 The Request Modification Methodology

The *RM-rules* take into account, in dealing with a request, not only the request by its own, but also information extracted from a context involving, among others, components like (i) the database (DB) conceptual and external schemes, (ii) the factual DB, (iii) a model of the application domain, and (iv) a *log* of the current session including the user requests and the answers the user have been presented with by the system.

RM-rules are classified as *dependent* upon or *independent* of the application domain, and, orthogonally, in accordance with the time in which they are applied, as:
- *pre* rules: preceding the execution of a command;
- *s_post* rules: following the successful execution of a command;
- *f_post* rules: following the unsuccessful execution of a command.

The above-mentioned classification has been described elsewhere [26,28]. Shortly, rules of the class *pre* can correct or complement a request. Rules of the class *s-post* can complement a request after its successful execution. Rules of the class *f_post* are called into use in the case of failure in the execution of a user request. They can produce and execute an *alternative* request, which allows the achievement of the same goal of the original request, or, when that is not possible, the achievement of an alternative goal related in a consistent way with the original one. If there is not any alternative, or if all the alternatives fail, if the failure is due to a *removable obstacle*, specific f_post rules can propose that the system monitor alerts the user when the obstacle ceases to exist. On the other hand, if the obstacles are known to be of a persistent nature, specific f_post rules can, at least, generate and display an *explanation* of the failure.

RM-rules of the classes *s_post* and *f_post* are further specialized into the (sub-) classes *s_post_query, s_post_info, f_post_alt,* and *f_post_comp*. The justification for the splitting of the *s_post* and *f_post* classes is given by the fact that there are RM-rules [28] whose execution ends with the proposal of an additional query (*s_post_query* in our extension) and others in which alternative queries are offered (*f_post_alt* in the current extension). Others are responsible for the production of additional relevant information (*s_post_info*) or for trying to compensate for the failure in the execution of a query (*f_post_comp*). It can take place, in the compensation, the output of an explanation for the failure.

At the end of the successful execution of a request, *template rules* direct the *editing* of the information included in an answer, so that the user be presented with the information in a more friendly way. It is allowed to take place, in the editing, the omission of uninteresting or unauthorized items.

The basic RM-rules of the methodology are gathered in one of the modules of the system architecture (see [28]). Notwithstanding this fact, the application designer can introduce new ones in the context of the application specification. For the purpose of introducing RM-rules, there are general standards to be followed for each of the above-mentioned classes. In each of those standards, the user is expected to define an action to be executed at the time the rule is activated. Its execution can cause the activation of specific modules, each of them including specific schemes implementing some form of cooperativeness from the system to the user. As an example, the module RECV of the system architecture contains an implementation of specific error-recovering schemes [28].

2.3   Cooperative Query-Execution Commands

The following is the basic *cooperative query-execution command*, provided by the methodology:

```
query (<query-expression>, <information>)
```

The parameters <query-expression> and <information> are Prolog expressions involving one or more facts from the DB. The <query-expression> can be a single fact, a conjunction of facts or a second-order predicate. The last option - second-order predicate - allows the recovering of a list of answers related to the query fact specified in the predicate.

In addition to the above-mentioned *query* command, we have introduced the command *query_on*, which allows the presentation of queries in a more general level. The syntax is:

```
query_on(C)
```

where C stands for a "general concept", which should be either an entity or a relationship class. The predicate above calls an specific structuring predicate which activates the RECV module to build up a query following the syntax for facts of the methodology. The query is then submitted to the system query processor, through the calling of a predicate semantically equivalent to the *query* command.

An essential element of our framework, specially in the context of the RM-rules, is the session *log*, in which a record of the interaction between the system and its user is kept. The log is formed by Prolog clauses defining specific predicates such as *was_queried*, *was_told*, *select_ans_qry*, to name a few. See [29] for details.

2.4 Processing the user Requests

According to the NICE methodology, specific schemes have been adopted for the processing of RM-rules against users' requests. Essentially, for each entered request, one or more rules are automatically activated. We discuss each introduced scheme in the following.

In the processing of rules of the type *pre* against user queries, the *successive* scheme has been taken into account in [26,28]. This scheme can be represented as shown in the sequel (for a single goal):

$$Q_0 \rightarrow Q_1 \rightarrow Q_2 \rightarrow ... \rightarrow Q_n$$

where Q_0 is the original query; $\rightarrow$ indicates a possible transformation; and Q_n is the transformed query.

At least two points can be raised up with respect to this strategy:
1. It can happen that some of the intermediate queries - Q_1, Q_2, ..., Q_{n-1} - be more interesting for the purpose of cooperativeness than the final transformed query Q_n.
2. As pointed out before, the query Q_0 is submitted through the issuing of the command *query*(Q_0), which activates the query processor of the system. Differently, the transformed query, Q_n, is directly processed against the underlying database in [26,28].

With respect to (i) above, in the current implementation the query expressions, in the sequence of query transformations from Q_0 to Q_n, are collected into a list from which a menu is constructed to query the user about the most appropriated question to query about. An extended query-the-user facility [31] is used in this process.

Now, in what (ii) is of concern, the chosen query, after the pre-processing process, is also submitted to the query processor of the system. This corresponds to a more general (and more natural) approach and makes it easier the management of all the question-answering process.

Now we turn our attention to another scheme of the methodology, namely the *cumulative* scheme. Let Q_a be the answered query after the pre-processing process. According to the solution presented in [26,28], one constructs a list containing all Q_s such that $Q_a \rightarrow Q_s$ is a valid transformation with respect to some *s-post* rule. The result list is included as part of the answer to the original query. In the current solution we are primarily interested in the transformations such that Q_s is a query expression representing a possible subsequent question. All those questions are collected into a list and a menu is presented to the user, allowing him to choose an additional query (if he wants to!). In agreement with the strategy for the *successive* scheme, the chosen query is submitted to the system query processor. Another important aspect of the pos-processing phase is the identification and presentation of additional relevant information, related to the answered question. In this case the *cumulative* scheme as initially proposed is appropriated.

In the case of failure in the execution of a user query, one searches for an *alternative* query whose execution ends in success. This strategy is defined as *alternative scheme* in [26]. If not one alternative has been encountered, the system tries to *compensate* for the failure, i. e., to present the user with appropriate messages and/or to generate an explanation of the failure.

Taking into account the proposed modification for the *successive* and *cumulative* schemes, outlined above, it has been necessary to consider, in the context of the *alternative* scheme, in the case in which the current (failed) query has been chosen from a menu, the possibility of identifying some alternative query from the previously presented menu. Here again the user is queried about the convenience of trying some of the other queries on the menu. From this point on, the system follows the same strategy of [26,28]. If necessary, it proceeds trying to find alternatives through the activation of specific *f_post* rules. If the attempt ends in failure, it tries to compensate for the failure, by means of the calling of other specific *f_post* rules.

The algorithms for the processing of user requests are described in [29].

3 Running the Prototype

We present some sample queries in the Appendix, based on the specification of an academic database application [29]. The notation used in the examples is Prolog-like [32].

The system, in the case of wrong query expressions, tries to correct them with respect to the conceptual schema. Next, a menu containing all possible query transformations, with respect to some specific *pre* rules, is presented to the user. After the successful execution of the input query, the system structures a menu containing possible subsequent queries, which are obtained taking into account the conceptual level information, the domain restrictions, and the introduced *constraining* rules. In the case of failure, if the failure is "reasonable" with respect to some specific *missing_info* clause, an appropriate message is displayed. If a failing query has been chosen from a menu, as the user could be interested in the other entries (queries), those ones are again suggested to him on a new menu.

The important point in the examples is that the system tries to establish, from the user input query, a dialogue in which not only it tries to answer the original query, as well as it tries to identify possible subsequent queries, which are then suggested to the user.

4 General Remarks

In this paper, we have described a methodology for question-answering in which the system tries to establish, from an input query, a controlled dialogue with its user. In the dialogue, the system tries to identify possible subsequent queries, which are then proposed to the user. The control aspect of the dialogue is based (implicitly) on the way of representing concepts in the knowledge base, on domain restrictions, and (explicitly) on specific constraining rules.

Unlike the emphasis followed in [26,28], in accordance with a very important point with respect to the system development was the investigation of new request modification rules, we are now more concerned with the proposal and implementation of a question answering model, structured over the NICE kernel. In this way our work is related to [22]. In fact, as one can see in [26,28], it is not possible (and not even easy!) to introduce a large number of really expressive request-modification rules. In this aspect we argue that the most important point with respect to the proposal of a question answering model is to investigate how one can improve the existing conceptual structures, and even to introduce new ones. Recall that the conceptual structures take part in the knowledge base specification, which represents the data semantics.

One could argue that a critical aspect with respect to the rule-based request modification, specially in what pre-rules are of concern, is related to efficiency, as the query transformation can cause a "delay" in the presentation of the query answer to the end user. It is important to stress, with respect to this aspect that the rule modification approach, as considered in the NICE system, is flexible enough to allow the designer to deal with efficiency aspects. In this way, one can inspect the actions associated with some specific pre-rules and see if it is possible to consider them in the context of rules either of the type s_post or of the type f_post. Notwithstanding that possibility, some pre-rules are really of importance for the purpose of cooperativeness: one could mention, for instance, those ones concerned with the verification of the request correctness with respect to the conceptual schema specification.

References

1. Bolc, L. & Jarke, M. (eds.). Cooperative Interfaces to Information Systems. Springer-Verlag (1986).
2. Allen, J.F. & Perrault, C.R. *Analyzing intentions in utterances*. Artificial Intelligence 15, 3, 143-178 (1980).
3. Goodman, B.A. & Litman, D.J. *On the Interaction between Plan Recognition and Intelligent Interfaces*. In: User Modeling and User-Adapted Interaction, 2(1-2), pp. 55-82 (1992).
4. Kautz, H.A. *A Formal Theory of Plan Recognition*. PhD thesis, The University of Rochester, Rochester, NY (1987).
5. Litman, D.J. & Allen, J.F. *A Plan Recognition Model for Subdialogues in Conversations*. Cognitive Science 11, Pages 163-200 (1987).
6. Motro, A. *Query generalization: a technique for handling query failure*. Proc. First International Workshop on Expert Database Systems (1984) 314-325.
7. Motro, A. *FLEX: A Tolerant and Cooperative User Interface to Databases*. IEEE Transactions on Knowledge and Data Engineering, Vol. 2, No. 2, pp. 231-246 (1990)
8. Cheikes, B. *Monitor Offers on a Dynamic Database: The search for relevance*. Technical Report CIS-85-43, Dept. of Computer and Information Science, University of Pennsylvania, October, 1985.

9. Mays, E. *A Temporal Logic for Reasoning about Changing Data Bases in the Context of Natural Language Question-Answering.* In: Kerschberg, L. (ed.) Expert Database Systems. New York: Benjamin Cummings, 1985.

10. Imielinski, T. *Intelligent Query Answering in Rule Based Systems.* Journal of Logic Programming, 4:229-257 (1987).

11. Motro, A. *Using Integrity Constraints to Provide Intensional Answers to Relational Queries.* Proceedings of the Fifteenth International Conference on Very Large Data Bases, Amsterdam, August (1989).

12. Allen, R.B. *User Models: theory, method, and practice.* Int. J. Man-Machine Studies, 32, 511-543 (1990).

13. Hemerly, A. S. Fundamentos Lógicos para modelos de usuários em ambientes cooperativos. PhD thesis, Dept. de Informática, PUC/RJ (1995).

14. Kobsa, A. & Wahlster, W. (eds.). User Models in Dialog Systems. Springer-Verlag (1989).

15. Rich, E. *Users are individuals: individualizing user models.* Int. J. Man-Machine Studies, 18, 199-214 (1983).

16. Cuppens, F. & Demolombe, R. *Cooperative answering: a methodology to provide intelligent access to databases.* In: Proc. of the Second International Conference on Expert Database Systems. L. Kerschberg (ed.). Benjamin/Cummings (1989) 621-643.

17. Chu, W.W.; Yang, H.; Chiang, K.; Minock, M.; Chow, G.; Larson, C. *CoBase: A Scalable and Extensible Cooperative Information System.* Journal of Intelligent Information Systems, Vol. 6, Number 2/3 (1996), pp. 223-259.

18. Minock, M.; Chu, W. W. *Explanation for Cooperative Information Systems.* In Proceedings of the Ninth International Symposium on Methodologies for Inteligent Systems, Baltimore, MD, 1996.

19. Godfrey, P., Minker, J. & Novik, L. *An Architecture for a Cooperative Database System.* Proceedings of the 1994 International Conference on Applications of Databases, Vadstena, Sweden, June 1994.

20. Kaplan, S.J. *Cooperative Responses from a Portable Natural Language Query System.* Artificial Intelligence, 19 (1982), Pages 165-187.

21. Godfrey, P. *Minimization in Cooperative Response to Failing Database Queries.* Int'l Journal of Cooperative Information Systems (IJCIS), World Scientific Publishing, 6(2):95-149 (1997).

22. Graesser, A. C. , Gordon, S. E. & Brainerd, L. E. *QUEST: A Model of Question Answering.* Computers Math. Applic. Vol. 23, No. 6-9, pp. 733-745, 1992.

23. Webber, B.L. *Questions, Answers and Responses: Interacting with Knowledge Base Systems.* In: On knowledge base management systems. Brodie, M.L. & Mylopoulos, J. (eds.). Springer-Verlag (1986).

24. Han, J.; Huang, Y.; Cercone, N.; Fu, Y. Fu: Intelligent Query Answering by Knowledge Discovery Techniques. IEEE TKDE 8(3): 373-390 (1996)

25. Motro, A. Cooperative Database Systems. International Journal of Intelligent Systems, Vol. 11, No. 10, October 1996, pp. 717-732.

26. Hemerly, A.S., Casanova, M.A. & Furtado, A.L. *Cooperative behaviour through request modification.* Proc. 10th Int'l. Conf. on the Entity-Relationship Approach, San Mateo, CA, USA (1991) 607-621.

27. Sena, G.J. Um modelo de sistema cooperativo baseado na modificação de solicitações de consulta e de atualização. PhD thesis, Dept. de Informática, PUC/RJ (1992).

28.Sena, G.J. Cooperative Environments for the use of Information Systems: description of the NICE project and a proposal of extensions to its present-day version. Technical Report 001/96, UNESP/Guaratinguetá/DMA (1996).

29.Sena, G. J.; Furtado, A.L. Cooperative Interfaces to Databases: Towards an Extended Version of the NICE System. Technical Report 001/98, UNESP/Guaratinguetá/DMA (1998).

30.Hull, R. & King, R. *Semantic Database Modeling: Survey, Applications, and Research Issues.* ACM Computing Surveys, Vol. 19, No. 3, pp. 201-260 (1987).

31.Sena, G.J.; Furtado, A.L. *An Extended Query-the-User Tool for Expert Systems.* Proceedings of the Fourth World Congress on Expert Systems, ITESM Mexico City Campus, March 16-20 (1998), pp. 355-362.

32.Marcus, C. Prolog Programming. Addison-Wesley Pub. Co. (1986).

Appendix: Clausal Notation and Query Examples

Clausal Notation. To give some insight in the notation adopted in the prototype, we present in the sequel the syntax for some of the concepts of a NICE application. We begin with the syntax for the *entity* and *relationship* classes, and for the attributes.

    entity(E,K).
    relationship(R,[E1,...,En]).
    is_a(E1,E2).
    attribute(E,A).attribute(R,A).

where E, E1, E2,...,En are entity classes, R is a relationship class, K is a domain from which the key values for instances of E are to be taken, and A is an attribute. Some examples are given in the sequel:

    entity(student,s_numb).entity(teacher,t_numb).
    chairman is_a teacher.
    relationship(takes,[student,class]).relationship(takes_part_in,[subject,course]).
    relationship(subject_classes,[subject,class]).
    relationship(assigned_to_class,[teacher,class]).
    attribute(subject,credits).attribute(has_taken,grade).

At the object level, we have the following syntax for the *facts*:

    E&&K. E&&K\A(V).
    R#PL. R#PL\A(V).

where V stands for a value from domain A, PL designates the list [E1&&K1,...,En&&Kn], called the relationship participant list, each Ei&&Ki, i=1,...,n, representing an entity class instance. Some examples are shown below:

    course&&comp.subject&&sb1.
    lab&&sb2.teacher&&t1.
    class&&cl2.subject&&sb1\credits(3).
    subject_classes#[subject&&sb1,class&&cl2].
    is_able_to_teach#[teacher&&t1,subject&&sb1].
    assigned_to_class#[teacher&&t2,class&&cl2].takes#[student&&s2,class&&cl1].

Query Examples. To illustrate the prototype behavior, we present two simple query examples in the sequel. The user entries below are italicized.

?- query_on(subject).
subject && V1
Attribute(s) of entity subject : credits sb_name
I can try to solve any of the queries in the sequel:
choose from the following:
(1) subject && V1
(2) subject && V1 \ credits(V2)
(3) subject && V1 \ sb_name(V3)
   Answer is **1** .
Would you like to try to get more information about or related to any of the facts in the sequel?
choose from the following:
(1) subject && sb1
(2) subject && sb2
(3) subject && sb3
(4) subject && sb4
(5) subject && sb5
   Answer is **3**.
Maybe you can be interested in obtaining
information concerning the (template)
facts in the sequel:
I can try to solve any of the queries in the sequel:
choose from the following:
(1) prerequisite_of # [subject && sb3,subject && V1]
(2) subject_classes # [subject && sb3,class && V2]
(3) is_able_to_teach # [teacher && V3,subject && sb3]
(4) assigned_to_class # [teacher && V4,class && cl4]
   Answer is **4** .
...s_pos processing...
...failure...
A teacher has not been yet assigned to the specified class
Would you like me to try to solve any of the other queries in the sequel ?
choose from the following:
(1) prerequisite_of # [subject && sb3,subject && V1]
(2) subject_classes # [subject && sb3,class && V2]
(3) is_able_to_teach # [teacher && V3,subject && sb3]
   Answer is **3**.

subject && sb1
subject && sb2
subject && sb3
subject && sb4

subject && sb5
is_able_to_teach # [teacher && t2,subject && sb3]

?- query_on(title).
What concept do you want, in fact, to query about?
choose from the following:
(1) student
(2) subject
(3) class
(4) course
(5) lab
(6) teacher
(7) classroom
(8) takes
(9) has_taken
(10) prerequisite_of
(11) takes_part_in
(12) subject_classes
(13) is_able_to_teach
(14) assigned_to_class
(15) reserved_for_classes
   Answer is **2**.

subject && V1
Attribute(s) of entity subject : credits sb_name
I can try to solve any of the queries in the sequel:
choose from the following:
(1) subject && V1
(2) subject && V1 \ credits(V2)
(3) subject && V1 \ sb_name(V3)
   Answer is **1** .

From this point on, the interaction is the same as shown in the previous query.

Answers About Validity and Completeness of Data: Formal Definitions, Usefulness and Computation Technique

Robert Demolombe

ONERA-CERT, 2 Avenue E. Belin BP 4025, 31055 Toulouse, France,
e-mail: Robert.Demolombe@cert.fr

Abstract. We present here a continuation of our work presented in [Dem97] . We recall definitions of valid subsets or complete subsets of a database, and the modal logic that is used for reasoning about assumptions on validity and completeness, in order to characterise subsets of a standard answer that are either valid or complete. We formally define several forms of answers that are either extensional or intensional. Then, we analyse which kinds of anwers are really useful for users. Finally, we present an automated deduction method to compute these answers. This method is based on SOL-deduction, which has been designed for classical logic, and we show how it can be adapted to our modal logic.

1 Introduction

In this paper is presented a continuation of a work that has already been published in [Dem97] (see also [CDJ94,DJ94,Dem96]). We have considered situations where databases, or distributed database, or information sources, in general, may, or may not, be reliable in regard to stored data. Here we have restricted the scope to databases.

It is assumed that some parts of the database are valid or complete in the sense introduced by A. Motro in [Mot86,Mot89]. If we consider, for example, a database that contains data about bank agencies: their location, the fact that they are open or close, that accounts are negative, etc, it can be assumed, for example, that data about open agencies are valid, and data about downtown agencies are complete.

Property of validity intuitively means that if it is stored in the database that some bank is open, then this fact is "guaranteed" to be true. Property of completeness means that if it is "guaranteed" that some bank agency is located downtown, then this fact is stored in the database.

In this situation, if some user asks to the database what are agencies not located downtown, it is not obvious to see how assumptions about validity and completeness can be combined to characterise what parts of the answer are guaranteed to be either valid or complete.

For that purpose a formal modal logic has been defined in [Dem97] which is briefly recalled in section 2. In section 3 we analyse different forms of answers about validity and completeness, and circumstances where they are useful. Finally, in section 4 is presented an automated deduction technique that has been implemented to compute that kinds of answers.

2   Background on validity and completeness of data

In [Dem97] we have defined a modal logic (see [Che88]) that has been used to give a formal definition to the fact that a given subset of a database is reliable either in regard to validity or in regard to completeness of data. In this section we briefly recall these definitions.

In the axiomatic definition of our logic we have all the axiom schema of classical propositional calculus, and the inference rule Modus Ponens.

To characterise database content we use the modal operator B, and sentences of the kind Bp, where p is a sentence of a classical propositional calculus language, intuitively mean that p is a consequence of sentences stored in the database. The axiomatic of B is defined by the following axiom schemas:

$(K1)$ $B(p \rightarrow q) \rightarrow (Bp \rightarrow Bq)$

$(D1)$ $\neg((Bp) \wedge (B(\neg p)))$

and inference rule of necessitation (Nec) $\dfrac{\vdash p}{\vdash Bp}$.

To characterise what the system which manages the database believes, we have introduced another modal operator K, and sentences of the kind Kp intuitively mean that the system "strongly believes" p. We do not say that the system knows p because we consider that we are in a context where no information can be taken as true in an absolute sense. However, we want to be able to make a distinction between beliefs, for which we accept that they may be wrong beliefs, and strong beliefs for which we have the same behaviour as for knowledge. That is, strong beliefs are irrevocably considered as true beliefs [1]. This intuitive meaning is formally expressed by axiom schema (T'). The axiomatic for K is defined by the following axiom schemas:

$(K2)$ $K(p \rightarrow q) \rightarrow (Kp \rightarrow Kq)$

$(D2)$ $\neg((Kp) \wedge (K(\neg p)))$

(T') $K(Kp \rightarrow p)$

and inference rule of necessitation (Nec) $\dfrac{\vdash p}{\vdash Kp}$.

The fact that strong beliefs are a particular kind of beliefs is expressed by the axiom schema:

(KB) $Kp \rightarrow Bp$

Finally, we have two axiom schemas (OBS1) and (OBS2) to express the fact that the database system has a **complete** knowledge of database content. That is, he knows what is, and what is not, in the database.

$(OBS1)$ $Bp \rightarrow K(Bp)$

---

[1] In the context of relational databases, a similar distinction is made between integrity constraints, that correspond to strong beliefs, and the rest of the database, that corresponds to beliefs.

$(OBS2)$ $\neg Bp \rightarrow K(\neg Bp)$

Notice that these two axioms do not imply that database content is a complete representation of the world.

In the following we extend the language used to represent database content from propositional calculus to first order calculus. However, we accept the Domain Closure Axiom, as it is usually the case in database context, and quantified formulas can be seen as ground conjunctions or ground disjunctions. Then, from a theoretical point of view, we are in fact in the field of propositional calculus.

The two modal operators we have presented in previous paragraph can be used to define the notions of reliable data in regard to validity or in regard to completeness [2]. Sentence $RV(p(x))$ means that the database system strongly believes that every sentence of the form $p(x)$ which is believed by the database is true in the world. Sentence $RC(p(x))$ means that the database system strongly believes that every sentence of the form $p(x)$ which is true in the world is believed by the database. In formal terms we have:

$$RV(p(x)) \stackrel{\text{def}}{=} K(\forall x(Bp(x) \rightarrow p(x)))$$

$$RC(p(x)) \stackrel{\text{def}}{=} K(\forall x(p(x) \rightarrow Bp(x)))$$

A given database state db is represented by a set of first order formulas, and a set of assumptions mdb about subsets of the database that are reliable for validity or completenes is represented by a set of sentences of the form $RV(p(x))$ or $RC(p(x))$. From db we define dbb that represents database content in terms of beliefs. We have:

$$dbb = \{Bp \; : \; \vdash db \rightarrow p\} \cup \{\neg Bp \; : \; \nvdash db \rightarrow p\}$$

3 Different sorts of answers

From a formal point view we can define several kinds of answers that inform users about parts of the answers that are either valid or complete. In this section we first present these formal definitions, and then we analyse which ones are really useful for users.

---

[2] Words "validity" and "completeness" are used in different contexts wheres they have different meanings. In formal logics they refer to the links between axiomatics and semantics. It is said that the axiomatics is valid (or sound) iff for every sentence p, $\vdash$ p implies $\models$ p, and it is said that it is complete iff for every sentence p, $\models$ p implies $\vdash$ p. In another context, it is said that a deduction strategy is complete iff for every sentence p, if p is a logical consequence of a theory T, then p can be derived from T using this strategy, and the strategy is said to be valid (or sound) iff for every sentence p, if p can be derived from p using this strategy, then p is a logical consequence of T.

3.1 Formal definitions of answers

Definitions are given in the logical framework presented in section 2.

Standard answers

The standard answer s to query $q(x)$ is defined by:

$$s = \{a \; : \; \vdash dbb \rightarrow Bq(a)\}$$

The standard answer is the set of individuals such that the database believes that they satisfy $q(x)$.

Extensional answer about validity

The extensional answer about validity ev to query $q(x)$ is defined by:

$$ev = \{a \; : \; \vdash mdb \wedge dbb \rightarrow Kq(a)\}$$

The answer ev is the set of individuals such that the database strongly believes that they satisfy $q(x)$.

Intensional answer about validity

The intensional answer about validity iv to query $q(x)$ is defined by:

$$\begin{aligned} iv = \{q'(x) \; : \; & \vdash mdb \rightarrow RV(q'(x))\} \text{ and} \\ & \vdash \forall x(q'(x) \rightarrow q(x)) \text{ and} \\ & q'(x) \text{ is maximal for implication}\} \end{aligned}$$

The answer iv is a set of sentences that characterise valid parts of the standard answer in terms of properties instead of a characterisation in terms of a set of individuals.

The condition "$q'(x)$ is maximal for implication" could be reformulated in more formal terms, it means that for every $q'(x)$ in iv there is no other sentence $q''(x)$ in iv such that $q''(x)$ logically implies $q'(x)$.

If $q'(x)$ is in iv, by definition of RV we have (1) $\forall x K(Bq'(x) \rightarrow q'(x))$. Since we have $\vdash \forall x(q'(x) \rightarrow q(x))$ we also have $\vdash \forall x K(q'(x) \rightarrow q(x))$, and from (1) we can infer (2) $\forall x K(Bq'(x) \rightarrow q(x))$.

Then, if for some individual a we have $Bq'(a)$, by (OBS1) we have $KBq'(a)$, and from (2) we can infer $Kq(a)$, and from (KB) we infer $Bq(a)$. That means that a is in s and it is also in ev.

Intensional answer about completeness

The intensional answer about completeness $ic-$ to query $q(x)$ is defined by:

$$\begin{aligned} ic- = \{q'(x) \; : \; & \vdash mdb \rightarrow RC(q'(x))\} \text{ and} \\ & \vdash \forall x(q'(x) \rightarrow q(x)) \text{ and} \\ & q'(x) \text{ is maximal for implication}\} \end{aligned}$$

The answer $ic-$ gives an intensional characterisation of subsets of the standard answer that are complete.

If $q'(x)$ is $ic-$, by definition of RC we have (1) $\forall x K(q'(x) \rightarrow Bq'(x))$, and from $\vdash \forall x(q'(x) \rightarrow q(x))$ we have (2) $\vdash \forall x(Bq'(x) \rightarrow Bq(x))$ and (3)

$\vdash \forall x K(Bq'(x) \rightarrow Bq(x))$. Then from (1) and (3) we have (4) $\forall x K(q'(x) \rightarrow Bq(x))$, and, by contraposition we have (5) $\forall x K(\neg Bq(x) \rightarrow \neg q'(x))$.

Then, if for a given individual a we have $\neg Bq(a)$, from (OBS2) we have $K\neg Bq(a)$, and by (5) we have $K\neg q'(a)$.

The intensional answer about completeness $ic+$ to query $q(x)$ is defined by:

$$ic+ = \{q'(x) \ : \ \vdash mdb \rightarrow RC(q'(x))\} \text{ and}$$
$$\vdash \forall x(q(x) \rightarrow q'(x)) \text{ and}$$
$$q'(x) \text{ is minimal for implication}\}$$

The answer $ic+$ gives an intensional characterisation of supersets of the standard answer that are complete.

If $q'(x)$ is in $ic+$, by definition of RC we have (1) $\forall x K(q'(x) \rightarrow Bq'(x))$, and from $\vdash \forall x(q(x) \rightarrow q'(x))$ we have (2) $\vdash \forall x K(q(x) \rightarrow q'(x))$. Then, from (1) and (2) we have (3) $\forall x K(q(x) \rightarrow Bq'(x))$, and, by contraposition, we have (4) $\forall x K(\neg Bq'(x) \rightarrow \neg q(x))$.

Then, if for a given individual we have $\neg Bq'(a)$, from (OBS2) we have $K\neg Bq'(a)$, and by (4) we have $K\neg q(a)$.

Extensional answer about completeness

The extensional answers about completeness $ec-$ and $ec+$ give the extension of intensional answers about completeness. Their definitions are:

$$ec- = \{a \ : \ \vdash dbb \rightarrow Bq'(a)\} \text{ and } q'(x) \text{ is in } ic-\}$$

$$ec+ = \{a \ : \ \vdash dbb \rightarrow Bq'(a)\} \text{ and } q'(x) \text{ is in } ic+ \}$$

3.2 Useful answers

The different kinds of answers are analysed in function of what users know.

Validity answers

There is no doubt about usefulness of extensional answers about validity.

For intensional answers we have to analyse the point more carefully. Let's consider an example where predicate "$agency(x)$" means that x is a bank agency, "$open(x)$" means that the agency x is open, and "$bank(x,y)$" means that x is an agency of bank y. We consider a user who is looking for an open agency and asks the query $q_1(x)$ below:

$q_1(x) = agency(x) \wedge open(x)$

which means: *what are open bank agencies?*. Suppose that in the intensional answer about validity iv we have $q'_1(x)$ below:

$q'_1(x) = agency(x) \wedge open(x) \wedge bank(x, BE)$

which means: *the answer is valid for all the agencies of Bank of Europe*. In fact, as we have shown in previous paragraph, we have $Bq'_1(a)$ implies $Kq_1(a)$, which means that the answer is guaranteed valid not for agencies that **are** agencies of the Bank of Europe, but for agencies such that the database **believes that they are** agencies of the Bank of Europe. So, if a user ignores what are these latter agencies stored in the database he cannot make use of the intensional answer. Except, if the database is complete for Bank of Europe agencies, and the user knows what are these agencies.

In more formal terms, if the intensional answer is of the form $q_1(x) \wedge cond(x)$, it is useful only if we have $RC(cond(x))$ and the user knows the extension of $Kcond(x)$.

Completeness answers

We first consider the extensional answers. If the standard answer to a query is $s = \{a, b, c, d, e, f\}$ and an extensional answer about completeness is $ec- = \{a, c, d\}$, what does it means that $ec-$ is complete? In fact the notion of completeness for a set is defined with respect to another set. Here, completeness means that for some intensional answer $q'(x)$ in $ic-$, all the elements that are guaranteed to satisfy $q'(x)$, in the sense $Kq'(x)$, are in $ec-$. So, if the user ignores what is the sentence $q'(x)$, he cannot know with respect to what $ec-$ is complete.

For instance, for query $q_1(x)$ we may have in $ic-$ the sentence $q_1''(x) = q_1(x) \wedge downtown(x)$. In that case, $ec-$ is useful only if the user knows that $ec-$ contains all the open agencies that are downtown.

The conclusion here is that extensional answers about completeness have to be completed with corresponding intensional answers about completeness. The same conclusion holds for answers of the kind $ec+$.

Let's analyse now usefulness of intensional answers.

We consider the same query $q_1(x)$ and we assume that $q_1'(x)$ is in $ic-$. From formal results shown in previous paragraph, if there is an agency, for instance g, which is not in the standard answer, that is such that we have $\neg Bq_1(g)$, then we have $K\neg q_1'(g)$. That means that for g user is guaranteed that it is not an open agency of the Bank of Europe. This information alone is not really useful, because it may be that g is not open, or that g is not an agency of the Bank of Europe. However, if in addition user knows that g is an agency of the Bank of Europe, then he can infer that g is not open.

In general, if $q_1'(x) = q_1(x) \wedge cond(x)$ is in $ic-$, for an individual a which is not in s (i.e. $\neg Bq_1(a)$), if the user knows that $cond(a)$ is true , he is guaranteed that a does not satisfy $q_1(x)$, in the sense $K\neg q_1(a)$.

Let's consider now the query $q_2(x) = agency(x) \wedge open(x) \wedge bank(x, BE)$. If we have in $ic+$ the sentence $q_2'(x) = agency(x) \wedge open(x)$, which guarantees that the database is complete for all the open agencies, from previous formal results, if some agency g is not in s, and the answer to the query $q_2'(g)$ is "no" (i.e. $\neg Bq_2'(g)$), then user is guaranteed that g does not satisfy $q_2(x)$ (i.e. $K\neg q_2(g)$). Here again this information is useful only if user knows that g is an agency of Bank of Europe.

Notice that the different kinds of answers about completeness allow to infer reliable negative information.

4 Automated deduction technique to compute answers

SOL-deduction

In this section is presented the automated deduction technique called SOL-deduction which is used to compute several sorts of answers [3]. This technique has been defined for first order classical logic, but we shall see how it can be used for the modal logic presented in previous sections.

SOL-deduction is based on SOL-resolution, an inference rule designed by K. Inoue [Ino91,Ino92a,Ino92b] to generate logical consequences of a first order theory represented by a set of clauses Σ [4]. One of the most important features of this inference rule is that it allows to concentrate consequence generation on clauses that satisfy some given property. For instance, to generate clauses formed only with positive literals, or clauses whose number of literals is less than or equal to a given fixed value.

We have no room here to give a formal presentation of SOL-resolution, so it will be presented through semi-formal definitions and examples (formal definitions can be found in [Ino92a]).

The property that can be used to restrict consequence generation has to characterise a "stable production field". A "production field" P is a pair $< L, Cond >$, where L is a subset of the literals of a given first order language, and $Cond$ is a certain property to be satisfied by clauses. For instance L may be the set of literals formed with two given predicate symbols. A production field is stable if for two any clauses C and D such that C subsumes D, D belongs to P only if C belongs to P.

We can check that the production field mentionned before is stable. Indeed, if D only contains the two fixed predicate symbols, and C subsumes D, then C also only contains these predicate symbols. At the opposite if the property would be that a clause contains at least one literal formed with a given predicate symbol, then the production field would not be stable.

To define SOL-derivations K. Inoue introduces the notion of "structured clause". A structured clause is a pair $< P, Q >$, where P is a set of literals and Q is an ordered set of literals. SOL-derivations are lists of structured clauses that start with a clause of the form $< [], C >$ and end with a clause of the form $< S, [] >$, and such that $< P_{i+1}, Q_{i+1} >$ can be generated from $< P_i, Q_i >$ by applying one the of the following rules:

   a) if l is the leftmost literal in Q_i:

      1) if $P_i \cup \{l\}$ is in the production field P, then P_{i+1} is $P_i \cup \{l\}$
      and R_{i+1} is obtained by removing l from Q_i,

      2) if there is a clause B_i in $\Sigma \cup \{C\}$ that contains

---

[3] Concepts of validity and completenes have also been implemented by Motro in the PANORAMA system [Mot96]. The technique he uses is based on an original extension of relational algebra, where tuples give an intensional representation of valid subsets or complete subsets. The technique is restricted to positive conjunctive queries.

[4] Even if SOL is used for cosequence generation, its strategy, like SL resolution, is of the kind of "backward chaining" strategies.

a literal which can be resolved with l with mgu θ, then
P_{i+1} is $P_i\theta$, and $\boldsymbol{R}_{i+1}$ is obtained by concatenating $\boldsymbol{B}_i\theta$
to $\boldsymbol{Q}_i\theta$,removing the reduced literal in $B_i\theta$, and framing $l\theta$,
3) if
    i) P_i or $\boldsymbol{Q}_i$ contains an unframed literal k different from l
    or another occurence of l, or
    ii) $\boldsymbol{Q}_i$ contains a framed literal $\neg k$,
and l and k are unifiable by mgu θ,
then $P_{i+1} = P_i\theta$ and $\boldsymbol{R}_{i+1}$ is obtained from
$\boldsymbol{Q}_i\theta$ by deleting $l\theta$,
b) $\boldsymbol{Q}_{i+1}$ is obtained from $\boldsymbol{R}_{i+1}$ by deleting every
framed literal not preceeded by an unframed literal.

The intuitive idea is to isolate in the part P of structured clauses the subset
of the literals in a standard clause that satisfies property $Cond$. At the end of a
derivation, since part Q is empty we obtain a consequence P that satisfies $Cond$.

Application of SOL-deduction to compute answers

We first consider computation of intensional answers about validity. We are
looking for formulas $q'(x)$ such that $\vdash mdb \rightarrow RV(q'(x))$, and $q'(x)$ implies $q(x)$,
and $q'(x)$ is maximal for implication.

Since, for every sentence in mdb and for $RV(q'(x))$, sentences are in the
scope of the modal operator K, in virtue of properties of K we can remove these
occurences of K. Let's call mdb' the set of sentences obtained from mdb after
removing K. Then, the problem is equivalent to find $q'(x)$ such that:

$$\vdash mdb' \rightarrow \forall x(Bq'(x) \rightarrow q'(x))$$

where mdb' is a set of sentences of the form $\forall x(Bf(x) \rightarrow f(x))$ or $\forall x(g(x) \rightarrow Bg(x))$ [5].

Then, the problem is to find sentences $f_1, \ldots, f_i$ and $g_1, \ldots, g_j$ such that
$\forall x(Bf_1(x) \rightarrow f_1(x))$, ...
, $\forall x(Bf_i(x) \rightarrow f_i(x))$, $\forall x(g_1(x) \rightarrow Bg_1(x))$, ... , $\forall x(g_j(x) \rightarrow Bg_j(x))$ are in
mdb', and we have:
$\vdash \forall x((f_1(x) \wedge \ldots \wedge f_i(x) \wedge \neg g_1(x) \wedge \ldots \wedge \neg g_j(x)) \rightarrow q(x))$
Indeed, in that case we have:
$\vdash \forall x(Bf_1(x) \wedge \ldots \wedge Bf_i(x) \wedge \neg Bg_1(x) \wedge \ldots \wedge \neg Bg_j(x) \rightarrow q(x))$
So, if we accept the Closed World Assumption, as people do in the context
of Relational databases when answers are computed by using relational algebra,
or SQL like languages, we have $\neg Bg$ equivalent to $B\neg g$, and therefore we have:
$\vdash \forall x(Bf_1(x) \wedge \ldots \wedge Bf_i(x) \wedge B\neg g_1(x) \wedge \ldots \wedge B\neg g_j(x) \rightarrow q(x))$
and
$\vdash \forall x(B(f_1(x) \wedge \ldots \wedge f_i(x) \wedge \neg g_1(x) \wedge \ldots \wedge \neg g_j(x)) \rightarrow q(x))$
That means that $q'(x) = f_1(x) \wedge \ldots \wedge f_i(x) \wedge \neg g_1(x) \wedge \ldots \wedge \neg g_j(x)$ is an
intensional answer about validity.

---

[5] Notice that $\forall x(g(x) \rightarrow Bg(x))$ is equivalent to $\forall x(\neg Bg(x) \rightarrow \neg g(x))$.

To use SOL-deduction we first consider modal operator B as a first order predicate $believes(x)$, and we transform sentences into clauses. Let the clausal form of $f(x)$ and $\neg g(x)$ be defined by:

$$\vdash \forall x(f(x) \leftrightarrow c_1(x) \wedge \dots c_s(x)) \vdash \forall x(\neg g(x) \leftrightarrow d_1(x) \wedge \dots \wedge d_t(x))$$

where the c_is and d_js are clauses. We define Σ as the following set of clauses:

- if $\forall x(Bf(x) \rightarrow f(x))$ is in mdb', the set of clauses
$\neg believes(f(x)) \vee c_1(x), \dots , \neg believes(f(x)) \vee c_s(x)$ is in Σ,

- if $\forall x(g(x) \rightarrow Bg(x))$ is in mdb', the set of clauses
$d_1(x) \vee believes(g(x)), \dots ,d_t(x) \vee believes(g(x))$ is in Σ,

and there is no other clause in Σ.

We consider the production field where L is the set of literals formed with the predicate $believes(x)$, and the property $Cond$ is that every literal in a clause is formed with the predicate $believes(x)$. We can easily check that this production field is stable.

For the top clause $< [], C >$ we have $C = \neg q(x_0)$, where x_0 is a Skolem constant.

If, at the end of a SOL-deduction we get the clause $< D, [] >$, the clause D is of the form $\neg believes(f_1(x_0)) \vee \dots \vee \neg believes(f_i(x_0)) \vee believes(g_1(x_0)) \vee \dots \vee believes(g_i(x_0))$, and we have:

$$\Sigma \vdash \forall x(believes(f_1(x_0)) \wedge \dots \wedge believes(f_i(x_0)) \wedge \neg believes(g_1(x_0)) \wedge \dots \wedge \neg believes(g_i(x_0)) \rightarrow q(x))$$

Moreover, if consequences obtained by SOL-deduction which are subsumed by other consequences are removed, the intensional anwer we get is maximal for implication.

Now, if we consider the computation of extensional answers about validity, we just have to compute the answer to the following query $q'(x)$:

$$q'(x) = f_1(x) \wedge \dots \wedge f_i(x) \wedge \neg g_1(x) \wedge \dots \wedge \neg g_j(x)$$

For the computation of intensional answers about completeness $ci+$ that are a super set of the query, we can use SOL-deduction in a similar way.

The property $\vdash mdb \rightarrow RC(q'(x))$ is reformulated into $\vdash mdb' \rightarrow \forall x(q'(x) \rightarrow Bq'(x))$, which is equivalent to $\vdash mdb' \rightarrow \forall x(\neg Bq'(x) \rightarrow \neg q'(x))$. We also have property $\vdash \forall x(q(x) \rightarrow q'(x))$ which is equivalent to $\vdash \forall x(\neg q'(x) \rightarrow \neg q(x))$. Then, we have to find sentences $q'(x)$ such that $\vdash mdb' \rightarrow \forall x(\neg Bq'(x) \rightarrow \neg q(x))$. Here again, if we accept that $\neg Bg$ is equivalent to $B\neg g$, the property is equivalent to $\vdash mdb' \rightarrow \forall x(B\neg q'(x) \rightarrow \neg q(x))$, which is of the same form as property that characterises intensional answers about validity and can be computed in the same way from the top clause $C = q(x_0)$.

5   Conclusion

We have shown that not every kind of answer is useful for users. Extensional answers about validity ev are always useful. Usefulness of intensional answers depends on what user knows, and extensional answers about completeness are useless if they are not completed by their intensional correspondants.

A prototype of SOL-deduction has been implemented by Laurence Cholvy [CD97a,CD97b] which we have used to test our method on several examples. Response times were rather good. For intensional answers of the kind $ic-$ we cannot use the method presented in section 4 and we have to investigate this issue in future works.

Acknowledgements. This work has been supported by *Centre National d'Etudes des Télécommunications (CNET)* in the context of contract CNET/ONERA-CERT 96 1B 317.

References

[CD97a] L. Cholvy and R. Demolombe. Génération de réponses non-standard dans le contexte d'un dialogue coopératif. Phase 1.2 Définition et caractérisation des procédures élémentaires et génériques permettant de calculer les réponses coopératives. Technical Report 2, ONERA-CERT-DTIM, 1997.

[CD97b] L. Cholvy and R. Demolombe. Génération de réponses non-standard dans le contexte d'un dialogue coopératif. Phase 1.3 Mise en oeuvre des procédures élaborées lors de la phase 1.2. Technical Report 3, ONERA-CERT-DTIM, 1997.

[CDJ94] L. Cholvy, R. Demolombe, and A.J.I. Jones. Reasoning about the safety of information: from logical formalization to operational definition. In *Proc. of 8th International Symposium on Methodologies for Intelligent Systems*, 1994.

[Che88] B. F. Chellas. *Modal Logic: An introduction.* Cambridge University Press, 1988.

[Dem96] R. Demolombe. Validity Queries and Completeness Queries. In *Proc. of 9th International Symposium on Methodologies for Intelligent Systems*, 1996.

[Dem97] R. Demolombe. Answering queries about validity and completeness of data: from modal logic to relational algebra. In T. Andreasen, H. Christiansen, and H. L. Larsen, editors, *Flexible Query Answering Systems.* Kluwer Academic Publishers, 1997.

[DJ94] R. Demolombe and A.J.I. Jones. Deriving answers to safety queries. In R. Demolombe and T. Imielinski, editors, *Nonstandard queries and nonstandard answers.* Oxford University Press, 1994.

[Ino91] K. Inoue. Consequence-Finding Based on Oredered Linear Resolution. In *Proc. of International Joint Conference on Artificial Intelligence*, Sydney, 1991.

[Ino92a] K. Inoue. Linear Resolution for Consequence Finding. *Artificial intelligence, an International Journal*, 56, 1992.

[Ino92b] K. Inoue. *Studies on Abductive and Nonmonotonic Reasoning.* PhD thesis, Kyoto University, 1992.

[Mot86] A. Motro. Completeness information and its application to query processing. In *Proc. of 12th International Conference on Very Large Data Bases*, 1986.

[Mot89] A. Motro. Integrity = validity + completeness. *ACM TODS*, 14(4), 1989.

[Mot96] A. Motro. PANORAMA: a Database System that Annotates Its Answers to Queries with their Properties. *Journal of Intelligent Information Systems*, 7, 1996.

Progress Report on the Disjunctive Deductive Database System `dlv` *

Thomas Eiter[b], Nicola Leone[a] **, Cristinel Mateis[a],
Gerald Pfeifer[a], and Francesco Scarcello[c]

[a]Institut für Informationssysteme, TU Wien
A-1040 Wien, Austria

[b]Institut für Informatik, Universität Gießen
Arndtstrasse 2, D-35392 Gießen

[c]ISI-CNR, c/o DEIS Universitá della Calabria
I-87030 Rende, Italy

{*eiter,leone,mateis,pfeifer,scarcell*} *@dbai.tuwien.ac.at*

Abstract. `dlv` is a deductive database system, based on disjunctive logic programming, which offers front-ends to several advanced KR formalisms. The system has been developed since the end of 1996 at Technische Universität Wien in an ongoing project funded by the Austrian Science Funds (FWF).

Recent comparisons have shown that `dlv` is nowadays a state-of-the-art implementation of disjunctive logic programming. A major strength of dlv are its advanced knowledge modelling features. Its kernel language extends disjunctive logic programming by strong negation (*a la* Gelfond and Lifschitz) and integrity constraints; furthermore, front-ends for the database language SQL3 and for diagnostic reasoning are available. Suitable interfaces allow `dlv` users to utilize base relations which are stored in external commercial database systems.

This paper provides an overview of the `dlv` system and describes recent advances in its implementation. In particular, the recent implementation of incremental techniques for program evaluation, as well as the use of relational join optimization strategies appear particularly relevant for deductive database applications. These techniques are suitably extended in `dlv` for the efficient instantiation of nonmonotonic programs.

Benchmarks on problems from different domains are also reported to give a feeling of the current system performance.

1 Introduction

Deductive databases extend relational database systems by the inferential power of logic programming. Their study has been one of the major activities of database researchers

---

* Partially supported by *FWF (Austrian Science Funds)* under the project P11580-MAT "A Query System for Disjunctive Deductive Databases" and by the Italian MURST under the project for Italia-Austria cooperation *Advanced Formalisms and Systems for Nonmonotonic Reasoning*.

** Please address correspondence to this author.

in the second half of the eighties. Besides important theoretical results, this study has led to the implementation of a number of deductive database systems supporting logic programming and its extensions as the query language [2, 4, 15, 20, 22]. Recently, the idea of incorporating disjunction in the deductive database languages has stimulated a renewed interest in this area, since deductive databases with disjunction, called *Disjunctive Deductive Databases (DDDBs)*, seem to be well suited to perform nonmonotonic reasoning tasks which are strongly needed in the field of Artificial Intelligence. Thus, during the last years, much research has been done concerning semantics and complexity of Disjunctive Deductive Databases. Interesting studies on the expressive power of DDDBs [8] have also shown that some concrete real world problems cannot be represented by (∨-free) deductive databases, while they can be represented by DDDBs. Among these problems we can mention Strategic Companies from the business domain (that we describe in Section 2.1), the famous Travelling Salesman Problem from the field of optimization, and even the problem of finding a minimum size key of a relation (i.e., a key with minimum number of attributes) from the domain of databases. Nevertheless, while DDDBs are now generally considered a powerful tool for common-sense reasoning and knowledge representation, there has been a shortage of actual (let alone efficient) implementations ([24, 1]).

This paper focuses on the DDDB system dlv (datalog with disjunction) currently developed at TU Wien in the *FWF project P11580-MAT "A Query System for Disjunctive Deductive Databases"*. A major strength of dlv are the advanced knowledge representation languages it supports. Its kernel language extends disjunctive logic programming by strong negation (*a* la Gelfond and Lifschitz) and integrity constraints; furthermore, front-ends for the database language SQL3 and for diagnostic reasoning are available. Suitable interfaces allow dlv users to access relations stored in external commercial database systems, so that dlv can be also used as an advanced interface to relational databases.

In Section 2, we will describe the languages supported by the system and address knowledge representation issues, showing how very sophisticated (and computationally hard) queries can be easily yet elegantly specified in dlv.

In Section 3 we will address implementation issues. In particular, we will first present the overall architecture of dlv. We will then describe some optimization techniques that have been recently incorporated in dlv, and finally report some benchmarks to give a feeling of the current system performance.

A previous version of the system, that does not include the optimization techniques presented here, has been described in [9, 6] and compared to other systems in [10]. For up-to-date information and a download of dlv, please visit the project homepage at http://www.dbai.tuwien.ac.at/proj/dlv/.

2 The Languages of dlv

2.1 Extended Disjunctive Logic Programming

This is the native interface of the system and offers the full power of the internal language of dlv: function-free disjunctive logic programs extended by allowing both integrity constraints and strong negation [11].

The presence of these constructs makes our language well-suited to easily represent a wide range of problems in a natural and highly declarative way.

A dlv rule has the following form:

$$L_1 \vee \ldots \vee L_k : - L_{k+1}, \ldots, L_m, not\ L_{m+1}, \ldots, not\ L_n$$

where $1 \leq k \leq m \leq n$ and each L_i is a literal, i.e., an atom $a(t_1, \ldots, t_o)$ or its "classical" negation $\tilde{a}(t_1, \ldots, t_o)$, a being the predicate name of that atom, and each t_i $(1 \leq i \leq o)$ being either a constant or a variable. The convention on names is the one of Prolog.

An *(integrity) constraint* is like a rule with $k = 0$ and $n \geq 1$. A dlv program P is a pair $< R, IC >$, where R is a set of dlv rules and IC a set of constraints. A *stable model* of P is any consistent answer set of R [11] satisfying all constraints in IC.

We next present some sample problems, drawn from different domains, and their encodings in the native language of dlv. This should give an idea about the use of the language for knowledge representation and reasoning. Some of these problems will be used as benchmarks to evaluate the performances of the system.

Example 1 (Reachability). connected(_, _), find for each city C in the database the cities which are reachable from C.

This is a classical deductive database example; we provide here the single recursive version.

```
reaches(X,Y)  :- connected(X,Y).
reaches(X,Y)  :- reaches(X,U), connected(U,Y).
```

Example 2 (Graph 3-colorability). Given a graph, represented by facts of the form node(_) and edge(_, _), assign each node one of three colors such that no two adjacent nodes have the same color.

3-colorability is a classical NP-complete problem. In *dlv*, it can be encoded in a very easy and natural way by means of disjunction and constraints:

```
col(X,r) V col(X,g) V col(X,b) : - node(X).
:- edge(X,Y), col(X,C), col(Y,C).
```

The disjunctive rule nondeterministically chooses a color for each node X in the graph; the constraint enforces that the choices are legal.

Example 3 (Prime Implicants). Find the prime implicants of a propositional CNF formula $\Phi = \bigwedge_{i=1}^{n}(d_{i1} \vee \ldots \vee d_{ic_i})$, where the $d_{i,j}$ are literals over the variables $x_1, \ldots, x_m$.

Recall that a *prime implicant* of Φ is a consistent conjunction I of literals such that $I \models \Phi$ and for no subformula I' of I we have $I' \models \Phi$. As easily seen, a prime implicant exists if and only if Φ is satisfiable. Thus, finding a prime implicant of Φ subsumes the satisfiability problem for Φ.

The representation in dlv is natural and simple. Here, true negation in the language plays a key role. We may use a literal translation of Φ into a dlv program P:

$$d_{11} \vee \ldots \vee d_{1c_1}. \qquad \ldots \qquad d_{n1} \vee \ldots \vee d_{nc_n}.$$

It is easy to see that the stable models of P correspond 1-1 to the prime implicants of Φ.

Example 4 (Strategic Companies). The strategic companies problem is from [3]; it is, to the best of our knowledge, the only Σ_2^P-complete KR problem from the business domain. No experimental results for any Σ_2^P-complete KR problems are known.

Briefly, a holding owns companies, each of which produces some goods. Moreover, several companies may have jointly control over another company. Now, some companies should be sold, under the constraint that all goods can be still produced, and that no company is sold which would still be controlled by the holding after the transaction. A company is *strategic*, if it belongs to a *strategic set*, which is a minimal set of companies satisfying these constraints. Those sets are expressed by the following natural program:

```
strategic(C1) v strategic(C2) :-
           produced_by(P,C1,C2).
strategic(C) :-
           controlled_by(C,C1,C2,C3),
           strategic(C1),
           strategic(C2),
           strategic(C3).
```

Here strategic(C) means that C is strategic, produced_by($P, C1, C2$) that product P is produced by companies $C1$ and $C2$, and controlled_by($C, C1, C2, C3$) that C is jointly controlled by $C1, C2$ and $C3$; we have adopted here from [3] that each product is produced by at most two companies and each company may be controlled by consortia of at most three other companies each.

The problem is to find out the set of all strategic companies (i.e., under brave reasoning, for which C the fact strategic(C) is true).

Note that this problem can not be expressed by a fixed normal logic program *uniformly on all collections* produced_by($p, c1, c2$) and controlled_by($c, c1, c2, c3$) (unless $NP = \Sigma_2^P$, an unlikely event).

2.2 Brave and Cautious Reasoning

The frontends for brave and cautious reasoning are an extension of the native interface described above. In addition to the program, the user also specifies a query, which is essentially the body of a rule followed by a question mark:

$$b_1, \ldots, \ b_m, \ \text{not } b_{m+1}, \ldots, \ \text{not } b_n \ ?$$

where each b_i $(1 \le i \le n)$ is a ground literal.

The brave reasoning frontend is invoked by the -FB command line option. If the query Q evaluates to true in at least one stable model M, then the system replies: "Q is bravely true, evidenced by M", i.e., returns a stable model that witnesses this fact; otherwise the answer is "Q is bravely false".

Similarly, the cautious frontend is invoked by -FC, and the system answers "Q is cautiously true" if and only if Q is true in all stable models. In case of a negative answer, we get: "Q is cautiously false, evidenced by M", where M is a stable model witnessing the falsity of Q.

2.3 SQL3

This frontend provides the possibility to use (a subset of) SQL3 query expressions, that are internally translated into the native system language. Since the SQL3 standard has not been completed yet, we resorted to the current working draft [25]. The system automatically invokes the SQL frontend for input files whose names carry the extension .sql.

First of all, since there are no column names in datalog, we have to include a construct that creates a connection between the parameters of a datalog predicate and the column names of an SQL table:

```
DATALOG SCHEMA { Relationname({Columnname} [,...]) } [,...];
```

The following grammar describes the query expressions which currently can be handled by the following SQL frontend:

```
[ WITH [RECURSIVE]
  { Relationname [ ( { Columnname } [, ... ] ) ]
    AS ( QueryExpression ) }
  [, ... ]
]

{ SELECT { [(Cor-)Relationname .] Columnname } [,...]
  FROM { Relationname [ [AS] Correlationname] } [,...]
  [ WHERE { [(Cor-)Relationname .] Columnname =
            [(Cor-)Relationname .] Columnname } [AND...]]]}
[ UNION ... ] ;
```

Here, "{ *item* } [*connective*...]" represents a list of *items*, separated by *connectives*; "[*expression*]" means that *expression* is optional; words in capital letters are keywords; QueryExpression refers to a construct as described above (without the trailing semicolon).

Observe that query expressions have in general two parts: A definition part (the WITH clause), and a query part.

Example 5 (List of Materials). Consider the canonical list of materials query:

```
DATALOG SCHEMA consists_of(major,minor);

WITH RECURSIVE listofmaterials(major,minor) AS
    (SELECT c.major, c.minor FROM consists_of AS c
     UNION
     SELECT c1.major, c2.minor
       FROM consists_of AS c1, listofmaterials AS c2
       WHERE c1.minor = c2.major
    )
SELECT major, minor FROM listofmaterials;
```

This query is translated into

```
listofmaterials(A, B) :- consists_of(A, B).
listofmaterials(A, B) :- consists_of(A, C),
                         listofmaterials(C, B).
sql2dl__intern0(A, B) :- listofmaterials(A, B).
```

and the elements of `sql2dl__intern0` are printed as the result. Here the first two rules represent the definition part and the last rule corresponds to the query part of the query expression.

(A rule and an internal predicate name for the query part have to be generated because in general queries may consist of several parts, connected by set operators like UNION.)

We are currently implementing furher features of the languages defined in [25], in particular set operators EXCEPT and INTERSECT, explicit joins, and additional comparison predicates like IN, $<$ and $>$. (To support the latter, we will also add arithmetic built-in predicates to our language.)

2.4 Diagnostic Reasoning

`dlv` provides two kind of diagnosis frontends: the *abductive diagnosis* frontend [21, 7], and the *Reiter's diagnosis* frontend [23].

Abduction, first studied by Peirce [18], is an important kind of reasoning, having wide applicability in different areas of computer science; in particular, it has been recognized as an important principle of common-sense reasoning.

Abductive diagnosis deals with the problem of finding an explanation (diagnosis) for observations (symptoms), based on a theory, which is in our framework represented by a logic program as in [13, 12]. Roughly speaking, abduction is an inverse of modus ponens: Given the clause $a \leftarrow b$ and the observation a, abduction concludes b as a possible explanation of a. Following [7, 13, 12], a *diagnostic problem* can be formally described as a tuple $\mathbf{P} = \langle Hyp, Obs, T \rangle$, where Hyp is a set of ground atoms (called *hypotheses*), Obs is a set of ground literals (called *manifestations* or *observations*), and T is a logic program. An *explanation (diagnosis)* for $\mathbf{P}$ is a subset $E \subseteq Hyp$ which satisfies the following property:

$T \cup E$ implies *Obs* under brave reasoning, i.e., there exists a stable model M of $T \cup E$, where all literals in *Obs* are true.

In general, a diagnostic problem may have no, a single, or several explanations. In accordance with Occam's principle of parsimony [19], which states that from two explanations the simpler is preferable, some minimality criterion is usually imposed on diagnoses. A widely used criterion is *Subset Minimality*, stating that a solution A is preferable to a solution B if $A \subset B$. According to this criterion, the acceptable solutions of **P** are restricted to the minimal explanations (they are considered to the most likely ones). Another criterion works under the assumption of *Single Error* and considers only elementary diagnoses (which consist of a single atom).

Example 6 (Keys Finding). Consider a relation scheme consisting of attributes *Class, Teacher, Hour, Room, Student* on which the following functional dependencies hold:

$$Teacher \leftarrow Class$$
$$Class \leftarrow Hour, Room$$
$$Room \leftarrow Hour, Teacher$$
$$Room \leftarrow Hour, Student$$

Finding the keys of this relation can be modeled as an abductibe problem as follows. Consider the abductive diagnostic problem $\mathbf{P}_{keys} = \langle H, O, T_{keys} \rangle$, where the theory T_{keys} is:

$$Teacher : - Class$$
$$Class : - Hour, Room$$
$$Room : - Hour, Teacher$$
$$Room : - Hour, Student$$
$$Cover : - Teacher, Class, Hour, Room, Student;$$

it encodes the functional dependencies and states that we have covered the relation if *all* attributes have been (transitively) implied.
The hypotheses are the attributes of the relation scheme:

$$H = \{Class, Teacher, Hour, Room, Student\}.$$

and, the set of observations is $O = \{cover\}$.

We have that every diagnosis is a covering of the relation. In particular, every minimal diagnosis is a key and vice versa. $\{Hour, Student\}$ is the only minimal diagnosis which is indeed the only key of the relation. Possible single error diagnoses would correspond to single attribute keys.

Our frontend for *abductive diagnosis* currently supports three different modes: general diagnosis, where all diagnoses are computed, subset minimal diagnosis[1], and single failure diagnosis. These modes are invoked by the command line options -FD, -FDmin and -FDsingle, respectively.

---

[1] For positive non-disjunctive theories only.

The diagnostic theory obeys the syntax described in Section 2.1. Hypothesis (resp. observations) are lists of atoms (resp. literals) separated by a dot (.) and are stored in files whose names carry the extension .hyp (resp. .obs).

Basically, the diagnostic frontend works as follows: After reading the input, disjunctive rules for guessing possible diagnosis candidates are generated from the hypotheses, while the observations become constraints that forbid the generation of inconsistent diagnoses. In subset-minimal diagnosis case, further rules are added for pruning non-minimal solutions. Finally, the grounding (and subsequently the MG etc.) are invoked, and for each reported stable model, the corresponding diagnosis is returned. The frontend for *consistency-based diagnosis* as described by Reiter [23] works similarly. The command line options are -FR, -FRmin and -FRsingle, respectively.

3   Implementation Issues

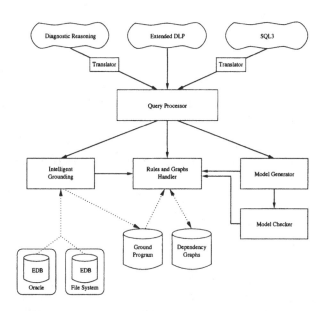

Fig. 1. Overall Architecture of the System

3.1   System Architecture

An outline of the general architecture of our system is depicted in Figure 1.

At the heart of the system lies the *Query Processor*. It controls the execution of the entire system and – in collaboration with the integrated frontends – it performs some pre-processing on the input and post-processing on the generated models, respectively.

Upon startup, the Query Processor reads the – possibly non-ground – input program and hands it over to the *Rules and Graphs Handler*, which splits it into subprograms.

Together with relational database tables, provided by an Oracle database or ASCII text files, the subprograms are then submitted to the *Intelligent Grounding Module*, which efficiently generates a subset of the grounded input program that has exactly the same stable models as the full program, but is much smaller in general.

The Query Processor then again invokes the Rules and Graphs Handler, which generates two partitionings of the ground(ed) program. They are used by the *Model Generator* (MG) and the *Model Checker*, respectively, and enable a modular evaluation of the program. This often yields a tremendous speedup.

Finally, the Model Generator is started. It generates one candidate for a stable model and invokes the Model Checker to verify whether it is indeed a stable model. Upon success, control is returned to the Query Processor, which performs post-processing and possibly invokes the MG to look for further models.

More details on the Intelligent Grounding and the Model Checker can be found in [16, 9].

3.2 Efficient Instantiation

In this section, we present the intelligent grounding (IG) module of the dlv system. The aim of IG is twofold:

 (i) to evaluate (∨-free) stratified programs components, and
(ii) to generate the instantiation of disjunctive or unstratified components (if the input program is disjunctive or unstratified)

In order to efficiently evaluate stratified programs (components), we use two principal techniques from classical deductive databases and from relational database optimization theory. The one is an improved version of the generalized semi-naive evaluation technique is linear and non-linear recursive rules. The other obtains an efficient evaluation of rules bodies (especially in case of large relations) using relational join optimization techniques (for more, see the end of this section).

If the input program is normal (i.e., ∨-free) and stratified, the IG completely evaluates the program and no further module is employed after the grounding; the program has a single stable model, namely the set of atoms returned by the instantiation procedure.

If the input program is either disjunctive or unstratified, then the instantiation procedure does not completely evaluate the program. However, the optimisation techniques mentioned above are useful to efficiently generate the instantiation of the non-monotonic part of the program. Two aspects are crucial for the instantiation:

(a) the number of generated ground rules, and
(b) the time needed to generate the grounding.

The size of the grounding generated is important because it strongly influences the computation time of the other modules of the system. A slower instantiation procedure generating a smaller grounding may be preferable to a faster one that generates a large grounding. However, the time needed by the former can not be ignored; otherwise, we could not really have a gain in computation time.

The main reason of large groundings, even for small-sized input programs, is that each atom of a rule in $\mathcal{P}$ may be instantiated to many atoms in B_{LP}, which leads to combinatorial explosion. However, in a reasonable program semantics, most of these atoms may not be derivable whatsoever, and hence such instantiations do not render applicable rules. We present an algorithm which generates ground instances of rules containing only atoms which can possibly be derived from $\mathcal{P}$. Denote for a rule r by $H(r)$, $B^+(r)$, and $B^-(r)$ its head, not-free part and not-part, respectively. We associate to $\mathcal{P}$ the dependency graph $G_{\mathcal{P}}$. The nodes of $G_{\mathcal{P}}$ are the predicates appearing in the head of the rules with non-empty body, and $G_{\mathcal{P}}$ has an arc from a node q to a node p iff there exists a rule $r \in \mathcal{P}$ such that $p \in H(r)$ and $q \in B^+(r)$.

A simple way to optimize (a) is to employ the collapsed dependency graph $\widehat{G_{\mathcal{P}}}$ associated to $\mathcal{P}$ which results from $G_{\mathcal{P}}$ by collapsing each maximal strongly connected component into a single node. Note that every node of $\widehat{G_{\mathcal{P}}}$ is a set of nodes of $G_{\mathcal{P}}$.

The optimization of (b) is realized through the techniques of the relational and deductive database optimization mentioned above.

Let $\mathcal{P}$ be a non-ground program and C a node of the graph $\widehat{G_{\mathcal{P}}}$. We denote by $recursive\_rules_{\mathcal{P}}(C)$ the set of the rules r of $\mathcal{P}$ s.t. predicates from C occur both in $H(r)$ and in $B^+(r)$, and by $exit\_rules_{\mathcal{P}}(C)$ the remaining set of rules r of $\mathcal{P}$ having a predicate from C in $H(r)$. Moreover, we say that a rule r of $\mathcal{P}$ is *total* if either (i) r is a fact, or (ii) r is normal stratified and every body literal is defined only by total rules. An atom is total if all rules defining it are total.

Recall that we assume that $\mathcal{P}$ is *safe*, i.e. all variables of a rule r appear in $B^+(r)$. Consequently, in order to instantiate a rule r, we merely have to instantiate $B^+(r)$, which uniquely determines the instance of r. We define the grounding of r w.r.t. a set of ground atoms $NF \subseteq B_{LP}$, denoted by $ground(r, NF)$, as the set of ground instances r' of r s.t. $B^+(r') \subseteq NF$. The set $ground(r, NF)$ is computed by the function *Evaluate* which is described at the end of this section.

Figure 2 outlines the algorithm *Instantiate*, which computes a ground program $\Pi \cup T$, where Π is the set of ground rules and T is the set of ground atoms derived from $\mathcal{P}$ (the ground rules with an empty body), having the same stable models as $\mathcal{P}$. $EDB_{\mathcal{P}}$ and $IDB_{\mathcal{P}}$ denote the extensional and intensional database of $\mathcal{P}$, respectively.

Initially, *Instantiate* sets $NF = EDB_{\mathcal{P}}$, $T = EDB_{\mathcal{P}}$ and $\Pi = \emptyset$. Then, it removes a node C from $\widehat{G_{\mathcal{P}}}$ which has no incoming arc (i.e., a source), and generates all instances r' of rules r defining predicates in C. This is done by calls to the Procedure *InstantiateRule*. However, the procedure does not generate all ground instances; rather, it generates only rules r' in $ground(r, NF)$ such that every negative total literal in $B^-(r')$ is true w.r.t. T. First, we add $H(r')$ to NF because each atom in $H(r')$ can possibly be derived. We then remove all positive literals (all negative total literals) in T from $B^+(r')$ (from $B^-(r')$). Finally, if the head of r' is disjunction-free and its body became empty after simplifications, then $H(r')$ is inserted into T, otherwise the simplified r' is added to Π.

In order to compute such an r', the function *Evaluate* proceeds by matching the atoms in $B^+(r)$ one by one with atoms in NF and binding the free variables accordingly in each step, as in the case of the relational join operation. If $r \in exit\_rules_{\mathcal{P}}(C)$, the set

ΔNF is irrelevant. If r is a linear recursive rule, the semi-naive optimization technique is used and the recursive body atom is matched only with atoms in ΔNF; all non-recursive atoms are matched with atoms in NF. If r is a non-linear recursive rule, an improved generalized semi-naive technique is used.

An efficient heuristics is to start with positive literals whose predicate occurs infrequently in NF (ΔNF) and whose variables we find in several body literals. Therefore, before starting the matching of the atoms in $B^+(r)$ one by one, we first order the positive literals of the body by the increasing cardinality of their ground occurrences in NF (ΔNF) and by the decreasing number of their shared variables. The positive literals with unique variables are placed at the end of the re-order rule body, even if the cardinalities of their ground occurrences in NF (ΔNF) are small. This is because in this case, the join operation with the rest of the body literals is equivalent to their cartesian product.

We describe next how the function *Evaluate* proceeds when r is an exit rule or a linear recursive rule.

At the i-th step, all literals L_j, $1 \le j < i$, are already matched and we try to match the i-th body literal L_i. Note that some variables of L_i could already be bounded, due to the previous steps. There are two possibilities: (i) L_i can be matched with some atom in NF (if $L_i \notin C$) or in ΔNF (if $L_i \in C$). If L_i is not the last body literal, we compute the matching of L_i and try to match the literal L_{i+1}. If L_i is the last body literal, we add the new ground instance of r to $ground(r, NF)$ and try to match L_i with another atom. (ii) L_i can not be matched with any atom in NF (if $L_i \notin C$) or in ΔNF (if $L_i \in C$). If L_i is the first body literal ($i = 1$), no further ground instance of r can be derived and the function *Evaluate* exits and returns the set $ground(r, NF)$. If $i > 1$, we backtrack to the previous literal L_{i-1} and try to match it with another atom in NF (if $L_{i-1} \notin C$) or in ΔNF (if $L_{i-1} \in C$).

If r is a non-linear recursive rule, the function *Evaluate* proceeds in a similar way. We need to mark one recursive body literal at a time. Each time the matching of the first body literal fails (in the case of the exit rule or linear recursive rule, the function would exit and return the set $ground(r, NF)$), we unmark the current marked recursive body literal, we mark the next recursive body literal and the same steps as in the case of exit rule or linear recursive rule are followed, with some differences: (i) the marked recursive body literal can be matched only with atoms in ΔNF, (ii) the recursive body literals left of the marked recursive body literal can be matched only with atoms in $NF - \Delta NF$, and (iii) the recursive body literals right of the marked recursive body literal can be matched only with atoms in NF. The classical generalized semi-naive technique makes no difference between the recursive body literals left or right of the marked recursive body literal, and it therefore generates duplicated ground instances. Our improvement avoids to generate the same ground rule more than once. The function *Evaluate* exits only when the matching of the first body literal fails and there is no other recursive body literal to be marked. For efficiency reasons, first non-recursive rules are instantiated once and for all. Then, the recursive rules are repeatedly instantiated until NF remains unchanged.

After that, the next source is processed until $\widehat{G_P}$ becomes empty. Each time we pick up a source C from $\widehat{G_P}$ to be processed, and then all possible derivable ground instances of C are generated once and for all at this step, by using the ground instances of the sources processed previously. In this way, we optimize (a), i.e. we generate only ground rules whose head contains atoms which can possibly be derived from $\mathcal{P}$.

Note that if $\mathcal{P}$ is a normal ($\vee$-free) stratified program, the grounding is empty because the body of all ground rules is empty and their head atom is added to T.

Procedure *Instantiate*($\mathcal{P}$: Safe_Program; **var** Π: GroundProgram; **var** T: SetOfAtoms)
var C: SetOfPredicates; NF, $NF1$, ΔNF: SetOfAtoms;
begin
    $NF := EDB_\mathcal{P}$; $T := EDB_\mathcal{P}$; $\Pi := \emptyset$;
    $\widehat{G_\mathcal{P}} :=$ collapsed dependency graph of $\mathcal{P}$;
    while $\widehat{G_\mathcal{P}} \neq \emptyset$ **do**
        Remove a node C of $\widehat{G_\mathcal{P}}$ without incoming edges;
        $NF1 := NF$;
        for each $r \in exit\_rules_\mathcal{P}(C)$ **do**
            InstantiateRule($\mathcal{P}, r, \emptyset, NF, T, \Pi$);
        $\Delta NF := NF - NF1$;
        repeat
            $NF1 := NF$;
            for each $r \in recursive\_rules_\mathcal{P}(C)$ **do**
                InstantiateRule($\mathcal{P}, r, \Delta NF, NF, T, \Pi$);
            $\Delta NF := NF - NF1$;
        until $\Delta NF = \emptyset$
    end_while
end_function;

Procedure *InstantiateRule*($\mathcal{P}$: Safe_Program; r: Rule; ΔNF: SetOfAtoms;
                                      var NF, T: SetOfAtoms;
                                      var Π: GroundProgram)
var H : SetOfAtoms; B^+, B^-: SetOfLiterals;
begin
    for each instance $H \leftarrow B^+, B^-$ of r in *Evaluate*($r, \Delta NF, NF$) **do**
        if $(\neg.B^- \cap T = \emptyset) \wedge (H \cap T = \emptyset)$ **then**
            $NF := NF \cup H$;
            Remove all positive literals in T from B^+;
            Remove all negative literals $\neg\, q$ from B^- s.t. q is total and $q \notin T$;
            if $(B^+ = \emptyset) \wedge (|H| = 1)$ **then**
                $T := T \cup H$
            else
                $\Pi := \Pi \cup \{H \leftarrow B^+, B^-\}$
            end_if
        end_if
end_procedure;

Fig. 2. Algorithm for computation of the (simplified) instantiated program

Example 7. Consider the following program $\mathcal{P}$, where a is an EDB predicate

$$p(1,2) \vee p(2,3) \leftarrow \qquad\qquad q(X) \vee q(Z) \leftarrow p(X,Y), p(Y,Z), \neg t(Y)$$
$$t(X) \leftarrow a(X) \qquad\qquad\qquad t(X) \leftarrow q(X), p(Y,X)$$

and suppose $EDB_{\mathcal{P}} = \{a(2)\}$. Then, *Instantiate* computes the set of ground atoms $T = \{a(2), t(2)\}$ and the following ground program Π of $\mathcal{P}$:

$$p(1,2) \vee p(2,3) \leftarrow \qquad q(1) \vee q(3) \leftarrow p(1,2), p(2,3), \neg t(2)$$
$$t(3) \leftarrow q(3), p(2,3)$$

Evaluation of node $\{p\}$ yields the upper left rule of Π, and $NF = \{a(2), p(1,2), p(2,3)\}$. We then evaluate the node $\{q\}$ and get the upper right rule of Π, while NF becomes $\{a(2), p(1,2), p(2,3), q(1), q(3)\}$. Finally, we consider the node $\{t\}$. The rule $t(X) \leftarrow a(X)$ yields $t(2) \leftarrow$ and $t(2)$ is added to T and NF, while Π remains unchanged; the rule $t(X) \leftarrow q(X), p(Y, X)$ yields $t(3) \leftarrow q(3), p(2,3)$.

Note that $ground(\mathcal{P})$ contains $1 + 3 + 27 + 9 = 40$ instances of the rules, while *Instantiate* generates only 3 rules. □

Theorem 1. *Let $\mathcal{P}$ be a safe program, and Π, T be the output parameters returned by* Instantiate($\mathcal{P}, \Pi, T$). *Then*

1. *$\mathcal{P}$ and $\Pi \cup T$ have exactly the same stable models;*
2. *if $\mathcal{P}$ is a $\vee$-free stratified program, then $\Pi = \emptyset$ (and T is the stable model of $\mathcal{P}$).*

3.3 Some Benchmarks

In this section we report some experimental results on the dlv system. Running times are taken over benchmark problems from different domains and should give a feeling of the current performance of the system. The problems we considered are: Reachability (Example 1), 3-Colorability (Example 2) and Strategic Companies (Example 4).

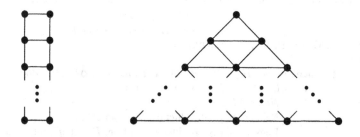

Fig. 3. Ladder Graph (left) and Simplex Graph (right)

The results of our experiments are displayed in Figure 4. They were run on a SUN Ultra 1/143 under Solaris 2.6 using version 2.91.14 (980315) of the egcs C++ compiler.

For **Reachability**, we used a map of 127 cities in the US, as provided by the Stanford Graphbase ([14]). Instances have been generated by varying a parameter k; in the instance for k a pairs of cities with distance less than k are directly connected.

The results are displayed in two upmost tables of Figure 4. The x-axis of the left diagram shows the number n of direct connections among cities (i.e., the size – number

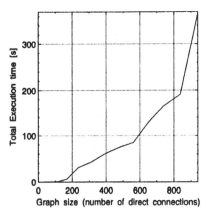
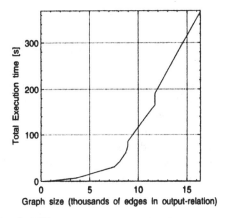

Results for **Reachability**

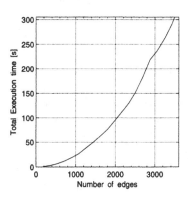
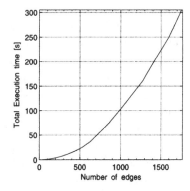

Results for **3-COL Ladder Graphs**   Results for **3-COL Simplex Graphs**

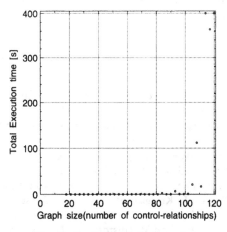

Results for **Strategic Companies**

Fig. 4. Experimental Results

of tuples – of the input relation). while the y-axis shows the total time taken by the system to compute the output relation. In the right diagram, the x-axis refers to the size (i.e., number of tuples) of the output. When the number of direct connections grows, the graph becomes very dense and we have a very high number of transitive connections in the result. A database instance consisting of nearly 600 direct connections, yielding some 10000 transitive connections, is processed in less than 2 minutes. When the graph becomes very dense, the performance gets worse, as for 1000 direct connections (15000 tuples in the output) dlv takes approximately 5 minutes. This encourages ongoing work on advanced data structures that are needed to efficiently support data-intensive applications. Nevertheless, it should be considered that **Reachability** is mainly a grounding and forward chaining benchmark which is not in the primary application domain of dlv.

For **Graph 3-Colorability,** we have considered two classes of graphs, namely *ladder graphs* and *simplex graphs* (see Figure 3). 3-Colorability on both classes has been used to evaluate the performance of other deductive systems, namely DeReS [5] and Smodels [17].

The results show that dlv is very efficient and scales well on these examples, as its advanced nonmonotonic inference mechanisms can be exploited there.

For **Strategic Companies,** we have generated instances for n companies and $3n$ products. Each company is controlled by one to five companies (Two consortia have to have at least one member in common), where the actual number of companies is uniform randomly chosen. On average there are 1.5 controlled_by relations per company.

The results for dlv are interesting if you consider that this problem is Σ_2^P-complete. On the x-axis we report the number of controlled_by relationships among couples of companies. Up to roughly 100, the evaluation is very fast. Then very hard instances can be met, but this is not surprising because of the high computational complexity of the problem.

We believe that further similar tests will prove useful to better understand the complex nature of Σ_2^P-hard problems.

References

1. C. Aravindan, J. Dix, and I. Niemelä. Dislop: A research project on disjunctive logic programming. *AI Communications,* 10(3/4):151–165, 1997.
2. F. Cacace, S. Ceri, S. Crespi-Reghizzi, L. Tanca, and R. Zicari. Integrating Object-Oriented Data Modeling with a Rule-Based Programming Paradigm. In *Proceedings of 1990 ACM-SIGMOD International Conference,* pages 225–236, Atlantic City, NJ, May 1990.
3. M. Cadoli, T. Eiter, and G. Gottlob. Default Logic as a Query Language. *IEEE Transactions on Knowledge and Data Engineering,* 9(3):448–463, May/June 1997.
4. D. Chimenti, R. Gamboa, R. Krishnamurthy, S. Naqvi, S. Tsur, and C. Zaniolo. The LDL System Prototype. *IEEE Transactions on Knowledge and Data Engineering,* 2(1), 1990.
5. P. Cholewiński, V. W. Marek, and M. Truszczyński. Default Reasoning System DeReS. In *Proceedings of International Conference on Principles of Knowledge Representation and Reasoning (KR '96),* Cambridge, Massachusetts, USA, 1996.

6. S. Citrigno, T. Eiter, W. Faber, G. Gottlob, C. Koch, N. Leone, C. Mateis, G. Pfeifer, and F. Scarcello. The dlv System: Model Generator and Application Frontends. In *Proceedings of the 12th Workshop on Logic Programming (WLP '97), Research Report PMS-FB10*, pages 128–137, München, Germany, September 1997. LMU München.

7. T. Eiter, G. Gottlob, and N. Leone. Abduction From Logic Programs: Semantics and Complexity. *Theoretical Computer Science*, 189(1–2):129–177, December 1997.

8. T. Eiter, G. Gottlob, and H. Mannila. Disjunctive Datalog. *ACM Transactions on Database Systems*, 22(3):315–363, September 1997.

9. T. Eiter, N. Leone, C. Mateis, G. Pfeifer, and F. Scarcello. A Deductive System for Nonmonotonic Reasoning. In J. Dix, U. Furbach, and A. Nerode, editors, *Proceedings of the 4th International Conference on Logic Programming and Nonmonotonic Reasoning (LPNMR '97)*, number 1265 in Lecture Notes in AI (LNAI), Berlin, 1997. Springer.

10. T. Eiter, N. Leone, C. Mateis, G. Pfeifer, and F. Scarcello. The KR System dlv: Progress Report, Comparisons and Benchmarks. Technical report, Institut für Informationssysteme, TU Wien, 1998.

11. M. Gelfond and V. Lifschitz. Classical Negation in Logic Programs and Disjunctive Databases. *New Generation Computing*, 9:365–385, 1991.

12. A. Kakas, R. Kowalski, and F. Toni. Abductive Logic Programming. *Journal of Logic and Computation*, 1993.

13. A. Kakas and P. Mancarella. Database Updates Through Abduction. In *Proceedings VLDB-90*, pages 650–661, 1990.

14. D. E. Knuth. *The Stanford GraphBase : a platform for combinatorial computing*. ACM Press, New York, 1994.

15. N. Leone and P. Rullo. BQM: A System Integrating Logic, Objects, and Non-Monotonic Reasoning. In *Invited Paper on 7th IEEE International Conference on Tools with Artificial Intelligence*, Washington, November 1995.

16. N. Leone, P. Rullo, and F. Scarcello. Disjunctive stable models: Unfounded sets, fixpoint semantics and computation. *Information and Computation*, 135(2):69–112, June 1997.

17. I. Niemelä and P. Simons. Efficient Implementation of the Well-founded and Stable Model Semantics. In *Proceedings of the 1996 Joint International Conference and Symposium on Logic Programming*, pages 289–303, Bonn, Germany, Sept. 1996.

18. C. S. Peirce. Abduction and induction. In J. Buchler, editor, *Philosophical Writings of Peirce*, chapter 11. Dover, New York, 1955.

19. Y. Peng and J. Reggia. *Abductive Inference Models for Diagnostic Problem Solving*. Symbolic Computation – Artificial Intelligence. Springer, 1990.

20. G. Phipps, M. A. Derr, and K. Ross. Glue-NAIL!: A Deductive Database System. In *Proceedings ACM-SIGMOD Conference on Management of Data*, pages 308–317, 1991.

21. D. Poole. Explanation and Prediction: An Architecture for Default and Abductive Reasoning. *Computational Intelligence*, 5(1):97–110, 1989.

22. R. Ramakrishnan, D. Srivastava, and S. Sudarshan. CORAL – Control, Relations and Logic. In *Proceedings of the 18th VLDB Conference*, Vancouver, British Columbia, Canada, 1992.

23. R. Reiter. A Theory of Diagnosis From First Principles. *Artificial Intelligence*, 32:57–95, 1987.

24. D. Seipel and H. Thöne. DisLog – A System for Reasoning in Disjunctive Deductive Databases. In *Proceedings International Workshop on the Deductive Approach to Information Systems and Databases (DAISD'94)*, 1994.

25. A. X3H2 and I. DBL. (ISO-ANSI Working Draft) Foundation (SQL/Foundation) [ISO DBL:LGW-008 / ANSI X3H2-97-030], Apr. 1997. Temporarily available at `ftp://jerry.ece.umassd.edu/isowg3/dbl/BASEdocs/public/sqlfound.txt`.

A Server for Fuzzy SQL Queries

José Galindo[1]   Juan M. Medina[2]   Olga Pons[2]   Juan C. Cubero[2]

[1] Dpto. Lenguajes y Ciencias de la Computación, Universidad de Málaga.
29071 Málaga (Spain). ppgg@lcc.uma.es
[2] Dpto. Ciencias de la Computación e I.A., Universidad de Granada.
18071 Granada (Spain). {medina,opc,carlos}@decsai.ugr.es

Abstract. The client-server model is being used mostly in the actual DataBase Management Systems (DBMS). However, these DBMS do not allow either to make flexible queries to the database or to store vague information in it. We have developed a FSQL Server for a Fuzzy Relational Database (FRDB). The FSQL language (Fuzzy SQL) is an extension of the SQL language that allows us to write flexible conditions in our queries. This Server has been developed for Oracle, following the model GEFRED, a theoric model for FRDB that includes fuzzy attributes to store vague information in the tables. The FSQL Server allows us to make flexible queries about traditional (crisp) or fuzzy attributes and we can use linguistic labels defined on any attribute.

KEYWORDS: Information Storage and Retrieval, Flexible and Fuzzy Queries, Fuzzy Relational Databases, Fuzzy SQL.

1 Introduction

The relational model was developed by E.F. Codd of IBM and published in 1970 in [6]. This model is the most used at present. In a theoric level, there exists many FRDB systems that, based on the relational model, they extend it in order to allow storing and/or treating vague and uncertain information.

In [16], Tahani presented a system to carry out fuzzy queries in a classic relational database. More recently, this topic has been widely studied by P. Bosc et al. [1].

Buckles and Petry presented in [2] their database model, in which they used similarity relations among a finite set of possible values for an attribute. This model was extended in [3] to store fuzzy numbers.

In order to store possibility distributions (in Zadeh's sense [20]) Umano and Fukami published their model in [17, 18], with a fuzzy relational algebra [19]. Later, other models appeared like the Prade-Testemale model [14, 15] and the Zemankova-Kandel model [21].

In [12, 13], the GEFRED model was proposed for FRDB. The GEFRED model represents a synthesis among the different models which have appeared to deal with the problem of the representation and management of fuzzy information in relational databases. One of the main advantages of this model is that it consists of a general abstraction which allows us to deal with different approaches, even when these may seem disparate.

Together with GEFRED, a fuzzy relational algebra was defined and in [9] a fuzzy relational calculus is defined. Both query languages allow the performance of fuzzy queries and they retrieve a table in which every attribute of every tuple may have a fulfilment degree associated. This fulfilment degree indicates the level with which this concrete value has satisfied the query condition and it is between 0 (condition not satisfied) and 1 (condition totally satisfied).

We present here an architecture that implements the model GEFRED for one of the commercial DataBase Management Systems (DBMS) most frequently used at present: Oracle. We have programmed a FRDB server that answers queries in a particular language, FSQL (Fuzzy SQL). This query language allows the writing of flexible queries, fulfilment degrees and thresholds, fuzzy constants... and other options that are very useful in making flexible queries in a FRDB.

2 Preliminary concepts about GEFRED

The GEFRED model is based on the definition which is called *Generalized Fuzzy Domain (D)* and *Generalized Fuzzy Relation (R)*, which include classic domains and classic relations respectively.

Definition 1. *If U is the discourse domain or universe, $\widetilde{\mathcal{P}}(U)$ is the set of all possibility distributions defined for U, including those which define the* Unknown *and* Undefined *types (types 8 and 9), and* NULL *is another type defined below (type 10) therefore, we define the* **Generalized Fuzzy Domain** *as $D \subseteq \widetilde{\mathcal{P}}(U) \cup$* NULL. *The* **Unknown**, **Undefined** *and* **NULL** *types are defined according to Umano, Fukami et al. [7, 18]. Then, all data types that can be represented are in table 1.*

Definition 2. *A **Generalized Fuzzy Relation**, R, is given by two sets: "Head" $(\mathcal{H})$ and "Body" $(\mathcal{B})$, $R = (\mathcal{H}, \mathcal{B})$, defined as: The "Head" consists of a fixed set of attribute-domain-compatibility terns (where the last is optional), $\mathcal{H} = \{(A_1 : D_1 [, C_1]), \ldots, (A_n : D_n [, C_n])\}$ where each attribute A_j has an underlined fuzzy domain, not necessarily different, D_j (j=1,2,...,n). C_j is a "compatibility attribute" which takes values in the range [0,1]. The "Body" consists of a set of different generalized fuzzy tuples, where each tuple is composed of a set of attribute-value-degree terns (the degree is optional), $\mathcal{B} = \{(A_1 : \widetilde{d}_{i1} [, c_{i1}]), \ldots, (A_n : \widetilde{d}_{in} [, c_{in}])\}$ with $i = 1, 2, \ldots, m$, where m is the number of tuples in the relation, and where $\widetilde{d}_{ij}$ represents the domain value for the tuple i and the attribute A_j, and c_{ij} is the compatibility degree associated with this value.* $\square$

The comparison operators are also redefined in order to be adapted to the fuzzy nature of our data. For example, the "Possibly Equal" comparator is defined in the following equation for possibility distributions where $\widetilde{p}, \widetilde{p'} \in D$, and their associated possibility distributions are $\pi_{\widetilde{p}}$ and $\pi_{\widetilde{p'}}$ respectively. U is the discourse domain underlying the generalized fuzzy domain D (see definition 1):

1. A single scalar (e.g. Size=Big, represented by the possibility of distribution 1/Big).
2. A single number (e.g. Age=28, represented by the possibility of distribution 1/28).
3. A set of mutually exclusive possible scalar assignations
   (e.g. Behaviour={Bad,Good}, represented by {1/Bad,1/Good}).
4. A set of mutually exclusive possible numeric assignations
   (e.g. Age= {20, 21}, represented by {1/20, 1/21}).
5. A possibility distribution in a scalar domain
6. A possibility distribution in a numeric domain
   (e.g. Age= {0.4/23, 1.0/24, 0.8/25}, fuzzy numbers or linguistic labels).
7. A real number belonging to [0, 1], referring to the degree of matching
   (e.g. Quality=0.9).
8. An **Unknown** value with possibility distribution
   Unknown={1/d : d ∈ D} on domain D, considered.
9. An **Undefined** value with possibility distribution
   Undefined={0/d : d ∈ D} on domain D, considered.
10. A **NULL** value given by **NULL**={1/Unknown,1/Undefined}.

Table 1. Data types for the FRDB.

$$\Theta^=(\widetilde{p},\widetilde{p'}) = \sup_{d\in U} \min\left(\pi_{\widetilde{p}}(d), \pi_{\widetilde{p'}}(d)\right) \tag{1}$$

We can define a similarity relation between two scalars (with a non ordered domain), in order to compare them.

On these definitions, GEFRED redefines the relational algebraic operators in the so-called **Generalized Fuzzy Relational Algebra**: Union, Intersection, Difference, Cartesian Product, Projection, Selection, Join and Quotient. These operators are defined giving the head and body of a generalized fuzzy relation which will be the result of the operation. All these operators are defined in [12] and [13], but the quotient is defined in [8].

In a relation (definition 2), the **compatibility degree** for an attribute value is obtained by manipulation processes performed on that relation and it indicates the degree to which that value has satisfied the operation performed on it.

3 FSQL (Fuzzy SQL)

The FSQL language extends the SQL language [4,5] to allow flexible queries. We have extended the SELECT command in order for it to express flexible queries and, due to its complex format, we only show here an abstract with the main extensions to this command:

- **Linguistic Labels**: If an attribute is capable of fuzzy treatment then linguistic labels can be defined on it. These labels will be preceded with the symbol $ to distinguish them easily. There are two types of labels and they will be used in different fuzzy attribute types:

1. Labels for attributes with an ordered underlined fuzzy domain: Every label of this type has associated a trapezoidal possibility distribution like the figure 1. So, for example, we can define labels $Very_Short, $Short, $Normal, $Tall and $Very_Tall on the Height attributed to a person. For example, we can set a possibility distribution for label $Tall with the values a=175, b=180, c=195 y d=200 (in centimeters).

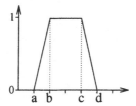

Fig. 1. Trapezoidal possibility distribution.

2. Labels for attributes with a non ordered domain (scalars of types 1, 3 and 5 in table 1): Here, there is a similarity relation defined between each two labels in the domain. The similarity degree is in the interval [0,1]. For example, for the Hair_Colour attributed to a person, we can define that labels $Fair and $Red_Haired are similar with a 0.6 degree.

– **Fuzzy Comparators**: Besides the typical comparators (=, >...), FSQL includes the fuzzy comparators in table 2. Like in SQL, fuzzy comparators compare one column with one constant or two columns of the same type.

Comparator for:		
Possibility	Necessity	Significance
FEQ	NFEQ	Fuzzy EQual (Possibly/Necessarily Equal)
FGT	NFGT	Fuzzy Greater Than
FGEQ	NFGEQ	Fuzzy Greater or Equal
FLT	NFLT	Fuzzy Less Than
FLEQ	NFLEQ	Fuzzy Less or Equal
MGT	NMGT	Much Greater Than
MLT	NMLT	Much Less Than

Table 2. Fuzzy Comparators for FSQL (Fuzzy SQL).

Possibility comparators are more general than necessity comparators are. Then, necessity comparators retrieve less tuples and these comply with the conditions necessarily. In [11], the definitions of all the comparators can be found with some examples of queries and their results. For example, FEQ uses de equation 1 and NFEQ uses the following equation:

$$\Theta^{\text{NFEQ}}(\tilde{p}, \tilde{p'}) = \inf_{d \in U} \max\left(1 - \pi_{\tilde{p}}(d), \pi_{\tilde{p'}}(d)\right) \tag{2}$$

- **Fulfilment thresholds** (γ): For each simple condition a fulfilment threshold may be established (default is 1). with the format:

$$\text{<condition>} \quad \text{THOLD} \quad \gamma.$$

indicating that the condition must be satisfied with minimum degree $\gamma \in [0,1]$ to be considered. The reserved word THOLD is optional and may be substituted by a traditional crisp comparator ($=, \leq ...$), modifying the query meaning. The word THOLD is equivalent to using the crisp comparator $\geq$.

Example 1. Give me all persons with fair hair (in minimum degree 0.5) that they are possibly taller than label $Tall (in minimum degree 0.8):

```
SELECT * FROM Person WHERE Hair   FEQ $Fair THOLD 0.5 AND
                           Height FGT $Tall THOLD 0.8
```

If we are looking for persons that are necessarily taller than label $Tall, then we use the fuzzy comparator NFGT instead of FGT.   □

- **Function** CDEG(<attribute>): It shows a column with the fulfilment degree of the condition of the query, for a specific attribute, which is expressed between brackets as the argument. If logic operators appear, the calculation of this compatibility degree is carried out following table 3. We use the minimum T-norm and the maximum T-conorm, but the user may change these values by default modifying only a view (FSQL_NOTANDOR). In this view the user can set the function to use for every logic operator (NOT, AND, OR). Obviously, that function must be implemented in the FSQL Server or may be implemented by the user himself.

<Condition>	CDEG(<Condition>)
<cond1> AND <cond2>	min(CDEG(<cond1>),CDEG(<cond2>))
<cond1> OR <cond2>	max(CDEG(<cond1>),CDEG(<cond2>))
NOT <cond1>	1 - CDEG(<cond1>)

Table 3. Default computation for function CDEG with logic operators in FSQL.

If the argument of the function CDEG is an attribute, then the function CDEG only uses the conditions that includes that attribute. We can use CDEG(*) to obtain the fulfilment degree of each tuple (with all of its attributes, not just one of them) in the condition.

- **Character %**: It is similar to the character * of SQL but this one also includes the columns for the fulfilment degrees of the attributes in which they are relevant. In the result you will also find the function CDEG applied to each and every one of the fuzzy attributes which appear in the condition. If we want to obtain in example 1 two more columns with the degrees of CDEG(Hair) and CDEG(Height), we would only have to replace * by %. Of course, this character may be also used with the format [[scheme.]table.]%, as for example: Person.%.

– **Fuzzy Constants**: In FSQL we can use the fuzzy constants as detailled in table 4. See examples 1 and 2.

F. Constant	Significance
UNKNOWN	Unknown value but the attribute is applicable (type 8 in table 1).
UNDEFINED	The attribute is not applicable or it is meaningless (type 9 in table 1).
NULL	Total ignorance: We know nothing about it (type 10 in table 1).
$[a,b,c,d]	Fuzzy trapezoid ($a \leq b \leq c \leq d$): See figure 1.
$label	Linguistic Label: It may be a trapezoid or a scalar (defined in FMB).
[n,m]	Interval "Between n and m" (a=b=n and c=d=m).
#n	Fuzzy value "Approximately n" (b=c=n and n-a=d-n=margin).

Table 4. Fuzzy constants that may be used in FSQL queries.

– **Condition with** IS: Another kind of condition we can use has the next format:

```
<Fuzzy_Attribute>  IS  [NOT]  (UNKNOWN | UNDEFINED | NULL)
```

Remarks concerning the condition with IS:
- This condition (without NOT) will be true if the left fuzzy attribute value (<Fuzzy_Attribute>) is the fuzzy constant placed on the right.
- If the attribute is not fuzzy and the constant is NULL, this constant will be understood in the way given by the DBMS.
- If FEQ is used instead of IS, the compatibility degree between attribute and constant is compared (equation 1) and not only when the attribute is *equal* to the constant.

Example 2. A query, which shows a compatibility degree, uses a trapezoidal constant and avoids the UNKNOWN values, could possibly be:

```
SELECT  City,CDEG(Inhabitants)
FROM    Population
WHERE   Country='Spain' AND
        Inhabitants FGEQ $[200,350,650,800] .75 AND
        Inhabitants IS NOT UNKNOWN
```

Remarks concerning the example:

– The minimum threshold is set at 0.75. The word THOLD not appear because it is optional.
– As we are using the comparator FGEQ, the c and d values of the trapezoid will not be used, i.e., if inhabitants equals or exceeds 350, the degree will be 1. Naturally, if the inhabitants is equal to or less than 200 the degree will be zero.

– If a spanish city has in the Inhabitants attribute the possibility distribution $[50,150,200,350], its fulfilment degree of the condition will be 0.5 and it will not appear in the final result, because the minimum has been set at 0.75.   □

Thus, in order to make FSQL queries are especially flexible, in every simple condition, we can modify the following three already defined important elements:

1. **Fuzzy Comparators** (table 2), overcoat changing between possibility and necessity.
2. **Thresholds**, in order to retrieve only the *most important* items.
3. **Comparators instead of word** THOLD, to modify the query meaning, e.g. to retrieve the *least important* items.
4. **Fuzzy constant** (Table 4): If the right part of a simple condition is a fuzzy constant this may be flexibly modified in order to better achieve the target.

4 FRDB Architecture

The FRDB and the FSQL Server [10] have been implemented using an already existing DBMS. Basically this involves three consequences:

1. The system will be slower than if it were programmed at a lower level.
2. The task is made much more simple (we do not have to program the DBMS).
3. We obtain all the advantages of the DBMS host (security, efficiency...) without our Server having to taking them into account.

The DBMS chosen was Oracle, because of its changeability, its large extension and its ability to program packages (with functions and procedures) internal to the system, in its own language, PL/SQL, which turns out to be quite efficient (more than others we have tested: Pro*C...). Of course, this architecture can be implemented in other DBMS. Basically, the architecture of the FRDB with the FSQL Server is made up by:

1. **Data**: Traditional Database and Fuzzy Meta-knowledge Base.
2. **FSQL Server**.
3. **FSQL Client**.

4.1 Data: Traditional Database and Fuzzy Meta-knowledge Base

The data can be classified in two categories:

– **Traditional Database**: They are data from our relations with a special format to store the fuzzy attribute values. The fuzzy attributes are classified by the system in 3 types:
  - Fuzzy Attributes **Type 1**: These attributes are totally crisp (traditional), but they have some linguistic trapezoidal labels defined on them, which allow us to make the query conditions for these attributes more flexible. Besides, we can use all constants in table 4 in the query conditions with these fuzzy attributes.

- Fuzzy Attributes **Type 2**: These attributes admit crisp data as well as possibility distributions over an ordered underlying domain. With these attributes we can store and use all the constants we see in table 4.
- Fuzzy Attributes **Type 3**: They are the types 1, 3 and 5 of table 1. These attributes have not an ordered underlying domain, for instance the hair colour in example 1. On these attributes some labels are defined and on these labels a similarity relation has yet to be defined. With these attributes we can only use the fuzzy comparator FEQ, as they have no relation of order. Obviously we cannot store or use the constants fuzzy trapezoid, interval and approximate value of table 4.

- **Fuzzy Meta-knowledge Base** (FMB): It stores information about the FRDB in a relational format. It stores attributes which admit fuzzy treatment and it will store different information for each one of them, depending on their type:

  - Fuzzy Attributes **Type 1**: In order to use crisp attributes in flexible queries we will only have to declare them as being a fuzzy attribute type 1 and store the following data in the FMB:
    - ⋆ Trapezoidal linguistic labels: Name of the label and a, b, c and d values (as in figure 1).
    - ⋆ Value for the margin of the approximate values (see table 4).
    - ⋆ Minimum distance in order to consider two values *very* separated (used in comparators MGT/NMGT and MLT/NMLT).
  - Fuzzy Attributes **Type 2**: As well as declare them as being a fuzzy attribute type 2, these attributes have to store the same data in the FMB as the fuzzy attributes type 1.
  - Fuzzy Attributes **Type 3**: They store in the FMB their linguistic labels, the similarity degree amongst themselves and the compatibility between attributes of this type, i.e., the attributes that use the same labels and that can be compared amongst themselves.

4.2 FSQL Server

It has been programmed entirely in PL/SQL and it includes 3 kinds of functions:

- **Translation Function** (FSQL2SQL): It carries out a lexical, syntactic and semantic analysis of the FSQL query. If errors, of any kind whatsoever, are found, it will generate a table with all the found errors. If there are no errors, the FSQL query is translated into a standard SQL sentence. The resulting SQL sentence includes reference to the following kinds of functions.
- **Representation Functions**: These functions are used to show the fuzzy attributes in a comprehensible way for the user and not in the internally used format.
- **Fuzzy Comparison Functions**: They are utilized to compare the fuzzy values and to calculate the compatibility degrees (CDEG function).

The Translation Function, summarizing, what it does is to replace the fuzzy attributes of the SELECT by calls to Representation Functions, the fuzzy conditions by calls to the Fuzzy Comparison Functions and the CDEG functions by calls to the Fuzzy Comparison Functions and other functions if there exists some logic operators (default functions are shown in table 3).

4.3 FSQL Client

It is an independent program which serves as an interface between the user and the FSQL Server. The user introduces the FSQL query and the client program communicates with the server and with the database in order to obtain the final results. The Translation Function of the FSQL Server is the only function that is to be executed directly by the client. We have developed a FSQL Client for Windows 95 and NT, called FQ (Fuzzy Queries).

5 Calling to the FSQL Server

We summarized the use process of the FSQL Server in the diagram in figure 2. In short, for a FSQL query the following steps are taken:

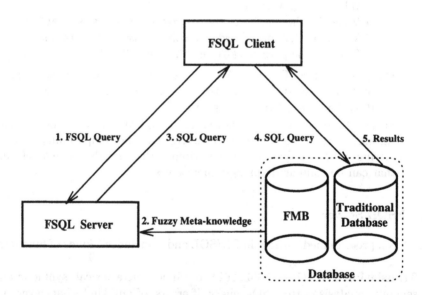

Fig. 2. Basic Architecture for the FRDB with the FSQL Server.

1. The FSQL Client program sends the FSQL query to the FSQL Server.
2. The FSQL Server analizes the query and, if it is correct, generates a SQL sentence, starting from the original query. In this step, the FSQL Server uses the information of the FMB.

3. Once the query has been generated in SQL, the client program will read it.
4. The client program will send the SQL query to any database, which is coherent with the FMB. In the execution of this query, functions of the FSQL Server will be used (Representation and Fuzzy Comparison Functions).
5. Finally, the client will receive the resulting data and it will show them.

Steps number 3 and 4 could have been eliminated to increase the efficiency but, in the way we have presented, we achieve an independence between the Traslation phase (steps number 1, 2 and 3) and the Consultation phase (steps number 4 and 5). That way, if we make use of a local database with FSQL Server and FMB, we will be able to translate our sentences locally and send the translated queries to a remote database, avoiding this way that the network is overcharged with error messages, translated queries... This way, the remote database would not have to have the Translation Function installed.

6 Conclusions

We have presented a FSQL Server, which extends an Oracle database so that it can be consulted in a flexible way through a language that is very similar to the popular SQL: The Fuzzy SQL (**FSQL**) language.

Besides, the main advantage of the used model is that it allows storing many types of fuzzy data (table 1). Then, the FSQL Server does the representation and the fuzzy comparison of these fuzzy data possible.

The presented architecture is not ideal for a final product, but it allows us to evaluate the possibilities of a FRDB on a practical level and not only on a theoretical one. Let us hope the DBMS incorporate soon new types of internal data which allow storing fuzzy values and fuzzy processing of these values. In this line of thinking the object-oriented databases could cooperate quite a lot.

However, the carried out tests prove that the FSQL Server is very fast, being able to be used as a real time server. Obviously, if the query is very complicated and we have a very large database, even if the translation is fast, the information recovery may be a little slow, since if the condition is long then the DBMS would carry out many operations.

Presently, we are working on the creation of a FSQL Client that can be executed through Internet (in Java). We are also working to apply this architecture in some real applications.

The usefulness of this Server is clear, since it can even be used in traditional databases, using only fuzzy attributes type 1, but we would like to underline the possibilities it could offer when used in combination with Data Mining techniques (classification...).

References

1. P. Bosc, O. Pivert, K. Farquhar, "Integrating Fuzzy Queries into an Existing Database Management System: An Example". International Journal of Intelligent Systems, Vol. 9, 475–492 (1994).

2. B.P. Buckles, F.E. Petry, "A Fuzzy Representation of Data for Relational Databases". Fuzzy Sets and Systems 7, 213–226 (1982).
3. B.P. Buckles, F.E. Petry, "Extending the Fuzzy Database with Fuzzy Numbers". Information Sciences 34, 145–155 (1984).
4. D.D. Chamberlin, R.F. Boyce, "SEQUEL: A Structured English Query Language". Proc. ACM SIGMOD Workshop on Data Description. Access and Control, 1974.
5. D.D. Chamberlin et al., "SEQUEL 2: A Unified Approach to Data Definition, Manipulation and Control". IBM J. R&D 20, num. 6, November, 1976.
6. E.F. Codd, "A Relational Model of Data for Large Shared Data Bases". Communications of the ACM, 13, no. 6, 377–387, June 1970.
7. S. Fukami, M. Umano, M. Muzimoto, H. Tanaka, "Fuzzy Database Retrieval and Manipulation Language", IEICE Technical Reports, Vol. 78, N° 233, pp. 65–72, AL-78-85 (Automata and Language) (1979).
8. J. Galindo, J.M. Medina, M.C. Aranda, "Una solución al problema de la División Relacional Difusa". VII Congreso Español sobre Tecnologías y Lógica Fuzzy (ESTYLF'97). Tarragona (Spain), September 1997.
9. J. Galindo, J.M. Medina, J.C. Cubero, "How to Obtain the Fulfilment Degrees of a Query using Fuzzy Relational Calculus". To appear in "Knowledge management in Fuzzy Databases". Eds. O. Pons, M.A. Vila and J. Kacprzyk. Ed. Physica-Verlag, 1998.
10. J. Galindo, J.M. Medina, O. Pons, M.A. Vila, J.C. Cubero, "A prototype for a fuzzy relational database". Demo session in the 6th International Conference on Extending Database Technology, Valencia (Spain), March 1998.
11. J. Galindo, J.M. Medina, A. Vila, O. Pons, "Fuzzy Comparators for Flexible Queries to Databases". Iberoamerican Conference on Artificial Intelligence, IB-ERAMIA'98, Lisbon (Portugal), October 1998.
12. J.M. Medina, O. Pons, M.A. Vila, "GEFRED. A Generalized Model of Fuzzy Relational Databases". Information Sciences, 76(1–2), 87–109 (1994).
13. J.M. Medina R., "Bases de Datos relacionales difusas. Modelo teórico y aspectos de su implementación". Ph. Doctoral Thesis, University of Granada, May 1994.
14. H. Prade, C. Testemale, "Generalizing Database Relational Algebra for the Treatment of Incomplete or Uncertain Information and Vague Queries". Information Sciences 34, 115–143 (1984).
15. H. Prade, C. Testemale, "Fuzzy Relational Databases: Representational issues and Reduction Using Similarity Measures". J. Am. Soc. Information Sciences 38(2), 118–126 (1987).
16. V. Tahani, "A Conceptual Framework for Fuzzy Query Processing–A Step toward Very Intelligent Database Systems". Information Process. Management, 13, 289–303 (1977).
17. M. Umano, S. Fukami, M. Mizumoto, K. Tanaka, "Retrieval Processing from Fuzzy Databases". Technical Reports of IECE of Japan, Vol 80, No. 204 (on Automata and Languages), pp. 45–54, AL80-50 (1980).
18. M. Umano, "Freedom-O: A Fuzzy Database System". Fuzzy Information and Decision Processes. Gupta-Sanchez edit. North-Holand Pub. Comp. (1982).
19. M. Umano, S. Fukami, "Fuzzy Relational Algebra for Possibility-Distribution-Fuzzy Relational Model of Fuzzy Data". Journal of Intelligent Information Systems, 3, 7–27 (1994).
20. L.A. Zadeh, "Fuzzy Sets as a Basis for a Theory of Possibility". Fuzzy Sets and Systems, 1, 3–28 (1978).
21. M. Zemankova-Leech, A. Kandel, "Fuzzy Relational Databases – A Key to Expert Systems". Köln, Germany, TÜV Rheinland (1984).

Query Answering in Nondeterministic, Nonmonotonic Logic Databases

Fosca Giannotti[1], Giuseppe Manco[1], Mirco Nanni[2] and Dino Pedreschi[2]

[1] CNUCE Institute of CNR, Via S. Maria 36, 56125 Pisa, Italy
email: F.Giannotti@cnuce.cnr.it, G.Manco@guest.cnuce.cnr.it
[2] Dipartimento di Informatica, Università di Pisa, C.so Italia 40, 56125 Pisa, Italy
email: {nnanni,pedre}@DI.Unipi.IT

Abstract. We consider in this paper an extension of Datalog with mechanisms for temporal, non monotonic and non deterministic reasoning, which we refer to as Datalog++. We show, by means of examples, its flexibility in expressing queries of increasing difficulty, up to aggregates and data cube. Also, we show how iterated fixpoint and stable model semantics can be combined to the purpose of clarifying the semantics of Datalog++ programs, and supporting their efficient execution. On this basis, the design of appropriate optimization techniques for Datalog++ is also briefly discussed.

1 Introduction

Motivations. The name **Datalog++** is used in this paper to refer to Datalog extended with mechanisms supporting:

- *temporal* reasoning, by means of temporal, or *stage*, arguments of relations, ranging over a discrete temporal domain, in the style of Datalog$_{1S}$ [5];
- *non monotonic* reasoning, by means of a form of stratified negation w.r.t. the stage arguments, called *XY-stratification* [20];
- *non deterministic* reasoning, by means of the non deterministic **choice** construct [9].

Datalog++, which is essentially a fragment of $\mathcal{LDL}$++ [2], and is advocated in [21, Chap. 10], revealed a highly expressive language, with applications in diverse areas such as AI planning [4], active databases [19], object databases [8], semistructured information management and Web restructuring [8]. However, a thorough study of the semantics of Datalog++ is still missing, which provides a basis to sound and efficient implementations and optimization techniques. A preliminary study of the semantics for a generalization of Datalog++ is sketched in [4], but their approach presents some inconveniences that are fixed in this paper.

Objective. The goal of this paper is twofold:

- to illustrate the adequacy of Datalog++ for flexible query answering, and
- to provide a declarative semantics for Datalog++, which accommodates and integrates the temporal, non monotonic and non deterministic mechanisms, and which makes it viable an efficient implementation.

We proceed as follows:

1. a natural, non effective, semantics for Datalog++ is assigned using the notion of a *stable model*;
2. an effective semantics is then assigned using an iterative procedure which exploits the stratification induced by the progression of the temporal argument;
3. in the main result of this paper, we show that 1. and 2. are equivalent, provided that a natural syntactic restriction is fulfilled, which imposes a disciplined use of the temporal argument within the *choice* construct.

On the basis of this result, we finally sketch a discussion on a repertoire of optimization techniques, especially tailored for Datalog++. In particular, we discuss how it is possible to support efficient history-insensitive temporal reasoning by means of real side-effects during the iterated computation [14].

Related Work. Non determinism is introduced in deductive databases by means of the **choice** construct. The original proposal in [12] was later revised in [18], and refined in [9]. These studies exposed the close relationship connecting non monotonic reasoning with non deterministic constructs, leading to the definition of a stable model semantics for **choice**. While the declarative semantics of **choice** is based on *stable model* semantics which is untractable in general, **choice** is amenable to efficient implementations, and it is actually supported in the logic database language $\mathcal{LDL}$ [15] and its evolution $\mathcal{LDL}++$ [2].

On the other side, stratification has been a crucial notion for the introduction of non monotonic reasoning in deductive databases. From the original idea in [1] of a static stratification based on predicate dependencies, stratified negation has been refined to deal with dynamic notions, as in the case of locally stratified programs [16] and modularly stratified programs [17]. Dynamic, or local, stratification has a close connection with temporal reasoning, as the progression of time points yields an obvious stratification of programs—consider for instance $Datalog_{1S}$ [5]. It is therefore natural that non monotonic and temporal reasoning are combined in several deductive database languages, such as those in [13], [11], [8], [21, Chap. 10].

However, a striking mismatch is apparent between the above two lines of research: non determinism leads to a multiplicity of (stable) models, whereas stratification leads to a unique (perfect) model. So far, no comprehensive study has addressed the combination of the two lines, which occurs in Datalog++, and which requires the development of a *non deterministic iterated fixpoint* procedure. We notice however the mentioned exception of [4], where an approach to this problem is sketched with reference to locally stratified programs augmented with `choice`. In the present paper, we present instead a thorough treatment of Datalog++ programs, and repair an inconvenience of the approach in [4] concerning the incompleteness of the iterated fixpoint procedure.

2 Query Answering with Datalog++

Datalog, the basis of deductive databases, is essentially a friendly, uniform syntax to express relational queries, and to extend the query facilities of the relational calculus with recursion. Datalog's simplicity in expressing complex queries impacted on the database technology, and nowadays recursive queries/views have become part of the SQL3 standard. Recursive queries find natural applications in all areas of information systems where computing transitive closures or traversals is an issue, such as in bill-of-materials problems, route or plan formation, graph traversals, and so on.

However, it is widely recognized that the expressiveness of Datalog's (recursive) rules is limited, and several extension, along various directions, have been proposed. In this paper, we address in particular two such directions, namely nondeterministic and nonmonotonic reasoning, supported respectively by the `choice` construct and the notion of XY-stratification. We introduce these mechanism by means of a few examples, which are meant to point out the enhanced query capabilities. The extended Datalog query language is referred to with the name **Datalog++**.

Non deterministic choice. The `choice` construct is used to non deterministically select subsets of answers to queries, which obey a specified FD constraint. For instance, the rule

$$\text{st\_ad(St, Ad)} \leftarrow \text{major(St, Area), faculty(Ad, Area), choice((St), (Ad))}.$$

assigns to each student a unique, arbitrary advisor from the same area, since the `choice` goal constrains the `st_ad` relation to obey the FD (St → Ad). Therefore, if the base relation `major` is formed by the tuples $\{\langle \text{smith, db} \rangle, \langle \text{gray, se} \rangle\}$ and the base relation `faculty` is formed by the tuples $\{\langle \text{brown, db} \rangle, \langle \text{scott, db} \rangle,$ $\langle \text{miller, se} \rangle\}$, then there are two possible outcomes for the query `st_ad(St, Ad)`: either $\{\langle \text{smith, brown} \rangle, \langle \text{gray, miller} \rangle\}$ or $\{\langle \text{smith, scott} \rangle, \langle \text{gray, miller} \rangle\}$. In practical systems, such as $\mathcal{LDL}++$, one of these two solutions is computed and presented as a result.

Semantics of choice. The semantics of `choice` is assigned using the so-called *stable model* semantics of Datalog¬ programs, a concept originating from autoepistemic logic, which was applied to the study of negation in Horn clause languages by Gelfond and Lifschitz [6]. To define the notion of a stable model we need to introduce a transformation H which, given an interpretation I, maps a Datalog¬ program P into a positive Datalog program $H(P, I)$:

$$H(P, I) = \{A \leftarrow B_1, \ldots, B_n \mid A \leftarrow B_1, \ldots, B_n, \neg C_1, \ldots, \neg C_m \in ground(P)$$
$$\wedge \{C_1, \ldots, C_m\} \cap I = \emptyset\}$$

Next, we define:

$$S_P(I) = T_{H(P,I)} \uparrow \omega$$

Then, M is said to be a *stable model* of P if $S_P(M) = M$. In general, Datalog¬ programs may have zero, one or many stable models. The multiplicity of stable models can be exploited to give a declarative account of non determinism.

We can in fact define the *stable version* of a program P, $SV(P)$, to be the program transformation where all the references to the **choice** atom in a rule $r : H \leftarrow B, \mathtt{choice}(X, Y)$ are replaced by the atom $\mathtt{chosen}_r(X, Y)$, and define the $\mathtt{chosen}_r$ predicate with the following rules:

> $\mathtt{chosen}_r(X, Y) \leftarrow B, \neg\mathtt{diffchoice}_r(X, Y).$
> $\mathtt{diffchoice}_r(X, Y) \leftarrow \mathtt{chosen}_r(X, Y'), Y \neq Y'.$

where, for any fixed value of X, each choice for Y inhibits all the other possible ones via $\mathtt{diffchoice}_r$, so that in the stable models of $SV(P)$ there is (only) one of them. Notice that, by construction, each occurrence of a **choice** atom has its own pair of **chosen** and **diffchoice** atoms, thus bounding the scope of the atom to the rule it appears in. The various stable models of the transformed program $SV(P)$ correspond to the possible outcomes of the original **choice** query.

Recursion, choice, and aggregation. In the student/advisor example, the **choice** construct is used to compute nondeterministic, nonrecursive queries. However, **choice** can be combined with recursion, as in the following rules which compute an arbitrary ordering of a given relation **r**:

> $\mathtt{ord\_r}(\mathtt{root}, \mathtt{root}).$
> $\mathtt{ord\_r}(X, Y) \leftarrow \mathtt{ord\_r}(\_, X), \mathtt{r}(Y), \mathtt{choice}(X, Y), \mathtt{choice}(Y, X).$

Here **root** is a fresh constant, conveniently used to simplify the program. If the base relation **r** is formed by k tuples, then there are $k!$ possible outcomes for the query $\mathtt{ord\_r}(X, Y)$, namely a set:

$$\{\mathtt{ord\_r}(\mathtt{root}, \mathtt{root}), \mathtt{ord\_r}(\mathtt{root}, t_1), \mathtt{ord\_r}(t_1, t_2), \ldots, \mathtt{ord\_r}(t_{k-1}, t_k)\}$$

for each permutation $\{t_1, \ldots, t_k\}$ of the tuples of **r**. Therefore, in each possible outcome of the mentioned query, the relation **ord_r** is a total (intransitive) ordering of the tuples of **r**. The double **choice** constraint in the recursive rule specifies that the successor and predecessor of each tuple of **r** is unique.

Interestingly, **choice** can be employed to compute new *deterministic* queries, which are inexpressible in Datalog, as well as in pure relational calculus. A remarkable example is the capability of expressing distributive *aggregates* (i.e., aggregates computable by means of a distributive and associative operator), as in the following program which computes the sum aggregate over a relation **r**, which uses an arbitrary ordering of **r** computed by **ord_r**:

> $\mathtt{sum\_r}(\mathtt{root}, 0).$
> $\mathtt{sum\_r}(Y, N) \leftarrow \mathtt{sum\_r}(X, M), \mathtt{ord\_r}(X, Y), \mathtt{plus}(N, M, Y).$
>
> $\mathtt{total\_sum\_r}(N) \leftarrow \mathtt{agg\_r}(X, N), \neg\mathtt{ord\_r}(X, \_).$

Here, $\mathtt{sum\_r(X,N)}$ is used to accumulate in $\mathtt{N}$ the summation up to $\mathtt{X}$, with respect to the order given by $\mathtt{ord\_r}$. Therefore, the total sum is reconstructed from $\mathtt{sum\_r(X,N)}$ when $\mathtt{X}$ is the last tuple in the order. Notice the use of (stratified) negation to the purpose of selecting the last tuple.

The predicate $\mathtt{plus}$ is the binary operator '+', so that $\mathtt{plus(N,M,Y)}$ corresponds to '$N = M + Y$'. The query $\mathtt{total\_sum\_r(N)}$ is deterministic, in the sense that the value of the summation is independent from the particular order adopted, as $+$ is commutative and associative. Notice that the hypotesis to have such a built-in is obviously an extension of Datalog, whose semantics is in this moment not relevant for the purpose of the presentation. Indeed, we might adopt the very unpractical hypotesis to base it on a finite extensional definition of a domain of integers.

In practical languages, such as $\mathcal{LDL}$++, some syntactic sugar for aggregation is used as an abbreviation of the above program [20]:

$$\mathtt{total\_sum\_r(sum < X >) \leftarrow r(X).}$$

Stage arguments and XY-programs. On the basis of this simple example, more sophisticated forms of aggregation, such as *datacube* and other OLAP functions, can be built. As an example, consider a relation

$$\mathtt{sales(Date, Department, Sale)}$$

and the problem of aggregating sales along the dimensions $\mathtt{Date}$ and $\mathtt{Department}$. Three aggregation patterns are then possible, corresponding to the various facets of the datacube:

$$< \mathtt{Date}, * >, \quad < *, \mathtt{Department} >, \quad < *, * >$$

Each $*$ corresponds to a dimension along with aggregation is performed. The first pattern corresponds to the aggregation (summation) of sales at a given date in all departments, and analogously for the second pattern. The third pattern corresponds to the aggregation of sales along all dimensions. In general, aggregations along n dimensions can be computed in many ways, starting from any aggregation along m dimensions, with $m < n$. A careful choice of a plan of aggregation can minimize the number of required operations to compute the whole datacube. The following program, which combines aggregation and recursion, implements the above idea, and introduces two other features of Datalog++.

$$\mathtt{cuboid(0, Date, Department, Sale)) \leftarrow sales(Date, Department, Sale).}$$
$$\mathtt{cuboid(I + 1, Dim'1, Dim'2, sum < S >) \leftarrow}$$
$$\mathtt{\quad cuboid(I, Dim1, Dim2, S), path(Dim1, Dim2, Dim'1, Dim'2).}$$

$$\mathtt{path(Date, Department, Date, *) \leftarrow Department \neq *, Date \neq *.}$$
$$\mathtt{path(Date, Department, *, Department) \leftarrow Department \neq *, Date \neq *.}$$
$$\mathtt{path(*, Department, *, *) \leftarrow Department \neq *.}$$

$$\mathtt{cube(Dim1, Dim2, S) \leftarrow cuboid(\_, Dim1, Dim2, S).}$$

Here, relation **path** specifies the execution plan for computing aggregations along I dimensions starting from a specific aggregation along $I - 1$ dimensions. In the example, we decided that the aggregation $< *, * >$ should be computed starting from $< *, \texttt{Department} >$, as presumably there are a few departments and many dates. Using complex objects, such as lists, the datacube example can be generalized to an arbitrary number of dimensions.

A thorough account on programming with nondeterminism in deductive databases can be found in [7, 10].

Stage arguments. One of the features of Datalog++ introduced by the datacube example is the *stage argument*: the first argument of relation **cuboid** is a natural number, called a *stage*. In a Peano-style syntax, stages have a unique operator, $. + 1$ (or $s(.)$). Datalog extended with stages is known as $Datalog_{1S}$ [5]. In the datacube example, the stage argument counts the number of dimensions along with aggregation is performed. More generally, stage arguments convey temporal information. The following simple example in pure $Datalog_{1S}$ show how to express that trains from Pisa to Genoa depart every other hour, from 8:00 until 22:00.

```
before22(21).
before22(H) ← before22(H + 1).

leaves(8, pisa, genoa).
leaves(H + 2, pisa, genoa) ← leaves(H, pisa, genoa), before22(H).
```

XY-programs. Another notion used in the datacube example is that of XY-programs originally introduced in [20]. The language of such programs is a subset of $Datalog_{1S}^{\neg}$, which admits a disciplined form of negation, using the stage argument to obtain a natural stratification. A general definition of XY-programs is the following. A set P of rules defining mutually recursive predicates, is an XY-program if it satisfies the following conditions:

1. each recursive predicate has a distinguished stage argument;
2. every recursive rule r is either an X-rule or a Y-rule, where:
   - r is an X-rule when the stage argument in every recursive predicates in r is the same variable,
   - r is a Y-rule when (i) the head of r has a stage argument $s(J)$, where J is a variable, (ii) some goal of r has J as its stage argument, and (iii) the remaining recursive goals have either J or $s(J)$ as their stage argument.

Intuitively, in the rules of XY-programs, an atom $p(J, \_)$ denotes the extension of relation **p** at the current stage (present time) J, whereas an atom $p(s(J), \_)$ denotes the extension of relation **p** at the next stage (future time) $s(J)$. By using a different *primed* predicate symbol p' in the $p(s(J), \_)$ atoms, we obtain the so-called *primed version* of an XY-program. We say that an XY-program is *XY-stratified* if its primed version is a stratified program. Intuitively, if the dependency graph of the primed version has no cycles through negated edges, then it is possible to obtain an ordering on the original rules modulo the stage arguments. As a consequence, an XY-stratified program is also locally stratified, and has therefore a unique stable model that coincides with its perfect model [16].

Let P be an XY-stratified program. Then, for each $i > 0$, define P_i as

$$P_i = \{r[s^i(nil)/I] \mid r \in P, I \text{ is the stage argument of the head of } r\}$$

i.e., P_i is the set of rule instances of P that define the predicates with stage argument $s^i(nil) = i$. Then the iterated fixpoint procedure for computing the (unique) minimal model of P can be defined as follows:

1. compute M_0 as the minimal model of P_0;
2. for each $j > 0$ compute M_j as the minimal model of $P_j \cup M_{j-1}$.

Notice that for each $j \geq 0$, P_j is stratified by the definition, and hence its perfect model M_j is computable via an iterated fixpoint procedure.

The following version of the *seminaive* graph-reachability program, discussed in [20], is an example of (XY-stratified) XY-program, which computes all nodes of a graph **g** reachable from a given node **a**:

```
delta(0, a).
delta(s(I), Y) ← delta(I, X), g(X, Y), ¬all(I, Y).
all(I, X) ← delta(I, X).
all(s(I), X) ← all(I, X), delta(s(I), _).
```

Observe the use of negation, which is not stratified in the usual sense (**delta** and **all** are mutually recursive), although it is stratified modulo the stage. In the outcome of the seminaive program, **all(n, b)** means that **b** is a node reachable from a in graph **g**. At each stage **i**, **delta(i, c)** means that **c** is a newly reached node, and **i** is also the length of the shortest path from **a** to **c**; using relation **delta** to propagate the search avoids unnecessary recomputations.

Datalog++. In this paper, we use the name Datalog++ to refer to the language of XY-programs augmented with **choice** goals. Combining the two mechanisms is natural in many examples. The datacube program discussed above is one such examples: it is indeed an XY-programs which uses aggregation, which is in turn based on **choice**. Other instances are the AI planning programs discussed in [4], the semantics for active databases in [19], the approach to semistructured information management and Web restructuring of [8], the reformulation of concurrent programs such as the alternating bit protocol and the readers-writers problems studied in [3]. Other small-scale examples are presented later in this paper.

The rest of this paper is devoted to show how the semantics of **choice**, which uses a nonstratified form of negation, can be reconciled with that of XY-programs, which use a form of stratified negation. This will also lead to a viable operational (fixpoint) semantics, and several promising optimizations.

3   A Semantics for Datalog++

When choice constructs are allowed in XY-programs, a multiplicity of stable models exists for any given program, and therefore it is needed to clarify how this phenomenon combines with the iterated fixpoint semantics of choice-free XY-programs.

Given a (possibly infinite) program P, consider a (possibly infinite) topological sort of its distinct recursive cliques $Q_1 \prec Q_2 \ldots \prec Q_i \prec \ldots$, induced by the dependency relation over the predicates of P. Given an interpretation I, we use the notation I_i to denote the subset of atoms of I whose predicate symbols are predicates defined in clique Q_i.

Define the stranformation $Q_i^{red(I)}$ of each clique Q_i within the given topological ordering, as a self-contained program which takes into account the information deduced by the previous cliques, on the basis of the interpretation I. The idea underlying the transformation is to remove from the clique all the dependencies induced by the predicates which are defined in lower cliques.

Example 1. Consider the program $P = \{p \leftarrow q, r. \quad q \leftarrow r, t. \quad r \leftarrow q, s.\}$ and the cliques $Q_1 = \{q \leftarrow r, t. \quad r \leftarrow q, s.\}$ and $Q_2 = \{p \leftarrow q, r.\}$. Now, consider the interpretation $I = \{s, q, r\}$. Then $Q_1^{red} = \{q \leftarrow r, t. \quad r \leftarrow q, s.\}$ and $Q_2^{red} = \{p \leftarrow .\}$. $\qquad\square$

It can be shown [8] that an arbitrary Datalog¬ program has a stable model if and only if each its approximating clique, according to the given topological sort, has a *local* stable model.

We turn now our attention to XY-programs. The result of instantiating the clauses of an XY-program P with all possible values (natural numbers) of the stage argument, yields a new program $SG(P)$ (for *stage ground*). More precisely, $SG(P) = \bigcup_{i \geq 0} P_i$, where P_i is the i-th stage instance of P (already defined in section 2).

Next, we introduce, for any XY-program P, its modified version $SO(P)$ (for *stage-out*), defined by $SO(P) = \bigcup_{i \geq 0} SO(P)_i$ where $SO(P)_i$ is obtained from the program fragment P_i of $SG(P)$ by extracting the stage arguments from any atom, and adding it to the predicate symbol of the atom. Similarly, the modified version $SO(I)$ of an interpretation I is defined. Therefore, the atom $p(i, x)$ is in I iff the atom $p_i(x)$ is in $SO(I)$, where i is the value in the stage argument position of relation p.

Finally, it is possible to define an iterative procedure to construct an arbitrary stable model M of P as the union of the interpretations $M_0, M_1, \ldots$ defined as follows:

Definition 1 (Iterated stable model procedure.). *Given a Program P, the interpretation $M = \bigcup_{i \geq 0} M_i$ is called an* iterated stable model *of P, where:*

Base case. *M_0 is a stable model of the bottom clique $SO(P)_0$.*

Induction case. *For $i > 0$, M_i is a stable model of $SO(P)_i^{red(M^{(i-1)})}$, i.e. the clique $SO(P)_i$ reduced with respect to $M_0 \cup \cdots \cup M_{i-1}$.* $\qquad\square$

It should be observed that this construction is close to the procedure called *iterated choice fixpoint* in [4]. Also, following the approach of [10], each local stable model M_i can in turn be efficiently constructed by a non deterministic fixpoint computation, in polynomial time.

The following example shows a computation with the iterated stable model procedure.

Example 2. Consider the following Datalog++ version of the *seminaive* program, discussed in [20], which non-deterministically computes a maximal path from node a over a graph g:

```
delta(0, a).
delta(s(I), Y) ← delta(I, X), g(X, Y), ¬all(I, Y), choice((I, X), Y).
all(I, X) ← delta(I, X).
all(s(I), X) ← all(I, X), delta(s(I), _).
```

Assume that the graph is given by $g = \{\langle a, b\rangle, \langle b, c\rangle, \langle b, d\rangle, \langle d, e\rangle\}$. The following interpretations are carried out at each stage of the iterated stable model procedure:

1. $I_0 = \{delta_0(a), all_0(a)\}$.
2. $I_1 = \{all_1(a), all_1(b), delta_1(b)\}$.
3. $I_2^1 = \{all_2(a), all_2(b), delta_2(c), all_2(c)\}$,
   $I_2^2 = \{all_2(a), all_2(b), delta_2(d), all_2(d)\}$
4. $I_3^1 = \emptyset$, $I_3^2 = \{all_3(a), all_3(b), all_3(d), delta_3(e), all_3(e)\}$
5. $I_j = \emptyset$ for $j > 3$.

We conclude that there are two stable models for the program: $I^1 = I_0 \cup I_1 \cup I_2^1$ and $I^2 = I_0 \cup I_1 \cup I_2^2 \cup I_3^2$. □

Unfortunately, the desired result that the notions of stable model and iterated stable model coincide does not hold in full generality, in the sense that the iterative procedure is not complete for arbitrary Datalog++ programs. In fact, as demonstrated by the example below, an undisciplined use of choice in Datalog++ programs may cause the presence of stable models that cannot be computed incrementally over the hierarchy of cliques.

Example 3. Consider the following simple Datalog++ program P:

```
q(0, a).
q(s(I), b) ← q(I, a).
p(I, X) ← q(I, X), choice((), X).
```

In the stable version $SV(P)$ of P, the rule defining predicate p is replaced by:

```
p(I, X) ← q(I, X), chosen(X).
chosen(X) ← q(I, X), ¬diffchoice(X).
diffchoice(X) ← chosen(Y), Y ≠ X.
```

It is readily checked that $SV(P)$ admits two stable models, namely $\{q(0, a), q(s(0), b), p(0, a)\}$ and $\{q(0, a), q(s(0), b), p(s(0), b)\}$, but only the first model is an iterated stable models, and therefore the second model cannot be computed using the *iterated choice fixpoint* of [4]. □

The technical reason for this problem is that the free use of the **choice** construct inhibits the possibility of defining a topological sort on $SO(P)$ based on the value of the stage argument. In the example 3, the predicate dependency relation of $SO(SV(P))$ induces a dependency among stage i and the stages $j > i$, because of the dependency of the **chosen** predicate from the predicates q_i for all stages $i \geq 0$.

To prevent this problem, it is suffices to require that **choice** goals refer the stage argument I in the domain of the associated functional dependency. The Datalog++ programs which comply with this constraint are called *choice-safe*. The following is a way to turn the program of example 3 into a choice-safe program (with a different semantics):

$$p(I, X) \leftarrow q(I, X), choice(I, X).$$

This syntactic restriction, moreover, does not compromise the expressiveness of the query language, in that it is possible to simulate within this restriction many practical uses of **choice** (see [14]).

The above considerations are summarized in the following result of the paper.

Theorem 1 (Correctness and completeness).
Let P be a choice-safe Datalog++ program and I an interpretation. Then I is a stable model of P iff it is an iterated stable model of P. □

4 Optimization of Datalog++ queries

A systematic study of query optimization techniques is needed to achieve realistic implementations of the iterated stable model procedure. In this section we sketch the direction along with our research is developing. The key idea is to exploit the particular syntactic structure due to the temporal arguments.

Forgetful-fixpoint computations. In many applications (e.g., modeling updates and active rules [19,8]) queries are issued with reference to the final stage only (which represents the commit state of the database). Such queries often exhibit the form $p(I, X), \neg p(s(I), \_)$, with the intended meaning "find the value X of p in the final state of p". This implies that (i) when computing the next stage, we can forget all the preceding states but the last one (see [20]), and (ii) if a stage I such that $p(I, X), \neg p(s(I), \_)$ is unique, we can stop the computation process once the above query is satisfied. For instance, the program in example 2 with the query $delta(I, X), \neg delta(s(I), \_)$ computes the last node visited in a (non deterministically chosen) maximal path starting from a. To answer this query, it suffices to consider either the partial model I_2^1 or the partial model I_3^2, and hence we can discard the previous partial models during the computation.

Another interesting case occurs when the answer to the query is distributed along the stages, e.g., when we are interested in the answer to a query such as delta(_, X), which ignores the stage argument. In this case, we can collect the partial answers via a gathering predicate defined with a copy-rule. For instance, the all predicate in example 2 collects all the nodes reachable from a in the selected path. Then the query all(I, X), ¬all(s(I), _), which is amenable for the described optimization, is equivalent to the query delta(_, X), which on the contrary does not allow it. Therefore, by (possibly) modifying the program with copy-rules for the all predicate, we can apply systematically the space optimized forgetful-fixpoint.

Delta-fixpoint computations. We already mentioned the presence of a *copy-rule* in example 2:

all(s(I), X) ← all(I, X), delta(s(I), _).

Its effect is that of copying all the tuples from the stage I to the next one, if any. We can avoid such useless space occupation, by maintaining for each stage only the modifications which are to be applied to the original relation in order to obtain the actual version. For example, the above rule represents no modification at all, and hence it should not have any effect; indeed, it suffices to keep track of the additions to the original database dictated by the other rule:

all(I, X) ← delta(I, X).

which can be realized by a supplementary relation all$^+$ containing, at each stage, the new tuples produced. If we replace the *copy-rule* with a *delete-rule* of the form:

all(s(I), X) ← all(I, X), delta(s(I), _), ¬q(X).

we need simply to keep track of the negative contribution due to literal ¬q(X), which can be stored in a relation all$^-$. Each all(I, ...) can then be obtained by integrating all(0, ...) with all the all$^+$(J, ...) and all$^-$(J, ...) atoms, with $J \leq I$.

Side-effect computations. A direct combination of the previous two techniques gives rise to a form of *side-effect* computation. Let us consider, as an example, the nondeterministic ordering of an array performed by swapping at each step any two elements which violate ordering. Here, the array $a = \langle a_1, \cdots, a_n \rangle$ is represented by the relation a with extension a(1, a$_1$), ..., a(n, a$_n$).

ar(0, P, Y) ← a(P, Y).
swp(I, P1, P2) ← ar(I, P1, X), ar(I, P2, Y), X > Y,
          P1 < P2, choice((I), (P1, P2)).
ar(s(I), P, X) ← ar(I, P, X), ¬swp(I, P, _), ¬swp(I, _, P), swp(I, _, _).

$$ar(s(I), P, X) \leftarrow ar(I, P1, X), swp(I, P1, P).$$
$$ar(s(I), P, X) \leftarrow ar(I, P1, X), swp(I, P, P1).$$
$$?ar(I, X, Y), \neg ar(s(I), \_, \_)$$

At each stage i we non deterministically select an unordered pair x, y of elements, delete the array atoms ar(i, p1, x) and ar(i, p2, y) where they appear, and add the new atoms ar(s(i), p1, y) and ar(s(i), p2, x) representing the swapped pair. The query allows a forgetful-fixpoint computation (in particular, stage selected by the query is unique), and the definition of predicate ar is composed by delete-rules and an add-rules. This means that at each step we can (i) forget the previously computed stages (but the last), and (ii) avoid copying most of relation ar, keeping track only of the deletions and additions to be performed. If the requested update are immediately performed, the execution of the proposed program, then, boils down to the efficient iterative computation of the following (non deterministic) Pascal-like program:

$$\textbf{while } \exists I \ a[I] > a[I+1] \textbf{ do } swap(a[I], a[I+1]) \textbf{ od}$$

Magic Sets. A second line of research investigates how to gear classic optimizations, such as magic sets, to Datalog++. These rewriting techniques are in fact incompatible with the structure of XY-programs, in that the magic version of an XY-program is not, in general, an XY-program. Adaptations of such techniques to Datalog++ are currently under investigation.

References

1. K. R. Apt, H. Blair, and A. Walker. Towards a theory of declarative knowledge. In J. Minker, editor, *Proc. Workshop on Found. of Deductive Databases and Logic Programming*, pages 89–148. Morgan Kaufman, 1988.
2. N. Arni, K. Ong, S. Tsur, and C. Zaniolo. $\mathcal{LDL}$++: A Second Generation Deductive Databases Systems. Technical report, MCC Corporation, 1993.
3. F. Bonchi. Verification of Datalog++ programs (in Italian). Master's thesis, Department of Computer Science University of Pisa, 1998.
4. A. Brogi, V. S. Subrahmanian, and C. Zaniolo. The Logic of Totally and Partially Ordered Plans: a Deductive Database Approach. *Annals of Mathematics in Artificial Intelligence*, 19:59–96, 1997.
5. J. Chomicki. Temporal deductive databases. In A. Tansel, J. Clifford, S. Gadia, S. Jajodia, A. Segev, and R. Snodgrass, editors, *Temporal Databases: Theory, Design and Implementation*, pages 294–320. Benjamin Cummings, 1993.
6. M Gelfond and V. Lifchitz. The Stable Model Semantics for logic programming. In *Proc. of the 5th Int. Conf. on Logic Programming*, pages 1070–1080, 1988.
7. F. Giannotti, S. Greco, D. Saccà, and C. Zaniolo. Programming with non Determinism in Deductive Databases. *Annals of Mathematics in Artificial Intelligence*, 19:97–125, 1997.
8. F. Giannotti, G. Manco, and D. Pedreschi. A Deductive Data Model for Representing and Querying Semistructured Data. In *Proc. 5th Int. Conf. on Deductive and Object-Oriented Databases (DOOD97)*, December 1997.

9. F. Giannotti, D. Pedreschi, D. Saccà, and C. Zaniolo. Non-Determinism in Deductive Databases. In *Proc. 2nd Int. Conf. on Deductive and Object-Oriented Databases (DOOD91)*, volume 566 of *Lecture Notes in Computer Science*, pages 129–146, 1991.

10. F. Giannotti, D. Pedreschi, and C. Zaniolo. Semantics and Expressive Power of Non Deterministic Constructs for Deductive Databases. Technical Report C96-04, The CNUCE Institute, 1996. Submitted.

11. D. Kemp, K. Ramamohanarao, and P. Stuckey. ELS programs and the efficient evaluation of non-stratified programs by transformation to ELS. In *Proc. 4th Int. Conf. on Deductive and Object-Oriented Databases (DOOD95)*, pages 91–108, 1995.

12. R. Krishnamurthy and S. Naqvi. Non-deterministic Choice in Datalog. In *Proc. 3rd Int. Conf. on Data and Knowledge Bases*, pages 416–424, 1988.

13. B. Lüdascher, U. Hamann, and G. Lausen. A logical framework for active rules. In *Proc. 7th COMAD Int. Conf. on Management of Data*. Tata McGraw-Hill, 1995.

14. M. Nanni. Nondeterminism and XY-Stratification in Deductive Databases (in Italian). Master's thesis, Department of Computer Science University of Pisa, 1997.

15. S. Naqvi and S. Tsur. *A Logic Language for Data and Knowledge Bases*. Computer Science Press, 1989.

16. T. C. Przymusinski. Every logic program has a natural stratification and an iterated fix point model. In *Proc. 8th ACM PODS Symposium on Principles of Database Systems*, pages 11–21, 1989.

17. K. A. Ross. Modular Stratification and Magic Sets for Datalog Program with Negation. *Journal of ACM*, 41(6):1216–1266, November 1994.

18. D. Saccà and C. Zaniolo. Stable Models and Non-determinism in Logic Programs with Negation. In *Proceedings of the ACM Symposium on Principles of Database Systems*, pages 205–217, 1990.

19. C. Zaniolo. Active Database Rules with Transaction Conscious Stable Model Semantics. In *Proc. 4th Int. Conf. on Deductive and Object-Oriented Databases (DOOD95)*, volume 1013 of *Lecture Notes in Computer Science*, pages 55–72, 1995.

20. C. Zaniolo, N. Arni, and K. Ong. Negation and Aggregates in Recursive Rules: The $\mathcal{LDL}++$ Approach. In *Proc. 3rd Int. Conf. on Deductive and Object-Oriented Databases (DOOD93)*, volume 760 of *Lecture Notes in Computer Science*, 1993.

21. C. Zaniolo, S. Ceri, C. Faloutsos, R.T Snodgrass, V.S. Subrahmanian, and R. Zicari. *Advanced Database Systems*. Morgan Kaufman, 1997.

Optimization of Logic Queries*
with MIN and MAX Predicates

Sergio Greco,[1] Carlo Zaniolo[2] and Sumit Ganguly[3]

[1] DEIS, Univ. della Calabria, 87030 Rende, Italy
greco@si.deis.unical.it
[2] Computer Science Dept., Univ. of California, Los Angeles, CA 90024
zaniolo@cs.ucla.edu
[3] Dept. of Computer Science, Rutgers University, New Brunswick, NJ 08903
sumit@cs.rutgers.edu

Abstract. We propose an algorithm for pushing *min* and *max* aggregates into recursive predicates, while preserving query equivalence under certain monotonicity constraints. The transformed query is often safe when the original one is not, and more efficient than the original query when this is safe.

1 Introduction

The program in Example 1, below, gives a declarative formulation of the shortest path problem. Given a weighted directed graph represented as a base relation arc, where all edge weights are nonnegative, the predicate path computes the set of all triples (X, Y, C) such that there is a path from node X to node Y whose cost is C. The predicate sh_path(X,Y,C) is intended to yield all the triples (X,Y,C) such that C is the least cost among all paths from node X to node Y.

Example 1. Stratified shortest path.

$$\text{sh\_path}(X, Y, C) \leftarrow \min(C, (X, Y), \text{path}(X, Y, C)).$$

$$\text{path}(X, Y, C) \leftarrow \text{arc}(X, Y, C).$$
$$\text{path}(X, Y, C) \leftarrow \text{path}(X, Z, C1), \text{arc}(Z, Y, C2), C = C1 + C2. \qquad \blacksquare$$

A precise semantics can be assigned to our program, by simply viewing the first rule containing the *min* predicate as a short hand for the following two rules:

$$\text{sh\_path}(X, Y, C) \leftarrow \text{path}(X, Y, C), \neg\text{a\_lesser\_path}(X, Y, C).$$

$$\text{a\_lesser\_path}(X, Y, C) \leftarrow \text{path}(X, Y, C'), C' < C.$$

where a_lesser_path is a new predicate symbol not appearing elsewhere in the program. This has formal semantics, inasmuch as by rewriting the min predicates by means of negation, we get a stratified program [1]. However, a straightforward evaluation of such a stratified program would materialize the predicate

---

* The work of the first author has been supported by the project MURST 40 % "".

path(X,Y,C) and then choose the smallest cost tuple for every X and Y. There are two problems with this approach: first, it is very inefficient, and second, the computation could be non-terminating if the relation arc is cyclic. To solve these problems, one begins by observing that all minimum paths of length $n+1$, because the weights are nonnegative, can be generated from the minimum paths of length n. Thus, the *min* predicate can be pushed into recursion, in such a way that the generation of new paths is interleaved with the computation of shortest paths, yielding the program of Example 2.

Example 2. Unstratified shortest path.

$$\text{path}(X, Y, C) \leftarrow \text{arc}(X, Y, C).$$
$$\text{path}(X, Y, C) \leftarrow \text{sh\_path}(X, Z, C1), \text{arc}(Z, Y, C2), C = C1 + C2.$$
$$\text{sh\_path}(X, Y, C) \leftarrow \min(C, (X, Y), \text{path}(X, Y, C)). \qquad \blacksquare$$

Unfortunately, as we attempt to give a meaning to Example 2 by rewriting it using negation, as in the previous example, we obtain a non-stratified program, with all the open semantic and computational issues therewith. These problems, widely recognized by deductive database researchers, have been the subject of recent works [2,3,5,7–10,14,16,18,21]. Although our discussion deals explicitly only with *min* programs, the symmetric properties of *max* programs follow by duality.

Here we use Datalog to study how min and max aggregates are propagated down into queries, since this simplies the presentation; however, similar techniques can be applied directly to the optimization of recursive SQL queries.

Observe that stratified aggregation has very high expressive power on ordered domains [11] and, therefore, queries should be written by using stratified aggregates which have clear and intuitive semantics. Moreover, the computation of queries with stratified *min* and *max* aggregates tend to be inefficient; however, the computation of queries with unstratified min and max aggregates can be very efficient, since useless branches can now be pruned early in the computation. In particular, a very efficient algorithm for the computation of monotonic queries with unstratified min and max aggregates was presented in [5]. Therefore, we are seeking techniques to rewrite stratified queries into equivalent unstratified ones.

2 Syntax and Semantics

The notion of a minimum naturally assumes the existence of a domain of constants over which a total order is defined. Formally, we assume the existence of an alphabet of constants, functions and predicates symbols. We assume also that there are a built-in set of constants D, called *cost domain*, two built-in binary predicates $<$ and $\leq$, and built-in functions whose arguments are elements of D. In our examples, we will use the cost domain of real numbers, where the built-in predicates $<$ and $\leq$ are the usual operators defined for real numbers and the built-in functions are the usual arithmetics operators $(+, -, *, \text{etc.})$.

We assume the basic concepts of terms, atom, Horn program, (Herbrand) interpretation and (Herbrand) model of logic programming.

Definition 1. A *special atom* is of the form $min(C, S, Q)$ where:

1. Q is an atom of first order logic, called *minimized atom*,
2. S is a set of variables, appearing as arguments Q, called *grouping variables*,
3. $C \notin S$ is a variable, appearing as argument of Q, called the *cost variable*. Cost variables can only take values from the cost domain. ∎

A *min atom* is either a special atom or an atom of first order logic (standard atom). A min rule is of the form $A \leftarrow B_1, ..., B_n$ where A is a standard atom and $B_1, ..., B_n$ are min atoms. A *ruleset* is a finite set of min rules. A *(min) program* is defined by a ruleset P, its underlying cost domain D_P plus an additional constraint defining the subrange of the cost domain whose values can be assigned to cost arguments; this subrange will be called the *valid cost sub-domain*. Both Examples 1 and 2 are min program.

A *(min) query* Q is a pair $\langle g(X), P \rangle$ where P is a min program program, g is a predicate symbol in P, say with arity $n \geq 0$, and X is a list of n variables; the atom $g(X)$ is said query-goal. Given a database D, the *answer* of Q on D, denoted by $Q(D)$, is the set of relations on g denoted as $A_g = \{M(g)|M$ is a (minimal) model defining the semantics of $P \cup D\}$. We say that two queries Q_1 and Q_2 are equivalent ($Q_1 \equiv Q_2$) if for each database D the answers of Q_1 and Q_2 on D are the same. Given a query $\langle g(X), P \rangle$ and a predicate p appearing in P, we say that p is reachable from g if g depends on p. A predicate g depends on a predicate q if there is a rule r such that g appear in the head and p in the body, or there is a predicates q such that g depends on q and q depends on p. Moreover, we say that a rule r is reachable from a predicate g(or equivalently, g depends on r) if the head predicate symbol of r is reachable from g.

For the sake of simplicity we consider min programs without negation. The extension to programs with stratified negation is straightforward.

Without loss of generality we assume that min rules are either standard Horn rules or non-Horn rules of the form

$$H \leftarrow min(C, S, Q)$$

where H and Q are standard atoms.

The semantics of a min program is defined by taking a min program P and defining a first order formula $foe(P)$, called the first order extension of P, obtained by replacing every occurrence of special atoms

$$min(C, S, q(\bar{Y}, C))$$

by the pair of goals

$$q(\bar{Y}, C), \quad \neg a\_lesser\_q(\bar{Y}, C)$$

The distinguished *a_lesser_q* predicate is defined by the additional rule of the form:

$$a\_lesser\_q(\bar{Y}, C) \leftarrow q(\bar{X}, C'), \ C' < C.$$

where an argument variable in $\bar{X}$ coincides with the corresponding variable in $\bar{Y}$ if this variable appears in the grouping set S and is a new variable otherwise. The variable C' is new and corresponds to the variable C.

For instance, the meaning of Example 2 is defined by the following program:

Example 3. The standard program defining the meaning of Example 2 is

```
path(X, Y, C) ← arc(X, Y, C).
path(X, Y, C) ← sh_path(X, Z, C1), arc(Z, Y, C2), C = C1 + C2.

sh_path(X, Y, C) ← path(X, Y, C), ¬a_lesser_path(X, Y, C).

a_lesser_path(X, Y, C) ← path(X, Y, C'), C' < C.
```
■

Since we view a min-program simply as a shorthand of $foe(P)$, we will say that M is an interpretation (resp. a (minimal) model) for P, when M is an interpretation (resp. a (minimal) model) for $foe(P)$. Therefore, we can define the semantics of min-programs by using concepts such as stratification, well founded model and stable models, developed for logic programs with negation.

We can now proceed and define classes of min programs which, because of their syntactic structure and stratification conditions induced by the underlying cost-domain, have a total well-founded model which coincides with the unique stable models and with the perfect model which defines the semantics of (locally) stratified programs.

We will assume that certain database predicates arguments called *cost arguments* can only take values from the cost domain, or a subset of this domain called a *valid cost sub-domain*. In most examples of this paper, we will assume that the set of nonnegative numbers is our valid cost sub-domain. The presence of database goals with cost arguments, and the fact that built-in predicates can be true only if their arguments are from the cost domain, implies that certain arguments in the derived predicates also belong to the cost domain.

We point out that the notion of valid cost domain is motivated by the fact that programs satisfy some particular properties only if we consider a subset of the cost domain.

A *valid instantiation* of a rule r in a program $foe(P)$ is a ground instance of r that is obtained by replacing all the variables of r with ground terms from $U_{foe(P)} \cup D'_P$ where (i) D'_P is a valid cost subdomain, and (ii) each goal corresponding to a built-in predicate is true. Thus valid instantiations will not contain a goal such as $3 > 4 + 1$ which is false and thus inconsequential. The valid instantiation of program $foe(P)$ is simply the set of all valid instantiations of all rules of $foe(P)$. The *valid dependency graph* of a program $foe(P)$, denoted G_P, is a directed graph whose nodes are ground atoms of $foe(P)$. In G_P, there is an arc from a node A to another node B if there is a valid instantiation of some rule r in $foe(P)$ such that A appears in the body and B appears in the head of r; moreover if A appears negated then the arc is marked, and will be said to be negative. The *immediate consequence operator* T_P is defined as

$$T_P(I) = \{q \mid \exists q \leftarrow p_1, ..., p_n \in ground(P) \text{ and } p_1, ..., p_n \in I\}.$$

We now formally introduce the definition of cost argument.

Definition 2. Let P be a min program, and let $det(P)$ denote the program obtained from $foe(P)$ by

1. removing all the **a_lesser** rules and
2. removing all **a_lesser** goals from the bodies of the rules.

The i-th argument of a predicate q of P, is said to be a *cost argument* if the i-th argument of every q-atom in $T_{det(P)}^{\infty}(\emptyset)$ belongs to the cost domain. Moreover, a predicate q that has a cost argument will be called a *cost predicate*.

∎

Thus, given a min program P it is possible to divide the predicate symbols appearing in P into the two distinguished sets of cost predicates and standard predicates. We will only consider programs where each recursive set of predicates consists of cost predicates (called *min clique*) or standard predicates (called *standard clique*). Standard cliques are computed by using the classical fixpoint computation whereas min cliques are computed by using special algorithms such as the greedy fixpoint of [5]. Predicates that appear inside special atoms will be called *minimized predicates*.

3 Propagation of min predicates

In this section, we present an algorithm for transforming monotonic-min programs into *query-equivalent* programs which can be more efficiently evaluated using the semi-naive greedy operator G_P [5].

We associate adornments to minimized cost predicates by assigning to each of their arguments, one of the three labels u, e, or m as follows:

1. the cost argument is labeled m
2. an argument not containing in the set of grouping variables is labeled e
3. an argument appearing in the set of grouping variables is labeled u.

Consider, for instance, the min atom $min(C, (X, Y), p(X, Z, Y, C))$. The adorned atom associated with the minimized atom is $p^{ueum}(X, Z, Y, C)$.

Observe that u-variables and e-variables are, respectively, universally and existentially quantified in the foe expansion of the min predicates. Observe also that grouping variables correspond, in non-recursive queries, to arguments appearing in the "GROUP BY" section in SQL queries.

Predicates that are not minimized will then be assigned the default adornment ϵ. For instance, in Example 1, the adornment for both sh_path is ϵ whereas the adornment for $path$ is uum.

Thus, we use the concept of *adornments* to abbreviate minimized predicates. The basic component of the transformation algorithm is the propagation of an adornment for the head of a rule into the body of the rule. We discuss this for Horn rules and non-Horn rules next.

3.1 Propagating Adornments into Horn Rules

Consider the following rule for which we wish to propagate the adornment uum for p into the body of the rule.

$$p(X, Z, C) \leftarrow q(X, Y, C1), \ s(Y, Z, C2), \ C = C1 + C2.$$

In this case, a particular tuple $p(X, Z, C)$ is a *possible* candidate member of p^{uum} provided that the conjunction $q^{uum}(X, Y, C1) \wedge s^{uum}(Y, Z, C2)$ is true. Clearly, this condition is necessary but not sufficient, since, the combination of two tuples from q^{uum} and s^{uum} may not result in a tuple for p^{uum}. This motivates us to introduce a new *surrogate* predicate cp^{uum} (the name for the surrogate predicate symbol is obtained by prefixing c to the name of the predicate and by superscripting the adornment) whose definition is intended to collect the set of candidate minimum tuples for the given adornment. Thus the propagation of the adornment uum in the above rule results in the following rule:

$$cp^{uum}(X, Z, C) \leftarrow q^{uum}(X, Y, C1), \ s^{uum}(Y, Z, C2), \ C = C1 + C2.$$

If there are multiple rules that define the predicate p, we generate one such adorned rule for each of the rules. Consequently, we define p^{uum} as the minimum over cp^{uum} as follows:

$$p^{uum}(X, Z, C) \leftarrow \min(C, (X, Z), cp^{uum}(X, Z, C)).$$

The above rule is called the *minima definition* of p, in terms of the surrogate predicate cp^{uum} for the adornment uum. In this manner, we generate the *adorned definition* of a predicate for a given adornment, which is the union of the adorned rules for the predicate and the minima definition of the predicate in terms of the surrogate predicate for that adornment.

Adorning variables by u

In the above example, the variable Y is shared by both $q(X, Y, C1)$ and $s(Y, Z, C2)$ in the body of the rule. It is safe to adorn Y as u in both the q and s predicates in the body. However, in general, it is not safe to adorn Y as e in either or both the predicates. Suppose that, for instance, we adorn Y by e in $q(X, Y, C1)$ and by u in $s(Y, Z, C2)$. This would give the following adorned rule

$$\overline{cp}^{uum}(X, Z, C) \leftarrow q^{uem}(X, Y, C1), \ s^{uum}(Y, Z, C2), \ C = C1 + C2.$$

It should be clear that $\overline{cp}^{uum}$ may be a proper subset of cp^{uum} since corresponding to the Y values in $q^{uem}(X, Y, C1)$, there may not be any Y values in $s(Y, Z, C2)$ (and therefore in $s^{uum}(Y, Z, C2)$[1]). Hence *shared variables in the body of a rule are adorned as u.*

Furthermore, consider the variables X and Z in the body and whose adornments are prescribed as u in the head. These variables are not shared in the body. In general, *variables that are adorned as u in the head are adorned as u in the body*, irrespective of whether they are shared or not.

---

[1] unless s is total in its first argument.

Adorning variables by e

Consider the following rule and the adornment uem to be propagated in the body:

$$p(X, Z, C) \leftarrow q(X, U, C1), \; s(W, Z, C2), \; C = C1 + C2.$$

Clearly, X must be adorned as u since it is so adorned in the head. Let us now consider the variables U and W. These variables are neither shared nor do they appear in the head. We adorn these variables by e, since their values are inconsequential. The variable Z in the body is also adorned as e since, it appears only once in the body and is adorned as e in the head. Thus, *variables that appear only once in the body and do not appear in the head are adorned as e. Variables that appear only once in the head as e and appear only once as in the body are adorned as e.*

Monotonicity of the cost predicate in the body

We now consider the constraints that the cost predicate must satisfy in order to propagate adornments. Consider the following rule, which is identical to the one considered previously except for the cost predicate, and the adornment uum (same as before).

$$p(X, Z, C) \leftarrow q(X, Y, C1), \; s(Y, Z, C2), \; C = C1 + (C2 \bmod 5).$$

However, in this case, the adornment cannot be propagated into the body predicate $s(Y, Z, C2)$ since the minimum value of $C2$ (as an integer) may not necessarily imply the minimum contribution of $(C2 \bmod 5)$ to C. However, the cost variable for the head is a non-decreasing monotonic function of the cost variable for the q-predicate and hence the adornment can be propagated into the q-predicate. The adorned rule for this case is

$$cp^{uum}(X, Z, C) \leftarrow q^{uum}(X, Y, C1), \; s(Y, Z, C2), \; C = C1 + (C2 \bmod 5).$$

This example shows that some body predicates may stay unadorned and are called unadornable predicates. All adornments to unadornable predicates resulting from the application of the previous rules are ignored.

Totality of the cost predicate in the body

We now consider the issue of totality of the cost predicate that is raised by the following example.

$$p(X, Z, C) \leftarrow q(X, Y, C1), \; s(Y, Z, C2), \; C = \log(C1 + C2 - 5).$$

Suppose that (as before) we wish to propagate the adornment uum into the body. In this case, however, it is not possible to propagate the adornment into any of the body predicates. Suppose that for a certain X, Y and Z, the minimum value for $C1$ is 2 and for $C2$ is 2. However, $C = \log(-1)$ is undefined. Hence, the adorned rule for this example is

$$cp^{uum}(X, Z, C) \leftarrow q(X, Y, C1), \; s(Y, Z, C2), \; C = \log(C1 + C2 - 5).$$

We formally define total mappings below.

Definition 3. *Let P be a min program with cost domain D_P and valid cost subdomain C_P. Let $f(X_1, \ldots, X_n)$ be an n-ary function on the cost domains. We say that the equality goal $Y = f(X_1, \ldots, X_n)$ defines a total monotonic mapping from X_i, $(1 \le i \le n)$ to Y when the following two conditions are satisfied:*

totality: *if $X_1, \ldots, X_n \in C_P$ then $f(X_1, \ldots, X_n) \in C_P$, and*
monotonicity: *if $X_1, \ldots X_n, U, V \in C_P$ and $V \le U$ then*
$$f(X_1, \ldots, X_{i-1}, V, X_{i+1}, \ldots, X_n) \le f(X_1, \ldots, X_{i-1}, U, X_{i+1}, \ldots, X_n) .$$ ∎

The rules for propagating adornments into the body of Horn rules are summarized below. We use the following running example:

Example 4.

$$cp^{uem}(X, Y, C) \leftarrow q(X, Z, N1, C1), \ r(Z, Y, N2, C2), \ s(Z, W, C3),$$
$$N1 = N2+1, \ C = C1+C2+(C3 \bmod 5).$$

where the last goal in the body of the rule define a total monotonic mapping from C1 and C2 ro C; the mapping from C3 to C is not monotonic. ∎

Propagation of adornments

Given a rule r with head predicate $p(\bar{X}, C)$, we denote with $B(r)$ the set of cost predicates in the body of r and with $TC(r)$ the set of cost predicates in $B(r)$ such that for each $q(\bar{Y}, C') \in B(r)$ there is a total-monotonic mapping from C' to C and C' is a variable not appearing in any other predicate in $B(r)$. In our example $TC(r) = \{q(X, Z, N1, C1), r(Z, Y, N2, C2)\}$ and $B(r) = TC(r) \cup \{s(Z, W, C3)\}$.

Given a variable X we denote with $\phi(X)$ the set of variables containing X plus all variables whose values depend on the value of X, i.e., all variables which are connected to X through some relational condition. For instance, in Example 4 we have $\phi(N1) = \{N1, N2\}$.

1. Predicates in $B(r) - TC(r)$ are adorned with the empty adornment ϵ. We call such predicates *non adorned predicates*.
2. Predicates in $TC(r)$ are adorned with the an adornment $\alpha \ne \epsilon$. We call such predicates *adorned predicates*. Each predicate $q(X_1, \ldots, X_n, C) \in TC(r)$, where C is the variable denoting the cost argument, is adorned as follows:
   (a) The cost argument C is labeled with m ($C1$ and $C2$ in Example 4);
   (b) Each variable labeled as u in the head is labeled as u in the body (X in Example 4).
   (c) Each variable X_i $(i \le 1 \le n)$ is labeled as u if there is a variable in $\phi(X_i)$ appearing in some other non built-in goal ($Z, N1$ and $N2$ in Example 4).
   (d) Each variable X_i $(i \le 1 \le n)$ which has not be labeled by m or u in steps $a - -c$ is labeled as e (This is the case of Y in Example 4.)

The adorned rule for the Example 4 is:

$$cp^{uem}(X, Y, C) \leftarrow q^{uuum}(X, Z, N1, C1), \ r^{ueum}(Z, Y, N2, C2), \ s(Z, W, C3),$$
$$N1 = N2+1, \ C = C1+C2+C3+(C3 \bmod 5).$$

Minima Definition of a predicate in terms of its surrogate predicate

Given a Horn clause with head predicate symbol p, the above rules generate the adorned version of each rule defining p, for a given adornment α. The adorned version of each rule defines a surrogate predicate cp^α. We complete the minima definition of p in terms of cp^α for the adornment α by introducing the following rule in the transformed program:

$$p^\alpha(X_1, ..., X_n) \leftarrow min(X_i, W, cp^\alpha(X_1, ..., X_n)).$$

where X_i is the cost argument and W is the set of variables adorned as u in α. The above rule is denoted by $mindef(p, cp^\alpha, \alpha)$ and is read as the minima definition of p in terms of cp^α as determined by the adornment α.

3.2 Propagating Adornments into Non-Horn rules

In this section, we discuss how to propagate an adornment into the body of a non-Horn rule.

Consider the following non-Horn rule.

$$p(X, Y, C) \leftarrow min(C, (X), q(X, Y, Z, C)).$$

The above rule may be rewritten as

$$p(X, Y, C) \leftarrow q^{ueem}(X, Y, Z, C).$$

where the definition of q^{ueem} is obtained using a surrogate predicate cq^{ueem} and the rules for propagation (see Section 3.1). Now suppose that the adornment for the head to be propagated is uem. Then, the adorned rule is

$$p^{uem}(X, Y, C) \leftarrow q^{ueem}(X, Y, Z, C).$$

This example shows that if all variables adorned as u in the body are also adorned as u in the head, then no change is made to the body. This further implies that if the adornment for the head is uum, then the body of the adorned rule remains unchanged, as follows:

$$p^{uum}(X, Y, C) \leftarrow q^{ueem}(X, Y, Z, C).$$

Indeed, while the adornment uum requires the minima for every value of X and Y, the body of the original rule, whose adornment is $ueem$, returns minima for X alone. Hence, Y is adorned as e in the body. If the adornment is eum, then the adorned rule is

$$p^{eum}(X, Y, C) \leftarrow q^{eeem}(X, Y, Z, C).$$

The rules for propagating an adornment α into a non-Horn rule

$$r : p(X_1, \ldots, X_n) \leftarrow min(Y_i, W, q(Y_1, \ldots, Y_n)).$$

are as follows:

1. First, the non-Horn rule is replaced by the following rule

$$p^\alpha(X_1, \ldots, X_n) \leftarrow q^\beta(Y_1, \ldots, Y_n).$$

   where β is the adornment corresponding to the min-predicate of the body.

2. Then, we construct the adornment γ for the body of the rule as follows: the variable Y_i denoting the cost-argument is labeled as m; a variable is labeled as e in γ if it is labeled as e in α or in β; the remaining variables are labeled as u^2. The adorned rule is

$$p^\alpha(X_1, \ldots, X_n) \leftarrow q^\gamma(Y_1, \ldots, Y_n).$$

3.3 Adorned definition of predicates

So far, we have discussed how to propagate an adornment for the head of a rule into the body to generate the adorned version of the rule.

For derived predicates, the *adorned definition* of a predicate p, for an adornment α, is the set of all rules defining the surrogate predicate cp^α and the minima definition of p in terms of cp^α for the adornment α.

If p is a base predicate, then the adorned definition of p w.r.t. the adornment α is the minima definition p in terms of p for the adornment α, i.e.,

$$p^\alpha(X_1, \ldots, X_n) \leftarrow min(X_i, W, p(X_1, \ldots, X_n)).$$

where X_i is the variable adorned as m in α and W is the set of variables adorned as u in α.

For sake of simplicity, we introduce the symbol ϵ, denoting the empty adornment. The minima definition of any predicate p in terms of another predicate q for ϵ is the empty set of rules. For propagating adornments from the head to the body of a rule, the adornment ϵ is considered as an abbreviation for the adornment that labels all variables (except the cost variable) by u and the cost variable by m.

We illustrate the adorned definition of predicates by the following example.

Example 5. Consider the program of Example 1. The adorned definition of the predicate **sh_path** *w.r.t. the adornment ϵ is:*

$$adorn\text{-}pred(\textbf{sh\_path}, \epsilon) = \{ \ \textbf{sh\_path}^\epsilon(\textbf{X}, \textbf{Y}, \textbf{C}) \leftarrow \textbf{path}^{\textbf{uum}}(\textbf{X}, \textbf{Y}, \textbf{C}). \ \}$$

Thus the adorned definition of the predicate **path** *appearing in the program with the adornment uum is*

$$adorn\text{-}pred(\textbf{path}, uum) = \left\{ \begin{array}{l} \textbf{cpath}^{\textbf{uum}}(\textbf{X}, \textbf{Y}, \textbf{C}) \leftarrow \textbf{arc}^{\textbf{uum}}(\textbf{X}, \textbf{Y}, \textbf{C}). \\ \textbf{cpath}^{\textbf{uum}}(\textbf{X}, \textbf{Y}, \textbf{C}) \leftarrow \textbf{path}^{\textbf{uum}}(\textbf{X}, \textbf{Z}, \textbf{C1}), \textbf{arc}^{\textbf{uum}}(\textbf{Z}, \textbf{Y}, \textbf{C2}), \\ \qquad\qquad\qquad \textbf{C} = \textbf{C1}+\textbf{C2}. \\ \textbf{path}^{\textbf{uum}}(\textbf{X}, \textbf{Y}, \textbf{C}) \leftarrow min(\textbf{C}, (\textbf{X}, \textbf{Y}), \textbf{cpath}^{\textbf{uum}}(\textbf{X}, \textbf{Y}, \textbf{C})). \end{array} \right\}$$

---

[2] We assume that there are not repeating variables in the head or in the body of canonical non-Horn rules

whereas the adorned definition of the predicate **arc** *appearing in the program with the adornment uum is*

$$adorn\text{-}pred(\mathbf{arc}, uum) = \{ \ \mathbf{arc}^{uum}(\mathbf{X}, \mathbf{Y}, \mathbf{C}) \leftarrow \min(\mathbf{C}, (\mathbf{X}, \mathbf{Y}), \mathbf{arc}(\mathbf{X}, \mathbf{Y}, \mathbf{C})).\} \quad \blacksquare$$

We now formally define the adorned definition of a predicate p, w.r.t. a given adornment α. In order to do so, we use the following terminology.

1. *adorn-rule*(r, α) is the adorned rule obtained by propagating the adornment α for the head of r into the body of r.
2. *mindef*(p, q, α) denotes the rule that defines p as the minima of q for the adornment α.

The adorned definition of a predicate p w.r.t. an adornment α, denoted by *adorn-pred*(p, α) is equal to

- *mindef*(p, p, α), if p is a base predicate
- $\{adorn\text{-}rule(r, \alpha) \mid r$ defines $p\} \cup \{mindef(p, cp^{\alpha}, \alpha)\}$, otherwise.

3.4 Algorithm for Adorning a Program

In this section, we discuss an algorithm that generates an adorned program from a given min-program and a query predicate.

The algorithm begins by generating the adorned definition of the query predicate, whose symbol we assume to be q. This may generate new adorned predicate symbols. The adorned definitions of these predicate symbols are (recursively) included in the adorned program until no new adorned predicate symbol remains.

General min-programs may have predicates without cost arguments, or predicates whose cost arguments are either non-monotonic or are not total. These predicates may not yield any adorned definitions during the propagation algorithm. Hence, the definition of such predicates must be included in the adorned program.

A simple way of achieving this is to initiate the adornment propagation algorithm with the query predicate symbol q and the adornment ϵ. After all adorned definitions are generated, the set of rules reachable from q^{ϵ} form the adorned program. Finally, in the adorned program, all occurrences of q^{ϵ} are replaced by q. We illustrate the algorithm by means of the following example.

Example 6. Consider the following program P, reproduced from Example 1.

$$\mathbf{sh\_path}(\mathbf{X}, \mathbf{Y}, \mathbf{C}) \leftarrow \min(\mathbf{C}, (\mathbf{X}, \mathbf{Y}), \mathbf{path}(\mathbf{X}, \mathbf{Y}, \mathbf{C})).$$

$$\mathbf{path}(\mathbf{X}, \mathbf{Y}, \mathbf{C}) \leftarrow \mathbf{arc}(\mathbf{X}, \mathbf{Y}, \mathbf{C}).$$
$$\mathbf{path}(\mathbf{X}, \mathbf{Y}, \mathbf{C}) \leftarrow \mathbf{path}(\mathbf{X}, \mathbf{Z}, \mathbf{C1}), \mathbf{arc}(\mathbf{Z}, \mathbf{Y}, \mathbf{C2}),$$
$$\mathbf{path}(\mathbf{X}, \mathbf{Y}, \mathbf{C}) \leftarrow \mathbf{C} = \mathbf{C1} + \mathbf{C2}.$$

Suppose that the query predicate symbol is **sh_path**. We begin the propagation algorithm with the adornment ϵ for **sh_path**. By propagating the adornment ϵ

into the only rule that defines **sh_path**, we obtain the following rule, which is included in P.

$$\text{sh\_path}^{\epsilon}(X, Y, C) \leftarrow \text{path}^{\text{uum}}(X, Y, C).$$

However, a new adorned predicate symbol **path^{uum}** is obtained. Hence, we now include the adorned definition of **path^{uum}** into P, which is as follows.

$$\text{cpath}^{\text{uum}}(X, Y, C) \leftarrow \text{path}^{\text{uum}}(X, Z, C1), \text{arc}^{\text{uum}}(Z, Y, C2), C = C1 + C2.$$
$$\text{cpath}^{\text{uum}}(X, Y, C) \leftarrow \text{arc}^{\text{uum}}(X, Y, C).$$
$$\text{path}^{\text{uum}}(X, Y, C) \leftarrow \min(C, (X, Y), \text{cpath}^{\text{uum}}(X, Y, C)).$$

A new adorned symbol **arc^{uum}** is generated, whose adorned definition is included in P.

$$\text{arc}^{\text{uum}}(X, Y, C) \leftarrow \min(C, (X, Y), \text{arc}(X, Y, C)).$$

We now obtain the set of rules in P that are reachable from **sh_path$^{\epsilon}$**, which is listed below.

$$\text{sh\_path}^{\epsilon}(X, Y, C) \leftarrow \text{path}^{\text{uum}}(X, Y, C).$$

$$\text{cpath}^{\text{uum}}(X, Y, C) \leftarrow \text{path}^{\text{uum}}(X, Z, C1), \text{arc}^{\text{uum}}(Z, Y, C2), C = C1 + C2.$$
$$\text{cpath}^{\text{uum}}(X, Y, C) \leftarrow \text{arc}^{\text{uum}}(X, Y, C).$$

$$\text{path}^{\text{uum}}(X, Y, C) \leftarrow \min(C, (X, Y), \text{cpath}^{\text{uum}}(X, Y, C)).$$

$$\text{arc}^{\text{uum}}(X, Y, C) \leftarrow \min(C, (X, Y), \text{arc}(X, Y, C)).$$

Thus, the original rules which are not reachable from **sh_path$^{\epsilon}$** are not included in the adorned program. The final adorned program is obtained by replacing **sh_path$^{\epsilon}$** in the above program by **sh_path**. ∎

The algorithm which propagates min predicates is reported in Figure 1 where the variables S and T contain, respectively, the set of predicate symbols to be adorned and the set of predicate symbols already adorned; $body(r)$ denotes the set of atoms in the body of a rule r.

3.5 Query Equivalence of Original and Adorned Programs

In this section, we characterize the query equivalence between the given program and the adorned program obtained as the output of Algorithm 1.

Note that Algorithm 1 includes the adorned definition of predicates into a given program P at each iteration. Hence, until termination, there is at least one adorned predicate symbol in P which is not defined in P, making it "incomplete". In order to prove the equivalence of the adorned program and the original program, we begin by completing the definition of such incomplete programs.

The *adorn-completion(P)*, for a given set of rules P, is P union with $mindef(p, p, \alpha)$, for every p^{α} which appears in the body of some rule in P but is undefined in P, that is, for each undefined n-ary predicate symbol p^{α} a rule of the form

Algorithm 1. *Propagation of Min Predicates*
Input: Min program P and a goal $q(t)$.
Output: Adorned min program;
var $S, T, new\text{-}pred$: set of predicate symbols;
      p : predicate symbol;
      α: adornment;
begin
      $S := \{q^\epsilon\}$; $T := \emptyset$;
      while $S \neq \emptyset$ **do**
            Choose an arbitrary predicate $p^\alpha \in S$;
            Include $adorn\text{-}pred(p, \alpha)$ in P;
            $new\text{-}pred = \{p^\alpha \mid p^\alpha \in body(r)$ for rule $r \in adorn\text{-}pred(p, \alpha)\} - T$;
            $S := S \cup new\text{-}pred$;
            $S := S - \{p^\alpha\}$; $T := T \cup \{p^\alpha\}$;
      end while
      $Q :=$ set of rules reachable from q^ϵ;
      return Q after replacing q^ϵ in Q by q;
end.

— **Figure 1.** *Propagation of Min Predicates* —

$$p^\alpha(X_1, ..., X_n) \leftarrow min(X_i, W, p(X_1, ..., X_n))$$

where X_i is the cost argument and W is the set of variables adorned as u in α is added to *adorn-completion*(P).

Lemma 1. *Let P be a set of rules with query predicate symbol q and a predicate symbol p reachable from q. Let $Q = P \cup adorn\text{-}pred(p, \alpha)$. Then*

$$adorn\text{-}completion(P) \equiv_q adorn\text{-}completion(Q)$$

Proof. Follows from the construction of the adorned rules.   ■

The following lemma discusses the special case when the adornment for propagation is ϵ.

Lemma 2. *Let P be a set of rules with query predicate symbol q. Let Q be the set of rules obtained by determining the set of rules in $P \cup adorn\text{-}pred(q, \epsilon)$ that are reachable from q^ϵ, and then replacing q^ϵ by q. Then*

$$adorn\text{-}completion(P) \equiv_q adorn\text{-}completion(Q)$$

Proof. Follows from the conventions for the ϵ adornment and the construction of adorned rules.   ■

Essentially, Lemma 2 states that query equivalence is preserved at the first iteration step of Algorithm 1 and Lemma 1 states that query equivalence is preserved at each subsequent iteration step of Algorithm 1. The following theorem formally states the query equivalence of the original and the adorned program.

Theorem 1. *Let* $Q_1 = \langle q, P_1 \rangle$ *be an aggregate stratified query and let* $Q_2 = \langle q^{\epsilon}, P_2 \rangle$ *be the query generated by Algorithm 1, then*

1. $foe(P_2)$ has a total well-founded model, and
2. $Q_1 \equiv Q_2$ under the well-founded semantics. ∎

Observe that $foe(P_1)$ in the above theorem is stratified and its perfect model coincide with the (total) well-founded model and with the unique total stable model. Moreover, $foe(P_2)$ has a total well-founded model which coincide with its unique total stable model. In the following example we present the completion of the adorned program at the various steps.

Example 7. Consider the program of Example 1 and the query $sh\_path(X, Y, C)$. In the first step the program P_1 consists of the rules in P plus the adorned rule;

$r_1 : \quad \text{sh\_path}^{\epsilon}(\text{X}, \text{Y}, \text{C}) \leftarrow \text{path}^{\text{uum}}(\text{X}, \text{Y}, \text{C}).$

In the adorn-completion of P_1 consists of P_1 plus the rule

$$path^{uum}(X, Y, C) \leftarrow min(C, (X, Y), path(X, Y, C)).$$

At the nest step, the algorithm generates the program P_2 (*adorn-completion*(P_1)) obtained by adding to P_1 the rules

$r_2 : \quad \text{cpath}^{\text{uum}}(\text{X}, \text{Y}, \text{C}) \leftarrow \text{arc}^{\text{uum}}(\text{X}, \text{Y}, \text{C}).$
$r_3 : \quad \text{cpath}^{\text{uum}}(\text{X}, \text{Y}, \text{C}) \leftarrow \text{path}^{\text{uum}}(\text{X}, \text{Z}, \text{C1}), \text{arc}^{\text{uum}}(\text{Z}, \text{Y}, \text{C2}), \text{C} = \text{C1}+\text{C2}.$
$r_4 : \quad \text{path}^{\text{uum}}(\text{X}, \text{Y}, \text{C}) \leftarrow \text{min}(\text{C}, (\text{X}, \text{Y}), \text{cpath}^{\text{uum}}(\text{X}, \text{Y}, \text{C})).$

The program *adorn* − *completion*(P_2) is obtained by adding to P_2 the rules

$$arc^{uum}(X, Y, C) \leftarrow min(C, (X, Y), arc(X, Y, C)).$$

At the third and final step, the algorithm generates the new program P_3 by adding to P_2 the rule

$r_5 : \quad \text{arc}^{\text{uum}}(\text{X}, \text{Y}, \text{C}) \leftarrow \text{min}(\text{C}, (\text{X}, \text{Y}), \text{arc}(\text{X}, \text{Y}, \text{C})).$

The adorn-completion of P_3 coincides with P_3 since all adorned predicates are defined. Observe that at each step the queries $(\text{sh-path}^{\epsilon}(\text{X}, \text{Y}, \text{C}), P_i)$ and $(\text{sh-path}(\text{X}, \text{Y}, \text{C}), P)$ are equivalent. ∎

4 Conclusion

In this paper, we have presented techniques for the propagation of extrema predicates into recursive logic programs. The main contribution consists of a precise algorithm for the propagation of *min* and *max* predicates into logic programs. The propagation of such meta-level predicates permits the efficient computation, by using a variation of the seminaive fixpoint, called seminaive greedy fixpoint [5], of logic programs with *min* and *max* predicates. In [5] it has been shown that the computation of the single source shortest path program of Example 1, after the propagation of the *min* predicates, has the same complexity of the celebrated Dijkstra's algorithm. The technique presented in the paper can be also extended to programs presenting different forms of monotonicity such as XY-stratification [22] and modular stratification [13].

References

1. K. Apt, H. Blair, and A. Walker. Towards a theory of declarative programming. In (*Foundations of Deductive Databases and Logic Programming* (Minker, ed.), 1988.
2. M.P. Consens and A.O. Mendelzon. Low complexity aggregation in graphlog and Datalog. Theoretical Computer Science, 1993.
3. S. W. Dietrich. Shortest Path by Approximation in Logic Programs. *ACM Letters on Programming Languages and Systems* Vol 1, No, 2, pages 119–137, June 1992,.
4. S. J. Finkelstein, N. Mattos, I.S. Mumick and H. Pirahesh. Expressing Recursive Queries in SQL. *ISO - IEC JTC1/SC21 WG3 DBL MCI Tec. Rep.*, March, 1996.
5. S. Ganguly, S. Greco, and C. Zaniolo. Extrema predicates in deductive databases. *J. Computer and System Science*, 1995.
6. M. Gelfond and V. Lifschitz. The stable model semantics of logic programming. In *Proc. of the Fifth Intern. Conf. on Logic Programming*, pages 1070–1080, 1988.
7. S. Greco, S. Ganguly, and C. Zaniolo. Greedy by Choice. *Proc. Eleventh ACM PODS Conf.*, pages 109–118, 1991.
8. S. Greco, D. Saccà, and C. Zaniolo. Dynamic Programming optimization for Logic Programs with Aggregates. *Proc. Int. Logic Progr. Symp.*, pages 109–118, 1993.
9. D. Kemp and P. Stuckey. Semantics of Logic Programs with Aggregates. In *Proc. of the 1991 Intern. Symposium on Logic Programming*, pages 387–341, 1991.
10. I.S. Mumick, H. Pirahesh, and R. Ramakrishnan. The magic of duplicates and aggregates. In *Proc. 16th Conf. on Very Large Data Bases*, pages 264–277, 1990.
11. I.S. Mumick, and O. Shmueli. How Expressive is Stratified Aggregation. In *Annals of Mathematics and Artificial Intelligence*, 1995.
12. H. Przymusinska and T.C. Przymusinski. Weakly perfect model semantics for logic programs. In *Proc. Fifth Intern. Conf. on Logic Progr.*, pages 1106–1120, 1988.
13. K. Ross. A Procedural Semantics for the Well-Founded Negation in Logic Programs. In *Proc. ACM Symp. on Principles of Database Systems*, pages 22-33, 1989.
14. K. Ross and Y. Sagiv. Monotonic Aggregation in Deductive Databases. *Proc. Eleventh ACM PODS Conf.*, 1992.
15. D. Saccà and C. Zaniolo. Stable models and non-determinism in logic programs with negation. In *Proc. of the Ninth ACM PODS Conf.*, pages 205–217, 1990.
16. S. Sudarshan and R. Ramakrishnan. Aggregation and relevance in deductive databases. In *Proc. of the 17th Conf. on Very Large Data Bases*, 1991.
17. R. Ramakrishnan, D. Srivastava, and S. Sudarshan. CORAL: Control, Relations and Logic. In *Proc. of Intl. Conf. on Very Large Data Bases*, 1992.
18. S. Sudarshan, D. Srivastava, R. Ramakrishnan and C. Beeri, Extending Well-Founded and Valid Semantics for Aggregation, In *Proc. of the Int. Logic Programming Symposium*, pages 591-608, 1992.
19. J. Ullman. *Principles of Data and Knowledge-Base Systems*, volume 1 and 2. Computer Science Press, New York, 1988.
20. A. Van Gelder, K.A. Ross, and J.S. Schlipf. The well-founded semantics for general logic programs. *Journal of ACM*, 38(3):620–650, 1991.
21. A. Van Gelder. Foundation of Aggregation in Deductive Databases In *Proceedings of the Third Int. Conf. on Deductive and O-O Databases*, Phoenix, AZ, 1993.
22. C. Zaniolo, N. Arni, and K. Ong. Negation and aggregates in recursive rules: the LDL++ approach, In *Proc. Int. Conf. od Deductive and Object Oriented Databases*, pp. 204-221, 1993.

Searching for General Documents

Kai Korpimies and Esko Ukkonen

Department of Computer Science, PO BOX 26 FIN-00014 University of Helsinki,
Finland.
Kai.Korpimies@cs.helsinki.fi
Esko.Ukkonen@cs.helsinki.fi

Abstract. Search agents provide effective means to find information in
the World-Wide Web based on user-submitted queries. As more and more
information becomes available and queries therefore should be more precise, there's a growing need for navigational tools. This paper introduces
a new relevance measure called *contextual relevance* which is based on
an analysis of term occurrence frequency in documents matching a user-
submitted query. We suggest this measure could be used to focus queries
into those documents which most generally describe the contents of the
matching documents.

1 Introduction and Motivation

Search agents in the World-Wide Web provide references to documents which
satisfy queries written in some specific query language. Typically the query
operands are terms, while the operations may include for instance the Boolean
ones. Sometimes it's also possible to indicate the relative importance of each
query operand with weights. Together with a reference, the agents usually return information on the degree of the referred document's relevance to the query.
This relevance is determined by a term-based comparison of the query and the
agent's document index. The comparison may also take into account the semantic relationships between terms based on some statistical analysis of term
co-occurrences (such as *Latent Semantic Indexing*; see [1]) or manually compiled
thesauri.

If the user's information needs are focused into a sufficiently abstract or
general topic, the query formulation is not always easy. The search agent requires
the topic to be described with a small number of characteristical terms; if general
terms are used, the precision of the retrieval may suffer. The user may not know
the subject and even if he is able to use specific terms, which have relatively
large indexing value and describe some easily recognisable aspects of the more
general topic, the agent finds the documents focusing into these specific aspects
most relevant and the user may still have to browse through the possibly very
long ranked list of references in order to arrive at the documents which satisfy
his more general information needs.

As an example, suppose a user is looking for a document with a general introduction to *information retrieval*. A simple query with the phrase "information

retrieval" may return a large amount of references to documents which describe some specific aspects of information retrieval, or research projects on information retrieval, or some more or less unrelated topic. The documents, which give a general account of the different information retrieval -related things are not necessarily found most relevant by the search agent. The documents are instead scored based on the number of occurrences of the phrase "information retrieval".

Simple keyword search is not enough: if a term is found in a document, it does not follow that the document would give general information about the subject. One might also argue that this problem is especially relevant in the very rich and heterogeneous environment of the World-Wide Web with its millions of personal homepages, lists and hypertext links (see also [2]). A global analysis of semantic term relations such as Latent Semantic Analysis suffers from problems linked to term *polysemy*: terms may have different meanings in different contexts. In query-based information retrieval one obvious context calling for special analysis is the set of documents satisfying the query, for example, the documents containing the phrase "information retrieval". A question we try to answer is: how can we find the documents which most *generally* correspond to the contents of the documents which match a given query? A document is general in respect to a query if its contents are shared by many of the matching documents. Thus we suggest a navigational process which combines querying and a term occurrence frequency -based analysis of the results.

The paper is organized as follows: in Sect. 2, we present an intuitive illustration of *contextual relevance* for terms and documents and discuss its relation to relevance feedback. Contextual document relevance is a measure for the generality of the document in respect to a query. The formal definitions and an algorithm for contextual document relevance assessment follow in Sect. 3. A small experiment on document generality is described in Sect. 4. In Sect. 5 we pose the question whether contextual relevance could be useful also in cluster-based navigation.

2 An Illustration

Intuitively, what we have in mind is illustrated in Fig. 1 where documents $D_1, \ldots, D_4$ matching a query Q are represented as sets of terms. We argue that the terms in the intersection of the four sets are likely to describe the *shared or general topics* of the documents better than the other terms, especially if they are rare in the documents which do not match the query Q (in which case they may also indicate well the relevance of documents to the query). We call these terms *contextually relevant* to query Q. We also argue that the terms found only in a small subset of the matching documents are more likely to specify the shared or general contents of the corresponding documents into some more or less narrow direction of their own.

Clearly the document D_3 is best characterised by the contextually relevant terms because it contains all of them, unlike the three others. We argue that it is likely to describe the general aspects shared by the four documents. Hence document D_3 should get the highest value of contextual relevance to query Q.

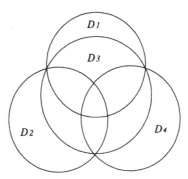

Fig. 1. Intuitive contextual relevance

As a more concrete example, suppose a user wants to know what *acid rain* is, that is, he is looking for a general document on the subject. If he submitted a simple query with the phrase "acid rain", and the search agent used simple keyword matching, the retrieved documents would have at least one phrase in common, namely "acid rain". In the World-Wide Web, at the time of writing, their number would be counted in tens of thousands and they would form a very heterogeneous group. There would be a number of documents describing *the chemical substances and reactions* linked to the phenomenon (like sulfurs for example), other documents describing the causes for acid rain like traffic, factories and volcanoes. There would also be documents describing the *effects* on plants, soil and lakes and documents telling about the *remedies* like liming etc. These topics are bound to be touched in a large number of acid rain documents while less general topics such as some individual research projects or situations in some distinct geographical areas are not likely to be discussed so extensively. Linked with each topic, there are a number of keywords such as the ones mentioned earlier: *sulfurs, traffic, factories, volcanoes, plants, soil, lakes, liming.* Some of these terms co-occur frequently with the phrase "acid rain" while others are frequent in the whole collection of documents. The former are especially good to indicate that the topic is linked with acid rain and should be mentioned in a general document describing the chemical reactions, the causes and effects and remedies of acid rain. We made a small experiment with acid rain documents with rather encouraging results described in Sect. 4.

An assessment procedure for contextual document relevance is sketched in Fig. 2. Based on a query Q a set R of matching documents is identified together with a set Q' of contextually relevant terms (arrows 1 and 2). The next step (arrow 3) is to arrive at the set R' of the contextually relevant documents by studying the occurrences of the terms in the set Q'. Finally the references are given to the user in the order of contextual relevance.

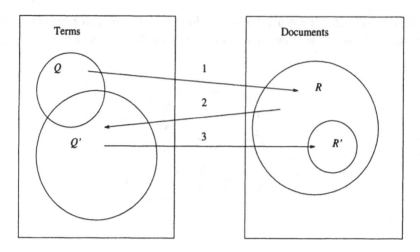

Fig. 2. Assessing contextual relevance

It is essential to note that the procedure above is rather general in that the set R can be identified in various ways using different query languages and evaluation schemes. Possibilities include *Vector Space Model, Boolean operations* (see e.g. [5]) and the *Probabilistic Model* (see e.g. [6]). After this first phase, the analysis as presented here is based on the Vector Space Model.

Our general approach is related to some aspects of *automatic relevance feedback*, but there are also fundamental differences. We are interested in automatically identifying the documents which generally describe a more or less broad topic defined in the query. That is, we make the assumption that the most general documents on the topic satisfy the *information needs* of the user. This would serve users with not much prior knowledge about the search topic in a rich and heterogeneous environment such as the World-Wide Web. In automatic relevance feedback, on the other hand, the queries are redirected based on user interaction, possibly outside the set R of retrieved documents: the intuitive relevance of the retrieved documents is assessed by the user based on his information needs, whatever they may be, and a set of good keywords is automatically identified from the chosen documents. A new query is formed with these keywords (see e.g. [5] and [4]). In our approach, the contextual term relevance is based on the documents in R without user interaction in Steps 2 and 3. Because the set R is of central importance to us, we take also the degree to which each document satisfies the query Q into account. In automatic relevance feedback this is of secondary importance.

3 Contextual Relevance

In a more rigorous analysis we have to take into account the different weights terms have in the documents matching the query and in the rest of the collection, together with the degrees to which the documents satisfy the query. Let us begin by introducing some basic notation to be used here.

3.1 Notation and the Vector Space Model

Using Vector Space Model, both the query Q and all documents D_i in the collection of n documents $D_1, \ldots, D_n$ are seen as *term vectors* with *term weights*. That is, $Q = (q_1, \ldots, q_t)$ and each $D_i = (w_{i1}, w_{i2}, \ldots, w_{it})$ where t is the total number of terms. The weight w_{ij} is often defined to be the frequency of occurrence of the term t_j in the document D_i while the weights q_i may be given by the user to indicate the relative importance of the terms.

The *relevance* of a document D_i to a query Q, $rel(Q, D_i)$, is based on the similarity between the query and document vectors. Let us define $rel(Q, D_i) \in [0, 1]$ for all documents D_i and queries Q. It is important to notice that this doesn't here refer to the more *intuitive or subjective relevance* which measures how well a document satisfies the *information needs* of the user.

One commonly used measure for the similarity between the query and document vectors is the *Cosine coefficient* (see e.g. [5]):

$$rel(Q, D_i) = \frac{\sum_{j=1}^{t} w_{ij} q_j}{\sqrt{\sum_{j=1}^{t} w_{ij}^2 \sum_{j=1}^{t} q_j^2}} \tag{1}$$

3.2 Contextual Term Relevance

Using the notation introduced in the previous section, the evidence for the contextual relevance of a term t_j to query Q can be considered to be

$$\sum_{i=1}^{n} w_{ij} rel(Q, D_i) \tag{2}$$

To arrive at the contextual relevance measure of Definition 1, we have to normalise the evidence by taking the document frequency df of the terms into account, which we here interpret to be the collection-wide sum of term weights.

$$df_j = \sum_{i=1}^{n} w_{ij} \tag{3}$$

Definition 1. (contextual term relevance)

$$crel(Q, t_j) = \frac{\sum_{i=1}^{n} w_{ij} rel(Q, D_i)}{\sum_{i=1}^{n} w_{ij}} \tag{4}$$

If a term t_j is found in sufficiently many documents, it's considered to be a *'stop word'* with little or no indexing value (see e.g. [5]). The contextual relevance of these terms is small according to Definition 1.

If the query language used in the original query for example allows Boolean operations and Q is an AND-statement, the operand terms are likely to be contextually relevant as they are found in all of the documents which match Q, but this depends on their frequency in the whole collection. Given a query $Q : t_r$ AND t_s, and supposing that the frequency of occurrence of both t_r and t_s in the documents which match the query is equal, it follows: $crel(Q, t_r) > crel(Q, t_s)$ iff $\sum_{i=1}^{n} w_{it_r} < \sum_{i=1}^{n} w_{it_s}$.

3.3 Contextual Document Relevance

First we present a procedure for contextual document relevance assessment implementing the intuitive procedure presented in Sect. 2. After that, we briefly consider the possibilities for query expansion and the need for document clustering.

A Procedure for Assessing the Contextual Document Relevance. Given the following:

- A *term-document matrix* W where documents $D_1, \ldots, D_n$ are represented as rows $D_i = (w_{i1}, \ldots, w_{it})$ of weights w_{ij} indicating the weight of term t_j in document D_i
- A threshold value α
- To improve efficiency, the sums of weights for all terms $t_1, \ldots, t_t$ in the whole collection obtained from the term-document matrix W

1. The user submits a query Q
2. $rel(Q, D_i)$ is assessed for each document $D_1, \ldots, D_n$
3. The contextual relevance $crel(Q, t_j)$ is assessed according to Definition 1 for all terms t_j appearing in the documents D_i for which $rel(Q, D_i) > \alpha$
4. The contextual relevance $crel(Q, D_i)$ is assessed according to Definition 2 (below) for each document D_i for which $rel(Q, D_i) > \alpha$
5. A list of document references ranked in the order of contextual relevance is given to the user

In Step 4 the task is to find the documents best characterised by the contextually relevant terms. The contextual relevance of all terms $t_1, \ldots, t_t$ can be seen as a vector $(crel(Q, t_1), crel(Q, t_2), \ldots, crel(Q, t_t))$ which suggests a similarity measure like the commonly used Cosine coefficient (see Sect. 3.1) to calculate the similarity between this vector and the vectors representing the documents which match the query Q.

The Cosine coefficient is normalised. Here one has to ask what are general documents like: is a document likely to be less general if it uses also contextually less relevant vocabulary *in addition* to the contextually relevant terms? We decided against this and used the unnormalised inner product of the vectors.

The inner product relies on term weights in documents and the degrees of contextual term relevance. It is debatable, whether we should use threshold values to make either both vectors or one of them binary. Intuitively, a general document has to touch many topics linked to the subject of the query and it is not enough that it describes in detail a single topic with much contextual relevance (like *liming* as a means of *desulphurisation* in our *acid rain* -experiment described in Sect. 4). On the other hand, the topics have to be closely related to the subject, which would suggest the use of non-binary vectors. Our acid rain -experiment demonstrated that the clearly poorest measure for the intuitive document generality was the inner product of non-binary vectors: it couldn't be used to identify the general documents. The peak performance for the inner product of binary vectors was good as the contextual relevance of general documents was 386 % of that of the non-general documents. This, however, depended largely on the choice of the threshold value used in the binarizing of the contextual term relevance vector. Using binary document vectors and non-binary contextual term relevance vector as in Definition 2 provided the best results.

Definition 2. (contextual document relevance)

$$crel(Q, D_i) = \sum_{j=1}^{t} crel(Q, t_j) w'_{ij} \tag{5}$$

where $w'_{ij} = 1$ if $w_{ij} > 0$, otherwise $w'_{ij} = 0$

Efficiency. After the initial document retrieval (Steps 1 and 2 or the first arrow in Fig. 2), Steps 3 and 4 have running time O(NT) where N is the number of documents for which $rel(Q, D_i) > \alpha$ while T is the number of terms in these documents. As discussed before, and demonstrated in Sect. 4, another threshold value could also be considered in Step 4: contextual document relevance could be assessed with only those terms which are contextually relevant enough. While this is quite necessary with the binary inner product, it also seemed to very slightly improve the results arrived at with Definition 2.

Contextual Relevance of Other Documents. As suggested above, contextual relevance can be used to identify the general documents from the set of documents R which match the query Q. However, it is essential to note that the contextual relevance can be assessed for a potentially large number of other documents as well. Contextual relevance is defined and can be evaluated for all terms occurring in at least one retrieved document, not only for terms that are found in, say, all of the retrieved documents. Therefore, the set of documents with some degree of contextual relevance is likely to be much larger and at least as large as the set of documents with some relevance to the original query. If the process is iterated until the contextual relevance of the documents converges (the contextual term relevance is assessed based on contextually relevant documents and so forth), the contextual relevance can be assessed for all documents which have directly or indirectly some common terms with the documents relevant to the original query.

Need for Clustering. As the documents which are most "average" in the context defined by the query are found contextually most relevant, the approach as defined above does not necessarily give good results in a situation, where the retrieved documents form clusters different enough from each other. Consider for example two document clusters with no or very few terms in common or a large document cluster overshadowing a smaller one. A solution is to analyse the contexts corresponding to these clusters separately.

4 Experimental Results

The large-scale experimental testing of the above scheme is under way. Meanwhile, we conducted a preliminary experiment on contextual term and document relevance with a search agent in the World-Wide Web. We supposed a user wished to have general information on acid rain: an introduction to the phenomenon with its causes, effects and remedies explained (see also Sect. 2). A straight-forward query with the phrase "acid rain" produced about 30 000 references to WWW-pages with clearly no general accounts amongst the documents on top of the ranked list.

Next we picked up from the retrieved documents a number of terms in a random manner. In Table 1 are some of the terms, the number of documents using them as given by the search agent (second column) and the frequences of their co-occurrence with the phrase "acid rain" (third column, titled freq. in R). The table is sorted according to the last column which gives the frequency of each term t_j in acid rain documents divided by their overall frequency. These $rf(Q, t_j)$ values approximate the contextual term relevance values $crel(Q, t_j)$ of Definition 1. The table shows only the very top of the term list: terms which scored lower than 0.0121 were excluded from the table. The terms with the lowest scores weren't particularly closely associated with acid rain: *name, information, auto, title, comments* etc.

The next step was to assess the contextual relevance of a number of documents randomly chosen from the top part of the ranking list the search agent had provided, together with some documents giving a general overview of acid rain (an introduction to the phenomenon with an explanation of causes and effects). Our sample of the general documents was small, seven pieces. The average size of the non-general documents was about 20 KB while that of the general documents was about 12 KB. The results are in Table 2. The columns titled term % give the average number of terms t_j with $rf(Q, t_j)$ above the threshold for both the general and non-general documents expressed as the percentage of all terms studied. This corresponds to the binary inner product discussed in Sect. 3. The columns titled $rf(Q, t_j)sum$ show the average rf-sums for terms above the

Table 1. The contextually most relevant terms as found through approximation

t_j	freq. of t_j	freq. in R	$rf(Q, t_j)$
desulphurisation	792	59	0.0745
unpolluted	4535	167	0.0368
sulfur	166750	5842	0.0350
leached	7432	206	0.0277
liming	10480	195	0.0186
ecosystems	222315	4072	0.0183
carbonic	14600	263	0.0180
ozone	531901	8837	0.0166
plankton	35139	534	0.0152
nitrates	28197	411	0.0146
pollution	1074227	15544	0.0145
emissions	637753	8732	0.0137
erosion	287380	3864	0.0134
forests	517886	6530	0.0126
pollutant	97965	1213	0.0124
ecological	446326	5422	0.0121
atmospheric	541195	6574	0.0121

threshold found in each group of documents. This corresponds to the inner product of binary document and non-binary contextual term relevance vectors (the latter approximated with the rf-values). We also experimented with non-binary document vectors, but the results were poor, partly explained by the fact that we didn't take document length into account for the reasons explained in Sect. 3. Fig. 3 illustrates how many percents better did the general documents score with different threshold values using these two measures.

Table 2. Contextually relevant terms in the test documents

threshold	term % non-general	general	%	$rf(Q, t_j)sum$ non-general	general	%
0.0003	14.8	35.0	236	0.07	0.24	355
0.0015	7.9	26.9	342	0.06	0.23	379
0.0050	4.0	15.4	386	0.05	0.20	393
0.0100	2.8	9.0	327	0.04	0.15	365

The standard deviations of the rf-sums were 0.05 for both the general and non-general documents using threshold 0.005. The non-general documents with consistently best scores listed on one hand acid rain -related hypertext links and on the other hand described legislation connected with pollution and acid rain.

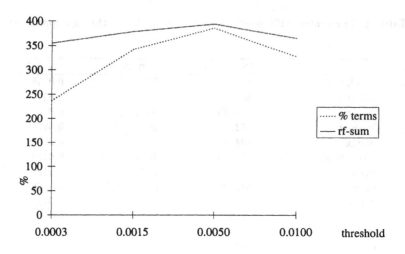

Fig. 3. Identifying general documents with threshold values

In all, based on our limited experiment, it seems that with the binary inner product there was a fall after a steady increase. This seems quite consistent with the experimental research done in the field of relevance feedback (see [4]). The rf-sum didn't depend so much on the threshold choice and provided in our experiment consistently better results. Furthermore, it seems likely that the threshold value giving the optimal performance for the binary inner product depends on the query and the collection (compare with [4]).

5 Further Research

As discussed in Sect. 3, the approach would in some cases benefit from clustering. In query-based IR, clustering can be used to suggest some possibilities for query re-directing to the user. This kind of clustering can be directed at terms or documents and it can be global or based primarily on the documents retrieved by a query. While the global clustering has been researched more extensively, also the latter approach has been demonstrated effective in [3]: with a technique called *Scatter/Gather* the user could navigate by choosing some of the clusters found from amongst the documents retrieved by a query. All clustering algorithms require some kind of a distance or similarity measure which usually depends on term or phrase co-occurrences (see e.g. [7] and [2]), possibly corrected with some collection-wide or global semantic analysis. Based on this, objects (e.g. documents) resembling each other are clustered together.

Clustering could be seen complimentary to the introduced approach which can be used to focus the query into the most general documents among the retrieved ones. This raises the question whether there are other connections between the two approaches. In IR, the clustering algorithms are typically used with a set of objects: an object either belongs to the set or it doesn't. It can be argued, that if the starting point for clustering is a query, document clustering should take into account the degree to which each retrieved document satisfies the query ($rel(Q, D_i)$ for each retrieved document D_i). One way to accomplish this is to use the contextual term relevance values in the document similarity measure. Assuming that the contextually less relevant terms are likely to specify the general or shared contents of the retrieved documents into their own directions, one can argue, that the presence of such terms in more than one of the retrieved documents provides important evidence for the similarity of these documents *within the context defined by the initial query*. Thus the less a term is contextually relevant, that is, the more irrelevant it contextually is, the more weight it should have in the similarity measure used in clustering. If the contextual irrelevance of a term t_j to a query Q is $cirr(Q, t_j)$, the Cosine coefficient could be used as follows:

$$csim(D_r, D_s) = \frac{\sum_{j=1}^{t} w_{rj} w_{sj} cirr(Q, t_j)}{\sqrt{\sum_{j=1}^{t} w_{rj}^2 \sum_{j=1}^{t} w_{sj}^2}} \qquad (6)$$

It can also be argued that within each cluster, the terms which most generally describe it are contextually most relevant. This could perhaps be used in cluster contents descriptions and making cluster combinations based on user choice.

6 Conclusions

We have introduced a new relevance measure, the contextual relevance, which can be assessed both for terms and documents. Contextual document relevance can be used to find the documents which most generally describe the topic of a user-submitted query. The measure is based on a combined analysis of the degree to which documents satisfy the query and term co-occurrence frequency. While the general method for contextual relevance assessment can be used with a number of different retrieval models, we have mainly used Vector Space Model in our paper. We also suggested that contextual term irrelevance could perhaps be used in document similarity measures needed in query-based document clustering for navigational purposes. Large-scale experimental results are still under way, but our preliminary experiment on identifying general documents was rather encouraging.

References

1. S. Deerwester, S. T. Dumais, T. K. Landauer, G. W. Furn & R. A. Harshman: "Indexing by Latent Semantic Analysis". Journal of the Society of Information Science 41 (6): 391 - 407, 1990.

2. X. Fu, K. J. Hammond & R. Burke: "ECHO: An Information Gathering Agent". Technical Report TR-96-18. The University of Chicago, Computer Science Department 1996.

3. M. A. Hearst & J. O. Pedersen: "Reexamining the Cluster Hypothesis: Scatter/Gather on Retrieval Results". In Proc. of the 19th Annual International ACM SIGIR Conference on Research and Development in Information Retrieval. Zurich, Switzerland 1996.

4. M. Magennis & C. J. van Rijsbergen: "The potential and actual effectiveness of interactive query expansion". In Proc. of the 20th International ACM SIGIR Conference on Research and Development in Information Retrieval. Philahelphia, Pennsylvania 1997.

5. Gerald Salton: "Automatic text processing: the transformation, analysis, and retrieval of information by computer". Addison-Wesley, Reading, MA, 1989.

6. H. R. Turtle: "Inference Networks for Document Retrieval". Ph. D. thesis, University of Massachusetts, 1990.

7. O. Zamir, O. Etzioni, O. Madani & R. M. Karp: "Fast and Intuitive Clustering of Web Documents". In Proc. the Third International Conference on Knowledge Discovery and Data Mining. Newport Beach, CA, 1997.

Low Retrieval Remote Querying Dialogue with Fuzzy Conceptual, Syntactical and Linguistical Unification

P. Kriško[3], P. Marcinčák[3], P. Mihók[2], J. Sabol[1], P. Vojtáš[3]

[1] VSŽ Informatika AS, Košice, Slovakia
[2] Department of Geometry and Algebra
[3] Department of Computer Science*
Faculty of Sciences, P. J. Šafárik University, Jesenná 5, 041 54 Košice, Slovakia

Abstract. In this paper we present a proposal of a flexible query answering system based on fuzzy logic. We introduce a fuzzy logic programming with a threshold cut and with connectives being arbitrary conjunctors, disjunctors (i.e. they do not need to be associative) and implicators. We use three types of unification: first of syntactical strings based on a similarity relation; second based on linguistic variables; third based on fuzzy conceptual lattices. Our systems assumes a fuzzy logic programming interpreter runs at the remote site. We propose a query dialogue where user can specify thresholds, number of truth values, finite (linear) approximations of fuzzy sets and connectives which are subject of tuning and learning, fuzzy conceptual lattice, fuzzy similarity relations and the form of answer required. This is intended to lower communication (retrieval) complexity. We present a computational (procedural) semantics which is sound and complete wrt. to declarative semantic.

1 Introduction

In this paper we present a proposal of a flexible query answering system based on fuzzy logic. To meet the requirement of answering rather intention of a query than the precise query, we use fuzzy unification: both linguistic, syntactic and conceptual. We assume the search engine (and domain knowledge) is described by a fuzzy logic program (IF-THEN rules, over a crisp or fuzzy database of facts, (see section 6 with historical remarks).

The fuzzy logic program (with built in fuzzy unification and confidence factor threshold cut) is assumed to be run at the remote site with the database to be queried. This fuzzy logic program has user defined flexible parameters: thresholds, fuzzy set of linguistic variables, tunable many valued connectives, fuzzy conceptual lattice and similarity relation for syntactical strings. For lower information retrieval we propose a querying dialogue, where user specifies (some

---

* e-mail: vojtas@kosice.upjs.sk, phone (+421 95) 62 209 49, fax (+421 95) 62 221 24
This work was supported by the grant 2/4375/97 of the Slovak Grant Agency for Science and the last author by A. von Humboldt Stiftung Germany.

of these) parameters and the form of the answer required . The whole calculation and database operation is assumed to be run at remote site. Only when a reasonable number of relevant information is found, can be downloaded.

For higher efficiency, our logic can be finitely valued and connectives can be finite approximations of t-norms (which need not to be associative). For historical remarks, comparison of our work with previous works and conclusions we refer to the last section.

2 Example

We present here an illustrative example from the domain of ecological problems of a huge enterprise (motivated by [26]).

Notice that in the following, introduced names can appear in abbreviated form when repeated.

The task is to find relevant information about huge companies which had recently severe ecological problems, and to specify what kind of environment was hit at most.

The manager's task has to be translated to a database (resp. logic programming) language. A thesaurus like conceptual lattice can help us for finding keywords connected to task. Assume we have found a remote database with attributes

eco(Company, Size, Year, Price, Links_To_Documents)

and the intended meaning of attributes and domains is:

Company = name of the company - alphanumerical string

Size = size of the company by the number of employee - integer

Price = total price of the ecological accident in billions - integer or linguistic variable

Year = year of the accident - integer

Links_To_Documents = links to text files - alphanumerical string

2.1 Transaction 1.

After a classical SQL query

OF SELECT SIZE >20 000 AND PRICE > 10 AND YEAR >1992
we can get no answer, and after a new query

OF SELECT SIZE >10 000 AND PRICE >5 AND YEAR >1982
we can get an enormous number of answers.

2.2 Transaction 2.

We send to remote site fuzzy sets describing membership functions of linguistic variables μ_{hc} for huge company, μ_{hp} for high price and μ_r for recently, e.g.

recently: (1982, 0) (1983, 0.2) (1984, 0.4) (1985, 0.6)

$$(1986, 0.8) \ (1987, 0.9) \ (1988, 0.9) \ (1989, 1), \ ...$$

and we expect that an entry eco(company, size, year, price, links_to_documents) fulfills our query with confidence $\min(\mu_{hc}(\text{size}), \mu_r(\text{year}), \mu_{hp}(\text{price}))$, where min is here the Gödel's conjunction, which can be also a subject of tuning. First we would like to know how many entries there are with the confidence factor cf

	$cf = 1$ and we get	0 entries, after tuning 0 entries
$0.8 \le cf < 1$	100	0
$0.6 \le cf < 0.8$	500	50
$0.3 \le cf < 0.6$	1000	600

(tuning could have used e.g. product conjunction instead of min).

2.3 Transaction 3.

We are searching for relevant answers/data (this is not knowledge mining). Results of the search so far are entries in database eco where last attribute are links to (possibly huge amount of) data in text files. Our task now is to specify, based on this text files, what kind of environment was hit at most.

For further search we use logic programming rules with incorporated values from a fuzzy conceptual lattice FCL and (an another) context dependent fuzzy conceptual lattice CD-FCL. This comes from linguistic sciences and can contain information like

$$FCL(\text{water\_dam} \ \le \ \text{river}) = 0.8$$
$$CD - FCL(eco\_acc, soil \le river) = 0.4$$
$$CD - FCL(eco\_acc, rain \le soil) = 0.8$$
$$CD - FCL(eco\_acc, air \le rain) = 0.6$$

If we have background knowledge about the field of context described by program rules, then FCL can be used on names of predicates e.g. river(x) can be unified with water_dam(x) influenced by cf=0.8.

Our search rule is the following

```
search(eco_acc, eco_links)←
    ←— select_document(document, eco_links)&
        select_concept(concept, domain(CD-FCL(eco_acc)))&
        degree_of_occurrence(val_deg_occ, concept, document)&
        append(occurrence(document, concept).with cf = val_deg_occ)
```

Append saves result of this rule in a fuzzy database of facts of our logic program. It runs through all combinations of names of documents and concepts e.g. occurrence(viena_report, river).with cf = 0.3.

This is used to calculate relevance of the concept river by aggregation of all degrees of occurrence of all concepts lying bellow "river" in FCL and CD-FCL through all documents. For this aggregation of degrees of occurrence we use disjunction in the body of our rule

relevance(river)⟵

⟵ occurrence(document, river)∨
select_bellow(concept 1, dom(FCL($\leq$ river))), occ(doc, conc1)∨
select_bellow(concept 2, dom(CD-FCL(eco_acc, $\leq$ river))),
occ(doc, conc2)

and we get e.g. relevance(river) = 0.9 which together with previous result gives the entry with highest confidence to be

eco(Tshernobyl, 11 000, 1984, 15, river) with $cf = 0.79$.

2.4 Transaction 4.

Now we get suspicion that lot of these entries can denote the same accident but they can differ in some attributes, e.g. because russian names can have different writing.

So asking for fuzzy equality we can get the answer, that between these 50 entries with cf between 0.6 and 0.8 is the truth value of the equality of their entries with the above one e.g.

$cf = 1$	1
$0.8 \leq cf < 1$	30
$0.6 \leq cf < 0.8$	10
$0.3 \leq cf < 0.6$	5
$0 \leq cf < 0.3$	4

where the most similar entries are e.g.

eco(Tshernobyl, 10 000, 1986, about_10, river)

eco(Tsernobilj, 12 000, 1986, more_than_10, lake)

eco(Cernobyl, 11 000, 1986, 20, water_dam)

and an example of those having the smallest equality grade can be e.g.

eco(United Oil, 20 000, 1991, 5, pacific)

Now we see, there are two major ecological accidents of huge companies happened recently. The first has more entries because it had more publicity and because of different ways of transcription of russian names and because lack of free access to information different sources could give different information.

Our model proposes at remote site there is a possibility to run a java based interpreter of our fuzzy logic program with access to data (which can be at remote site distributed) and which communicates with the user via a net browser in html language.

For related work we refer e.g.to [15] and [28] and several contributions to this volume, e.g. [1], [8], [18] and [19].

3 The theory

In what follows we develop the theory of fuzzy logic programming with extended unification, namely its declarative and procedural part.

In the picture

$$\text{real data} \longleftrightarrow \text{declarative part} \longleftrightarrow \text{procedural part}$$

the declarative part of our theory (truth functional fuzzy logic) should correspond to the real world (and fuzzy sets, rules, connectives, similarity relations and conceptual lattices can be tuned and/or learned in order to fit data better).

The procedural part (our fuzzy logic computation) is first coupled with the declarative part through our proofs of soundness and completeness. Hence computed answers coincide with declarative part and hence should fit real world data (and prompting for new learning, tuning etc).

3.1 The language

Our language is a language of predicate calculus, without function symbols and with several sorts of variables (attributes) and constants (domain of attribute) grouped into two groups

1) Those being of syntactical nature $Var^s_1, \ldots, Var^s_k$ and $Con^s_1, \ldots, Con^s_k$

2) Those being possible domains of linguistic variables (we call them linguistic sorts) $Var^l_1, \ldots, Var^l_m$ and $Con^l_1, \ldots, Con^l_m$.

For each sort of variables (both syntactic and linguistic) there are symbols for different fuzzy equalities e.g. $=^s_i, =^l_j$.

For each linguistic sort of variables there are unary symbols for fuzzy subsets $\mu^i_1, \ldots, \mu^i_{n_i}$ (e.g. huge_company, high_price,...).

Further part of our language are predicate symbols of specified arity, i.e. of n-tuples of sorts of variables $ar =< X_1, \ldots, X_n >$.

As a metalevel, we have for every n-tuple of sorts of variables a fuzzy lattice on names of predicate symbols of same arity.

3.2 Structures

Assume moreover our language contains several rationality preserving connectives: conjunctions $\&_1$, $\&_2$, ...,$\&_k$, disjunctions $\vee_1$, $\vee_2$, ...,$\vee_l$ and implications $\to_1$, $\to_2$, ...,$\to_m$ and a negation $\neg$. Truth value functions for conjunctions are assumed to be lower continuous conjunctors (i.e. fulfilling all properties of a t-norm except of associativity), similarly for disjunctions there are disjunctors, for implications we have implicators (see the book [17]).

We follow closely Lloyd's and Apt's presentation (and even notation) ([20], [3]). Herbrand base B_L consists of all ground atoms. An n-ary predicate symbol can be interpreted as a fuzzy subset of $Con^{ar} = Con^{X_1} \times \ldots Con^{X_n}$, i.e. as a mapping from Con^{ar} into the unit interval $[0, 1]$. Glueing all these together we get a many sorted Herbrand interpretation namely a mapping $f : B_L \to [0, 1]$.

For purposes of this paper a theory is a partial mapping P assigning formulas rational numbers from $(0,1]$. Partiality of the mapping P we understand as of being defined constantly zero outside of the domain $dom(P)$. A single axiom we often denote as $(\varphi, P(\varphi))$ or $\varphi.cf = P(\varphi)$.

An interpretation f is a model of a theory P if for all formulas $\varphi \in dom(P)$ we have

$$f(\varphi) \geq P(\varphi).$$

3.3 Modus ponens based on conjunctors

For our application we have to decide what are reasonable implications and how do we evaluate logic programming computation with uncertain rules. Our starting point is the fuzzy modus ponens (see historical remarks), which syntactically looks like

$$\frac{(B, x), (B \to A, y)}{(A, C_\to(x, y))}$$

Assertion $MP(C, \mathcal{I})$ means: C is a conjunctor, $\mathcal{I}$ is an implicator then from $f(B) \geq x$ and $f(B \to A) = \mathcal{I}(f(B), f(A)) \geq y$ follows that $f(A) \geq C(x, y)$.

According to S. Gottwald ([12]) we can define following properties of functions of two real variables

$\Phi1(\mathcal{I})$ iff $\mathcal{I}$ is nonincreasing in the first and nondecreasing in the second coordinate.

$\Phi2(C, \mathcal{I})$ iff $C(x, \mathcal{I}(x, y)) \leq y$

$\Phi3(C, \mathcal{I})$ iff $\mathcal{I}(x, C(x, y)) \geq y$

Note that $\Phi2(C, \mathcal{I})$ implies $MP(C, \mathcal{I})$. More on this see [17].

4 Semantics of fuzzy logic programming

4.1 Declarative semantics

To have the possibility to aggregate various witnesses for same conclusion we allow bodies of our rules to contain disjunctions. A formula B is called a body if it is a disjunction (possibly multiple different disjunctions) of several (possibly different) conjunctions of atoms with only exception, we assume our bodies do not contain names for fuzzy subsets of variables of linguistic sort. That is we allow fuzzy linguistic variables only in Queries (this restriction concerns only this theoretical part, because it is out of the scope of this paper to give a theory of unification for fuzzy sets here). Typically a body looks like

$$\vee \left([\&_1(B_1, \&_2(B_2, B_3))], [\&_3(C_1, \&_4(C_2, C_3))]\right).$$

Warning, the usual Prolog notation does not apply. A colon , in body does not denote a conjunction, it only separates inputs of a connective written in a prefix notation.

A rule is a formula of form $A \leftarrow B$, where B is a body and A is an atom. Here $\leftarrow$ means a true implication, because in arbitrary many valued logic we do not have DNF description of implication. An atom is also called a fact (typically an element of a Herbrand base B_L). A fuzzy logic program P is a theory $P :$ $Formulas \longrightarrow [0,1] \cap Q$ such that $dom(P) = P^{-1}(0,1]$ is finite and consists of rules and facts. Query (or a goal) is again an atom (positive) intended as a question A? prompting the system (we do not have refutation here).

Definition 1. *A pair $(x; \theta)$ consisting of a real number $0 < x \leq 1$ and a substitution θ is a **correct answer** for a program P and a query A? wrt a theory T if for arbitrary interpretation $f : B_L \rightarrow [0,1]$ which is a models of both P and the theory T we have $f(\forall(A\theta)) \geq x$.*

4.2 Procedural semantics of fuzzy logic programming

What follows is a certain generalization of fuzzy unification (see historical comments and work of T. Alsinet [2]). First we define admissible rules which act on tuples of words in the alphabet A_P and substitutions. A_P is the disjoint union of alphabets of the language of the program $dom(P)$ without implications and enlarged by names for rationals. Moreover for every implication $\rightarrow$ we have in A_P a conjunctor $C_\rightarrow$, intended for evaluating modus ponens with $\rightarrow$. Note that the fact that implications are not in A_P is important, because implications are very often not lower semicontinuous and we need assumption of lower semicontinuity of connectives in A_P later.

Note that in these rules we mix the syntactical part of the classical resolution with bookkeeping history of the computation in order to be able at the end to compute the value of the confidence of the answer.

We define admissible rules as follows:

Rule 1. Assume that along the computation we obtained a goal with selected atom being

$$A(s, l, \mu, c, \ldots)\vartheta$$

where s is a syntactical constant, l a constant from linguistic domain, μ a fuzzy linguistic variable, c a concept and ϑ substitutions made so far.

If we find a rule (fact)

$$A_1(s_1, l_1, l_2, c_1, \ldots) \longleftarrow_c B.cf = q$$

with head of same arity as A is, then we can continue the inference with the goal where $A(s, l, \mu, c, \ldots)\vartheta$ is replaced by the following expression

$$C\left(q, (A_1 \leq^{ar} A)\&(s =^s s_1)\&(l =^l l_1)\&\mu(l_2)\&(c_1 \leq c)\&B\right)\vartheta\theta.$$

Here

C is the conjunctor evaluating modus ponens with implication of the rule,

q is the confidence factor of the rule (fact) used,

$(A_1 \leq^{ar} A)$ is the fuzzy conceptual lattice value of concepts which are names of predicates,

$(s =^s s_1)$ is the truth value of fuzzy syntactical equality of s and s_1,

$(l =^l l_1)$ is the truth value of fuzzy linguistic equality of l and l_1,

$(c \leq c_1)$ is again a fuzzy conceptual lattice value of concepts considered as elements of domain of attribute.

For instance, if the body B is empty, this rule gives the truth value of how does an entry A_1 in a fuzzy database fit the query(goal) A.

Rule 2. From $\vee(A, B)$ infer $\vee(0, B)$ or $\vee(A, 0)$.

We need this rule, because if one branch of the program fails, hence no aggregation of multiple answers is possible, we can still calculate remaining branch.

Rule 3. If the word does not contain any predicate symbols rewrite all connectives by respective truth value functions and calculate the value of the expression - this is the computed answer.

Definition 2. *Let P be a program and A is a goal. A pair $(r; \theta)$ consisting of a rational number r and a substitution θ is said to be a* **computed answer** *if there is a sequence $G_0, \ldots, G_n$ such that*

1. *every G_i is a pair consisting of a word in A_P and a substitution*
2. $G_0 = (A, \mathrm{id})$
3. *every G_{i+1} is inferred from G_i by one of admissible rules (between lines we do not forget the usual Prolog renaming of variables along derivation).*
4. $G_n = (r; \theta')$ *and* $\theta = \theta'$ *restricted to variables of A*

Example. Just to illustrate computational procedure of our procedural semantics we give a simple program in propositional logic (hence without unification). Consider a program P with rules (connectives are in prefix notation).

$A \leftarrow \vee\, ([\&_1(B_1, \&_2(B_2, B_3))], [\&_3(C_1, \&_4(C_2, C_3))]).cf = a$

$B_1 \leftarrow_1 \&_3(D_1, D_2).cf = b_1$

$C_2 \leftarrow_2 \&_2(E_1, E_2).cf = c_2$

and the database $B_2.cf = b_2$, $B_3.cf = b_3$, $C_1.cf = c_1$, $C_3.cf = c_3$, $D_1.cf = d_1$, $D_2.cf = d_2$, $E_1.cf = e_1$, $E_2.cf = e_2$.

The question (consultation) A? leads to computation which resembles classical Prolog, we have just to remember (via a bookkeeping) confidence factors for the final evaluation of the confidence of the answer (see also graded proofs of P. Hájek ([13])):

$\mathcal{C}(a, \vee([\&_1(B_1, \&_2(B_2, B_3))], [\&_3(C_1, \&_4(C_2, C_3))])$

$\mathcal{C}(a, \vee([\&_1(C_1(b_1, \&_3(D_1, D_2)), \&_2(B_2, B_3))], [\&_3(C_1, \&_4(C_2, C_3))])$

$\mathcal{C}(a, \vee([\&_1(C_1(b_1, \&_3(D_1, D_2)), \&_2(B_2, B_3))],$
$\qquad\qquad [\&_3(C_1, \&_4(C_2(c_2, \&_2(E_1, E_2)), C_3))])$

$\cdots\cdots$

$\mathcal{C}(a, \vee^{\cdot}([\&_1^{\cdot}(C_1(b_1, \&_3^{\cdot}(d_1, d_2)), \&_2^{\cdot}(b_2, b_3))],$
$\qquad\qquad [\&_3^{\cdot}(c_1, \&_4^{\cdot}(C_2(c_2, \&_2^{\cdot}(e_1, e_2)), c_3))])$

the last expression is the confidence factor of the answer YES to the query A?

4.3 Soundness of semantics

Denote by $Eq(P)$ the theory P extended by axioms of equality for all fuzzy equalities involved in the language of program P and $ConEq(P)$ a further extension of $Eq(P)$ with axioms for fuzzy lattices $(\forall x)(p_1(x) \longrightarrow p_2(x)).cf = (p_1 \leq^{ar} p_2)$ (if p_1, p_2 are concept names of predicates) and with $(A(c_1) \to A(c_2)).cf = (c_1 \leq c_2)$ (if c_1, c_2 are concepts in domain of a predicate A).

Theorem 1. *Every computed answer for a fuzzy definite program P and A is a correct answer wrt the theory $ConEq(P)$.*

Proof. Is similar to that of [20]. Take a goal A with a computation of length $k + 1$ starting with a rule $P(A \leftarrow B) = q$. Suppose that the result holds for all computed answers due to computations of length $\leq k$. For each atom D from the body B there is a computation of length $\leq k$, hence computed answer $d \leq f(D)$ in every model of P. But then $f(B) \geq b$ computed answer for whole body, because conjunctions and disjunctions are monotone in both coordinates. Hence as f being a model of P means $f(A \leftarrow B) \geq P(A \leftarrow B) = q$ and by the soundness of modus ponens we get $f(A) \geq C(q, b)$.

In the case of conceptual unification we use axioms from $ConEq(P)$.

4.4 Fixpoint theory and completeness.

Consider the lattice

$$F_P = \{f : f \text{ is a mapping from } B_P \text{ into } [0, 1]\}$$

with coordinatewise lattice ordering. In [30] there was developed fixpoint theory for propositional fuzzy logic programs.

We state here without proof that for syntactic and linguistic unification we have a fixpoint theory of fuzzy logic programs over the above mentioned lattice. Moreover we have the following:

Theorem 2. *Assume our logic program does not contain conceptual unification (i.e. our fuzzy lattice gives values constantly 0) and negation and for all implications we have $\Phi 1 - 3(C_i, \mathcal{I}_i)$ and all truth value functions in A_P are lower semicontinuous. Then for every answer (x, Θ) for P and A? which is correct wrt the theory $Eq(P)$ and for every $\epsilon > 0$ there is a computed answer (r, ϑ) for P and A? such that $x - \epsilon < r$ and $\Theta = \vartheta\gamma$ (for some γ).*

5 Cutting the search tree and finite approximations

Now we come to an important point in our theory, which enables us to create efficient implementations. Namely we show how to implement a sound (green) cut and finite approximations of connectives and truth values (assuming our theory does not have negation).

The idea of the cut is, that at a certain point of computation we already have a part of computed confidence factor value and the rest (so far unresolved predicate symbols) can in the best case have truth value 1 (due to some future computations). So if we are interested only in computed answers which are above certain threshold we can replace at each step all atoms by 1 we get an upper estimation of the final confidence (because conjunctions and disjunctions are monotone). If this upper estimation is below our threshold we can cut the computation because the final result can not be above the threshold. So our admissible rues will look like:

Metarule with cut. If the estimated value of the outcome of the rule is above the threshold then do the inference, else cut the computation.

User defined preciseness. In almost all real world applications we do not need to work with infinitely valued logic (there is always a border of resolution, exactness or even real world domains are finite). Although we developed our theory for the infinite case (just because it is mathematically easier) we can now notice that having finitely many truth values we can take all our connectives be partially constant functions which take only these values (and still are lower continuous). So we can decide ourselves how exact our computation (querying) should be and still inside this finitely valued theory we are sound and complete.

On the other side when we do not worry about infinitely values we have another possibility to enhance efficiency. Namely we can take our structures to be linear approximations (triangulations of data learned). So the computational complexity of our object entering the computed answer formula can be very low.

6   Historical remarks and conclusions

Paper [9] of D. Dubois , J. Lang and H. Prade contains an overview of fuzzy logic programming until'91. Recently J. F. Baldwin, T. P. Martin and P. W. Pilsworth [4] implemented the FRIL-system based on mass assignment. Completeness of fuzzy logic programming was proved for Lukasiewicz logic by K. Klawonn and K. Kruse [16] and by P. Vojtáš and L. Paulík [29] and for Gödel logic by M. Mukaidono and H. Kikuchi [21].

Besides resolution and refutation two sorts of fuzzy modus ponens are used in fuzzy logic programming. Fuzzy modus ponens in syntactical narrow sense dates to works of J. Pavelka [23] and S. Gottwald [12], see also book of P. Hájek [13]. Generalized fuzzy modus ponens dealing with interpolation of knowledge was introduced by L. A. Zadeh in [31]. Modus ponens generating functions are well known since the work of E. Trilas and L. Valverde [27] and D. Dubois and H. Prade [10]. For an overview we refer to a book of P. E. Klement, R. Mesiar and E. Pap [17].

All these approaches work with connectives of classical many valued logic of Lukasiewicz, Gödel and/or product logic. Nevertheless E. Naito, J. Ozawa, I. Hayashi and N. Wakami in [22] showed on a real application in a hotel reservation system that classical many valued connectives are not always sufficient to describe real world data, especially different user stereotypes and/or environments. They also presented a procedure for learning connectives from (sample) data.

As already mentioned, fuzzy logic was also used in querying (see e.g. J. Kacprzyk and S. Zadrozny [15] and M. Trompf, D. Baum, H. Janstetter and A. Weckert [28]). Fuzzy querying is closely connected to fuzzy unification and fuzzy databases. There are several approaches e.g. similarity based of B. P. Buckles and F. E. Petry [6], fuzzy relational based of J. F. Baldwin and S. O. Zhou [5], possibilistic of H. Prade and C. Testemale [25], probabilistic P. Hájek, F. Esteva and L. Godo [14]. For an overview of these and combined approaches see P. Bosc, J. Kacprzyk [7] and F. E. Petry [24]. Crisp conceptual lattices with connection to information systems were introduced and studied by B. Gantner and R. Wille [11], see also C. Carpineto and G. Romano ([8]). Another approaches to this phenomena are in following contributions in this volume: query subsumption of M. Al-Qasem ([1]), contextual relevance measure of K. Korpimies and E. Ukkonen ([18]) and association rules of Y. Liu et al ([19]).

We use above mentioned fuzzy logic programming with modus ponens in narrow sense and we extend it with arbitrary connectives motivated by Naito, Ozawa, Hayashi and Wakami [22]. For propositional logic it was done in [30]. Our unification uses above similarity and fuzzy relational approaches and we extend it with a fuzzy generalization of conceptual lattices of Gantner and Wille [11]. For such a generalized fuzzy logic programming we prove soundness and completeness. We use client_server architecture: the logic program supporting querying runs at remote site. We use estimation of confidence factor of answers for a threshold cut and for reduction of communication complexity. Our system allows disjunction in body of rules, which enables us to aggregate partial confidences witnessing the final relevance of the query answer.

Conclusions:

- we present a proposal of a flexible querying system based on sound and complete fuzzy logic programming

- the decision which information is most relevant is done at the remote site with the help of fuzzy conceptual lattice. This lowers the communication complexity

- connectives are also tunable, which gives an another possibility the system to be flexible and to be tuned to fit real data.

References

1. M. Al-Qasem, S. M. Deen. Query subsumption, this volume
2. T. Alsinet. Fuzzy unification degree. Preprint 97
3. K. R. Apt. logic Programming. In Handbook of Theoretical Computer Science. Elsevier 1990, 493–574
4. J. F. Baldwin, T. P. Martin, P. W. Pilsworth. FRIL: Fuzzy and Evidential Reasoning in Artificial Intelligence. John Willey Sons, 1995
5. J. F. Baldwin, S. O. Zhou. A fuzzy relational inference language. Fuzzy Sets and Systems 14, 155–174

6. B. P. Buckles, F. E. Petry. Fuzzy databases and their applications. In Fuzzy Information and Decision Process, M. Gupta et al. eds. North Holland New York 1982, 361–371

7. P. Bosc, J. Kacprzyk. Fuzziness in Database Management Systems. Physica Verlag, Heidelberg 1995

8. C. Carpineto, G. Romano. Effective reformulation of boolean queries with concept lattices, this volume

9. D. Dubois, J. Lang, H. Prade. Fuzzy sets in approximate reasoning. Part 2: Logic approaches. Fuzzy Sets and Systems 40 (1991) 203–244

10. D. Dubois, H. Prade. Fuzzy logic and the generalized modus ponens revisited. Cybernetics and Systems 15 (1984) 293–331

11. B. Gantner, R. Wille. Formale Begrifsanalyse. Math. Grundlagen. Springer 1996

12. S. Gottwald. Fuzzy Sets and Fuzzy Logic, Vieweg 1993

13. P. Hájek. Metamathematics of Fuzzy Logic. Kluwer, Dodrecht 1998

14. P. Hájek, F. Esteva, L. Godo. Fuzzy logic and probability. In Proc. Uncertainty in Artificial Intelligence. P. Besnard and S. Hanko eds. Montreal 1995, 237–244

15. J. Kacprzyk, S. Zadrozny. A fuzzy querying interface for www environment, In Proc. IFSA'97, M. Mareš et al eds. Academia, Prague 1997, 285–290

16. K. Klawonn, K. Kruse. A Lukasiewicz logic based Prolog. Mathware Soft Comput. 1 (1994) 5–29

17. P.E. Klement, R. Mesiar, E. Pap. Triangular Norms. Book in preparation

18. K. Korpimies, E. Ukkonen. Searching for general documents, this volume

19. Y. Liu, H. Chen, J. X. Yu, N. Ohto. Using stem rules to define document retrieval queries, this volume

20. J. W. Lloyd. Foundations of Logic Programming. Springer Berlin, 1987

21. M. Mukaidono, H. Kikuchi. Foundations of fuzzy logic programming. In Advances in Fuzzy Systems. Vol.1. P. Z. Wang, K. F. Loe eds. World Science Publ. Singapore 1995, 225–244

22. E. Naito, J. Ozawa, I. Hayashi, N. Wakami. A proposal of a fuzzy connective with learning function, in [7], 345–364

23. J. Pavelka. On fuzzy logic I, II, III. Zeitschrift Math. Logik Grundl. Math. 25 (1979) 45–52, 119–134, 447–464

24. F. E. Petry. Fuzzy Databases - Principles and Applications. Kluwer Dodrecht 1997

25. H. Prade, C. Testemale. Generalizing database relational algebra for the treatment of incomplete/uncertain information and vague queries. Proc 2nd NAFIPS Workshop, New York 1983

26. J. Sabol, L.Kvaska, M. Antal, J. Sirota. The new information system STEELMAN (in slovak) AT&P Journal 2 (1997) 6–8

27. E. Trillas, L. Valverde. An inquiry on t-indistinguishability operator. In Aspects of Vagueness, H. Skala et al. eds. Reidel Dodrecht, 1984, 231–256

28. M. Trompf, D. Baum, H. Janstetter, A. Weckert. Crisp and fuzzy search in product databases for Online Applications. In Proc. EUFIT'97, H. J. Zimmermann ed. Verlag Mainz Wissenschaftsverlag, Aachen, 1997. pp. 57–61

29. P. Vojtáš, L. Paulík. Logic programming in RPL and RQL. In Proc. Sofsem 95, M. Bartošek et al. eds. LNCS 1012 Springer 1995, 487–492

30. P. Vojtáš. Fuzzy reasoning with flexible t-operators. Proc. IFSA'97, M. Mareš et al eds. Academia Prague 1997, 345–350

31. L. A. Zadeh. On the analysis of large scale systems. In Systems Approaches and Environment Processes Götingen 1974, H. Gabbinger ed. Vanderhoek and Rupprecht, 1974, 23–37

Knowledge Discovery for Flexible Querying

Henrik L. Larsen, Troels Andreasen, and Henning Christiansen

Department of Computer Science
Roskilde University, DK-4000 Roskilde
{hll, troels, henning}@ruc.dk

Abstract. We present an approach to flexible querying by exploiting similarity knowledge hidden in the information base. The knowledge represents associations between the terms used in descriptions of objects. Central to our approach is a method for mining the database for similarity knowledge, representing this knowledge in a fuzzy relation, and utilizing it in softening of the query. The approach has been implemented, and an experiment has been carried out on a real-world bibliographic database. The experiments demonstrated that without much sophistication in the system, we can automatically to derive domain knowledge that corresponds to human intuition, and utilize this knowledge to obtain a considerable increase in the quality of the search system.

1 Introduction

An increasing number of users access an increasing amount of information with a decreasing insight knowledge about the domains of the information accessed. Indeed, the need of effective solutions to flexible, intuitive querying-answering systems is already obvious, and it becomes increasingly important to provide such solutions, allowing everyday's user find their way trough a mess of information available, in particular through the Internet. For a representative collection of approaches to flexible query-answering we refer to [1–3].

Fuzzy evaluation of queries introduces a flexibility that, as compared to conventional evaluation, brings query-answering a great deal closer to the ideal of human dialog. This flexibility is partly manifested in fuzzy notions available for query specification, and partly in the inclusion and ranking of similar, but non-matching objects in the answer. Since both the interpretation of fuzzy query concepts, and the determination of similar objects, draw on the ability to compare and order values, fuzzy query evaluation is heavily dependent on measures of similarity and on ordering defined for attribute domains underlying the database.

Furthermore, for the flexibility to be apparent from the users point of view, the similarity measure applied must correspond to the user's perception of the attribute domain. That is, two values in an attribute domain are similar to the degree that replacing the one value for the other in an object does not change the user's potential interest in the object. For instance, the two prices of a home, 110,000$ and 115,000$ are rather similar, as are the meanings of the terms 'summer cottage' and 'weekend cottage'.

In numerical domains the similarity measure may often be specified as a function of the distance. For non-numerical domains, such as the domain of subject terms of documents, the similarity measure may in general be represented by a fuzzy relation that is reflexive and asymmetric. Such a relation is depicted by a directed fuzzy graph; when the vertices represent terms, and the edges the (directed) similarity between terms, we refer to such a graph as a *fuzzy term net*.

A central issue in knowledge engineering for flexible querying systems, is the acquisition of the similarity knowledge. Sources for such may include domain experts, and existing ontologies (including thesauri and lexicons). However, other important sources are the information bases queried, and observed user behavior, possibly including feedback from users. To exploit the latter sources, the similarity knowledge must be discovered (or learned) from the set of instances considered. Although similarity knowledge obtained by discovery tends to be less precise, due to its emperical basis, than knowledge aquired from domain experts and ontologies, it has the advantage that it may be applied dynamically to reflect the current use as represented in the information base and by the users of the querying system.

In this paper, we present an approach to discovering and utilizing knowledge in information bases. Especially the discovery aspect, which is also touched upon in [4, 5], is important, since flexible approaches depends on available, useful domain knowledge, and we actually can derive such knowledge from the information base. Of major interest in our approach are domains of words used in describing properties of objects, thus domains with at least no inherent useful ordering. In a library database these may be authors' keywords, librarians' keywords, and words appearing in titles, notes, abstracts or other textual attributes attached to objects.

2 Fuzzy term nets in representation of similarity

We distinguish between two kinds of similarity on domains of words (or terms): thesaurus-like and association-like similarity. A *thesaurus-like* similarity notion relates words with respect to meaning; similar words are words with overlapping meaning, as exemplified in Figure 1(a). The structure depicts a synonym relation, or, more precisely, 'a kind of' relation, on the domain; in the example, for instance that a house is a kind of home. An *association-like* similarity notion relates words with respect to use or ideally with respect to natural human association, as exemplified in Figure 1(b), where a given word points to other words that are similar with respect to the context in which they are applied. We refer to such structures as term nets. Obviously we obtain a generalization when allowing term relationships to be graded, that is, when allowing for fuzzy term nets. A fuzzy term net representing an association structure is referred to as an *associative term net* . The fuzzy relation represented by such a net, reflects the vagueness of the term relationships, and the associated uncertainty due to its emperical basis. For any pair of terms (A, B), the derived strength of a relationship from A to B, $s(A, B)$, is taken as an estimate of the degree to which A is associated

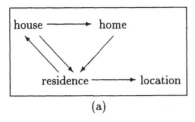
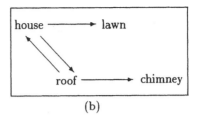

| (a) | (b) |

Fig. 1. Term similarity structures: (a) a thesaurus structure, (b) an association structure

to B, such that $s(A, B) > s(A, C)$ indicates that A is associated stronger to B than to C.

In the following, we present an approach to flexible querying using discovered similarity knowledge represented by associative term nets. The approach was tested using an experimental prototype for querying in bibliographic databases. The databases used in the experiments were all extracted from real library databases. Most of these databases had a complex database scheme from which we extracted a subset relevant to the purpose of the investigation, as described by the following unnormalized database scheme:

```
bib_entity(Author*, Title, Year, Type, Note*, Keyword*)
```

where * indicates a multi-value field. In the following, we shall consider only bibliographic entity ('bib_entity') objects of type 'book', and only the single-value attribute Title, and the multi-value attribute Keyword. Since the keywords are chosen from a controlled vocabulary of words (terms), and attached to books by librarians, not by authors, we have a high degree of homogeneity in the keyword characterizations of objects.

Our approach to flexible querying extends conventional crisp query evaluation in two respects, namely: (1) fuzzy interpretation of single constraints (criteria): weakening such that similar values also are considered, and (2) fuzzy aggregation of single constraints in the compound query, relaxing conjunction "as much a necessary" towards disjunction. First, we introduce the associative term net derived from the database. This net is the basis for the similarity relation and thus for the fuzzy interpretation of single constraints. We then present the use of the net in query evaluation, and give examples of queries evaluated against the small database used in an experiment.

3 Discovery of term associations

The most important attribute domains in bibliographic databases are the sets of words used in different descriptions of objects in the database, e.g., in titles, abstracts, notes, related keywords, and, even, in the author names. Our main interest is the association similarity between words (or terms), and a major issue here is how to establish the term association net representing this similarity.

Since we did not have access to any useful manually created association networks, apart from the available library classification systems, and since these constitute only very sparse networks, we focused on automatically discovery of associations by, so to say, mining data in the database. For the experiment discussed in this paper, we have chosen to build a network based on librarian keywords (terms) with no influence on associations from words as used in other attributes describing objects. Thus, even titles are ignored when associating terms.

The association relation $s(\Delta, \Delta)$, where Δ is the set of terms in the Keywords domain, is defined as follows,

$$s(A, B) = \begin{cases} 0 & \|\Omega_A\| = 0 \\ \frac{\|\Omega_A \cap \Omega_B\|}{\|\Omega_A\|} & \|\Omega_A\| > 0 \end{cases} \tag{1}$$

where Ω denotes the set of documents represented in the database, and Ω_X denotes the subset which applies the term X in the description of the document. By this definition, the relation is reflexive, and asymmetric. Thus, in the example illustrated by Figure 2(a), we have

$$s(A, B) = \frac{7}{7+3} = 0.70$$

$$s(B, A) = \frac{7}{7+21} = 0.25$$

The corresponding edges in the association term net are depicted in Figure 2(b).

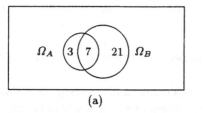

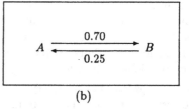

(a)   (b)

Fig. 2. Illustration of term association computation and representation: (a) frequencies of A and B, (b) resulting term associations

As an example of similarity knowledge derived in this way, consider the small section of the association term net, derived from the database in the experiment, as shown in Figure 3.

Since the approach is—as far as similarity of words used in query constraints are concerned—solely based on term associations as described above, an interesting question is: What is the kind of these associations, and how can its meaning be described? The intention is to capture relations that resemble relevant aspects of human associations. As compared to the other extreme to achieve this; knowledge acquisition by interviewing an expert in the domain in question, one major drawback appears to be the following: Words that are closely related by

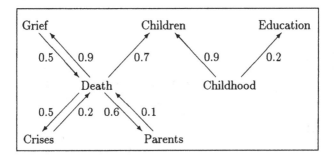

Fig. 3. A small section of the term association net derived from the database

association may also be closely related by meaning, as, for instance, 'parent' and 'mother'. When two words are closely related by meaning, a document will typically apply only one of these words, and therefore the system would not capture the association between the two words. However, since our term association net is based only on words attached from a controlled set, where each word in this set is carefully chosen to be with a distinct meaning—and thus "close meaning" is a rare phenomenon—this drawback has only little influence on the quality of the resulting association net.

Normally, we would expect an association relation to be transitive to some degree—if a house relates to a garage and a garage to a car, then we may also perceive that the house relates to the car. Even so, it appears wrong to impose transitivity on the associations obtained from mining, as suggested in our approach. Assume that there is a is a strong relation from house to garage, a strong relation from garage to car, and a weaker relation from house to car. In this situation we would expect all three relations to be reflected by the associations derived from statistics on the use of the words. Therefore, to strengthen the relationships through transitivity of the relation, is likely to lead to less intuitive results.

4 Using term associations in flexible querying

4.1 Definition of the flexible query-answer

We consider user queries expressed as a list of criteria $C_1, \ldots, C_n$ that all should be satisfied as much as possible. A criterion C_i represents a constraint on the domain of an attribute referred to by the criterion. For the experiment we considered criteria of the form *keyword* $= X$, where X is some term in the domain of keywords. Hence, queries are are expressed on the form $Q = X_1$ and $\ldots$ and X_n. Since our major objective was to explore to which extent mined knowledge may be meaningful and useful for query evaluation, we deliberately chose simple knowledge aggregation operators, such as the max operator and the arithmetic mean, without allowing for importance weighting of criteria. More sophisticated operators for query evaluation have been studied elsewhere (see, for instance, [6–8]) and leave space for further improvements.

A query is evaluated under two thresholds, δ_C and δ_Q, which delimit the extend to which a single constraint (criterion), respectively the query aggregation, can be relaxed. A constraint is relaxed through expanding the criterion term to a disjunction of all terms that the criterion term associates to, with a strength of at least δ_C. Notice, that this disjunction always contains the criterion term itself. The satisfaction of a criterion term by an object is the maximum of the satisfaction of the terms in its expansion. The overall satisfaction of the query is determined as the arithmetic mean of the satisfaction of the criterion terms; only objects that satisfy the query to at least the degree δ_Q are included in the answer. Formally, the answer to a query $Q = X_1$ and ... and X_n, with the thresholds δ_C and δ_Q, posed to a collection Ω is set defined by:

$$\text{Answer}(\Omega|Q) = \{(\omega, \sigma) \mid \omega \in \Omega, \ \sigma = \text{score}(Q|\omega), \ \sigma \geq \delta_Q\} \tag{2}$$

with

$$\text{score}(Q|\omega) = \frac{1}{n} \sum_{i=1}^{n} \gamma_i \tag{3}$$

and

$$\gamma_i = \begin{cases} 0 & \max_{Y \in \Delta_\omega} s(X_i, Y) < \delta_C \\ \max_{Y \in \Delta_\omega} s(X_i, Y) & \text{otherwise} \end{cases} \tag{4}$$

where Δ_ω is the set of terms represented as the value of the attribute Keyword of the object ω.

We notice that the max operator is just instance of the t-conorms that may be applied in Formula def:cscore. We may argue that a stronger t-conorm, such as the algebraic sum, defined by $g(a, b) = a + b - ab$ will provide a better measure. Similarly, the arithmetic mean is an instance of the averaging operators that may be applied in Formula def:qscore, and we may argue that a weaker operator, closer to the min operator, will improve the correctness of the measure. For the latter, we may apply an an OWA operator [9] with a higher degree of *andness*, say, 0.75, than the arithmetic mean which, when modeled by an OWA operator, has the *andness* 0.5.

4.2   On the effect of the thresholds on the answer

The relaxaton of the criterion terms $X_1, \ldots, X_n$ replaces each X_i by a disjunction of the set of terms which it is associated to with a strength of at least δ_C, that is, the set defined by

$$r_{s, \delta_C}(X_i) = \{(Y, \beta) \mid Y \in \Delta, \ \beta = s(X_i, Y), \ \beta \geq \delta_C\} \tag{5}$$

Thus, lowering δ_C allows more terms to be included in the set, and, thereby, more objects to satisfy the criterion. For illustration, consider the query

$$Q = \text{Death and Childhood}$$

When referring to Figure 3 we get for $\delta_C = 0.8$:

$$r_{s,0.8}(\text{Death}) = \quad \{\,(\text{Death}, 1), \quad (\text{Grief}, 0.9)\,\}$$

$$r_{s,0.8}(\text{Childhood}) = \{\,(\text{Childhood}, 1), \quad (\text{Children}, 0.9)\,\}$$

while $\delta_C = 0.6$ leads to

$$r_{s,0.8}(\text{Death}) = \quad \{\,(\text{Death}, 1), \quad (\text{Grief}, 0.9),$$
$$(\text{Children}, 0.7), \quad (\text{Parents}, 0.6)\,\}$$

$$r_{s,0.8}(\text{Childhood}) = \{\,(\text{Childhood}, 1), \quad (\text{Children}, 0.9)\,\}$$

Thus, by Formula 3, an object ω with the Keyword attribute value $\Delta_\omega = \{\text{Parents}, \text{Childhood}\}$ satisfies the criterion Death to dergee 0.6 (through Parents), and the criterion Childhood to degree 1 (through Childhood). We obtain as the overall score in the query $Q = $ 'Death and Childhood' as the arithmetic mean of the two satisfactions, namely $(0.6 + 1)/2 = 0.8$. In Table 1 we show for different levels of the overall score the subsets of keywords yielding this score when applied as the value Δ_ω of the Keyword attribute of an object ω.

Table 1. Scores in $Q = $ 'Death and Childhood' by objects described by the keywords in one of the subsets

Category	Score	Values of the Keyword attribute
1	1.00	{Death, Childhood}
2	0.95	{Death, Children}, {Grief, Childhood}
3	0.90	{Grief, Children}
4	0.85	{Children, Childhood}
5	0.80	{Parents, Childhood}, {Children}
...		
N	0.50	{Death},{Childhood}
$N+1$	0.45	{Grief}, {Children}
...		

Now, setting thresholds $\delta_Q = 1$ and $\delta_C = 1$ results in only Category 1 objects, that is, the same answer as we would obtain to the crisp Boolean query 'Death AND Childhood'. Keeping $\delta_Q = 1$ and lowering δ_C do not change anything since the score falls below 1 if just one criterion is satisfied below 1. Keeping $\delta_C = 1$ and setting $\delta_Q = 0.5$ lead to an answer consisting of Category 1 and Category N objects, that is, the same answer as we would obtain to the crisp Boolean query 'Death OR Childhood'. Setting $\delta_Q = 0.85$ and $\delta_C = 0.7$ (or lower) lead to Category 1–4 objects in the answer.

4.3 An example from flexible querying in a set of real data

To give an impression of how this works in practice, an answer to the query $Q = $ 'Death and Childhood' is shown in Table 2. The query is evaluated on a database containing about 6,000 objects that was also the basis for the applied association term net exemplified by a small subset in Figure 3. Without relaxing the query—that is, with $\delta_Q = 1$ and $\delta_C = 1$, corresponding to the crisp Boolean query 'Death AND Childhood'—the answer is empty. For the answer shown, the chosen thresholds are $\delta_Q = 0.80$ and $\delta_C = 0.80$. Only titles and scores for the books are listed.

Table 2. Answer to 'Death and Childhood', when evaluated on the database in the experiment

Score	Title of the book
0.95	Only a broken heart knows
0.95	Baby's death—"life's always right"
0.95	We have lost a child
0.95	Loosing a child
0.95	Cot death
0.95	When parents die
0.95	To say good-bye
0.95	We have lost a child
0.95	A year without Steve
0.95	Taking leave
0.95	Grief and care in school
0.89	Can I die during the night
0.89	Children's grief
0.89	Children and grief

Where the crisp query gave an empty answer, and would have required tedious trail and error from the user's side, the flexible query evaluation gave immediately a set of obvious relevant books, in fact with a very high recall and a high precision. These results even surprised the experienced librarians associated to the project team. We should emphasize that the database used in the experiment is not a "fake". The content is descriptions of real world books on issues related to children, school and education. All descriptions are made by librarians, that have carefully examined the books and in this connection chosen distinct, describing keywords from a controlled vocabulary. The resulting association term net is in a sense really the work of the librarians. However, they are not aware that they have been doing this work. What they see is only their description. The term net however, is, so to say, a description of their descriptions.

5 Concluding remarks

We have presented ideas and preliminary results from an ongoing research project on applying fuzzy query evaluation based on domain knowledge derived from the database state. The functions used for grading objects in the answer and for building the networks are deliberately chosen as simple, partly because we want the principles to be as easily comprehensible as possible, and partly because further research has to be done to reveal properties that make functions suitable and more accurate.

In this paper we have shown only one example of a query result. However, we have developed a system, which is frequently tested by and discussed with librarians, who agree that the association based query relaxation in general leads to relevant additional objects.

The experiments performed have demonstrated that under certain assumptions on quality of data, mining for associations leads to results that support better answers to queries. Also, we consider the resulting association term net as valuable additional information, that may be of interest, not only to the casual user of the system, but also potentially to the professionals with insight knowledge of the domain, because the network constitute a kind of inversion of data and therefore may exploit patterns that are otherwise hidden even from experts.

Acknowledgment

This research was supported in part by the Danish Library Center Inc., and the Danish Natural Science Research Council (SNF).

References

1. Larsen, H.L., Andreasen, T. (eds.): *Flexible Query-Answering Systems.* Proceedings of the first workshop (FQAS'94). Datalogiske Skrifter No. 58, Roskilde University, 1995.
2. Christiansen, H., Larsen, H.L., Andreasen, T. (eds.): *Flexible Query-Answering Systems.* Proceedings of the second workshop (FQAS'94). Datalogiske Skrifter No. 62, Roskilde University, 1996.
3. Andreasen, T., Christiansen, H., Larsen T. (eds.): *Flexible Query Answering Systems.* Kluwer Aademic Publishers, Boston/Dordrecht/London, 1997.
4. Andreasen, T.: *Dynamic Conditions.* Datalogiske Skrifter, No. 50, Roskilde University, 1994.
5. Andreasen, T.: On flexible query answering from combined cooperative and fuzzy approaches. In: *Proc. 6'th IFSA, Sao Paulo, Brazil, 1995.*
6. Larsen, H.L., Yager, R.R.: The use of fuzzy relational thesauri for classificatory problem solving in information retrieval and expert systems. *IEEE J. on System, Man, and Cybernetics* **23**(1):31–41 (1993).
7. Larsen, H.L., Yager, R.R.: Query Fuzzification for Internet Information retrieval. In D. Dubois, H. Prade, R.R. Yager, Eds., *Fuzzy Information Engineering: A Guided Tour of Applications,* John Wiley & Sons, pp. 291–310, 1996.
8. Yager, R.R., Larsen, H.L.: Retrieving Information by Fuzzification of Queries. em International Journal of Intelligent Information Systems **2** (4) (1993).
9. Yager, R.R.: On ordered weighted averaging aggregation operators in multicriteria decision making. em IEEE Transactions on Systems, Man and Cybernetics **18** (1):183–190 (1988).

Question Answering with Textual CBR

Mario Lenz, André Hübner, and Mirjam Kunze

Dept. of Computer Science, Humboldt University Berlin, D-10099 Berlin,
{lenz,huebner,kunze}@informatik.hu-berlin.de

Abstract. In this paper, we show how case-based reasoning (CBR) techniques can be applied to document retrieval. The fundamental idea is to automatically convert textual documents into appropriate case representations and use these to retrieve relevant documents in a problem situation. In contrast to Information Retrieval techniques, we assume that a Textual CBR system focuses on a particular domain and thus can employ knowledge from that domain. We give an overview over our approach to Textual CBR, describe a particular application project, and evaluate the performance of the system.
Keywords: Case-Based Reasoning, Textual CBR, Information Retrieval.

1   Introduction

Case-based reasoning (CBR) is concerned with the reuse of knowledge obtained during earlier problem solving episodes. In a problem situation, the key idea is to look for *similar* problem descriptions from the past and to utilize the solution that worked for this past problem. In this sense, CBR models the cognitive idea of *experience*. Obviously, this paradigm implies that a case base is available containing these *experiences*.

Traditionally, CBR has been concerned with more structured domains where cases can be encoded in terms of attribute-value vectors, sets of features, graphs and so on. In practice, however, an enormous amount of the above mentioned experiences is available as natural language texts only. Typical examples are manuals of technical equipment, documentations, reports by physicians, and, of course, the widely-used collections of Frequently Asked Questions (FAQ). Consequently, CBR researchers started to address the issue of knowledge contained in textual documents recently.

In this paper, we describe how CBR techniques can be used to build question answering systems. For this, we first describe the characteristics of a typical application area and then present our approach of Textual CBR. To illustrate the application of this technique, we describe in some detail a project performed in an industrial setting. Finally, we discuss related work and briefly evaluate the behavior of the system.

2   A Typical Application Area: The Hotline

Today it is becoming more and more difficult to sell products without a reliable and efficient customer support. This is true both, for industrial equipment as well as for highly complex software systems. The reason for this is that maintenance costs often exceed the initial value and thus become a decision criterion of customers [12]. Consequently, many companies establish so-called *help desks* and *hotlines* which the customer may contact in case of a problem.

2.1 Characteristics of hotline and help desk applications

Generally, applications such as help desks and hotlines can be characterized as follows:

- A hotline will always focus on a specific domain, e.g., on some type of technical devices, on a set of software components etc. This implies that no topics outside this domain will be dealt with and a *general world understanding* is not required.
- Because of the limitation to a specific domain, a number of highly specific terms will be used such as names of components, functions and modules.
- Naturally, a hotline will rely very much on textual documents such as FAQs, documentations, and error reports. Also, the customers' queries will be given in free text plus some additional information such as names of hardware components, software release numbers etc.
- The term *hotline* does not mean that customer enquiries have to be handled within seconds. Rather, finding the answers to problems usually involves a complex problem analysis and thus may take some time. Nevertheless, questions concerning problems that have been solved before should, of course, be answered rapidly.

Consequently, there is an urgent need for systems which can support the hotline staff in retrieving relevant documents in a specific problem context. For this, techniques are required which support the search for documents given a user's question, i.e. on the one hand they have to handle natural language texts, on the other hand these techniques must be flexible enough to cope with paraphrased documents which have essentially the same semantics.

2.2 Limitations of IR models

When trying to recall relevant textual documents, usually Information Retrieval (IR) techniques [16] are applied. In the context of the above sketched hotline scenario, however, a major limitation of IR models is that knowledge, such as domain-specific terms and the relationships among these, can hardly be utilized when searching the document collection. A pure keyword-based search, on the other hand, is not powerful enough to provide a flexible question answering system. For example, virtually any natural language text can be paraphrased such that nearly every keyword is changed but the semantics of the entire expression is still very close to the original text.

Another limitation of IR techniques is that they have problems in dealing with *semi-structured* documents, i.e. documents for which a certain structure can be assumed. As an example consider the widely used FAQ collections where each entry is in fact a question-answer pair. Also, in the hotline scenario documents typically contain pieces of knowledge which should be encoded using a more structured representation, such as attribute-value pairs – and a specific type of similarity measure can usually be applied to compare different attribute values.

3 Textual CBR

As mentioned before, the fundamental idea of CBR is to recall relevant cases from earlier problem solving episodes in a problem context [1]. In terms of a question answering system, this means that relevant documents should be recalled as answers to a question posed by some user.

3.1 The knowledge of a CBR system

A crucial difference to the above sketched IR models is that CBR is a knowledge-based technique – hence any CBR system explicitly allows (*even:* requires) the integration of semantic knowledge. Consequently, during knowledge acquisition a domain model has to be build which describes the essential properties of the domain, the entities which one is talking about, and their relationships (most important: similarity). This domain model certainly will include a domain specific thesaurus (as in some advanced IR models) but may go beyond this type of knowledge by considering structural and topological relationships too. For example, knowledge about technical devices and how they relate to each other can not be captured in a traditional thesaurus.

In terms of the knowledge container model [14], every piece of knowledge can be represented in one (or more) of the following categories:

(a) the collection of cases;
(b) the definition of an index vocabulary for cases;
(c) the construction of a similarity measure;
(d) the specification of adaptation knowledge.

In this paper, we will assume that **(a)** documents are available which can serve as the basis for a case base and **(d)** adaptation is of limited use only. Consequently, the most important knowledge containers are **(b)** the index vocabulary describing which term are used in the domain and **(c)** the similarity measure relating the various terms to each other. In particular, a *semantic* similarity measure of CBR systems will contain *additional* knowledge as a supplement to the other knowledge containers.

A more detailed comparison of IR models and Textual CBR is given in [9].

3.2 The CBR-ANSWERS project

Within the CBR-ANSWERS project we addressed the application of CBR techniques in situations like the hotline scenario. In addition to the properties given in

Section 2, we further assume that a knowledge engineering process is performed in order to model the application domain and to fill the knowledge containers of the CBR system.

The basic idea behind Textual CBR is to consider documents as cases and compare these cases in terms of similarity. The assumption then is that similar documents express related information needs and hence a highly similar document is likely to be useful for answering a user's question. However, *similarity* of documents is not based merely on a common set of keywords but rather on the similarity measure constructed during knowledge acquisition.

Case structure and case representation. In order to access the information contained in the textual documents, each document is converted into a single case. This process is performed automatically, i.e. no manual case authoring has to be performed.

For case representation, we used the *Case Retrieval Net* (CRN) model [10] where each case is described by a set of *Information Entities* (IEs). Each IE captures a specific case feature. The set of all IEs may be further distinguished according to specific types, such as

- keywords such as *billing*;
- domain-specific expressions, such as *Customer Administration Module*, which would not normally be considered as a single keyword but have a specific meaning;
- special codes, numbers etc. which refer to a particular object in the domain;
- attribute-value pairs, like *Version=1.1*;
- further attributes required for domain modeling.

As the set of IEs is required for case representation, it has to be constructed during the knowledge engineering process. For example,

- existing documents may be investigated for determining useful keywords;
- domain experts have to be interviewed to get an understanding of the application domain;
- manuals and documentations may provide useful insights;
- glossaries and such will contain lists of domain-specific terms.

Note that this process should not be limited to statistic methods but rather should put as much emphasis as possible on knowledge elicitation.

Given an IE dictionary, each document is converted into a properly structured case by *parsing* the document and trying to locate IEs in the text. Note, however, that *parsing* here is a highly complicated process. In fact, it is a mapping of textual parts to IEs which includes

- recognition of keywords and phrases, including their grammatical variations, abbreviations etc.;
- special functionality to identify and interpret codes, numbers and so on;
- a simple kind of Information Extraction [15] in order to obtain some structural information in the form of attribute-value pairs.

An important feature of the CRN model is that IEs may be compared in terms of similarity. Again, a proper similarity specification has to be developed during knowledge engineering. For the keywords and phrases a tool like WORDNET [13] appears to be highly useful as it provides information on how different terms relate to each other. Unfortunately, WORDNET is only available for English. What's more, it will not cover domain-specific terms. The specification of their relationships is again a result of a careful knowledge acquisition process.

Similarity and retrieval. Once the documents have been converted into cases, similarity of cases is computed based on the similarity of the constituing IEs, i.e. the similarity of a case F to a query Q is defined as:

$$SIM(Q, C) = \sum_{e_i \in Q} \sum_{e_j \in C} sim(e_i, e_j) \tag{1}$$

where e_i and e_j are the IEs used to represent the query Q and the case C, respectively. The function sim specifies the *local* similarity of any two IEs. The sum realizes a composite similarity measure so that each part of the case that is activated contributes to the overall achieved similarity of this case.

To get a better understanding of how the various types of IEs contribute to case similarity, it is helpful to sketch how the similarity function of Equation 1 is composed according to the types of IEs which really influence each other. In more detail, the overall similarity measure takes into account

- similarity based on common keywords;
- similarity based on common domain-specific terms;
- similarity based on related keywords and specific terms;
- similarity based on attribute values as specified in the documents;
- similarity based on attribute values obtained during automatic Information Extraction.

Note that in that order the components of the similarity function become more and more knowledge-intensive. In Section 5.1 we will show how these components contribute to the overall performance of the system.

The retrieval process directly utlizes the IEs of cases and their similarity relationships as they are encoded by means of a Case Retrieval Net. In particular, efficiency and flexibility are valuable benefits of this model [10].

General system architecture. Figure 1 shows the principle architecture of the CBR-ANSWERS system. The entire system is implemented in a Client-Server architecture. When using the system, two separate phases must be distinguished

(1) an off-line process during which the above described *parsing* takes place and the actual case memory is constructed;

(2) an on-line process of actually querying the system.

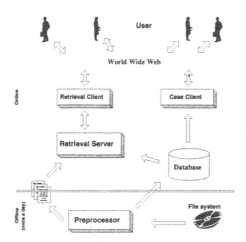

Fig. 1. Architecture of the CBR-ANSWERS system

The easiest way to access the system is via World Wide Web, but of course other clients may be used as well.

Besides the components required for the retrieval process itself, CBR-ANSWERS includes a number of additional modules which will vary depending on the particular application. As an example, Figure 1 shows the *Case Client* and a *Database* which are utilized to display the documents which the user requested.

4 Applications

In recent months, the CBR-ANSWERS system has been used in three application projects. Firstly, the FALLQ project has been a specific implementation providing hotline support for LHS, a company developing billing systems for telecommunication services [11]. The application scenario here is very close to the general hotline scenario as sketched in Section 2.

Secondly, the EXPERIENCEBOOK is a knowledge management tool on the basis of CBR-ANSWERS for the system administrators of the Department of Computer Science at Humboldt University [7]. It serves as an *external memory* in that it allows to maintain a *corporate Know How* among the group of system administrators. Another specific property of the EXPERIENCEBOOK is that the experts themselves are the users of the system, i.e. they query the system when facing problems and they provide some part of the input to the system by inserting new documents.

4.1 The AUTOMATIC HOTLINE

Finally, CBR-ANSWERS serves as the basic model for a project being performed in cooperation with Siemens AG, in particular with the customer support group of *Automation & Drives*. We will explore this project here in some detail.

Again the objective is similar to the hotline scenario described in Section 2, i.e. the goal is to answer questions posed by customers by reusing knowledge contained in FAQs and such.

A major difference, however, is that the hotline staff should be contacted only if a user's question can not be answered by showing them specific documents (cf. Figure 2). More precisely, the process model of the AUTOMATIC HOTLINE is such that the customers use a specific WWW site to describe their problems in terms of a textual query, some information on the particular domain they are requesting help for, and possibly information on the devices involved. Given this, a provided document collection is searched and the best matching documents are presented to the user assuming that highly similar documents will very likely be helpful in answering the users' requests. Only if this does not yield a solution to the problem the hotline staff is contacted and asked for help. Finally, if they answer the request, this is added to the document collection and thus the *Automatic Hotline* automatically acquires new knowledge and extends its scope of handable requests.

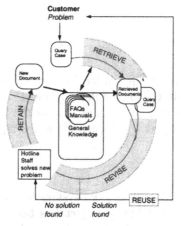

Fig. 2. Process model of the AUTOMATIC HOTLINE based on the R^4 model [1]

The AUTOMATIC HOTLINE directly utilizes a number of document types which are available at Siemens. These include usual FAQs, *Informal Notes* on recently observed problems as a simple verbal description of these problems and *User Information Notes*. While all three document types basically contain the same information, there is a difference in reliability. As the name indicates, *Informal Notes* are just draft notes which may give hints but are not trustworthy. On the other hand, FAQs express well-established knowledge resulting from frequent usage. In that range, *User Information Notes* are somewhere in between.

In fact, customers may already browse these documents when facing some problem (www.ad.siemens.de/support/html_00). The *Automatic Hotline* based on CBR-ANSWERS provides means of intelligently searching and analyzing these documents rather than browsing numerous directories. This is becoming more and more important as the devices shipped to customers are becoming more and more complex and – as a result of putting more emphasis on customer support – the number of FAQs etc. is steadily growing.

A key property distinguishing the AUTOMATIC HOTLINE in particular from the FALLQ project is that several languages have to be supported by the system. In a first stage, a focus is set on German rather than English texts. This implies additional effort because German grammar is much more complicated and even more irregular than English.

Later on English and other languages will be supported, too. Then, the approach of CBR-ANSWERS has the major advantage that textual documents are converted to cases represented by sets of IEs. These IEs are, in fact, some kind of *symbols* having a certain meaning in the real world. Consequently, it is possible to reuse exactly the same symbols including their similarity relationships for another language[1]. The only thing required is a description of how these symbols can be derived given the texts, that is a language-specific *parsing* method. Basically this should utilize a translation of the general purpose terms while specific terms, such as names of functions, devices, and modules, remain unchanged.

5 Discussion

5.1 Evaluation

Evaluation methodology. Despite the users' acceptance of the systems implemented by adapting CBR-ANSWERS to the above mentioned applications, a theoretical evaluation is required to clearly show advantages and disadvantages of the approach. For this purpose, measures similar to those known from the IR community should obviously be used. However, there are some crucial differences with respect to the underlying assumptions:

Firstly, measures like *precision* and *recall* generally assume that for a set of test queries relevance judgments are known. In our projects, this appeared to be a major drawback as these projects were performed in highly specialized domains where relevance judgment is possible only by a domain expert. What's more, one can easily imagine that it is hard, if not impossible, to get these experts perform a task which is mainly interesting from an academic point of view.

Secondly, the original *recall* measures the percentage of the retrieved relevant documents with respect to all relevant ones. In the hotline scenario, however, the goal is not to retrieve *all* relevant items but rather to answer a query successfully. Hence, *one* relevant document is sufficient (for a similar discussion see [2]).

Concerning the second problem, we modified the notion of *recall* such that for a single query *recall* is 1.0 if a relevant document has been retrieved, and 0 otherwise.

The first problem was harder to overcome. To construct a set of queries for evaluation, we utilized the following observation: While relevance judgments can

---

[1] Remember that CBR-ANSWERS is operating in a very specific domain only and that a general world understanding is not necessary.

only be given by a domain expert, virtually every one can determine whether two queries have a similar semantics. Consequently, we randomly selected a set of FAQs and changed their question components in several steps, from minor grammatical variations to complete reformulations. In the latter case, we changed as many expressions as possible but kept the names of devices, modules, components etc.

An example of such a reformulation might be:

Original query:
In what modus do I have to shoot the 128 KByte EPROM for the CPU-944?
Modified query:
How do I have to run the 944 CPU for shooting a 128 KB EPROM?

As this example shows, the semantics of the query may change slightly. But in any case, the answer to the original query will still answer the modified one.

When applying this procedure, one knows which FAQs are relevant for each of the modified queries. In most situations it was just the original document, but in about 25 percent a second relevant FAQ could be found as nearly exactly the same FAQ occurred in a different context again.

Based on this, we built a set of test queries from the AUTOMATIC HOTLINE domain and used this test set for a number of performance tests. In particular, the ablation study described in the following provides useful insights into the behavior of the system.

Ablation Study. As described in Section 3.2, the similarity measure implemented in CBR-ANSWERS generally consists of several components with varying degree of knowledge contained. To determine the contribution of each component, we performed an ablation study by subsequently eliminating higher level components.

In Figure 3 some of the results obtained from evaluating the CBR-ANSWERS system with the SIMATIC domain are shown. As the *precision–recall* curve shows, the performance of the system degrades if less knowledge is integrated into the similarity measure.

More precisely, the performance is degrading if more and more knowledge intensive components are eliminated:

– If no *Information Extraction* is performed, the system's performance degrades only slightly (curve 1 vs. curve 2).
– If the domain structure is not used to filter out similar documents from completely other areas[2], the same *recall* values are achieved at a lower level of *precision* (curve 1 vs. curve 3).
– Another step can be observed if structural information contained in the documents is not considered (curve not shown here).

---

[2] Note that in the AUTOMATIC HOTLINE application documents may describe related observations – but as they apply to different components, such a document is of no use if it describes a behavior of a different component.

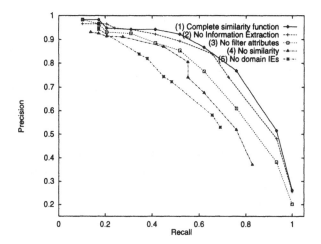

Fig. 3. Results of the ablation study

- If the similarity of index terms is not considered, the performance further degrades (curve 3 vs. curve 4).
- Finally, a major loss in performance results if the domain-specific terms are removed from the set of IEs (curve 4 vs. curve 5).

In fact, the performance of the system is as expected. Another observation which is not shown in Figure 3 was that performance further degrades if structural information, such as attribute-value pairs describing release numbers of devices etc., is not represented explicitly but handled as ordinary text.

5.2 Related Work

As mentioned before, some other projects recently addressed topics concerned with Textual CBR. The **FAQFinder** project [2] is probably the most similar approach to CBR-ANSWERS. FAQFinder, too, applies CBR in combination with other techniques to document management. In particular, the goal is to answer questions by retrieving relevant FAQs from USENET news groups. It uses WORDNET [13] to base its reasoning on a semantic knowledge base.

A crucial difference to CBR-ANSWERS is that FAQFinder does not focus on a specific domain. Instead, it applies a two stage process:

- In the first step, a shallow analysis mainly of the keywords contained in the query is used to infer the most likely news groups related to the request.
- After the user has selected one of the presented news groups, a more sophisticated analysis of the related FAQ file starts to compare the contained FAQs with the user's query.

CBR-ANSWERS assumes an even stronger focus on a specific domain. In particular, all the systems derived from the CBR-ANSWERS model have been designed specifically for the particular application. For example, in technical areas a lot of terms exist that would hardly be represented in WORDNET. That's why, a careful knowledge engineering process has been performed to employ domain-specific knowledge for similarity assessment. In FAQFinder, on the contrary, the semantic base (i.e. WORDNET) is the same for all news group topics and knowledge specific to a single domain can not be incorporated.

SPIRE uses a completely different approach for dealing with textual cases [3, 4]. Based on the observation from the field of IR that people have problems in formulating *good queries* to IR systems, the idea behind SPIRE is to use a combination of CBR and IR technology: A user's request for some information is analyzed by means of a CBR module. As a result, a small number of relevant cases representing text documents are selected and sent to the INQUERY retrieval engine. Consequently, CBR is in fact used as an interface to IR.

5.3   Open issues

An obvious weakness of the CBR-ANSWERS system is the explicit assumption that documents are similar if they are represented by similar IEs. As these are obtained from the textual representation, there is a certain danger that a minor variation of the text completely changes the semantics but is not recognized by the parsing process. Sophisticated Natural Language Processing (NLP) techniques providing a high-level representation of texts might be considered a possible solution to this problem. However, we experienced that most NLP techniques have problems when it comes to real-world texts: Firstly, they are computationally too expensive to be applied to larger text collections. In the FALLQ application briefly described in Section 4, for example, the system currently has to handle approximately 40,000 documents each varying between several lines and 3 or 4 pages of text. Secondly, most of these NLP techniques only work with small dictionaries and (even worse) are not robust when unknown terms are encountered. Thirdly, many documents contain pieces of text which does not follow a proper grammar structure but rather consists of informal notes, brief statements and so on.

Consequently, we concentrated on so-called *shallow* NLP techniques, such as *Part-Of-Speech* tagging. These are both, efficient and robust, and still may provide useful information, for example, for the Information Extraction process. Nevertheless, further improvements are required here.

Another major problem is maintenance of the system. As explained above, a sophisticated knowledge engineering process is required, e.g., for constructing the IE dictionary and for specifying an appropriate similarity measure. Currently, hardly any support is provided for these tasks. Future work here will address both, intelligent interfaces enabling the user to specify and change the behavior of the system, and automatic methods of knowledge acquisition probably originating in the areas of Machine Learning and Information Extraction.

Acknowledgments

The authors want to thank all the people who have been involved in the Textual CBR projects discussed in this paper, in particular Hans-Dieter Burkhard, Thomas Ritz, Alexander Glintschert, and Marlies Gollnick.

References

1. Agnar Aamodt and Enric Plaza, 'Case-based reasoning: foundational issues, methodological variations, and system approaches', *AI Communications*, 7(1), 39–59, (1994).
2. Robin Burke, Kristian Hammond, Vladimir Kulyukin, Steven Lytinen, Noriko Tomuro, and Scott Schoenberg, 'Question Answering from Frequently Asked Question Files', *AI Magazine*, 18(2), 57–66, (1997).
3. Jody J Daniels, *Retrieval of Passages for Information Reduction*, Ph.D. dissertation, University of Massachusetts at Amherst, 1997.
4. Jody J Daniels and Edwina L Rissland, 'What You Saw Is What You Want: Using Cases to Seed Information', In Leake and Plaza [8], pp. 325–336.
5. Lothar Gierl and Mario Lenz, eds. *Proceedings 6th German Workshop on Case-Based Reasoning*, IMIB Series Vol. 7, Rostock, 1998. Inst. fuer Medizinische Informatik und Biometrie, University of Rostock.
6. Günther Görz and Steffen Hölldobler, eds. *KI-96: Advances in Artificial Intelligence*, Lecture Notes in Artificial Intelligence, 1137. Springer Verlag, 1996.
7. Mirjam Kunze and Andre Hübner, 'CBR on Semi-structured Documents: The ExperienceBook and the FAllQ Project', in *Proceedings 6th German Workshop on CBR*, (1998).
8. David B Leake and Enric Plaza, eds. *Case-Based Reasoning Research and Development, Proceedings ICCBR-97*, Lecture Notes in Artificial Intelligence, 1266. Springer Verlag, 1997.
9. Mario Lenz, 'Textual CBR and Information Retrieval – A Comparison', In Gierl and Lenz [5].
10. Mario Lenz and Hans-Dieter Burkhard, 'Case Retrieval Nets: Basic ideas and extensions', In Görz and Hölldobler [6], pp. 227–239.
11. Mario Lenz and Hans-Dieter Burkhard, 'CBR for Document Retrieval - The FALLQ Project', In Leake and Plaza [8], pp. 84–93.
12. Mario Lenz, Hans-Dieter Burkhard, Petra Pirk, Eric Auriol, and Michel Manago, 'CBR for Diagnosis and Decision Support', *AI Communications*, 9(3), 138–146, (1996).
13. G A Miller, 'WORDNET: A lexical database for english', *Communications of the ACM*, 38(11), 39–41, (1995).
14. Michael M. Richter. The knowledge contained in similarity measures. Invited Talk at ICCBR-95, 1995. http://wwwagr.informatik.uni-kl.de/~lsa/CBR/Richericcbr95remarks.html.
15. Ellen Riloff and Wendy Lehnert, 'Information extraction as a basis for high-precision text classification', *ACM Transactions on Information Systems*, 12(3), 296–333, (1994).
16. Gerard Salton and M. McGill, *Introduction to Modern Information Retrieval*, McGraw-Hill, New York, 1983.

Using Stem Rules to Refine Document Retrieval Queries

Ye Liu[1], Hanxiong Chen[2], Jeffrey Xu Yu[3] and Nobuo Ohbo[1]

[1] Institute of Electronic & Information Science,
University of Tsukuba, Tsukuba, Japan 305.
[2] Tsukuba International University, Manabe 6, Tsuchiura, Japan 300.
[3] Department of Computer Science, Australian National University,
Canberra, ACT 0200, Australia.

Abstract. In this paper, a data mining approach for query refinement is proposed using Association Rules (ARs) among keywords being extracted from a document database. When a query is under-specified or contains ambiguous keywords, a set of association rules will be displayed to assist the user to choose additional keywords in order to refine his/her original query. To the best of our knowledge, no reported study has discussed on how to screen the number of documents being retrieved using ARs. The issues we are concerned in this paper are as follows. First, an AR, $X \Rightarrow Y$, with high confidence will intend to show that the number of documents that contain both sets of keywords X and Y is large. Therefore, the effectiveness of using minimum support and minimum confidence to screen documents can be little. To address this issue, maximum support and maximum confidence are used. Second, a large number of rules will be stored in a rule base, and will be displayed at run time in response to a user query. In order to reduce the number of rules, in this paper, we introduce two co-related concepts: "stem rule" and "coverage". The stem rules are the rules by which other rules can be derived. A set of keywords is said to be a coverage of a set of documents if these documents can be retrieved using the same set of keywords. A minimum coverage can reduce the number of keywords to cover a certain number of documents, and therefore can assist to reduce the number of rules to be managed. In order to demonstrate the applicability of the proposed method, we have built an interactive interface, and a medium-sized document database is maintained. The effectiveness of using ARs to screen will be addressed in this paper as well.

Keywords Information Retrieval, Query Refinement, Data Mining, Stem Rule, and Keyword Coverage.

1 Introduction

Due to the rapid growth of on-line documents, the difficulty users are facing is that a large number of irrelevant documents will be returned when a query is under-specified or contains ambiguous keywords. However, the task of formulating an effective query is difficult in the sense that it requires users, without any knowledge about the collection of documents, to predict the keywords that will appear in the documents the users want to have. Therefore, it is highly desirable that a system can support query refinement by adding appropriate keywords to the keywords initially submitted by the users. Query expansion [Peat91] and query feedback [Salt90] were proposed to make use of relationships such as similarity between keywords. In brief, the technique of query expansion is based on an association hypothesis which states: if an index term is good at discriminating relevant from non-relevant documents then any closely associated index term is also likely to be good at this. On the other hand, the relevance feedback in [Salt90] is a method in which queries are modified using the keywords obtained from the result set of documents if they have high similarity to the keywords used in the queries. However, these approaches have the difficulties to differentiate between relevant and non-relevant documents, because the keywords with higher similarities intend to include the similar documents.

Like the methods proposed in [Salt90,Peat91], our approach is based on co-occurrence of keywords. Unlike these approaches, we use Association Rules (AR), and we focus on screening retrieval results, which is also a main difference between our approach and [Andr98]'s. ARs are based on a statistical method in which the support makes rules meet certain frequency and the confidence describes degree of relation. The confidence also indicates that relationships are not symmetric, as confidences of $X \Rightarrow Y$ and $Y \Rightarrow X$ are often different from each other. It is very important that, unlike the similarity and co-occurrence, association rules are not symmetric.

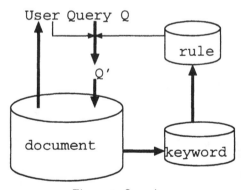

Figure 1: Overview

In this paper we present a query refinement method for a document retrieval system in which ARs among keywords mined in large document databases are used. A document has a keyword list. A query is given as a set of keywords, and the documents that contain all of the keywords in the given query will be retrieved. Such a keyword list has the same role as a transaction – which is a list of items – in a sale transaction database. An AR in the form of $\{X \Rightarrow Y, \ C\%\}$ means that a document that contains all of the keywords in X also contains all those keywords in Y, with confidence $C\%$. ARs are mined based on the concept of support and confidence.

In our scheme, ARs are used to refine a query. The overview of this process is illustrated in Figure 1. First, the keywords will be extracted from a document database. ARs are mined for those keywords which have a good screening effect. ARs are stored and managed in a rule base. Second, the system selects from the rule base association rules with respect to the user's query. The association rules will be displayed including the support and the confidence for each association rule. Third, the user who submits his/her query can make a decision based on the association rules together with their support and confidence to refine his/her original query. This process will be carried out repeatedly until the user successfully refine his/her query. The two issues that we are mainly concerned with in this paper are as follows.

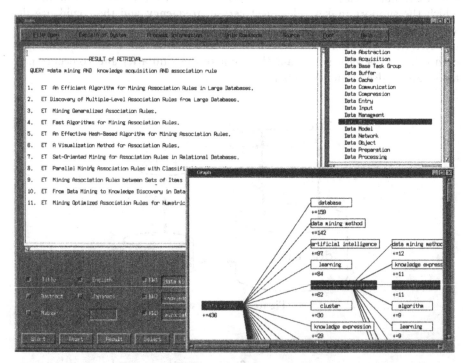

Figure 2: An Example of Query Refinement

- **Issue 1:** In [Agra93,Fayy96,Han95,Sava95,Srik96], ARs are defined as ones whose support and confidence exceed given thresholds called a minimum support and a minimum confidence. Given a query containing a set of keywords Q. When an AR $\{X \Rightarrow Y, \%C\}$ with a high confidence is picked up, the keywords included in Y will be added to a submitted query Q. However, when the AR has a high confidence, the effectiveness of screening of the number of documents being retrieved is very small. In the example of Figure 2, suppose that a user wants to retrieve documents on the topics of data mining, using a keyword "data mining". This user can get 436 hits. If his/her query is refined by adding "database", then the number of documents being retrieved is 159. It can be seen that the added keyword "database" can only screen little because the confidence is high between these two keywords. On the contrary, the keywords, "knowledge acquisition" and "association rule", are always associated to data mining. By adding these two keywords into the original query, the number of documents being retrieved is screened to 11. To address this issue, maximum support and maximum confidence are proposed to be used in conjunction with minimum support and minimum confidence.
- **Issue 2:** The second issue is that too many rules will be generated. If the number of keywords in a document database is k, then a naive method must check $k \times (k - 1)$ combinations to generate all ARs between two keywords, and so on. Finally, it must check exponential combinations for generating all ARs.

  To avoid a large number of rules being generated, *stem rules* are introduced by which the other association rules can be derived. Furthermore, a co-related concept, called *coverage*, is proposed. A set of keywords is said to be a coverage of a set of documents if these documents can be retrieved using the same set of keywords. A minimum coverage is the smallest set of keywords to cover the documents. With the concept of stem rules and coverage, the number of ARs can be reduced to a feasible level, and it can ensure that all documents can be covered.

Two classical factors, *recall* and *precision* ([Naga90]), are often used to evaluate an information retrieval system. The two factors are defined as follows. Let Eq be a set of documents in an information system, and let Rq be an appropriate set of documents that should be retrieved for a query Q. Suppose that the information system executes the query Q from Eq. And supposed that the result is a set of documents and is denoted Eq'. The recall and precision are defined as $|Eq'|/|Rq|$ and $|Eq'|/|Eq|$, respectively. Recently, [Véle97] independently notes the same problem we are targeting[Chen97] that too many documents will be retrieved by a query which is under-specified or contains ambiguous terms. The solution proposed in [Véle97] is an algorithms called RMAP which provides suggestions to refine the user query by calculating ranks of terms. In Comparison with the experiments in [Véle97], our system guarantees the coverage to be 100%. That is, we greatly reduce the candidates a user can choose to refine his/her query without lost any documents he/she wants to access. On the other hand, unlike [Peat91,Salt90] which automatically refine an user query, our interactive interface enhances the precision because the user interactively chooses what he/she want to refine his query.

The rest of this paper is organized as follows. The preliminaries of this study is given in Section 2. Section 3 and Section 4 will discuss the stem rules and the coverage, respectively. Section 5 gives an outline of our prototype system and addresses experimental results using ARs. Section 6 concludes our discussion.

2 Preliminaries

In this section, we give the notations that we will use in the following discussions in brief. Let $\mathcal{D}$ and $\mathcal{K}$ be a set of documents and a set of keywords, respectively. An operation ρ, which extracts keywords from a document $d \in \mathcal{D}$, is defined as $\rho(d) = \{k \mid (k \in \mathcal{K}) \wedge (k$ is a keyword included in $d)\}$. Furthermore, let $D \subset \mathcal{D}$. $\bigcup_{d \in D} \rho(d)$ is denoted by $\rho(D)$, and in particular $\rho(\mathcal{D}) = \mathcal{K}$. A query is a set of keywords Q ($\subset \mathcal{K}$). A query evaluation will retrieve all the documents that contain all the given keywords in Q, and is defined as $\sigma(Q) = \{d \mid d \in \mathcal{D} \wedge Q \subseteq \rho(d)\}$. Let X and Y be subsets of $\mathcal{K}$. The support and the confidence of a rule, $X \Rightarrow Y$, are calculated as follows.

$$Spt(X \Rightarrow Y) = Pr(X \cup Y)$$
$$Cnf(X \Rightarrow Y) = Pr(X|Y) = Pr(X \cup Y)/Pr(X)$$

Here, $Pr(K) \triangleq |\sigma(K)|/|\mathcal{D}|$ where $K \subset \mathcal{K}$. In particular, $Spt(X) = Pr(X)$. Given a document database $\mathcal{D}$, algorithm 1 retrieves all keywords contained and in the same time, calculates the support for each keyword.

Algorithm 1 Counting Supports

Input: a set of documents $\mathcal{D}$.
Output: a set of keywords and a support for each keyword in the set.

```
let K = ∅;
foreach d ∈ D do
    calculate ρ(d);
    foreach k ∈ ρ(d) do
        if k ∈ K then
            Spt(k) = Spt(k) + 1;
        else
            K = K ∪ {k};
            Spt(k) = 1;
        endif
endfor
```
---

3 Stem Rules

In order to reduce the total number of rules that we need to store and to process, a set of *stem rules* are introduced. The stem rules are the only rules that we need to store in the rule base. All the other applicable association rules can be generated from the stem rules at run time instead of being generated from scratch. In addition to the minimal support as used in [Fayy96,Han95,Sava95,Srik96], we first define the maximum support and the maximum confidence for the purposes of query refinement.

Definition 1 Base Condition: *A rule, $X \Rightarrow Y$, satisfies a base condition if and only if*

$$\theta_{s_l} < Spt(X \Rightarrow Y) < \theta_{s_u}$$
$$Cnf(X \Rightarrow Y) < \theta_{c_u}$$

Here, θ_{s_l}, θ_{s_u} and θ_{c_u} are minimum support, maximum support and maximum confidence of the rule, respectively.

Definition 2 Stem Rule: *Given two rules r_1 and r_2. If r_1 satisfying the base condition implies that r_2 satisfies the same base condition, we say that rule r_2 is derived from rule r_1. A stem rule is a rule that can not be derived by any rules. In particular, for a stem rule, $X \Rightarrow Y$, there exists $d \in \mathcal{D}$ such that $X \cup Y \subset \rho(d)$.*

This definition restricts the keywords of a rule to appear in at least one document. This restriction is natural because in keyword retrievals, if a set of keywords does not appear in any documents, then the retrievals by this set of keywords will get no hits.

Property 1 *The following properties are used to exclude non-stem rules.*

a) $\forall K \subset \mathcal{K}, 0 \le |\sigma(K)| \le |\mathcal{D}|$ and $0 \le Pr(K) \le 1$;
b) $K \subset K' \subseteq \mathcal{K}$ implies $Pr(K) \ge Pr(K')$ and $\sigma(K') \subseteq \sigma(K)$;
c) Let $X \subseteq X'$, and $Y \subseteq Y'$. $Spt(X \Rightarrow Y) < \theta_s$ implies $Spt(X \Rightarrow Y') < \theta_s$, $Spt(X' \Rightarrow Y) < \theta_s$, and $Spt(X' \Rightarrow Y') < \theta_s$;
d) $Cnf(X \Rightarrow Y) < \theta_{c_u}$ implies $Cnf(X \Rightarrow Y') < \theta_{c_u}$;
e) If $(X \Rightarrow Y)$ satisfies the base condition, then $(X \Rightarrow Y')$ satisfies the base condition.
f) Let $\Delta X \subseteq \mathcal{K}$. If $(X \Rightarrow Y)$ meets the base conditions, then $(X - \Delta X \Rightarrow Y \cup \Delta X)$ meets the base conditions.

The following Algorithm 2 extracts a set of stem rules from a document database $\mathcal{D}$. First, a candidate set of rules, "Cand", will be generated in Algorithm 2. Second, a set of stem rules is generated from "Cand". An r is added to "Cand" again even if its confidence greater than θ_c because r may derive other stem rules. In other words, r can not be excluded at this point of time because the inverses of d) and f) of Property 1 do not hold.

Unlike Agrawal's algorithm in ([Agra93]) which computes 1-Itemsets, 2-Itemsets, ..., n-Itemsets from a set of items $\mathcal{K}$, we generate a set of stem rules from each document instead. At the step of computing n-Itemsets for each n, the complexity of Agrawal's algorithm is $O(_nC_{|\mathcal{K}|})$, because all combinations of items (keywords) $\mathcal{K}$ must be checked. However, on the other hand, the time complexity of our algorithm is $O(_nC_{|\rho(d)|})$, because we only need to check keywords in a document.

Algorithm 2 Generation of Stem Rules

Input: A set of documents $\mathcal{D}$.
Output: A set of Stem Rules, R_s.

```
let Cand = ∅;
let R_s = ∅ be a set of Stem Rules;
foreach d ∈ D do
    calculate ρ(d);
    foreach X ⊂ ρ(d) do
        if θ_s_l < Spt(X) < θ_s_u then
            Append X ⇒ ∅ to Cand;
        endif
    endforeach
endforeach
while Cand ≠ ∅ do
    remove a rule X ⇒ Y from Cand;
    foreach k ∈ X do
        let r = (X − {k} ⇒ Y ∪ {k})
        if Cnf(r) < θ_c_u and r cannot be derived from R_s then
            add r to R_s;
            delete those rules which can be derived from r from Cand;
        else
            add r to Cand;
        endif
    endforeach
endwhile
```

---

4   Coverage

Definition 3 Coverage: *Let K and D be a subset of $\mathcal{K}$ and a subset of $\mathcal{D}$, respectively. We say that K covers D, or K is a coverage of D, iff*

$$D \subseteq \bigcup_{k \in K} \sigma(k)$$

In a similar fashion, K is also called a coverage of K' ($\subseteq K$) iff

$$\bigcup_{k \in K'} \sigma(k) \subseteq \bigcup_{k \in K} \sigma(k)$$

By the definition, $\mathcal{K}$ is a coverage of $\mathcal{D}$, and $\rho(D)$ is a coverage of D. We also say a set of rules, R, covers D if $\bigcup_{X \Rightarrow Y \in R}(X \cup Y)$ covers D. A minimum coverage is defined as follows in order to exclude redundant keywords from the rule space.

Definition 4 Minimum Coverage: *A set of keywords, K, is called a minimum coverage of D iff D can not be covered by any $K' \subset K$.*

Due to space limitation, we give the following remark without proof. This property guarantees the consistency of processing based on stem rule and coverage. In other words, coverage can be generated by using stem rule.

Property 2 *Let R_s be a set of stem rules. R_s covers a set of documents each of which contains more than one keyword, and at least one of the keywords has the support over θ_{s_1}.*

$$\bigcup_{(X \Rightarrow Y) \in R_s} (X \cup Y)$$

covers $D = \{d \mid (|\rho(d)| > 1) \wedge \exists k \in \rho(d)(spt(k) \geq \theta_{s_1})\}$.

The following Algorithm 3 calculates a minimum coverage for a query which contains a set of keywords, K_0.

Algorithm 3 Minimum Coverage

Input: A query containing a set of keywords K_0.
Output: A minimum coverage $\underline{K}$ for K_0.

let $D = \emptyset$;
let $\mathcal{K} = \emptyset$;
calculate $D_0 = \cup_{k \in K_0}\sigma(k)$;
let $RK = \rho(D_0)$;
sort RK in ascending order based on the supports of its keywords;
while $RK \neq \emptyset$ **and** $D \neq D_0$ **do**
    select k_0 such that $Spt(k_0) = \min_{k \in RK}\{Spt(k) \mid Spt(k) > \theta_{s_1}\}$;
    $RK = RK - \{k_0\}$;
    $D = D \cup \sigma(k_0)$;
    $\underline{K} = \underline{K} \cup \{k_0\}$;
    foreach $k \in RK$ **do**
        $\sigma(k) = \sigma(k) - \sigma(k_0)$;
    endforeach
endwhile

---

5 A Prototype System

We have implemented a prototype system in an UNIX environment, and its graphical user interface is shown in Figure 2. An user query Q will be refined in an interactive way. The prototype system displays the structure of stem rules in response to the user's original query. The user can reference the support and the confidence attached to the the rules to decide the keywords he/she wants to be included in his/her original query. The structure displayed supports conjunction and disjunction refinement. Keywords in a path of the structure mean a conjunction, and keywords in a same layer of the tree mean a disjunction.

Our prototype system currently supports a medium-sized document database of electric engineering documents. The number of all documents is 40,000 ($|\mathcal{D}| = 40,000$), and 16717 keywords are extracted from the document database ($|\mathcal{K}| = \rho(\mathcal{D}) = 16717$). Though in section 2, the support of a keyword set K is defined as $Spt(K) = Pr(K) = |\sigma(K)|/|\mathcal{D}|$, we use intuitively $|\sigma(K)|$ to stand for the support of K in the following because $|\mathcal{D}| = 40,000$ is always fix.

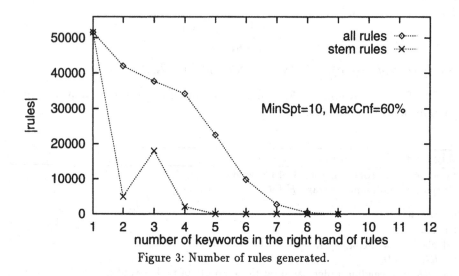

Figure 3: Number of rules generated.

We analyze the distribution of keywords in the document database. The maximum number of keywords in a document is 33 and minimum number of it is 3. In other words, a document contains at least 3 keywords and at most 33 keywords. Most of the documents contain less than 15 keywords ($|\rho(d)| < 15$). Therefore, the rule base will be small because the stem rules are generated based on the combinations of $\rho(d)$. We also find that two-thirds of the keywords have supports less than 10 documents (or $0.025\% = 10/40,000$). Especially at points where the supports are greater than 200 documents, there rarely exist more than two keywords. The smaller the threshold of the minimum support (θ_{s_l}) is, the larger the size of the rule base is. Using a large θ_{s_l} can reduce the size of the rule base but it may result that stem keywords do not cover all documents. The minimum support we use to build the coverage is 5 documents (0.0125%).

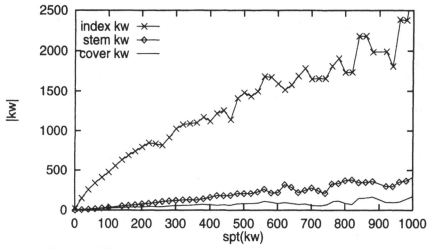

Figure 4: The supports v.s. the number of associated keywords.

The numbers of rules we generated are shown in Figure 3. In this experiment, the threstholds of minimum support, maximum support and maximum confidence are set to $\theta_{s_l} = 0.025\%$, $\theta_{s_u} = 5\%$ and $\theta_{c_u} = 60\%$, respectively. In the figure, the number of rules is counted according to the number of keywords used in the rules. From Figure 3, it can be seen that both Agrawal's algorithm and our algorithm will generate the same 50000 rules when there is only one keyword. This is because that no combination of keywords is needed in both algorithms. However, for any large number of keywords, when all combinations of keywords must be checked, Agrawal's algorithm needs to generate totally about 150,000 rules while our algorithm only generates 20,000 rules. From Figure 3, it can be concluded that even an extremely small θ_{s_l} can reduce the size of rule base considerably, and can be effective for screening.

Figure 4 illustrates the numbers of the three different keyword candidates when keywords have certain supports. In this figure, "index kw", "stem kw" and "cover kw" are the index keywords, the stem keywords and the coverage keywords, respectively. For an instance, when the support, $spt(kw)$, is 300, it can be seen that on average a keyword of support 300 will be associated with about 1000 other keywords. Using stem rules, the number of stem keywords can be reduced to less than 10%. If coverage keyword candidates are used additionally, the number is reduced to half of stem keywords. This means that users can select from much less candidates to refine their queries.

As suggested in [Buck95], we also submit queries and investigate the relationship between precision and recall. Figure 5 shows the superiority of our approach using ARs over both traditional data mining approach and the approach using similarity. In this figure, "Cover", "MinSpt" and "Similar" stand for the retrieval of using coverage approach, traditional data mining approach with minimun support and the approach of using similarity, respectively. It can be seen that "Cover" always has higher recall and precision than other two approaches because our system guarantees the coverage to be 100% and a user can interactively choose what he/she wants in order to refine his/her query. Fixing recalls, the precisions of our approach are up to 15% higher than those of the other two. Fixing the precisions, the recalls of our approach are up to 20% higher than those of the other two approaches.

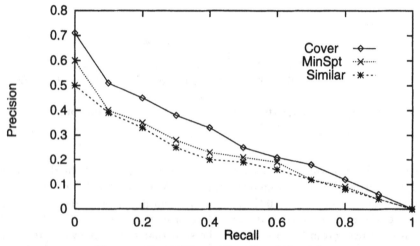

Figure 5: Comparison of Recall and Precision.

6 Conclusion

We propose a query refinement method for a document retrieval system. This query refinement is based on mining ARs among keywords from a document database. Users are able to refine their queries by scanning keyword candidates through a graphical user interface. Two concepts of *Stem Rule* and *Coverage* are introduced, in order to reduce the size of the rule base. Our experimental results confirm the effectiveness of our system. In this paper, we show the effectiveness of the stem rules and the minimum coverage of keywords.

As future work, we will investigate the sizes of rules and the effectiveness of these rules for the precision. Also, we are planning to use clustering as a technique for query refinement in conjunction with association rules.

References

[Agra93] R. Agrawal, T.Imielinski and A.Swami: Mining Association Rules between Sets of Items in Large Databases. *ACM SIGMOD'93*, pp.207-216, Washington, DC, USA.

[Alla95] J.Allan: Relevance Feedback With Too Much Data. *ACM SIGIR'95*, pp.337-343, Seattll, WA, USA.

[Andr98] T. Andreasen, H. L. Larsen, & H. Christiansen: Term Associations and Flexible Querying. *Proc. FQAS'98, International Conference on Flexible Query Answering Systems*, May 13-15, 1998, Roskilde, Danmark. *Lecture Notes in Artificial Intelligence*, Springer-Verlag 1998 (this volume).

[Buck95] C. Buckley *et al.* Automatic query expansion using SMART : TREC 3. In D. K. Harman *ed.* Overview of the 3rd Text REtrieval Conference. NIST Special Publication, 1995.

[Chen94] C.M.Chen and N.Roussopoulos: Adaptive Selectivity Estimation Using Query Feedback. *ACM SIGMOD'94*, pp.161-172, Minneapolis, Minnesota, USA.

[Chen97] H.Chen, Y.Liu & N. Ohbo: Keyword Document Retrieval by Data Mining. IPSJ SIG Notes, Vol.97(64), pp.227-232, Sapporo, Japan, 1997 (in Japanese)

[Fayy96] U.Fayyad, G.Piatestsky & P.Smyth: From Data Mining to Knowledge Discovery in Databases. *The 3rd Knowledge Discovery and Data Mining*, pp.37-53, California, USA, 1996.

[Han95] J.Han and Y.Fu: Discovery of Multiple-Level Association Rules from Large Databases. *21st VLDB*, pp.420-431, Zurich, Swizerland, 1995.

[Naga90] M. Nagao *et al. ed.* Encyclopedic Dictionary of Computer Science. ISBN4-00-080074-4, pp.215, 1990(in Japanese).

[Peat91] H.J.Peat and P.Willett: The Limitations of Term Co-Occurrence Data for Data for Query Expansion in Document Retrieval Systems. *Journal of The American Society for Information Science*, vol.42(5), pp.378-383, 1991.

[Sava95] A.Savasere, E.Omiecinski and S.Navathe: An Efficient Algorithm for Mining Association Rules in Large Databases. *21st VLDB*, pp.432-444, Zurich, Swizerland, 1995.

[Salt90] G. Salton and C. Buckley: Improving Retrieval Performance By Relevance Feedback. *Journal of The American Society for Information Science*, vol.41(4), pp.288-297, 1990.

[Srik96] R.Srikant and R.Agrawal: Mining Quantitative Association Rules in Large Relational Tables. *ACM SIGMOD'96*, pp.1-12, Montreal, Canada, 1996.

[Xu96] Jinxi Xu and W.Bruce Croft: Query Expansion Using Local and Global Document Analysis. *ACM SIGIR'96*, pp.4-11, Zurich, Switzerland, 1996.

[Véle97] B. Vélez, *et al*: Fast and Effective Query Refinement. *ACM SIGIR'*97, pp.6-15, Philadelphia, PA, USA 1997.

Application of Fuzzy Rule Induction to Data Mining

Christophe Marsala

LIP6, Université Pierre et Marie Curie,
4 place Jussieu,
75252 Paris cedex 05, FRANCE.
Christophe.Marsala@lip6.fr

Abstract. In this paper, a data mining process to induce a set of fuzzy rules from a database is presented. This process is based on the construction of fuzzy decision trees. We present a method to construct fuzzy decision trees and a method to use them to classify new examples. In presence of databases, prerequisites for training sets are introduced to generate a good subset of data that will enable us to construct a fuzzy decision tree. Moreover, we present different kinds of rules that can be induced by means of the construction of a decision tree, and we discuss some possible uses of such knowledge.

1 Introduction

Nowadays, a large amount of data is contained in a lot of databases. These data represent an important source of potential knowledge which is highly interesting for us to use. However, the extraction of this knowledge from these databases is very difficult. A solution is to mine databases in order to induce such knowledge [1, 10]. Automated data mining is a very interesting process to induce knowledge from such databases. A particular instance of such knowledge is represented by fuzzy knowledge.

We study induction of a set of fuzzy rules from a database, the inductive learning scheme. Such kind of induced rules can be introduced to optimize the query process of the database [8, 16] or to deduce decisions from data [2, 3, 11, 12]. Many works have been done on the topics of inducing rules from database, but the introduction of fuzzy set theory in the process of induction of rules is more recent.

In the induction of knowledge from data, difficulties appear when considering data described by means of numeric-symbolic values. This kind of values is very important to handle because it is very close to human knowledge and rules with such values are usually more understandable and explainable than rules with numerical values. The introduction of fuzzy set theory enables us to handle such values. This leads us to the construction of a set of fuzzy rules by means of the construction of *fuzzy decision trees* (FDT). A decision tree is a summarization of the knowledge that lies in a set of data in the sense that it represents this knowledge in an explainable form. Moreover, new descriptions can be classified into classes by means of decision rules. In the case of FDTs, the structure of knowledge is more general. It enables us to use numerical or symbolic values, representing fuzzy modalities, during both the learning phase (construction of a tree) and the generalization phase, when classifying new cases.

A problem arises when considering the construction of FDTs from a database. The structure of a database, for instance a relational database, is too complex and must be simplified into a training set to construct a tree. In this case, the characterization of a *good* training set must be considered to ask a query on the database and to recover a set of data.

There exist several kinds of rules that can be induced and obtained from a database. FDTs enable us to obtain various kinds of such rules.

This paper is composed as follows: in Section 2, the construction and the utilization of FDTs are briefly presented. In Section 3, we introduce the problem of the generation of a good training set from a database, we present some criteria for a set of data to be considered as a good training set and we propose solutions to use FDTs to induce various kinds of knowledge from a database. Finally, we present some perspectives for this work.

2 Fuzzy Decision Trees

A decision tree is a natural structure of knowledge. Each node in such a tree is associated with a test on the values of an attribute, each edge from a node is labeled with a particular value of the attribute, and each leaf of the tree is associated with a value of the class. A decision tree is equivalent to a set of IF...THEN rules. Each path in the tree is associated with a rule, where premises are composed by the tests of the encountered nodes, and the conclusion of the rule is composed by the class associated with the leaf of the path.

Edges can be labeled by so-called numeric-symbolic values. A numeric-symbolic attribute is an attribute whose values can be either numeric or symbolic linked with a numerical variable. For instance, the size of a person can be considered as a numeric-symbolic attribute: either a numerical value, as "1.72 meters", or a numeric-symbolic value such as "tall" is associated with the size. Such kind of values leads to the generalization of decision trees into *fuzzy decision trees* [4,6,15,17,18]. An example of FDT is given in Figure1. With this tree, constructed by means of our software *Salammbô* [13], the type of an iris flower can be recognized when knowing particular values for a set of attributes. A remark can be made about the possible occurrence of several modalities of an attribute in the same branch. An attribute is discretized in two modalities several times with different thresholds for these modalities depending on the current training subset of examples associated with that node.

FDTs enable us to use numeric-symbolic values either during their construction or when classifying new cases. The use of fuzzy set theory enhances the understandability of decision trees when considering numerical attributes. More-

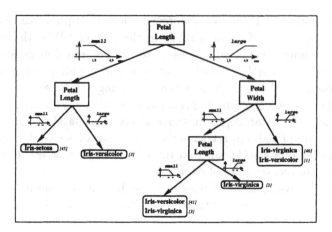

Fig. 1. A fuzzy decision tree

over, we have proven in [13] that the fuzziness leads to a better robustness when classifying new cases.

2.1 Learning Phase: Construction of a Fuzzy Decision Tree

A decision tree can be constructed from a set of examples by *inductive learning*. Inductive learning is a process to generalize knowledge from the observation of a given phenomenon. It is based on a set of *examples*, called the *training set*. Each example is a case already solved or completely known, associated with a pair [description, class] where the *description* is a set of pairs [attribute, value] which is the available knowledge. The aim of inductive learning is to infer knowledge in order to be able to associate any forthcoming description with its presumed class. A common process of inductive learning is the construction of decision trees from a given set of examples [7, 14].

Most of the algorithms to build decision trees, the Top Down Induction of Decision Trees (TDIDT) algorithms, proceed in the same way. The decision tree is built from its root to its leaves. The training set is successively split by means of a question on the value of a chosen attribute (the divide and conquer strategy).

Let $\mathcal{E}$ be a training set composed by a set of examples t_i. Each t_i is defined by a value $t_i[A_j]$ for each attribute A_j of a set of attributes $\mathcal{A}$. A particular attribute $C \in \mathcal{A}$ is highlighted and considered as the class to learn. The TDIDT algorithm to build decision trees is the following:

1. *Select* an attribute $A_j \in \mathcal{A}$, $A_j \neq C$, with m_j modalities $\{v_{j1}, ..., v_{jm_j}\}$. This attribute will be used to split the training set $\mathcal{E}$ into several subsets. A node $\eta(A_j)$ is created in the tree. It is labeled with a test on the value of A_j.
2. *Split* the training set $\mathcal{E}$ by means of the selected attribute A_j. As many subsets $\mathcal{E}_{jl}$ as modalities v_{jl} are created:

$$\mathcal{E} = \bigcup_{l=1,...,m_j} \mathcal{E}_{jl} \quad \text{with} \quad \mathcal{E}_{jl} = \{t_i \in \mathcal{E} \mid t_i[A_j] = v_{jl}\}$$

Each value v_{jl} of the attribute labels an edge from the node $\eta(A_j)$, this edge leads to the corresponding subset $\mathcal{E}_{jl}$. In the case of numeric-symbolic attributes, the partition of $\mathcal{E} = \mathcal{E}_{j1} \cup ... \cup \mathcal{E}_{jm_j}$ can be fuzzy when each $\mathcal{E}_{ji}$ is a fuzzy set of the set $\mathcal{F}$ of elements of $\mathcal{E}$ in adequation with the value v_{ji} of attribute A_j (i.e. $\mathcal{F} = \{t_i \in \mathcal{E} \mid \mu_{v_{jl}}(t_i[A_j]) > 0\}$ if $t_i[A_j]$ is numerical) and examples belonging to the intersection $\mathcal{E}_{ji} \cap \mathcal{E}_{jk}$ should be distributed by means of a splitting strategy.

3. *Check* if the stopping criterion is fulfilled by each subset $\mathcal{E}_{jl}$. A leaf is created from a subset that fulfills this criterion. This leaf is associated with the class of this subset.

4. Start again in step 1 with all the subsets that do not fulfill the stopping criterion.

At each step of this algorithm, a parameter of the algorithm has to be selected: a measure of discrimination, a splitting strategy, a stopping criterion.

Measure of Discrimination. The choice of an attribute is done by means of a measure of discrimination. It enables us to measure the power of discrimination of an attribute A_j relatively to the class C. It evaluates to which extent the values of this attribute are linked with each modality of the class. Thus, all the attributes can be compared in order to select the best one to split the training set. In the process of construction of decision trees, the choice of the best attribute by means of a measure of discrimination is a heuristic that enables us to optimize the tree being built. This heuristic should minimize the size of the tree and introduces a semantic coherence of the tests that label the nodes of the tree. The question associated with a node will be the more pertinent in order to discover the value of the class.

A measure of discrimination must be defined specifically in order to construct FDTs from a set of examples described by means of numeric-symbolic attributes. It has to take into account the degrees of membership to a fuzzy value for each example of the training set. The most commonly used measure of discrimination in the presence of fuzzy values is an extension of the Shannon entropy, the so-called star entropy [15]:

$$H_S^*(C|A_j) = - \sum_{l=1}^{m_j} P^*(V_{jl}) \sum_{k=1}^{K} P^*(C_k|V_{jl}) \log(P^*(C_k|V_{jl}))$$

where $V_{jl} = \{t_i \in \mathcal{E} \mid t_i[A_j] = v_{jl}\}$ and $C_k = \{t_i \in \mathcal{E} \mid t_i(C) = c_k\}$. This measure is obtained from the classical Shannon measure of entropy by substituting the Zadeh's probability measure P^* of fuzzy events [19] to the classical probability. Let $\mathcal{V} = \{x_1, ..., x_n\}$ be a fuzzy set defined by its membership function μ, each element x_i from $\mathcal{V}$ is associated with a classic probability measure of occurrence $P(x_i)$. $\mathcal{V}$ is considered as a fuzzy event. The *probability of the fuzzy event* $\mathcal{V}$ is defined by Zadeh as:

$$P^*(\mathcal{V}) = \sum_{i=1}^{n} \mu(x_i)P(x_i)$$

Splitting Strategy. The splitting strategy defines how the training set will be split by a question on the value of an attribute. In the case of numerical or symbolic attribute, each modality v_{jl} of an attribute A_j defines a subset $\mathcal{E}_{jl}$ of the training set, composed by the examples that possess value v_{jl} for A_j for $l = 1 \ldots m_j$.

In the case of numeric-symbolic attributes, a common solution is to distribute the examples in all the subsets $\mathcal{E}_{ji}$ with their degree of membership to the fuzzy value v_{ji}. Secondly, a close strategy is to distribute the examples in the same way but to give a membership degree equal to 1 to all the examples in the intersection $\mathcal{E}_{jl} \cap \mathcal{E}_{jk}$ to reflect their membership to both subsets. However, a drawback of this strategy is to duplicate the most imprecise, uncertain or noisy examples of the training set. A third strategy is to use α-cuts for each fuzzy set. For instance, with $\alpha = \frac{1}{2}$, the following crisp partition is created: $\forall l = 1, \ldots m_j$, $\mathcal{E}_{jl} = \{t_i \in \mathcal{E} \mid \mu_{v_{ji}}(t_i[A_j]) \geq \frac{1}{2}\}$. A last solution can be to create an additional specific subset with all examples from this intersection. Thus, it will lead to the construction of a specific edge from the current node, and so, to the construction of a specific subtree to discriminate these examples.

Stopping Criterion. The stopping criterion T enables to know if a subsets of $\mathcal{E}$ is homogeneous with regard to the class. The process of construction of the decision tree will stop the development of a path on a suitable set. The stopping criterion can be for instance defined as one of the following strategies:

- All the examples of $\mathcal{E}$, or at least a *majority* of examples, are associated with the same class. Usually, the stopping criterion T is linked with the measure of discrimination used in step 1 of the algorithm. The notion of *majority* is evaluated by means of a threshold for the value of the measure of discrimination. The smaller the value of the measure of discrimination, the more homogeneous the training set with regard to the class.
- The number of examples in $\mathcal{E}$ is too small to justify a split of $\mathcal{E}$.
- There is no more attribute to use. This stopping criterion is used when we accept only one node associated with an attribute on a path of the tree.

The stopping criterion for the construction of FDTs is very similar to the stopping criterion in the classic case. The impurity of the current training set with respect to the repartition of the classes can be measured either by the measure of discrimination used in step 1 of the algorithm, which is fuzzy, or by another one, fuzzy or not.

2.2 Classifying With a Fuzzy Decision Tree

As mentioned, a path of the tree is equivalent to an IF...THEN rule. The premises for such a rule r are composed by tests on values of attributes, and the conclusion is the value of the class that labels the leaf of the path:

$$\text{if } A_{l_1} = v_{l_1} \text{ and } \ldots \text{and } A_{l_p} = v_{l_p} \text{ then } C = c_k$$

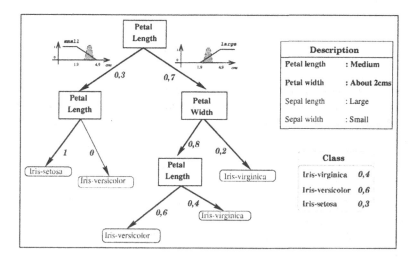

Fig. 2. Classification with a fuzzy decision tree

In a FDT, a leaf can be labeled by a set of values $\{c_1, \ldots, c_K\}$ for the class, each value c_j associated with a weight computed during the learning phase. Thus, a path of a FDT is equivalent to the following rule:

$$\text{if } A_{l_1} = v_{l_1} \text{ and } \ldots \text{ and } A_{l_p} = v_{l_p} \text{ then}$$
$$C = c_1 \text{ with the degree } P^*(c_1|(v_{l_1}, \ldots v_{l_p})) \text{ and } \ldots$$
$$\text{and } C = c_K \text{ with the degree } P^*(c_K|(v_{l_1}, \ldots v_{l_p}))$$

A new example e to classify is described by means of values for each attribute $\{A_1 = w_1; \ldots; A_n = w_n\}$. This description is compared with the premises of the rule r by means of a measure of satisfiability [5] enabling us to value the satisfiability of any observed modality w to the edge modality v. The measure of satisfiability used in the software *Salammbô* is:

$$\mathbf{Deg}(w, v) = \frac{\int_X \mu_{w \cap v}\, dx}{\int_X \mu_w\, dx} \quad \text{if} \quad \int_X \mu_w\, dx \neq 0 \tag{1}$$

where μ_w is the membership function associated with the modality w, $\mu_{w \cap v}$ is the membership function associated with the intersection $w \cap v$ between the modality w and the modality v, X is the universe of values where μ_w and $\mu_{w \cap v}$ are defined.

For each premise, a degree of satisfiability $\mathbf{Deg}(w_{l_i}, v_{l_i})$ is computed for the corresponding value w_{l_i}. Finally, given a rule r, a description is associated with the class c_j with a *final degree* of satisfiability $\mathbf{Fdeg}_r(c_j)$ that corresponds to the satisfiability of the description to the premises of the rule r weighted by the conditional probability for c_j according to the rule r in order to take into account the confidence of the rule:

$$\mathbf{Fdeg}_r(c_j) = \top_{i\,=\,1\ldots p}\mathbf{Deg}(w_{l_i}, v_{l_i}).P^*(c_j|(v_{l_1}, v_{l_2}, \ldots v_{l_p}))$$

Final degrees computed from all the rules are aggregated by means of a triangular conorm $\perp$ (for instance, the *maximum* triangular conorm) to obtain a single degree of satisfiability $\mathbf{Fdeg}(c_j)$. If n_ρ is the number of rules given by the FDT:

$$\mathbf{Fdeg}(c_j) = \perp_{r\,=\,1\ldots n_\rho}\mathbf{Fdeg}_r(c_j)$$

For each value of the class, the description e is associated with such a degree of satisfiability $\mathbf{Fdeg}(c_j)$ for each class c_j computed from the whole set of rules. The class c_e associated with e can be chosen as the class with the higher degree of satisfiability:

$$\mathbf{FDeg}(c_e) = \max_{j=1\ldots K}\mathbf{FDeg}c_j)$$

We used such a process of aggregation of degrees in order to have meaningful values of degrees for each class.

The whole process of classification is summarized in Figure2. A given example, the *description* of which described by means of fuzzy values, must be classified. Each of its values for corresponding attribute are compared with each value labeling a vertex in the tree. The value of this degree is reported on the corresponding edge of the tree. The final degree for each class is computed as mentioned and is reported on the figure.

2.3   Construction of Fuzzy Partitions

The process of construction of FDTs is based on the knowledge of a fuzzy partition for each numerical attribute. However, it can be difficult to possess such fuzzy partition. We propose an automatic method of construction of a fuzzy partition from a set of values for a numeric-symbolic attribute [13,9].

This method is based on the utilization of the mathematical morphology theory implemented by means of the formal language theory. Kernels of concordant values of a numerical attribute related to the values of the class can be found. Fuzzy modalities induced from a set of numerical values of an attribute are linked with the repartition of the values of the class related to the numerical attribute. Thus a contextual partitioning of an attribute is done that enables us to obtain the best partition related to the attribute with respect to the class.

This method can be used, without the process of construction of FDTs, to construct fuzzy partitions on the universe of values of numerical attribute, when the required fuzzy modalities must be linked with values of another attribute. More details can be found in [13,9].

3 Fuzzy Decision Trees to Mine Knowledge

A database is a complex structure of data. It cannot be considered as a classical training set to construct decision trees without any previous treatment. Such a treatment, that enables us to extract simpler data from the database, is made by means of appropriate queries.

In this part, we present several kinds of knowledge that can be induced from a training set by means of the construction of a decision tree: classification rule, characterization rule or association rule. After that, we present some utilizations of such induced set of rules.

3.1 Training Set

First of all, as mentioned in Section 2, the construction of a decision tree requires a training set. The database, either relational or more complex, cannot be used as a training set. For instance, a relational database is a set of tables linked each other by means of relations while a decision tree can only be constructed from a single table. A training set can be constructed from a subset of the database by means of a query that enables us to extract a pertinent subset of data.

For instance, let us place ourselves in a concrete problem. Let an industrial company database composed of the following relations.

CUSTOMERS(num-customer#, country, address)

COMMANDS(num-command#, date, num-customer#, amount)

PRODUCTS(num-Product#, unit-price, num-provider#, number-available)

A-COMMAND(num-command#, unit-price, quantity, num-Product#, discount)

This database is related to the products of the company and their customers. An appropriate query to build a training set from this database is:

SELECT
CUSTOMERS.country, A-COMMAND.num-Product, PRODUCTS.unit-price,
A-COMMAND.quantity, A-COMMAND.discount, COMMANDS.amount,
FROM
CUSTOMERS, A-COMMAND, COMMANDS, PRODUCTS
WHERE
A-COMMAND.num-command = COMMANDS.num-command
AND CUSTOMERS.num-customer = COMMANDS.num-customer
AND PRODUCTS.num-Product = A-COMMAND.num-Product

This query will produce a single table that will be used as a training set.

Now, the problem is to ask such a query to obtain a *good* training set to induce knowledge. In our scheme, a training set is considered as *good* when it enables us to induce *coherent* rules. The two prerequisites to induce such rules are:

- for each attribute, examples of the training set cover a consequent range of values.
- given a particular attribute, the *class*, in the training set, examples from each class are sufficient to induce classification rules or characterization rules.

Table 1. Example of Training set

Country	num-Prod.	U-price	Quant.	Disc.	Amount
Italy	17	135.00	4	No	540.00
Canada	64	115.00	15	Yes	6584.75
Denmark	18	218.50	12	Yes	2490.90
France	19	32.00	15	No	10263.40
France	40	64.00	30	No	5740.00
Italy	41	33.50	3	No	459.00

The consequent range of values is a guaranty for constructing a decision tree that will possess a high level of generality. The number of examples from each class ensures us that no particular case will be forgotten in the induction process.

3.2 Different Kinds of Rules Induced From Databases

Let $\mathcal{E}$ be a good training set composed by examples, each example is described by means of values for a set of attributes $\mathcal{A}$. Values for such attributes can be symbolic, numerical or numeric-symbolic. From this training set, different kinds of rules will be induced.

Classification Rules. We are first interested in *classification rules* induced from a database. The purpose is to construct a classifier from $\mathcal{E}$, for instance a set of rules, to recognize a particular attribute $\mathcal{C} \in \mathcal{A}$, the class, by means of a subset of attributes of $\mathcal{A}$. With a classifier, a value for the class can be associated to any forthcoming description.

A decision tree is such a classifier and the construction of a decision tree from $\mathcal{E}$ enables us to obtain a set of classification rules.

For instance, let us consider that the class to recognize is the French country for a customer, given modalities for the attributes of his command (Table1). The FDT constructed by our software *Salammbô* is presented in Figure3.

Thus, a classification rule that enables us to recognize a command from France is: *if the quantity is important and the amount is low, then the command comes from France (1.0)*.

A new command (for instance, *the quantity is medium and the amount is average*) can be associated with a class by means of such rules.

The explainability of FDT is highlighted here more than in the case of classical decision trees that handle numerical attributes. A fuzzy modality is more understandable than a threshold on the universe of numerical values of an attribute. Moreover, FDTs appear smaller than classical trees for a given problem.

Characterization Rules. *Characterization rules* can also be induced from a database. From $\mathcal{E}$, the purpose is to find characterizations based on elements of $\mathcal{A}$ that discriminate a particular attribute $\mathcal{C}$.

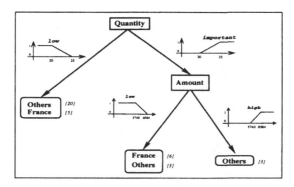

Fig. 3. Example of fuzzy decision tree

Such rules can also be deduced from a decision tree by regrouping all the paths that end on a leaf labeled by the same value of the class. Thus, the decision that labels a leaf is characterized by the values of the attributes occurring in the nodes of all these paths.

For instance, a characterization rule can be *French commands possess an important quantity and a low amount.*

Association Rules. Finally, *association rules* are also induced from a database [2, 3]. In this case, there is no particular highlighted attribute from $\mathcal{A}$. The aim is to find rules that describe the examples of $\mathcal{E}$ in pointing out association rules between values of attributes of $\mathcal{A}$. Association rules can be considered as a particular form of classification rules [12].

To induce a set of such rules from a training set, several trees can be generated in varying the attribute selected as the class. The values of attributes appearing on a path of the decision tree can be considered as linked to determine the class. In the tree, each path is associated with a degree deduced from the number of training examples that lead to the construction of this path. A threshold can be fixed to preserve all paths with high degrees.

For instance, for *French commands*, an association rule is induced between the *important* modality for attribute *Quantity* and the *low* modality for attribute *amount.*

Moreover, association is induced by means of the method of construction of fuzzy partitions. This method enables us to determine fuzzy modalities for a numerical attribute related to the repartition of the values of a given class. Thus, an association between values of numerical attributes and values of the class is taken into account to generate a fuzzy modality for this attribute.

3.3 A New Knowledge For the Database

The induced rule base is a new form of knowledge that can be associated with the database. This knowledge can be used in different ways.

First of all, it enables us to improve the querying process of the database. Such a set of induced fuzzy rules can be associated with a database as a knowledge base. Such a knowledge base can be used to help answering frequent queries. A quick response can be found for a query on the value of an attribute. It can also lower the conditions on the values of attributes for a query, before the process of examination of the database [8].

Moreover, the rules induced by means of a FDT take advantage of the fuzziness of their values to take into account new numeric-symbolic values for attributes. The method of classification with such a set of fuzzy rules is a good way to handle new values for attributes.

Secondly, a set of fuzzy rules induced by means of the construction of a FDT is completely expressible. It can be used as a new knowledge on the domain of the database, and it can be understood by any expert of this domain. For instance, numerical attributes can be discretized in more explainable fuzzy modalities.

4 Conclusion

In this paper, we present an inductive method to construct FDTs from a training set of data. This method is based on an automatic method of construction of fuzzy modalities that enables us to generate fuzzy values from a set of numerical values. A method is also presented to use a FDT to classify a new description.

Our aim is to use FDTs to mine knowledge, as a fuzzy rule base, from a relational database. In this case, we highlight the problem of the generation of a good training set to induce such knowledge. We propose some prerequisites for such training sets that have to be taken into account in the query process of the database to construct a good subset of data.

Given a good training set, we present different kinds of rules that can be induced by means of the construction of a decision tree, and we discuss some possible use of such knowledge.

In future works, we will focus on the characterizations of good training sets in order to automate the construction of a training set from a database.

5 Acknowledgement

The author wishes to thank here Nara Martini Bigolin for her valuable help during the preparation of this paper and for all the very fruitful comments that enabled him to develop part 3 of this paper.

References

1. P. Adriaans and D. Zantinge. *Data mining.* Addison-Wesley, 1996.
2. R. Agrawal, T. Imielinski, and A. Swami. Database mining: A performance perspective. *IEEE Transactions on Knowledge and Data Engineering*, 5(6):914–925, December 1993.

3. R. Agrawal, T. Imielinski, and A. Swami. Mining association rules between sets of items in large databases. In *Proceedings of the ACM-SIGMOD International Confference on Management of Data*, pages 207–216, Washington DC, USA, May 1993.

4. B. Bouchon-Meunier, C. Marsala, and M. Ramdani. Learning from imperfect data. In D. Dubois, H. Prade, and R. R. Yager, editors, *Fuzzy Information Engineering: a Guided Tour of Applications*, pages 139–148. John Wileys and Sons, 1997.

5. B. Bouchon-Meunier, M. Rifqi, and S. Bothorel. Towards general measures of comparison of objects. *Fuzzy Sets and Systems*, 84(2):143–153, December 1996.

6. X. Boyen and L. Wehenkel. Automatic induction of continuous decision trees. In *Proceedings of the 6th International Conference IPMU*, volume 1, pages 419–424, Granada, Spain, july 1996.

7. L. Breiman, J. H. Friedman, R. A. Olshen, and C. J. Stone. *Classification And Regression Trees*. Chapman and Hall, New York, 1984.

8. I. A. Chen. Query answering using discovered rules. In S. Y. W. Su, editor, *Proceedinds of the 12th International Conference on Data Engineering*, pages 402–411, New Orleans, Louisiana, USA, February 1996. IEEE Computer Society Press.

9. C. Marsala, B. Bouchon-Meunier. Fuzzy partioning using mathematical morphology in a learning scheme. In *Proceedings of the 5th IEEE Int. Conf. on Fuzzy Systems*, volume 2, pages 1512–1517, New Orleans, USA, September 1996.

10. J. Han and Y. Fu. Exploration of the power of attribute-oriented induction in data mining. In U. M. Fayyad, G. Piatetsky-Shapiro, P. Smyth, and R. Uthurusamy, editors, *Knowledge discovery and data mining*, chapter 16, pages 151–170. AAAI Press – MIT Press, 1996.

11. X. Hu and N. Cercone. Mining knowledge rules from databases: A rough set approach. In S. Y. W. Su, editor, *Proceedinds of the 12th International Conference on Data Engineering*, pages 96–105, New Orleans, Louisiana, USA, February 1996. IEEE Computer Society Press.

12. B. Lent, A. Swami, and J. Widom. Clustering association rules. In *Proceedinds of the 13th International Conference on Data Engineering*, pages 220–231, Birmingham, UK, April 1997. IEEE Computer Society Press.

13. C. Marsala. *Apprentissage inductif en présence de données imprécises : construction et utilisation d'arbres de décision flous*. Thèse de doctorat, Université Pierre et Marie Curie, Paris, France, Janvier 1998. Rapport LIP6 n° 1998/014.

14. J. R. Quinlan. Induction of decision trees. *Machine Learning*, 1(1):86–106, 1986.

15. M. Ramdani. Une approche floue pour traiter les valeurs numériques en apprentissage. In *Journées Francophones d'apprentissage et d'explication des connaissances*, 1992.

16. S. Shekhar, B. Hamidzadeh, A. Kohli, and M. Coyle. Learning transformation rules for semantic query optimization: A data-driven approach. *IEEE Transactions on Knowledge and Data Engineering*, 5(6):950–964, December 1993.

17. M. Umano, H. Okamoto, I. Hatono, H. Tamura, F. Kawachi, S. Umedzu, and J. Kinoshita. Fuzzy decision trees by fuzzy ID3 algorithm and its application to diagnosis systems. In *Proceedings of the 3rd IEEE Conference on Fuzzy Systems*, volume 3, pages 2113–2118, Orlando, june 1994.

18. Y. Yuan and M. J. Shaw. Induction of fuzzy decision trees. *Fuzzy Sets and systems*, 69:125–139, 1995.

19. L. A. Zadeh. Probability measures of fuzzy events. *Journal Math. Anal. Applic.*, 23, 1968. reprinted in "*Fuzzy Sets and Applications: selected papers by L. A. Zadeh*", R. R. Yager, S. Ovchinnikov, R. M. Tong and H. T. Nguyen eds, pp. 45–51.

Applying Genetic Algorithms to the Feature Selection Problem in Information Retrieval

María J. Martín-Bautista, María-Amparo Vila

Department of Computer Science and Artificial Intelligence
Granada University, Avda. Andalucía s/n, 18071 Granada, Spain.
e-mail: {mbautista, vila}@decsai.ugr.es

Abstract. The demand of accuracy and speed in the Information Retrieval processes has revealed the necessity of a good classification of the large collection of documents existing in databases and Web servers. The representation of documents in the vector space model with terms as features offers the possibility of application of Machine Learning techniques. A filter method to select the most relevant features before the classification process is presented in this paper. A Genetic Algorithm (GA) is used as a powerful tool to search solutions in the domain of relevant features. Implementation and some preliminary experiments have been realized. The application of this technique to the vector space model in Information Retrieval is outlined as future work.

1   Introduction

The information explosion caused by the expansion of the communications has promoted the creation of large information stores. The classification and hierarchization of these data warehouses have become a pressing need, specially in processes of Information Retrieval.

The classification problem has been widely studied in others disciplines such as Numerical Taxonomy and Machine Learning, and many techniques generated in these fields are being exported to solve the problems of classification and rules generation in Data Mining and Knowledge Discovery in large databases.

One of the first stages of the classification process is the Feature Selection (FS), by means of which the complexity of the problem is reduced by the elimination of irrelevant features to consider later in the classification stage. This paper concerns to this problem: the developed model deals with the selection of the most relevant features in classification processes by utilizing a Genetic Algorithm (GA). The possible solutions of the problem, e.g. the sets of most relevant features, are coded into the chromosomes by binary alphabet, with 0 and 1 representing the absence or presence of a the feature in the set solution, respectively.

The initial results in the experimentation with our model reveal GAs as a powerful tool to reduce the dimensionality of classification problems. A future application to very large sets, and specially, to documents in the vector space model is also outlined.

The paper is organized as follows: in next section, an introduction to the feature selection problem and the most known methods are given. A preliminary study of this problem in the framework of Information Retrieval is outlined in section 3. In section 4, a survey of the application of GAs to the problem is studied; our genetic model to selection of features is explained in section 5 and the experimental results of the developed system are shown in section 6. Finally, some concluding remarks and future trends are presented in section 7.

2 Feature Selection

Several approaches attempting to solve the feature selection problem have been presented in some fields of Artificial Intelligence, such as Machine Learning and Pattern Recognition. Moreover, its application scope has extended to other fields such as Data Mining and Knowledge Discovery, in which the efficiency of most of the processes tends to be reduced by the presence of irrelevant features.

The FS problem may be formulate as follows: Let us consider a set of items or examples represented by means of a set F of variables or features. These items are to be distributed in different classes and the objective is to find a subset R of features with the property of being relevant regarding this classification.

In the literature, there have been several definitions of relevance. Roughly speaking, a feature is considered as relevant if it has the discriminatory power to distinguish between examples belonging to different classes in a degree higher than a fixed threshold.

The first experiments about FS have been realized in Machine Learning, where most of the methods of classification and reduction of the features set have been proposed [2]. These methods may be classified in two categories [5]:

- *Filter Methods*, which are applied before the classification, and its evaluation does not depend on the classification but usually based on different measures of distance between the examples.
- *Wrapper Methods* that are applied while the classification or rather, their goodness is based on the result of the classification by a certain method.

This last category of methods presents, in general, the best performance, due to the use of the error of the classification algorithm as a measure of the accuracy and efficiency of the method. However, the drawbacks of these methods are significant as well:

⟨ As the feature selection depends on the classification algorithm, we loose generality because of the behaviour of the classification algorithm in terms of accuracy and efficiency. Furthermore, the selection of a classification method slightly suitable for a certain problem may give rise to choose or eliminate features wrongly.

⟨ The computational time employed by this sort of methods is excessive. The problem may get worse exponentially with the size of the sample set and the number of features. Furthermore, it may turn into a tough problem, specially when Soft Computing techniques such as GAs and Neural Networks are used to solve it when the sets of examples and/or features are large.

This is the main reason to use a filter method, as it treats the problem feature selection in broad outline.

3 Feature Selection in Information Retrieval

The classification of documents in Web servers and documentary databases is a determinant aspect in Information Retrieval. The efficiency of the different methods utilized in query and matching processes is usually diminished by a poor categorization of the documents.

As most of the techniques used in documentary classification are determined by the occurrences of the words (terms) appearing in the documents, the fixing of the set of most relevant terms seems to be an important stage in this process.

One of the most remarkable model of representation of documents is the vector space model [6], in which the terms of queries and documents are the components of vectors. These terms may be viewed as features which binary values 0 and 1 indicate the absence or presence of a term in the document, respectively.

Hence, a collection of documents may be a multidimensional space of vectors. The application of the traditional Machine Learning techniques of classification is overwhelmed with this complexity and a previous process of feature selection in order to reduce the dimensionality becomes an ineludible task.

The problem of FS in the framework of documentary databases, therefore, can be studied from two points of view. If the documents are not previously classified, the selection of the most relevant features (terms in documents) give us those terms which describe the documents better. On the other hand, if ther is a previous classification of the documents, a selection of the features would carry out the search of the most discriminant terms, that is, those terms which allow to distinguish the different existent classes in a later stage.

4 Applying GAs to Feature Selection

GAs is an adaptive search technique which improvement over random and local search methods have been demonstrated [3]. In a GA, a population of individuals representing possible space solutions is maintained through several generations. Each individual is evaluated in each generation based on its fitness with respect to the considered function to minimize or maximize. New individuals are produced by the selection, crossover and mutation of the fittest individuals. Through the generations, the population is led to the space of the better solutions in the given domain.

In this approach, a Filter Method to reduce the features set by using GA is developed. Other approaches with GAs to solve this problem have been proposed in the literature, but they may be considered as Wrapper Methods, since they used the error of a classification algorithm as the fitness function to minimize.

There is a main reason to justify the use of the GA in a Filter Model instead of a Wrapper one. The computational time of the GAs is quite high; therefore, the combination of GAs and a classification method is not so efficiently, moreover if we take into account that a run of the classification algorithm would be needed every time that the GA population is evaluated. If the sample set is not very big, and the number of features is not very high, as tends to be in Machine Learning, the GAs in Wrapper Methods are quite useful, since the system usually classify or learn at the same time that the selection of the features occurs. However, there are two cases where the GAs in a Filter Method is highly recommended to use instead of a Wrapper Method:

⟨   When the sample set is very large or/and the number of features is disproportionate, as usually happens in other fields such as Information Retrieval and Data Mining.

⟨   When the sample set is classified previously, and we are looking for those features that gives us the classification. In this case, the Wrapper Method would be not so useful as we may not know the classification method utilized, and the use of a specific classification algorithm as fitness function could lead us to wrong results.

5   The Genetic Model of Feature Selection

5.1   Problem Formulation

Let $E = e_1, e_2, ..., e_m$ be a set of examples to classify, where each example i is represented by a set of features $F_i = f_{i1}, f_{i2}, ..., f_{in}$. Thus, the presence or absence of a feature j in a certain example i is determined by a binary code as follows:

⟨ $f_{ij} = 0$, if the jth feature is presented in the example i, and

⟨ $f_{ij} = 1$, if the jth feature is not presented in the example i.

Let suppose now a population of chromosomes $C_1, ..., C_p$ with binary coding, where each chromosome represents a potential solution of the problem, that is, a minimal relevant set of features for a certain sample set. Therefore, the position j of the hth chromosome will be 1 if the jth feature is selected as relevant; and will be 0 if the feature j is not considered as relevant in the set. Hence, the length of the chromosome will be the number of features of the sample set. Regarding the number of chromosomes into the population, it will be determined by the size of the sample set, the number of known or expected classes and the number of features, as it will be explained further on.

In the following paragraphs, the elements concerning a definition of a GA will be presented. In all of them, the main idea to consider is the knowledge about the classes of the sample set, that is, a classification a priori of the examples. Based on this previous classification, the initialization of the population as well as the fitness function may be modified.

5.2 Initialization of the Population

In the first generation of the GA, the chromosomes may be created based on the sample set. In GAs, the first population is usually generated randomly but, as the chromosomes reflect the differences among the examples, it seems reasonable to initializate the population starting from chromosomes related to the sample set. In this sense, there may be four different ways to generate the initial population:

Initialization 1 (I1). Each chromosome is an example selected randomly.

Initialization 2 (I2). For each chromosome, two examples are selected randomly, and the XOR between them will be calculated to generate the chromosome. As we are dealing with a binary alphabet, a gene in the chromosome will be 1 if the feature of this position is able to distinguish between the two selected examples, and 0 otherwise.

Initialization 3 (I3). Just like the previous initialization, the chromosome is determined by the XOR of two examples, but the pairs of examples must belong to different classes.

A previous classification of the sample set is not considered in Initialization 1 and Initialization 2 so, both are valid when the classes are known or not. However, Initialization 3 depends on the classification a priori. As for the size of the population, if the sample set is not quite large, the first population could contain the sample set several times in Initialization 1, or just a multiple of the number of the examples in the other cases.

5.3 Fitness Function

The use of binary codification in the chromosomes reveals that the relevance of the features will take part in the fitness function. In the case of real codification, every position in the chromosome may represent the relevance of that feature, and a threshold may be established to consider the most relevant ones.

The general idea to calculate the adaptation of the chromosomes, is the use of a measure of distance between a chromosome and the vector resulting from the comparison of two examples of the sample set as follows:

Let e_i, $e_j \in E$, with i, $j \leq card(E)$ and $i \neq j$, be two examples to compare, and let $v_{i,j}(x)$ be the discriminatory vector calculated as the logical operator XOR of e_i and e_j, that is:

$$v_{i,j}(x) = \begin{cases} 0 & if \ e_i(x) = e_j(x) \\ 1 & if \ e_i(x) \neq e_j(x) \end{cases} \tag{1}$$

where $x \leq n$, with n being the number of features (length of the chromosomes).

Each position of the vector v represents the capacity of a particular feature to discriminate two specific examples. Therefore, a chromosome will fit better if the features selected, that is, the positions where a 1 is placed into the chromosome, coincide with those features that discriminate the examples, that is, the positions of 1 in the discriminatory vector. Based in the difference of the chromosome and the discriminatory vector, the Hamming Distance between them may be calculated as a first approach to the fitness function:

$$d_y = \sum_{x=1}^{n} \left| C_y(x) - v_h(x) \right| \tag{2}$$

where $y \leq p$ and $h \leq t$, with p being the size of the population and t representing the number of discriminatory vectors generated, and n representing the number of features.

This measure evaluates the overall features in a chromosome, but a weight to give more importance to those features that have discriminated more pairs of examples is needed. Thus, in order to have an individual evaluation of every feature, a vector $g(x)$ is calculated by the accumulation of each discriminatory vector $v_{i,j}(x)$ generated:

$$g(x) = \sum_{h=1}^{t} \left(v_{i,j}(x) \right)_h, \quad x = 1, \ldots, n \tag{3}$$

Therefore, the fitness function may be weighed by the accumulated capacity of discrimination of every feature as follows:

$$d_y = \frac{\sum_{x=1}^{n} \left(\left| C_y(x) - v_h(x) \right| \cdot \left(1 - \frac{g(x)}{\sum_{x=1}^{n} g(x)} \right) \right)}{n} \qquad (4)$$

Hence, the discriminatory capacity of the chromosome itself and not only the similarity between the chromosome and the discriminatory vector must be evaluated. This capability of the chromosome is calculated by adding the accumulated discriminatory values of every feature presented into the chromosome, that is, those positions equal to 1, as it is shown below:

$$q_y = \frac{\sum_{x=1}^{n} \left(C_y(x) \cdot g(x) \right)}{\sum_{x=1}^{n} g(x)} \qquad (5)$$

As the q_y value is higher, the better is the chromosome. Thus, to minimize the fitness function, the capacity of the chromosome is added in the following way:

$$p_y = d_y + (1 - q_y) \qquad (6)$$

Based on this definition of fitness function, there may be several ways to evaluate the population. Mainly, it depends on the knowledge of a previous classification of the examples. As the discriminatory vector is obtained from two examples of the sample set, it seems reasonable to select examples belonging to different classes. Thus, if the sample set is classified a priori, there would be several ways to select the two examples, as is shown below:

Evaluation 1 (E1). If a previous classification of the examples does not exist, the discriminatory vector may be calculated from the random selection of a different pair of examples each time.

Evaluation 2 (E2). A pair of examples is selected randomly from a pair-pool of all the possible pairs of examples (e_i, e_j), where e_i and e_j belong to different classes. For sample sets of two classes, only a discriminatory vector will be resulted. The generalization to k classes would bring about $k \cdot (k-1)/2$ different discriminatory vectors. In this case, a partial fitness p_y^r value, with $r = 1,...,k \cdot (k-1)/2$ would be calculated for each discriminatory vector between examples from different classes each time. The overall fitness value would be obtained by the average of all the partial fitness values as follows:

$$p_y = \frac{\sum\limits_{r=1}^{k \cdot (k-1)/2} p_y^r}{k \cdot (k-1)/2} \tag{7}$$

where p_y^r is calculated as (6).

Based on the number of generations, the number of possible pair, the size of the population, and the length of the chromosome, the evaluation of the population with the same pair could be realized through several generations.

6   Implementation and Experimentation

In order to analyzed the behaviour of the GA in datasets with both irrelevant and correlated features, an artificial dataset called CorrAL coming from Machine Learning has been selected. CorrAL dataset [4] has 32 instances classified in two classes. (A_0, A_1, B_0, B_1, I, C) are the features of the examples, where A_0, A_1, B_0, B_1 are relevant, I is irrelevant and C is correlated to the class label 75% of the time.

6.1   GA Parameters

The genetic operators selected have been: the linear ranking as scheme of selection probabilities [1], the one-point crossover and the standard mutation [3]. The mutation probability is 0.001 and the crossover probability is 0.6. The size of the population depends of the initialization method selected. The number of iterations is at least, 50.

The algorithm has been run three times for every combination of an evaluation and an initialization method, each one with a different seed for the random number generator.

6.2   Results

The experiments have been realized with populations of different sizes. When the population size is equal to the number of examples (32), the E2 evaluation method seems to work much more better than E1 (see Fig. 1) as was expected. However, both methods show a poor behaviour as they need a high number of generations to find the optimal solution. This fact could be due to the lack of diversity in the population because of the little size of the population. As for the iteration methods, I3 presents the best performance and I1 the worst.

In the second case, where the population size is 64, the E1 evaluation works better than the E2 evaluation. As the size of the population increases, the diversity is higher, so the average of iterations in both methods decrease considerably. The iteration methods keep the same order in the performance.

The good results in the second case lead us to test if an increase of the size of the population improves the system performance. However, when the population size is 96, there is not an appreciable difference in the behaviour of the system. The ranking of the iteration methods is the same, and again the E1 evaluation method is better than E2.

However, if we focus on the I3 as initialization method, which is the one with the best performance in all the cases, it can be observed that the results from E1 and E2 are similar when the population size is doubled or tripled.

Population Size	E1		E2		Avg.
N° Examples	I1	992	I1	310	651
	I2	680	I2	390	535
	I3	750	I3	195	472,5
	Avg.	807,3	Avg.	298,3	
2*(N°Examples)	I1	82	I1	578	330
	I2	55	I2	170	112,5
	I3	62	I3	77	69,5
	Avg.	66,3	Avg.	275	
3*(N°Examples)	I1	216	I1	155	185,5
	I2	116	I2	93	104,5
	I3	69	I3	75	72
	Avg.	133,6	Avg.	107,6	

Fig. 1.   Irrelevance   Evaluation.

7   Summary and Future Work

In this paper we presented the use of a genetic algorithm for selecting features in the framework of Information Retrieval. The size of the databases and the large number of documents to retrieve in web servers lead us to develop our system as a filter method to select the most relevant features before the classification process.

As the fitness function, a similarity measure between the chromosomes, representing sets of features, and the discriminatory vector resulting from the comparison of examples of the sample set was considered.

Preliminary tests had been realized by using a Machine Learning dataset which have allowed us to compare the different methods proposed for the initialization and evaluation of the population.

Results have shown that the better initialization method is the I3, which generated the chromosomes from the XOR operator between a random pair of examples belonging to different classes. When a previous classification is not provided, the I2 method should be used. As for the evaluation methods, they do not seem to present an uniform behaviour when the size of the population is changed.

However, when the population size is doubled or tripled, E1 and E2 have a similar performance. In both cases, the number of iterations of the pair E1-I3 is slightly less than the iterations of E2-I3. This fact could be due to differences in the target of both evaluations. On the one hand, the E1 evaluation method attempts to discriminate the examples without taking into account the classes. On the other hand, E2 is more restrictive as it tries to discriminate between classes, which justifies that E1 utilizes less generations to find the solution. In any case, the short computation time needed to reach the solution, whichever the evaluation method, reveals the goodness of the presented approach.

As future work, some experiments in larger set of examples have to be realized. The future application of this approach to documentary databases will lead the algorithm to search in a much higher solutions space, where a regular difference among the evaluation methods can be set.

The use of the vector space model as representation of the documents in terms of presence and absence of features facilitates us the task of codification of the features in the chromosomes. A way to deal with the frecuency of the terms in the document as an additional measure in the fitness function must be considered as well.

References

1. Baker, J.E. Adaptive Selection Methods for Genetic Algorithms. In *Proc. on the First International Conference on Genetic Algorithms and their applications*, pp.101-111, Grefenstette, J.J. (ed). Hillsdale, New Jersey: Lawrence Earlbaum, 1985.
2. Dash, M and Liu, H. Feature Selection for Classification. In *Intelligent Data Analysis, vol. 1, no. 3*, 1997.
3. Holland, J.H. *Adaptation in Natural and Artificial Systems*. Massachusetts: MIT Press, 1992.
4. John, G.H., Kohavi, R. and Pfleger, K. Irrelevant Features and the Subset Selection Problem. In *Proc. of the Eleventh International Conference on Machine Learning*, pp.121-129. San Francisco, CA: Morgan Kauffmann Publishers, 1994.
5. Langley, P. Selection of Relevant Features in Machine Learning. In *Proc. of the AAAI Fall Symposium on Relevance*. New Orleans, LA: AAAI Press, 1994.
6. Salton, G and McGill, M.J. *Introduction to Modern Information Retrieval*. New York: McGraw-Hill, 1983.

An Overview of Cooperative Answering in Databases *

Jack Minker

Department of Computer Science and Institute of Advanced Computer Studies
University of Maryland, College Park

Abstract

The field of cooperative answering goes back to work started by Joshi and Webber [12] in natural language processing in the early 1980s at the University of
Pennsylvania. The work was applied to databases and information systems at
the University of Pennsylvania by Kaplan [14,15] and Mays [17]. Other early
work at the University of Pennsylvania and at other universities is discussed in
[25,13,26,16,18,24]. Databases and knowledge base systems are often difficult
to use because they do not attempt to cooperate with their users. A database
or a knowledge base query system provides literal answers to queries posed to
them. Such answers to queries may not always be the best answers. Instead,
an answer with extra or alternative information may be more useful and less
misleading to a user.

This lecture surveys foundational work that has been done toward developing
database and knowledge base systems with the ability to exhibit cooperative
behavior. In the 1970s, Grice [11] proposed maxims of cooperative conversation.
These maxims provide the starting point for the field of cooperative answering.

To develop a general system for data and knowledge bases, it is important to
specify both the sources of information needed to provide cooperative behaviors,
and what constitutes cooperative behavior. Several sources of knowledge apply:
the basic knowledge in a system is given by explicit data, referred to as data
in a relational database, or facts (extensional data) in a deductive database;
by general rules that permit new relations (or new predicates) to be developed
from existing data, referred to as views in relational databases and as intensional
data in deductive databases; and by integrity constraints that must be consistent
with the extensional and intensional data. Integrity constraints may be obtained
either through the user or the database administrator, or by a data mining
capability. Whereas integrity constraints must be consistent with every instance
of the database schema, another source of knowledge is state constraints, which
may apply to the current state, and need not apply to a subsequent state upon
update. Two additional sources of knowledge arise from information about the
users. One describes the class of the user, for example, an engineer or a child,
each of whom expect different kinds of answers to queries, and user constraints

---

* Invited Paper, Flexible Question Answering Systems, May 13-15, 1998, Roskilde,
Denmark

that must be satisfied. User constraints need not be consistent with the database, but reflect the interests, preferences and desires of the user.

Alternative cooperative behaviors are explained and illustrated by examples. The cooperative behaviors discussed are:

1. *Misconceptions.* A misconception is a query for which it is not possible, in any state of the database to have an answer.
2. *State Misconceptions.* A state misconception is a query for which it is not possible to have an answer, given the current state of the database.
3. *False Presuppositions.* A query has a false presupposition when it fails to have an answer, but is neither a misconception nor a state misconception.
4. *Intensional Answer.* An intensional answer is a generalization of a query which provides a rule that satisfies the query, but does not necessarily provide data that satisfies the query.
5. *Relaxed Answer.* A relaxed answer to a query is an answer that may or may not satisfy the original query, but provides an alternative answer that may meet the needs of the user.
6. *Scalar Implicature.* A scalar implicature is a range that may meet the query.
7. *User Goals, Inferences and Preferences.* User goals, interests and preferences should be adhered to when answering a query.

A brief description is provided of three systems that have been implemented, which exhibit cooperative behavior for relational and deductive databases. The systems and their features are:

1. *Cooperative AnsweRing Meta INterpreter (CARMIN)*, developed at the University of Maryland by Minker and his students [9, 8, 10].
   (a) Misconceptions.
   (b) State Misconceptions
   (c) False Presuppositions
   (d) Intensional Answers
   (e) Relaxed Answers
   (f) User Goals, Interests and Limited Preferences
2. *CoBase*, developed at UCLA by Chu and his students [3, 2, 1, 4, 5]. A language, *CoSQL* has been implemented and interfaced with an existing database (Oracle) and SQL.
   (a) Intensional Answers
   (b) Relaxed Answers
   (c) User Goals, Inferences and Preferences
3. *FLEX*, developed at George Mason University by Motro [23, 19–22].
   (a) Well Formedness Test of Queries and Automatic Modification
   (b) Relaxed Queries
   (c) False Presuppositions

For a discussion of the state-of-the-art of cooperative answering systems, see [6]. A description of work on relaxation in cooperative answering systems is given in [7].

A functional description is provided of a cooperative database system. It is currently possible to develop a cooperative capability that interfaces with any of the existing database systems. Since proposed and future versions of relational databases will include capabilities to handle recursion and semantic query optimization, the ability to include cooperative capabilities will, in the not too distant future, be incorporated into such systems.

References

1. W. W. Chu and Q. Chen. A structured approach for cooperative query answering. *IEEE Transactions on Knowledge and Data Engineering*, 6(5), Oct. 1994.
2. W. W. Chu, Q. Chen, and A. Y. Hwang. Query answering via cooperative data inference. *Journal of Intelligent Information Systems (JIIS)*, 3(1):57–87, Feb. 1994.
3. W. W. Chu, Q. Chen, and R.-C. Lee. Cooperative query answering via type abstraction hierarchy. In S. M. Deen, editor, *Cooperating Knowledge Based Systems 1990*, pages 271–290. Springer-Verlag, University of Keele, U.K., 1991.
4. W. W. Chu, Q. Chen, and M. A. Merzbacher. CoBase: A cooperative database system. In R. Demolombe and T. Imielinski, editors, *Nonstandard Queries and Nonstandard Answers*, Studies in Logic and Computation 3, chapter 2, pages 41–73. Clarendon Press, Oxford, 1994.
5. W. W. Chu, H. Yang, K. Chiang, M. Minock, G. Chow, and C. Larson. CoBase: A scalable and extensible cooperative information system. *Journal of Intelligent Information Systems (JIIS)*, 6(2/3):223–259, May 1996.
6. T. Gaasterland, P. Godfrey, and J. Minker. An overview of cooperative answering. *Journal of Intelligent Information Systems*, 1(2):123–157, 1992. Invited paper.
7. T. Gaasterland, P. Godfrey, and J. Minker. Relaxation as a platform for cooperative answering. *Journal of Intelligent Information Systems*, 1:293–321, 1992.
8. T. Gaasterland, P. Godfrey, J. Minker, and L. Novik. A cooperative answering system. In A. Voronkov, editor, *Proceedings of the Logic Programming and Automated Reasoning Conference*, Lecture Notes in Artificial Intelligence 624, pages 478–480. Springer-Verlag, St. Petersburg, Russia, July 1992.
9. T. Gaasterland, P. Godfrey, J. Minker, and L. Novik. Cooperative answers in database systems. In *Proceedings of the Space Operations, Applications, and Research Conference*, Houston, Texas, Aug. 1992.
10. P. Godfrey, J. Minker, and L. Novik. An architecture for a cooperative database system. In W. Litwin and T. Risch, editors, *Proceedings of the First International Conference on Applications of Databases*, Lecture Notes in Computer Science 819, pages 3–24. Springer Verlag, Vadstena, Sweden, June 1994.
11. H. Grice. Logic and Conversation. In P. Cole and J. Morgan, editors, *Syntax and Semantics*. Academic Press, 1975.
12. A. Joshi, B. Webber, and I. Sag, editors. *Elements of Discourse Understanding*. Cambridge University Press, 1981.
13. A. K. Joshi, B. L. Webber, and R. M. Weischedel. Living up to expectations: Computing expert responses. In *Proceedings of the National Conference on Artificial Intelligence*, pages 169–175, University of Texas at Austin, Aug. 1984. The American Association for Artificial Intelligence.
14. S. J. Kaplan. Appropriate responses to inappropriate questions. In Joshi et al. [12], pages 127–144.

15. S. J. Kaplan. Cooperative responses from a portable natural language query system. *Artificial Intelligence*, 19(2):165–187, Oct. 1982.

16. W. Lehnert. A computational theory of human question answering. In Joshi et al. [12], pages 145–176.

17. E. Mays. Correcting misconceptions about database structure. In *Proceedings of the CSCSI '80*, 1980.

18. K. McKeown. *Generating Natural Language Text in Response to Questions about Database Queries*. PhD thesis, University of Pennsylvania, 1982.

19. A. Motro. Extending the relational model to support goal queries. In *Proceedings from the First International Workshop on Expert Database Systems*, pages 129–150. Benjamin/Cummings, 1986.

20. A. Motro. SEAVE: A mechanism for verifying user presuppositions in query systems. *ACM Transactions on Office Information Systems*, 4(4):312–330, October 1986.

21. A. Motro. Using constraints to provide intensional answers to relational queries. In *Proceedings of the Fifteenth International Conference on Very Large Data Bases*, Aug. 1989.

22. A. Motro. FLEX: A tolerant and cooperative user interface to databases. *IEEE Transactions on Knowledge and Data Engineering*, 2(2):231–246, June 1990.

23. A. Motro. Panorama: A database system that annotates its answers to queries with their properties. *Journal of Intelligent Information Systems (JIIS)*, 7(1):51–74, Sept. 1996.

24. M. E. Pollack. Generating expert answers through goal inference. Technical report, SRI International, Stanford, California, Oct. 1983.

25. M. E. Pollack, J. Hirschberg, and B. Webber. User participation in the reasoning processes of expert systems. In *Proceedings of the American Association of Artificial Intelligence*, 1982.

26. B. L. Webber and E. Mays. Varieties of user misconceptions: Detection and correction. In *Proceedings of the Eighth International Joint Conference on Artificial Intelligence*, pages 650–652, Karlsruhe, Germany, Aug. 1983.

Automatic Generation of Trigger Rules for Integrity Enforcement in Relational Databases with View Definition

Laura Mota-Herranz and Matilde Celma-Giménez

Departamento de Sistemas Informáticos y Computación,
Universidad Politécnica de Valencia,
Camino de Vera s/n, 46022 Valencia (Spain)
{lmota,mcelma}@dsic.upv.es
http://www.dsic.upv.es

Abstract. In this paper, we propose a method for integrity enforcement in relational databases with view definition using the production rule mechanism provided by active database systems. The method generates a set of trigger rules at compile-time. This set of rules can repair at run-time the inconsistency produced by some transactions by executing a simple update over the extensional database. We also propose a logic metaprogram which implements the method.

1 Introduction

An integrity constraint is a condition that the database is required to satisfy at all times. If the evolution through time of a database is described by a sequence of states where, given a state, the following state is obtained by the execution of a transaction, then the database must not be allowed to reach a state in which some integrity constraint is violated. The traditional behaviour of database systems when a transaction containing one or more violating updates occurs is to roll back the transaction in its entirety. This simple rejection is obviously unsatisfactory for most real databases due to the fact that rolling back the transaction can imply undoing a lot of updates, even though the violations can be repaired with other updates.

There are two alternative approaches to solving this problem. In the first approach, a set of safe transactions is designed from the database scheme. These transactions never lead the database to an inconsistent state and are the only ones allowed to users [8]. The second approach allows the user to run any transaction but, in this case, the database scheme includes what to do when a violation is detected. Therefore, when a transaction leads the database to an inconsistent state, instead of rolling back the transaction which yields the initial state, the system executes a *repair transaction* that leads the database to a consistent state [3–5, 7, 10].

The work we present in this paper is centered on the second approach. We propose a method that computes actions capable of repairing the consistency in a deductive database[1] when the database has reached an inconsistent state in which some integrity constraint is violated. We will use techniques and tools of active database systems. We will also make use of the results of solving the problems of *simplified integrity checking* and *view updating*. The paper has been organized as follows. Section 2 describes the framework and introduces an illustrative example. Section 3 presents a first solution based on examples. Section 4 presents the language used to define the repairs focusing on both their syntax and semantics. Section 5 includes a logic metaprogram that implements the proposed solution. Finally, in section 6, we comment on our future work.

2   The Framework

In this section we present the framework of the method.

1. Let (R, IC) be a deductive database scheme where: R is a relational language [9] with disjoint sets of base predicates and derived predicates, and $IC \subseteq \{W_i : W_i$ is a closed formula in R, $1 \leq i \leq n\}$ is the set of integrity constraints.
2. Let $D = EDB \cup IDB$ be a database state where EDB is the extensional database and IDB is the intensional database:
   - $EDB \subseteq \{A : A$ is a ground atom over a base predicate$\}$
   - $IDB \subseteq \{A \leftarrow L_1 \wedge \ldots \wedge L_n : A$ is an atom over a derived predicate and L_i is a literal$\}$
   and let $comp(D)$ be the first order theory which represents the state D in the completion semantics [6].
3. Let D be a database state which satisfies every integrity constraint W in IC. This means that $comp(D) \models W$.
4. Let $\{\leftarrow inc_i : inc_i \leftarrow \neg W_i, 1 \leq i \leq n\}$ be the set of integrity constraints in denial form where inc_i ($1 \leq i \leq n$) is a predicate symbol of zero arity that does not occur in the database scheme.
5. Let $D \cup \{inc_i \leftarrow \neg W_i\}$ have a hierarchical, allowed and strict normal form [1] (for the sake of simplicity, we will refer to this normal form as D).
6. Let a transaction be a set of update operations over base predicates which have one of the following patterns: $ins(A)$ or $del(A)$ where A is a ground atom over a base predicate.

Example 1. Let D be a database state with the following deductive rules (the extensions of the base predicates $\{d, f, g, h, j, k, l, m, q, s, t\}$ are not specified because they are not necessary for the purpose of the example):

1. $p(x_1, y_1) \leftarrow q(x_1, y_1) \wedge s(z_1, y_1) \wedge \neg r(x_1, z_1)$
2. $p(x_2, y_2) \leftarrow l(x_2, y_2) \wedge \neg j(x_2, y_2)$
3. $r(x_3, y_3) \leftarrow h(x_3, y_3) \wedge t(y_3, z_3) \wedge \neg n(y_3, z_3)$

---

[1] Since we are going to use deductive rules to define the views, from now on, we will use the expression "deductive database" instead of "relational database with view definition".

4. $n(x_4, y_4) \leftarrow d(x_4, y_4) \wedge g(x_4, z_4) \wedge \neg f(x_4, z_4)$

5. $inc \leftarrow k(x_5, y_5) \wedge p(x_5, y_5)$

And, let $W = \forall x_5 \forall y_5 \ (k(x_5, y_5) \rightarrow \neg p(x_5, y_5))$ be an integrity constraint whose denial form is $\leftarrow inc$ (where inc is defined by rule 5).

3   The Method Based on Examples

In the approach we propose, the system reacts autonomously when the database has reached an inconsistent state. The reaction consists of a sequence of database updates, which we will call *repairs*. These updates remove constraint violations progressively until the database reaches a final state, which satisfies every integrity constraint. If this is not possible, the system must abort the transaction leading the database to the initial state that there was before the execution of the user's transaction.

The question is now, how can we specify the reactive behaviour of the system? Obviously, the system has to react when some integrity constraint is violated. This circumstance can only happen when some database updates are executed. Consequently, the system will react when one operation that can violate an integrity constraint is executed; then it will check if the integrity constraint has actually been violated; and, finally it will execute a repair. It is easy to see that a smart way of specifying this behaviour is by means of the trigger rules (also called Event-Condition-Action rules) of the active systems. Therefore, the method we propose will generate a set of trigger rules for each integrity constraint. These rules, which we call *repair rules*, have an operation that can violate the constraint as event and an operation that can remove the violation as action.

In this section we will show how the method generates these rules automatically from the database scheme. If W_i is an integrity constraint whose denial form is $\leftarrow inc_i$ (where $inc_i \leftarrow \neg W_i$) and taking previous assumptions (from 1 to 6) into account, then W_i is violated when the execution of a user's transaction induces the insertion of the inconsistency atom inc_i. Therefore, the problem of automatically generating repair rules for the constraint W_i can be viewed as a special case of the problem of updating a deductive database[2].

Let us consider a method, M, which solves the updates by generating transactions which only update the extensional database. Then, in a very general way, the problem of automatic generation of repair rules can be solved in two steps:

– Step 1: compute an operation O_j over a base predicate that can induce an insertion for the inconsistency atom inc_i. This can be achieved using the method M with input request $ins(inc_i)$.

---

[2] This problem can be stated as follows: "Given a database state D and an update $insert(G)$ (resp. $delete(G)$) where G is a well-formed formula that D does not satisfy (resp. satisfies), find a transaction T such that the state obtained after applying T to D satisfies G (resp. does not satisfy)".

- Step 2: compute an operation O_k over a base predicate that can induce a deletion for the inconsistency atom inc_i. Using the above method with input request $del(inc_i)$ we can obtain the operation O_k. This operation has to be *compatible* with $O_j{}^3$.

Let us refer back to the example 1. It is easy to determine that, deletions of facts from predicate j can suppose the violation of the constraint W by inducing the insertion of the atom inc through rules 2 and 5. We can also determine that deletions from predicate l can repair the integrity by inducing the deletion of the atom inc. Then we can define the following rule to repair the violation of the integrity constraint W (where E represents the event part of the rule, C represents the condition part, and A represents the action part):

Rule R_0 : $E : del(j(x_2, y_2))$ $C : inc$ $A : del(l(x_2, y_2))$

Notice that the evaluation of the condition of this rule can be very costly. It uses the rule 1 in spite of the fact that, if the initial state was consistent, then the insertion of the atom inc can only be induced by rule 2 when the event $del(j(x, y))$ has happened. Taking this information into account, we can rewrite the rule as follows:

Rule R_0 : $E : del(j(x_2, y_2))$ $C : k(x_2, y_2) \wedge l(x_2, y_2)$ $A : del(l(x_2, y_2))$

In accordance with these ideas, in the remainder of the section we will illustrate how we can automatically generate the repair rules in the database example at compile-time. For this purpose, we construct the *dependency graph* for the predicates of the database. The nodes in this graph are predicates and the arcs are doubly labeled with a deductive rule and with a sign ($+$ or $-$). The graph has an arc from node A to node B labeled with $(r, +)$ (resp. $(r, -)$) if the predicate B appears in the head of a rule whose body contains the predicate A in a positive (resp. negative) literal. The following figure shows the dependency graph for the database scheme of the example:

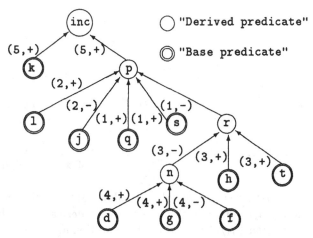

---

[3] We will say that the operation $ins(L)$ is compatible with $del(N)$ if $L \neq N$.

To illustrate how we can obtain the repair rules from this graph, we will study three paths from a base predicate to the inconsistency predicate.

– Path 1: from predicate k to inc

<u>Condition after</u>   (inc)

$p(x_5,y_5)$ $(5,+)$ ↑ inc←$k(x_5,y_5)\wedge p(x_5,y_5)$
                    (k)

From this path we can deduce the following: "the insertion of an instance of $k(x_5, y_5)$, say $k(a, b)$, induces the insertion of a derivation path for the atom inc if $p(a, b)$ is *satisfied after* the operation occurs".

– Path 2: from predicate q to inc

<u>Condition after</u>   (inc)

$k(x_5,y_5)\theta_1$ $(5,+)$ ↑(inc←$p(x_5,y_5)\wedge k(x_5,y_5))\theta_1$
                           (p)   unified by $\theta_1=\{x_5/x_1,y_5/y_1\}$

$(s(z_1,y_1)\wedge\neg r(x_1,z_1))\theta_1$ $(1,+)$ ↑(p(x_1,y_1)←$q(x_1,y_1)\wedge s(z_1,y_1)\wedge\neg r(x_1,z_1))\theta_1$
                           (q)

Again, from this path, we can deduce that: "the insertion of an instance of $q(x_1, y_1)$, say $q(a, b)$, induces the insertion of a derivation path for $p(a, b)$ if there is a substitution $\{z_1/c\}$ such that the condition $s(c, b) \wedge \neg r(a, c)$ is *satisfied after* the operation occurs; and the insertion of $p(a, b)$ induces the insertion of a derivation path for inc if $k(a, b)$ is *satisfied after* the operation occurs". Generalizing, we can conclude that the insertion of an instance of $q(x_1, y_1)$ induces the insertion of inc if $k(x_1, y_1) \wedge s(z_1, y_1) \wedge \neg r(x_1, z_1)$ is *satisfied after* the operation occurs (where this condition has been obtained by correctly applying the substitutions to the body of the rules).

– Path 3: from predicate f to inc

<u>Condition after</u>   (inc)

$k(x_5,y_5)\theta_1$

$(5,+)$ ↑(inc←$p(x_5,y_5)\wedge k(x_5,y_5))\theta_1$
     (p) $\theta_1 = \{x_5/x_3,y_5/y_1\}$

$(q(x_1,y_1)\wedge s(z_1,y_1))\theta_2\theta_1$

$(1,-)$ ↑(p(x_1,y_1)←$q(x_1,y_1)\wedge s(z_1,y_1)\wedge$
     (r) $\neg r(x_1,z_1))\theta_2\theta_1$
              $\theta_2 = \{x_1/x_3,z_1/x_4\}$

$\neg r(x_3,y_3)\theta_3\theta_2\theta_1$

$(3,-)$ ↑(r(x_3,y_3)←$h(x_3,y_3)\wedge t(y_3,z_3)\wedge$
     (n) $\neg n(y_3,z_3))\theta_3\theta_2\theta_1$
              $\theta_3 = \{y_3/x_4,z_3/y_4\}$

$(d(x_4,y_4)\wedge g(x_4,z_4))\theta_3\theta_2\theta_1$

$(4,-)$ ↑(n(x_4,y_4)←$d(x_4,y_4)\wedge g(x_4,z_4)\wedge$
     (f) $\neg f(x_4,z_4))\theta_3\theta_2\theta_1$

Finally, from this path we can conclude the following: "the deletion of an instance of $f(x_4, z_4)$, say $f(a, b)$, induces the insertion of a derivation path for $n(a, c)$ if there is a substitution $\{y_4/c\}$ such that the condition $d(a, c) \wedge g(a, b)$ is *satisfied after* the operation occurs. The insertion of $n(a, c)$ induces the deletion of an instance of $r(x_3, a)$, say $r(d, a)$, if there is not another derivation path for this atom, i.e. if $\neg r(d, a)$ is *satisfied after* the operation. The deletion of $r(d, a)$ induces the insertion of $p(d, e)$ if there is a substitution $\{y_1/e\}$ such that the condition $q(d, e) \land s(a, e)$ is *satisfied after* the operation occurs. Finally, the insertion of $p(d, e)$ induces the insertion of *inc* if $k(d, e)$ is *satisfied after* the operation". In summary, the deletion of $f(a, b)$, induces the insertion of a derivation path for *inc* if $k(d, e) \land q(d, e) \land s(a, e) \land \neg r(d, a) \land d(a, c) \land g(a, b)$ is *satisfied after* the operation. This condition can be simplified if we remove the conjunction $d(a, c) \land g(a, b)$ from it (this simplification is possible because, if the condition contains the literal $\neg r(d, a)$, then it is not necessary to check $d(a, c) \land g(a, b)$). Generalizing, we can conclude that the deletion of an instance of $f(x_4, z_4)$ can induce the insertion of *inc* if the condition $k(x_3, y_1) \land q(x_3, y_1) \land s(x_4, y_1) \land \neg r(x_3, x_4)$ (obtained by correctly applying the substitutions) is *satisfied after* the operation.

Then, how can we use these ideas to generate the repair rules? Obviously, every path in the graph from a base predicate to an inconsistency predicate represents a possible violation of the constraint represented by that inconsistency predicate. We can determine the update which can induce that violation from the leaf in the path. If the leaf is the predicate A and the path to the inconsistency predicate is positive (resp. negative), then, the violating updates are insertions (resp. deletions) of ground atoms built with the predicate A[4]. On the other hand, the conjunction that we have called *Condition after* represents a condition which must be satisfied after the operation occurs in order to ensure that the update has actually induced an inconsistency. Notice that the *Condition after* is only generated from the body of the rules that appear in the path between the inconsistency predicate and the first negative literal over a derived predicate.

In accordance with these ideas and without considering still the action part of the rules, the repair rules generated from the paths 1, 2 and 3 are the following:

Rule R_1 : $E : ins(k(x_5, y_5))$ $C : p(x_5, y_5)$ $A :?$

Rule R_2 : $E : ins(q(x_1, y_1))$ $C : k(x_1, y_1) \land s(z_1, y_1) \land \neg r(x_1, z_1)$ $A :?$

Rule R_3 : $E : del(f(x_4, z_4))$
$C : k(x_3, y_1) \land q(x_3, y_1) \land s(x_4, y_1) \land \neg r(x_3, x_4)$ $A :?$

The condition of these rules can be simplified unfolding atoms over derived predicates. Accordingly, we can rewrite the rule R_1 as the two following rules:

Rule R_{11} : $E : ins(k(x_5, y_5))$ $C : l(x_5, y_5) \land \neg j(x_5, y_5)$ $A :?$

Rule R_{12} : $E : ins(k(x_5, y_5))$ $C : q(x_5, y_5) \land s(z_1, y_5) \land \neg r(x_5, z_1)$ $A :?$

Once we have shown how it is possible to generate the events and the conditions of the rules, we are going to illustrate how to find an action for the rule from its condition. Let $C = L_1 \land \ldots \land L_n$ be the condition of one of these rules. Then, there are three possibilities for each literal L_i ($1 \leq i \leq n$):

---

[4] A path is positive if there is an even number of minus signs or no minus signs in the arcs of the path. A path is negative if there is an odd number of minus signs in the arcs of the path.

- L_i is a base positive literal: the operation $del(L_i)$ could falsify C so this operation can be used as a repair action of the rule.
- L_i is a base negative literal, $L_i = \neg A_i$: the operation $ins(A_i)$ could falsify C so it can be considered as a repair action of the rule.
- L_i is a derived negative literal, $L_i = \neg A_i$: in this case, we cannot consider operations over this literal because it is a derived one. So, we have to find the operations over base literals that can falsify L_i (by inducing insertions in the atom A_i). These operations can be the action of the rule.

For instance, from the condition in rule R_{11} we can deduce that the updates $ins(j(x_5, y_5))$ and $del(l(x_5, y_5))$ are two potential actions for the rule. With these actions we can generate the following rules:

$$Rule\, R_{111} : E : ins(k(x_5, y_5))\ C : l(x_5, y_5) \wedge \neg j(x_5, y_5)\ A : del(l(x_5, y_5))$$

$$Rule\, R_{112} : E : ins(k(x_5, y_5))\ C : l(x_5, y_5) \wedge \neg j(x_5, y_5)\ A : ins(j(x_5, y_5))$$

Now we focus on the rule R_2. The possible actions for this rule are $\{del(k(x_1, y_1)), del(s(z_1, y_1))\} \cup \{updates\ which\ induce\ an\ insertion\ into\ r(x_1, z_1)\}$. However, how can we determine the updates over base predicates which could induce an insertion into $r(x_1, z_1)$? Obviously, we can follow the approach used before when we looked for updates that could induce the insertion of an inconsistency atom. Let us consider the subgraph of the dependency graph having as root the predicate r. If we study the paths in this subgraph as we did before, we can determine the set of updates which can induce the insertion of $r(x_1, z_1)$. Let us consider the following path.

- Path 4: from predicate f to r

Condition before	Condition after	
		(r)
	$(h(x_3,y_3) \wedge t(y_3,z_3))\theta_1$	$\uparrow (r(x_3,y_3) \leftarrow h(x_3,y_3) \wedge$
	$(3,-)$	$\neg n(y_3,z_3) \wedge t(y_3,z_3))\theta_1$
		(n)
		$\theta_1 = \{y_3/x_4, z_3/y_4\}$
$(d(x_4,y_4) \wedge g(x_4,z_4))\theta_1$	$\neg n(x_4,y_4)\theta_1$	$\uparrow (n(x_4,y_4) \leftarrow d(x_4,y_4) \wedge$
	$(4,-)$	$\neg f(x_4,z_4) \wedge g(x_4,z_4))\theta_1$
		(f)

From this path, we can conclude that if we want to insert a derivation path for an instance of $r(x_3, x_4)$, for example $r(d, a)$, we could insert an instance of $f(a, z_4)$ for a substitution for the variable z_4. But, how can we find this substitution? By studying the path, we realize that "the insertion of an instance of $f(a, z_4)$, say $f(a, b)$, induces the deletion of a derivation path for those instances of $n(a, y_4)$ such that the condition $d(a, y_4) \wedge g(a, b)$ was *satisfied before* the operation occurs". So, the conjunction that we have called *Condition before* can help us to find the substitution for z_4 and to instantiate the action $ins(f(a, z_4))$. However, the deletion of these instances of $n(a, y_4)$ will only be real if the condition $\neg n(a, y_4)$ is *satisfied after* the operation. Finally, the deletion from $n(x_4, y_4)$ induces the insertion in $r(x_3, x_4)$ if the condition $h(x_3, x_4) \wedge t(x_4, y_4)$ is *satisfied after* the operation. In general, the insertion of an instance of $f(x_4, z_4)$ can induce the insertion of instances of $r(x_3, x_4)$ if $h(x_3, x_4) \wedge t(x_4, y_4) \wedge \neg n(x_4, y_4)$ is *satisfied after* the operation.

Therefore, in the most general case, the action of a repair rule will be a tuple with three components: (CB, O, CA). This tuple must be interpreted as follows: "CB is a condition that must be evaluated in the state previous to the operation to instantiate O; O is an operation which properly constitutes the action of the rule; and CA is a condition that will be evaluated in the state reached after the operation in order to ensure that the rule actually has repaired a violation". Finally, we can generate the following rule from the rule R_2:

$$\text{Rule } R_{21}: \quad E : ins(q(x_1, y_1)) \quad C : k(x_1, y_1) \wedge s(z_1, y_1) \wedge \neg r(x_1, z_1)$$
$$A : CB = d(z_1, y_4) \wedge g(z_1, z_4),$$
$$O = ins(f(z_1, z_4))$$
$$CA = h(x_1, z_1) \wedge t(z_1, y_4) \wedge \neg n(z_1, y_4)$$

To conclude, let us suppose that a transaction has executed the operation $ins(q(a, b))$. This operation triggers the rule R_{21} because it unifies with the event of the rule with the substitution $\{x_1/a, y_1/b\}$; in order to determine if the action of the rule must be executed it is necessary to evaluate the condition $k(a, b) \wedge s(z_1, b) \wedge \neg r(a, z_1)$ in the new state. Let us suppose that this condition is satisfied for the substitution $\{z_1/c\}$, then the action which must be executed is: $(CB = d(c, y_4) \wedge g(c, z_4), O = ins(f(c, z_4)), CA = h(a, c) \wedge t(c, y_4) \wedge \neg n(c, y_4))$. Let us suppose again that: 1) the evaluation of $d(c, y_4) \wedge g(c, z_4)$ in the state previous to the operation obtains the substitution $\{y_4/d, z_4/e\}$ and 2) the condition $h(a, c) \wedge t(c, d) \wedge \neg n(c, d)$ is satisfied in the new state. Then the operation $ins(f(c, e))$ repairs one violation induced by $ins(q(a, b))$.

Summarizing what we have presented in this section, we propose a method that generates trigger rules which enforce the consistency in a deductive database. The method is based on the following guidelines:

- The event and the condition of the rules are obtained from the dependency graph by studying the paths from a base predicate to an inconsistency predicate.
- The conditions are unfolded using the deductive rules.
- The action of the rule is generated from its condition identifying operations which can make the condition false.

4 Repair Rule Language

In this section, we introduce a language for expressing repair rules in the context of deductive databases. After formally defining the syntax of the rules, we specify the execution semantics of the rule language.

4.1 Syntax

Before providing a formal definition for repair rule language, let us introduce the concepts of *operation* and *condition* as follows:

- Operation: let P be a base predicate and t_i $(1 \leq i \leq n)$ be either a variable or a constant. Then, an operation is one expression in the following set: $\{ins(P(t_1, \ldots, t_n)), del(P(t_1, \ldots, t_n)), abort\}$
- Condition: a condition is the special predicate *true* or a conjunction of literals where derived predicates are always negated.

Now, we define a repair rule R as a structure with four elements (INC, E, C, Γ) where:

1) INC is the inconsistency atom associated to the constraint that the rule is going to enforce;

2) E is an operation which is different from *abort*, which causes the rule to be *triggered*;

3) C is the condition of the rule. This condition is checked when the rule is triggered; and

4) Γ represents the action part of the rule and is a tuple $\Gamma = (CB, O, CA)$ where CB is a condition that tries to instantiate action O when necessary, O is an operation which properly constitutes the action of the rule, and CA is a condition that will be used to ensure that the action has actually repaired a violation.

4.2 Semantics

While the defined rule language prescribes what can be specified in each repair rule, the rule execution semantics prescribes how the system behaves once a set of rules has been defined. In this first version, we consider a simple model in which the rule execution is tuple-oriented and the rule processing granularity is transaction bounded.

It is said that a rule R is *triggered* if there is a variable substitution that unifies R's event with an operation. It is also said that a rule R is *relevant* if it is triggered and its condition is satisfied.

We specify the execution semantics of the rules operationally. First, we need to state the meaning of the elementary database operations. Let O be a ground updating operation. The meaning of O is a transformation from a database state D $(D = EDB \cup IDB)$ to a database state D' $(D' = O(D))$ defined as follows:

- if $O = ins(P(t_1, \ldots, t_n))$ then $D' = EDB \cup \{P(t_1, \ldots, t_n)\} \cup IDB$
- if $O = del(P(t_1, \ldots, t_n))$ then $D' = EDB - \{P(t_1, \ldots, t_n)\} \cup IDB$
- if $O = abort$ then D' is the state $D_{initial}$ that existed before the occurrence of the user's transaction.

Based on these definitions, the operational semantics of the system is defined in terms of state transitions following the ideas in [3]. Given a state D_i, a set of repair rules $\Re$ and a transaction T_i, a state transition is the application of the *production step* (shown below) to D_i in order to generate a new database state D_{i+1} and a new transaction T_{i+1}. A *computation* is the process of repeating the application of the production step until one of the following situations is reached:

- Case 1: there is at least one rule with the operation *abort* as action. This means that the system is not able to enforce the consistency of the database.
- Case 2: there are no relevant rules. This means that the new state satisfies every integrity constraint.
- Case 3: there are relevant rules but the last production step has not changed the transaction. This means that the system is not able to enforce the consistency of the database.

The production step is embodied in the following algorithm:

INPUT: $D_i, T_i, \Re$;   OUTPUT: D_{i+1}, T_{i+1}
BEGIN
  $R_t = \{R\beta | R \in \Re$ and β is a mgu between the event of R and some operation in $T_i\}$
  $R_r = \{R\alpha | R \in R_t, R = (INC, E, C, CB, O, CA)$ and there is a
          SLDNF-refutation for $D_i \cup \{\leftarrow C\}$ with computed answer $\alpha\}$
  /*R_t is the set of triggered rules and R_r is the set of relevant rules*/
  IF $R_r = \phi$
  THEN $D_{i+1} := D_i; T_{i+1} := T_i$ /*Case 2*/
  /* T_i includes the user's transaction and the operations executed by the system*/
  ELSE IF there is a rule in R_r with $O = abort$
          THEN $D_{i+1} := D_{initial}; T_{i+1} := \{ \}$ /* Case 1 */
          ELSE select a rule $r = (INC, E, C, CB, O, CA)$ from R_r;
              IF there is a computed answer θ for $D_i \cup \{\leftarrow CB\}$ AND
                there is a computed answer for $(O\theta)(D_i) \cup \{\leftarrow CA\theta\}$ AND
                $(O\theta)$ is ground AND $(O\theta)$ is compatible with each update in T_i
              THEN $D_{i+1} := (O\theta)(D_i); T_{i+1} := T_i \cup (O\theta)$
                  /*The action of the rule is applied to the input state*/
                  /*The transaction is extended with the action of the rule*/
              ELSE $D_{i+1} := D_i; T_{i+1} := T_i$ /* Case 3 */
              ENDIF
          ENDIF
  ENDIF
END.

This execution semantics is coupled with the user's transaction as follows: state D_0 is the result of the application of a user's transaction, say T, to some original state $D_{initial}$ which holds every assumption presented in section 2. Then, a computation applied to D_0 leads to a final state D_{final}. The transaction that leads from the state $D_{initial}$ to the state D_{final} includes the user's transaction and all the operations executed by the system.

5   Automatic Generation of Repair Rules

In order to completely define the method we have presented, we propose a logic metaprogram [2], which uses the deductive rules to compute a set of repair rules. We will only present the definition of the more interesting predicates here. First we will explain the meaning of the predicates:

- *Base(L)*: holds if the predicate associated with the literal L is base.

- *Derived(L)*: holds if the predicate associated with the literal L is derived.
- *IncPred(L)*: holds if the predicate associated with the literal L is an inconsistency predicate.
- *PosLit(L)*: holds if the literal L is positive.
- *Compatible(O1,O2)*: holds if the operations $O1$ and $O2$ are compatible.
- *Rule(H $\Leftarrow$ B)*: holds if there is a deductive rule $(H \Leftarrow B)$ in IDB.
- *Component(L,C,R)*: holds if the literal L appears in the conjunction C with the rest of the conjunction being in R.
- *Appear(L,C)*: holds if the literal L appears in the conjunction C.
- *Unfold(C1,C2)*: generates the condition $C1$ from a condition $C2$ using the set of deductive rules.
- *Insert(P,E,CB,CA)*: holds if the event E induces an insertion in the predicate associated with P when the condition CB is satisfied before the event happens, and, if the condition CA is satisfied after the event happens.
- *Delete(P,E,CB,CA)*: holds if the event E induces a deletion over the predicate associated with P when the condition CB is satisfied before the event happens, and, if the condition CA is satisfied after the event happens.
- *MakeRule(I,E,C,CB,A,CA)*: generates repair rules as explained in section 3.

The rules that define the last three predicates are the following:

Insert(P,ins(E),true,Rest)	$\leftarrow$	Rule($P \Leftarrow B$) $\wedge$ Component(E,B,Rest) $\wedge$ PosLit(E) $\wedge$ Base(E)
Insert(P,del(E),true,Rest)	$\leftarrow$	Rule($P \Leftarrow B$) $\wedge$ Component(noE,B,Rest) $\wedge$ Base(E)
Inse__(P,E,CB,Rest&CA)	$\leftarrow$	Rule($P \Leftarrow B$) $\wedge$ Component(M,B,Rest) $\wedge$ PosLit(M) $\wedge$ Derived(M) $\wedge$ Insert(M,E,CB,CA)
Insert(P,E,CB,B)	$\leftarrow$	Rule($P \Leftarrow B$) $\wedge$ Component(noM,B,Rest) $\wedge$ Derived(M) $\wedge$ Delete(M,E,CB,CA)
Delete(P,ins(E),Rest,true)	$\leftarrow$	Rule($P \Leftarrow B$) $\wedge$ Component(noE,B,Rest) $\wedge$ Base(E)
Delete(P,del(E),Rest,true)	$\leftarrow$	Rule($P \Leftarrow B$) $\wedge$ Component(E,B,Rest) $\wedge$ PosLit(E) $\wedge$ Base(E)
Delete(P,E,CB&Rest,CA)	$\leftarrow$	Rule($P \Leftarrow B$) $\wedge$ Component(M,B,Rest) $\wedge$ PosLit(M) $\wedge$ Derived(M) $\wedge$ Delete(M,E,CB,CA)
Delete(P,E,CB&Rest,CA)	$\leftarrow$	Rule($P \Leftarrow B$) $\wedge$ Component(noM,B,Rest) $\wedge$ Derived(M) $\wedge$ Insert(M,E,CB,CA)
MakeRule(I,E,true,true,abort,true)	$\leftarrow$	IncPred(I) $\wedge$ Insert(I,E,CB,CA) $\wedge$ Unfold(true,CA)
MakeRule(I,E,C,true,del(L),true)	$\leftarrow$	IncPred(I) $\wedge$ Insert(I,E,CB,CA) $\wedge$ Unfold(C,CA) $\wedge$ Appear(L,C) $\wedge$ PosLit(L)
MakeRule(I,E,C,true,ins(L),true)	$\leftarrow$	IncPred(I) $\wedge$ Insert(I,E,CB,CA) $\wedge$ Unfold(C,CA) $\wedge$ Appear(noL,C) $\wedge$ Base(L)
MakeRule(I,E,C,CB,O,CA)	$\leftarrow$	IncPred(I) $\wedge$ Insert(I,E,CB1,CA1) $\wedge$ Unfold(C,CA1) $\wedge$ Appear(noM,C) $\wedge$ Derived(M) $\wedge$ Insert(M,O,CB,CA) $\wedge$ Compatible(O,E)

6 Conclusions

In this paper we have presented a method for generating a set of production rules for integrity enforcement (repair rules) in the context of an active and deductive system. The main features of the method are: 1) it works for deductive databases, 2) the set of repair rules is generated at compile-time, and 3) inconsistency is repaired using simple base updates (the repair rules only perform one update over a base predicate).

The advantage of using simple updates is that the change made by the rules is minimal. However, the disadvantage is that repairs consisting of more than one operation, which can be easily computed, are not considered by the method. Future extensions of this work deal with this problem.

Acknowledgments

The authors would like to thank Hendrik Decker for his helpful comments on previous versions of this paper.

References

1. M. Celma. *Comprobación de la integridad en bases de datos deductivas: un método basado en el almacenamiento de los caminos de derivación.* PhD thesis, DSIC (UPV), 1992.
2. M. Celma, J.C. Casamayor, L. Mota, M.A. Pastor, and F. Marqués. A derivation Path Recording Method for Integrity Checking in Deductive Databases. In *2nd International Workshop on the Deductive Approach to Information Systems and Databases*, pages 15–17, Aiguablava (Catalunya), 1991.
3. S. Ceri, P. Fraternali, S. Paraboschi, and L. Tanca. Automatic generation of Production Rules for Integrity Maintenance. *ACM Transactions on Database Systems*, 19(3), 1994.
4. S. Ceri and J. Widom. Deriving production rules for constraint maintenance. In *Proc. of the 16th Int. Conf. on VLDB*, 1990.
5. M. Gertz. An extensible Framework for Repairing Constraint Violations. 1996. Internet.
6. J.W. Lloyd. *Foundations of Logic Programming.* Springer-Verlag, Berlin, 1987.
7. G. Moerkotte and P.C. Lockemann. Reactive Consistency Control in Deductive Databases. *ACM Transactions on Database Systems*, 16(4):671–702, 1991.
8. J. Pastor. Extending the Synthesis of Updates Transaction Programs to handle Existential Rules in Deductive Databases. In *Proc. of the 17th Int. Conf. on VLDB*, 1991.
9. R. Reiter. Towards a Logical Reconstruction of Relational Database Theory. In M.L. Brodie, J.L. Mylopoulus, and J.W. Schmit, editors, *On Conceptual Modelling*, Lecture Notes in Computer Science. Springer-Verlag, Berlin, 1984.
10. B. Wütrich. On Update and Inconsistency Repairing in Knowledge Bases. In *Proc. of the 9th IEEE Int. Conf. on Data Engineering*, Vienna (Austria), 1993.

Estimating the Quality of Databases

Amihai Motro[1] and Igor Rakov[2]

[1] Information and Software Engineering Department
George Mason University, Fairfax, VA 22030, USA,
ami@gmu.edu, http://www.ise.gmu.edu/~ami

[2] General Electric Information Services
401 N. Washington Street MNB1D, Rockville, MD 20850, USA
igor.rakov@geis.ge.com

Abstract. With more and more electronic information sources becoming widely available, the issue of the quality of these often-competing sources has become germane. We propose a standard for specifying the quality of databases, which is based on the dual concepts of data soundness and data completeness. The relational model of data is extended by associating a quality specification with each relation instance, and by extending its algebra to calculate the quality specifications of derived relation instances. This provides a method for calculating the quality of answers to arbitrary queries from the overall quality specification of the database. We show practical methods for estimating the initial quality specifications of given databases, and we report on experiments that test the validity of our methods. Finally, we describe how quality estimations are being applied in the Multiplex multidatabase system to resolve cross-database inconsistencies.

1 Data Quality

What is it? Data quality has several dimensions. The most common dimension is *soundness*: whether the data available are the true values. Data soundness is often referred to as correctness, precision, accuracy, or validity. Another common dimension of data quality is its *completeness*: whether all the data are available. In the terminology of databases, data completeness refers to both the completeness of files (no records are missing), and to the completeness of records (all fields are known for each record). Soundness and completeness are two orthogonal dimensions, in the sense that they are concerned with completely separate aspects of data quality [6]. Other important dimensions often discussed are *consistency* and *currency*. Consistency (often referred to as integrity) assumes specific *constraints* that state the proper relationships among different data elements are known, and considers whether these constraints are satisfied by the data. Currency considers whether the data are up-to-date, reflecting the most recent values. For additional discussion of various quality dimensions, see [3, 12].

What can be done about it? Concerns about data quality can be addressed in three ways: Protection, measurement, and improvement. The focus of the first approach is on *prevention*. It advocates careful handling of data at every phase, from acquisition to application. In some respects, this approach is modeled after quality control methods in production processes [12]. The second approach focuses on the *estimation* of quality. A data quality measure is adopted, and the quality of the data is estimated in accordance to this measure. The third approach is the most ambitious. Data quality may be improved by identifying obvious errors in the data ("outlying values"), and either removing these values, or substituting them (as well as values that are missing altogether) with more probable values. This approach is often referred to as data *cleansing* or *scrubbing* [1].

In this paper we consider only the dimensions of data soundness and data completeness, and we focus on data quality estimation. The advantages of data quality estimation are threefold. Clearly, decision-making is improved when the quality of the data used in the decision process is known. To this end, it is important to be able to determine the quality of specific data within a given database (see Section 4). In the presence of alternative sources of information, quality estimates suggest the source that should be preferred (see Section 6). Finally, information is a commodity, and its value (price) should be based on its quality.

This paper presents an overview of the issues and the solutions proposed. For a more complete treatment the reader is referred to [8] and [9]. Our treatment of the issues is in the context of relational databases, and we assume the standard definitions of the relational model.

In Sections 2 and 3 we propose a standard for specifying the quality of relational databases, which is based on data soundness and data completeness, and we explain how such quality specifications may be estimated. Quality specifications are associated with each relation instance of the database, and may be considered an extension of the relational model. Suitably, the relational algebra is extended as well, to calculate the quality specifications of derived relation instances. This provides a method for estimating the quality of answers to arbitrary queries (Section 4). In section 5 we report on experiments that were carried out to test the validity of our methods, and in section 6 we describe how quality estimations are being applied in the Multiplex multidatabase system to resolve cross-database inconsistencies. Additional research directions are discussed briefly in Section 7.

2 Simple Quality Estimation

A database and the real world that it models can be formalized as two *instances* of the same database scheme. We denote the *actual* (stored) database instance D, and we denote the *ideal* (real-world) database instance W. Of course, W is a hypothetical instance which is unavailable. The stored instance D is an *approximation* of the ideal instance W.

How good is this approximation? Clearly, the answer to this question would provide a measure of the quality of the given database.

To determine the goodness of the approximation we must measure the *similarity* of two database instances. Since each instance is a set (of tuples), we can use measures that compare two sets of elements. One such measure is based on two components as follows (X denotes the cardinality of a set X:

- Soundness (of the database relative to the real world): $\frac{|D \cap W|}{|D|}$
- Completeness (of the database relative to the real world): $\frac{|D \cap W|}{|W|}$

Soundness measures the proportion of the stored information that is true, and completeness measures the proportion of the true information that is stored. These measures are similar to the *precision* and *recall* measures in the field of information retrieval, where they are used to rate the goodness of answers extracted from an information source in response to queries [10].

Note that each intersection element (a database tuple that is also in the real world instance) contributes to both soundness and completeness. Similarly, when a database tuple and a real world tuple differ (even in a single attribute), both soundness and completeness are affected adversely. Consider, for example, a relation Employee consisting of 20 attributes, and assume that the stored instance and the ideal instance each have 100 tuples. Assume further that the two instances are identical in all values except in the Date_of_Birth attribute, where half the values are incorrect. Soundness and completeness will both measure 0.5, whereas intuitively the quality is much higher.

A simple improvement is to *decompose* all relations to smaller units of information. A relation $(A_1, \ldots, A_n)$, in which A_1 is the key attribute, is decomposed to n relations of two attributes each: $(A_1, A_i), i = 1, \ldots, n$. Comparing decomposed instances provides measures that are more refined. In the above example, soundness and completeness will both measure 0.975.

As both D and W may be very large, the estimations of soundness and completeness should be based on *samples* of D and W.

Estimating Soundness. To determine the proportion of the stored information that is true, the following procedure is used:

1. Sample D.
2. For each $x \in D_{\text{sample}}$ determine if $x \in W$.
3. Calculate the soundness estimate as the number of "hits" divided by the sample size $|D_{\text{sample}}|$.

Step 1, sampling a database, is simple. But Step 2 is difficult: we need to determine the presence of database elements in W without actually constructing it. This is accomplished by *human verification* of the sample elements.

Estimating Completeness. To determine the proportion of the true information that is stored, the following procedure is used:

1. Sample W.
2. For each $x \in W_{\text{sample}}$ determine if $x \in D$.
3. Calculate the completeness estimate as the number of "hits" divided by the sample size $|W_{\text{sample}}|$.

Step 2, verifying the presence of elements in the database, is simple. But Step 1 is difficult: we need to sample W without actually constructing it. This may be interpreted as constructing a *fair challenge* to the database by using various resources (e.g., by judicious sampling of alternative databases).

The soundness and completeness estimates obtained by these procedures amount to a *simple quality specification* for the database.

3   Refined Quality Estimation

Information sources are rarely of uniform quality. An information source may provide information of excellent quality on one topic, and information of poor quality on another topic. Hence, the *overall* quality estimations described in the previous section may prove to be very crude estimates of the quality of *specific* data.

A substantial improvement over these methods is to *partition* the database into areas that are highly homogeneous with respect to their quality: any subarea of a highly homogeneous area would maintain roughly the same quality as the initial area. These partitions, and the corresponding quality measurements of their components, would provide a more *refined* quality specification for the database. Formal definitions for "areas" and "homogeneity" follow.

"Areas" and "subareas" are defined with *views*. Views may involve selection and projection (projections must retain the key attributes). *Homogeneity (with respect to soundness)* of a view v is defined as the average soundness difference between the given view and all its possible subviews:

$$H_S(v) = 1/N \sum_{i=1}^{N} |s(v) - s(v_i)|$$

where $v_1, \ldots, v_n$ are the possible subviews of v, and $s(v)$ is the soundness of v. A low homogeneity measure indicates that the view is highly homogeneous. It can be shown that perfect homogeneity, $H_S(v) = 0$, is achieved only when the view elements are all true or all false. A threshold value of H is used to assure that all the views of a partition are highly homogeneous. Homogeneity with respect to completeness is defined analogously.

The homogeneity measure H is easy to rationalize, but is expensive to compute. Our overall approach, however, does not depend on a specific measure, and cheaper-to-compute measures could be substituted. The alternative homogeneity measure that we use is the *Gini Index*, known from statistical classification theory [2, 4]. The Gini index for the soundness of a view v is

$$2p_0 \cdot p_1 = 2p_1(1 - p_1) = 2p_0(1 - p_0)$$

where p_0 is the proportion of the incorrect elements in v, and p_1 is the proportion of the correct elements in v. The Gini index for the completeness of a view is defined analogously.

A view v would be considered *highly homogeneous* if all the possible ways of splitting v into two subviews v_1 and v_2 will not yield substantial (i.e., above some threshold) improvement in the homogeneity. The improvement in homogeneity is measured by the difference between the Gini index of the view v and the combined Gini index of the subviews v_1 and v_2:

$$\Delta G = G(v) - \alpha_1 G(v_1) - \alpha_2 G(v_2)$$

where $G(v)$ is the Gini index of v, and $\alpha_i = |v_i|/|v|$.

A recursive algorithm for finding highly homogeneous views is outlined below. Note that the algorithm must be performed separately for soundness and completeness, and that it is repeated for for each relation. Note also that it is performed only on samples. The partition views that are discovered by the algorithm are considered to projections (that retain key attributes) and selections.

Algorithm for Finding Quality Specifications

- **Input**: A sample of the relation; a threshold value.
- **Output**: A set of views on the relation that are highly homogeneous with respect to a quality measure.
- **Step 1**: Label the relation as the root node, and place it in a queue Q.
- **Step 2**: Retrieve the next node from Q, and make it the current node v.
- **Step 3**: Consider all the possible splits of v into two subnodes v_1 and v_2 and measure the reduction ΔG of each split.
- **Step 4**: Select a split that maximizes the reduction, and split v.
- **Step 5**: If the reduction of this split is greater than the threshold value, place v_1 and v_2 in Q. Otherwise, make v a leaf node and go to Step 6.
- **Step 6**: If Q is not empty, go to Step 2. Otherwise, stop.

The threshold value is needed to prevent splitting down to individual elements. Admittedly, Step 3 is computationally expensive and should be refined to reduce search space and make use of heuristic information.

The highly homogeneous partitions obtained with this algorithm and the soundness or completeness estimates of their views amount to a *refined quality specification* for the given database.

4 Estimating the Quality of Answers to Queries

An important application of database quality specifications is to infer from them quality specifications for answers issued from the database in response to arbitrary queries.

To this end we consider each query as a *chain* of individual relational operations. Each relational operation is extended to produce (in addition to the standard result) a *quality specification of the result*. Consequently, each operation in the chain receives a quality specification from the previous operation and uses it to derive a quality specification for the next operation. This allows us to calculate quality specifications of sequences of relational operations (i.e., general queries). The relational operations that have been considered so far are Cartesian product and a combined selection-projection operation.

In other words, the traditional relational model is *extended* to include quality specifications for each relation instance, and the traditional relational algebra is extended to derive quality specifications of the results of its operations. These extensions assume that all quality specifications use views that are perfectly homogeneous; i.e., each of their subviews inherits the very same quality.

At the final step, the *overall quality* of the answer is computed from the final quality specification as follows. The views of a quality specification *partition* the answer. Hence, each answer is partitioned into views with known (inherited) quality. The overall quality is then computed as a weighted sum of the quality of these views. If we have only *estimates* of quality, then the *variance* of these estimates is also calculated. The details of these extensions to the relational model may be found in [8] and [9].

Quality specifications require partitions whose views are highly homogeneous. (A requirement for perfect homogeneity may result in views that contain very few tuples, yielding specifications that have impractically large number of views.) On the other hand, the extensions to the relational algebra assumed that the partition views are perfectly homogeneous. Nonetheless, it can be shown that these extensions are still acceptable; namely, the result of a projection-selection on a highly homogeneous view will be (with high probability) also highly homogeneous, and the homogeneity of the result of a Cartesian product will be close to the largest (worst) of the homogeneities of the input views.

5 Experimentation

The viability and performance of the approach and methods described in Sections 3 and 4 were tested in an experiment. The experiment used synthetic data and was limited to selection-projection queries (i.e., without Cartesian products). Only soundness was considered.

For this experiment a simple interactive tooolkit was constructed. The toolkit leads its users through the following steps:[1]

1. The user selects a data set, an error pattern, and a sampling rate.
2. The data set is sampled.
3. A quality (soundness) specification is derived.
4. The user submits an arbitrary query.
5. The answer is computed.
6. The quality of the answer is estimated.
7. The estimate is compared with the actual quality.

---

[1] The toolkit can be tried at
http://www.ise.gmu.edu/~irakov/quality/experiment.html.

The pre-assignment of errors to the selected data set in Step 1 is the only deviation from the actual estimation process proposed in Section 3 and 4. It has two obvious advantages: it allows skipping the manual verification, and it provides the actual quality (normally unavailable) for comparison.

The measure of performance used in comparing the estimated quality to the actual quality is the *relative error*; i.e., the difference between the computed quality and the actual quality, divided by the actual quality.

Our experimentation lead to several observations. As expected, the error decreases as the sample size increases. Also, the error decreases as the answer cardinality increases. Determining the optimal threshold value for the discovery of the homogeneous views is less straightforward; our experiments indicate that it is often in the range 0.3–0.5. With sample size of about 15% and answer cardinality of about 400 tuples, the relative error is in the range of 4%–6%.

6 Application: Harmonization of Inconsistencies

In recent years there has been overwhelming interest in the problem of multidatabase integration: How to provide integrated access to a collection of autonomous and heterogeneous databases [5, 11]. The usual focus in systems that address this problem is the resolution of *intensional inconsistencies*: How to reconcile the schematic differences among the participating databases (this issue is known as semantic heterogeneity). The *Multiplex* project [7] also addresses the problem of *extensional inconsistencies*: How to reconcile the data differences among the participating databases. Specifically, Multiplex does not assume that overlapping information sources are mutually consistent, and it focuses on methods for *harmonizing* inconsistent answers into a single authoritative answer.[2]

The architecture of Multiplex centers on a global database scheme that is specified in the relational model. Individual information providers may define any number of *views* over this global scheme, committing to provide the contents of these views opon request. The participating systems may have vastly different architectures (i.e., not necessarily relational), but they must deliver their contributions in the form of tables, which extend the global views that they agreed to provide. A query over the global relations must then be translated into an equivalent query over the contributed view definitions. Possibly, some queries might not have a translation, because some of the information they target has not been provided by any source; such queries would be given only *partial answers*. On the other hand, it is possible that some queries would have *multiple answers*, because some of the information they target is provided by more than one source; such answers would require *harmonization*.

Essentially, the Multiplex approach is to allow a multidatabase designer to specify a-priori a *conflict resolution strategy* whenever the potential for inconsistencies exists (i.e., whenever the definitions of the contributed views overlap). One important option in this strategy (among many other options) is to base the resolution on the quality of the alternatives.

---

[2] The Multiplex server is available at http://www.ise.gmu.edu/~multiplex.

Assume a query Q has multiple answers $A_1, \ldots A_n$. Assume first that there is no information regarding their quality; i.e., each answer is presented by its source as if it is sound and complete. This may be formalized as each answer being presented as both sound and complete: $s(A_i) = 1.0$ and $c(A_i) = 1.0$ for $i = 1, \ldots, n$. Obviously, unless these answers are identical, these soundness and completeness claims are mutually inconsistent.

An intuitive heuristic is to let the answer providers *vote* on the complete answer space $\bigcup_{i=1}^{n} A_i$ as follows:

1. If $x \in A_i$ then provider i votes "yes" on x (an expression of the claimed soundness of A_i).
2. If $x \notin A_i$ then provider i votes "no" on x (an expression of the claimed completeness of A_i).

Where x is an element of the answer space. Define:

1. $L = \{x | x \text{ received only "yes" votes}\}$
2. $U = \{x | x \text{ received at least one "yes" vote}\}$

The true answer A is "sandwiched" between L and U: $L \subseteq A \subseteq U$. Hence, L and U constitute a *lower bound* and an *upper bound* for the true answer A. This "interval" conforms nicely with how unknown values are estimated in other disciplines. If desired, it is possible to create in-between layers E_i, as well

$$E_i = \{x | x \text{ received at least } i \text{ "yes" votes}\}$$

thus providing "tiers" within the largest estimate U.

Assume now that each answer A_i has its individual quality specifications: $s(A_i) = s_i$ and $c(A_i) = c_i$. Using probabilistic arguments, the voting scheme is extended:

1. If $x \in A_i$ then provider i votes on x

$$P(x \in A | x \in A_i) = s_i$$

2. If $x \notin A_i$ then provider i votes on x

$$P(x \in A | x \notin A_i) = \frac{(s_i/c_i) - s_i}{(n/|A_i|) - 1}$$

where n is the size of the entire answer space.

Votes are then combined to provide *ranking* of the tuples in the answer space. This is useful for handling queries that pre-specify the desired answer cardinality.

7 Research Directions

We introduced a new model for data quality in relational databases, which is based on the dual measures of soundness and completeness. This model extends the relational model by assigning each relation instance a quality specification, and by extending the relational algebra to calculate the quality specifications of derived relation instances. The principal purpose of this model is to provide answers to arbitrary queries with estimations of their quality. We described an algorithm for deriving initial quality specifications for the stored relations from samples whose quality had been established manually. And we described how quality estimations are being applied in the Multiplex multidatabase system to resolve cross-database inconsistencies.

There are many issues that require further investigation, and we mention here three research directions.

We discussed the advantage of considering the correctness of individual attributes over the correctness of entire tuples. Still, an individual value is either correct or incorrect, and, when incorrect, we do not consider the amount by which it deviates from the true value. A possible extension of this work is to generalize our quality specifications and extend our quality estimations so that they consider the *similarity* of the stored values to the real values.

Because of the cost of establishing quality estimations, our methods are most suitable for static information. When the information is dynamic, it would be advisable to timestamp the estimations at the time that they were obtained and attach these timestamps to all quality inferences. One may also consider the automatic attenuation of quality estimations as time progresses.

The cost of establishing quality estimations is due mainly to the human effort that it requires. An attractive alternative is to develop methods that "discover" the quality "automatically" (or, more accurately, with only limited human guidance). A possible direction is to draw on techniques that have been developed for data mining and knowledge discovery.

Acknowledgement. This work was supported in part by DARPA grant N0060-96-D-3202.

References

1. Bort, J.: Scrubbing dirty data. *InfoWorld*, 17(51), December 1995.
2. Breiman, L., Friedman, J., Olshen, R., and Stone, Ch.: *Classification and Regression Trees*. Wadsworth International Group, 1984.
3. Fox, C., Levitin, A., and Redman, T.: The notion of data and its quality dimensions. *Information processing and management*, 30(1), 1994.
4. Chen, M. C., McNamee, L., and Matloff, N.: Selectivity estimation using homogeneity measurement. *Proceeding of the International Conference on Data Engineering*, 1990.
5. Hurson, A.R., Bright, M.W., Pakzad, S.: *Multidatabases: An Advanced Solution to Global Information Sharing*, IEEE Computer Society Press, 1993.

6. Motro, A.: Integrity = validity + completeness. *ACM Transactions on Database Systems*, 14(4):480–502, December 1989.

7. Motro, A: Multiplex: A Formal Model for Multidatabases and Its Implementation. Technical Report ISSE-TR-95-103, Department of Information and Software Engineering, George Mason University, March 1995.

8. Motro, A., Rakov, I: Not all answers are equally good: Estimating the quality of database answers. In *Flexible Answering Systems* (T. Andreasen, H. Christiansen, and H.L. Larsen, Editors), Kluwer Academic Publishers, 1997, 1–21.

9. Rakov, I: *Data quality and Its Use for Reconciling Inconsistencies in Multidatabase Environments*, Ph.D. Dissertation, George Mason University, May 1998.

10. G. Salton and M. J. McGill: *Introduction to Modern Information Retrieval*. McGraw-Hill, New York, New York, 1983.

11. Wiederhold, G. (Ed.): Special Issue of the Journal of Intelligent Information Systems, 6(2-3), June 1996.

12. Wang, R., Storey, V., and Firth, Ch.: A framework for analysis of data quality research. *IEEE Transactions on Knowledge and Data Engineering*, 7(4), August 1995.

Querying Clocked Databases

Mehmet A. Orgun[1] and Chuchang Liu[2]

[1] Department of Computing, Macquarie University, NSW 2109, Australia
[2] Information Technology Division, Defence Science and Technology Organisation,
PO Box 1500, Salisbury, SA 5108, Australia

Abstract. We propose a temporal extension of Datalog which can be used to
model and query temporal databases with relations based on multiple clocks. The
extension, called Clocked Temporal Datalog, is based on a clocked temporal logic
in which each formula can be assigned a separate clock. A Clocked Temporal Datalog program consists of three parts: (1) a clock definition, (2) a clock assignment,
and (3) a program body. The clock definition specifies all the available clocks. The
clock assignment assigns to each predicate defined in the program body a clock
from the clock definition. The meaning of the program body naturally depends
on the provided clock definition and assignment. Therefore a Clocked Temporal
Datalog program models intensionally a clocked (temporal) database in which
each relation is defined over a clock.

1 Introduction

While there is not a wealth of reported research on deductive database systems for temporal data, temporal databases based on the relational model have been extensively studied in the literature; we refer the reader to the survey of Özsoyoğlu and Snodgrass [13].
Temporal extensions based on logic programming are also considered, for instance, by
Chomicki and Imieliński [4], Baudinet et al [2] and Böhlen and Marti [3]. These proposals are concerned with modeling and querying infinite temporal data in logic languages
(such as extensions of DATALOG) in which predicates are extended with explicit time
parameters. A temporal extension of Datalog is considered by Orgun [11], based on the
function-free subset of the temporal language Chronolog [12]. These languages, however, are not designed to deal with multiple granularities and/or multiple clocks, but
they make the representation of infinite temporal information possible and often enable
a more compact representation of finite information. They also improve the expressivity
of query languages for temporal data.

One important issue is that the relations in a temporal database are not necessarily
defined on the same granularity of time, and it seems unnatural to force them all onto
a prescribed notion of time. Doing so would lead to semantic mismatches [6, 7]. Ladkin [7] recognized that distinct granularities cannot be mixed, and developed an algebra
where the granularity of the source time-stamps is considered. Wiederhold, Jajodia and
Litwin [15] also recognized the problem, and provided an algebra in which data with
multiple granularities are converted to a uniform model of data based on time intervals. Gagne and Plaice [6] propose a temporal deductive database system whose model
is based on a dense model of time rather than a discrete model. Dyreson and Snodgrass [5] extended SQL-92 to support mixed granularities with respect to a granularity

lattice. There are also some other recent works extending the relational model and algebra to deal with multiple granularities, for instance, another calendar-based approach is proposed by Lee et al [8].

In this paper, we first propose a model for clocked databases in which relations are defined over multiple time-lines or more precisely, multiple histories. We then consider a deductive system for clocked databases, featuring a clocked temporal extension of Datalog. Clocked Temporal Datalog is based on TLC [9], a temporal logic which can be used to model and reason about events defined over multiple clocks. A Clocked Temporal Datalog program in its own right models intensionally a clocked database in which each relation is defined over a clock. Clocked Temporal Datalog can also be used as a deductive front-end to clocked databases to enhance the expressivity of their query languages. Through programmable clock definitions, temporal data in a clocked database can also be viewed, manipulated and summarized at different granularities.

In TLC, each formula can be assigned a clock which is a subsequence of a discrete time-line. In TLC, a calendar-dependent partitioning of the time-line is not assumed, and hence granularity conversion operators are not required. Our approach is therefore more restrictive in modelling granularity than some others reported in the literature, however, it does not require a predetermined granularity lattice, it involves programmable clock definitions, and it is grounded in temporal logic. Temporal logic [14] provides a clean framework in which the temporal properties of certain applications databases can be formalized, studied, and then generalized and applied in other application domains.

The paper is organised as follows. Section 2 discusses a model for clocked databases. Section 3 gives a brief introduction to TLC. Section 4 introduces Clocked Temporal Datalog. Section 5 presents the declarative semantics of Clocked Temporal Datalog programs and establishes the connection between clocked databases and programs.

2 A Model for Clocked Databases

A clocked database consists of three components: (1) a set of relation symbols, (2) a clock assignment, and (3) a relation mapping. The clock assignment assigns a clock to each relation symbol; the relation mapping assigns to each relation symbol a clocked relation defined over its clock.

In the following, we denote the set of natural numbers $\{0, 1, 2, 3, \ldots\}$ by ω.

Definition 1 (Clocks). *A clock is a strictly increasing sequence of natural numbers. The global clock gc is the sequence of natural numbers: $\langle 0, 1, 2, 3, \ldots \rangle$. The empty clock is the empty sequence: $\langle \rangle$.*

Let ck be a clock. We write $t \in ck$ if t occurs in ck (t is a moment on clock ck). We now define the rank of a moment on a given clock.

Definition 2. *Given a clock $ck = \langle t_0, t_1, t_2, \ldots \rangle$ we define the rank of t_n on ck to be n, written as $rank(t_n, ck) = n$. Inversely, we write $t_n = ck^{(n)}$, which means that t_n is the moment in time on ck whose rank is n.*

We have an ordering relation on clocks defined as follows.

Definition 3 ($\sqsubseteq$). *For any given clocks ck_1 and ck_2, we write $ck_1 \sqsubseteq ck_2$ if for all $t \in ck_1$, we have $t \in ck_2$. If $ck_1 \sqsubseteq ck_2$ then we also say that ck_1 is a sub-clock of ck_2.*

It can be shown that the set of clocks, denoted by CK, with the ordering $\sqsubseteq$, is a complete lattice in which the global clock is the maximum element and the empty clock is the minimum element.

We now define two operations on clocks that correspond to the greatest lower bound (g.l.b) and least upper bound (l.u.b.) of clocks with respect to $\sqsubseteq$.

Definition 4 ($\sqcap, \sqcup$). *Let $ck_1, ck_2 \in$ CK. We define two operations on clocks as follows: $ck_1 \sqcap ck_2 \equiv g.l.b.\{ck_1, ck_2\}$ and $ck_1 \sqcup ck_2 \equiv l.u.b.\{ck_1, ck_2\}$.*

Let $\mathbf{D}$ be a domain of values of interest. Let $\mathbf{D}^n$ denote the n-folded Cartesian product of $\mathbf{D}$, and $P(\mathbf{D}^n)$ the set of all subsets of $\mathbf{D}^n$. We denote the set of all functions from set X to set Y by $[X \rightarrow Y]$.

Definition 5 (**Clocked relations**). *Let $ck \in$ CK. A clocked relation with arity n is a map from ck to $P(\mathbf{D}^n)$. The set of clocked relations is denoted by $\bigcup_{n \in \omega} \bigcup_{ck \in CK} [ck \rightarrow P(\mathbf{D}^n)]$.*

Let R be the set of relation symbols we are allowed to have in a clocked database. A clock assignment tells us those times at which each relation symbol has a defined value. Note that we also write r/n for a relation symbol r with arity n.

Definition 6. *A clock assignment α is a map from R to CK, that is, $\alpha \in [R \rightarrow CK]$. The clock associated with a relation symbol $r/n \in R$ over α is denoted by $\alpha(r/n)$.*

Definition 7 (**Clocked database**). *Let R be a set of relation symbols, and α a clock assignment. A clocked database DB is a triple $\langle R, \alpha, \mu \rangle$ where μ assigns a clocked relation over $\alpha(r/n)$ to all $r/n \in R$.*

We write $\mu(r/n)$ to denote the clocked relation which is assigned to r/n by μ; $\mu(r/n)$ is in fact a map from $\alpha(r/n)$ to $P(\mathbf{D}^n)$. Intuitively, μ tells us the value associated with a relation symbol whenever it is defined.

3 Temporal Logic with Clocks

Temporal Logic with Clocks (TLC) is an extension of temporal logic in which each predicate symbol is associated with a clock [9]. In this section, we first extend TLC with an additional temporal operator, namely fby, and then give a brief introduction to its syntax and semantics.

In the vocabulary of TLC, apart from variables, constants and predicate symbols, we also have propositional connectives: $\neg$, $\vee$ and $\wedge$, universal quantifier: $\forall$, three temporal operators: first, next, and fby, and punctuation symbols: "(" and ")". In TLC, the definition of terms is as usual. The other connectives $\rightarrow$, $\leftrightarrow$ and the quantifier $\exists$ can be derived from the primitive connectives and universal quantifier as usual.

The intuitive meaning of the temporal operators is as follows: (1) first A: A is true at the initial moment in time, (2) next A: A is true at the next moment in time, and (3) *A* fby *B*: *A* is true at the initial moment in time and from then on *B* is true. It should be kept in mind that these readings are relative to the given formula clocks (see below). We write next [n] for n successive applications of next. If n $= 0$, then next [n] is the empty string.

3.1 Clock calculus

We use a clock assignment to assign a clock to each predicate symbol. The clock of a formula may also be determined by the clocks of the subformulas appearing it through a clock calculus.

Definition 8. *A clock assignment α is a map from the set SP of predicate symbols to the set CK of clocks, that is, $\alpha \in [SP \to CK]$. The notation $\alpha(p)$ denotes the clock which is associated with a predicate symbol p on α.*

Definition 9. *Let A be a formula and α a clock assignment. The clock associated with A, denoted as $\alpha^*(A)$, is defined inductively as follows:*

- *If A is an atomic formula $p(e_1, \ldots, e_n)$, then $\alpha^*(A) = \alpha(p)$.*
- *If $A = \neg B$, first B, $(\forall x)B$ or $(\exists x)B$ then $\alpha^*(A) = \alpha^*(B)$.*
- *If $A = B \wedge C$, $B \vee C$, $B \to C$ or $B \leftrightarrow C$, then $\alpha^*(A) = \alpha^*(B) \sqcap \alpha^*(C)$.*
- *If $A = $ next B, then (1) $\alpha^*(A) = \langle t_0, \ldots, t_{n-1} \rangle$ when $\alpha^*(B) = \langle t_0, \ldots, t_n \rangle$ is non-empty and finite; (2) $\alpha^*(A) = \alpha^*(B)$ when $\alpha^*(B)$ is infinite or empty.*
- *If $A = B$ fby C, then $\alpha^*(A) = \langle b_0, c_k, c_{k+1}, \ldots \rangle$ where $\alpha^*(B) = \langle b_0, b_1, \ldots \rangle$ and $\alpha^*(C) = \langle c_0, c_1, \ldots, c_{k-1}, c_k, c_{k+1}, c_{k+2}, \ldots \rangle$ and $c_{k-1} \le b_0 < c_k$ for some $k \ge 0$.*

The following definitions will also be very useful in developing the declarative semantics of Clocked Temporal Datalog programs.

Definition 10. *Temporal atoms are defined inductively as follows:*

- *Any atomic formula is a temporal atom.*
- *If A is a temporal atom then so are* first *A and* next *A.*

Definition 11. *A temporal atom is fixed-time if it has an application of* first *followed by a number of applications of* next; *otherwise it is open. A formula is fixed-time if all atoms contained in it are fixed-time; otherwise it is open.*

3.2 Semantics

Let $\mathcal{B} = \langle \{ \text{false}, \text{true} \}, \le \rangle$ denote a Boolean algebra of truth values with the ordering **false** $\le$ **true** and the following standard operations:

- **comp** $= \{ \text{true} \mapsto \text{false}, \text{false} \mapsto \text{true} \}$ (complementation),
- $X \times Y = $ the g.l.b. of $\{ X, Y \}$ with respect to $\le$,
- $X + Y = $ the l.u.b. of $\{ X, Y \}$ with respect to $\le$.

At a given time $t \in \omega$, the value of a formula can be **true, false** or undefined, depending on the clocks of predicate symbols appearing in it. A temporal interpretation together with a clock assignment assigns meanings to all the basic elements of *TLC*.

Definition 12. *A temporal interpretation I on a given clock assignment α of TLC comprises a non-empty domain* **D** *over which the variables range, together with for each variable, an element of* **D***; for each term an element of* **D***; and for each n-ary predicate symbol p/n, a clocked relation of $\alpha(p/n) \to P(\mathbf{D}^n)$.*

We denote the clocked relation represented by p/n on I over α by $I(p/n)$. To refer to the value of p/n at a particular moment in time, we use the notation $I(p/n)(t)$. For any $t \in \alpha(p)$, the value $I(p/n)(t)$ is naturally defined; for any $t \notin \alpha(p)$, the value $I(p/n)(t)$ is not defined.

In the following, the notation $[\![A]\!]_{\alpha,I}^t$ is used to denote the value of A under interpretation I on clock assignment α at moment t.

Definition 13. *Let I be a temporal interpretation on a given clock assignment α of TLC. For any formula A of TLC, $[\![A]\!]_{\alpha,I}^t \stackrel{\text{def}}{=} [\![A]\!]_{\alpha^*(A),I}^t$ whenever $t \in \alpha^*(A)$. The function $[\![A]\!]_{\alpha,I}^t$ is defined inductively as follows:*

(1) *If e is a term, then $[\![e]\!]_{\alpha,I}^t = I(e) \in \mathbf{D}$.*

(2) *For any n-ary predicate symbol p and terms $e_1, \ldots, e_n$,*
$[\![p(e_1, \ldots, e_n)]\!]_{\alpha^*(p(e_1,\ldots,e_n)),I}^t = $ **true** *if $\langle [\![e_1]\!]_{\alpha,I}^t, \ldots, [\![e_n]\!]_{\alpha,I}^t \rangle \in I(p)(t)$;* **false** *otherwise.*

(3) *For any formula of the form $\neg A$, $[\![\neg A]\!]_{\alpha^*(\neg A),I}^t = \mathbf{comp}([\![A]\!]_{\alpha^*(A),I}^t)$.*

(4) *For any formula of the form $A \wedge B$, $[\![A \wedge B]\!]_{\alpha^*(A \wedge B),I}^t = [\![A]\!]_{\alpha^*(A),I}^t \times [\![B]\!]_{\alpha^*(B),I}^t$.*

(5) *For any formula of the form $A \vee B$, $[\![A \vee B]\!]_{\alpha^*(A \vee B),I}^t = [\![A]\!]_{\alpha^*(A),I}^t + [\![B]\!]_{\alpha^*(B),I}^t$.*

(6) *For any formula of the form $(\forall x)A$, $[\![(\forall x)A]\!]_{\alpha^*((\forall x)A),I}^t = $ **true** $if [\![A]\!]_{\alpha^*(A),I[d/x]}^t = $ **true** *for all $d \in \mathbf{D}$ where the interpretation $I[d/x]$ is just like I except that the varible x is assigned the value d in $I[d/x]$;* **false** *otherwise.*

(7) *For any formula of the form* first A, $[\![\text{first } A]\!]_{\alpha^*(\text{first } A),I}^t = [\![A]\!]_{\alpha^*(A),I}^s$ *where $s = \alpha^*(\text{first } A)^{(0)}$.*

(8) *For any formula of the form* next A, $[\![\text{next} A]\!]_{\alpha^*(\text{next } A),I}^t = [\![A]\!]_{\alpha^*(A),I}^s$ *where $s = \alpha^*(\text{next } A)^{(n+1)}$ and $n = rank(t, \alpha^*(\text{next } A))$.*

(9) *For any formula of the form A* fby B, $[\![A \text{ fby } B]\!]_{\alpha^*(A \text{ fby } B),I}^t = [\![A]\!]_{\alpha^*(A),I}^t$ *if $rank(t, \alpha^*(A \text{ fby } B)) = 0$; otherwise, $[\![A \text{ fby } B]\!]_{\alpha^*(A \text{ fby } B),I}^t = [\![B]\!]_{\alpha^*(B),I}^s$ where $s = \alpha^*(B)^{(n-1)}$ and $n = rank(t, \alpha^*(A \text{ fby } B))$.*

Let $\models_{I,\alpha} A$ denote the fact that A is true under I on clock assignment α, in other words, $[\![A]\!]_{\alpha,I}^t = [\![A]\!]_{\alpha^*(A),I}^t = $ **true** for all $t \in \alpha^*(A)$. We also use the notation $\models_\alpha A$ to denote the fact that $\models_{I,\alpha} A$ for any temporal interpretation I over clock assignment α. In particular, if $\models_{I,\alpha} A$, then we say that the temporal interpretation I on α is a model of the formula A and use $\models A$ to denote the fact that for any interpretation I and any clock assignment α we have $\models_{I,\alpha} A$.

Axioms and rules of inference of TLC can be found in [9]. The version of TLC presented in this paper would have additional axioms and rules to formalize the temporal operator fby. We omit the details.

4 Clocked Temporal Datalog

A Clocked Temporal Datalog program consists of three components: $P = \langle P_c, P_a, P_b \rangle$ where P_c, P_a and P_b are the clock definition, the clock assignment and the program body of the program P. The clock definition P_c specifies all the available clocks. The clock assignment P_a assigns to each predicate defined in the program body a clock from the clock definition. The main point is that the clock assignment α of P_b is totally determined by P_c and P_a.

The basic building blocks of Clocked Temporal Datalog programs are temporal atoms and temporal units. The formal definitions of temporal units and program clauses are given below.

Definition 14 (Temporal units).

- *A temporal atom is a temporal unit.*
- *If $A_1, \ldots, A_m$ and $B_1, \ldots, B_n$ (for $m, n \geq 1$) are temporal units, then so is $(A_1, \ldots, A_m)$ fby $(B_1, \ldots, B_n)$.*

Definition 15 (Program clauses).

- *A program clause in P_c and P_b is of the form A <- $B_1, \ldots, B_n$ where A is a temporal atom and all B_i's are temporal units. If $n = 0$, then the program clause is also called a fact.*
- *A program clause in P_a is of the form* assign(p, ck_i) *where p is a predicate symbol defined in P_b and ck_i is a predicate symbol with arity 1 defined in P_c.*

All the predicates in P_c are assumed to be defined on the global clock gc. It should be noted that P_c, except for temporal operator fby, is just like a program of Chronolog [12], a temporal logic programming language with temporal operators first and next only. In the underlying temporal logic of Chronolog, the timeline is modeled by the sequence of natural numbers, i.e., the global clock gc. P_a is a Prolog program; a clause such as assign$(p/n, cki)$ in P_a says that ck_i is the clock associated with the predicate symbol p/n defined in P_b.

Since P_c is a program, the definition of each ck_i in general may or may not "represent" an actual clock. To ensure that it does, we stipulate that each ck_i satisfy the following clock constraints:

Definition 16 (clock constraints [9]).

- *For any successful query* first next[m] $ck_i(X)$, *we have that* $m \leq X$.
- *For any pair of successful fixed-time queries* first next[m] $ck_i(X)$ *and* first next[m] $ck_i(Y)$, *we have that* $X = Y$.
- *For any pair of successful fixed-time queries* first next[m] $ck_i(X)$ *and* first next[n] $ck_i(Y)$, *if* $m < n$, *then* $X < Y$.

The first constraint says that the rank of a moment on a clock is not greater than the moment. The last two constraints ensure that clocks are linear and monotonic. When the second constraint is relaxed, we may have branching time.

We now give an example program (clocked database). Suppose that there is a library which only holds books. Book acquisitions are dealt with at the end of each week. We may define the following predicates (among others):

```
stock(X):              book X is in stock.
acquisition(X): book X has been acquired by the library.
onloan(X):             book X in on loan.
```

An incomplete program for the library is given below:

```
% CLOCK DEFINITION %
ck1(N) <- N = 0 fby (ck1(M), N is M+1).
ck2(N) <- ck1(M), N is M*7.

% CLOCK ASSIGNMENT %
assign(stock,ck1).
assign(acquisition,ck2).
assign(onloan,ck1).

% PROGRAM BODY %
first stock(mobbydick).
first next stock(the_hobbit).
next stock(X) <- stock(X).
stock(X) <- acquisition(X).
first next acquisition(war_and_peace).
first next[2] acquisition(germinal).
...
```

The clock definition defines two clocks, i.e., ck1 and ck2. Here ck1 represents the clock $\langle 0, 1, 2, 3, \ldots \rangle$ in which each moment can be interpreted as a day. Then ck2 can be interpreted as representing weeks (or, say mondays), i.e., $\langle 0, 7, 14, 21, \ldots \rangle$. At time $t = 0$, the left-hand-side of fby in the clause for ck1 is used; therefore the initial value for ck1 is 0. At times $t > 0$, the right-hand-side of fby is used; therefore the subsequent values for ck1 are determined by the previous value for ck1 plus 1.

The clock assignment assigns clocks for the predicate symbols defined in the program body, for instance, the clock of stock is ck1.

The program body includes facts to define the initial stock in the library and some rules. Once a book is in stock, it remains in stock forever. Since predicates stock and acquisition are defined over ck1 and ck2 respectively and these clocks synchronize at 0, 7, 14 etc., the book war_and_peace is included in stock at time 7, the book germinal at time 14 and so on.

Suppose that we want to find which books are in stock at time 1:

```
<- first next stock(X).
```

The answers to the goal are X = mobbydick, X = the_hobbit and so on. We now ask "which books are in stock at the end of week 1?":

```
<- first next[7] stock(X).
```

Then the answers will include all those books which are already in stock from time 0 to time 7 plus all the books acquired until time 7, eg, X = mobbydick, X = war_and_peace and so on.

If all atoms of a goal are fixed-time, then the goal is a fixed-time goal; otherwise it is an open goal. An open goal stands for a series of independent fixed-time goals. For example, the open goal `<- stock(X)` stands for a series of independent fixed-time goals of form `<- first next[n] stock(X)` for all $t \in$ ck1 where $n = rank(t, \text{ck1})$. Answers to fixed-time goals can be obtained by using a clocked extension of SLD-resolution [9].

5 Declarative Semantics

This section develops the meaning (declarative semantics) of Clocked Temporal Datalog programs based on an extension of the declarative semantics of Chronolog(MC) programs [9]. The meaning of the program body of a Clocked Temporal Datalog program is naturally presented as the meaning of the program.

5.1 Semantics of clock definitions

Let $P = \langle P_c, P_a, P_b \rangle$ be a Clocked Temporal Datalog program. The clock assignment P_a is a set of facts, i.e. a Prolog program. The semantics results for Prolog programs can be found in Lloyd [10]. P_c is an ordinary Chronolog program [12], except for temporal operator fby. Although fby allows us to define some predicate more succinctly, it does not really add any expressive power to the language when all the predicates are defined over the global clock. The following result will thus allow us to benefit from the declarative semantics of Choronolog programs:

Lemma 1. *Let* $P = \langle P_c, P_a, P_b \rangle$ *be a Clocked Temporal Datalog program. Then* P_c *is equivalent to an* fby-*free program* P'_c.

Proof. We sketch an informal proof. Let α be a clock assignment that assigns gc to each predicate symbol. Without any loss of generality, consider the following program clause: $C = A$ `<-` B_1 fby B_2. We have that $\alpha^*(C) = \alpha^*(A$ `<-` B_1 fby $B_2) = gc$. By the semantics of fby, at time 0, the value of A is determined by the value of B_1; at all times > 0, the value of A is determined by the previous value of B_2. Therefore the clause C is equivalent to the two clauses given below:

$$C1 = \text{first } A \text{ <- first } B_1.$$
$$C2 = \text{next } A \text{ <- } B_2.$$

It is easy to verify that $C1$ is applicable at time 0; and $C2$ is applicable at all times > 0. Nested fby's can be eliminated in a similar manner. ∎

The declarative semantics of P_c can be developed in terms of temporal Herbrand models as follows. The results given below applies to fby-free clock definitions, and by lemma 1 they apply to any clock definition of Clocked Temporal Datalog.

The Herbrand universe of P_c, denoted by U_c, is generated by constants and function symbols that appear in P_c. Note that the Herbrand universes of P_c and P'_c coincide. The Herbrand base B_c of P_c consists of all those fixed-time temporal atoms generated by predicate symbols appearing in P_c with terms in U_c used as arguments. Subsets of B_c are regarded as temporal Herbrand interpretations of P_c. Note that the Herbrand bases of P_c and P'_c also coincide.

Let I be a temporal interpretation of P_c with U_c as its domain. Let α be a clock assignment which maps each predicate symbol defined in P_c to gc. Then I is identified with a subset H of B_c by the following. For all $t \in \alpha(p)$:

$$[\![p(e_1,\ldots,e_n)]\!]_{\alpha,I}^t = \textbf{true} \text{ iff } \texttt{first next}[t]\, p(e_1,\ldots,e_n) \in H.$$
$$[\![p(e_1,\ldots,e_n)]\!]_{\alpha,I}^t = \textbf{false} \text{ iff } \texttt{first next}[t]\, p(e_1,\ldots,e_n) \notin H.$$

Orgun and Wadge [12] showed that the minimum temporal Herbrand model of a Chronolog program exists, and it consists of all the logical consequences of the program. We denote the minimum model of P_c by $\mathcal{M}(P_c)$. The following result follows from lemma 1 and analogous results for Chronolog [12].

Theorem 1. *Let* $P = \langle P_c, P_a, P_b \rangle$ *be a Clocked Temporal Datalog program. Let* α *be a clock assignment which maps each predicate symbol defined in* P_c *to* gc. *Then we have:* $\mathcal{M}(P_c) = \mathcal{M}(P_c') = \{A \in B_c | P_c' \models_\alpha A\}$.

Given a program $P = \langle P_c, P_a, P_b \rangle$, we now show that the clock assignment of α of P_b can be obtained from P_c and P_a if all the clock constraints are satisfied. We first have the following sufficiency result which states that if a clock definition in P_c satisfies the clock constraints, then it represents an actual clock in CK.

Lemma 2. *Let* $P = \langle P_c, P_a, P_b \rangle$ *be a Clocked Temporal Datalog program. For each predicate symbol* $\texttt{cki}$ *defined in* P_c' *with a clause of the form* $\texttt{assign(cki,p/n)}$ *in* P_a, *if* $\texttt{cki}$ *satisfies the clock constraints with respect to* $\mathcal{M}(P_c)$, *then the clock represented by* $\texttt{cki}$ *is given as:* $\langle t\,|\,\texttt{first next}[k]\,\,\texttt{cki}(t) \in \mathcal{M}(P_c) \rangle_{k \in \omega}$.

Definition 17. *Let* $P = \langle P_c, P_a, P_b \rangle$ *be a Clocked Temporal Datalog program and* $\mathcal{SP}$ *the set of predicate symbols appearing in* P_b. *Let* $CP = \{cki \mid \texttt{assign(p,cki)} \in P_a \text{ and } p \in \mathcal{SP}\}$. *We call* P_c *and* P_a *an admissible clock definition if the following conditions are satisfied:*

- *each* $\texttt{cki} \in CP$ *is defined as a unary predicate in* P_c
- *each* $\texttt{cki} \in CP$ *satisfies the clock constraints with respect to* $\mathcal{M}(P_c)$
- *each* $p \in \mathcal{SP}$ *occurs in at most one clause of the form* $\texttt{assign(p,cki)} \in P_a$

The clock assignment α of P_b determined by an admissible P_c and P_a, can be recovered as follows. For all $p \in \mathcal{SP}$:

- $\alpha(p) = \langle t\,|\,\texttt{first next}(k)\,\,\texttt{cki}(t) \in \mathcal{M}(P_c) \rangle_{k \in \omega}$ if $\texttt{assign(p,cki)} \in P_a$ (this case is provided by lemma 2);
- $\alpha(p) = \langle 0, 1, 2, 3, \ldots \rangle = gc$ if p is not assigned a clock in P_a (default).

In general, there is no easy way of automatically checking whether clock constraints are satisfied by each clock definition. In [9], it is shown that a clock definition with some syntactic restrictions satisfies the clock constraints. However, the restrictions only allow a small set of periodic clock definitions, therefore, here we use the clock constraints in a prescriptive manner to restrict the admissibility of clock definitions. Note that it is the programmer's responsibility to ensure that clock definitions are admissible.

Programmable clock definitions are very flexible in specifying periodic as well as some non-periodic clocks. For instance, the following program clauses define a non-periodic Fibonacci-like clock, that is, $\langle 1, 2, 3, 5, 8, 13, \ldots \rangle$:

```
first cki(1).
first next cki(2).
next[2] cki(N) <- next cki(X), cki(Y), N is X+Y.
```

This clock definition would be ruled out by the restriction imposed in [9]. The restriction does not allow mutual clock definitions, such as the ones given below, either.

```
even(N) <- N = 0 fby (odd(M), N is M+1).
odd(N) <- even(M), N is M+1.
```

Here predicates even and odd define the sequences of even numbers and odd numbers over time, respectively.

5.2 Semantics of program bodies

Let $P = \langle P_c, P_a, P_b \rangle$ be a Clocked Temporal Datalog program. We know that P_b is true in a temporal interpretation I on a given clock assignment α if and only if all program clauses in P_b are true in I on α. If we can show that a program clause is true in I on α if and only if all fixed-time instances of the clause are true in I on α, then we can use the analogous results developed for Chronolog(MC) [9], restricted to its function-free subset. However, this result is not as straightforward as that for clock definitions.

A fixed-time instance of a program clause will only contain fixed-time temporal atoms. We refer the reader to [9] for details of fixed-time instances of fby-free program clauses. In P_b, we cannot directly eliminate the occurrences of fby's because the clocks of involved sub-formulas may be different. However, given a particular moment t on the clock of a program clause with fby, we have the knowledge of which side of the fby operator is involved at that time. Then, a fixed-time instance of the clause can be obtained by referring to the involved side of fby; the other side will simply be dropped from the instance. Nested fby's can be eliminated one at a time.

We therefore have the following result, which complements lemma 1:

Lemma 3. *Let* $P = \langle P_c, P_a, P_b \rangle$ *be a Clocked Temporal Datalog program. Then* P_b *is equivalent to an* fby-*free program* P_b'.

Let U_b denote the clocked Herbrand universe of P_b which is generated by constants and function symbols that appear in P_b. The clocked Herbrand base B_b of P_b consists of all those fixed-time temporal atoms generated by predicate symbols appearing in P_b with terms in U_b used as arguments. Again, the Herbrand universes of P_b and P_b' coincide; and so do their Herbrand bases. Let α be the clock assignment determined by P_c' and P_a and I a temporal interpretation of P_b with U_b as its domain. Then I is identified with a subset H of B_b by the following. For all $t \in \alpha(p)$:

$$[\![p(e_1,\ldots,e_n)]\!]_{\alpha,I}^t = \textbf{true} \text{ iff first next}(rank(t,\alpha(p)))\,p(e_1,\ldots,e_n) \in H.$$
$$[\![p(e_1,\ldots,e_n)]\!]_{\alpha,I}^t = \textbf{false} \text{ iff first next}(rank(t,\alpha(p)))\,p(e_1,\ldots,e_n) \notin H.$$

If $P = \langle P_c, P_a, P_b \rangle$ is a Clocked Temporal Datalog program with an admissible clock definition, then, $\langle P_c', P_a, P_b' \rangle$ is an equivalent Chronolog(MC) program, restricted to its function-free subset. Then, the following result follows from lemmas 1 and 3, and the analogous results for Chronolog(MC) programs [9].

Theorem 2. *Let* $P = \langle P_c, P_a, P_b \rangle$ *be a Clocked Temporal Datalog program, with an admissible clock definition. Then* $\langle P_c', P_a, P_b' \rangle$ *is a Chronolog(MC) program with an admissible clock definition. Let* α *be the clock assignment determined by* P_c' *and* P_a. *Then* $\mathcal{M}(P_b) = \mathcal{M}(P_b') = \{A \in B_b \mid P_b' \models_\alpha A\}$.

If Clocked Temporal Datalog is used to query a clocked database, the clocks of relations defined in a program will be determined by the clock assignment of the program, while the clocks of relations defined in the clocked database will be determined by the clock assignment of the database. We assume that the set of relation symbols in the clocked database are distinct from the set of predicate symbols defined in the program.

Let $P = \langle P_c, P_a, P_b \rangle$ be a Clocked Temporal Datalog program with an admissible clock definition, and $\mathsf{DB} = \langle R, \beta, \lambda \rangle$ a clocked database. Now P and DB together correspond to the clocked database $\mathsf{DB}' = \langle R \cup \mathcal{SP}, \alpha \cup \beta, \mu \rangle$ where

- $\mathcal{SP}$ is the set of predicate symbols that appear in P_b'.
- α is the clock determined by P_a and P_c.
- P_{db} is a set of facts (fixed-time temporal atoms) that correspond to the facts in the clocked database DB,
- μ is a map determined as follows. For any $p \in R$, $\mu(p) = \lambda(p)$. For any $p \in (\mathcal{SP} \setminus R)$, $\mu(p) = \{t \mapsto I(p)(t) \mid t \in \alpha(p)\}$ where I is the temporal interpretation over clock $\alpha \cup \beta$ identified with $\mathcal{M}(P_b \cup P_{db})$.

When a Clocked Temporal Datalog program is used on its own as a deductive clocked database, the clocked database the program models is a special case of the above definition with $R = \emptyset$, $\beta = \emptyset$ and $\lambda = \emptyset$.

Bottom-up evaluation strategies such as the fixed point computation are used to compute the entire minimum Herbrand model of a given Datalog program [1]. However, since a clocked database modeled by a Clocked Temporal Datalog program may contain clocked relations defined over infinite clocks, we can only compute finite portions of a given clocked database over any period of time, provided that the program is *temporally stratified* (that is, all future data is defined in terms of past and/or present data). We omit the details due to space limitations.

6 Concluding Remarks

We have proposed a deductive system for temporal data, based on the function-free subset of Chronolog(MC) [9], that can deal with granularity of time. Our interpretation of a granularity in the underlying model for time is a clock. However, if we interpret granularity as periodicity, our model is not yet quite satisfactory, because the following clocks are based on the same periodicity: $\langle 0, 7, 14, 21, \ldots \rangle$ and $\langle 1, 8, 15, 22, \ldots \rangle$ and yet they are interpreted as different granularities. We are planning to include in TLC some temporal operators to provide various alignments of clocks in a seamless manner.

A promising avenue of further research is to relax the second clock constraint to obtain branching time. Then, finding answers to a given goal would also involve finding a branch of time in which the goal can be proved. To the best of our knowledge, no other deductive system for temporal data offers such flexibility.

Acknowledgements

The work presented in this article is partly sponsored by an Australian Research Council (ARC) Grant. Thanks are due to two anonymous referees for their constructive comments and suggestions. The second author was based at Macquarie University while the research reported in this article was conducted.

References

1. K. R. Apt, H. A. Blair, and A. Walker. Towards a theory of declarative knowledge. In J. Minker, editor, *Foundations of Deductive Databases and Logic Programming*, pages 89–148. Morgan Kaufmann, Los Altos, Calif, 1988.
2. M. Baudinet, M. Niézette, and P. Wolper. On the representation of infinite temporal data and queries. In *Proceedings of the Tenth ACM SIGACT-SIGMOD-SIGART Symposium on Principles of Database Systems*, pages 280–290. The Association for Computing Machinery, 1991.
3. M. Böhlen and R. Marti. On the completeness of temporal database query languages. In D. M. Gabbay and H. J. Ohlbach, editors, *Proceedings of ICTL'94: The First International Conference on Temporal Logic*, volume 827 of *LNAI*, pages 283–300, Gustav Stresemann Institut, Bonn, Germany, 1994. Springer-Verlag.
4. J. Chomicki and T. Imieliński. Temporal deductive databases and infinite objects. In *Proceedings of the Seventh ACM SIGACT-SIGMOD-SIGART Symposium on Principles of Database Systems*, pages 61–73. The Association for Computing Machinery, 1988.
5. C. E. Dyreson and R. T. Snodgrass. Temporal granularity. In R. T. Snodgrass, editor, *The TSQL2 Temporal Query Language*, pages 347–383. Kluwer Academic Press, 1995.
6. J.-R. Gagné and J. Plaice. A non-standard temporal deductive database system. *Journal of Symbolic Computation*, 22(5&6), 1996.
7. P. Ladkin. *The Logic of Time Representation*. PhD thesis, University of California, Berkeley, California, USA, 1987.
8. J. Y. Lee, R. Elmasri, and J. Won. An integrated temporal data model incorporating time series concept. Department of Computer Science and Engineering, The University of Texas at Arlington, Texas, U.S.A., February 1997.
9. C. Liu and M. A. Orgun. Dealing with multiple granularity of time in temporal logic programming. *Journal of Symbolic Computation*, 22(5&6):699–720, 1996.
10. J. W. Lloyd. *Foundations of Logic Programming*. Springer-Verlag, 1984.
11. M. A. Orgun. On temporal deductive databases. *Computational Intelligence*, 12(2):235–259, 1996.
12. M. A. Orgun and W. W. Wadge. Theory and practice of temporal logic programming. In L. Fariñas del Cerro and M. Penttonen, editors, *Intensional Logics for Programming*, pages 23–50. Oxford University Press, 1992.
13. G. Özsoyoğlu and R. T. Snodgrass. Temporal and real-time databases: A survey. *IEEE Transactions on Knowledge and Data Engineering*, 7(4):513–532, August 1995.
14. J. van Benthem. Temporal logic. In D. M. Gabbay, C. J. Hogger, and J. A. Robinson, editors, *Handbook of Logic in Artificial Intelligence and Logic Programming*, volume 4. Oxford University Press, 1993.
15. G. Wiederhold, S. Jajodia, and W. Litwin. Dealing with granularity of time in temporal databases. In R. Andersen, J. A. Bubenko, and A . Sølvberg, editors, *Advanced Information Systems Engineering: Proceedings of the Third International Conference CAiSE'91*, pages 124–140, Trondheim, Norway, May 13–15 1991. Springer-Verlag.

Querying for Facts and Content in Hypermedia Documents

Thomas Rölleke, Norbert Fuhr

University of Dortmund

Abstract. Objects such as documents and databases contain knowledge about objects. We consider this knowledge as the *content* of objects. We represent the content of objects as *facts* about other objects.

We consider both documents and databases as *contexts* since in the context of these objects some knowledge is valid. This uniform view on documents and databases as contexts brings particular advantage for hypermedia applications. Databases knows about the structure of its hypermedia documents. Hypermedia documents mirror facts about objects. The facts about the structure of hypermedia documents are combined with the content of documents.

In this paper, we present the query facilities gained from the combination of factual and content knowledge. We point out the conceptual differences between factual and content-oriented querying. We combine both types of querying and gain a framework for querying hypermedia documents where we can query among both facts and content.

1 Introduction

Hypermedia documents are characterised by their structure. They consist of other documents and they bear links to other documents. For considering this structure for querying, we need to store facts about this structure. These facts are knowledge of a database, i. e. these facts form the content of a database.

Beside the structure, databases know relationships concerning documents, e. g. authors of documents. Also documents contain knowledge. They contain knowledge about relationships of objects, e. g. friendship relations. We consider both databases and documents as structured and information-bearing objects. We call these objects *contexts* since in the context of them some knowledge is valid.

This uniform view on databases and documents as contexts establishes novel query facilities. The knowledge of contexts is combined and we can query among this combined knowledge. For example, the knowledge of several documents about tourist attractions in Scotland can be combined in order to retrieve knowledge about the tourist attractions directly. Classical techniques for retrieving information from documents would only support querying for the documents that contain the desired information. We distinguish conceptually between content-oriented and factual querying. Content-oriented querying searches for objects that possess some knowledge, whereas factual querying searches for objects that satisfy some relationships. The framework of contexts supports the combination of both types of querying.

Basic IR (information retrieval) systems (e. g. [Salton 71], [Callan et al. 92]) are designed for content-oriented querying. Facts about documents, e. g. authors of documents, are treated like content. Typically, we loose the information whether a document is about or of a specific author. Database systems store attributes of documents. For example, the title of a document is treated as an attribute. In these systems, string matching operations on attribute values support content-oriented querying. The underlying data models lead to expressive query languages (see [Abiteboul et al. 97]). However, the content is represented as a set of strings; the semantics of the content is not captured formally.

[Newcomb et al. 91] and [Macleod 91] address the particular aspect of hypermedia documents: their structure has to be considered in storage and retrieval. [Meghini et al. 93] and [Chiaramella et al. 96] introduce IR models based on logic. The semantics of the content of documents can be modelled and expressive query formulation is supported. Our approach has been to extend database models for IR purposes. In [Fuhr & Rölleke 97], we presented a probabilistic relational algebra as a basis for integrating IR and database systems. We consider this integration as a presupposition for achieving hypermedia IR systems that can deal with large data sets (see [Rölleke & Fuhr 97]). In [Rölleke & Fuhr 96], we presented a logical framework for retrieving complex objects such as hypermedia documents. [Fuhr et al. 98] links this logical framework with basic IR functionalities.

This paper concentrates on the description of our querying framework. It is structured as follows:

- Section 2 depicts the aspects of *factual querying*.
- Section 3 extends the framework with *content-oriented querying*.
- Section 4 combines *factual and content-oriented querying*.

We restrict this paper to the non-probabilistic querying framework. In [Rölleke 98], the probabilistic extension is defined.

2 Factual Querying

Factual querying refers to facts about objects. Which facts do we store and which formalism should we use? In the following, we motivate five pillars for factual querying:

- Classification
- Attributes
- Conjunction
- Negation with incomplete knowledge
- Rules

In object-oriented data modelling *classification* and *attributes* are central concepts. The first refers to the grouping of objects into classes. For example, object doc1 is a member of class document. The second refers to the characterisation of objects by their attribute values. For example, object peter is the value of the attribute author of object doc1. For factual querying, we decide to store these two types of facts: classification facts and attribute facts. Then, a query can ask for the objects and attribute values that make a formula true.

For example, assume the following fact database:

```
sailor(peter)        % classification
doc1.author(peter)   % attribute
```

We can query now for all members of the class sailor:

```
?- sailor(X)
```

As a second query, we ask for all documents of author peter:

```
?- D.author(peter)
```

For classes and attributes, we use names (e. g. sailor and author). We consider classes and attributes as predicates. A class has one argument, an attribute has two arguments. In place of the arguments, variables are allowed.

For formulating a complex query, we support conjunction and negation. Consider a conjunctive query asking for all objects D for which the author is a sailor:

```
?- D.author(X) & sailor(X)
```

For achieving a flexible system with respect to negation, we add the possibility to choose an open-world-assumption (OWA) or a closed-world-assumption (CWA). A clause like CWA(author) means that we assume that all authors are known in the fact database. The query processing will assume the truth value false for each author proposition where no fact is given. For example, a formula "not author(mary)" will be true if the fact author(hugo) is not known. As default, we assume an OWA. For example, a formula "not sailor(mary)" is neither true nor false, if the fact sailor(mary) is not known. Consider the following database:

```
CWA(author)
peter.friend(mary)
```

For the attribute author, a CWA is applied, whereas for friend, an OWA is applied. A query with negation for the authorship of mary yields true.

```
?- not doc1.author(mary) % is true
```

If we would use a variable in place of mary, each constant of the database that is not specified in a fact as author value would make this formula true. Now, consider a query for the friendship between peter and paul:

```
?- not peter.friend(paul) % is unknown
```

This query yields unknown. If we would use a variable in place of paul, the result would be empty since the query formula is not true for any object. In general, the result contains only those objects for which the negation is explicitly specified to be true.

For formulating a disjunctive query, we use rules. Also, rules provide a means for generalisation. Consider first a disjunctive query for all objects that are landscape images or where the author is mary:

```
retrieve(D) :- landscape_image(D)
retrieve(D) :- D.author(mary)
?- retrieve(D)
```

We demonstrate the second usage usage of rules by generalising over the hierarchy of author attributes:

```
D.author(X) :- D.first_author(X)
```

Every first author of an object is also an author of the object.

Now, we define the introduced language. The language is based on two sets of terminal symbols: a set of names and a set of constants. Names start with a lowercase letter, constants are strings or numbers. The language is defined inductively:

Definition 1.

- *Each classification "class-name(obj-name)" is a proposition.*
- *Each attribute value assignment "obj-name.attr-name(value)" is a proposition where "value" is either a constant or a name.*
- *Each proposition is a formula.*
- *Each conjunction "ψ_1 & ψ_2" is a formula where ψ_1 and ψ_2 are formulae.*
- *Each negation "not φ" is a formula where φ is a proposition.*
- *An expression "CWA(name)" is a CWA-clause.*
- *An expression "head :- body" is a rule where "head" is a proposition and body is a formula.*

The language for factual querying is defined. Its semantics is presented in the preceding examples. The formal definition of the semantics is to be found in [Rölleke 98].

Structural knowledge about hypermedia documents can be represented as facts about documents. For example, attributes such as sections, references, etc. are used for storing facts about the structure of objects. Classification supports the grouping of objects according to their media type. For example, we assign each object to a media class such as video, image, etc. In the next section, we extend the definition of the query language for dealing with content-oriented querying.

3 Content-oriented Querying

First, we demonstrate content-oriented querying with atomic documents. In a second step, we integrate knowledge about the structure of documents.

3.1 Atomic Contexts

For content-oriented querying on atomic contexts, we concentrate in the following on the representation of content. Consider the following example of the representation of the atomic context (document) doc1:

```
doc1[ sailing    boats
      sailor(peter)    peter.friend(mary) ]
```

The content is represented by four facts. In addition to classification and attribute facts, we include here the classical content representation as known in information retrieval: terms. Like classes and attributes, we consider terms as predicates, but without any argument. The content representation tells us that doc1 is about sailing and boats. It knows (shows) that peter is a sailor and that mary is a friend of peter.

A content-oriented query asks for all objects that possess some knowledge. Consider the following example:

```
?- D[sailing & sailor(peter)]
```

We ask for all contexts (objects) in which the formula "sailing & sailor(peter)" is true.

Like in factual querying, we use rules for expressing a disjunctive query. A query for all contexts about sailing or boats becomes:

```
retrieve(D) :- D[sailing]
retrieve(D) :- D[boats]
?- retrieve(D)
```

We have introduced the concepts for content-oriented querying on atomic contexts. We extend the definition 1 of our query language as follows:

Definition 2.

- *Every name is a proposition.*
- *Every context clause "name[ψ]" is a formula where ψ is a formula.*

The nested structure of context clauses leads us to the next issue of querying: consider the structure of documents.

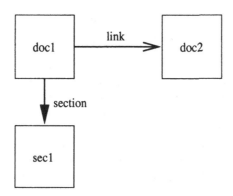

Fig. 1. Document with logical and link structure

3.2 Structured Contexts

Structured contexts are contexts that consist of other contexts. We use this aggregation of contexts for reflecting the structure of objects such as the logical structure.

Hypermedia documents are characterised by a logical structure and a link structure, i. e. documents consist of other documents and documents point to other documents. Consider the structured document in figure 1. On the database level, we could reflect this structure by attributes. Consider the following example:

```
doc1.section(sec1)
doc1.link(doc2)
```

Object sec1 is a section of doc1. Object doc1 is linked to object doc2. The different attribute names reflect the different semantics of the logical structure and the hypertext structure.

We use a nested context structure for reflecting the logical structure. The motivation behind is to answer a content-oriented query with an aggregated context. Consider the following nested context doc1:

```
doc1[sec1[ peter.friend(mary) ]
     sec2[ peter.friend(paul) ]
]
```

Object doc1 consists of two sub-objects: sec1 and sec2. Each sub-object possesses some knowledge. Here, some facts about friendship are presented. Now, we query for all contexts that know mary to be a friend of peter:

```
?- D[peter.friend(mary)]
```

We retrieve sec1 and doc1 since sec1 knows about the friendship relation and the knowledge of sec1 is propagated to doc1. Is is propagated, because sec1 is nested into doc1. A second query asks for a conjunction:

```
?- D[peter.friend(mary) & peter.friend(paul)]
```

This conjunction is only true in the aggregated context doc1, i. e. no single section on its own makes the formula true. Thus, the answer for a content-oriented query contains the smallest aggregated context that makes the content formula true. This feature is desirable for querying hypermedia documents which consist of several components and where the content of the whole document is determined by the content of its components.

When combining knowledge, we have to deal with inconsistent propositions. For example, one context claims a proposition to be true and the other claims it to be false. Assume, the context doc1 contains a third section where mary is not a friend of peter.

```
doc1[...
    sec3[ not peter.friend(mary) ]
]
```

Now, the proposition peter.friend(mary) is inconsistent on the level of doc1. However, this partial inconsistency does not destroy the querying facilities. Content-oriented querying remains reasonable for the true and false propositions of each context. In particular, the inconsistent propositions prevent the retrieval of the upper (large) contexts. The propagation of knowledge upwards the aggregation hierarchy and the ability to deal with inconsistencies allows us to retrieve the relevant entry points into hypermedia documents.

We have investigated content-oriented querying with respect to structured contexts. In the next section, we combine both factual and content-oriented querying.

4 Factual and Content-oriented Querying

Querying for hypermedia data often bears the problem that the raw data on its own does not reveal the semantical content. For example, an MPEG encoded video does hardly allow to deduce the semantical content. For querying among those kind of media data, we need to incorporate related data. For example, news videos can be retrieved if we can access related text articles.

The combination of factual and content-oriented querying supports the consideration of related data. Consider the following formulation of a retrieval rule:

```
retrieve(D) :- D.link(D1) & D1[ sailing & boats ]
```

Including this rule, we retrieve all objects D that are linked to objects D1 that are retrieved with respect to the content description.

A second benefit of the integrated representation of facts and content is the *augmentation* of knowledge. The knowledge of a super-objects such as a database is augmented by the knowledge of its sub-objects such as documents. We gain the possibility to query over the facts given in documents. For example, consider the query for all friends of peter:

```
doc1[sec1[ peter.friend(mary) ]
    sec2[ peter.friend(paul) ]
    sec3[ not peter.friend(mary) ]
]
?- peter.friend(X)
```

Assume that the database contains doc1. The factual query retrieves paul, but not mary. The knowledge of each sub-object is propagated upwards the aggregation hierarchy. Already on the level of doc1, the proposition peter.friend(mary) is inconsistent. The combination of the knowledge sources leads to a set of inconsistent propositions. However, reasonable querying remains possible among the true and false propositions of the database.

5 Conclusion

We have presented a querying language that makes the conceptual difference between factual and content-oriented querying explicit. However, both types of querying are represented in a uniform framework. The content of objects is represented as facts and rules.

Objects such as databases and documents are considered as contexts in which a logical program is specified. This uniform view on both databases and documents is of particular advantage for hypermedia documents. The logical program of the database contains structural information about hypermedia documents. Further-on, the nested structure of contexts reflects the structure of hypermedia documents and the answer for a query contains the smallest aggregated context that makes the query true.

We have implemented the introduced querying language on top of the relational logical Datalog model. We have added the means for dealing with the intrinsic uncertainty of knowledge. Probability values can be attached to facts, rules, and context clauses. The querying framework is applied for developing information systems that contain hypermedia documents.

References

[Abiteboul et al. 97] Abiteboul, S.; Cluet, S.; Christophides, V.; Milo, T.; Moerkotte, G.; Simeon, J. (1997). Querying documents in object databases. *International Journal on Digitial Libraries 1(1)*, pages 5–19.

[Callan et al. 92] Callan, J.; Croft, W.; Harding, S. (1992). The INQUERY Retrieval System. In: *Proceedings of the 3rd International Conference on Database and Expert Systems Applications*, pages 78–83.

[Chiaramella et al. 96] Chiaramella, Y.; Mulhem, P.; Fourel, F. (1996). *A Model for Multimedia Information Retrieval.* Technical report, FERMI ESPRIT BRA 8134, University of Glasgow.

[Fuhr & Rölleke 97] Fuhr, N.; Rölleke, T. (1997). A Probabilistic Relational Algebra for the Integration of Information Retrieval and Database Systems. *ACM Transactions on Information Systems 14(1)*, pages 32–66.

[Fuhr et al. 98] **Fuhr, N.; Gövert, N.; Rölleke, T.** (1998). DOLORES: A System for Logic-Based Retrieval of Multimedia Objects. In: *Proceedings of the 21st Annual International ACM SIGIR Conference on Research and Development in Information Retrieval.* ACM, New York.

[Macleod 91] **Macleod, A.** (1991). A Query Language for Retrieving Information from Hierarchic Text Structures. *The Computer Journal 34(3)*, pages 254–264.

[Meghini et al. 93] **Meghini, C.; Sebastiani, F.; Straccia, U.; Thanos, C.** (1993). A Model of Information Retrieval Based on a Terminological Logic. In: Korfhage, R.; Rasmussen, E.; Willett, P. (eds.): *Proceedings of the Sixteenth Annual International ACM SIGIR Conference on Research and Development in Information Retrieval,* pages 298–308. ACM, New York.

[Newcomb et al. 91] **Newcomb, S. R.; Kipp, N. A.; Newcomb, V. T.** (1991). The "HyTime" Hypermedia/Time-based Document Structuring Language. *Communications of the ACM 34(11)*, pages 67–83.

[Rölleke & Fuhr 96] **Rölleke, T.; Fuhr, N.** (1996). Retrieval of Complex Objects Using a Four-Valued Logic. In: Frei, H.-P.; Harmann, D.; Schäuble, P.; Wilkinson, R. (eds.): *Proceedings of the 19th International ACM SIGIR Conference on Research and Development in Information Retrieval,* pages 206–214. ACM, New York.

[Rölleke & Fuhr 97] **Rölleke, T.; Fuhr, N.** (1997). Probabilistic Reasoning for Large Scale Databases. In: Dittrich, K.; Geppert, A. (eds.): *Datenbanksysteme in Büro, Technik und Wissenschaft,* pages 118–132. Springer, Berlin et al.

[Rölleke 98] **Rölleke, T.** (1998). *Probabilistic Logical Representation and Retrieval of Complex Objects.* University of Dortmund. Dissertation (in preparation).

[Salton 71] **Salton, G. (ed.)** (1971). *The SMART Retrieval System - Experiments in Automatic Document Processing.* Prentice Hall, Englewood, Cliffs, New Jersey.

Querying Objects with Complex Static Structure

Iztok Savnik[1] and Zahir Tari[2]

[1] University of Ljubljana, Faculty of Computer and Information Science, Slovenia
[2] Royal Melbourne Institute of Technology, Department of Computer Science,
Australia

Abstract. This paper describes the database algebra QAL which serves
as the logical algebra in the query execution system of the Distributed
Object Kernel [25]. QAL is based on the concepts of the early functional query languages. It provides a simple functional semantics of the
language and the means to express complex queries in a step-by-step
manner. The operations of QAL are designed to allow simple and efficient manipulation of objects having complex classification or composition structure. The expressive power of QAL is presented through a
case-study consisting of a comprehensive set of examples of queries which
manipulate complex objects.

1   Introduction

Database management systems are employed for storing data in many novel
computer applications ranging from computer aided design, process control and
computer integrated manufacturing to software engineering, multimedia and Internet applications. Novel demands for the representation and manipulation of
the data in these applications include the needs to represent and query objects
having complex composition and/or classification structure.

In this paper we present the database algebra QAL [20] designed for the
manipulation of complex objects [14, 1]. QAL is used as the logical algebra [11] in
the query execution system of the Distributed Object Kernel [25] (abbr. DOK)
which is currently under development. DOK will serve as a platform for the
development of applications which involve heterogeneous distributed databases
storing business and multimedia data.

QAL evolved from the FQL family [6, 4, 17] of functional query languages
by generalising their operations for the manipulation of objects. Let us briefly
present the operations and the expressive power of QAL. Firstly, QAL includes
a set of operations, called *model-based operations*, which are derived from the
concepts used in the QAL's database model formalisation. They enable users
to inquire about the basic properties of objects from the extensional and the
intensional parts of the database including, however, the classification hierarchy
of objects. Secondly, the *declarative* operations of QAL are the functional operations defined on sets of objects. The declarative operations of QAL include
a group of higher-order functional operations which allow for a simple way of
expressing queries that manipulate composite objects.

The rest of the paper is organised as follows. Section 2 presents the formal view of the object-oriented data model which is used for the definition of the basic operations of the algebra. The complete set of QAL's operations is presented in Section 3. In Section 4 the use of QAL operations for expressing queries that manipulate objects with complex static structure is demonstrated through a case-study. Further, the main ideas used for the integration of QAL into the DOK are presented in Section 5. In Section 6 we present the related work. Finally, Section 7 gives a short conclusion.

2 Data Model

This section presents the main features of the object-oriented data model serving as a framework for the definition of the QAL algebra. The data model provides, in addition to the basic constructs of the object-oriented data model [3], a uniform view of the database by treating classes as abstract objects. In this respect, it is based on ideas introduced in the logic-based declarative language F-Logic [13]. The extended presentation of the data model can be found in [20].

2.1 Object Identifiers

An *object identifier* (abbr. *oid*) is a unique symbol which represents an entity from the real world[1]. An object identifier is either an *individual identifier* which represents a concrete entity, or a *class identifier* which represents an abstract concept.

The class identifier stands for a set of individual identifiers which represent the *interpretation* of a class identifier. Formally, the interpretation of a class identifier c is a set of individual identifiers denoted as $I_c(c)$; the elements of $I_c(c)$ are called the *members* of the class identifier c. The interpretations of two class identifiers are non-intersecting sets of object identifiers. Therefore, an individual identifier has exactly one parent class identifier.

The set of class identifiers is organised with respect to the partial ordering relationship *ISA_SUBCLASS* – this relationship is denoted as "$\preceq_i$". The partially ordered set of class identifiers is extended to include individual identifiers. A member of a given class identifier is related to this class identifier by the relationship $\preceq_i$. Formally, $o \in I_c(c) \implies o \preceq_i c$, where o represents an individual identifier and c is a class identifier.

The *inherited interpretation* [2, 24] of a class identifier c, denoted as $I_c^*(c)$, includes all *instances* of c, that is, the members of c and the members of $c's$ subclass identifiers. Formally, $I_c^*(c) = \bigcup_{c_j \preceq_i c \wedge c_j \in \mathcal{V}_c} I_c(c_j)$, where $\mathcal{V}_c$ denotes the set of all class identifiers of a given database.

---

[1] The object identifiers of QAL correspond to the so-called *logical id-s*, as introduced by Kifer et al. in [13].

2.2 O-Values

An o-value [2] is either: an oid; a set $\{o_1, \ldots, o_n\}$, where o_i-s represent o-values; or a tuple defined as $[A_1{:}o_1, \ldots, A_n{:}o_n]$, where o_i-s represent o-values and A_i-s are attribute names. An o-value can be either a ground o-value or a type o-value. A *ground o-value* includes only the individual identifiers and a *type o-value* includes only the class identifiers.

An example of a ground o-value is $[name{:}\text{"Jim"}, age{:}50, kids{:}\{ana, tom\}]$, representing the properties of a person. The string "Jim" and the integer number 50 are the simple identifiers which are usually called constants. Next, the component $\{ana, tom\}$ is the set of individual identifiers which represent kids, that is, the instances of the class identifier *person*. The type of the above o-value is, as it will be presented shortly, the type o-value $[name{:}string, age{:}int, kids{:}\{person\}]$, where the terms *string, int* and *person* represent class identifiers.

The interpretation of a type o-value t, denoted as $I(t)$, is a set of ground o-values which is defined as follows. Firstly, in the case that the type o-value t is a class identifier, its interpretation is $I(t) = I_c(t)$. Secondly, the interpretation of a tuple-structured type o-value is $I([a_1 : T_1, \ldots, a_n : T_n]) = \{[a_1 : o_1, \ldots, a_n : o_n]; o_i \in I(T_i), i \in [1..n]\}$. Finally, the interpretation of a set-structured type o-value is $I(\{S\}) = \{s; s \subseteq I(S)\}$. If a ground o-value v is an element of $I(t)$ than we say that t is the *type* of v.

The relationship $\preceq_i$ defined on identifiers is extended to relate o-values. The new relationship is denoted as $\preceq_o$; we refer to it as a *more_specific* relationship. Suppose we have two o-values v_1 and v_2. Firstly, if the o-values v_1 and v_2 are object identifiers then $v_1 \preceq_o v_2 \iff v_1 \preceq_i v_2$. Secondly, if $v_1 = \{s_1\}$ and $v_2 = \{s_2\}$ where s_1 and s_2 are o-values, then $v_1 \preceq_o v_2 \iff s_1 \preceq_o s_2$. Finally, if $v_1 = [a_1 : t_1 \ldots, a_k : t_k]$ and $v_2 = [b_1 : s_1 \ldots, b_n : s_n]$ where t_i-s and s_i-s are o-values and the attributes of v_1 and v_2 are ordered so that $a_i = b_j$ when $i = j$, then $v_1 \preceq_o v_2 \iff k \geq n \wedge \forall i (i \in [1..n] \wedge a_i = b_i \wedge t_i \preceq_o s_i)$. Note that the partial ordering relationship $\preceq_o$ relates type o-values as well as ground o-values.

In a similar way to the inherited interpretation of class identifiers, we introduce the *inherited interpretation* of type o-values. Given a type o-value t, its inherited interpretation includes the union of interpretations of the type o-value t and the interpretations of all type o-values more specific than t. Formally, $I^*(t) = \bigcup_{t_j \preceq_o t \wedge t_j \in \mathcal{V}_T} I(T_j)$, where $\mathcal{V}_T$ denotes the set of all type o-values of a given database. Finally, the *natural interpretation* of a type o-value t, denoted as $I^\circ(t)$, includes all o-values more specific than t. Formally, $I^\circ(t) = \{o; o \preceq_o t\}$.

2.3 Objects

An object is defined as a pair (i, v), where i is an object identifier and v its corresponding value. An object identifier is a reference to an object, and a *value* represents the state of object realised by *o-value*. Similarly as in the case of object identifiers, we differentiate between two types of objects: *class objects* and *individual objects*. A class object represents an abstract concept and acts as a representation of a set of individual objects which share similar static structure and behaviour.

2.4 Working Example

The examples in the following sections are based on a conceptual schema which describes a simplified University environment. We define the conceptual schema by listing the class objects and the relationships among class identifiers which define the inheritance hierarchy of classes.

```
(department,[dept_name:string,
            head:employee,
            staff:{employee}])
(course,[title:string,
        instructor:lecturer ])
(project,[pro_name:string,
         descr:string,
         participants:{employee},
         budget:integer ])
(person,[name:string,
        age:int,
        address:string,
        family:{person}])
(student,[courses:{course}])
```

```
(employee,[salary:int,
          manager:employee,
          projects:{project},
          dept:department])
(lecturer,[])
(assistant,[])
(student-assistant,[])
```

student $\preceq_i$ person
employee $\preceq_i$ person
lecturer $\preceq_i$ employee
assistant $\preceq_i$ lecturer
professor $\preceq_i$ lecturer
student-assistant $\preceq_i$ assistant
student-assistant $\preceq_i$ student

3 Operations of QAL Algebra

The QAL algebra is based on the previously presented object-oriented data model. It includes two types of operation: model-based operations and declarative operations. The *model-based operations* are used to access and manipulate the properties of individual and class objects represented by the constructs of the data model. The *declarative operations* of QAL are used for expressing declarative queries on databases. The model-based operations are in this context used to assist the declarative operations in expressing database queries.

3.1 Model-Based Operations

In this sub-section we define the operations that are derived from the constructs of the previously presented object-oriented database model. Some of the model-based operations, i.e. the valuation operation, the extension operations, the equality operation and the operation class_of, are defined similarly as in other query languages (see, e.g. [15, 13, 12, 7]). The model-based operations which are introduced by the algebra QAL are the poset comparison operations, the closure operations and the operations lub-set and glb-set.

Valuation operation: The value of the object referenced by an identifier o can be obtained by the valuation operation **val** i.e. the value of o is o.**val**. If the valuation operation is followed by attribute name, then it can be abbreviated by the operator "$\rightarrow$" as it is common in procedural programming languages.

Extension operations: On the basis of the ordinary interpretation I_c and the inherited interpretation I_c^* of class identifiers defined in Section 2, two types of extension operations are defined. Firstly, the operation `ext` maps a class identifier to the set of its members. Secondly, the operation `exts` maps a class identifier to the set of its instances.

Class_of: The operation `class_of` maps an individual identifier to its parent class identifier. It is defined as $x.\mathtt{class\_of} = c \iff x \in I(c)$.

Poset comparison operations: These operations allow for relating o-values with respect to the partial ordering of o-values $\preceq_o$ introduced in Sub-section 2.1. The poset comparison operations are: $\preceq_o$, $\prec_o$, $\succ_o$ and $\succeq_o$.

Closure operations: Given a class identifier c, the closure operations `subcl` and `supcl` are used to compute the set of more specific or more general class identifiers of the identifier c. While the comparison operations can serve merely for expressing relationships among object identifiers, the result of the closure operation is the set of class identifiers that can be further used in the query.

Nearest common more general and more specific objects: The operations `lub-set` and `glb-set` are defined to compute the nearest more general or more specific object identifiers of the argument set of object identifiers with respect to the relationship $\preceq_i$.

Equality: Two types of equality operations are provided. Firstly, the ordinary equality denoted as "==" is used to compare o-values. Secondly, the *deep equality* [23] denoted as "=" compares object identifiers on the basis of values of the corresponding objects.

3.2 Declarative operations

Every declarative operation of QAL is a function which manipulates a set of o-values called the *argument* of operation. The operations have a set (possible empty) of *parameters* which can be either the o-values or the queries. The result of the declarative operation is an o-value.

A QAL *query* is an expression $o.f_1 \ldots .f_n$, where o is an o-value represented as a constant or a variable, the dot operator "." represents the functional composition and $f_i's$ are QAL operations. The parameter queries of the QAL declarative operations can use the *identity* function `id` to refer to the elements of the set which is an argument of the declarative operation.

Apply: The operation `apply`(f) is used to evaluate a parameter function f on the elements of the argument set. The parameter function f can be an attribute, a method or another query.

Select: The operation `select`(P) is used to filter an argument set of o-values by using a parameter predicate P. The operations that can be used to in the predicate P are: the standard arithmetic relationships, the set membership and set inclusion operators, previously presented model-based operations and the boolean operations.

Set operations: QAL includes the standard set operations union, intersection and difference which are denoted as `union`, `intsc` and `differ`, respectively. The ordinary value equality "==" is used for computing the set operations.

Tuple: The operation $\text{tuple}(a_1 : f_1, \ldots, a_n : f_n)$ is a generalisation of the relational operation project. Given a set of o-values as an argument of the operation, a tuple is generated for each o-value from the argument set. The value of the attribute a_i is an o-value which is the result of the evaluation of the parameter query f_i.

Explicit Join: The operation $\text{ojoin}(f, a_1, a_2, P)$ [23] joins the argument set of o-values with the result of the query f using the predicate P. The parameters a_1 and a_2 are optional. In the case that any of the ojoin arguments is not a set of tuples, then the o-values from this argument set are treated as tuples including a single component labelled a_i. Except from this, ojoin is defined as the relational join operation.

Group: The operation $\text{group}(a : f, b : g)$ applies the functions f and g to each element of the argument set. The results of the function g are grouped into sets in accordance with the results of the function f. The result of the operation group is a set of pairs which include the value of f (labelled as a) and the set of results of g (labelled as b) that share the common value of f.

Unnest: Three operations are defined to be able to unnest arbitrarily structured o-values in the argument composite objects. In order to provide an unified view of the possible types of unnesting, we give the operations the same name. The QAL **unnest** operations are defined as follows. First, the operation **unnest** is used to flatten the set of sets [23]. Second, given a set of tuples, the operation $\text{unnest}(A)$ unnests a set-valued component A [23]. Finally, given a set of tuples that include a tuple-valued component A, the operation $\text{unnest}(A)$ flattens the nested tuple [1].

Apply_at: To be able to apply a query to any nested components of the o-values from the argument set, the functionality of the operation apply is extended by a new parameter that serves as a component selector. The operation $\text{apply\_at}(p, f)$ identifies the desired components by applying the *aggregation path* p to the o-values that are the elements of the argument set. The aggregation path is specified by a sequence of attributes separated by dot operators. The query f is evaluated on the identified components. The evaluation of the aggregation path serves solely for the identification of the component and does not restructure the argument complex object.

4 A Case-Study

So far, we have presented the operations of the QAL algebra. In this section we focus our attention on the use of operations for querying objects having complex static structure. Two types of queries are studied: (i) queries that use conceptual schemata, and (ii) queries that manipulate complex objects.

The natural interpretation I° presented in Section 2 is used for the definition of the semantics of o-values that appear in QAL queries. Note that an instance of a type o-value t can be any o-value which is more specific than t.

4.1 Using Conceptual Schemata for Querying Databases

Let us first define two general types of query which will later serve for the classification of queries which use the conceptual schemata. Firstly, the *intensional queries* are the queries the answers to which consist of the elements of the conceptual schema [19, 22]. Secondly, the *extensional queries* are conventional queries the answers to which consist solely of the extensional portion of the database.

The following types of query that use the conceptual schemata are presented. Firstly, the intensional queries allow for inquiring and reasoning about the properties of the conceptual schemata. Secondly, we present the extensional queries which include references to the intensional part of the database. Finally, the queries which generalise the results of the extensional queries are demonstrated.

Intensional Queries. The following query selects all subclasses of `person` which are more general than at least one of the classes `student-assistant` or `professor`. In general, such queries use the poset comparison operations and/or the operations `subcl` and `supcl` to select a subset of classes representing the conceptual schema. The result of the query is an o-value which is the instance of the type o-value {person}.

```
person.subcl.select( id ≻ₒ student-assistant or
                     id ≻ₒ professor );
```

The query presented below retrieves all classes at the top level of the class hierarchy[2], that is, the only superclass they have is `object`. The result of the query is an instance of the type o-value {object}.

```
object.subcl.select( id.supcl = {object} );
```

Extensional queries. The following query uses poset comparison operations to relate object identifiers. It retrieves the instances of the class identifier `person` which are more specific than the class identifier `lecturer` and, at the same time, more general than or equal to the class identifier `student_assistant`. The query result is an instance of the type o-value {person}.

```
person.exts.select( id ≺ₒ lecturer and
                    student_assistant ⪯ₒ id.class_of );
```

The following query demonstrates the use of the poset comparison operations for relating tuple structured o-values. It returns a set of o-values describing persons; each o-value must be more specific than the o-value [address: "Brisbane", family:{employee}, manager:instructor]. The result of the query is of type {[name:string, age:int, address:string, family:{person}]}.

```
person.exts.apply( id.val ).
            select( id ≺ₒ [ address: "Brisbane",
                            family: {employee},
                            manager: instructor ]);
```

---

[2] This query was originally presented in [9].

Generalisations of extensional queries. The query given below answers the following question: Which are the parent classes of employees who work in CSD and who are younger than 25? The query first filters the set of employees and then it applies the operation class_of to each element of the resulting set. The result of the query is an instance of the type o-value {employee}.

```
employee.exts.select( id->dept = csd and
                      id->age < 25 ).
         apply( id.class_of );
```

4.2 Querying complex objects

In this section, we present the use of QAL operations for the manipulation of complex objects. The presentation is based on the classification of operations on complex objects defined by Kim et al. in [14]. The following types of query which manipulate complex objects are presented.

Suppose that the argument of a query is a set of complex objects. Firstly, the set of complex objects can be filtered by specifying the selection condition on the values of simple and complex attributes of argument complex objects. The second type of query projects the selected attributes from the flat and/or nested levels of complex objects from the argument set. Next, we present queries which filter nested components of complex objects. Finally, the use of QAL operations for restructuring complex objects is demonstrated. All examples in this section are based on the class object department which is now redefined as follows.

```
(department,[dept_name: string,
            head: employee,
            staff: {[emp_name:string, address:string,
                    projects:{project}, family:{person}]}]);
```

Retrieval of complex objects. Let us first present a simple query that filters a set of complex objects. The following query selects all departments whose head is a member of the class professor or some more specific class. The result of the query is an instance of {department}.

```
department.ext.select( id->head.class_of ≼o professor );
```

A more complex case is retrieving complex objects by expressing the predicates on the nested components of complex objects. The predicates are specified by the use of nested queries. The query given below retrieves departments which are involved in the project identified by object identifier *pr*4. The result of the query is an o-value of type {department}.

```
department.ext.select( pr4 in id->staff.
                           apply( id.projects ).
                           unnest ));
```

Projecting Components of Complex Objects. Given a set of complex objects describing departments, the following query projects the value of the attribute head and the values of attributes that describe personal information about employees. This type of query is similar to the nested-relational operation project as defined in [8, 16]. The result of a query is an o-value of type {[head: employee, staff: {[name:string, address:string, family:{person}]}]}.

```
department.ext.tuple( head: id->head,
                      staff: id->staff.
                             tuple( name: id.emp_name,
                                    address: id.address,
                                    family: id.family ));
```

Filtering Nested Components of Complex Objects. The following query filters the nested components of o-values which describe departments. The nested component is identified using the aggregation path staff.family. The original set is replaced by the set of family members who are younger than 30. The query result is a set of o-values having the same structure as the o-values describing departments.

```
department.ext.apply( id.val ).
            apply_at( staff.family,
                      id.select( id->age < 30 ));
```

Restructuring Complex Objects. The first example demonstrates the use of QAL restructuring operations to realise the typical restructuring operations on NF^2 relations. The query unnests the attribute staff and attribute projects and, after, it groups the names of employees and departments by the projects in which they participate. The result is an instance of the type o-value {[pro_id: project, group: {[emp: string, dept: string]}]}.

```
department.ext.apply( id.val ).
            unnest( staff ).
            unnest( projects ).
            group( pro_id: id.projects,
                   group: id.tuple( emp: id.emp_name,
                                    dept: id.dept_name ));
```

The following example presents the query which restructures the nested components of complex objects. Given a set of complex objects describing departments, the query identifies the components that include a set of identifiers referring to projects and then replaces every occurrence of an oid with a tuple that contains the name and the budget of each project. The result is an instance of type {[dept_name: string, head: employee, staff: {[emp_name: string, address: string, projects: {[pro_name: string, budget: int]}, family: {person}]}]}.

```
department.ext.apply( id.val ).
            apply_at( staff.projects,
                    id.tuple( pro_name: id->pro_name,
                            budget: id->budget ));
```

5 The integration of QAL into DOK

The algebra QAL will serve as the *logical algebra* [11] in the distributed query processing system of DOK [25]. The *physical algebra* of the query processing system is based on the subset of QAL which is equivalent to the complete QAL algebra. It includes the operations that can be efficiently evaluated on distributed databases, and, for which there exists a set of well-defined rules used for the low-level distributed query optimisation.

The DOM+ [25] (Distributed Object Model), the data model of DOK, allows for the representation of different aspects of distributed databases using the usual constructs of object-oriented database model, the meta-objects, and the virtual objects. Firstly, the constructs of object-oriented database model provide the means for the representation of the classification, composition, inheritance and encapsulation abstractions in a local database. Secondly, the meta-objects serve for the representation of the object properties which relate to their role in a distributed environment, for example, the physical location of objects. Finally, the virtual classes and objects allow for the global view of the database in a distributed environments.

The model-based operations allow QAL to inquire about the relationships between different types of DOM+ objects in a comprehensible manner. They can serve for querying the relationships among virtual objects as well as more specific properties of objects at the local level, i.e. its static properties, types, etc. In addition, QAL allows for the uniform treatment of the data and the meta-data levels of the database [22]. Hence, the same language can be used to explore the data, the schema and the meta-data levels of databases.

The general direction of our approach to the manipulation of DOM+ objects is to provide the tools for simple and efficient definition of queries for the manipulation of virtual objects at the global repository, which is the abstract level of the representation of DOK objects. Furthermore, a user have to be provided with the means to manipulate other more detailed levels of the representations of DOM+ virtual objects, such as the implementation specifics, locations of objects, etc. However, the manipulation of such data may require more deep understanding of the DOK architecture.

6 Related work

The work on the QAL algebra has been influenced by the functional query language FQL proposed by Buneman and Frankel [6], by some of its descendants, that is, GDL [4] and O^2FDL [17], and by the functional database programming language FAD [10]. QAL subsumes the operations of FQL, i.e. the operations extension, restriction, selection and composition, as well as the extensions of FQL provided by the query languages GDL [4] and O^2FDL [17]. In contrast to FQL, QAL does not support recursion.

Further, the algebra QAL is closely related to the Query Algebra originally proposed by Shaw and Zdonik in [23]. This algebra has been further used as the basis for the EXCESS/EQUAL algebra and its query optimiser [18]. QAL shares many similarities with these algebras in some of the basic operations (i.e. select, tuple and set manipulation operations), while it differs significantly in the operations for restructuring complex objects and for querying nested components of complex objects. In addition, QAL includes a rich set of primitive operations which serve for querying database schemata.

Let us now very briefly present the work closely related to the two main problems addressed in the paper: the use of conceptual schema for querying databases, and querying complex objects. The problem of querying conceptual schema of object-oriented databases has, to our knowledge, not been addressed by recent database algebras. The query languages which include the constructs that allow for querying conceptual schemata and/or relationships between the schema and the instance portion of a database are: ORION [15], F-Logic [13], OSCAR [12], ODMG OQL [7] and P/FDM query language [9]. The related studies of the operations for querying composite (complex) objects include: [14] by Kim, [8] by Colby, [8] by Liu and [1] by Abiteboul. The comparison of the operations of QAL with the operations of the related database algebras and query languages can be found in [20, 21].

7 Concluding remarks

In this paper we presented the logical algebra of complex objects QAL which allows for expressing the queries on objects with complex static structure. We proposed a set of simple operations, referred to as model-based operations, which provide a uniform access to the intensional and the extensional portions of the database. The model-based operations are used for inquiring and reasoning about the properties of individual and class objects. Further, an operation called apply_at which is used for querying nested components of complex objects is introduced. Its semantics is simple and comprehensible, and it can serve as the base for the efficient implementation of queries that manipulate composite objects.

References

1. S. Abiteboul, C. Beeri, *On the Power of the Languages For the Manipulation of Complex Objects*, Verso Report No.4, INRIA, France, Dec. 1993.
2. S. Abiteboul, P.C. Kanellakis, *Object Identity as Query Language Primitive*, Proc. of the ACM Conf. on Management of Data, 1989.
3. M. Atkinson, et al. *The Object-Oriented Database Systems Manifesto*, Proc. of First Int'l Conf. Deductive and OO Databases, North Holland, 1989, pp. 40-57.

4. D.S. Batory, T.Y. Leung, T.E. Wise, *Implementation Concepts for an Extensible Data Model and Data Language*, ACM Trans. on Database Systems, 13(3), Sep 1988, pp. 231-262.

5. E. Bertino et al, *Object-Oriented Query Languages: The Notion and Issues*, IEEE Trans. on Knowledge and Data Engineering, 4(3), June 1992.

6. P. Buneman, R.E. Frankel, *FQL- A Functional Query Language*, Proc. of the ACM Conf. on Management of Data, 1979.

7. R.G.G. Cattell (Editor), *The Object Database Standard: ODMG-93*, Morgan Kaufmann Publishers, 1993.

8. L.S. Colby, *A Recursive Algebra and Query Optimization for Nested Relations*, Proc. of the ACM Conf. on Management of Data, 1989.

9. S.M. Embury, Z. Jiao, P.M.D. Gray, *Using Prolog to Provide Access to Metadata in an Object-Oriented Database*, Practical Application of Prolog, 1992.

10. S. Danforth, P. Valduriez, *A FAD for Data Intensive Applications*, IEEE Trans. on Knowledge and Data Engineering, 4(1), Feb. 1992.

11. G. Graefe, *Query Evaluation Techniques for Large Databases*, ACM Comp. Surveys, Vol.25, No.2, June 1993, pp. 73-170.

12. J. Göers, A. Heuer, *Definition and Application of Metaclasses in an Object-Oriented Database Model*, Technical Report, Dept. of Computer Science, Technical University of Clausthal, 1994.

13. M. Kifer, G. Lausen, J. Wu, *Logical Foundations of Object-Oriented and Frame-Based Languages*, Technical Report 93/06, Dept. of Computer Science, SUNY at Stony Brook.

14. W. Kim, H.-T. Chou, J. Banerjee, *Operations and Implementation of Complex Objects*, IEEE Trans. on Software Engineering , 14(7), July 1988.

15. W. Kim, et al., *Features of the ORION Object-Oriented Database System*, 11th Chapter in *Object-Oriented Concepts, Databases and Applications*, W.Kim (ed.).

16. L. Liu, *A formal approach to Structure, Algebra & Communications of Complex Objects*, Ph.D. thesis, Tilburg University, 1992.

17. M. Mannino, I.J. Choi. D.S. Batory, *The Object-Oriented Data Language*, IEEE Trans. on Software Engineering, 16(11), Nov. 1990.

18. G.A. Mitchell, *Extensible Query Processing in an Object-Oriented Database*, Ph.D. thesis, Brown University, 1993.

19. M.P. Papazoglou, *Unravelling the Semantics of Conceptual Schemas*, Communications of the ACM, Sept. 1995.

20. I. Savnik, Z. Tari, T. Mohorič, *QAL: A Query Algebra of Complex Objects*, Under revision for Data & Knowledge Eng. Journal, 1998.

21. I. Savnik, *A Query Language for Complex Database Objects*, Ph.D. thesis, University of Ljubljana, CSD Tech. Report, J.Stefan Institute, CSD-TR-95-6, Jun 1995.

22. I. Savnik, Z. Tari, *Querying Conceptual Schemata of Object-Oriented Databases*, Proc. of DEXA'96 Workshop, IEEE Comp. Society, 1996.

23. G.M. Shaw, S.B. Zdonik, *A Query Algebra for Object-Oriented Databases*, Proc. of IEEE Conf. on Data Engineering, 1990.

24. S.L. Vandenberg, *Algebras for Object-Oriented Query Languages*, Ph.D. thesis, Technical Report No. 1161, University of Wisconsin, July 1993.

25. Z. Tari, A. Zaslavsky, I. Savnik, *Supporting Cooperative Databases with Distributed Objects*, In "Parallel and Distributed Systems: Theory and Applications", J.L. Aguilar Castro (Editor), Int. Inst. of Information and Systemics, 1998, To appear.

An Alternating Well–Founded Semantics for Query Answering in Disjunctive Databases

Dietmar Seipel

University of Würzburg
Am Hubland, D – 97074 Würzburg, Germany
seipel@informatik.uni-wuerzburg.de
Tel. +49 931 888 5026, Fax. +49 931 888 4600

Abstract. The *well–founded semantics* has been introduced for normal databases (i.e. databases that may have default negation in their rule bodies, but do not have disjunctions). In this paper we propose an extension of the well–founded semantics to the disjunctive case. For this purpose we investigate the alternating fixpoint approach of Van Gelder, Ross and Schlipf [16], and develop a suitable generalization to the case of disjunctive rule heads.

Given a disjunctive database $\mathcal{P}$, the new *alternating well–founded semantics* derives a set $ADWFS_{\mathcal{P}}$ of partial Herbrand interpretations of $\mathcal{P}$. This set coincides with the set of minimal models if there are no default negations in the database. For general disjunctive databases it is always not empty (if all rule heads are non–empty), i.e. $ADWFS_{\mathcal{P}}$ is *consistent*. The alternating well–founded semantics is very useful for *query answering* in disjunctive databases. During a fixpoint computation the final set $ADWFS_{\mathcal{P}}$ is approximated by a sequence $(\mathcal{I}_n)_{n\in\mathbb{N}_0}$ of sets $\mathcal{I}_n$ of partial Herbrand interpretations. At any step of the fixpoint computation it holds: If the query already holds in $\mathcal{I}_n$, then the query will also hold in $ADWFS_{\mathcal{P}}$, and the computation can be terminated.

For other semantics like the semantics of stable and partial stable models, so far no computations are known that have this property.

Keywords

disjunctive logic programming, query answering, non–monotonic reasoning, well–founded semantics, handling inconsistency, program transformations

1 Introduction

The alternating fixpoint approach of Van Gelder, Ross and Schlipf [16] has been used for constructing the well–founded semantics of normal databases (without disjunctions). This approach constructs a partial Herbrand interpretation, the so–called *well–founded model* M_W of the database. M_W can be described by two sets of atoms: first, the set T_W of all atoms that are *true* in M_W, and secondly that set F_W of all atoms that are *false* in M_W. Rather than representing the

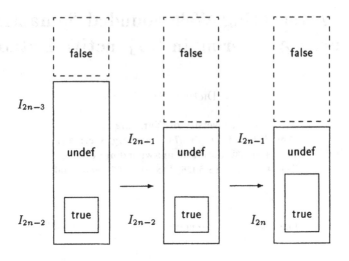

Fig. 1. The Alternating Fixpoint Approach

false atoms, the construction of M_W deals with the complement set U_W of all atoms that are not *false*, i.e. those atoms that are at least *undefined* in the truth ordering.

T_W and U_W are *approximated* by an alternating sequence $(I_n)_{n \in \mathbb{N}_0}$ of sets of atoms, such that the sets with even (odd) index monotonically approximate T_W (U_W) from below (above), cf. Figure 1. The sets I_n are defined by: $I_0 = \emptyset$, $I_{n+1} = \Gamma_P(I_n)$, for all $n \in \mathbb{N}_0$, where $\Gamma_P(I_n)$ is taken as the minimal Herbrand model of the Gelfond–Lifschitz transformation P^{I_n} of P w.r.t. I_n. Then it holds: $I_0 \subseteq \ldots \subseteq I_{2n-2} \subseteq I_{2n} \subseteq \ldots \subseteq T_W \subseteq U_W \subseteq I_{2n-1} \subseteq I_{2n-3} \subseteq \ldots \subseteq I_1$.

Quite frequently, *queries* to a database can be answered without computing the complete sequence $(I_n)_{n \in \mathbb{N}_0}$. For instance for the normal database

$$P = \{\, c, \; p \leftarrow c \wedge not\, d, \; q \leftarrow c \wedge not\, p, \; a \leftarrow not\, b, \; b \leftarrow not\, a \,\}$$

we get $I_0 = \emptyset$, $I_1 = \{a, b, c, p, q\}$, and $T_W = I_{2n} = \{c, p\}$, $U_W = I_{2n+1} = \{a, b, c, p\}$, for all $n \geq 1$. Already after having computed I_1 it becomes clear that the query "$Q = \neg d$" evaluates to true (i.e. d is false) under the well–founded semantics, and I_2 shows that the query "$Q = p$" evaluates to true. In the well–founded model M_W, the atoms "a" and "b" are undefined due to their negative mutual dependency in P.

2 Basic Definitions and Notations

Given a first order language $\mathcal{L}$, a *disjunctive database* P consists of logical inference rules of the form

$$r = A_1 \vee \ldots \vee A_k \leftarrow B_1 \wedge \ldots \wedge B_m \wedge not\, C_1 \wedge \ldots \wedge not\, C_n, \qquad (1)$$

where A_i $(1 \leq i \leq k)$, B_i $(1 \leq i \leq m)$, and C_i $(1 \leq i \leq n)$ are atoms in the language $\mathcal{L}$, $k, m, n \in \mathbb{N}_0$, and *not* is the negation–by–default operator.[1] For a rule r it is possible that $m = n = 0$; in this case, r is also called a *fact*. The set of all *ground instances* of the rules in $\mathcal{P}$ is denoted by *gnd* $(\mathcal{P})$. A rule r of the form (1) above is denoted for short as:

$$r = \alpha \leftarrow \beta \wedge not \cdot \gamma, \tag{2}$$

where $\alpha = A_1 \vee \ldots \vee A_k$, $\beta = B_1 \wedge \ldots \wedge B_m$, and $\gamma = C_1 \vee \ldots \vee C_n$.[2] An example for a disjunctive database is given by

$$\mathcal{P} = \{\, a \vee b,\ q \leftarrow b \wedge not\, a,\ p \leftarrow a \wedge not\, b\,\}.$$

Partial Herbrand Interpretations

A *partial (or three–valued) Herbrand interpretation* of a disjunctive database $\mathcal{P}$ is given by a truth function $I : HB_{\mathcal{P}} \rightarrow \{\, t, f, u\,\}$ that assigns one of the truth values t (true), f (false) or u (undefined) to the atoms of the Herbrand base $HB_{\mathcal{P}}$. By $\mathcal{HI}_{\mathcal{P}}$ we denote the set of all partial Herbrand interpretations of $\mathcal{P}$. $I \in \mathcal{HI}_{\mathcal{P}}$ is called a *total Herbrand interpretation*, if all atoms A are mapped to classical truth values t or f. For a partial Herbrand interpretation I we introduce the following notations:

$$I^t = \{\, A^t \mid A \in HB_{\mathcal{P}} \wedge I(A) = t\,\},$$
$$I^f = \{\, A^f \mid A \in HB_{\mathcal{P}} \wedge I(A) = f\,\},$$
$$I^u = \{\, A^u \mid A \in HB_{\mathcal{P}} \wedge (\, I(A) = t \vee I(A) = u\,)\,\}.$$

Using this notation, there are two ways of representing I as a set of annotated atoms, either by specifying the true and false atoms or by specifying the true and undefined atoms (cf. [14]):

tf–*Representation*: $I^{tf} = I^t \cup I^f$,
tu–*Representation*: $I^{tu} = I^t \cup I^u$.

Note that in the tu–representation every *true* atom A is recorded as A^t and as A^u. Note also that the tf–representation is essentially the same as the conventional representation of I as a *set of literals* (where $A^t \mapsto A$ and $A^f \mapsto \neg A$). For a set $\mathcal{I}$ of partial Herbrand interpretations we will use corresponding notations for $v \in \{\, tf, tu\,\}$: $\mathcal{I}^v = \{\, I^v \mid I \in \mathcal{I}\,\}$. By $\mathcal{I} =_v \mathcal{J}$, we denote that $\mathcal{I}^v = \mathcal{J}$. Consider for instance the Herbrand base $HB_{\mathcal{P}} = \{\, a, b, c, d, p, q\,\}$, and the partial Herbrand interpretation I, such that $I(c) = I(p) = t$, $I(d) = I(q) = f$, $I(a) = I(b) = u$. Then I can be represented in the following two ways:

$$I^{tf} = \{\, c^t, p^t, d^f, q^f\,\}, \quad I^{tu} = \{\, c^t, p^t, c^u, p^u, a^u, b^u\,\}.$$

---

[1] By $\mathbb{N}_+ = \{\, 1, 2, 3, \ldots\,\}$ we denote the set of positive natural numbers, whereas $\mathbb{N}_0 = \{\, 0, 1, 2, \ldots\,\}$.

[2] Note that γ is a disjunction, and, according to De Morgan's law, *not* $\cdot \gamma$ is taken to be a conjunction.

Truth Ordering and Knowledge Ordering

There are two common *partial orderings on truth values*, the truth ordering $\leq_t$ and the knowledge ordering $\leq_k$ (cf. [4]):

> *Truth Ordering:* $f \leq_t u,\ u \leq_t t,$
> *Knowledge Ordering:* $u \leq_k f,\ u \leq_k t.$

These orderings are generalized (pointwise) to partial Herbrand interpretations like follows: for $x \in \{t, k\}$, $I_1 \leq_x I_2$ iff $I_1(A) \leq_x I_2(A)$, for all $A \in HB_P$. Alternatively, the orderings can be characterized based on the tf–representation and the tu–representation, respectively:

$$I_1 \leq_k I_2 \text{ iff } I_1^{tf} \subseteq I_2^{tf}, \text{ and } I_1 \leq_t I_2 \text{ iff } I_1^{tu} \subseteq I_2^{tu}.$$

The orderings are generalized to sets of partial Herbrand interpretations like follows: for $x \in \{t, k\}$,

$$\mathcal{I}_1 \sqsubseteq_x \mathcal{I}_2, \text{ iff for all } I_2 \in \mathcal{I}_2 \text{ there exists } I_1 \in \mathcal{I}_1, \text{ such that } I_1 \leq_x I_2.$$

Finally, for a set $\mathcal{I}$ of partial Herbrand interpretations the minimal elements of $\mathcal{I}$ in the truth ordering and the knowledge ordering, respectively, are denoted by $min_t(\mathcal{I})$ and $min_k(\mathcal{I})$.

Models and Query Answering in Disjunctive Databases

A total Herbrand interpretation I of a disjunctive database $\mathcal{P}$ is a *model* of a ground rule $r = \alpha \leftarrow \beta \wedge not \cdot \gamma$, if it holds: if the rule body $\beta \wedge not \cdot \gamma$ is true in I, then also the rule head α must be true in I. For a partial Herbrand interpretation I this can be generalized by adding a second condition: if the rule body is undefined in I, then the rule head must be true or undefined. In other words, for a *partial model* of a ground rule r it must hold: $I(\alpha) \geq_t I(\beta) \wedge I(not \cdot \gamma)$, where the Boolean operations on truth values are given in Figure 2.

$\wedge$	t	f	u		$\vee$	t	f	u		$\neg$	
t	t	f	u		t	t	t	t		t	f
f	f	f	f		f	t	f	u		f	t
u	u	f	u		u	t	u	u		u	u

Fig. 2. Boolean operations in three–valued logic

For model–based semantics, one can compute the set $\mathcal{I}$ of intended models of the database, and one can also derive the set S of formulas that corresponds to $\mathcal{I}$ by means of *sceptical reasoning*. The formulas in S usually are taken from the following sets, which are called the *disjunctive, negative,* and the *general Herbrand base,* respectively:

$$DHB_\mathcal{P} = \{\, A_1 \lor \ldots \lor A_k \mid A_i \in HB_\mathcal{P},\ 1 \le i \le k,\ k \in \mathbb{N}_0 \,\},$$
$$NHB_\mathcal{P} = \{\, \neg A_1 \lor \ldots \lor \neg A_k \mid A_i \in HB_\mathcal{P},\ 1 \le i \le k,\ k \in \mathbb{N}_0 \,\},$$
$$GHB_\mathcal{P} = \{\, \alpha_d \lor \alpha_n \mid \alpha_d \in DHB_\mathcal{P},\ \alpha_n \in NHB_\mathcal{P} \,\}.$$

An *Herbrand state* is a set $S \subseteq GHB_\mathcal{P}$ of formulas. Sceptical reasoning with a set $\mathcal{I}$ of (partial) Herbrand interpretations consists in deriving the Herbrand state $STATE(S, \mathcal{I})$ of all disjunctions C in a given universe $S \subseteq GHB_\mathcal{P}$ which are satisfied by all interpretations in $\mathcal{I}$:

$$STATE(S, \mathcal{I}) = \{\, C \in S \mid \forall I \in \mathcal{I} : I \models C \,\}.$$

A *query* to a disjunctive database $\mathcal{P}$ is given by a disjunction $\mathcal{Q} \in GHB_\mathcal{P}$. Given a semantics and the corresponding set $\mathcal{I}$ of intended models of $\mathcal{P}$, then the answer to $\mathcal{Q}$ is yes iff $\mathcal{Q} \in STATE(GHB_\mathcal{P}, \mathcal{I})$. For the disjunctive database $\mathcal{P} = \{\, a \lor b,\ q \leftarrow b \land not\ a,\ p \leftarrow a \land not\ b \,\}$ the set of intended models would usually be the set $\mathcal{I}$ of *perfect models* (cf. [9]) since $\mathcal{P}$ is *stratified* (i.e. there is no recursion through negation in $\mathcal{P}$):

$$\mathcal{I} =_{\text{tf}} \{\, \{\, a^t, p^t, b^f, q^f \,\},\ \{\, b^t, q^t, a^f, p^f \,\} \,\}.$$

Thus, we can derive the disjunctions in the states (subsumed disjunctions are omitted)

$$STATE(DHB_\mathcal{P}, \mathcal{I}) = \{\, a \lor b,\ a \lor q,\ b \lor p,\ p \lor q \,\},$$
$$STATE(NHB_\mathcal{P}, \mathcal{I}) = \{\, \neg a \lor \neg b,\ \neg a \lor \neg q,\ \neg b \lor \neg p,\ \neg p \lor \neg q \,\}.$$

Besides the "pure" disjunctions in these Herbrand states, the general Herbrand state $STATE(GHB_\mathcal{P}, \mathcal{I})$ contains "mixed" disjunctions like $a \lor \neg p$ and $b \lor \neg q$.

3 The Alternating Fixpoint Approach

We will present a new alternating fixpoint approach that uses *annotated constraints* and *annotated databases* for constructing a new type of well–founded models for a disjunctive database $\mathcal{P}$.

The alternating fixpoint approach works on sets $\mathcal{I}$ of partial Herbrand interpretations, and extends them – w.r.t. the knowledge ordering – to other sets $\mathcal{J}$ of partial Herbrand interpretations, such that $\mathcal{I} \sqsubseteq_k \mathcal{J}$. It uses two operators $\Gamma_\mathcal{P}^\downarrow$ and $\Gamma_\mathcal{P}^\uparrow$, which take the partial Herbrand interpretations $I \in \mathcal{I}$ and extend them to other partial Herbrand interpretations J such that $I \le_k J$, cf. Figure 1. The two operators $\Gamma_\mathcal{P}^\downarrow$ and $\Gamma_\mathcal{P}^\uparrow$ alternatingly work on the true and the undefined atoms, respectively. For each partial Herbrand interpretation $I \in \mathcal{I}$:

1. the operator $\Gamma_\mathcal{P}^\downarrow$ computes new partial Herbrand interpretations J, such that $I^t = J^t$ and $I^u \supseteq J^u$, and
2. the operator $\Gamma_\mathcal{P}^\uparrow$ computes new partial Herbrand interpretations J, such that $I^u = J^u$ and $I^t \subseteq J^t$.

Annotated Constraints

For enforcing the properties given in 1. and 2. above we need the following sets $C^{\downarrow P,I}$ and $C^{\uparrow P,I}$ of constraints.

Definition 1. *(Annotated Constraints)*
For a disjunctive database P and $I \in \mathcal{HI}_P$ we define

$$C^{\downarrow P,I} = I^t \cup \{ A^u \leftarrow A^t \mid A \in HB_P \} \cup \{ \leftarrow A^u \mid A \in HB_P \wedge I(A) = f \},$$
$$C^{\uparrow P,I} = I^t \cup I^u \cup \{ \leftarrow A^t \mid A \in HB_P \wedge I(A) = f \}.$$

A partial Herbrand interpretation I is extended into another partial Herbrand interpretation J in two phases. When the decreased set J^u of undefined atoms is computed, then the constraints $\leftarrow A^u$ forbid the extended interpretation J to contain an annotated atom A^u that was not undefined (i.e. that was false) in I. When the increased set J^t of true atoms is computed, then the constraints $\leftarrow A^t$ forbid the extended interpretation J to contain any true atom that was not undefined (i.e. that was false) in I.

Annotated Databases

Given a truth value $v \in \{ t, u \}$, for a disjunction $\alpha = A_1 \vee \ldots \vee A_k$ and a conjunction $\beta = B_1 \wedge \ldots \wedge B_m$ of atoms we define $\alpha^v = A_1^v \vee \ldots \vee A_k^v$, $\beta^v = B_1^v \wedge \ldots \wedge B_m^v$. For a disjunctive rule $r = \alpha \leftarrow \beta \wedge not \cdot \gamma$ we define

$$r^u = \alpha^u \leftarrow \beta^u \wedge not \cdot \gamma^t,$$
$$r^t = \alpha^t \leftarrow \beta^t \wedge not \cdot \gamma^u.$$

For a disjunctive database P we define $P^u = \{ r^u \mid r \in P \}$, $P^t = \{ r^t \mid r \in P \}$, and the *annotated database* $P^{tu} = P^t \cup P^u \cup \{ A^u \leftarrow A^t \mid A \in HB_P \}$.
For instance, the disjunctive database

$$P = \{ a \vee b, \ q \leftarrow b \wedge not\, a, \ p \leftarrow a \wedge not\, b \},$$

is annotated like follows:

$$P^u = \{ a^u \vee b^u, \ q^u \leftarrow b^u \wedge not\, a^t, \ p^u \leftarrow a^u \wedge not\, b^t \},$$
$$P^t = \{ a^t \vee b^t, \ q^t \leftarrow b^t \wedge not\, a^u, \ p^t \leftarrow a^t \wedge not\, b^u \}.$$

For any total Herbrand interpretation I of P^{tu} we introduce the notation I^∇ for the partial Herbrand interpretation of P that is induced by I, i.e. for $A \in HB_P$

$$I^\nabla(A) = \begin{cases} t & \text{if } I(A^t) = t \\ u & \text{if } I(A^u) = t \text{ and } I(A^t) = f \\ f & \text{if } I(A^u) = f \end{cases}$$

For a set $\mathcal{I}$ of total Herbrand interpretations of the annotated database P^{tu}, let $\mathcal{I}^\nabla = \{ I^\nabla \mid I \in \mathcal{I} \}$.

Definition 2. *(Gelfond–Lifschitz Transformation)*
Let $\mathcal{P}$ be a disjunctive database $\mathcal{P}$ and $I \in \mathcal{H}_{\mathcal{I}\mathcal{P}}$.

(i) For $r = \alpha \leftarrow \beta \wedge not \cdot \gamma \in gnd(\mathcal{P})$ we define $r^I = \alpha \leftarrow \beta \wedge \neg I(\gamma)$. The *Gelfond–Lifschitz transformation* of $\mathcal{P}$ is $\mathcal{P}^I = \{ r^I \mid r \in gnd(\mathcal{P}) \}$.

(ii) The *Gelfond–Lifschitz transformations* $\mathcal{P}^{\downarrow I}$ and $\mathcal{P}^{\uparrow I}$ are defined by

$$\mathcal{P}^{\downarrow I} = (\mathcal{P}^u)^{(I^t)}, \quad \mathcal{P}^{\uparrow I} = (\mathcal{P}^t)^{(I^*)}.$$

The Operators $\Gamma_{\mathcal{P}}^{\downarrow}$ and $\Gamma_{\mathcal{P}}^{\uparrow}$

Based on the annotated databases we can define two operators that apply a certain model generation operator to sets of partial Herbrand interpretations, and then *minimize* the resulting sets of partial Herbrand interpretations in the *truth ordering*.

Definition 3. *(The Operators $\Gamma_{\mathcal{P}}^{\downarrow}$ and $\Gamma_{\mathcal{P}}^{\uparrow}$)*
Given a disjunctive database $\mathcal{P}$ and $\mathcal{I} \in 2^{\mathcal{H}_{\mathcal{I}\mathcal{P}}}$, the operators

$$\Gamma_{\mathcal{P}}^{\theta} : 2^{\mathcal{H}_{\mathcal{I}\mathcal{P}}} \to 2^{\mathcal{H}_{\mathcal{I}\mathcal{P}}}$$

for $\theta \in \{ \downarrow, \uparrow \}$ are defined by

$$\Gamma_{\mathcal{P}}^{\downarrow}(\mathcal{I}) = min_t(\bigcup_{I \in \mathcal{I}} \mathcal{MM}(\mathcal{P}^{\downarrow I} \cup \mathcal{C}^{\downarrow \mathcal{P}, I})^{\nabla}),$$

$$\Gamma_{\mathcal{P}}^{\uparrow}(\mathcal{I}) = min_t(\bigcup_{I \in \mathcal{I}} \mathcal{MM}(\mathcal{P}^{\uparrow I} \cup \mathcal{C}^{\uparrow \mathcal{P}, I})^{\nabla}).$$

In the definition above the operator $\mathcal{MM}$ derives a set of total Herbrand interpretations of an annotated database, which is then lifted to a a set of partial Herbrand interpretations of the original database.

Example 1. *($\Gamma_{\mathcal{P}}$-Operators)*
For the disjunctive database

$$\mathcal{P} = \{ a \vee b, \ q \leftarrow not \, a, \ p \leftarrow not \, b \},$$

the *alternating fixpoint approach* derives the following sets of partial Herbrand interpretations, where $\mathcal{I}_0 =_{tu} \{ A^u \mid A \in HB_{\mathcal{P}} \}$, $\mathcal{I}_{2n+1} = \Gamma_{\mathcal{P}}^{\downarrow}(\mathcal{I}_{2n})$, and $\mathcal{I}_{2n+2} = \Gamma_{\mathcal{P}}^{\uparrow}(\mathcal{I}_{2n+1})$, for $n \in \mathbb{N}_0$.

$$\mathcal{I}_0 =_{tu} \{ \{ a^u, b^u, p^u, q^u \} \},$$
$$\mathcal{I}_1 =_{tu} \{ \{ a^u, p^u, q^u \}, \{ b^u, p^u, q^u \} \},$$
$$\mathcal{I}_2 =_{tu} \{ \{ a^t, p^t, a^u, p^u, q^u \}, \{ b^t, q^t, b^u, p^u, q^u \} \},$$
$$\mathcal{I}_3 =_{tu} \{ \{ a^t, p^t, a^u, p^u \}, \{ b^t, q^t, b^u, q^u \} \},$$
$$\mathcal{I}_m = \mathcal{I}_3, \text{ for all } m \geq 3.$$

It turns out that $\mathcal{I}_3$ is the set of *perfect models* of $\mathcal{P}$.

The disjunctive database $\mathcal{P}$ of the following example is known from literature (cf. [11]). For $\mathcal{P}$ there are no *partial stable models*. With the new alternating fixpoint approach the set of minimal Herbrand models is computed as the semantics of $\mathcal{P}$.

Example 2. ($\Gamma_{\mathcal{P}}$-Operators)
For the disjunctive database

$$\mathcal{P} = \{\, a \vee b \vee c, \; a \leftarrow not\, b, \; b \leftarrow not\, c, \; c \leftarrow not\, a \,\},$$

the *alternating fixpoint approach* derives the following sets of partial Herbrand interpretations, where $\mathcal{I}_{2n+1} = \Gamma_{\mathcal{P}}^{\downarrow}(\mathcal{I}_{2n})$, and $\mathcal{I}_{2n+2} = \Gamma_{\mathcal{P}}^{\uparrow}(\mathcal{I}_{2n+1})$, for $n \in \mathbb{N}_0$.

$$
\begin{aligned}
\mathcal{I}_0 &=_{tu} \{\, \{\, a^u, b^u, c^u \,\} \,\}, \\
\mathcal{I}_1 &= \;\; \mathcal{I}_0, \\
\mathcal{I}_2 &=_{tu} \{\, \{\, a^t, a^u, b^u, c^u \,\}, \{\, b^t, a^u, b^u, c^u \,\}, \{\, c^t, a^u, b^u, c^u \,\} \,\}, \\
\mathcal{I}_3 &=_{tu} \{\, \{\, a^t, a^u, b^u \,\}, \{\, b^t, b^u, c^u \,\}, \{\, c^t, a^u, c^u \,\} \,\}, \\
\mathcal{I}_4 &=_{tu} \{\, \{\, a^t, b^t, a^u, b^u \,\}, \{\, b^t, c^t, b^u, c^u \,\}, \{\, a^t, c^t, a^u, c^u \,\} \,\}, \\
\mathcal{I}_m &= \;\; \mathcal{I}_4, \; \text{for all } m \geq 4.
\end{aligned}
$$

It turns out that $\mathcal{I}_4$ is the set of *minimal models* of $\mathcal{P}$.

Note that in general we do not get the minimal models. E.g. in Example 1 we got the set of perfect models of $\mathcal{P}$, and the third minimal model $I =_{tf} \{\, a^t, b^t, p^f, q^f \,\}$ was not derived.

Naive Alternating Fixpoint Computation

In the following we want to contrast the new alternating fixpoint computation scheme to another computation scheme, that we will call *naive*. The *naive alternating computation scheme* is just based on the Gelfond–Lifschitz transformation, and it does not use the annotated constraints. Furthermore, it works just on single sets of atoms, rather than on partial Herbrand interpretations. The naive computation scheme works as follows: $\mathcal{I}_0 = \{\, \emptyset \,\}$, $\mathcal{I}_{n+1} = \Gamma_{\mathcal{P}}(\mathcal{I}_n)$, for all $n \in \mathbb{N}_0$, where

$$\Gamma_{\mathcal{P}}(\mathcal{I}) = min_t\,(\bigcup_{I \in \mathcal{I}} \mathcal{MM}(\mathcal{P}^I)).$$

Note that for normal databases (i.e. databases without disjunctions) both approaches coincide, and they yield the well-known *well-founded semantics*. When there are no disjunctions in the database, then it is not necessary to explicitly enforce the annotated constraints, since they will be fulfilled automatically.

For disjunctive databases (i.e. databases with disjunctions and negations), however, the following example shows that the naive alternating computation approach may not give us an intuitive interpretation, whereas the alternating fixpoint approach does so.

Example 3. (Naive Alternating Fixpoint Computation)
In the naive alternating computation scheme we get the following results for the previous two example databases.

(i) For the disjunctive database

$$\mathcal{P} = \{\, a \vee b,\ q \leftarrow not\, a,\ p \leftarrow not\, b\,\},$$

we get the following sets of partial Herbrand interpretations, as described in Figure 3:

$$\mathcal{I}_0 = \{\,\emptyset\,\},$$
$$\mathcal{I}_1 = \{\,\{a, p, q\}, \{b, p, q\}\,\},$$
$$\mathcal{I}_2 = \{\,\{a, p\}, \{b, p\}, \{a, q\}, \{b, q\}\,\},$$
$$\mathcal{I}_m = \mathcal{I}_2,\ \text{for all } m \geq 2.$$

Here we do not get the set of perfect models, which we get with the alternating computation scheme. Instead we get two additional non–perfect interpretations $\{b, p\}$ and $\{a, q\}$, which certainly are not intended models of the database.[3]

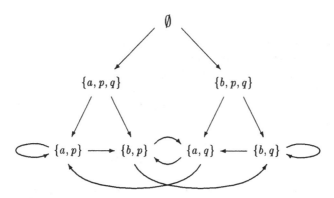

Fig. 3. Naive Computation

(ii) For the disjunctive database

$$\mathcal{P} = \{\, a \vee b \vee c,\ a \leftarrow not\, b,\ b \leftarrow not\, c,\ c \leftarrow not\, a\,\},$$

we get the following sets of partial Herbrand interpretations, as described in Figure 4:

$$\mathcal{I}_0 = \{\,\emptyset\,\},$$

---

[3] They are not even models of the database.

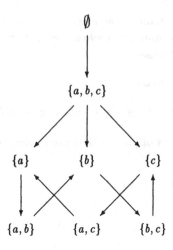

Fig. 4. Naive Computation

$$\mathcal{I}_1 = \{\,\{a,b,c\},\,\},$$
$$\mathcal{I}_2 = \{\,\{a\}, \{b\}, \{c\}\,\},$$
$$\mathcal{I}_3 = \{\,\{a,b\}, \{b,c\}, \{a,c\}\,\},$$
$$\mathcal{I}_{2n} = \mathcal{I}_2, \text{ for all } n \geq 1,$$
$$\mathcal{I}_{2n+1} = \mathcal{I}_3, \text{ for all } n \geq 1.$$

Here we do not get the set of minimal models, which we get with the alternating computation scheme. Also the computation does not reach a fixpoint. Instead it loops between the set $\mathcal{I}_3$ of minimal Herbrand models and a set $\mathcal{I}_2$ of three Herbrand interpretations $\{a\}$, $\{b\}$ and $\{c\}$, which are not even models of $\mathcal{P}$. In this approach the meaning of the derived set of partial Herbrand interpretations is not clear at all.

4 The Alternating Well–Founded Semantics A_{DWFS}

The composite application of the two operators $\Gamma_\mathcal{P}^\downarrow$ and $\Gamma_\mathcal{P}^\uparrow$ defines a new operator $F_\mathcal{P}$. The ordinal powers of the operator $F_\mathcal{P}$ correspond to a sequence of alternating applications of the operators $\Gamma_\mathcal{P}^\downarrow$ and $\Gamma_\mathcal{P}^\uparrow$.

Definition 4. *(The Operator $F_\mathcal{P}$)*
Given a disjunctive database $\mathcal{P}$ and $\mathcal{I} \in 2^{\mathcal{H}_{\mathcal{I}\mathcal{P}}}$.

(i) The operator

$$F_\mathcal{P} : 2^{\mathcal{H}_{\mathcal{I}\mathcal{P}}} \rightarrow 2^{\mathcal{H}_{\mathcal{I}\mathcal{P}}}$$

operates on sets $\mathcal{I} \in 2^{\mathcal{H}_{\mathcal{I}\mathcal{P}}}$ of partial Herbrand interpretations:

$$F_\mathcal{P}(\mathcal{I}) = \Gamma_\mathcal{P}^\uparrow(\,\Gamma_\mathcal{P}^\downarrow(\mathcal{I})\,).$$

(ii) The *ordinal powers* $F_P^{\uparrow \alpha}(\mathcal{I})$ are

$$F_P^{\uparrow 0}(\mathcal{I}) = \mathcal{I},$$
$$F_P^{\uparrow \alpha}(\mathcal{I}) = F_P(F_P^{\uparrow \alpha-1}(\mathcal{I})), \text{ for a successor ordinal } \alpha,$$
$$F_P^{\uparrow \alpha}(\mathcal{I}) = lub_k\{\, F_P^{\uparrow \beta}(\mathcal{I}) \mid \beta < \alpha \,\}, \text{ for a limit ordinal } \alpha,$$

where $lub_k(\mathcal{X})$ is the *least upper bound* of $\mathcal{X} \subseteq 2^{\mathcal{H}_{\mathcal{I}_P}}$ in the knowledge ordering $\sqsubseteq_k$.

(iii) The *ordinal powers* are $F_P \uparrow \alpha = F_P^{\uparrow \alpha}(\bot_F)$, where

$$\bot_F =_{tu} \{\, A^u \mid A \in HB_P \,\}$$

is the least element of $2^{\mathcal{H}_{\mathcal{I}_P}}$ in the knowledge ordering $\sqsubseteq_k$.

Example 4. (Disjunctive Well–Founded Models)
For the disjunctive database

$$\mathcal{P} = \{\, a \vee b, \; q \leftarrow not\ a, \; p \leftarrow not\ b \,\},$$

the *alternating fixpoint approach* derives the following sets of partial Herbrand interpretations:

$$F_P \uparrow 0 =_{tu} \{\, \{ a^u, b^u, p^u, q^u \} \,\},$$
$$F_P \uparrow 1 =_{tu} \{\, \{ a^t, p^t, a^u, p^u, q^u \}, \{ b^t, q^t, b^u, p^u, p^u \} \,\},$$
$$F_P \uparrow 2 =_{tu} \{\, \{ a^t, p^t, a^u, p^u \}, \{ b^t, q^t, b^u, p^u \} \,\},$$
$$F_P \uparrow n = \quad F_P \uparrow 2, \text{ for all } n \geq 2.$$

$F_P \uparrow 2$ is the set of *perfect models* of $\mathcal{P}$.

Monotonicity and Fixpoints of the Operators

For the operators $\Gamma_P^{\downarrow}$ and $\Gamma_P^{\uparrow}$ and a set $\mathcal{I}$ of partial Herbrand interpretations it holds $\mathcal{I} \sqsubseteq_k \Gamma_P^{\downarrow}(\mathcal{I})$ and $\mathcal{I} \sqsubseteq_k \Gamma_P^{\uparrow}(\mathcal{I})$. Thus, we also get

$$\mathcal{I} \sqsubseteq_k \Gamma_P^{\uparrow}(\,\Gamma_P^{\downarrow}(\mathcal{I})) = F_P(\mathcal{I}).$$

By transfinite induction it can be shown that the ordinal powers $F_P^{\uparrow \alpha}(\mathcal{I})$ form a chain in the knowledge ordering:

$$\alpha \leq \beta \Longrightarrow F_P^{\uparrow \alpha}(\mathcal{I}) \sqsubseteq_k F_P^{\uparrow \beta}(\mathcal{I}).$$

From this we can conclude that the operator F_P is *monotonic* on its ordinal powers. Thus, the ordinal powers $F_P \uparrow \alpha$ converge to a fixpoint[4] $F_P \uparrow \gamma$, where γ is called the *closure ordinal* of F_P.

---

[4] Note that this fixpoint is the least fixpoint of F_P when restricted to its ordinal powers, but it need not be the least fixpoint of F_P in general, since F_P is not monotonic in general.

Definition 5. *(The Alternating Disjunctive Well–Founded Semantics)*
Given a disjunctive database $\mathcal{P}$, the *alternating disjunctive well–founded semantics* of $\mathcal{P}$ is given by the set

$$ADWFS_\mathcal{P} = F_\mathcal{P} \uparrow \gamma,$$

where γ is the closure ordinal of $F_\mathcal{P}$. The partial Herbrand interpretations in $ADWFS_\mathcal{P}$ are called alternating disjunctive well–founded models.

Consistency

It can be shown that the *alternating fixpoint approach* will always derive a non–empty set of partial models for all disjunctive databases $\mathcal{P}$ without denial rules (i.e. rules with an empty rule head).

Theorem 1. *(Consistency of ADWFS)*
Let $\mathcal{P}$ be a disjunctive database, and let $I_0 =_{tf} \emptyset$. If $\mathcal{P}^{I_0}$ is logically consistent[5], then $ADWFS_\mathcal{P} \neq \emptyset$.

The semantics of *stable* and *partial stable* models (cf. [5, 6, 11]) are among the most prominent semantics for disjunctive databases. Unfortunately, there are databases which are logically consistent, but are inconsistent w.r.t. these semantics. For large databases, small inconsistent parts can prohibit the existence of (partial) stable models.

5 Conclusions

The disjunctive well–founded semantics has got quite a number of nice properties. If the databases are *normal*, then it is identical with the *well–founded* semantics. For *positive–disjunctive* databases (i.e. databases without default negation) it is identical with the *minimal model* semantics, and for *disjunctive* databases without denial rules there always exist well–founded models, i.e. the semantics is *consistent*.

The computation of alternating disjunctive well–founded models has been implemented within the system DISLOG for efficient reasoning in disjunctive databases, cf. [12].

In [14] a characterization of the *partial stable models* (cf. [11]) of a disjunctive database $\mathcal{P}$ in terms of the *total stable models* (cf. [6]) of the annotated database $\mathcal{P}^{tu}$ is given. Since the construction of $ADWFS_\mathcal{P}$ is essentially based on $\mathcal{P}^{tu}$, too, currently we are trying to investigate the relationship between the two different approaches.

Acknowledgement: The author would like to thank Jack Minker for his comments on earlier versions of this paper.

---

[5] I.e. $\mathcal{P}^\emptyset$ it has an Herbrand model, which is guaranteed if there are no denial rules in the database $\mathcal{P}$.

References

1. *S. Brass, J. Dix:* Characterizations of the Disjunctive Stable Semantics by Partial Evaluation, Proc. Third Intl. Conf. on Logic Programming an Non–Monotonic Reasoning (LPNMR'95), Springer LNAI 928, 1995, pp. 85-98, and: Journal of Logic Programming, vol. 32(3), 1997, pp. 207–228.
2. *T. Eiter, N. Leone, D. Sacca:* On the Partial Semantics for Disjunctive Deductive Databases, Annals of Mathematics and Artificial Intelligence, to appear.
3. *B.A. Davey, H.A. Priestley:* Introduction to Lattices and Order, Cambridge University Press, 1990.
4. *M. Fitting:* Bilattices and the Semantics of Logic Programs, Journal of Logic Programming, vol. 11, 1991, pp. 91–116.
5. *M. Gelfond, V. Lifschitz:* The Stable Model Semantics for Logic Programming, Proc. Fifth Intl. Conference and Symposium on Logic Programming (ICSLP'88), MIT Press, 1988, pp. 1070–1080.
6. *M. Gelfond, V. Lifschitz:* Classical Negation in Logic Programs and Disjunctive Databases, New Generation Computing, vol. 9, 1991, pp. 365–385.
7. *J.W. Lloyd:* Foundations of Logic Programming, second edition, Springer, 1987.
8. *J. Lobo, J. Minker, A. Rajasekar:* Foundations of Disjunctive Logic Programming, MIT Press, 1992.
9. *T.C. Przymusinski:* On the declarative semantics of Deductive Databases and Logic Programming, in: Foundations of Deductive Databases and Logic Programming, J. Minker ed., 1988, pp. 193–216.
10. *T.C. Przymusinski:* Extended Stable Semantics for Normal and Disjunctive Programs, Proc. Seventh Intl. Conference on Logic Programming, 1990, pp. 459–477.
11. *T.C. Przymusinski:* Stable Semantics for Disjunctive Programs, New Generation Computing, vol. 9, 1991, pp. 401–424.
12. *D. Seipel:* DISLOG – A Disjunctive Deductive Database Prototype, Proc. Twelfth Workshop on Logic Programming (WLP'97), 1997, pp. 136–143.
    DISLOG is available on the WWW at
    "http://www-info1.informatik.uni-wuerzburg.de/databases/DisLog".
13. *D. Seipel, J. Minker, C. Ruiz:* Model Generation and State Generation for Disjunctive Logic Programs, Journal of Logic Programming, vol. 32(1), 1997, pp. 48–69.
14. *D. Seipel, J. Minker, C. Ruiz:* A Characterization of Partial Stable Models for Disjunctive Deductive Databases, Proc. Intl. Logic Programming Symposium (ILPS'97), MIT Press, 1997, pp. 245–259.
15. *D. Seipel:* Partial Evidential Stable Models For Disjunctive Databases, Proc. Workshop on Logic Programming and Knowledge Representation (LPKR'97) at the International Symposium on Logic Programming 1997 (ILPS'97), 1997.
16. *A. Van Gelder, K.A. Ross, J.S. Schlipf:*, Unfounded Sets and Well–Founded Semantics for General Logic Programs, Proc. Seventh ACM Symposium on Principles of Database Systems, 1988, pp. 221–230.
17. *C. Witteveen, G. Brewka:* Skeptical Reason Maintenance and Belief Revision, Journal of Artificial Intelligence, vol. 61, 1993, pp. 1–36.
18. *J.H. You, L.Y. Yuan:* Three-Valued Formalisms of Logic Programming: Is It Needed ?, Proc. Ninth ACM Symposium on Principles of Database Systems (PODS'90), 1990, pp. 172–182.

Towards a Cooperative Question-Answering Model

Galeno J. de Sena[1] and Antonio L. Furtado[2]

[1]UNESP - Campus de Guaratinguetá, DMA, C.P. 205
CEP: 12500-000 GUARATINGETÁ - SP BRAZIL
gsena@feg.unesp.br
[2]PUC/RJ - Depto. de Informática, R. Marquês de São Vicente, 225
CEP: 22451-041 Rio de Janeiro - RJ BRAZIL
furtado@inf.puc-rio.br

Abstract. A model of question-answering is proposed in this paper. In the model, the system tries, from an input query, to establish a controlled dialogue with its user. In the dialogue, the system tries to identify and to suggest to the user new queries, related to the input query. The dialogue control is based on the structure of the concepts stored in the knowledge base, on domain restrictions, and on specific constraining rules. The system kernel is essentially an extended version of a cooperative interface for accessing data and knowledge bases.

1 Introduction and Works on Cooperativeness

We propose in this paper a model of question-answering in which the system, taking as the starting point an input query, tries to establish a controlled dialogue with its user. In the dialogue the system not only tries to answer the input query but also tries to identify and propose new queries. The aspect of dialogue control is based on the structure of the concepts stored in the knowledge base - essentially the way they are related among themselves, on domain restrictions, and on specific constraining rules.

A cooperative information system [1] tries to help its users with the achievement of their plans and goals. In other words, a cooperative system tries to do more than simply answering a query or applying an operation. Several works have given their contribution in specific aspects of cooperativeness. We comment about some of them briefly in the sequel.

For instance, with respect to the recognition of the user plans we could mention [2,3,4,5]. An algorithm for the generalization of a query expression in the case of failure has been introduced in [6]. One of the aspects considered in [7] is the error recovering of queries on the basis of the data semantics. Monitoring offers on the part of the system, with the corresponding activation of the associated "triggers" are taken into account in [8,9]. The works [10,11] deal with the aspect of intensional characterization of the resulting answer sets. User modeling is of concern for instance in [12,13,14,15]. A rule-based methodology for the transformation of the user query prior to its execution is presented in [16].

The COBASE system [17,18] makes use of structures for knowledge representation known as *type abstraction hierarchies*. The *Carmin* project [19] aims at developing a general framework for cooperativeness. A natural language based cooperative interface - named COOP - is described in [20]. The work [21] includes an algorithm, named ISHMAEL, for enumerating both minimal failing subqueries and maximal succeeding subqueries of a query, when the query fails. Other relevant works with a view to structuring question-answering systems are [22,23,24,25].

The NICE system [26,27,28] introduces a methodology for cooperative access to data and knowledge bases based on the modification of the user request - query or update, by means of the systematic application of request-modification rules (RM-rules) against the request. The methodology adopted in the NICE project allows the investigation of several research aspects, with a view to proposing and developing extensions to the system. The kernel of the question-answering model discussed in this paper is essentially a NICE-based methodology for cooperative question-answering. We will restrict ourselves to query requests in this paper.

The paper is organized as follows. In section 2 we present a brief description of the methodology. Next, in section 3, we give simple query examples illustrating the methodology. Section 4 concludes the paper. For a more formal description of the system as a whole, the interested reader should consult [29].

2 Description of the System

We describe in this section the main aspects of our system including the way of describing applications, the basis of the request modification methodology, the provided cooperative query-execution commands, and the way of processing the users' requests.

2.1 The Concepts of a NICE Application: Clausal Specification

We will present, in this section, the concepts that are relevant to the development of applications in the context of our system. In the appendix we explore some of the syntactical aspects of the specification. The reader is referred to [26,28] for a more formal discussion.

The conceptual model is essentially the Entity Relationship Model [30] with *is_a* hierarchies. Therefore, at the conceptual level, the application designer must introduce clauses for the *entity* and *relationship* classes, and for relating entity classes through *is_a* hierarchies. For each of the specified entity and relationship classes, one can introduce clauses defining its *attributes*. Domain values, which define the values for the attributes, should be introduced in specific *domain* clauses. Next, at the object level, *facts* can be specified. Each introduced fact corresponds to either an entity or a relationship class instance.

Consistent with the abstract data type approach, the operations allowed upon a DB are predefined. Each application-oriented operation is specified by a set of clauses indicating:

- the effects of the operation, i. e., the facts that are added to or removed from the DB as a consequence of the application of the operation;
- the preconditions of the application of the operation in terms of the facts that should hold or not in the DB.

Related to the application operations are the clauses of the definition of a predicate named *imposs*, used to specify a list expressing a conjunction of goals which must not hold in any state of the application, as it implies the violation of some of the integrity constraints.

The application designer can introduce, in the application specification, clauses characterizing the user classes of the application. In addition the designer may specify restrictions with respect to the operations allowed to each user class.

As it will be clear later, an important aspect of the current work is to allow the system to propose new questions, from the query submitted by the user. To identify possible subsequent queries, the system must know how the concepts are related among themselves. A natural and immediate way of constructing such queries is through the structure adopted for the knowledge base, more specifically, taking into account, mainly, the relationships explicitly stated in the knowledge base. The problem with this strategy is that the resulting number of queries can become really large. Thus, it is essential to try to constrain the set of possible following queries.

In the current prototype implementation, the constraining is done implicitly by the system - through the consideration of domain restrictions, and explicitly, through the introduction of clauses defining the predicate *constraining_rule*, whose general form is:

```
constraining_rule(RId,CF,UC,OQC,FQC,CC) :- condition.
```

where: *Rid*: is an identification of the rule; *CF*: is a constraining fact: it must be true at the time the rule is called into use; *UC*: provides the identification of the user class for which this rule is to be applied; *OQC*: is the original query concept, from which other queries will be proposed by the system; *FQC*: is a list of the following query concepts to structure the subsequent queries; and *CC*: is the constraining class, which could be either *complete* or *partial*, the first option meaning that only the concepts on the list FQC can be used to structure new queries, and the second one meaning that the system may consider additional concepts in the process of structuring the queries.

For example, in an academic database application, if a student, at the enrollment period, presents a question about *subject*, then the system may propose other questions related to the concepts included on a list of follow-up concepts. That list, which corresponds to the parameter *FQC*, could include, for instance, the concepts *prerequisite_of*, *subject_classes*, and so on.

There are situations in which it is reasonable that a fact is not present in the knowledge base. In those cases, one should not deal with the absence of the fact as an ordinary failure. Instead, it could be the case that only an appropriated message should be displayed. (On the contrary, the system would try to carry out a complete f_post processing (see section 2.2 below), in the sense of the NICE methodology.) To characterize such situations, one should introduce clauses defining the predicate *missing_info*, whose general form follows:

```
missing_info(Pred, Cond, Msg)  :- condition.
```

where: *Pred*: corresponds to the undefined predicate; *Cond*: specifies a condition which must be true at the time the rule is invoked; and *Msg*: is a message which will explain why the absence of *Pred* is reasonable in the context of the application of the rule.

For instance, in the academic database application, a specific *missing_info* clause may used to indicate that, at the enrollment period, a *teacher* has not yet been assigned to a specific *class* (of a *subject*).

2.2 The Request Modification Methodology

The *RM-rules* take into account, in dealing with a request, not only the request by its own, but also information extracted from a context involving, among others, components like (i) the database (DB) conceptual and external schemes, (ii) the factual DB, (iii) a model of the application domain, and (iv) a *log* of the current session including the user requests and the answers the user have been presented with by the system.

RM-rules are classified as *dependent* upon or *independent* of the application domain, and, orthogonally, in accordance with the time in which they are applied, as:

- *pre* rules: preceding the execution of a command;
- *s_post* rules: following the successful execution of a command;
- *f_post* rules: following the unsuccessful execution of a command.

The above-mentioned classification has been described elsewhere [26,28]. Shortly, rules of the class *pre* can correct or complement a request. Rules of the class *s-post* can complement a request after its successful execution. Rules of the class *f_post* are called into use in the case of failure in the execution of a user request. They can produce and execute an *alternative* request, which allows the achievement of the same goal of the original request, or, when that is not possible, the achievement of an alternative goal related in a consistent way with the original one. If there is not any alternative, or if all the alternatives fail, if the failure is due to a *removable obstacle*, specific f_post rules can propose that the system monitor alerts the user when the obstacle ceases to exist. On the other hand, if the obstacles are known to be of a persistent nature, specific f_post rules can, at least, generate and display an *explanation* of the failure.

RM-rules of the classes *s_post* and *f_post* are further specialized into the (sub-) classes *s_post_query, s_post_info, f_post_alt*, and *f_post_comp*. The justification for the splitting of the *s_post* and *f_post* classes is given by the fact that there are RM-rules [28] whose execution ends with the proposal of an additional query (*s_post_query* in our extension) and others in which alternative queries are offered (*f_post_alt* in the current extension). Others are responsible for the production of additional relevant information (*s_post_info*) or for trying to compensate for the failure in the execution of a query (*f_post_comp*). It can take place, in the compensation, the output of an explanation for the failure.

At the end of the successful execution of a request, *template rules* direct the *editing* of the information included in an answer, so that the user be presented with the information in a more friendly way. It is allowed to take place, in the editing, the omission of uninteresting or unauthorized items.

The basic RM-rules of the methodology are gathered in one of the modules of the system architecture (see [28]). Notwithstanding this fact, the application designer can introduce new ones in the context of the application specification. For the purpose of introducing RM-rules, there are general standards to be followed for each of the above-mentioned classes. In each of those standards, the user is expected to define an action to be executed at the time the rule is activated. Its execution can cause the activation of specific modules, each of them including specific schemes implementing some form of cooperativeness from the system to the user. As an example, the module RECV of the system architecture contains an implementation of specific error-recovering schemes [28].

2.3 Cooperative Query-Execution Commands

The following is the basic *cooperative query-execution command*, provided by the methodology:

```
query (<query-expression>, <information>)
```

The parameters <query-expression> and <information> are Prolog expressions involving one or more facts from the DB. The <query-expression> can be a single fact, a conjunction of facts or a second-order predicate. The last option - second-order predicate - allows the recovering of a list of answers related to the query fact specified in the predicate.

In addition to the above-mentioned *query* command, we have introduced the command *query_on*, which allows the presentation of queries in a more general level. The syntax is:

```
query_on(C)
```

where C stands for a "general concept", which should be either an entity or a relationship class. The predicate above calls an specific structuring predicate which activates the RECV module to build up a query following the syntax for facts of the methodology. The query is then submitted to the system query processor, through the calling of a predicate semantically equivalent to the *query* command.

An essential element of our framework, specially in the context of the RM-rules, is the session *log*, in which a record of the interaction between the system and its user is kept. The log is formed by Prolog clauses defining specific predicates such as *was_queried, was_told, select_ans_qry*, to name a few. See [29] for details.

2.4 Processing the user Requests

According to the NICE methodology, specific schemes have been adopted for the processing of RM-rules against users' requests. Essentially, for each entered request, one or more rules are automatically activated. We discuss each introduced scheme in the following.

In the processing of rules of the type *pre* against user queries, the *successive* scheme has been taken into account in [26,28]. This scheme can be represented as shown in the sequel (for a single goal):

$$Q_0 \to Q_1 \to Q_2 \to ... \to Q_n$$

where Q_0 is the original query; $\to$ indicates a possible transformation; and Q_n is the transformed query.

At least two points can be raised up with respect to this strategy:
1. It can happen that some of the intermediate queries - Q_1, Q_2, ..., Q_{n-1} - be more interesting for the purpose of cooperativeness than the final transformed query Q_n.
2. As pointed out before, the query Q_0 is submitted through the issuing of the command *query(Q_0)*, which activates the query processor of the system. Differently, the transformed query, Q_n, is directly processed against the underlying database in [26,28].

With respect to (i) above, in the current implementation the query expressions, in the sequence of query transformations from Q_0 to Q_n, are collected into a list from which a menu is constructed to query the user about the most appropriated question to query about. An extended query-the-user facility [31] is used in this process.

Now, in what (ii) is of concern, the chosen query, after the pre-processing process, is also submitted to the query processor of the system. This corresponds to a more general (and more natural) approach and makes it easier the management of all the question-answering process.

Now we turn our attention to another scheme of the methodology, namely the *cumulative* scheme. Let Q_a be the answered query after the pre-processing process. According to the solution presented in [26,28], one constructs a list containing all Q_s such that $Q_a \to Q_s$ is a valid transformation with respect to some *s-post* rule. The result list is included as part of the answer to the original query. In the current solution we are primarily interested in the transformations such that Q_s is a query expression representing a possible subsequent question. All those questions are collected into a list and a menu is presented to the user, allowing him to choose an additional query (if he wants to!). In agreement with the strategy for the *successive* scheme, the chosen query is submitted to the system query processor. Another important aspect of the pos-processing phase is the identification and presentation of additional relevant information, related to the answered question. In this case the *cumulative* scheme as initially proposed is appropriated.

In the case of failure in the execution of a user query, one searches for an *alternative* query whose execution ends in success. This strategy is defined as *alternative scheme* in [26]. If not one alternative has been encountered, the system tries to *compensate* for the failure, i. e., to present the user with appropriate messages and/or to generate an explanation of the failure.

Taking into account the proposed modification for the *successive* and *cumulative* schemes, outlined above, it has been necessary to consider, in the context of the *alternative* scheme, in the case in which the current (failed) query has been chosen from a menu, the possibility of identifying some alternative query from the previously presented menu. Here again the user is queried about the convenience of trying some of the other queries on the menu. From this point on, the system follows the same strategy of [26,28]. If necessary, it proceeds trying to find alternatives through the activation of specific *f_post* rules. If the attempt ends in failure, it tries to compensate for the failure, by means of the calling of other specific *f_post* rules.

The algorithms for the processing of user requests are described in [29].

3 Running the Prototype

We present some sample queries in the Appendix, based on the specification of an academic database application [29]. The notation used in the examples is Prolog-like [32].

The system, in the case of wrong query expressions, tries to correct them with respect to the conceptual schema. Next, a menu containing all possible query transformations, with respect to some specific *pre* rules, is presented to the user. After the successful execution of the input query, the system structures a menu containing possible subsequent queries, which are obtained taking into account the conceptual level information, the domain restrictions, and the introduced *constraining* rules. In the case of failure, if the failure is "reasonable" with respect to some specific *missing_info* clause, an appropriate message is displayed. If a failing query has been chosen from a menu, as the user could be interested in the other entries (queries), those ones are again suggested to him on a new menu.

The important point in the examples is that the system tries to establish, from the user input query, a dialogue in which not only it tries to answer the original query, as well as it tries to identify possible subsequent queries, which are then suggested to the user.

4 General Remarks

In this paper, we have described a methodology for question-answering in which the system tries to establish, from an input query, a controlled dialogue with its user. In the dialogue, the system tries to identify possible subsequent queries, which are then proposed to the user. The control aspect of the dialogue is based (implicitly) on the way of representing concepts in the knowledge base, on domain restrictions, and (explicitly) on specific constraining rules.

Unlike the emphasis followed in [26,28], in accordance with a very important point with respect to the system development was the investigation of new request modification rules, we are now more concerned with the proposal and implementation of a question answering model, structured over the NICE kernel. In this way our work is related to [22]. In fact, as one can see in [26,28], it is not possible (and not even easy!) to introduce a large number of really expressive request-modification rules. In this aspect we argue that the most important point with respect to the proposal of a question answering model is to investigate how one can improve the existing conceptual structures, and even to introduce new ones. Recall that the conceptual structures take part in the knowledge base specification, which represents the data semantics.

One could argue that a critical aspect with respect to the rule-based request modification, specially in what pre-rules are of concern, is related to efficiency, as the query transformation can cause a "delay" in the presentation of the query answer to the end user. It is important to stress, with respect to this aspect that the rule modification approach, as considered in the NICE system, is flexible enough to allow the designer to deal with efficiency aspects. In this way, one can inspect the actions associated with some specific pre-rules and see if it is possible to consider them in the context of rules either of the type s_post or of the type f_post. Notwithstanding that possibility, some pre-rules are really of importance for the purpose of cooperativeness: one could mention, for instance, those ones concerned with the verification of the request correctness with respect to the conceptual schema specification.

References

1. Bolc, L. & Jarke, M. (eds.). Cooperative Interfaces to Information Systems. Springer-Verlag (1986).
2. Allen, J.F. & Perrault, C.R. *Analyzing intentions in utterances.* Artificial Intelligence 15, 3, 143-178 (1980).
3. Goodman, B.A. & Litman, D.J. *On the Interaction between Plan Recognition and Intelligent Interfaces.* In: User Modeling and User-Adapted Interaction, 2(1-2), pp. 55-82 (1992).
4. Kautz, H.A. *A Formal Theory of Plan Recognition.* PhD thesis, The University of Rochester, Rochester, NY (1987).
5. Litman, D.J. & Allen, J.F. *A Plan Recognition Model for Subdialogues in Conversations.* Cognitive Science 11, Pages 163-200 (1987).
6. Motro, A. *Query generalization: a technique for handling query failure.* Proc. First International Workshop on Expert Database Systems (1984) 314-325.
7. Motro, A. *FLEX: A Tolerant and Cooperative User Interface to Databases.* IEEE Transactions on Knowledge and Data Engineering, Vol. 2, No. 2, pp. 231-246 (1990)

8. Cheikes, B. *Monitor Offers on a Dynamic Database: The search for relevance.* Technical Report CIS-85-43, Dept. of Computer and Information Science, University of Pennsylvania, October, 1985.
9. Mays, E. *A Temporal Logic for Reasoning about Changing Data Bases in the Context of Natural Language Question-Answering.* In: Kerschberg, L. (ed.) Expert Database Systems. New York: Benjamin Cummings, 1985.
10. Imielinski, T. *Intelligent Query Answering in Rule Based Systems.* Journal of Logic Programming, 4:229-257 (1987).
11. Motro, A. *Using Integrity Constraints to Provide Intensional Answers to Relational Queries.* Proceedings of the Fifteenth International Conference on Very Large Data Bases, Amsterdam, August (1989).
12. Allen, R.B. *User Models: theory, method, and practice.* Int. J. Man-Machine Studies, 32, 511-543 (1990).
13. Hemerly, A. S. Fundamentos Lógicos para modelos de usuários em ambientes cooperativos. PhD thesis, Dept. de Informática, PUC/RJ (1995).
14. Kobsa, A. & Wahlster, W. (eds.). User Models in Dialog Systems. Springer-Verlag (1989).
15. Rich, E. *Users are individuals: individualizing user models.* Int. J. Man-Machine Studies, 18, 199-214 (1983).
16. Cuppens, F. & Demolombe, R. *Cooperative answering: a methodology to provide intelligent access to databases.* In: Proc. of the Second International Conference on Expert Database Systems. L. Kerschberg (ed.). Benjamin/Cummings (1989) 621-643.
17. Chu, W.W.; Yang, H.; Chiang, K.; Minock, M.; Chow, G.; Larson, C. *CoBase: A Scalable and Extensible Cooperative Information System.* Journal of Intelligent Information Systems, Vol. 6, Number 2/3 (1996), pp. 223-259.
18. Minock, M.; Chu, W. W. *Explanation for Cooperative Information Systems.* In Proceedings of the Ninth International Symposium on Methodologies for Inteligent Systems, Baltimore, MD, 1996.
19. Godfrey, P., Minker, J. & Novik, L. *An Architecture for a Cooperative Database System.* Proceedings of the 1994 International Conference on Applications of Databases, Vadstena, Sweden, June 1994.
20. Kaplan, S.J. *Cooperative Responses from a Portable Natural Language Query System.* Artificial Intelligence, 19 (1982), Pages 165-187.
21. Godfrey, P. *Minimization in Cooperative Response to Failing Database Queries.* Int'l Journal of Cooperative Information Systems (IJCIS), World Scientific Publishing, 6(2):95-149 (1997).
22. Graesser, A. C. , Gordon, S. E. & Brainerd, L. E. *QUEST: A Model of Question Answering.* Computers Math. Applic. Vol. 23, No. 6-9, pp. 733-745, 1992.
23. Webber, B.L. *Questions, Answers and Responses: Interacting with Knowledge Base Systems.* In: On knowledge base management systems. Brodie, M.L. & Mylopoulos, J. (eds.). Springer-Verlag (1986).
24. Han, J.; Huang, Y.; Cercone, N.; Fu, Y. Fu: Intelligent Query Answering by Knowledge Discovery Techniques. IEEE TKDE 8(3): 373-390 (1996)
25. Motro, A. Cooperative Database Systems. International Journal of Intelligent Systems, Vol. 11, No. 10, October 1996, pp. 717-732.
26. Hemerly, A.S., Casanova, M.A. & Furtado, A.L. *Cooperative behaviour through request modification.* Proc. 10th Int'l. Conf. on the Entity-Relationship Approach, San Mateo, CA, USA (1991) 607-621.

27.Sena, G.J. Um modelo de sistema cooperativo baseado na modificação de solicitações de consulta e de atualização. PhD thesis, Dept. de Informática, PUC/RJ (1992).

28.Sena, G.J. Cooperative Environments for the use of Information Systems: description of the NICE project and a proposal of extensions to its present-day version. Technical Report 001/96, UNESP/Guaratinguetá/DMA (1996).

29.Sena, G. J.; Furtado, A.L. Cooperative Interfaces to Databases: Towards an Extended Version of the NICE System. Technical Report 001/98, UNESP/Guaratinguetá/DMA (1998).

30.Hull, R. & King, R. *Semantic Database Modeling: Survey, Applications, and Research Issues.* ACM Computing Surveys, Vol. 19, No. 3, pp. 201-260 (1987).

31.Sena, G.J.; Furtado, A.L. *An Extended Query-the-User Tool for Expert Systems.* Proceedings of the Fourth World Congress on Expert Systems, ITESM Mexico City Campus, March 16-20 (1998), pp. 355-362.

32.Marcus, C. Prolog Programming. Addison-Wesley Pub. Co. (1986).

Appendix: Clausal Notation and Query Examples

Clausal Notation. To give some insight in the notation adopted in the prototype, we present in the sequel the syntax for some of the concepts of a NICE application. We begin with the syntax for the *entity* and *relationship* classes, and for the attributes.

entity(E,K).

relationship(R,[E1,...,En]).

is_a(E1,E2).

attribute(E,A).attribute(R,A).

where E, E1, E2,...,En are entity classes, R is a relationship class, K is a domain from which the key values for instances of E are to be taken, and A is an attribute. Some examples are given in the sequel:

entity(student,s_numb).entity(teacher,t_numb).

chairman is_a teacher.

relationship(takes,[student,class]).relationship(takes_part_in,[subject,course]).

relationship(subject_classes,[subject,class]).

relationship(assigned_to_class,[teacher,class]).

attribute(subject,credits).attribute(has_taken,grade).

At the object level, we have the following syntax for the *facts*:

E&&K. E&&K\A(V).

R#PL. R#PL\A(V).

where V stands for a value from domain A, PL designates the list [E1&&K1,...,En&&Kn], called the relationship participant list, each Ei&&Ki, i=1,...,n, representing an entity class instance. Some examples are shown below:

course&&comp.subject&&sb1.

lab&&sb2.teacher&&t1.

class&&cl2.subject&&sb1\credits(3).

subject_classes#[subject&&sb1,class&&cl2].

is_able_to_teach#[teacher&&t1,subject&&sb1].

assigned_to_class#[teacher&&t2,class&&cl2].takes#[student&&s2,class&&cl1].

Query Examples. To illustrate the prototype behavior, we present two simple query examples in the sequel. The user entries below are italicized.

?- query_on(subject).
subject && V1
Attribute(s) of entity subject : credits sb_name
I can try to solve any of the queries in the sequel:
choose from the following:
(1) subject && V1
(2) subject && V1 \ credits(V2)
(3) subject && V1 \ sb_name(V3)
   Answer is **1** .
Would you like to try to get more information about or related to any of the facts in the sequel?
choose from the following:
(1) subject && sb1
(2) subject && sb2
(3) subject && sb3
(4) subject && sb4
(5) subject && sb5
   Answer is **3**.
Maybe you can be interested in obtaining
information concerning the (template)
facts in the sequel:
I can try to solve any of the queries in the sequel:
choose from the following:
(1) prerequisite_of # [subject && sb3,subject && V1]
(2) subject_classes # [subject && sb3,class && V2]
(3) is_able_to_teach # [teacher && V3,subject && sb3]
(4) assigned_to_class # [teacher && V4,class && cl4]
   Answer is **4** .
...s_pos processing...
...failure...
A teacher has not been yet assigned to the specified class
Would you like me to try to solve any of the other queries in the sequel ?
choose from the following:
(1) prerequisite_of # [subject && sb3,subject && V1]
(2) subject_classes # [subject && sb3,class && V2]
(3) is_able_to_teach # [teacher && V3,subject && sb3]
   Answer is **3**.

subject && sb1
subject && sb2

subject && sb3
subject && sb4
subject && sb5
is_able_to_teach # [teacher && t2,subject && sb3]

?- *query_on(title)*.
What concept do you want, in fact, to query about?
choose from the following:
(1) student
(2) subject
(3) class
(4) course
(5) lab
(6) teacher
(7) classroom
(8) takes
(9) has_taken
(10) prerequisite_of
(11) takes_part_in
(12) subject_classes
(13) is_able_to_teach
(14) assigned_to_class
(15) reserved_for_classes
  Answer is **2**.

subject && V1
Attribute(s) of entity subject : credits sb_name
I can try to solve any of the queries in the sequel:
choose from the following:
(1) subject && V1
(2) subject && V1 \ credits(V2)
(3) subject && V1 \ sb_name(V3)
  Answer is **1** .

From this point on, the interaction is the same as shown in the previous query.

Semantic Query Optimization through Abduction and Constraint Handling

Gerhard Wetzel

Logic Based Systems Lab, Department of Computer Science
Brooklyn College, NY 11210, USA,
gw@sci.brooklyn.cuny.edu
http://sci.brooklyn.cuny.edu/~gw

Francesca Toni
Department of Computing, Imperial College
London SW7 2BZ, UK,
ft@doc.ic.ac.uk
http://laotzu.doc.ic.ac.uk/UserPages/staff/ft/ft.html

Abstract. The use of integrity constraints to perform Semantic Query Optimization (SQO) in deductive databases can be formalized in a way similar to the use of integrity constraints in Abductive Logic Programming (ALP) and the use of Constraint Handling Rules in Constraint Logic Programming (CLP). Based on this observation and on the similar role played by, respectively, extensional, abducible and constraint predicates in SQO, ALP and CLP, we present a unified framework from which (variants of) SQO, ALP and CLP can be obtained as special instances. The framework relies on a proof procedure which combines backward reasoning with logic programming clauses and forward reasoning with integrity constraints.

1 Introduction

Semantic Query Optimization (SQO) in deductive databases uses implicit knowledge coded in Integrity Constraints (ICs) to transform queries into new queries that are easier to evaluate and ideally contain only atoms of extensional predicates. SQO sometimes allows for unsatisfiable queries to be rejected without accessing the database at all.

ICs in Abductive Logic Programming (ALP) and Constraint Handling Rules (CHRs) in Constraint Logic Programming (CLP) are used in a similar way as ICs in SQO. ALP aims at transforming given goals (observations) into new goals containing only atoms of abducible predicates (hypotheses). ICs are used to reject incompatible hypotheses. CLP aims at transforming given goals into new goals containing only atoms of constraint predicates. CHRs are used to program a user-defined constraint solver which simplifies constraints and checks them for satisfiability. CHRs can be viewed declaratively as ICs.

Based on the similar use of ICs and CHRs as well as of extensional, abducible and constraint predicates, we present a unified framework from which (variants of) SQO, ALP and CLP can be obtained as special instances. The framework relies on a proof procedure, originally defined for ALP, combining backward reasoning with logic programming clauses and forward reasoning with ICs.

The paper is organized as follows. Section 2 gives some background and examples on SQO, ALP and CLP and shows how the three areas are related to each other. Section 3 defines a unified framework in which the three areas are embedded. Section 4 defines the basic proof procedure for the unified framework and some possible extensions. Section 5 shows how SQO can be obtained as a special instance of the framework and its proof procedure. Section 6 gives some application examples.

This paper is based on [31, 32].

2 SQO, ALP, CLP

A logic program consists of clauses of the form

$H \leftarrow B_1 \wedge \ldots \wedge B_n$

where H is an atom, the B_i are literals and all variables are implicitly universally quantified from the outside. Any such clause is said to "define" the predicate of the atom H.

A deductive database is a logic program separated into an *extensional database* (EDB), consisting of unit clauses ($n = 0$), and an *intensional database* (IDB), consisting of any clauses. The predicates solely defined in the EDB are referred to as extensional, whereas the predicates defined in the IDB are referred to as intensional. The EDB is typically very large and therefore looking up information in the EDB during query answering may be computationally explosive. Thus, it is desirable to preprocess and optimize a given query to reduce the necessity of accessing the EDB during the query answering process. The area of research concerned with such query transformation is called **Semantic Query Optimization** (SQO, [3,4]). SQO uses implicit knowledge coded in *integrity constraints* (ICs) to transform queries into new queries that are easier to answer and ideally contain only atoms of extensional predicates. In some cases, SQO may allow the rejection of unsatisfiable queries without accessing the EDB at all.

Example 1. (SQO)
Query: `employee(X)` $\wedge$ `position(X,manager)` $\wedge$ `bonus(X,B)` $\wedge$ `B=0`
IC: `position(X,manager)` $\wedge$ `bonus(X,B)` $\rightarrow$ `B`$\neq$`0`
Let the predicates `employee`, `position` and `salary` be extensional. SQO uses the IC to show that the query has no answers without accessing the EDB. If PROLOG were used to process the query, it would have to look at every `employee` fact.

The use of ICs to optimize queries adds to their standard use of checking and maintaining consistency of dynamically changing databases. (For further work on the role and semantics of integrity constraints in deductive databases in general and in SQO in particular see [11] and the references therein.) ICs are used in a similar way in **Abductive Logic Programming** (ALP, [18,19]), to check and maintain consistency of dynamically generated explanations for observations. In ALP, predicates are either ordinary, processed by backward reasoning with clauses in a given logic program, or *abducible*, undefined in the given program. Explanations consist of atoms of abducible predicates only.

More formally, an abductive logic program consists of a logic program T, a set of ICs and a set of candidate abducible predicates. Δ is an *explanation* for an observation G if

(1) Δ consists of atoms of abducible predicates only
(2) $T \cup \Delta$ "entails" G
(3) $T \cup \Delta$ "satisfies" the ICs

The notions of entailment and IC satisfaction can be defined in numerous ways. At the very least IC satisfaction means that $T \cup \Delta$ is consistent with the ICs (*consistency view*). We will adopt a flexible "propertyhood view" in our unified framework (see section 3).

Example 2. (ALP)
Observation: **bird ∧ flies**
IC: **penguin ∧ flies → false.**
Let **penguin, albatross** and **flies** be abducible, and **bird** be defined by the logic program
  bird ← albatross
  bird ← penguin.
Then, {**albatross, flies**} is a consistent explanation for the observation, whereas {**penguin, flies**} is not.

In SQO, the optimization of a query by means of ICs may introduce new atoms of extensional predicates into the query. Analogously, in ALP, ICs may introduce abducibles into explanations. Thus the use of ICs in SQO and ALP is similar, with extensional, respectively intensional, predicates in SQO taking the role of abducible, respectively ordinary, predicates in ALP. This similarity was first noticed by Kakas [16,17].

Constraint Logic Programming (CLP, [13,14]) also considers two kinds of predicates, ordinary predicates, processed by backward reasoning with clauses in a given logic program, and *constraint* predicates, simplified and checked for satisfiability by a built-in constraint solver. A given goal is solved when it is reduced to a set of constraints that cannot be simplified further. Recently, ICs in the form of Constraint Handling Rules (CHRs, [7]) have been used to explicitly user-define the constraint solver.

Example 3. (CLP)
Goal: **X > 1 ∧ 1 > Y ∧ Y > X**
ICs: **X > Y ∧ Y > Z → X > Z**
  X > N ∧ N > X → false.
A CLP system employing a built-in constraint solver working either over a finite integer domain (such as **cc(FD)** [30]) or over the domain of real numbers

(CLP($\mathcal{R}$), [13]) does not need the explicit ICs as the constraint solver recognizes that the constraints in the goal are unsatisfiable over their respective domains.

If no built-in constraint solver is present, the ICs can be used as CHRs to determine the unsatisfiability of the goal: the first IC (transitivity) adds $X > Y \wedge 1 > X$ to the goal and then the second IC becomes applicable and generates **false**.

Note that PROLOG, which cannot make use of the ICs, would either refuse to process the uninstantiated arithmetic expressions or fail to terminate, if it tried to unfold an explicitly given definition of ">".

Based on the observation that extensional, abducible and constraint predicates are treated in similar ways in SQO, ALP and CLP and that the use of ICs plays a similar role in the three frameworks, in the next section we define a unified framework in which (variants of) SQO, ALP and CLP can be obtained as special instances. The framework's proof procedure (see section 4) can be used for the generation of optimized queries, explanations, sets of constraints for given queries, observations, goals.

3 Unified Framework and Semantics

Knowledge in the unified framework is represented by definitions and ICs. *(Iff) definitions* are of the form
$$H \leftrightarrow D_1 \vee \ldots \vee D_n$$
where H is an atom (different from **true** and **false**) and each D_i is a conjunction of literals. Variables in the head H are implicitly universally quantified from the outside, whereas variables in any of the disjuncts D_i but not appearing in the head H are implicitly existentially quantified in the disjunct. A definition is said to *define* the predicate of the atom H.

Definitions are used in place of conventional clauses in order to reduce the amount of non-deterministic search. There may still be several definitions for the same predicate, but we require that the head atoms H of different definitions must not unify. One (iff) definition corresponds to n (if) clauses in a logic program which define the same predicate and whose head atoms unify.

ICs are implications of the form
$$A_1 \wedge \ldots \wedge A_n \rightarrow B_1 \vee \ldots \vee B_m$$
where the A_i and B_j are atoms. Variables in ICs are implicitly universally quantified from the outside.

Note that an IC could be equivalently written as a *denial* implication
$$A_1 \wedge \ldots \wedge A_n \wedge \neg B_1 \wedge \ldots \wedge \neg B_m \rightarrow false$$
which, in a deductive database, could have the declarative meaning that if the A_i are entailed by the database and none of the B_j is, then the IC is violated. Procedurally, ICs can be given a forward reasoning interpretation: if the A_i hold, then "propagate" $B_1 \vee \ldots \vee B_m$. Interpreted in this way, ICs are similar to *if-then, condition-action* or *production rules* in Artificial Intelligence. Large-scale commercial AI applications like R1/XCON [26] make use of such rules.

While ICs can be transformed into normal logic programs [21] and thus potentially into definitions, operationally useful information may be lost in the transformation and the resulting program may not only be further from the specification (and thus harder to understand and to prove correct), but also less efficient to run.

Definitions and ICs may involve atoms of three kinds of predicates:

- *user-defined* predicates, defined by a set T_u of domain-specific, user-given definitions,
- *built-in* predicates, including equality as well as arithmetic inequality and arithmetic operators, defined by an implicit set T_b of definitions,
- *external* predicates, defined by an inaccessible (unknown) set T_e of definitions.

The union $T_u \cup T_b \cup T_e$ is denoted by T. The union $T_u \cup T_b$ of the accessible parts of the theory T is denoted by T'. The set of all ICs is denoted by IC.

User-defined predicates correspond to ordinary predicates in LP, ALP and CLP as well as intensional predicates in SQO. Built-in predicates correspond to equality in standard LP and ALP and to constraint predicates in CLP. Note that equality is the only constraint predicate in LP from a CLP point of view. The issue of built-in (constraint) predicates in deductive databases is often left open. External predicates correspond to abducibles in ALP and extensional predicates in SQO. The ALP instance of the framework can be thought of as generating those parts of an unknown theory T_e relevant to the given observation. In the SQO instance the theory T_e is the known EDB which remains inaccessible until the final optimized query has been formulated.

As T_e is inaccessible, information about external predicates is only provided by ICs. ICs are also used to provide information about accessible, user-defined or built-in predicates whenever it would be expensive to access T directly. Therefore, ICs can be thought of as approximations of the definitions in T.

In order to guarantee that ICs be sound approximations of T, we require that the ICs are *properties* of T, i.e. sentences true in all *intended models* of T, $T \models_{int} IC$ in short. The user chooses which models are intended.[1] Possible choices include the perfect, stable, and well-founded models of the logic program obtained by rewriting the iff definitions of T into if clauses. Often there is a more or less canonical choice, e.g. the unique minimal Herbrand model for Horn programs and the unique perfect model for locally stratified logic programs (the latter choice and restriction is made in [22]).

By allowing the user to choose the notion of intended model, we allow a higher degree of flexibility. Note that if a theory T and a set of ICs are given, then the user is limited in the choice of intended models, whereas if a theory T is given together with its intended models, then the user is limited in the choice of

---

[1] Subject to a few restrictions given in [31], e.g. T must have at least one intended model (which may, however, be three-valued) to rule out the case where everything is a trivial property of a theory without intended models.

ICs — in both cases the user has to ensure that $T \models_{int} IC$ holds. For example, if T contains only

    p ↔ p

and the intended model of T is the minimal Herbrand model of **p ← p**, then

    p → **false**

is a property of T and thus may be used as an IC.

The *initial goal* is a conjunction of literals with all variables being free. The computational task, whose formalization into a proof procedure is given in section 4, is to reduce the given initial goal to a disjunction of answers, which is equivalent to the initial goal in the sense that the goal and the disjunction are satisfied, in the intended models of T, by the same assignments to the free variables. Such answers are obtained by using definitions to "unfold" atomic goals to equivalent disjunctions of goals which can then be "split" using distributivity. Surrogate subgoals are introduced by "propagation" (resolution) with ICs. As in Operations Research, surrogate subgoals are logically redundant, but may be easier to solve.

An atom A is called *suspended*, if there is no accessible definition $H \leftrightarrow D_1 \vee \ldots \vee D_n$ such that A is an instance of H (i.e. $A = H\sigma$ for some substitution σ).[2] Otherwise A is called *reducible*.

Thus atoms of external predicates, whose definitions are inaccessible, are always suspended, whereas atoms of user-defined and built-in predicates are suspended if they are insufficiently instantiated to be an instance of the head of a definition. The way in which definitions are written can be used to control suspension of atoms and the amount of non-determinism in the search for answers.

Example 4. Let the user-defined predicate **p** be defined by the following two definitions:

    p(X,a) ↔ q(X)
    p(X,b) ↔ r(X)

Then **p(X,Y)** and **p(a,Y)** are suspended, but **p(X,a)** and **p(a,b)** are reducible. If the definition

    p(X,Y) ↔ (Y=a ∧ q(X)) ∨ (Y=b ∧ r(X))

were used instead, then atoms of **p** would never be suspended.

T_b is assumed to be such that atoms like **X<Y**, **X>0** and **plus(2,X,Y)** are suspended, but **1<0**, **1>0** and **plus(2,2,X)** are not suspended (and can be reduced to **false**, **true** and **X=4**, respectively).

ICs are used to process suspended goals. "Propagation" with ICs may add to the goals reducible atoms which can then be "unfolded".

The framework's declarative semantics introduces three different notions of answer so that the proof procedure can be sound with respect to at least the weakest notion (for any permissible choice of intended model). The strongest notion is that of *ideal answer*: A is an ideal answer to the initial goal G_0 if

---

[2] Note that there is either exactly one or no such definition since heads of different definitions are not allowed to unify.

(A1) A is a conjunction of suspended atoms and implications (whose atoms are also suspended)

(A2) $T \models_{int} \check{\forall}[G_0 \leftarrow A]$

(A3) $T \not\models_{int} \neg \exists A$

Here $\check{\forall}$ and $\exists$ denote the universal and existential closures, respectively, quantifying over all free variables.

Condition (A1) means that goals have to be "unfolded" as far as possible, i.e. until all subgoals are suspended. Condition (A2) says that the initial goal G_0 must follow from the answer A in all intended models of T, for the same assignments to the free variables in G_0. Condition (A3) requires A to be satisfiable in at least one intended model of T. This implies that $\mathcal{IC} \cup \tilde{\exists} A$ is consistent since we assume that $T \models_{int} \mathcal{IC}$ (and since T must have at least one intended model). This condition defines the *propertyhood view* of IC satisfaction. The propertyhood view allows a more flexible view of IC satisfaction than those approaches fixing the notion of intended models and requiring the integrity constraints to be true in either some or all models of the theory or database.

The given answer definition is idealistic since T contains the inaccessible part T_e which is not available (to the proof procedure) for checking the satisfiability condition (A3). In general all suspended atoms can only be checked for consistency using the ICs. Or, in SQO terminology, it is not normally possible to optimize away and thus reject a query that has no answers but satisfies the ICs without consulting the EDB.

Thus, in addition to ideal answers, two weaker answer notions are defined. A is a *good answer* to G_0 if (A1) and (A2) hold and

(A3$_g$) $T' \cup \mathcal{IC} \cup CET \cup \tilde{\exists} A$ is consistent (CET is Clark's Equality Theory [5])

The suspension of user-defined and built-in predicates in T' may still prevent the proof procedure from identifying violations of condition (A3$_g$). Therefore an even weaker third answer notion is introduced: A is a *weak answer* to G_0 if (A1) and (A2) hold and

(A3$_w$) $\mathcal{IC} \cup CET \cup \tilde{\exists} A$ is consistent

Every answer computed by the proof procedure presented in the next section satisfies conditions (A1), (A2) and at least condition (A3$_w$).

Note the similarity of the above conditions to the ALP answer definition given in section 2. In ALP the only suspended atoms are the abducible atoms, so condition (1) of the ALP answer definition is just a special case of condition (A1). Condition (2) and (A2) are similarly variants of each other. Conditions (A3), (A3$_g$) and (A3$_w$) are all different ways of formalizing the satisfiability condition (3).

In section 5 we will compare the notion of answer definition in the unified framework and the notion of optimized query in SQO.

4 Proof Procedure

This section describes a rather abstract (high-level) proof procedure for the unified framework which can be regarded as a generalization and simplification of two abductive proof procedures, the Iff Proof Procedure [8] and SLDNFA [6]. By mainly ignoring efficiency issues, the proposed proof procedure may serve as a scheme for a family of proof procedures which can be obtained as instances by restricting and extending the abstract procedure in different ways. Thus more specialized procedures for ALP, CLP and SQO may be obtained as required.

4.1 Basic operations

A *derivation* of a goal G_n from an initial goal G_0 is a finite sequence of goals $G_0, G_1, \ldots, G_n$ where G_1 is obtained from G_0 by conjoining all ICs to G_0, and, for $0 < i < n$, G_{i+1} is obtained from G_i by applying one of the following operations:

1. *Unfolding* replaces a reducible atom A, which is either a conjunct of the goal or is a condition of an implication in the goal, by its definition. I.e. if there is a substitution σ such that $A = H\sigma$ and $H \leftrightarrow D_1 \vee \ldots \vee D_m$ is an accessible definition in T, then replace A by $(D_1 \vee \ldots \vee D_m)\sigma$.

2. *Propagation* is a form of resolution. If a subgoal contains the conjuncts $p(s_1, \ldots, s_n) \wedge Cond \to Conc$ and $Susp \to p(t_1, \ldots, t_n)$, then the "resolvent" $Cond \wedge Susp \wedge (s_1 = t_1 \wedge \ldots \wedge s_n = t_n) \to Conc$ can be added to the subgoal. $Susp$ is (usually) a conjunction of suspended atoms; the equalities in the resulting implication may allow the instantiation of atoms in $Susp$ such that they can be further unfolded.

3. *Logical equivalence transformations* include splitting (replacing $(A \vee B) \wedge C$ by $(A \wedge C) \vee (B \wedge C)$), normalization of implications (replace $\neg A \wedge B \to C$ by $B \to A \vee C$ and replace $(A \vee B) \to C$ by $(A \to C) \wedge (B \to C)$), and logical simplifications such as the replacement of $A \wedge \mathbf{false}$ by $\mathbf{false}$ and of $\mathbf{true} \to A$ by A.[3]

4. *Equality rewriting* implements the unification algorithm and performs substitutions to deal with equality atoms introduced into the goal. The rewrite rules used are adapted from [8] and are based on [25]. Conceptually, equality rewriting may also be regarded as propagation with the CET axioms of Clark's Equality Theory, followed by deletion of the no longer needed, rewritten terms.

If there is a derivation of $G_n = D \vee Rest$ from an initial goal G_0 and the operations of the proof procedure have been exhaustively applied to the disjunct D of the goal G_n, then a *computed answer* to G_0 is extracted from D after omitting all implications in D which are ICs or could have been derived from ICs without taking the initial goal into account (see [31] for details and justifications) and transforming all remaining implications in D into denials. The latter ensures that no further steps of propagation (with atoms not present in D) could generate new conclusions.

---

[3] Except that the implication $\mathbf{true} \to A$ is not rewritten to A, if A contains a universally quantified variable. Related proof procedures impose range-restrictedness on definitions and ICs [8] or more complicated safety requirements on the operations.[6]

Example 5. Given the goal disjunct D

    p(a) ∧ q(a) ∧ [p(X) → q(X)]

the computed answer is

    p(a) ∧ q(a) ∧ [p(X) ∧ X≠a → false]

The denial expresses that p(X) must not hold for any X not equal to a. If further instances of p besides p(a) were true, then further instances of q would have to be true as well (but they might be defined as false in T).

The operations of the proof procedure are all sound in the sense that they derive goals which are equivalent in T, i.e.

$$T \models_{int} \tilde{\forall}[G_i \leftrightarrow G_{i+1}]$$

Every computed answer to G_0 is at least a weak answer to G_0. Under certain further assumptions (see [31]) soundness results with respect to the stronger answer notions are also obtainable. Refutation soundness (good and ideal answers are never rejected) can be proven. Completeness results (for every ideal answer there is a corresponding computed answer) are only obtainable for special cases and for extensions of the proof procedure.

4.2 Extensions

Constraint Propagation with Disjunctions (CPD) [31, 22] generalizes propagation so that it can be used within and across disjunct boundaries in goals. CPD can be viewed as a natural implementation, and in some sense generalization, of several methods of handling disjunctive constraints in CLP,[4] such as CHIP's forward-checking and look-ahead techniques, Generalized Propagation and Constructive Disjunction (see [31] for more details and references and [15] for an overview of handling disjunctive constraints in CLP).

More technical improvements of the proof procedure are needed with respect to the efficiency of propagation and its termination. Since propagation is defined as resolution, the problem of restricting propagation can be approached by looking at resolution restrictions proposed in the theorem-proving literature. Possible restrictions include P_1-resolution, which corresponds to the requirement that the expression *Susp* in the definition of propagation is empty, and hyper-resolution, which corresponds more closely to the forward reasoning interpretation of ICs (only apply an IC if all of its condition atoms can be shown to hold).

Another important extension of the proof procedure is the *deletion* operation. It interprets ICs as identifying logically redundant and operationally useless subgoals which can be removed to simplify the goal. Ideally, deletion should be applied automatically by the proof procedure, e.g. the atom X>0 should be deleted as soon as the atom X>1 is added to the goal, if the ICs contain transitivity

    X>Y ∧ Y>Z → X>Z

which is a property of the built-in definition of the ">" predicate. However, the same rule can be applied by propagation if the conclusion X>Z is operationally useful. Criteria have to be worked out when ICs are to be used for propagation and when for deletion. See [33] for more on the use of ICs as deletion rules.

---

[4] Note that, in our framework, any disjunction can function as a disjunctive constraint.

4.3 Implementation

PROCALOG [34], short for *PROgramming with Constraints and Abducibles in LOGic,* is a realization of the unified framework and proof procedure as a programming language. It includes several of the extensions proposed in section 4.2.

Two prototype implementations have been used in [31] to provide some computational results for solutions to sample CLP applications, e.g. the n-queens problem and a warehouse location problem. A more efficient implementation (based on one of the two prototypes) is currently being developed.

5 SQO as an instance of the unified framework

We refer to the logic-based approach to SQO in deductive databases proposed in [3, 4]. The aim of SQO is to transform a given query, by using the intensional database (IDB) and a given set of ICs, but without accessing the extensional database (EDB), into an equivalent query which consists only of EDB (and possibly built-in) atoms and satisfies the ICs.

In the unified framework, the IDB corresponds to the user-defined part T_u of the given theory T and the EDB corresponds to the inaccessible theory T_e. Whereas in conventional (deductive) databases the EDB is assumed to be an enumeration of ground facts, in the SQO instance of the unified framework the EDB (i.e. T_e) is not explicitly restricted in this way. Whereas in conventional (deductive) databases the IDB is assumed to be a logic program, in the SQO instance of the unified framework the IDB (T_u) is a set of (iff) definitions. We obtain an exact correspondence, if T_u is assumed to be in homogenized form, i.e. if T_u is the set of all definitions for intensional predicates in the completion of a logic program. The approach in [3, 4] restricts the IDB to a set of non-recursive Horn clauses without function symbols and assumes that the ICs are not recursive either. The unified framework does not impose any such restriction. These restrictions have also been partly lifted in further work on SQO such as [23] and [10]. In particular, the latter extends the original approach of [3, 4] to deal with negative literals in the IDB and in ICs as well as IDB clauses with disjunctive heads.

In the unified framework, built-in as well as extensional atoms can be part of the optimized queries. Some recent work, e.g. [29], attempts to apply constraint technology to databases in general and query optimization in particular, usually employing a conventional CLP approach with a built-in constraint solver rather than explicit rules for constraint handling. In our approach built-in (constraint) predicates are naturally accommodated via propagation with ICs and unfolding with T_b.

5.1 SQO semantics

The aim of SQO, to transform a given query into an equivalent query which consists only of EDB (and possibly built-in) atoms and satisfies the ICs, is a special case of the computational task in the unified framework, to reduce a given initial goal to an equivalent disjunction of computed answers, each consisting only of suspended atoms and satisfying the ICs. In fact, if we assume that T_u is in homogenized form, atoms of user-defined predicates are never suspended and only EDB atoms (and possibly built-ins) are suspended and belong to computed answers.

In order to illustrate how SQO fits in the unified framework's semantics, we now give a declarative semantics for SQO. Other work on SQO usually defines SQO only in operational terms, although the following relationship between the initial and the optimized query is implied. Given an initial query Q_0, the query Q is an *optimized query* of Q_0 if

(S1) Q consists of atoms of EDB predicates only (and possibly built-ins, if any)
(S2) $IDB \cup IC\,(\cup\, T_b) \models \tilde{\forall}[Q_0 \leftrightarrow Q]$
(S3) $IDB \cup IC\,(\cup\, T_b) \cup \tilde{\exists}Q$ is consistent

Condition (S1) is the SQO instance of condition (A1) in the unified framework's semantics. Approaches to incorporate into databases built-in predicates to deal with (in-)equality and arithmetics usually suspend atoms of those predicates in a way similar to the unified framework, thus allowing built-ins to become part of the final optimized query. Note that if T_u is not in homogenized form and if thus atoms of user-defined predicates may be suspended and become part of an answer, then we may obtain what has been called *intensional answers* in the database literature (e.g. see [28]). Our concept of suspension may be viewed as a generalization of the idea of intensional answers.

Condition (S2) corresponds to condition (A2) in the unified framework's semantics, with two differences: IC in (S2) replaces T_e (EDB) in (A2) and and the stronger equivalence $Q_0 \leftrightarrow Q$ in (S2) replaces the implication $G_0 \leftarrow A$ in (A2). The first difference reflects the fact that the EDB plays no role during query optimization, if not through the ICs. If the ICs are properties of IDB $\cup$ EDB, as required by the unified framework, this difference is not substantial. The second difference reflects the fact that the optimized query Q is actually a disjunction of sub-queries $Q_1 \vee \ldots \vee Q_m$ with each sub-query Q_i corresponding more closely to an answer A in the unified framework. In fact, if there are only finitely many answers $A_1, \ldots, A_n$, then their disjunction is equivalent, in the intended models of T, to the initial goal G_0:
$$T \models_{int} \tilde{\forall}[G_0 \leftrightarrow A_1 \vee \ldots \vee A_n]$$
However, in the general case, there might be infinitely many answers so that only an implication can be used. Note though that the formulation
$$T \models_{int} \tilde{\forall}[G_0 \leftrightarrow A \vee Rest]$$
where $Rest$ is some formula, is equivalent to (A2) and possibly closer to (S2).

Condition (S3) corresponds to the good answer condition (A3$_g$). If user-defined predicates are never suspended and equality is the only built-in predicate, then the proof procedure for the unified framework will only compute good answers. The analogue of the ideal answer condition (A3$_i$), which can be expressed in the SQO case as

$$IDB \cup EDB \models_{int} \tilde{\exists}Q$$

is not suitable, however, because in SQO the optimized query Q may not have any answers in the EDB.

5.2 Proof procedures for SQO

[3,4] propose a *two-phased compiled approach* consisting of a *compilation phase* and a *transformation phase*.

The compilation phase generates *semantically constrained axioms* which combine the information given in the IDB and the integrity constraints. For example, given the IDB

    p(X) ← a(X)
    p(X) ← b(X)

and the IC

    a(1) → false

the compilation phase generates the semantically constrained axiom

    p(X) ← a(X) ∧ X≠1

([3,4] uses a slightly different syntax). This is achieved using *partial subsumption*, an operation which is based on resolution between the bodies of IDB clauses and integrity constraints. The additional condition X≠1 is called a *residue* of the IC.

In the unified framework's proof procedure, everything happens at run-time, and there is no pre-compilation. However, the effects of partial subsumption are achieved by propagation (combined with unfolding). For example, if the given query is p(X), the unified framework's proof procedure generates the goal

    (a(X) ∧ X=1 → false) ∨ b(X)

by first unfolding the goal using the (homogenized) definition

    p(X) ↔ a(X) ∨ b(X)

and then applying propagation.

In practice the use of propagation instead of pre-compilation can have both advantages (no overhead as propagation can be restricted to atoms and implications actually "related" to the initial goal) and disadvantages (the same steps of propagation may have to be executed several times). More importantly, using propagation eliminates the restriction to non-recursive databases in an arguably simpler and more natural way than in the aforementioned extensions of SQO to recursive databases [23, 10].

In the second phase of SQO, the transformation phase, the query is modified by using the semantically constrained axioms obtained in the compilation phase as new clauses to unfold atoms in the given query and introducing the body of the axioms (after appropriate unification) into the new *semantically constrained query*. If more than one semantically constrained axiom unifies with a given query atom, then a disjunction of two semantically constrained subqueries is introduced.

In the unified framework, these query modifications correspond to unfolding (plus splitting, if needed) and equality rewriting. As [4] notice, query modification may lead to built-in expressions (equalities, inequalities, arithmetic operators etc.) becoming fully instantiated and thus evaluable. The unified framework's definitions of built-in predicates and suspension constitute a formalization and generalization of these concepts.

Evaluation of built-in atoms may lead to parts of the query becoming immediately unsatisfiable. Continuing the example given earlier in this section, if the initial query is p(1), then query modification using the semantically constrained axiom p(X) ← a(X) ∧ X≠1 yields the new semantically constrained query

(a(1) ∧ 1≠1) ∨ b(1).

The first disjunct contains an evaluable atom, 1≠1, which can be reduced to false. Thus the query can be reduced to the second disjunct and the final optimized query is b(1).

In the unified framework, given the initial goal p(1), unfolding yields the disjunction a(1) ∨ b(1). Propagation with the integrity constraint can then be applied to introduce false into the first disjunct, which is afterwards eliminated by logical equivalence transformation. The computed answer is again b(1).

The query transformation phase treats specially the residues that are added to IDB clauses when generating semantically constrained axioms in the compilation phase. Such special treatment is not required in the unified framework as propagation and logical equivalence transformation achieve the desired effects. There is one interesting special case in which a residue in the form of a "unit clause" is obtained. This corresponds to an implication true → A being derived by the unified framework's proof procedure. Then A could be added to the query as auxiliary information. However, if A already occurs as an atom in the query, then it could also be deleted from the query since the unit clause residue implies that the query atom will simply succeed. This relates to the issue of using integrity constraints sometimes for propagation and sometimes for deletion as mentioned in section 4.2.

6 Applications

The merits of the unified approach lie in its flexibility and its generality, reflected by the relatively few restrictions compared with existing versions of its instances (e.g. the restriction to non-recursive clauses in SQO).

As an example of the flexibility of the framework, consider the problem of configuring a computer system. The possible choices for the components (processor, monitor, memory, operating system, etc.) can be specified by definitions:

processor(X) ↔ (X = pentium) ∨ (X = sparc) ∨ ...

operating_system(X) ↔ (X = os2) ∨ (X = unix) ∨ ...

Dependencies, whether system constraints or personal preferences, between the different choices can be represented by ICs, in the form of both positive requirements and denials, e.g.

processor(sparc) → operating_system(unix)

processor(sparc) ∧ operating_system(os2) → false.

In SQO, processor and operating_system may be extensional and be regarded as inaccessible during query optimization. In the SQO instance of the framework, the query `processor(sparc) ∧ operating_system(os2)`

is rejected as inconsistent with the ICs without consulting the EDB.

In the CLP instance of the framework, the goal

`processor(X) ∧ operating_system(os2)`

results in the constraint `X=pentium` being derived as an answer (but not `X= sparc`).

In the ALP instance of the framework, the definitions of `processor` and `operating_system` might be regarded as unknown and the predicates treated as abducible. Given the observation `processor(sparc)`, the answer

`processor(sparc) ∧ operating_system(unix)`

is an abductive explanation which satisfies the ICs (whereas an answer containing `operating_system(os2)` does not).

Further examples of applications of the unified framework which are given in [31] include constraint satisfaction problems (such as n-queens and map coloring), Operations Research applications (such as job-shop scheduling and warehouse location problems) and an approach to configuration which bears some similarity to the CALOG framework are discussed in [31].

The use of ICs to improve the efficiency of logic (PROLOG) programs without having to abandon the original, natural specification is another interesting application of the framework. Again, see [31] for some examples.

7 Conclusion and Related Work

A unified framework for ALP, CLP and SQO has been presented. Variants of and procedures for ALP, CLP and SQO can be obtained as instances of the framework and its proof procedure. Further developments of the ALP and CLP aspects of this work can be found in [22]. The proof procedure presented in section 4 is a simplification and generalization of the abductive proof procedure presented in [8] and [9]. It is also closely related to SLDNFA, an abductive proof procedure defined in [6].

Previous proposals to relate ALP to deductive databases (and thus potentially to SQO) [16, 17] and to integrate ALP and CLP [20, 27] focused either on particular aspects of a combined framework or developed hybrid systems. Our unified framework can be instantiated to obtain (versions of) SQO, ALP and CLP as well as combinations of these frameworks. For example, the combination of SQO and the manipulation of built-in, constraint-like predicates is obtained as a by-product.

Recent activities in parallel with this work point to a convergence of related research. CHR^V [1] introduces disjunctions into the bodies of CHRs in a similar way as disjunctions are permitted in the bodies of definitions in the unified framework. Moreover, CHR^V is presented in this same volume as a "flexible query language" confirming the potential of CHRs for use in deductive database. Also in this volume, Bressan and Goh [2] apply abductive mechanisms to query optimization and implement them using CHRs. Although their formalism is different, the unified framework we have presented could be thought of as the general theory behind their work.

The framework and its implementations could lend themselves to many well-known problems and applications of Artificial Intelligence, especially problems with a large search space (where even a limited use of the CPD extensions can drastically reduce the search tree) and applications relying on knowledge representation in the form of condition-action (if-then) rules (where integrity constraints can often be used to model the rules in a logical way). The latter include expert systems for configuration problems or medical diagnosis.

Acknowledgements

We are grateful to Robert Kowalski for his collaboration in parts of this research. The first author is supported by ONR grant N00014-96-1-1057. The second author is supported by the UK EPSRC project "Logic-based multi-agent systems".

References

1. Abdennadher, S.; Schütz, H.: CHR$^\vee$: A Flexible Query Language. In this volume.
2. Bressan, S.; Goh, C. H.: Answering Queries in Context. In this volume.
3. Chakravarthy, U. S.; Grant, J.; Minker, J.: Foundations of Semantic Query Optimization for Deductive Databases. In: Minker, J. (ed.): *Foundations of Deductive Databases and Logic Programming*, pp. 243–273, Morgan Kaufmann 1988
4. Chakravarthy, U. S.; Grant, J.; Minker, J.: Logic-Based Approach to Semantic Query Optimization, *ACM Transactions on Database Systems* 15 (2), pp. 162–207, 1990
5. Clark, K. L.: Negation as failure. In: Gallaire, H.; Minker, J. (eds.): *Logic and Data Bases*, pp. 292–322, Plenum Press 1978
6. Denecker, M.; De Schreye, D.: SLDNFA: an abductive procedure for abductive logic programs, *Journal of Logic Programming* 34 (2), pp. 111–167, 1997
7. Frühwirth, T.: Constraint Handling Rules. In: Podelski, A. (ed.): *Constraint Programming: Basic and Trends*, pp. 90–107, LNCS 910, Springer Verlag 1995
8. Fung, T. H.: *Abduction by Deduction*. Ph.D. Thesis, Imperial College 1996
9. Fung, T. H.; Kowalski, R. A.: The Iff Proof Procedure for Abductive Logic Programs, *Journal of Logic Programming* 33 (2), pp. 151–165, 1997
10. Gaasterland, T.; Lobo, J.: Processing Negation and Disjunction in Logic Programs Through Integrity Constraints, *Journal of Intelligent Information Systems* 2, pp. 225–243, 1993
11. Godfrey, P.; Grant, J.; Gryz, J.; Minker, J.: Integrity Constraints: Semantics and Applications. To appear in: Chomicki, J.; Saake, G.: *Logics for Databases and Information Systems*, Kluwer 1998
12. Janson, S.; Haridi, S.: Programming Paradigms of the Andorra kernel language, Saraswat, V.; Ueda, K. (eds.): *Proc. of the Int. Symp. on Logic Programming*, pp. 167–186, MIT Press 1991
13. Jaffar, J.; Lassez, J.-L.: Constraint Logic Programming, *Proc. of the 14th ACM Symp. on the Principles of Programming Languages*, pp. 111–119, 1987
14. Jaffar, J.; Maher, M.: Constraint Logic Programming: A Survey, *Journal of Logic Programming* 19/20, pp. 503–581, 1994

15. Jourdan, J.; Sola, T.: The Versatility of Handling Disjunctions as Constraints. In: Bruynooghe, M.; Penjam, J. (eds.): *Proc. of the 5th Intern. Symp. on Programming Languages Implementation and Logic Programming*, pp. 60–74, Springer Verlag 1993

16. Kakas, A. C.: Deductive Databases as Theories of Belief, Technical Report, Imperial College, 1991

17. Kakas, A. C.: On the Evolution of Deductive Databases, Technical Report, Imperial College, 1991

18. Kakas, A. C.; Kowalski, R. A.; Toni, F.: Abductive Logic Programming, *Journal of Logic and Computation* 2 (6), pp. 719–770, 1992

19. Kakas, A. C.; Kowalski, R. A.; Toni, F.: The role of abduction in logic programming. To appear in: Gabbay, D. M. et al. (eds.): *Handbook of logic in Artificial Intelligence and Logic Programming*, vol. 5, pp. 235–324, Oxford University Press 1998

20. Kakas, A. C.; Michael, A.: Integrating Abductive and Constraint Logic Programming. In: Sterling, L. (ed.): *Proc. of the 12th Int. Conf. on Logic Programming*, pp. 399–413, MIT Press 1995

21. Kowalski, R. A.; Sadri, F.: Logic Programs with Exceptions. In: Warren, D. H. D.; Szeredi, P. (eds.): *Proc. of the 7th Int. Conf. on Logic Programming*, pp. 598–613, MIT Press 1990

22. Kowalski, R. A.; Toni, F.; Wetzel, G.: Executing Suspended Logic Programs, to appear in a special issue of *Fundamenta Informaticae* ed. by K. Apt.

23. Lakshmanan, L. V. S.; Missaoui, R.: Pushing Semantics into Recursion: A General Framework for Semantic Optimization of Recursive Queries. In: *Proc. of the Intern. Conf. on Data Engineering*, Taiwan, 1995

24. Manthey, R.; Bry, F.: SATCHMO: A Theorem Prover Implemented in PROLOG. In: Lusk, E.; Overbeek, R. (eds.): *Proc. of the 9th Conf. on Automated Deduction*, pp. 415–434, LNCS 310, Springer-Verlag 1988

25. Martelli, A., Montanari, U.: An efficient unification algorithm, *ACM Trans. on Prog. Lang. and Systems* 4 (2), pp. 258–282, 1982

26. McDermott, J.: R1: A Rule-Based Configurer of Computer Systems, *Artificial Intelligence* 19 (1), pp. 39–88, 1982

27. Maim, E.: Abduction and Constraint Logic Programming, In: Neumann, B. (ed.): *Proc. of the 10th European Conf. on Artificial Intelligence*, 1992

28. Pirotte, A.; Roelants, D.; Zimányi, E.: Controled generation of intensional answers, *IEEE Trans. on Knowledge and Data Engineering*, 3 (2), pp. 221–236, 1991

29. Ross, K. A.; Srivastava, D.; Stuckey, P. J.; Sudarshan, S.: Foundations of Aggregation Constraints, *Theoretical Computer Science* 193 (1–2), pp. 149-179, 1998

30. Van Hentenryck, P.; Saraswat, V. A.; Deville, Y.: Design, Implementation, and Evaluation of the Constraint Language cc(FD). In: Podelski, A. (ed.): *Constraint Programming: Basic and Trends*, pp. 293–316, Springer Verlag 1995

31. Wetzel, G.: *Abductive and Constraint Logic Programming*, Ph.D. thesis, Imperial College 1997

32. Wetzel, G.: A Unifying Framework for Abductive and Constraint Logic Programming. In: Bry, F.; Freitag, B.; Seipel, D. (eds.): *12th Workshop on Logic Programming (WLP'97)*, pp. 58–68, LMU München 1997

33. Wetzel, G.: Using Integrity Constraints as Deletion Rules. In A. Bonner et al. (eds): *Proceedings of the DYNAMICS'97 post-conference (ILPS'97) workshop on (Trans)Actions and Change in Logic Programming and Deductive Databases*

34. Wetzel, G.; Kowalski, R. A.; Toni, F.: PROCALOG — Programming with Constraints and Abducibles in Logic. In: Maher, M. (ed.): *Proc. of the 1996 Joint Int. Conf. and Symp. on Logic Programming*, p. 535

Implementing Fuzzy Querying via the Internet/WWW: Java Applets, ActiveX Controls and Cookies

Sławomir Zadrożny and Janusz Kacprzyk

Systems Research Institute
Polish Academy of Sciences
ul. Newelska 6
01-447 Warsaw
Poland
E-mail: kacprzyk@ibspan.waw.pl

Abstract. We discuss how tools developed in the framework of the Internet technology support the implementation of front-end user interfaces to database management systems (DBMSs) meant to operate via the Internet, mainly related to fuzzy querying. Some back-end implementation issues and examples are also discussed.

1 Introduction

The Internet is perceived as a herald of the Information Society. In such a new society the role of computerized information systems will certainly be constantly growing. When designing such computerized systems, specific features of the human nature should be taken into account. This definitely applies to querying interfaces, as they are a most visible part of a DBMS which in turn seem to be an indispensable component of any information systems. WWW creates a new framework for applications following the client-server paradigm, notably for the DBMSs, characterized by, e.g. a cross-platform availability, cheaper software maintenance and unified user interface. Thus, a WWW browser might be an attractive alternative for specialized database clients, and this way of accessing a database over the Internet (intranet) will be more and more popular.

This paper is based, first, on our previous works [16, 15, 5, 4, 6–8, 10, 12, 9, 14, 3, 20, 21] in which extensions to the traditional syntax and semantics of a querying language were proposed to accomodate flexible fuzzy terms, first for Xbase and then Microsoft Access. For the latter FQUERY for Access packages has been implemented by the authors. Then, fuzzy querying over the Internet/WWW was proposed by Kacprzyk and Zadrożny in [8, 11, 13], and this paper is a further step in this direction.

First, we discuss FQUERY for Access, and then we describe how such a querying system can be implemented using a WWW browser (Netscape Navigator and Microsoft Explorer).

2 FQUERY for Access package

FQUERY for Access [6–8, 10, 12, 9] makes it possible to use imprecise conditions in the queries to a traditional, crisp database. For example, in case of a real estate agency database we can use in the queries an imprecise term as *"low price"*. The problem is how to extend classic query languages (here: Microsoft Access's SQL) to be able to use such imprecise terms. Basically, the following issues have to be dealt with: (1) a proper formalism suitable for the representation and interpretation of imprecision, (2) corresponding changes to the syntax and semantics of a query language, (3) elicitation and manipulation of imprecise terms and queries containing them, and (4) providing some means for an appropriate processing of imprecise terms by a querying engine in question.

In FQUERY for Access, firstly, a fuzzy logic based approach to imprecise terms modeling is adopted with imprecise terms represented by fuzzy sets in appropriate universes, operations corresponding to t-norms and s-norms, etc. Secondly, into the syntax of the querying language *fuzzy values*, as in "price is **low**"; *fuzzy relations*, as in "land area is **much greater than** living area" and *linguistic quantifiers* (as in "**most** of the specified conditions should be met") are introduced. Then, all imprecise terms are defined and manipulated by the user within familiar, intuitive GUI of Microsoft Windows. Typical controls as well as charts, where applicable, are employed. Finally, the fuzzy querying engine is integrated with its (Access's) native one, at least from the user's viewpoint. An extra toolbar, shown in Figure 1, is provided to: maintain lists of imprecise terms, introduce them into a query, and start the querying. The querying is done by the Access's native engine.

3 Basics of the Internet/WWW

WWW is one of the most popular Internet service. Its implementation involves two types of software: (1) the client, i.e. a WWW browser (e.g., Microsoft Explorer or Netscape Navigator), and (2) the server, as, e.g., Microsoft Internet Information Server, Netscape's FastTrack or Apache.

In the simplest case the browser provides only rudimentary presentation services and the server is a file server. Currently available implementations of the WWW servers and browsers provide a much more extended functionality. In the former case, this may be the ability to execute other applications and deliver to the user appropriately encoded results (e.g., by using HTML), i.e. the WWW server may also be treated as an application server. This proceeds by using different techniques. Most of the servers support a simple mechanism, a *Common Gateway Interface* (CGI). This approach is standard, but not effective in terms of the host computer's resources usage. In case of browsers, some enhancements were introduced to the basic request-and-display principle. First of all, to make the CGI protocol really useful, some means of sending input data for server-based CGI-compliant applications have to be provided as, e.g., an extension to HTML called *forms*. The browser displays a HTML form using Microsoft Windows' *controls* or X-windows' *widgets*, such as a push button, listbox, etc. The

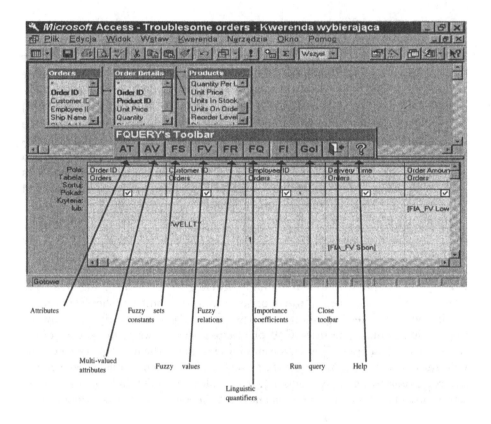

Fig. 1. FQUERY for Access's toolbar

data entered using these controls will be sent to the server with the request for a document – usually referring to some CGI application. The server will execute this application setting the data provided by the user as an input. Such data may be, e.g., a query which is used by the CGI-compliant program to fetch matching records from a database. The server catches the output of the executed application and sends it back to the browser.

The HTML forms provide therefore a basic level of interaction which may be used for the implementation of a fuzzy database querying – see, e.g., [8, 11, 13], but still lacks some important features.

Forms have become part of the HTML and are widely recognized by different browser implementations, even in a non-GUI environment (e.g., Lynx). Recent enhancements are much more sophisticated though less standardized. They allow to embed in a HTML page a code to be executed on the browser-side rather than on the server-side (as for CGI-compliant applications). The simplest technique is to use scripting languages, e.g. Microsoft's Visual Basic Script or Netscape's Javascript. The second technique is that specially prepared Java programs, *Java applets*, may be embedded in the HTML text. They are more powerful than script routines, however still limited in comparison to standalone Java programs, for security reasons. The third technique is *ActiveX controls* which are sent over the network in the binary ready-to-execute form, thus are faster in execution than applets which have to be interpreted. However, the ActiveX controls are currently limited to Windows, while Java applets are working on other platforms too, notably UNIX.

The HTTP protocol is state-less to keep the protocol simple and fast, thus it has no built-in mechanism for employing either the concept of a session or history of previous transactions, which may be important for, e.g., database management and querying. Some remedy is offered by *cookies*, i.e. pieces of text which may be sent by a server with the document requested by a browser. Then, subsequent browser's requests are accompanied with the same cookie acting as a session identifier.

4 Elicitation, storage and processing of imprecise terms in the Internet setting

The definitions of linguistic (fuzzy) terms may be stored at the server or browser side. The first solution is more consistent with WWW standards. The parameters of fuzzy terms may be stored in the same database as the data to be retrieved, in a separate database or even in flat files. It should be relatively easy for, e.g., a CGI-compliant application to handle this information at the server side. It may be a little bit cumbersome to achieve personalization of fuzzy terms in this approach. All definitions have to be stored at the server side so that, in case of multiple users, this may require an essential amount of extra disk space. Thus, storing of this information at the browser side would solve the question of personalization. Unfortunately, manipulation of data on a local disk at the browser side is considered as risky for security reasons. Presently, this may be achieved by using the ActiveX controls or cookies. The first option provides a full access to a local file system and may become acceptable in the future when security problems will be solved. The second option is fairly secure but local data handling is rather limited and even here standards do not exist. Anyway, the parameters of available fuzzy terms, predefined or defined by current and/or other users, have to be embedded in the user's querying interface through, e.g., HTML form controls or Java applets/ActiveX controls.

The database search and calculation of matching degrees for the records against a query may take place at the browser or server side. The former alternative implies a solution loosely connected with the WWW services and will be omitted here. The latter approach may be implemented using a CGI-compliant application – see, e.g., [8] – or a WWW server extensions using API; see, e.g., [2]. From the viewpoint of functionality of this "middle-ware" (gateway) application, the following classification may be proposed:

- the gateway fetches the rows from the database and only then evaluates the query against them,
- the handling of fuzziness is built into the DBMS, and the gateway just forwards the query and its results,

– the gateway itself manages the database, and the handling of fuzziness is a part of its regular query processing.

The first approach may be applied for virtually any DBMS. The whole fuzzy querying logic has to be implemented in the gateway. The second approach would be definitely most efficient though commercial DBMSs accepting fuzzy queries are not widely available yet. An example of such a solution may be found in [2]. The third approach may be well-suited for simple databases as, e.g., an XBase file (see [11]).

Finally, results of the query are to be displayed. Here, the features of the HTML perfectly fit the needs. The results may have the form of a list where each line consists of a value of a key field of the record with a matching degree od this record. Each such a line contains a hyperlink which brings to the screen the content of the whole record.

We will now present two pilot implementations of fuzzy querying over the Internet using some WWW-related tools and techniques mentioned above.

5 Implementation of fuzzy querying over the Internet

The first interface, with advanced client-side techniques will be illustrated on a WWW-based fuzzy querying interface for a database of Research, Technology and Development (RTD) institutions from Central and Eastern Europe (cf. [8, 11]). The second WWW based interface presented makes it possible to submit a query over the Internet to the fuzzy querying engine implemented by the FQUERY for Access add-on, and to display the results back on the user screen in the window of a WWW browser (cf. [2]).

5.1 WWW-based interface to a simple fuzzy querying back-end

The core of our first implementation of fuzzy querying over the Internet is an XBase file which contains descriptions of some Research, Technology and Development (RTD) institutions from Central and Eastern Europe constructed as a result of a research project for the support of cooperation between the scientific communities of the European Union and other European countries.

Each organization in the database is described by many attributes (fields), and the following attributes are selected to demonstrate the use of fuzzy terms in queries:

1. number of employees (*numerical*),
2. country (*single-valued*),
3. subjects of activity related to RTD (*multi-valued*), and
4. specific topics/know-how (*textual*).

The first field is numeric. Our fuzzy querying scheme is enriched with fuzzy values and fuzzy relations, and then fuzzy linguistic quantifiers. Here we will only illustrate them with examples of simple queries exemplified by: "Number of employees IS *small*", "Number of employees IS *much greater than* 100".

The second field is a text (string). Very often (also here) it may be natural to pose a question like: "Country IS IN *Central Europe*". The concept of "Central Europe" should be represented by a set, preferably fuzzy, as one can claim, that, e.g., Hungary belongs to this set for sure (to degree 1), Bulgaria does not belong to this set (to degree 0),and Slovenia belongs to this set but only to some degree, more than 0 but less than 1.

The third field is virtual, represented by a set of logical (Yes/No) fields. More precisely, there is a separate field corresponding to each possible subject of activity related to RTD in a given organization. A query may refer collectively to all these fields. Thus, we propose to treat all this fields as one, virtual multi-valued field. Dealing with a set of values, both in a record and a query, calls for soft measures of matching as the requirement that both sets are exactly equal is usually too rigid.

Finally, the fourth field is typical for information retrieval, i.e. it contains purely textual data. We do not propose any fuzzy extensions in this respect.

A WWW browser provides a framework for the user interface of our querying system. Basically, we use: (1) HTML forms, (2) Java applets, (3) JavaScript scripting, (4) frames , and (5) cookies.

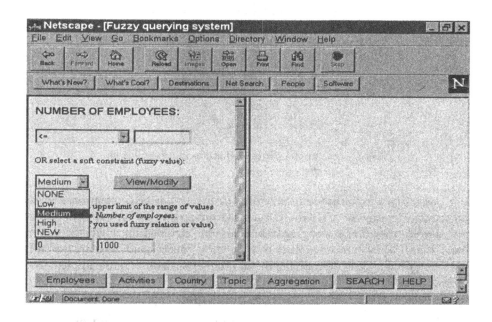

Fig. 2. Main screen of the interface

The main screen of our system is shown in Figure 2. There are three frames: the main frame, at the left, for specifying query criteria, the second frame for specifying membership functions for a fuzzy set employed in a query and for displaying help information, and the third frame, at the bottom, for quickly moving around the first frame.

In the main frame there is a HTML form with separate controls corresponding to particular fields mentioned previously. The numerical field "Number of employees" may be used in a query with fuzzy values or fuzzy relations. Figure 2 shows how a fuzzy value may be introduced into a query. The user may select a fuzzy value from a list which may be easily manipulated via typical tools of a graphical user interface (GUI). If a user contacts the system for the first time (i.e. there is no cookie at the client side), the list is short and contains only standard, predefined fuzzy values. The user can also define "own" fuzzy values which are stored at the browser side within the cookie and are then available. The definition, by selecting "NEW", is via a GUI shown in Figure 3, implemented as a Java applet. The definitions of fuzzy values, relations and quantifiers are stored and defined similarly using cookies and Java applets, respectively.

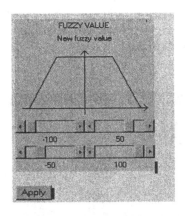

Fig. 3. Java applet for the definition of a fuzzy value

Classically, all conditions specified for the particular fields mentioned would be combined using the AND and OR logical connectives. In our querying system we allow for more flexible aggregation operators, representing linguistic quantifiers. Thus, the user may request that, e.g., "most" of the conditions are met. The user may define "own" quantifiers by an interaction with a graph implemented using a Java applet as in Figure 3.

At the server side we can distinguish two types of operations:

- a regular communication with a WWW browser due to the HTTP protocol done by the WWW server, and
- a dynamic generation of HTML documents and processing of a query by a set of CGI-compliant programs.

The whole processing is initiated by a browser requesting the "main document" of our querying system containing the query form. The browser request may be accompanied by the cookie comprising the definitions of user-specific fuzzy terms. The server simply sends the query form to the browser together with the cookie if one was present in the request. Now the browser side processing takes place, as described above. Finally, the user presses the "SEARCH" button and all information entered by the user is transmitted to the server. Then, the server initially processes the data according to the CGI specification and calls our main C program which makes the actual query processing and database search. In fact, all information about fuzzy terms possibly used in the query are contained in the data forwarded to this program by the WWW server. Thus, it has only to extract particular pieces of data, place them in its internal data structures and then start the search of the database. It fetches subsequent records and computes the matching degree. A partial fulfillment of the criteria by a record is possible. We start with the matching of particular conditions against the values of the attributes in a record. Then, the partial matching degrees are combined using an aggregation operator and we obtain an overall matching degree sought. Then, the records are ordered according to their matching degrees, and finally a HTML document containing the list of hyperlinks to the particular records is produced. More precisely, each hyperlink consists of the matching degree and the content of a pre-specified field of the record. All these hyperlinks lead to another C program which delivers the full content of the records selected.

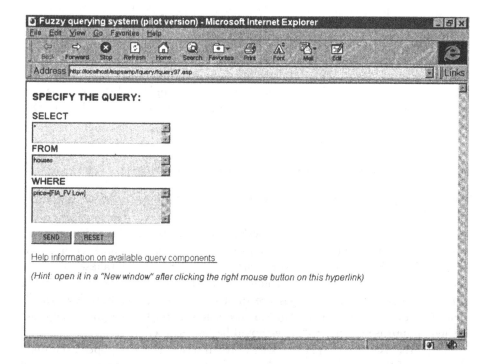

Fig. 4. Formulation of a simple condition in a query using the Microsoft Explorer

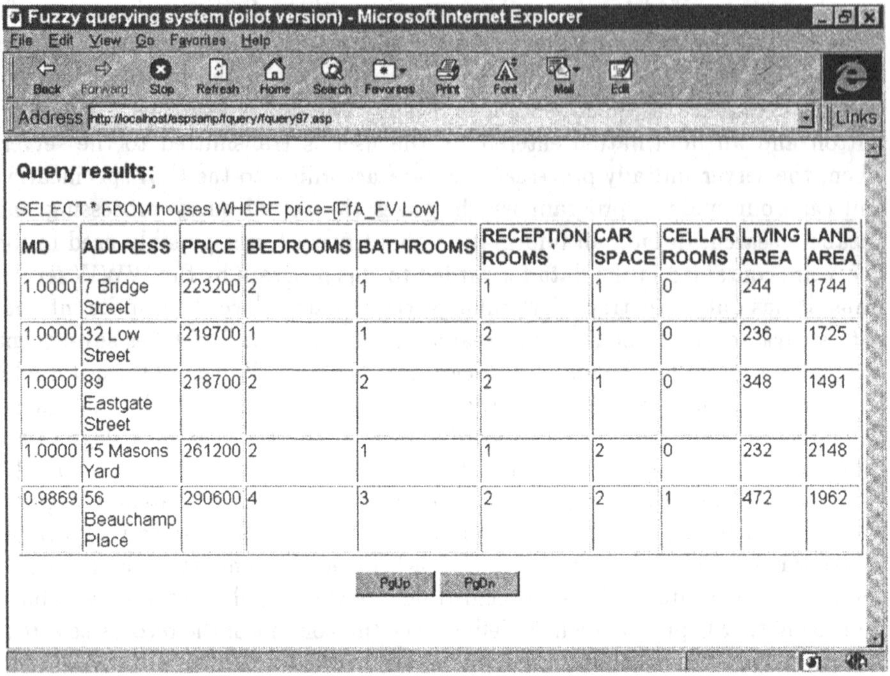

Query results:

SELECT * FROM houses WHERE price=[FfA_FV Low]

MD	ADDRESS	PRICE	BEDROOMS	BATHROOMS	RECEPTION ROOMS	CAR SPACE	CELLAR ROOMS	LIVING AREA	LAND AREA
1.0000	7 Bridge Street	223200	2	1	1	1	0	244	1744
1.0000	32 Low Street	219700	1	1	2	1	0	236	1725
1.0000	89 Eastgate Street	218700	2	2	2	1	0	348	1491
1.0000	15 Masons Yard	261200	2	1	1	2	0	232	2148
0.9869	56 Beauchamp Place	290600	4	3	2	2	1	472	1962

PgUp   PgDn

Fig. 5. Results of fuzzy querying over the Internet using the Microsoft Explorer

To summarize, at the server side we have the following components of our fuzzy querying system: (1) a database file (XBase format), (2) HTML pages for: query form (enhanced with JavaScript functions and applets), list of records and the contents of a selected record, (3) the searching program, and (4) the program displaying (reporting) records.

5.2 WWW-based interface to FQUERY for Access

The WWW-based interface presented here is meant to form a query containing fuzzy elements as discussed in Section 2 and submit it over the Internet to the fuzzy querying engine implemented by FQUERY for Access. Then, the query is processed as in the standalone case. The query results are sent back to the client and displayed by the browser. For example, in querying a database of houses for sale in a real estate agency, virtually all customers' requirements concerning preferred apartments and houses are imprecise as, e.g., "possibly low price", "more or less two bedrooms", "in the city center", etc. For simplicity, suppose a single imprecise condition "price should be low" is used.

First, the user, e.g., using the Microsoft's Internet Explorer, opens the main document of the querying system shown in Figure 4. It contains a simple query form. The same syntax and semantics applies as in Section 2, i.e., fuzzy elements may be employed as query parameters. To learn which fuzzy elements are available, the user can open another window where all fuzzy values, relations etc. currently defined are listed. After forming the query, the user sends it to the WWW server. This request, with query definition data, makes the server start script, written in VBScript, embedded in the associated document. It opens an appropriate database, and then executes the query. The query results are stored in a table, which is then used to create an HTML page sent back to the browser - see, e.g., Figure 5.

Concluding, the same fuzzy querying tool, FQUERY for Access, may be used in the desktop and Internet environment as well.

6 Concluding remarks

The purpose of this paper was to briefly present how tools developed in the framework of the Internet/WWW technology do support the implementation of fuzzy querying. The focus was on the front-end user interface, but some back-end implementation issues and examples were also discussed.

We hope that the Internet is a challenge for fuzzy querying and, at the same time, may give momentum to further research in this relevant field.

References

1. P. Bosc and J. Kacprzyk, editors. *Fuzziness in Database Management Systems*, Heidelberg, 1995. Physica–Verlag.
2. W. Dobrzyński, J. Kacprzyk, and S. Zadrożny. An example of fuzzy querying using microsoft' active server pages tools. In *Proceedings of Fifth European Congress on Intelligent Techniques and Soft Computing - EUFIT'97 (Aachen, Germany)*, volume 2, pages 1181–1185, 1997.
3. J. Kacprzyk. Fuzzy logic in dbmss and querying. In N.K. Kasabov and G. Coghill, editors, *Proceedings of Second New Zealand International Two-Stream Conference on Artificial Neural Networks and Expert Systems (Dunedin, New Zealand)*, pages 106 – 109, Los Alamitos, CA, USA, 1995. IEEE Computer Society Press.
4. J. Kacprzyk and S. Zadrożny. Fuzzy queries in microsoft access: toward a 'more intelligent' use of microsoft windows based dbmss. In *Proceedings of the 1994 Second Australian and New Zealand Conference on Intelligent Information Systems - ANZIIS'94 (Brisbane, Australia)*, pages 492 – 496, 1994.
5. J. Kacprzyk and S. Zadrożny. Fuzzy querying for microsoft access. In *Proceedings of the Third IEEE Conference on Fuzzy Systems (Orlando, USA)*, volume 1, pages 167–171, 1994.
6. J. Kacprzyk and S. Zadrożny. Fquery for access: fuzzy querying for a windows-based dbms. In P. Bosc and J. Kacprzyk, editors, *Fuzziness in Database Management Systems*, pages 415 – 433. Physica–Verlag, Heidelberg, 1995.
7. J. Kacprzyk and S. Zadrożny. Fuzzy queries in microsoft access v. 2. In *Proceedings of 6th International Fuzzy Systems Association World Congress (Sao Paolo, Brazil)*, volume II, pages 341 – 344, 1995.

8. J. Kacprzyk and S. Zadrożny. A fuzzy querying interface for a www-server-based relational dbms. In *Proceedings of IPMU'96 – 6th International Conference on Information Processing and Management of Uncertainty in Knowledge–Based Systems (Granada, Spain)*, volume 1, pages 19–24, 1996.

9. J. Kacprzyk and S. Zadrożny. Flexible querying using fuzzy logic: An implementation for microsoft access. In T. Andreasen, H. Christiansen, and H.L. Larsen, editors, *Flexible Query Answering Systems*, pages 247–275. Kluwer, Boston, 1997.

10. J. Kacprzyk and S. Zadrożny. Fuzzy queries in microsoft access v. 2. In D. Dubois, H. Prade, and R.R. Yager, editors, *Fuzzy Information Engineering – A Guided Tour of Applications*, pages 223 – 232. Wiley, New York, 1997.

11. J. Kacprzyk and S. Zadrożny. A fuzzy querying interface for a www environment. In *Proceedings of IFSA'97 – Seventh International Fuzzy Systems Association World Congress (Prague, Czech Rep.)*, volume IV, pages 285 – 290, Prague, 1997. Academia.

12. J. Kacprzyk and S. Zadrożny. Implementation of owa operators in fuzzy querying for microsoft access. In R.R. Yager and J. Kacprzyk, editors, *The Ordered Weighted Averaging Operators: Theory and Applications*, pages 293–306. Kluwer, Boston, 1997.

13. J. Kacprzyk and S. Zadrożny. Issues and solutions for fuzzy database querying over internet. In *Proceedings of Fifth European Congress on Intelligent Techniques and Soft Computing – EUFIT'97 (Aachen, Germany)*, volume 2, pages 1191–1195., 1997.

14. J. Kacprzyk, S. Zadrożny, and A. Ziółkowski. Fquery iii+: a 'human consistent' database querying system based on fuzzy logic with linguistic quantifiers. *Information Systems*, (6):443 – 453, 1989.

15. J. Kacprzyk and A. Ziółkowski. Database queries with fuzzy linguistic quantifiers. *IEEE Transactions on Systems, Man and Cybernetics (SMC)*, 16:474 – 479, 1986.

16. J. Kacprzyk and A. Ziółkowski. Retrieval from databases using queries with fuzzy linguistic quantifiers. In H. Prade and C.V. Negoita, editors, *Fuzzy Logics in Knowledge Engineering*, pages 46–57. Verlag TÜV Rheinland, Cologne, 1986.

17. J.M. Medina, J.C. Cubero, O. Pons, and M.A. Vila. Fuzzy search in internet: an architectural approach. In *Proceedings of IFSA'97 – Seventh International Fuzzy Systems Association World Congress (Prague, Czech Rep.)*, volume IV, pages 290 – 296, Prague, 1997. Academia.

18. F.E. Petry. *Fuzzy Databases: Principles and Applications*. Kluwer, Boston, 1996.

19. L.A. Zadeh. A computational approach to fuzzy quantifiers in natural languages. *Computers and Maths. with Appls.*, (9):149 – 184, 1983.

20. S. Zadrożny and J. Kacprzyk. Fuzzy querying using the 'query–by–example' option in a windows–based dbms. In *Proceedings of Third European Congress on Intelligent Techniques and Soft Computing – EUFIT'95 (Aachen, Germany)*, volume 2, pages 733–736, 1995.

21. S. Zadrożny and J. Kacprzyk. Multi–valued fields and values in fuzzy querying via fquery for access. In *Proceedings of FUZZ–IEEE'96 – Fifth International Conference on Fuzzy Systems (New Orleans, USA)*, volume 2, pages 1351 – 1357, 1996.

22. M. Zemankova and Kacprzyk J. The roles of fuzzy logic and management of uncertainty in building intelligent information systems. *Journal of Intelligent Information Systems*, (2):311–317, 1993.

Author Index

Springer
and the
environment

At Springer we firmly believe that an
international science publisher has a
special obligation to the environment,
and our corporate policies consistently
reflect this conviction.
We also expect our business partners –
paper mills, printers, packaging
manufacturers, etc. – to commit
themselves to using materials and
production processes that do not harm
the environment. The paper in this
book is made from low- or no-chlorine
pulp and is acid free, in conformance
with international standards for paper
permanency.

 Springer

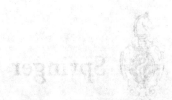

Lecture Notes in Artificial Intelligence (LNAI)

Lecture Notes in Computer Science